go ahead.

no one is watching you.

ALSO FROM PLASTIC FARM PRESS

PLASTIC FARM: SOWING SEEDS ON FERTILE SOIL

by Rafer Roberts
with Danielle Corsetto, Dennis Culver, Dave Morgan,
Wendi Strang-Frost and Jake Warrenfeltz
(this is the book you are currently holding)

PLASTIC FARM: FERTILIZER, an interlude in three aprils

by Rafer Roberts
with Wendi Strang-Frost and Jake Warrenfeltz

coming soon:

PLASTIC FARM: SEASONS OF GROWTH IN THE FIELDS OF DESPAIR

by Rafer Roberts
with Matt Dembicki, Chris Piers, Dale Rawlings, Mal Jones, Jim8Ball and more...

MISHIT: THE NON-PLASTIC COMICS OF RAFER ROBERTS

12 ANGRY LOVE POEMS

poetry by Nan "naniminx" Roberts

SEASONS OF THE SEVENTH CHILD

more (less angry) poetry by Nan "naniminx" Roberts

http://www.plasticfarm.com

 The comics contained within this book were originally printed in serialized form in Plastic Farm #1-12 and some were printed in oversized mini-comic form as Plastic Farm One, Two, Three and Four. These comics were orignally drawn to various aspect ratios. They are presented here in the artists' preferred format. No artists were harmed in the making of this comic, unless you count psychological damage, in which case I think I fucked some people up for life. FIRST PRINTING.
ISBN-13: 978-0-9814570-2-4 ISBN-10: 0-9814570-2-9

PLASTIC FARM

SOWING SEEDS ON FERTILE SOIL

written and mostly drawn by Rafer Roberts

For Nan.

Table Of Contents

Bonus Material

INTRODUCTIONS

To this revised edition:

You hold in your hands the revised edition of PLASTIC FARM: SOWING SEEDS ON FERTILE SOIL. To those of you experiencing this book for the first time: welcome and enjoy yourself. To those of you who have visited PLASTIC FARM before (and especially to those of you who bought the first edition of this collection): thank you, welcome back and I hope you enjoy the improvements.

Most of the improvements in this edition have to do with the lettering on the early chapters. I was a young punk when I started drawing PLASTIC FARM and didn't give a shit if people could actually read the words I was writing. Sloppy lettering? Don't cramp my style with your "legibility", grandpa! It didn't help that I was drawing at a much larger scale for printing on a much larger page size, and when it came time to re-format to fit standard comic size, the reduction was much higher than one would have liked. The result was nearly unreadable, which brings us to this edition.

This book is 6"x9" with a much larger gutter margin to accommodate the high page count. (Owners of the first edition of this book may recall a few panels being lost in the binding. I have worked to keep that from happening in this edition.) As such, the art reduction is higher. If I had left the original lettering alone it would be impossible to read any of these early chapters. So, over the course of a few weeks in early 2011, I re-lettered all of pages 1-96 and some of chapters 6, 8, and 13 for consistency's sake. I also modified a few pages of artwork to remove bleed that never really bled properly in order to facilitate better formatting.

What I did my best NOT to do, however, is to rewrite history despite the sometimes overwhelming desire to do so. I left nearly all of the original dialogue as written. In some cases I fixed grammar and spelling, but there are probably less than ten total instances where I even did that. As much as I wanted to redraw some of the early comics to improve them, I left them in place so that you get what was originally presented, warts and all. My mantra through this process was "What Would George Lucas Do?". When the times came where I wanted to change or fix something, I would ask myself that question, and then I would do the opposite.

So thanks again for your support. I hope you like what we've done here.

-Rafer Roberts
02.01.11

To those of you in the year 2050 and beyond:

What you hold in your hands is a primitive version of a book. As recently as 20 years ago, books were printed using a tacky permanent substance called "ink" on sheets of pulped trees referred to as "paper" (ask your grandparents about trees) and sold individually for reading and ownership. During these times, people would dedicate entire sections of their house (and in most towns, entire buildings called "libraries") for the storage and collection of books. In order to read a book, one would have to go to one of these libraries to "borrow" one (similar to renting one today) or purchase one at a variety of book selling buildings or through the old "internet". Once purchased, books would be kept on shelves within a person's home where each book could take up as much as two inches of shelf space. Many times these kept books would remain unread and would act as ornaments designed to impress visitors. Or, as history tells us, primitive books could be burned for heat in the Winter months (ask your grandparents about Winter) or for wiping away rectal residue. Some people, including the author of this volume, once made careers from printing books. All who did so are now long dead from a dozen types of cancers caused from common substances found in pre-EPA/OSHA regulated factories. Old printed books are a rarity today and finding this one outside of a museum is highly unlikely. Perhaps this was found in the basement of some condemned tenement building, or perhaps in the attic of some long dead relative, or in some old forgotten corner of a dusty antique store. In any case, this book is probably contaminated with black mold and is now slowly killing you.

To those of you reading this in the year 2590 and beyond:

Salutations and Celébré! Most wonderful luck be upon you for locating the last remaining un-changed un-manipulated version of the long ago thought lost Holy Book. Impressive find, and much power now becomes you. Crumbled the whole of the Plastic Church may be when this original truth is set before them. Set free shall be those Kamikazians who worship under the false pretense that their messiah rode upon a beastly tentacled sea slug. The Dinosaur is Truth. No more shall Raoulvians and Oden sects wage bloody war over which side of his face did the most glorious and benevolant Chester wear his scar. The Scar is Truth. Peace be among us. And lo, this book may set some of thine own false beliefs asunder. Remember your beliefs but forget them all the same. As the prophet once spake "flip your neck topper one-eighty and tend to your own fucking store" and so shall it be. All realities are one. All realities are yours. Use this book to restore peace to this war torn universe. Unite the tribes and set their minds free.

And wash your fucking hands. There has to be like 600 years worth of black mold all over this fucking thing.

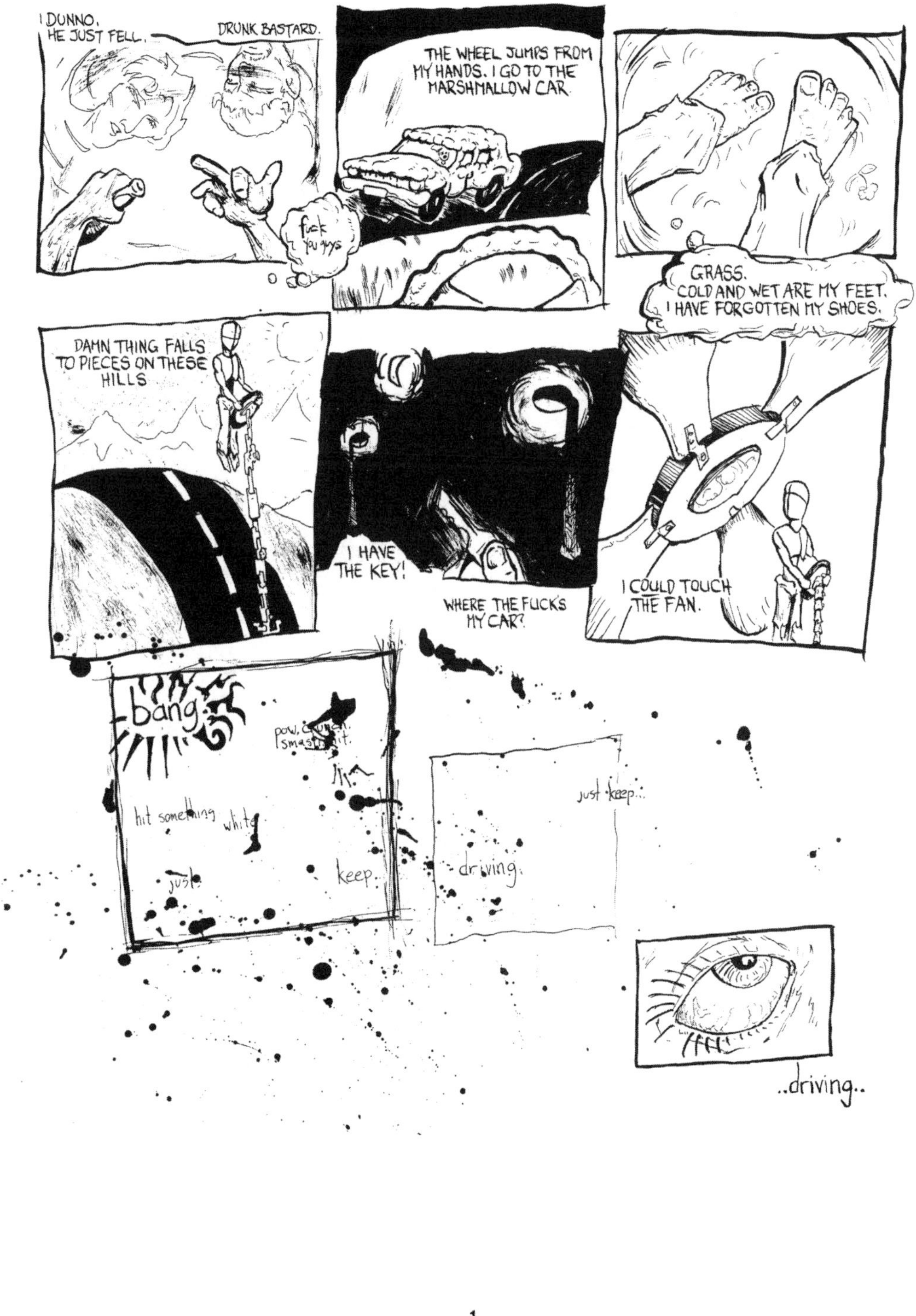
I DUNNO. HE JUST FELL.
DRUNK BASTARD.
fuck you guys
THE WHEEL JUMPS FROM MY HANDS. I GO TO THE MARSHMALLOW CAR.
GRASS. COLD AND WET ARE MY FEET. I HAVE FORGOTTEN MY SHOES.
DAMN THING FALLS TO PIECES ON THESE HILLS
I HAVE THE KEY!
WHERE THE FUCK'S MY CAR?
I COULD TOUCH THE FAN.
bang
hit something white
just
keep..
just keep..
driving.
..driving..

Plastic Farm

a comic

prolog

"nothing is true: everything is permitted"

-wsburroughs

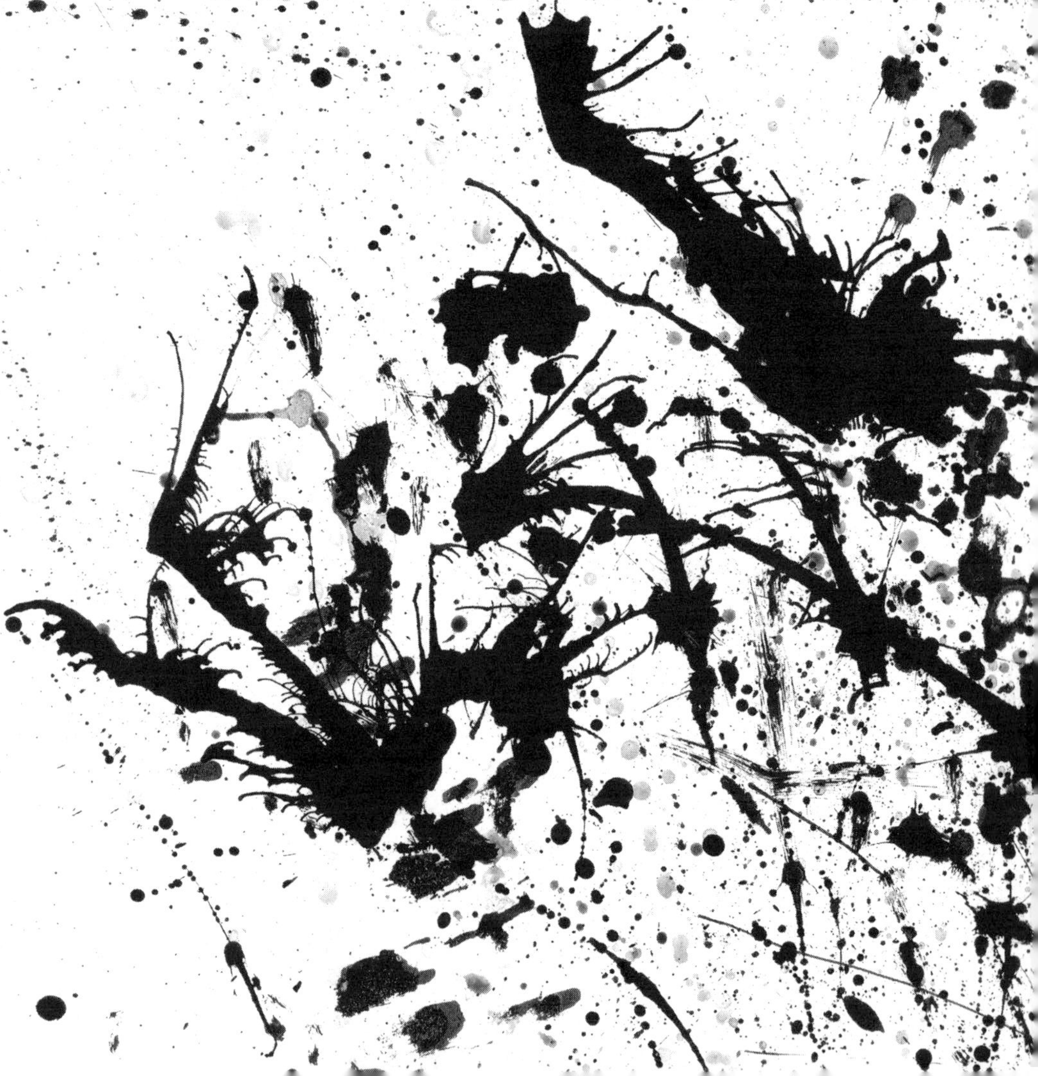

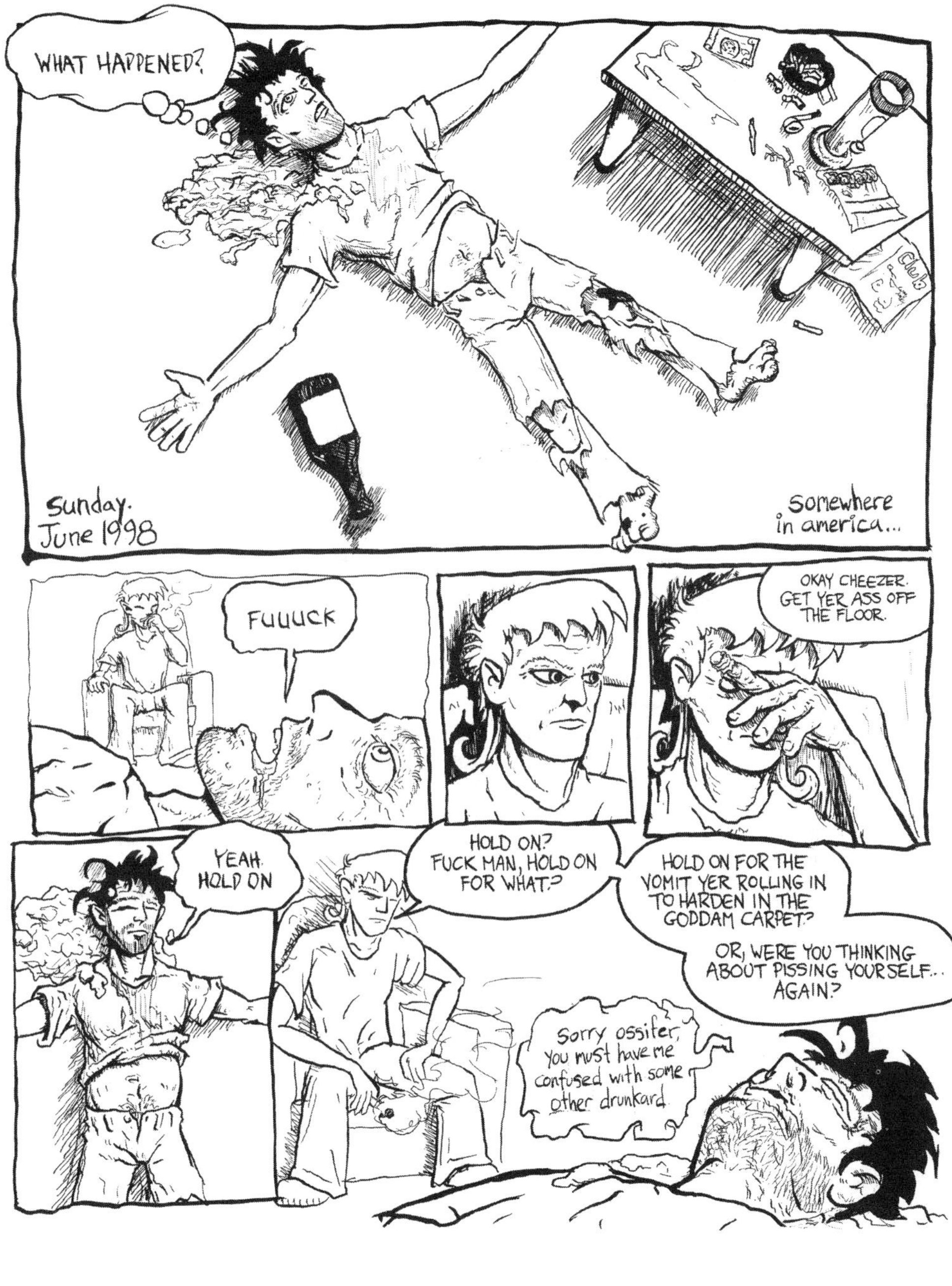
WHAT HAPPENED?
Sunday.
June 1998
Somewhere
in america...
Fuuuck
OKAY CHEEZER.
GET YER ASS OFF
THE FLOOR.
YEAH.
HOLD ON
HOLD ON?
FUCK MAN, HOLD ON
FOR WHAT?
HOLD ON FOR THE
VOMIT YER ROLLING IN
TO HARDEN IN THE
GODDAM CARPET?
OR, WERE YOU THINKING
ABOUT PISSING YOURSELF...
AGAIN?
Sorry ossifer,
you must have me
confused with some
other drunkard.

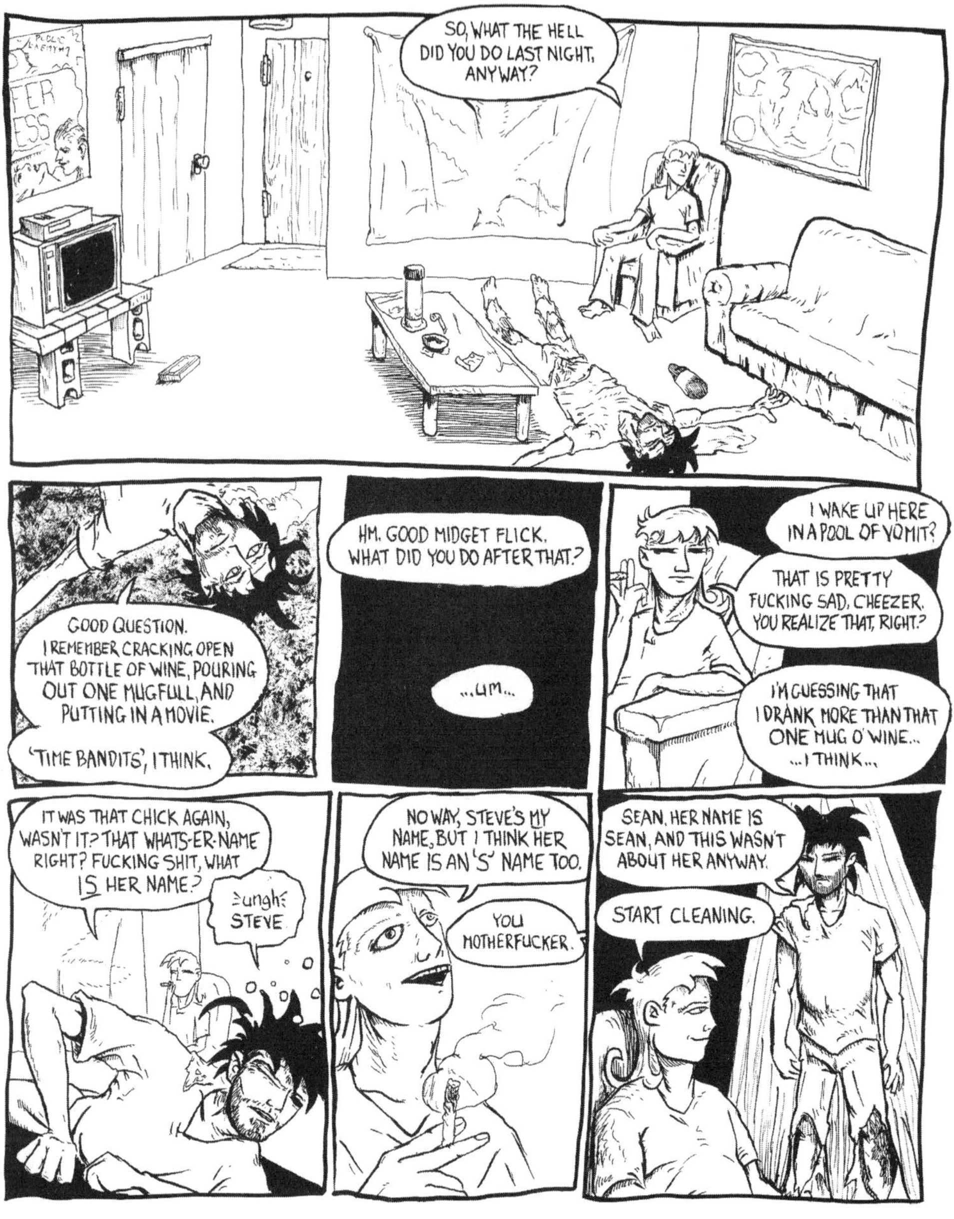
SO, WHAT THE HELL DID YOU DO LAST NIGHT, ANYWAY?
GOOD QUESTION. I REMEMBER CRACKING OPEN THAT BOTTLE OF WINE, POURING OUT ONE MUGFULL, AND PUTTING IN A MOVIE.
'TIME BANDITS', I THINK.
HM. GOOD MIDGET FLICK. WHAT DID YOU DO AFTER THAT?
...UM...
I WAKE UP HERE IN A POOL OF VOMIT?
THAT IS PRETTY FUCKING SAD, CHEEZER. YOU REALIZE THAT, RIGHT?
I'M GUESSING THAT I DRANK MORE THAN THAT ONE MUG O' WINE... ...I THINK...
IT WAS THAT CHICK AGAIN, WASN'T IT? THAT WHATS-ER-NAME RIGHT? FUCKING SHIT, WHAT IS HER NAME?
ungh STEVE
NO WAY, STEVE'S MY NAME, BUT I THINK HER NAME IS AN 'S' NAME TOO.
YOU MOTHERFUCKER.
SEAN. HER NAME IS SEAN, AND THIS WASN'T ABOUT HER ANYWAY.
START CLEANING.

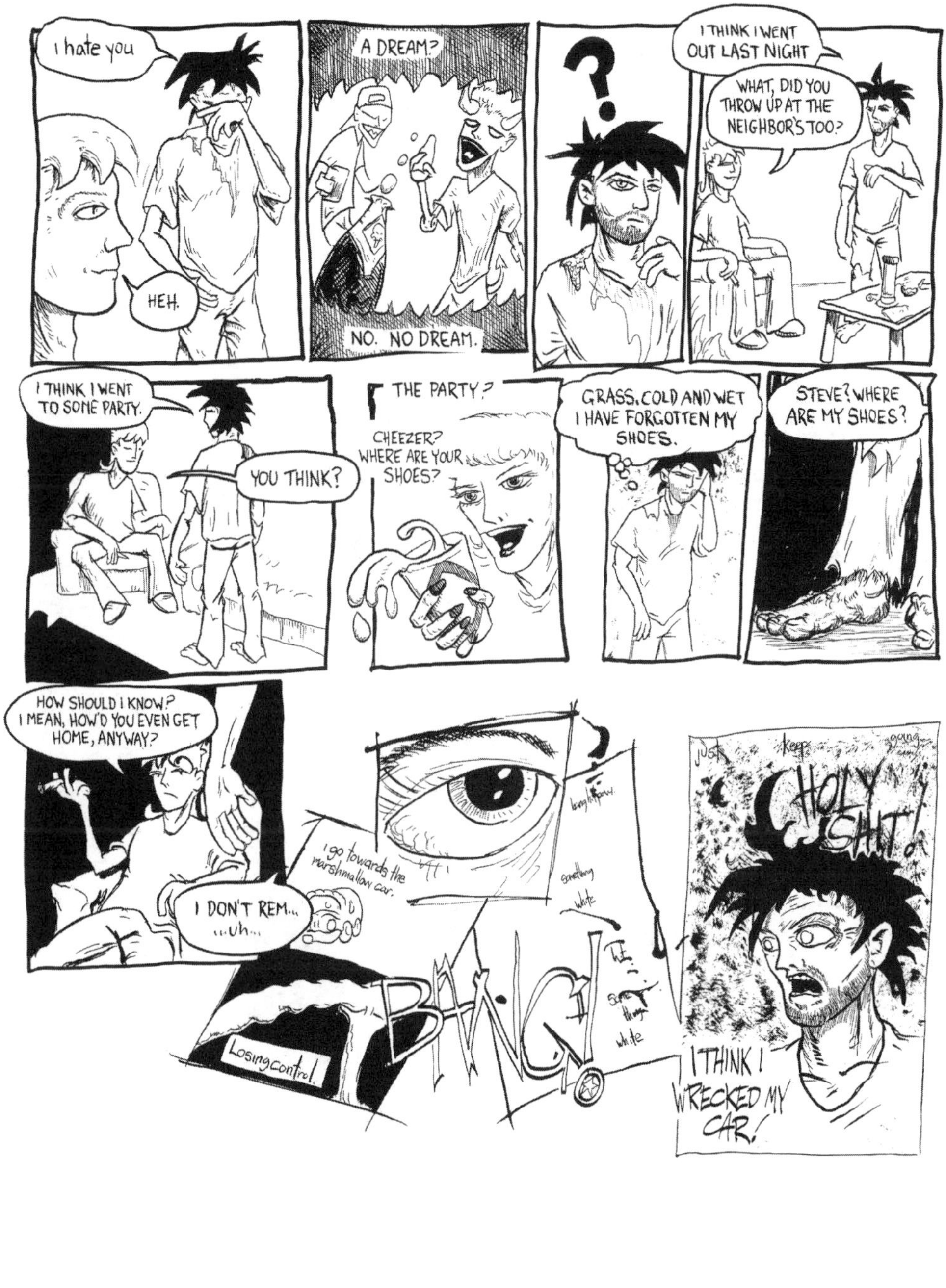

i hate you
HEH.
A DREAM?
NO. NO DREAM.
I THINK I WENT OUT LAST NIGHT
WHAT, DID YOU THROW UP AT THE NEIGHBOR'S TOO?
I THINK I WENT TO SOME PARTY.
YOU THINK?
THE PARTY?
CHEEZER? WHERE ARE YOUR SHOES?
GRASS, COLD AND WET I HAVE FORGOTTEN MY SHOES.
STEVE? WHERE ARE MY SHOES?
HOW SHOULD I KNOW? I MEAN, HOW'D YOU EVEN GET HOME, ANYWAY?
I DON'T REM... ...uh...
i go towards the marshmallow car.
something white
Losing control.
BANG!
some thing white
just keep going
HOLY SHIT!
I THINK I WRECKED MY CAR!

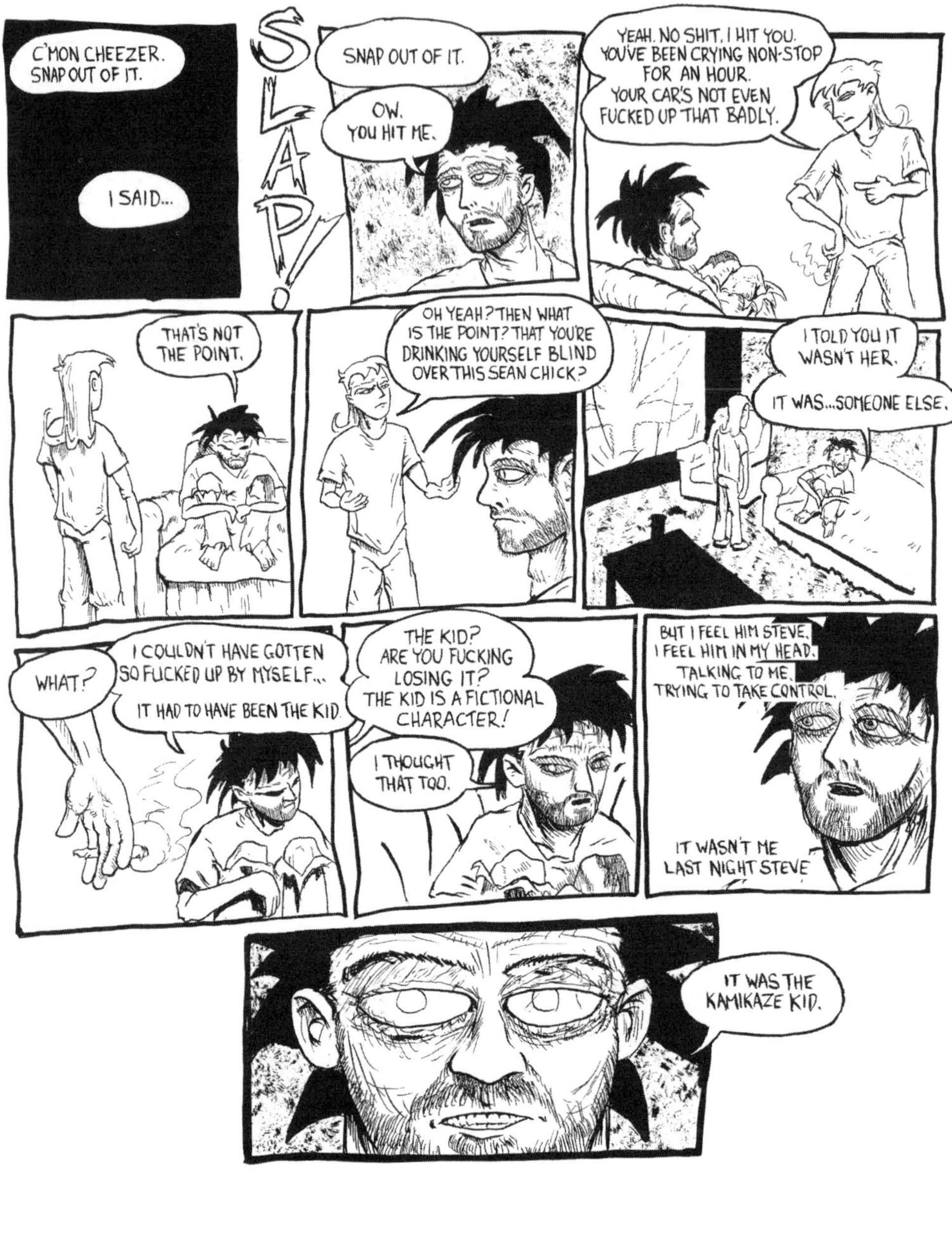
C'MON CHEEZER.
SNAP OUT OF IT.
I SAID...
SLAP!
SNAP OUT OF IT.
OW.
YOU HIT ME.
YEAH. NO SHIT, I HIT YOU.
YOU'VE BEEN CRYING NON-STOP
FOR AN HOUR.
YOUR CAR'S NOT EVEN
FUCKED UP THAT BADLY.
THAT'S NOT
THE POINT.
OH YEAH? THEN WHAT
IS THE POINT? THAT YOU'RE
DRINKING YOURSELF BLIND
OVER THIS SEAN CHICK?
I TOLD YOU IT
WASN'T HER.
IT WAS...SOMEONE ELSE.
WHAT?
I COULDN'T HAVE GOTTEN
SO FUCKED UP BY MYSELF...
IT HAD TO HAVE BEEN THE KID.
THE KID?
ARE YOU FUCKING
LOSING IT?
THE KID IS A FICTIONAL
CHARACTER!
I THOUGHT
THAT TOO.
BUT I FEEL HIM STEVE,
I FEEL HIM IN MY HEAD,
TALKING TO ME,
TRYING TO TAKE CONTROL.
IT WASN'T ME
LAST NIGHT STEVE
IT WAS THE
KAMIKAZE KID.

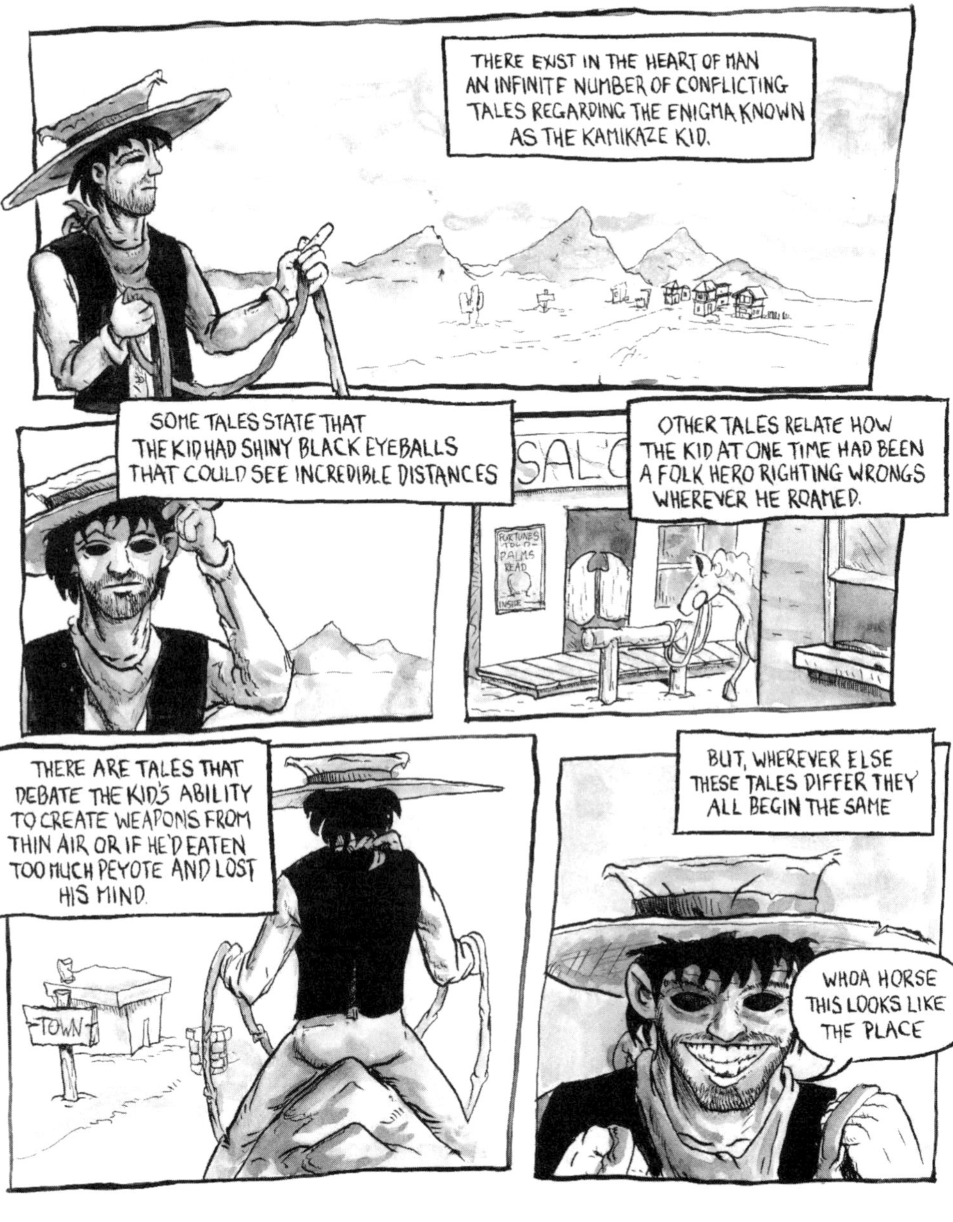
THERE EXIST IN THE HEART OF MAN AN INFINITE NUMBER OF CONFLICTING TALES REGARDING THE ENIGMA KNOWN AS THE KAMIKAZE KID.
SOME TALES STATE THAT THE KID HAD SHINY BLACK EYEBALLS THAT COULD SEE INCREDIBLE DISTANCES
OTHER TALES RELATE HOW THE KID AT ONE TIME HAD BEEN A FOLK HERO RIGHTING WRONGS WHEREVER HE ROAMED.
SAL
FORTUNES TOLD PALMS READ INSIDE
THERE ARE TALES THAT DEBATE THE KID'S ABILITY TO CREATE WEAPONS FROM THIN AIR OR IF HE'D EATEN TOO MUCH PEYOTE AND LOST HIS MIND.
TOWN
BUT, WHEREVER ELSE THESE TALES DIFFER THEY ALL BEGIN THE SAME
WHOA HORSE THIS LOOKS LIKE THE PLACE

"THE KAMIKAZE KID CAME INTO TOWN AT SUNSET RIDING UPON A GIANT DINOSAUR-LOOKING HELL-BEAST AND HEADED STRAIGHT FOR THE BAR..."

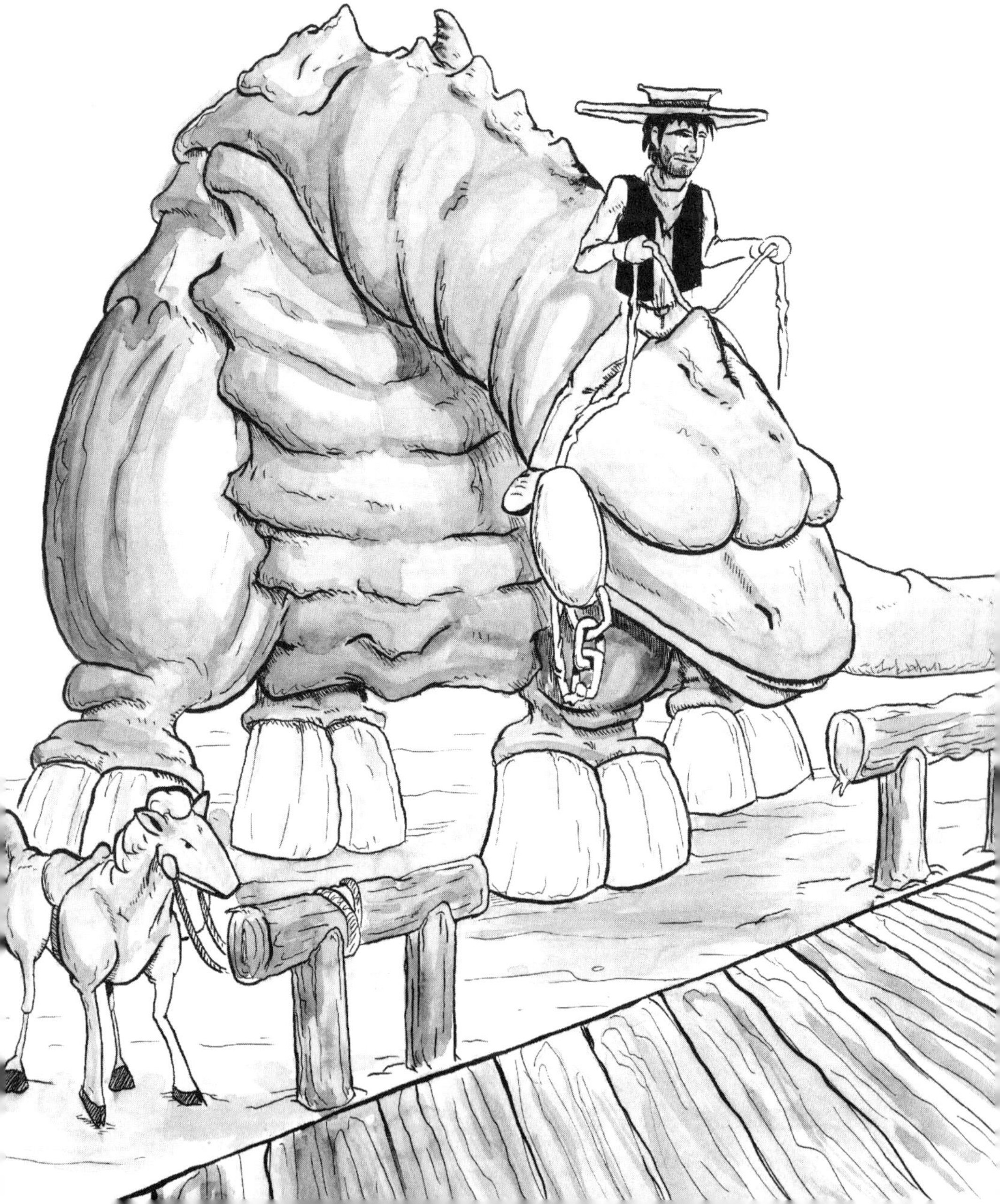

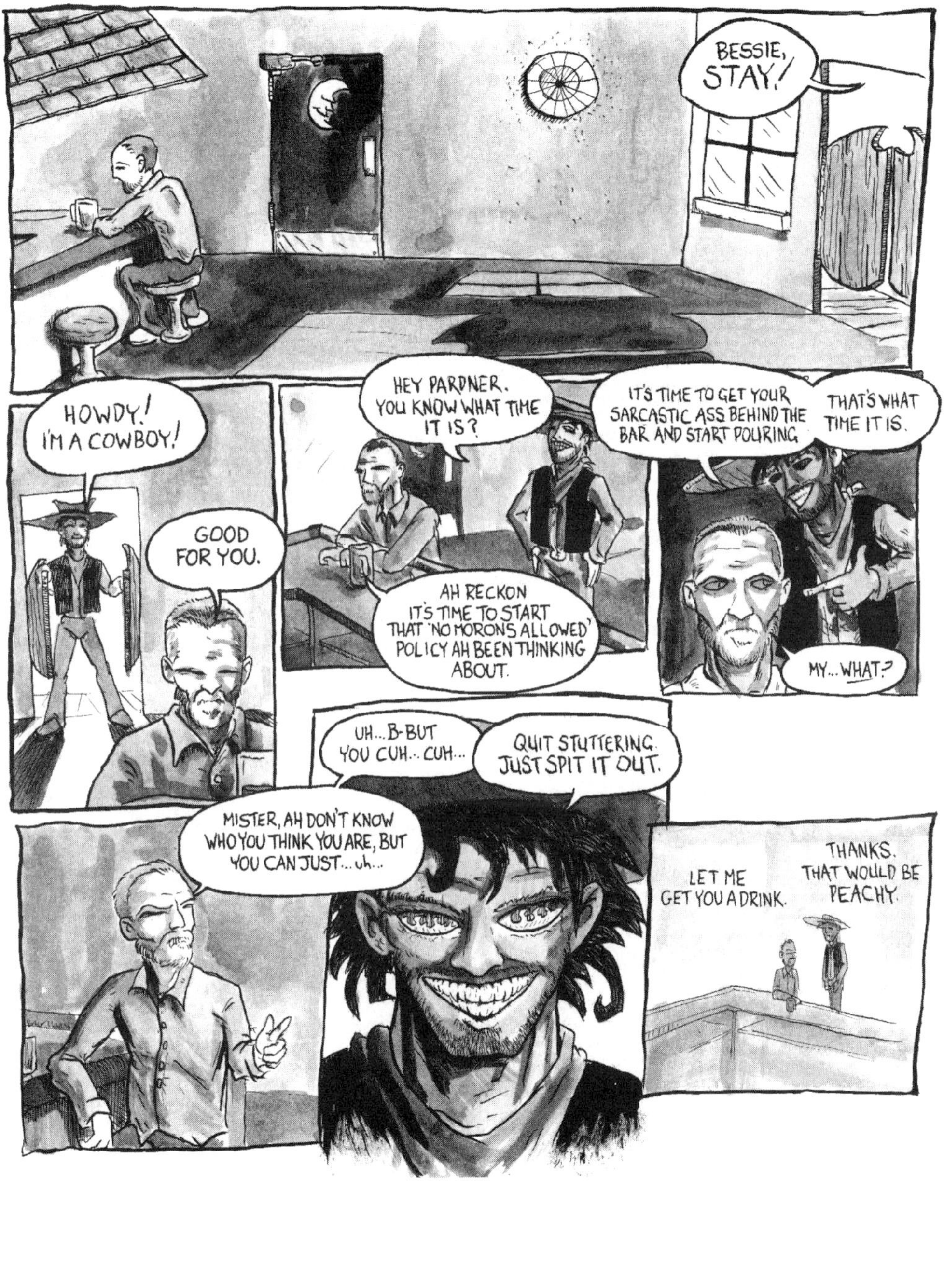
BESSIE, STAY!
HOWDY! I'M A COWBOY!
GOOD FOR YOU.
HEY PARDNER. YOU KNOW WHAT TIME IT IS?
AH RECKON IT'S TIME TO START THAT 'NO MORONS ALLOWED' POLICY AH BEEN THINKING ABOUT.
IT'S TIME TO GET YOUR SARCASTIC ASS BEHIND THE BAR AND START POURING.
THAT'S WHAT TIME IT IS.
MY... WHAT?
UH... B-BUT YOU CUH... CUH...
QUIT STUTTERING. JUST SPIT IT OUT.
MISTER, AH DON'T KNOW WHO YOU THINK YOU ARE, BUT YOU CAN JUST... uh...
LET ME GET YOU A DRINK.
THANKS. THAT WOULD BE PEACHY.

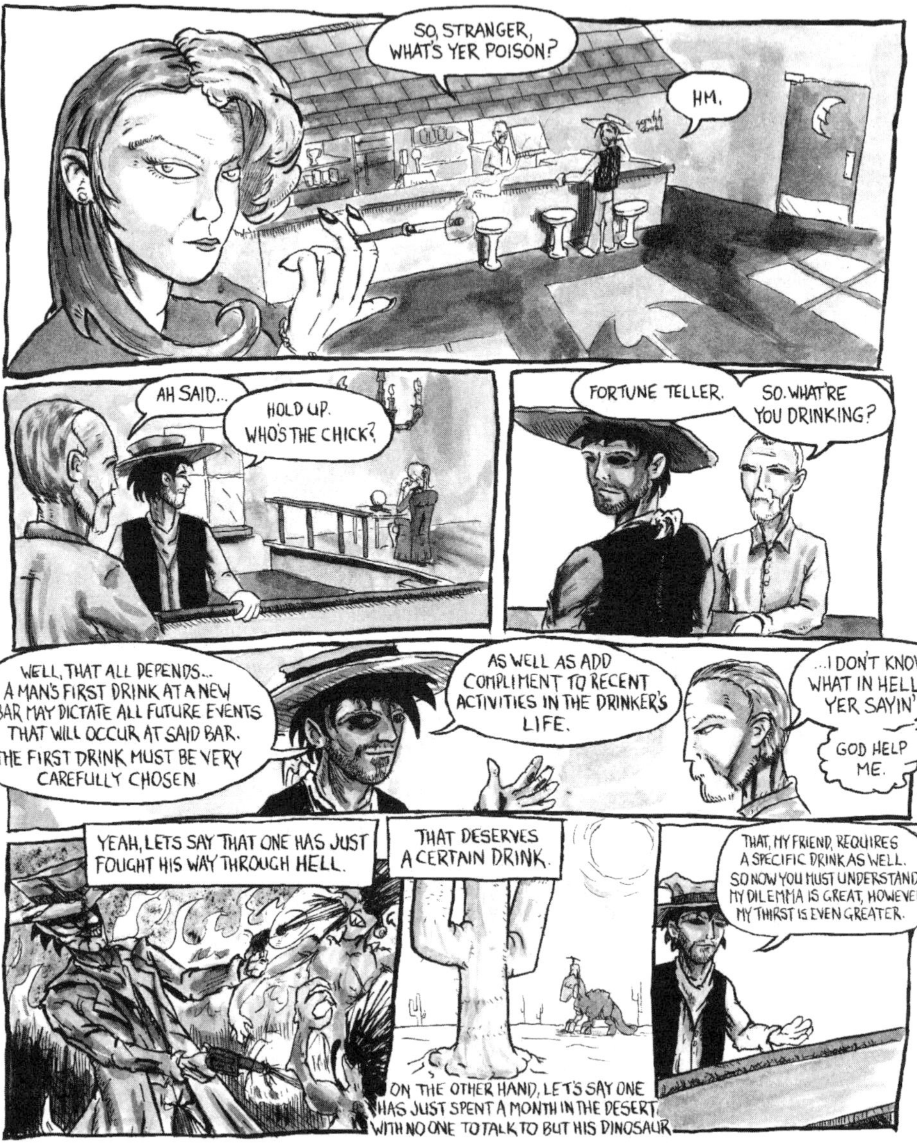
SO, STRANGER, WHAT'S YER POISON?
HM.
AH SAID...
HOLD UP. WHO'S THE CHICK?
FORTUNE TELLER.
SO. WHAT'RE YOU DRINKING?
WELL, THAT ALL DEPENDS... A MAN'S FIRST DRINK AT A NEW BAR MAY DICTATE ALL FUTURE EVENTS THAT WILL OCCUR AT SAID BAR. THE FIRST DRINK MUST BE VERY CAREFULLY CHOSEN.
AS WELL AS ADD COMPLIMENT TO RECENT ACTIVITIES IN THE DRINKER'S LIFE.
...I DON'T KNOW WHAT IN HELL YER SAYIN'
GOD HELP ME.
YEAH, LETS SAY THAT ONE HAS JUST FOUGHT HIS WAY THROUGH HELL.
THAT DESERVES A CERTAIN DRINK.
ON THE OTHER HAND, LET'S SAY ONE HAS JUST SPENT A MONTH IN THE DESERT WITH NO ONE TO TALK TO BUT HIS DINOSAUR
THAT, MY FRIEND, REQUIRES A SPECIFIC DRINK AS WELL. SO NOW YOU MUST UNDERSTAND MY DILEMMA IS GREAT, HOWEVER MY THIRST IS EVEN GREATER.

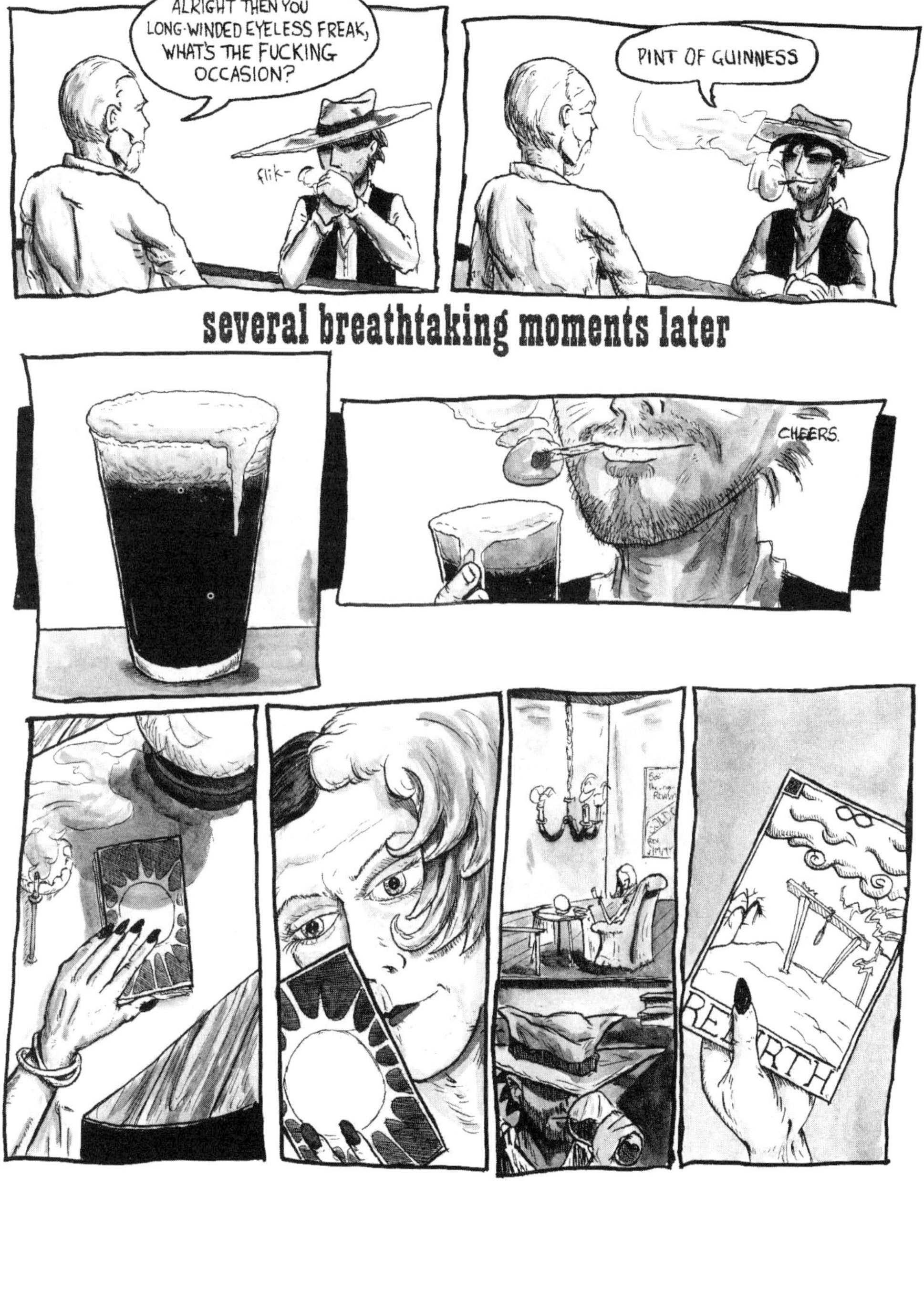
ALRIGHT THEN YOU LONG-WINDED EYELESS FREAK, WHAT'S THE FUCKING OCCASION?
flik-
PINT OF GUINNESS
several breathtaking moments later
CHEERS.

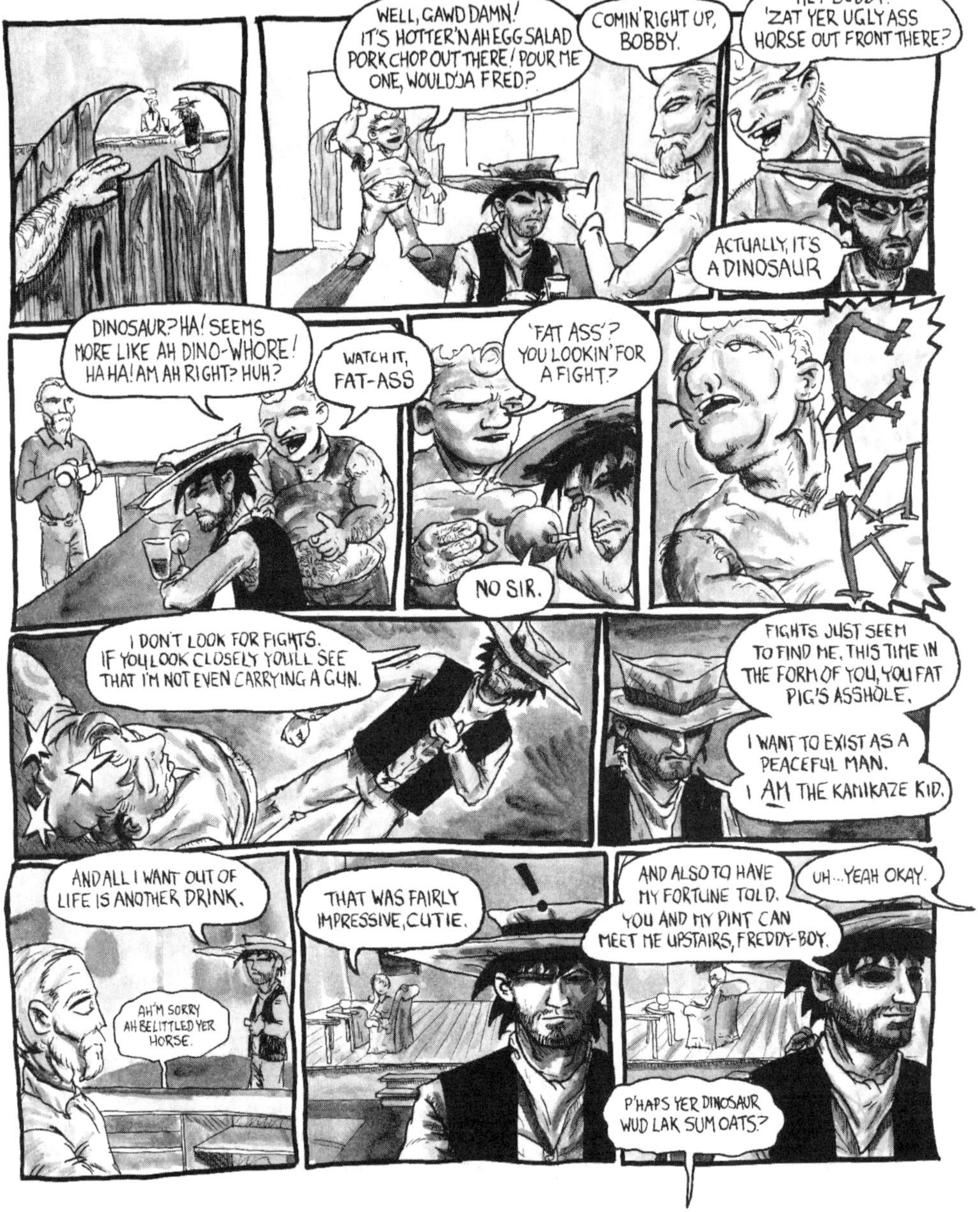
WELL, GAWD DAMN! IT'S HOTTER'N AH EGG SALAD PORK CHOP OUT THERE! POUR ME ONE, WOULD'JA FRED?
COMIN' RIGHT UP, BOBBY.
HEY BUDDY! 'ZAT YER UGLY ASS HORSE OUT FRONT THERE?
ACTUALLY, IT'S A DINOSAUR
DINOSAUR? HA! SEEMS MORE LIKE AH DINO-WHORE! HA HA! AM AH RIGHT? HUH?
WATCH IT, FAT-ASS
'FAT ASS'? YOU LOOKIN' FOR A FIGHT?
NO SIR.
I DON'T LOOK FOR FIGHTS. IF YOU LOOK CLOSELY YOU'LL SEE THAT I'M NOT EVEN CARRYING A GUN.
FIGHTS JUST SEEM TO FIND ME, THIS TIME IN THE FORM OF YOU, YOU FAT PIG'S ASSHOLE.
I WANT TO EXIST AS A PEACEFUL MAN.
I AM THE KAMIKAZE KID.
AND ALL I WANT OUT OF LIFE IS ANOTHER DRINK.
AH'M SORRY AH BELITTLED YER HORSE.
THAT WAS FAIRLY IMPRESSIVE, CUTIE.
!
AND ALSO TO HAVE MY FORTUNE TOLD. YOU AND MY PINT CAN MEET ME UPSTAIRS, FREDDY-BOY.
UH...YEAH OKAY.
P'HAPS YER DINOSAUR WUD LAK SUM OATS?

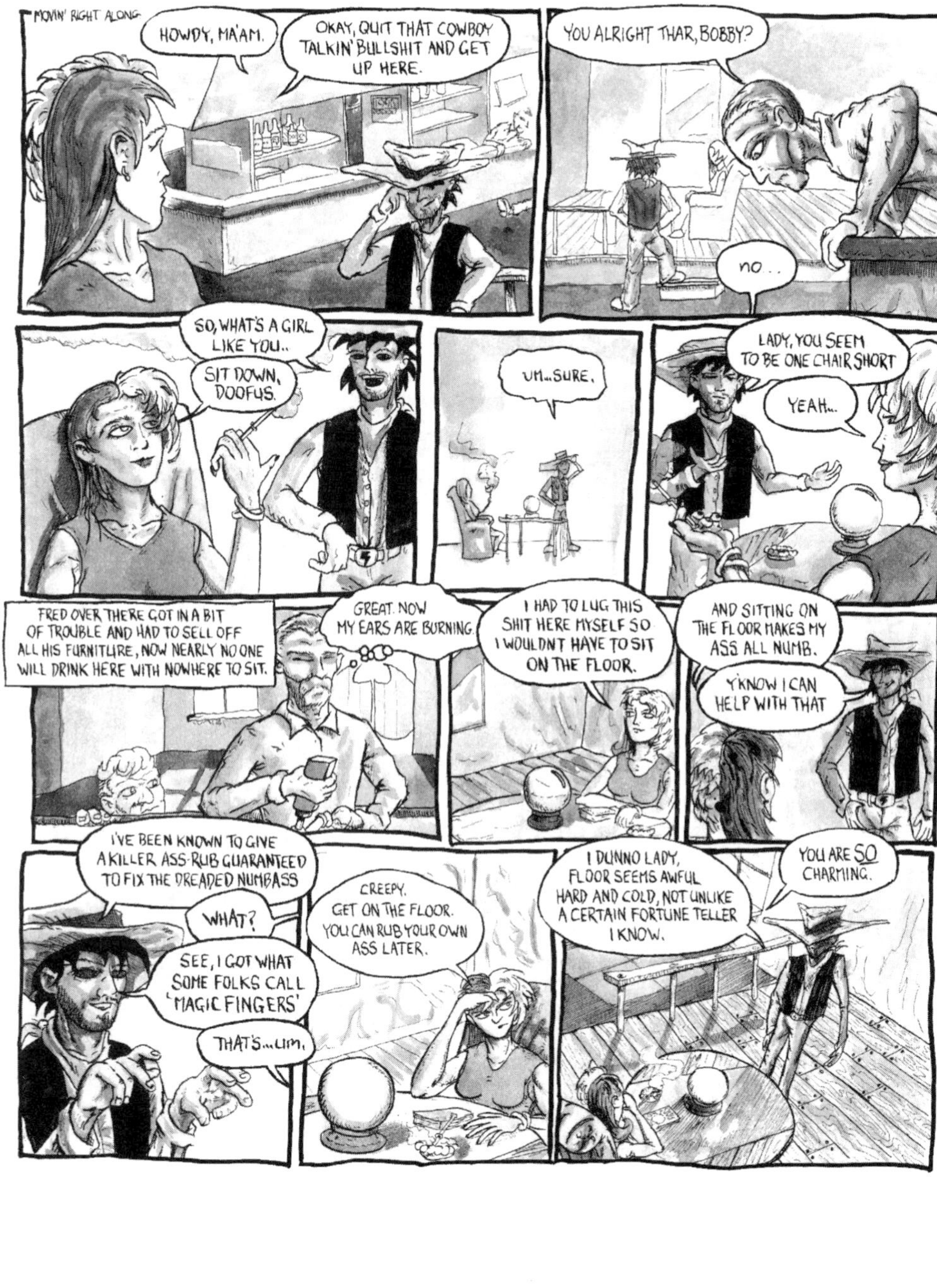
MOVIN' RIGHT ALONG
HOWDY, MA'AM.
OKAY, QUIT THAT COWBOY TALKIN' BULLSHIT AND GET UP HERE.
YOU ALRIGHT THAR, BOBBY?
no..
SO, WHAT'S A GIRL LIKE YOU..
SIT DOWN, DOOFUS.
UM...SURE.
LADY, YOU SEEM TO BE ONE CHAIR SHORT
YEAH..
FRED OVER THERE GOT IN A BIT OF TROUBLE AND HAD TO SELL OFF ALL HIS FURNITURE, NOW NEARLY NO ONE WILL DRINK HERE WITH NOWHERE TO SIT.
GREAT. NOW MY EARS ARE BURNING.
I HAD TO LUG THIS SHIT HERE MYSELF SO I WOULDN'T HAVE TO SIT ON THE FLOOR.
AND SITTING ON THE FLOOR MAKES MY ASS ALL NUMB.
Y'KNOW I CAN HELP WITH THAT
I'VE BEEN KNOWN TO GIVE A KILLER ASS-RUB GUARANTEED TO FIX THE DREADED NUMBASS
WHAT?
SEE, I GOT WHAT SOME FOLKS CALL 'MAGIC FINGERS'
THAT'S...UM,
CREEPY. GET ON THE FLOOR. YOU CAN RUB YOUR OWN ASS LATER.
I DUNNO LADY, FLOOR SEEMS AWFUL HARD AND COLD, NOT UNLIKE A CERTAIN FORTUNE TELLER I KNOW.
YOU ARE SO CHARMING.

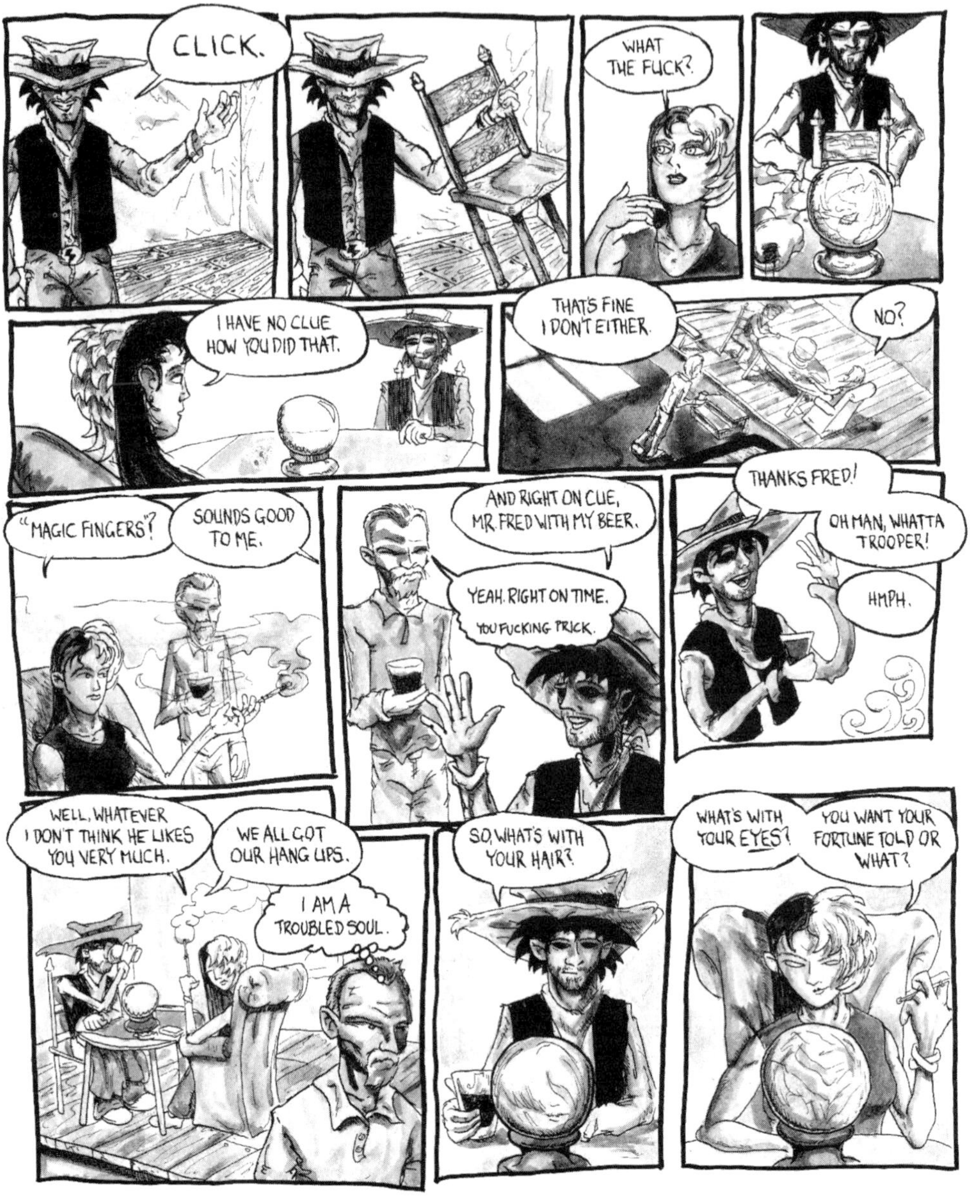
CLICK.
WHAT THE FUCK?
I HAVE NO CLUE HOW YOU DID THAT.
THAT'S FINE I DON'T EITHER.
NO?
"MAGIC FINGERS"?
SOUNDS GOOD TO ME.
AND RIGHT ON CUE, MR. FRED WITH MY BEER.
YEAH. RIGHT ON TIME.
YOU FUCKING PRICK.
THANKS FRED!
OH MAN, WHATTA TROOPER!
HMPH.
WELL, WHATEVER I DON'T THINK HE LIKES YOU VERY MUCH.
WE ALL GOT OUR HANG UPS.
I AM A TROUBLED SOUL.
SO, WHAT'S WITH YOUR HAIR?
WHAT'S WITH YOUR EYES?
YOU WANT YOUR FORTUNE TOLD OR WHAT?

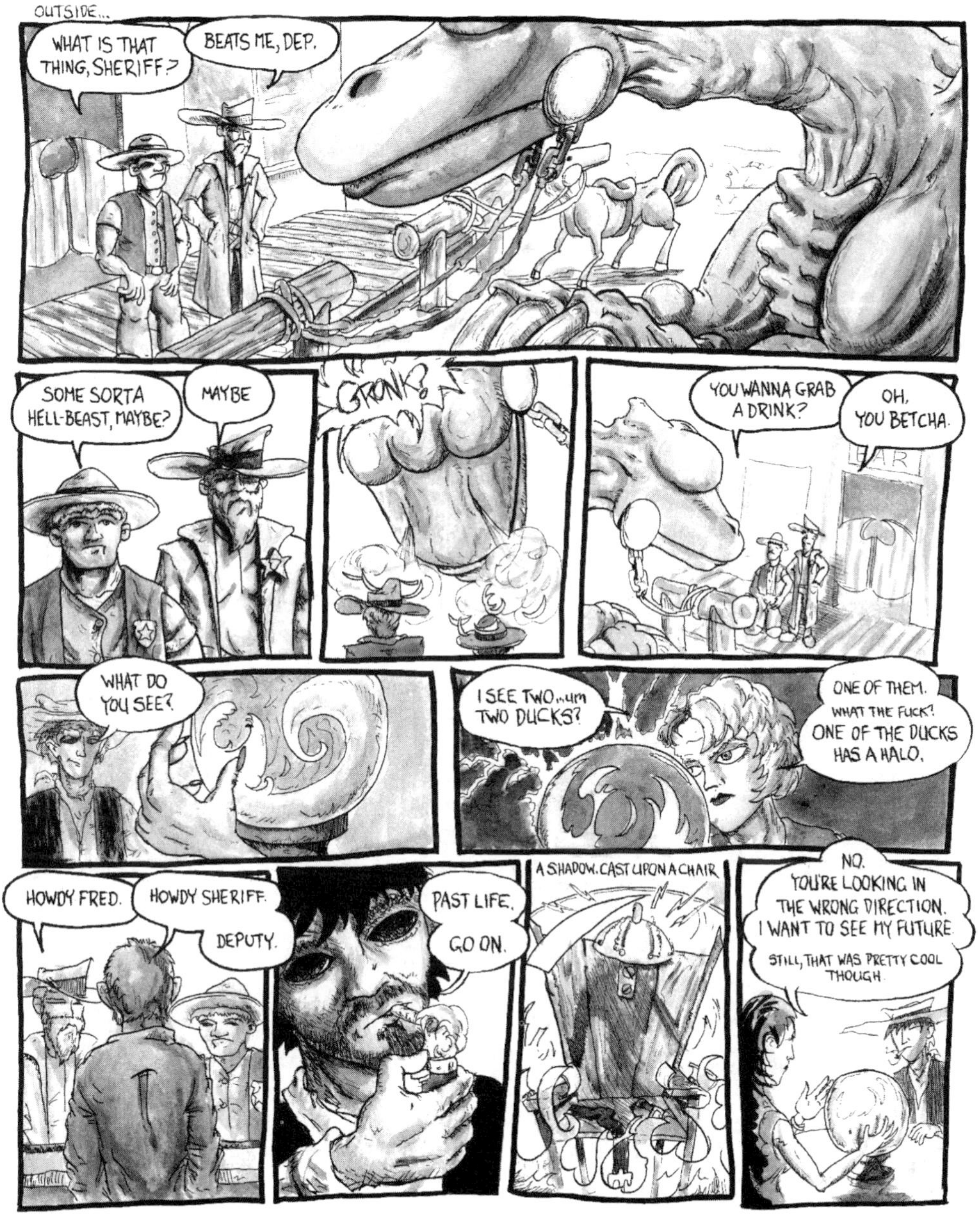
OUTSIDE...
WHAT IS THAT THING, SHERIFF?
BEATS ME, DEP.
SOME SORTA HELL-BEAST, MAYBE?
MAYBE
GRONK?
YOU WANNA GRAB A DRINK?
OH, YOU BETCHA.
BAR
WHAT DO YOU SEE?
I SEE TWO...um TWO DUCKS?
ONE OF THEM.
WHAT THE FUCK?
ONE OF THE DUCKS HAS A HALO.
HOWDY FRED.
HOWDY SHERIFF.
DEPUTY.
PAST LIFE.
GO ON.
A SHADOW, CAST UPON A CHAIR
NO. YOU'RE LOOKING IN THE WRONG DIRECTION. I WANT TO SEE MY FUTURE.
STILL, THAT WAS PRETTY COOL THOUGH.

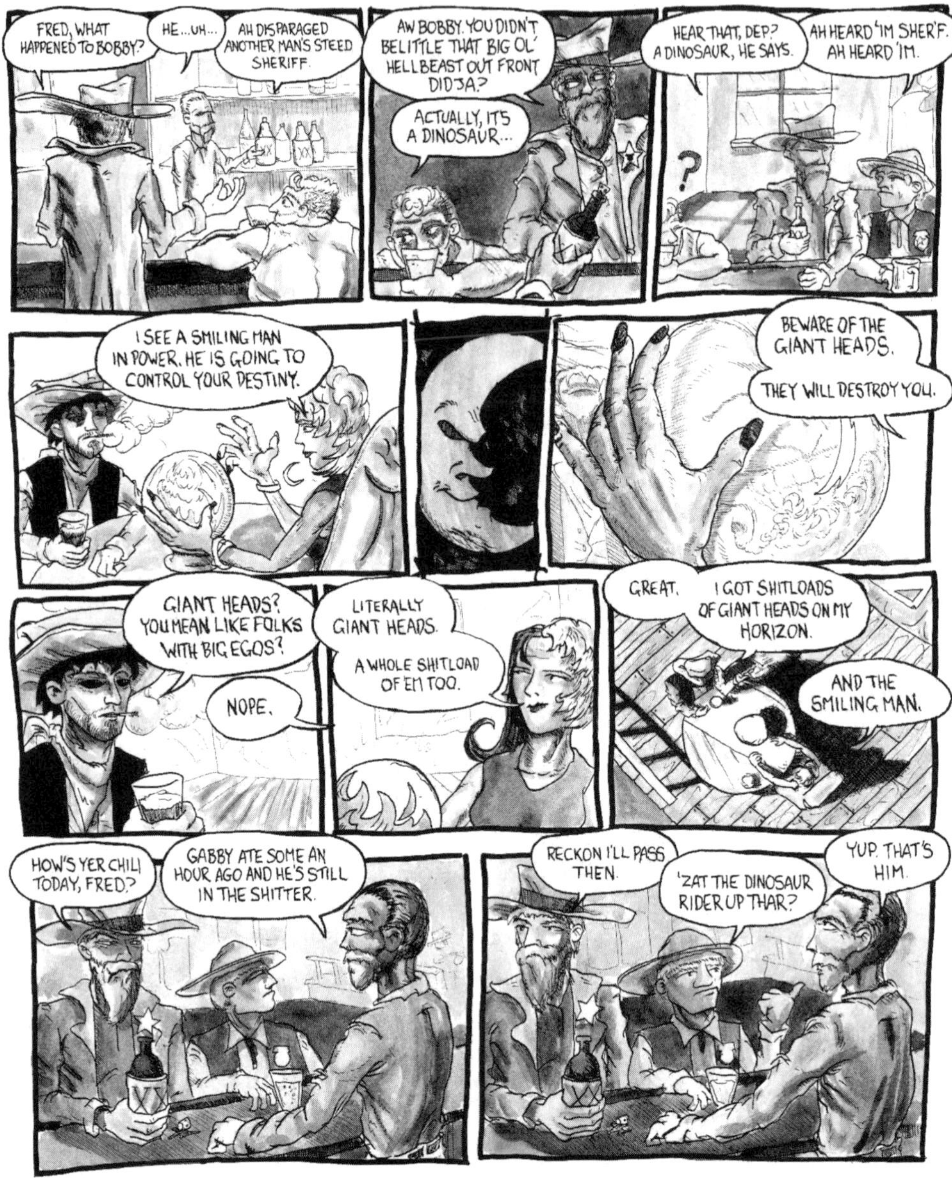
FRED, WHAT HAPPENED TO BOBBY?
HE...UH...
AH DISPARAGED ANOTHER MAN'S STEED SHERIFF.
AW BOBBY. YOU DIDN'T BELITTLE THAT BIG OL' HELLBEAST OUT FRONT DIDJA?
ACTUALLY, IT'S A DINOSAUR...
HEAR THAT, DEP? A DINOSAUR, HE SAYS.
AH HEARD 'IM SHER'F. AH HEARD 'IM.
?
I SEE A SMILING MAN IN POWER. HE IS GOING TO CONTROL YOUR DESTINY.
BEWARE OF THE GIANT HEADS.
THEY WILL DESTROY YOU.
GIANT HEADS? YOU MEAN LIKE FOLKS WITH BIG EGOS?
NOPE.
LITERALLY GIANT HEADS.
A WHOLE SHITLOAD OF 'EM TOO.
GREAT.
I GOT SHITLOADS OF GIANT HEADS ON MY HORIZON.
AND THE SMILING MAN.
HOW'S YER CHILI TODAY, FRED?
GABBY ATE SOME AN HOUR AGO AND HE'S STILL IN THE SHITTER.
RECKON I'LL PASS THEN.
'ZAT THE DINOSAUR RIDER UP THAR?
YUP. THAT'S HIM.

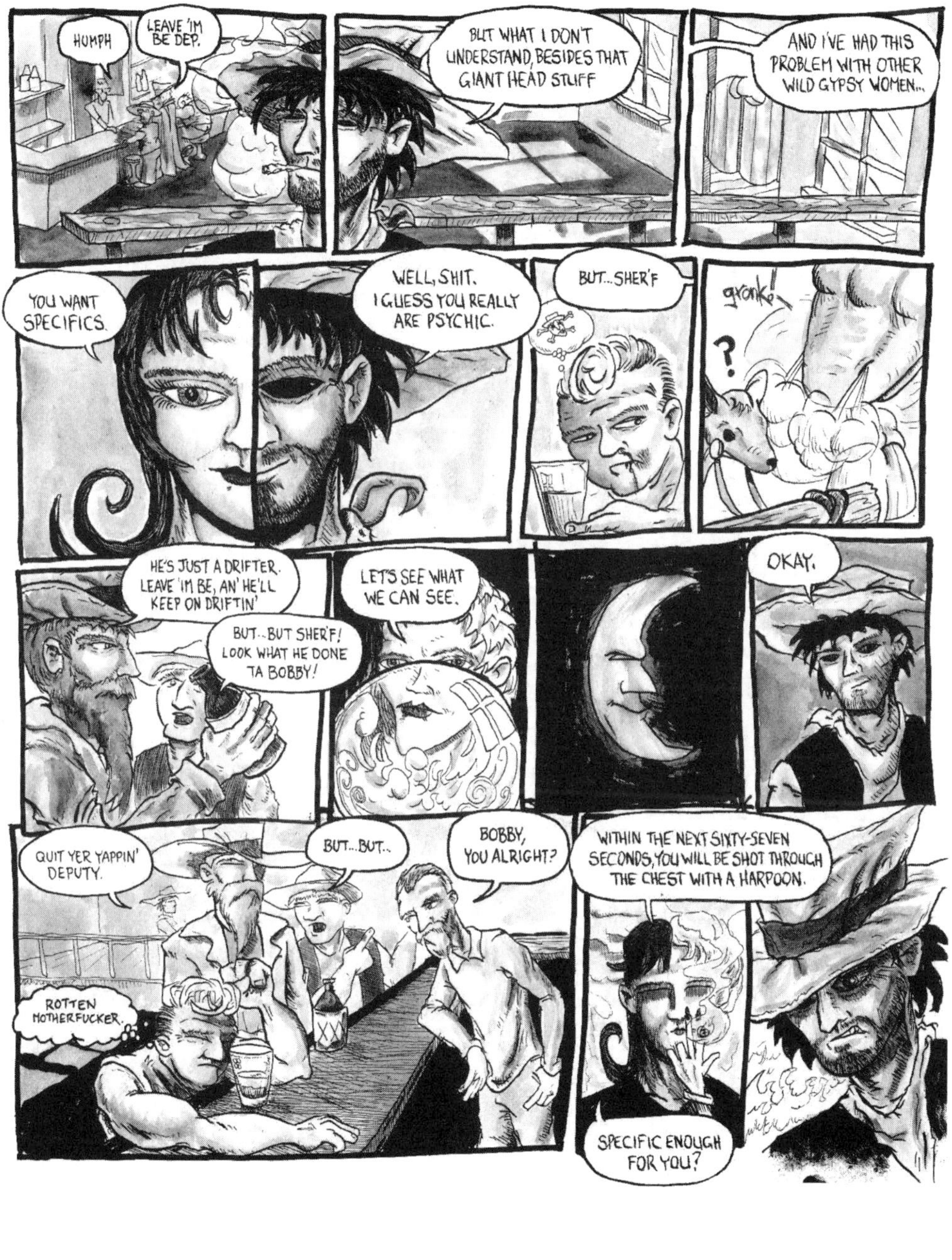
HUMPH
LEAVE 'IM BE DEP.
BUT WHAT I DON'T UNDERSTAND, BESIDES THAT GIANT HEAD STUFF
AND I'VE HAD THIS PROBLEM WITH OTHER WILD GYPSY WOMEN...
YOU WANT SPECIFICS.
WELL, SHIT. I GUESS YOU REALLY ARE PSYCHIC.
BUT...SHER'F
gronk!
?
HE'S JUST A DRIFTER. LEAVE 'IM BE, AN' HE'LL KEEP ON DRIFTIN'
BUT...BUT SHER'F! LOOK WHAT HE DONE TA BOBBY!
LET'S SEE WHAT WE CAN SEE.
OKAY.
QUIT YER YAPPIN' DEPUTY.
BUT...BUT..
BOBBY, YOU ALRIGHT?
ROTTEN MOTHERFUCKER.
WITHIN THE NEXT SIXTY-SEVEN SECONDS, YOU WILL BE SHOT THROUGH THE CHEST WITH A HARPOON.
SPECIFIC ENOUGH FOR YOU?

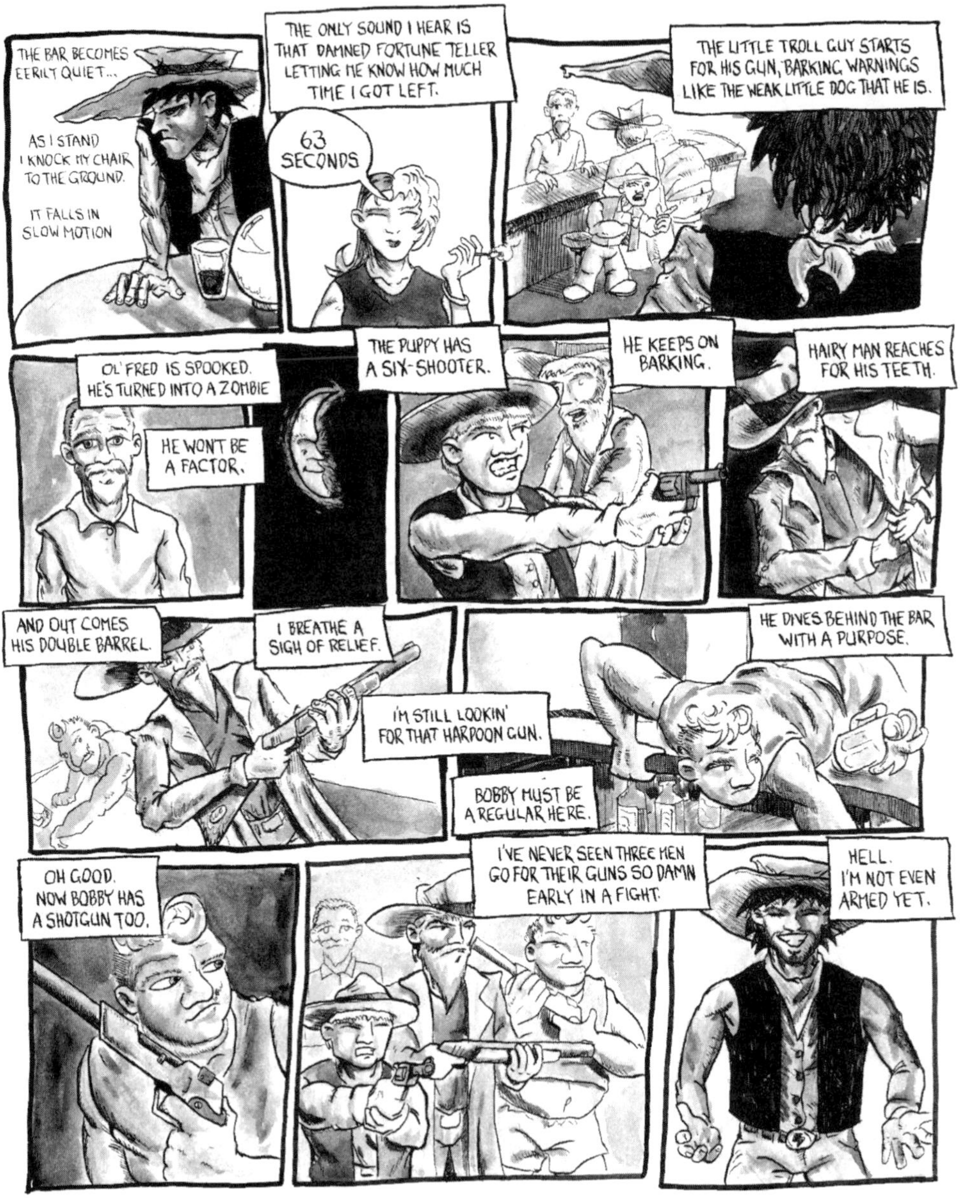
THE BAR BECOMES EERILY QUIET...
AS I STAND I KNOCK MY CHAIR TO THE GROUND.
IT FALLS IN SLOW MOTION
THE ONLY SOUND I HEAR IS THAT DAMNED FORTUNE TELLER LETTING ME KNOW HOW MUCH TIME I GOT LEFT.
63 SECONDS
THE LITTLE TROLL GUY STARTS FOR HIS GUN, BARKING WARNINGS LIKE THE WEAK LITTLE DOG THAT HE IS.
OL' FRED IS SPOOKED. HE'S TURNED INTO A ZOMBIE
HE WONT BE A FACTOR.
THE PUPPY HAS A SIX-SHOOTER.
HE KEEPS ON BARKING.
HAIRY MAN REACHES FOR HIS TEETH.
AND OUT COMES HIS DOUBLE BARREL.
I BREATHE A SIGH OF RELIEF.
I'M STILL LOOKIN' FOR THAT HARPOON GUN.
HE DIVES BEHIND THE BAR WITH A PURPOSE.
BOBBY MUST BE A REGULAR HERE.
OH GOOD. NOW BOBBY HAS A SHOTGUN TOO.
I'VE NEVER SEEN THREE MEN GO FOR THEIR GUNS SO DAMN EARLY IN A FIGHT.
HELL. I'M NOT EVEN ARMED YET.

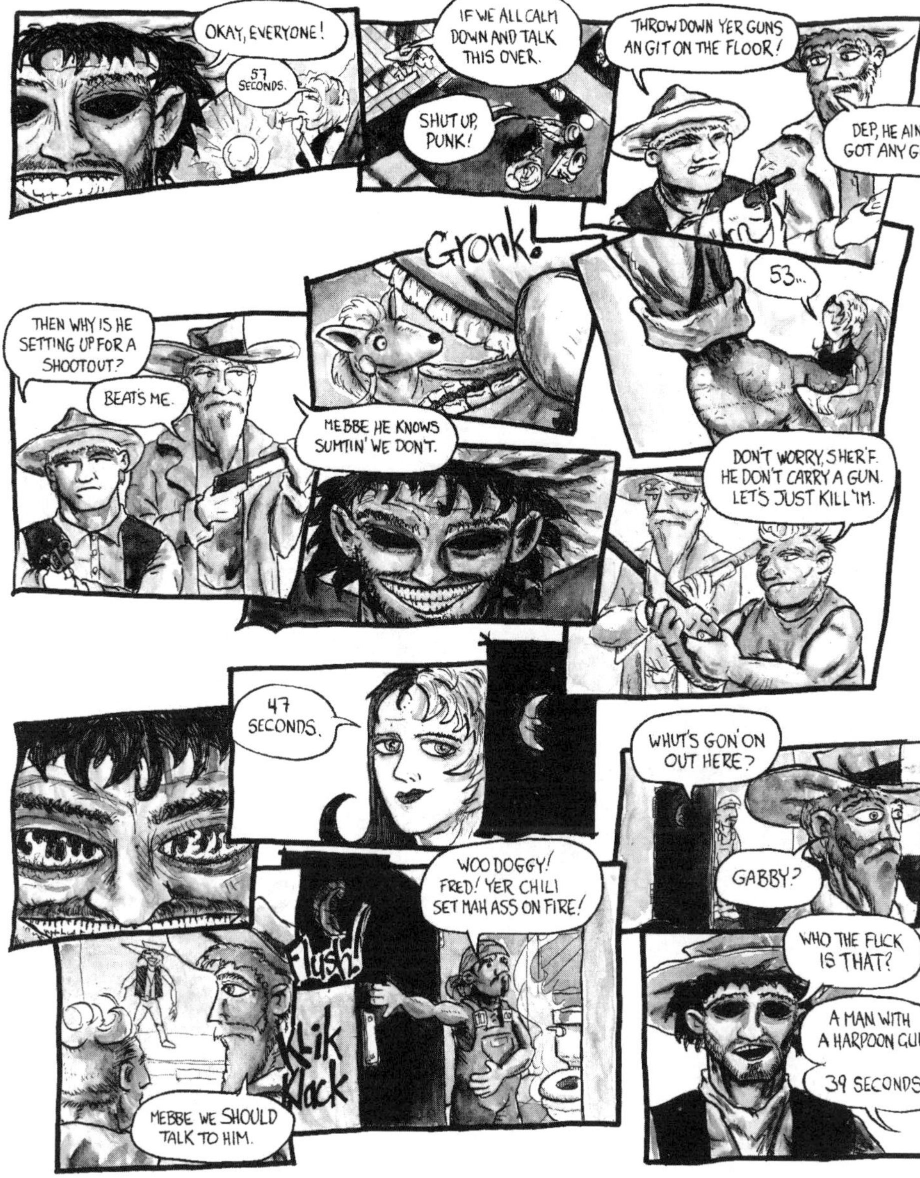
OKAY, EVERYONE!
57 SECONDS.
IF WE ALL CALM DOWN AND TALK THIS OVER.
SHUT UP, PUNK!
THROW DOWN YER GUNS AN GIT ON THE FLOOR!
DEP, HE AIN'T GOT ANY GUNS.
Gronk!
53...
THEN WHY IS HE SETTING UP FOR A SHOOTOUT?
BEAT'S ME.
MEBBE HE KNOWS SUMTIN' WE DON'T.
DON'T WORRY, SHER'F. HE DON'T CARRY A GUN. LET'S JUST KILL 'IM.
47 SECONDS.
WHUT'S GON'ON OUT HERE?
GABBY?
WOO DOGGY! FRED! YER CHILI SET MAH ASS ON FIRE!
Flush!
Klik Klack
MEBBE WE SHOULD TALK TO HIM.
WHO THE FUCK IS THAT?
A MAN WITH A HARPOON GUN.
39 SECONDS

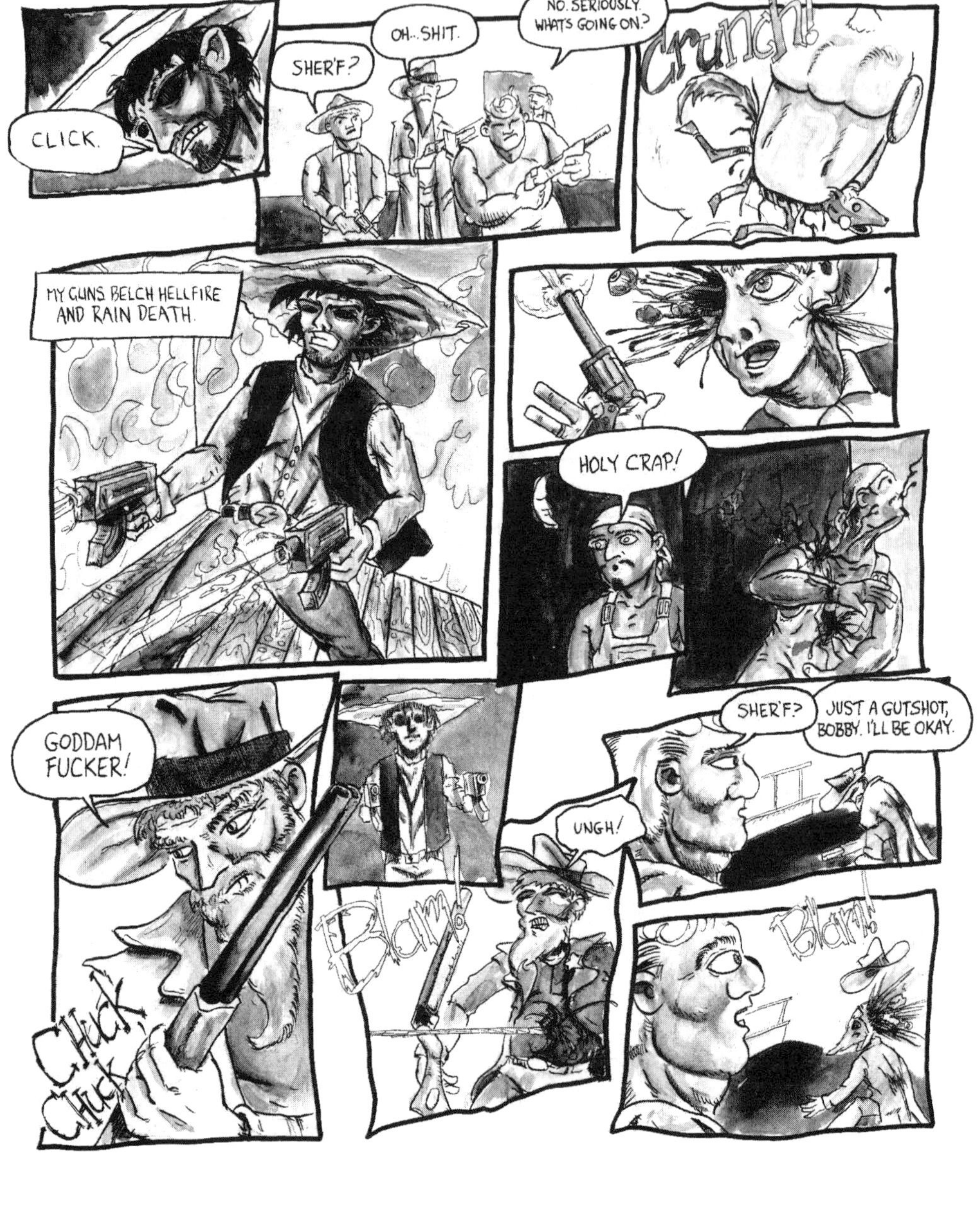
CLICK.
SHER'F?
OH.. SHIT.
NO. SERIOUSLY. WHAT'S GOING ON?
crunch!
MY GUNS BELCH HELLFIRE AND RAIN DEATH.
HOLY CRAP!
GODDAM FUCKER!
Chuck Chuck
Blam!
UNGH!
SHER'F?
JUST A GUTSHOT, BOBBY. I'LL BE OKAY.
Blam!

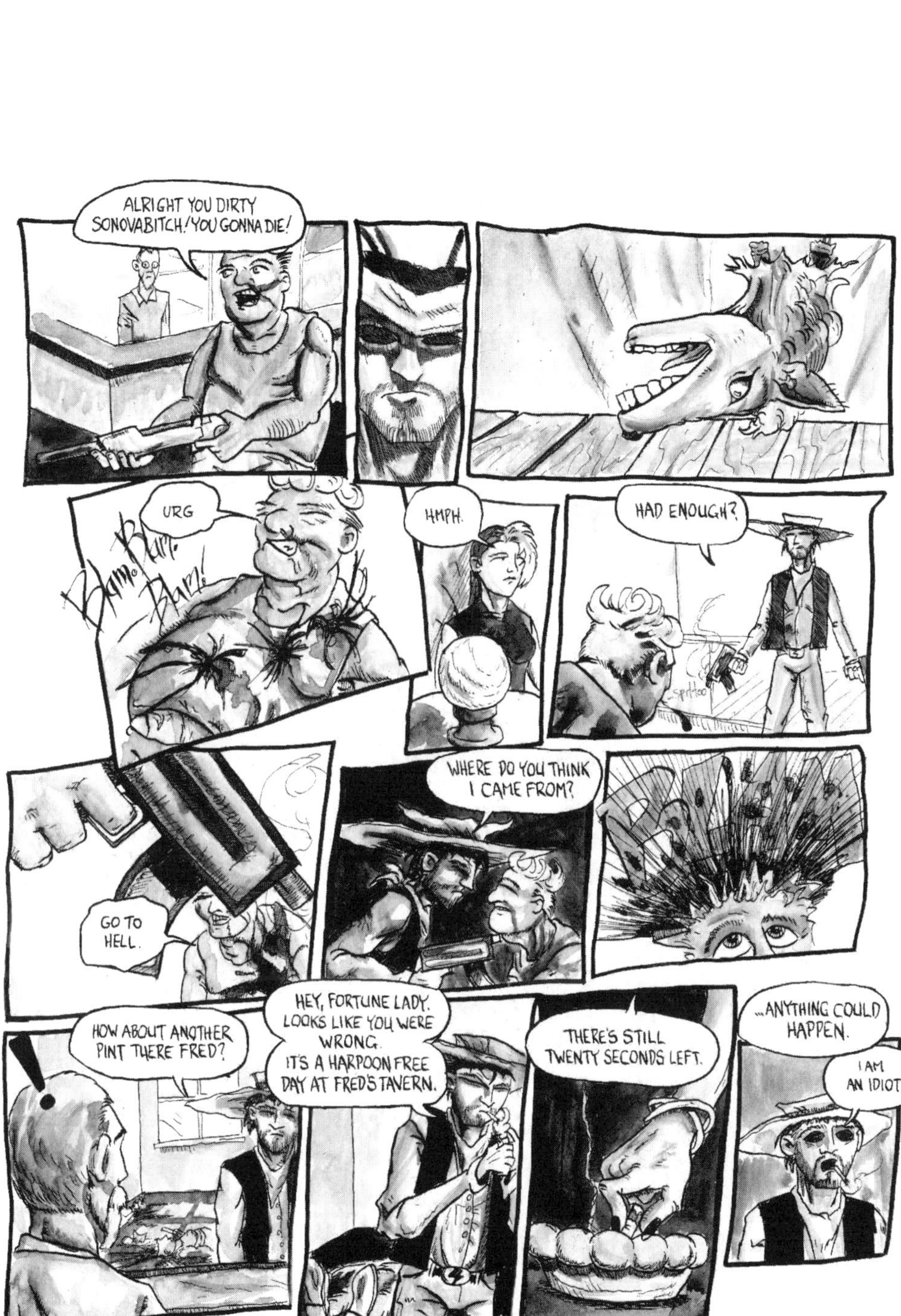
ALRIGHT YOU DIRTY SONOVABITCH! YOU GONNA DIE!
URG
Blam. Blam. Blam!
HMPH.
HAD ENOUGH?
GO TO HELL.
WHERE DO YOU THINK I CAME FROM?
HOW ABOUT ANOTHER PINT THERE FRED?
HEY, FORTUNE LADY. LOOKS LIKE YOU WERE WRONG. IT'S A HARPOON FREE DAY AT FRED'S TAVERN.
THERE'S STILL TWENTY SECONDS LEFT.
...ANYTHING COULD HAPPEN.
I AM AN IDIOT.

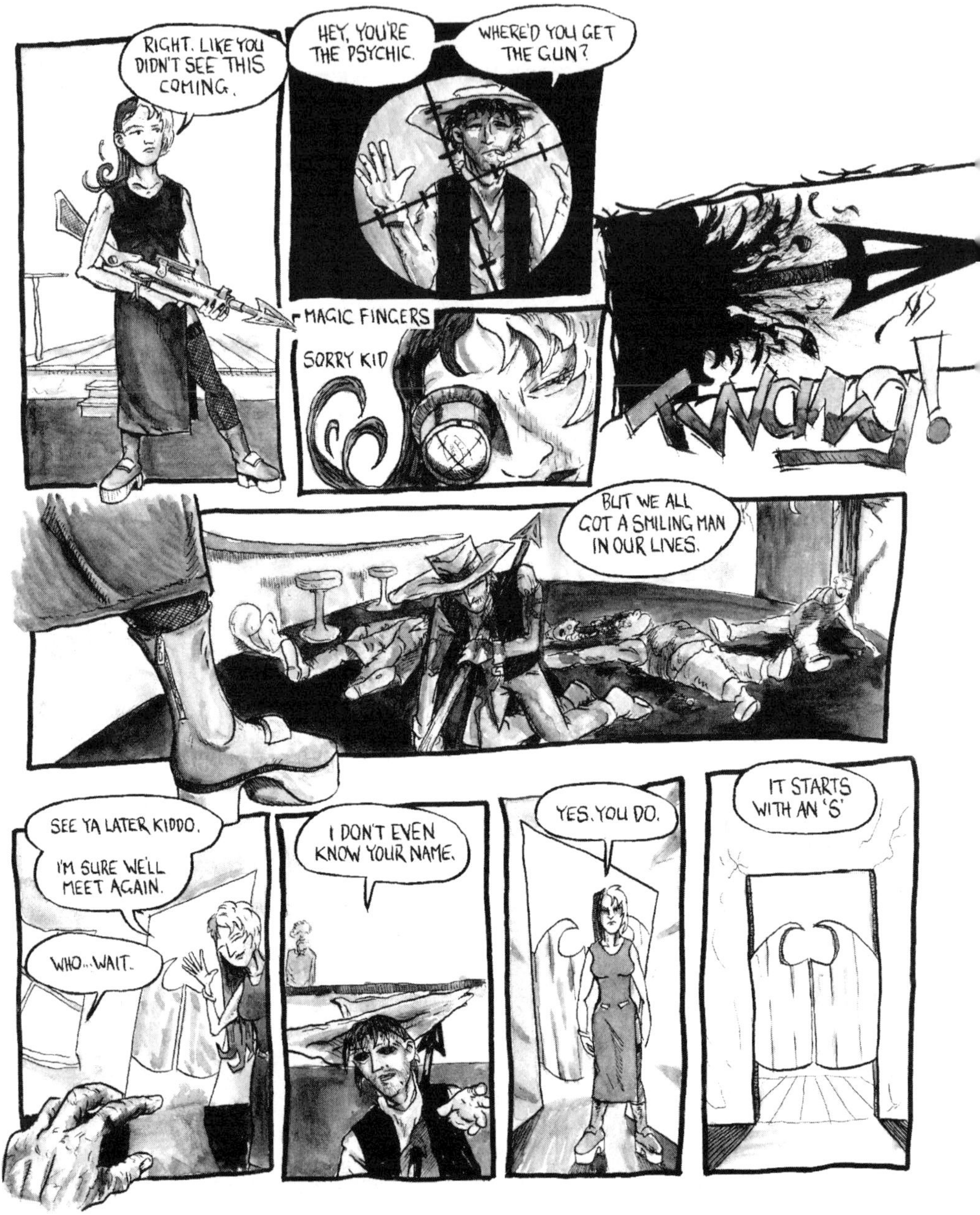
RIGHT. LIKE YOU DIDN'T SEE THIS COMING.
HEY, YOU'RE THE PSYCHIC.
WHERE'D YOU GET THE GUN?
MAGIC FINGERS
SORRY KID
TWANG!
BUT WE ALL GOT A SMILING MAN IN OUR LIVES.
SEE YA LATER KIDDO.
I'M SURE WE'LL MEET AGAIN.
WHO... WAIT.
I DON'T EVEN KNOW YOUR NAME.
YES. YOU DO.
IT STARTS WITH AN 'S'

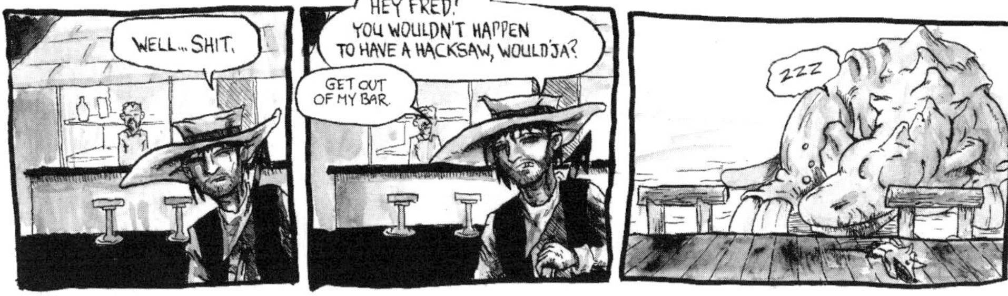
WELL... SHIT.
HEY FRED! YOU WOULDN'T HAPPEN TO HAVE A HACKSAW, WOULD'JA?
GET OUT OF MY BAR.
ZZZ

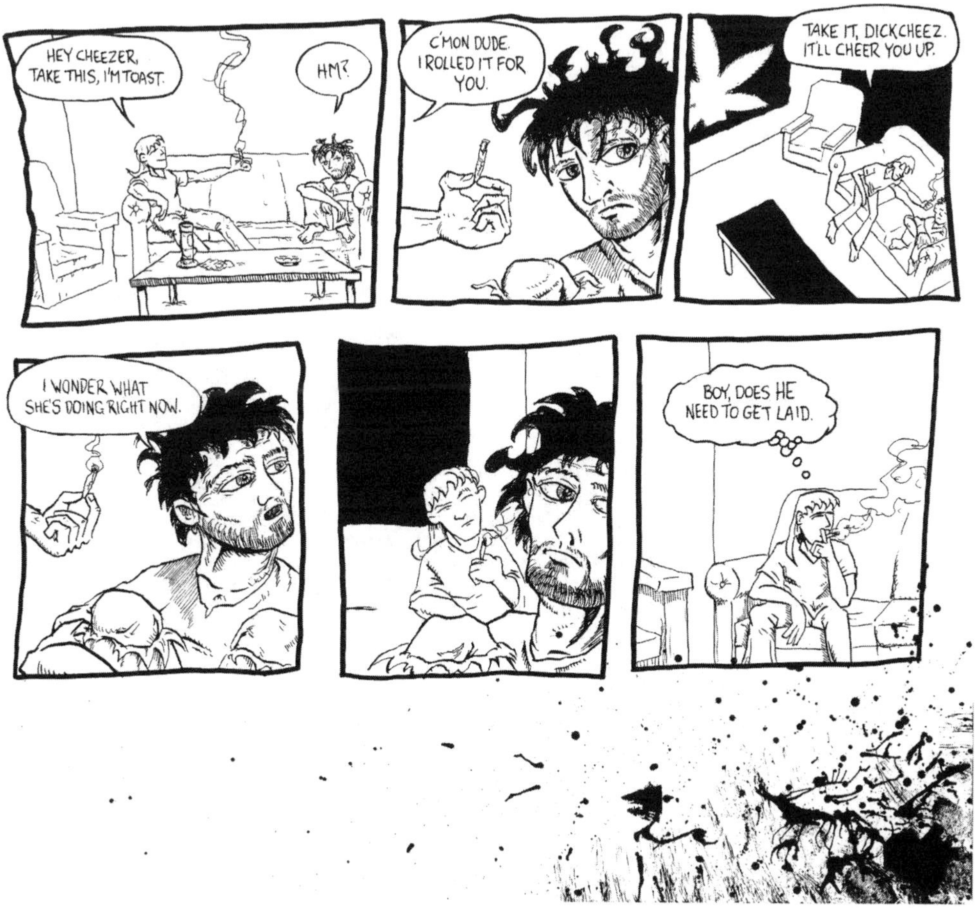
HEY CHEEZER, TAKE THIS, I'M TOAST.
HM?
C'MON DUDE. I ROLLED IT FOR YOU.
TAKE IT, DICKCHEEZ. IT'LL CHEER YOU UP.
I WONDER WHAT SHE'S DOING RIGHT NOW.
BOY, DOES HE NEED TO GET LAID.

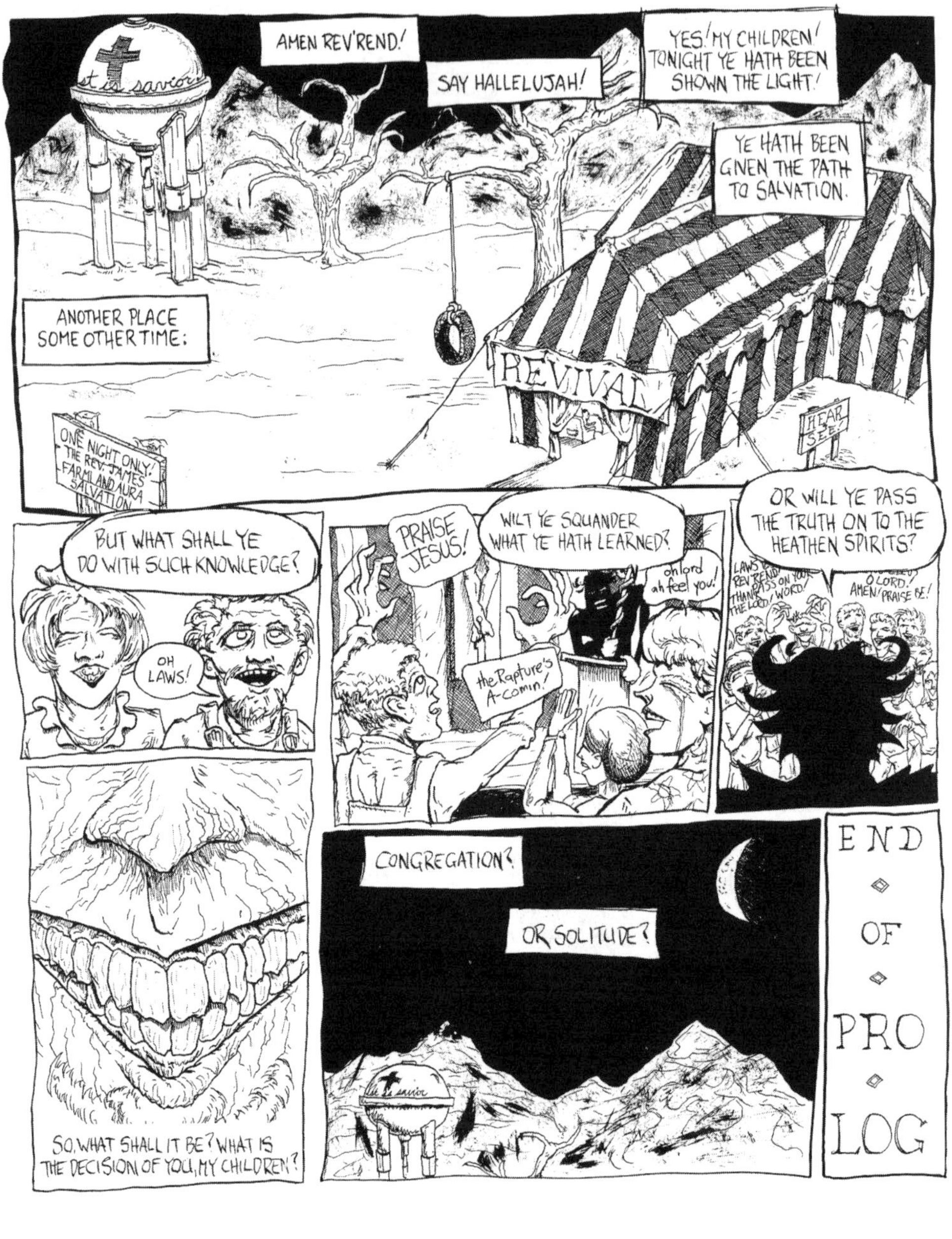

AMEN REV'REND!
SAY HALLELUJAH!
YES! MY CHILDREN! TONIGHT YE HATH BEEN SHOWN THE LIGHT!
YE HATH BEEN GIVEN THE PATH TO SALVATION.
ANOTHER PLACE SOME OTHER TIME:
REVIVAL
ONE NIGHT ONLY! THE REV. JAMES FARMLAND AURA SALVATION
HEAR SEE!
BUT WHAT SHALL YE DO WITH SUCH KNOWLEDGE?
OH LAWS!
PRAISE JESUS!
WILT YE SQUANDER WHAT YE HATH LEARNED?
oh lord ah feel you!
the Rapture's A-comin!
OR WILL YE PASS THE TRUTH ON TO THE HEATHEN SPIRITS?
LAWS REV'REND!
THANK THE LORD!
PASS ON YOUR WORD!
O LORD!
AMEN!
PRAISE BE!
SO, WHAT SHALL IT BE? WHAT IS THE DECISION OF YOU, MY CHILDREN?
CONGREGATION?
OR SOLITUDE?
END OF PRO LOG

PLASTIC FARM

PART ONE
SOWING SEEDS ON FERTILE SOIL

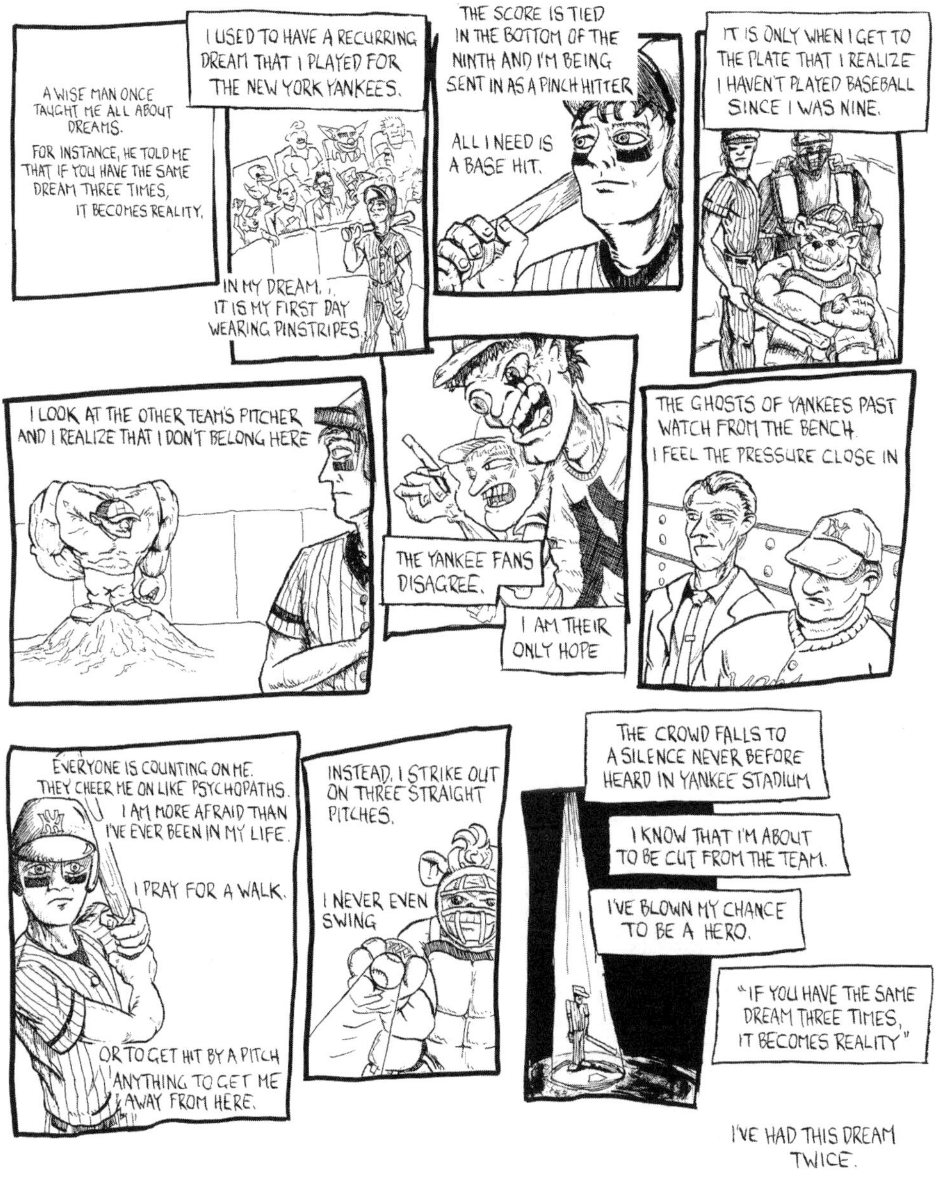
A WISE MAN ONCE TAUGHT ME ALL ABOUT DREAMS.
FOR INSTANCE, HE TOLD ME THAT IF YOU HAVE THE SAME DREAM THREE TIMES, IT BECOMES REALITY.
I USED TO HAVE A RECURRING DREAM THAT I PLAYED FOR THE NEW YORK YANKEES.
IN MY DREAM, IT IS MY FIRST DAY WEARING PINSTRIPES.
THE SCORE IS TIED IN THE BOTTOM OF THE NINTH AND I'M BEING SENT IN AS A PINCH HITTER
ALL I NEED IS A BASE HIT.
IT IS ONLY WHEN I GET TO THE PLATE THAT I REALIZE I HAVEN'T PLAYED BASEBALL SINCE I WAS NINE.
I LOOK AT THE OTHER TEAM'S PITCHER AND I REALIZE THAT I DON'T BELONG HERE
THE YANKEE FANS DISAGREE.
I AM THEIR ONLY HOPE
THE GHOSTS OF YANKEES PAST WATCH FROM THE BENCH.
I FEEL THE PRESSURE CLOSE IN
EVERYONE IS COUNTING ON ME. THEY CHEER ME ON LIKE PSYCHOPATHS.
I AM MORE AFRAID THAN I'VE EVER BEEN IN MY LIFE.
I PRAY FOR A WALK.
OR TO GET HIT BY A PITCH
ANYTHING TO GET ME AWAY FROM HERE.
INSTEAD, I STRIKE OUT ON THREE STRAIGHT PITCHES.
I NEVER EVEN SWING
THE CROWD FALLS TO A SILENCE NEVER BEFORE HEARD IN YANKEE STADIUM
I KNOW THAT I'M ABOUT TO BE CUT FROM THE TEAM.
I'VE BLOWN MY CHANCE TO BE A HERO.
"IF YOU HAVE THE SAME DREAM THREE TIMES, IT BECOMES REALITY"
I'VE HAD THIS DREAM TWICE.

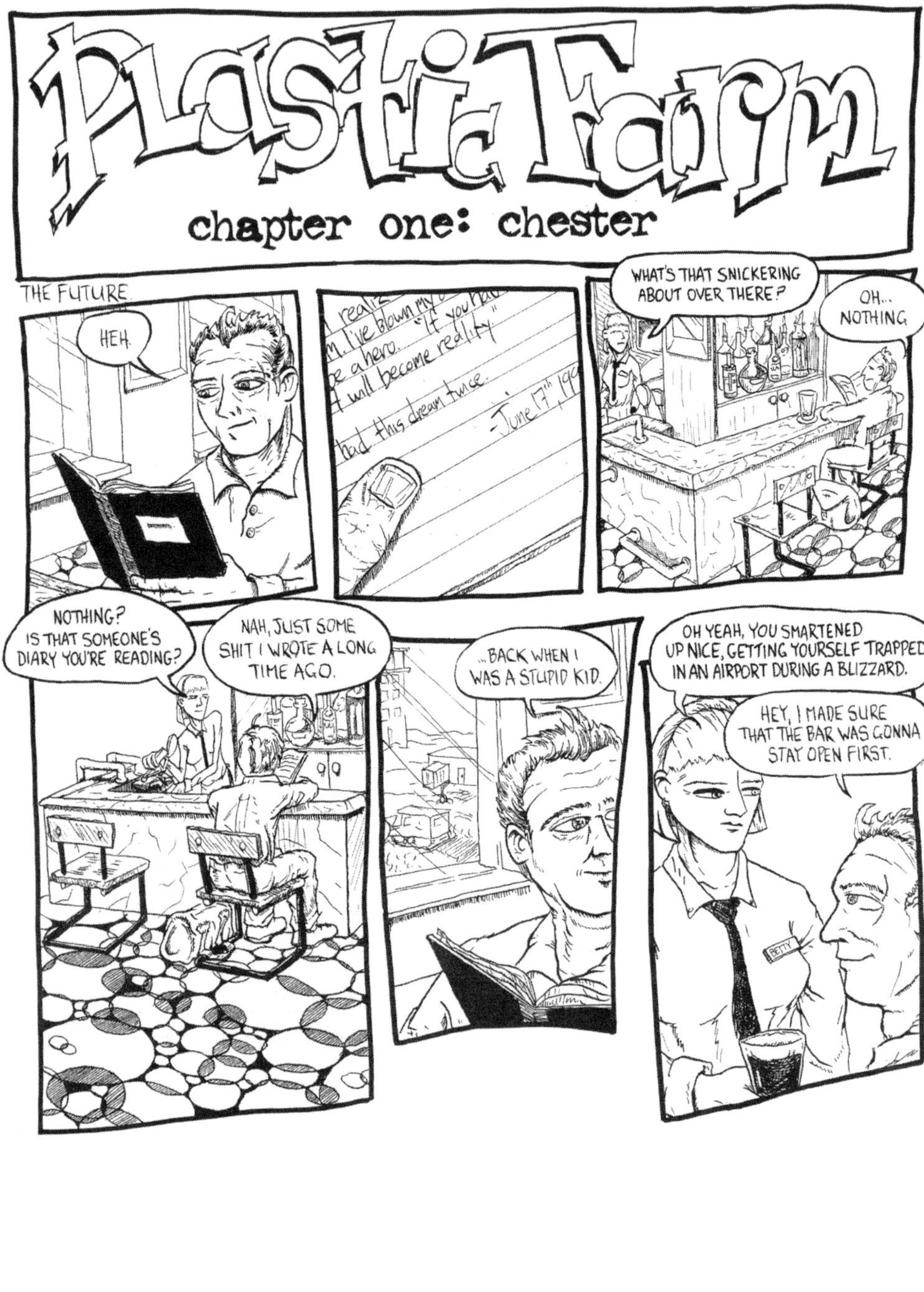
Plastic Farm
chapter one: chester
THE FUTURE.
HEH.
will become reality"
had this dream twice.
-June 17th
WHAT'S THAT SNICKERING ABOUT OVER THERE?
OH... NOTHING
NOTHING? IS THAT SOMEONE'S DIARY YOU'RE READING?
NAH, JUST SOME SHIT I WROTE A LONG TIME AGO.
...BACK WHEN I WAS A STUPID KID.
OH YEAH, YOU SMARTENED UP NICE, GETTING YOURSELF TRAPPED IN AN AIRPORT DURING A BLIZZARD.
HEY, I MADE SURE THAT THE BAR WAS GONNA STAY OPEN FIRST.
BETTY

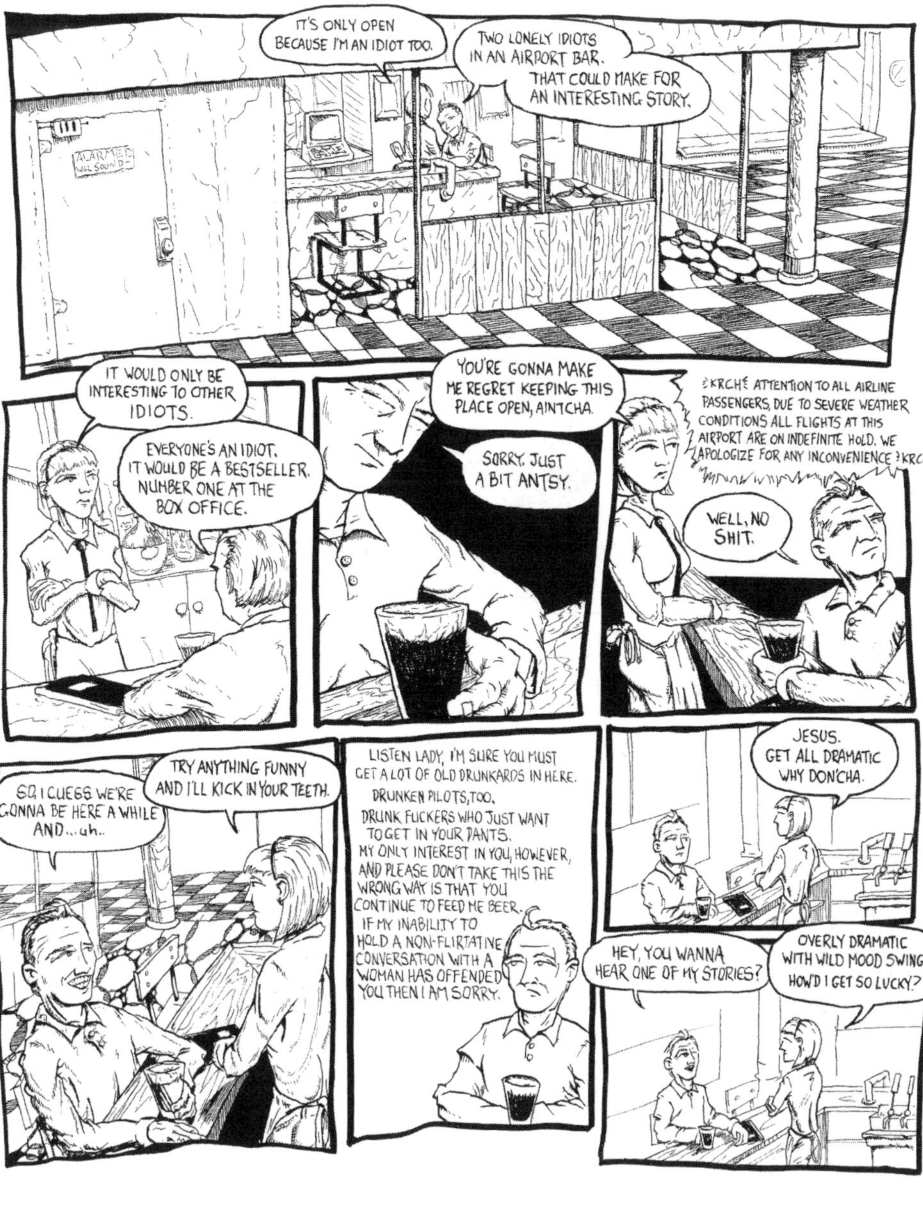
IT'S ONLY OPEN BECAUSE I'M AN IDIOT TOO.
TWO LONELY IDIOTS IN AN AIRPORT BAR.
THAT COULD MAKE FOR AN INTERESTING STORY.
ALARMED WILL SOUND
IT WOULD ONLY BE INTERESTING TO OTHER IDIOTS.
EVERYONE'S AN IDIOT. IT WOULD BE A BESTSELLER. NUMBER ONE AT THE BOX OFFICE.
YOU'RE GONNA MAKE ME REGRET KEEPING THIS PLACE OPEN, AINTCHA.
SORRY. JUST A BIT ANTSY.
KRCH ATTENTION TO ALL AIRLINE PASSENGERS, DUE TO SEVERE WEATHER CONDITIONS ALL FLIGHTS AT THIS AIRPORT ARE ON INDEFINITE HOLD. WE APOLOGIZE FOR ANY INCONVENIENCE KRCH
WELL, NO SHIT.
SO, I GUESS WE'RE GONNA BE HERE A WHILE AND...uh..
TRY ANYTHING FUNNY AND I'LL KICK IN YOUR TEETH.
LISTEN LADY, I'M SURE YOU MUST GET A LOT OF OLD DRUNKARDS IN HERE.
DRUNKEN PILOTS, TOO.
DRUNK FUCKERS WHO JUST WANT TO GET IN YOUR PANTS.
MY ONLY INTEREST IN YOU, HOWEVER, AND PLEASE DON'T TAKE THIS THE WRONG WAY IS THAT YOU CONTINUE TO FEED ME BEER.
IF MY INABILITY TO HOLD A NON-FLIRTATIVE CONVERSATION WITH A WOMAN HAS OFFENDED YOU THEN I AM SORRY.
JESUS. GET ALL DRAMATIC WHY DON'CHA.
HEY, YOU WANNA HEAR ONE OF MY STORIES?
OVERLY DRAMATIC WITH WILD MOOD SWINGS. HOW'D I GET SO LUCKY?

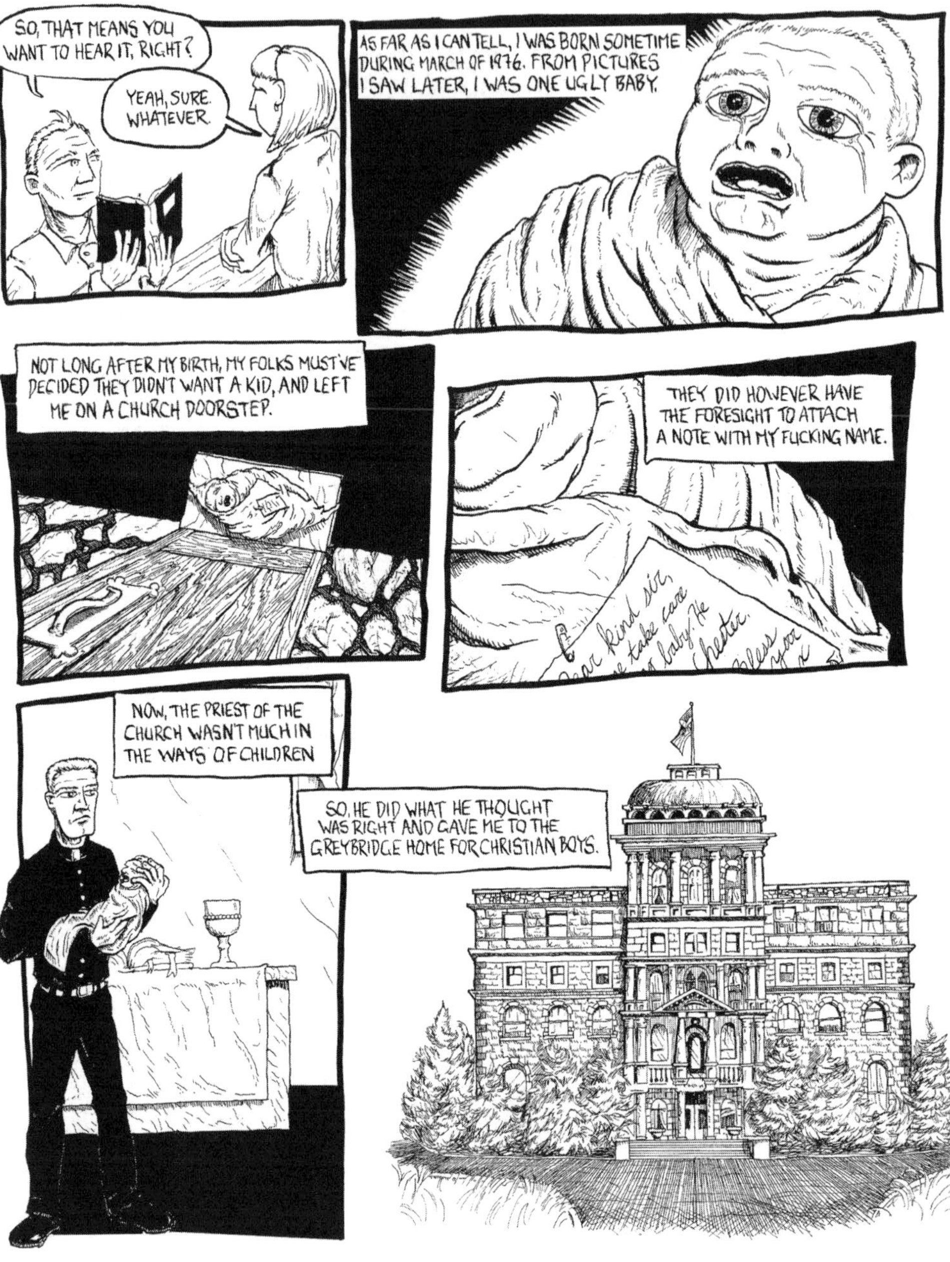
SO, THAT MEANS YOU WANT TO HEAR IT, RIGHT?
YEAH, SURE. WHATEVER.
AS FAR AS I CAN TELL, I WAS BORN SOMETIME DURING MARCH OF 1976. FROM PICTURES I SAW LATER, I WAS ONE UGLY BABY.
NOT LONG AFTER MY BIRTH, MY FOLKS MUST'VE DECIDED THEY DIDN'T WANT A KID, AND LEFT ME ON A CHURCH DOORSTEP.
THEY DID HOWEVER HAVE THE FORESIGHT TO ATTACH A NOTE WITH MY FUCKING NAME.
NOW, THE PRIEST OF THE CHURCH WASN'T MUCH IN THE WAYS OF CHILDREN
SO, HE DID WHAT HE THOUGHT WAS RIGHT AND GAVE ME TO THE GREYBRIDGE HOME FOR CHRISTIAN BOYS.

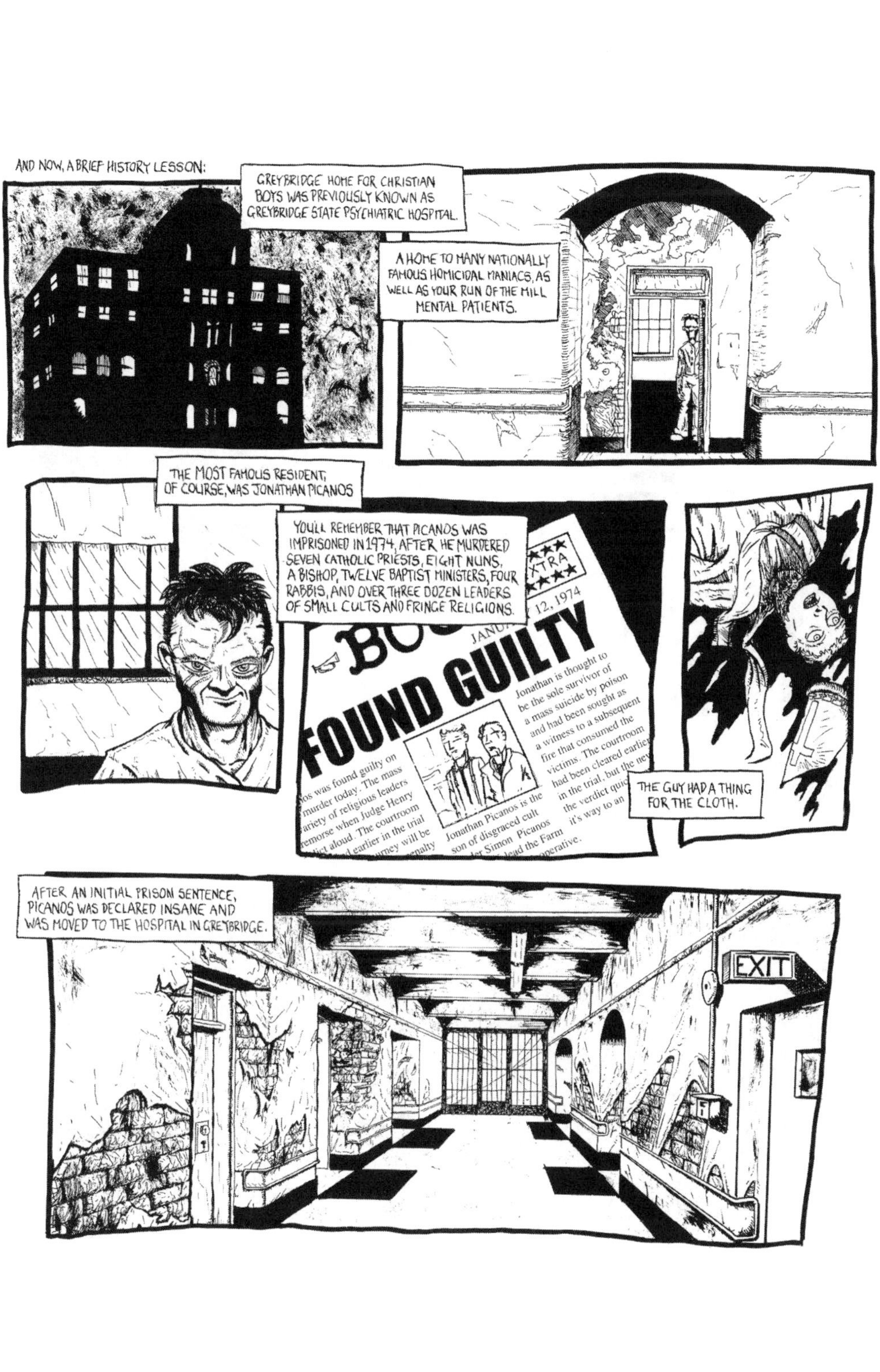
AND NOW, A BRIEF HISTORY LESSON:
GREYBRIDGE HOME FOR CHRISTIAN BOYS WAS PREVIOUSLY KNOWN AS GREYBRIDGE STATE PSYCHIATRIC HOSPITAL.
A HOME TO MANY NATIONALLY FAMOUS HOMICIDAL MANIACS, AS WELL AS YOUR RUN OF THE MILL MENTAL PATIENTS.
THE MOST FAMOUS RESIDENT, OF COURSE, WAS JONATHAN PICANOS
YOU'LL REMEMBER THAT PICANOS WAS IMPRISONED IN 1974, AFTER HE MURDERED SEVEN CATHOLIC PRIESTS, EIGHT NUNS, A BISHOP, TWELVE BAPTIST MINISTERS, FOUR RABBIS, AND OVER THREE DOZEN LEADERS OF SMALL CULTS AND FRINGE RELIGIONS.
12, 1974
FOUND GUILTY
Jonathan is thought to be the sole survivor of a mass suicide by poison and had been sought as a witness to a subsequent fire that consumed the victims. The courtroom had been cleared earlie
murder today. The mass
Jonathan Picanos is the son of disgraced cult
THE GUY HAD A THING FOR THE CLOTH.
AFTER AN INITIAL PRISON SENTENCE, PICANOS WAS DECLARED INSANE AND WAS MOVED TO THE HOSPITAL IN GREYBRIDGE.
EXIT

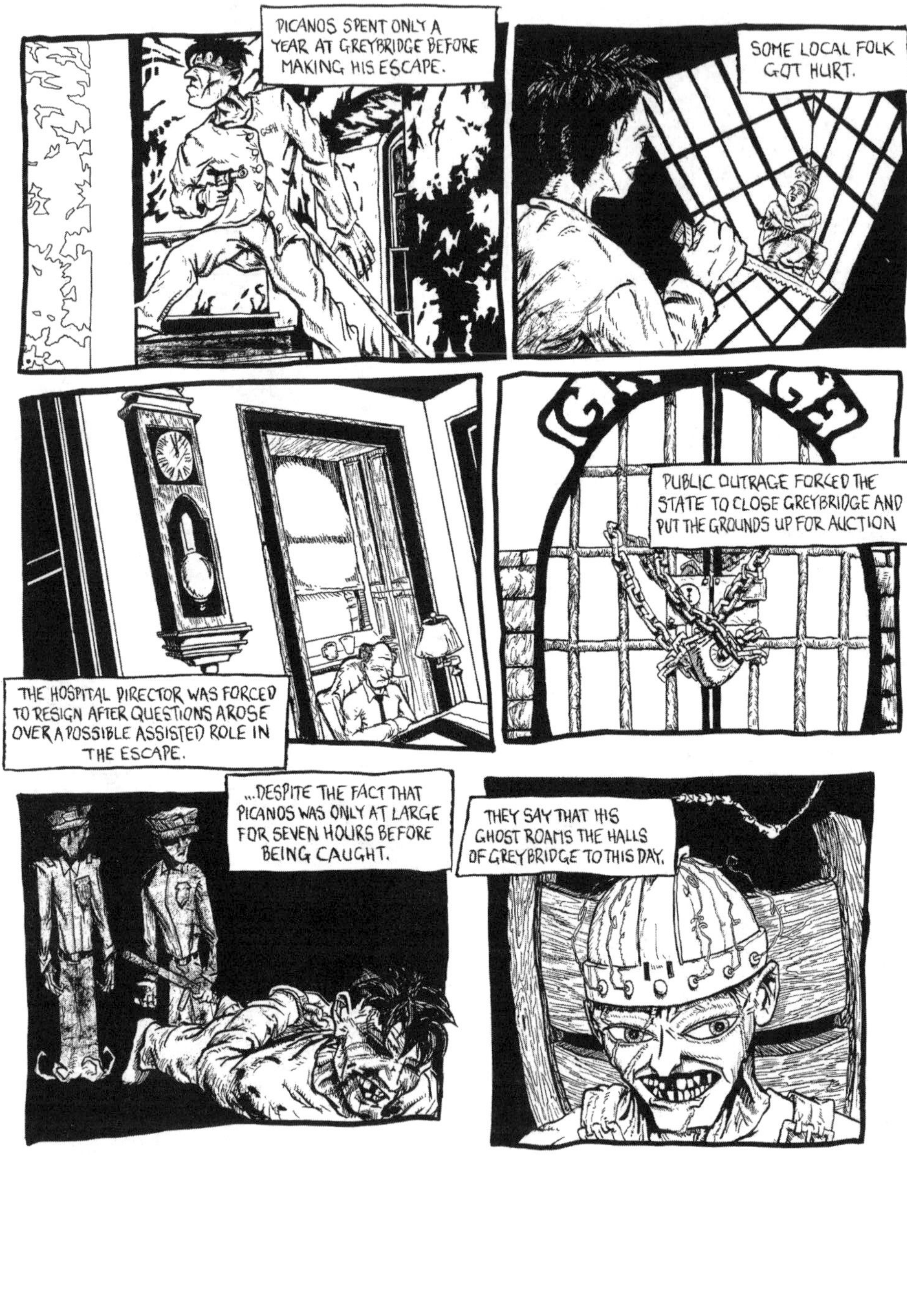
PICANOS SPENT ONLY A YEAR AT GREYBRIDGE BEFORE MAKING HIS ESCAPE.
SOME LOCAL FOLK GOT HURT.
THE HOSPITAL DIRECTOR WAS FORCED TO RESIGN AFTER QUESTIONS AROSE OVER A POSSIBLE ASSISTED ROLE IN THE ESCAPE.
PUBLIC OUTRAGE FORCED THE STATE TO CLOSE GREYBRIDGE AND PUT THE GROUNDS UP FOR AUCTION
...DESPITE THE FACT THAT PICANOS WAS ONLY AT LARGE FOR SEVEN HOURS BEFORE BEING CAUGHT.
THEY SAY THAT HIS GHOST ROAMS THE HALLS OF GREYBRIDGE TO THIS DAY.

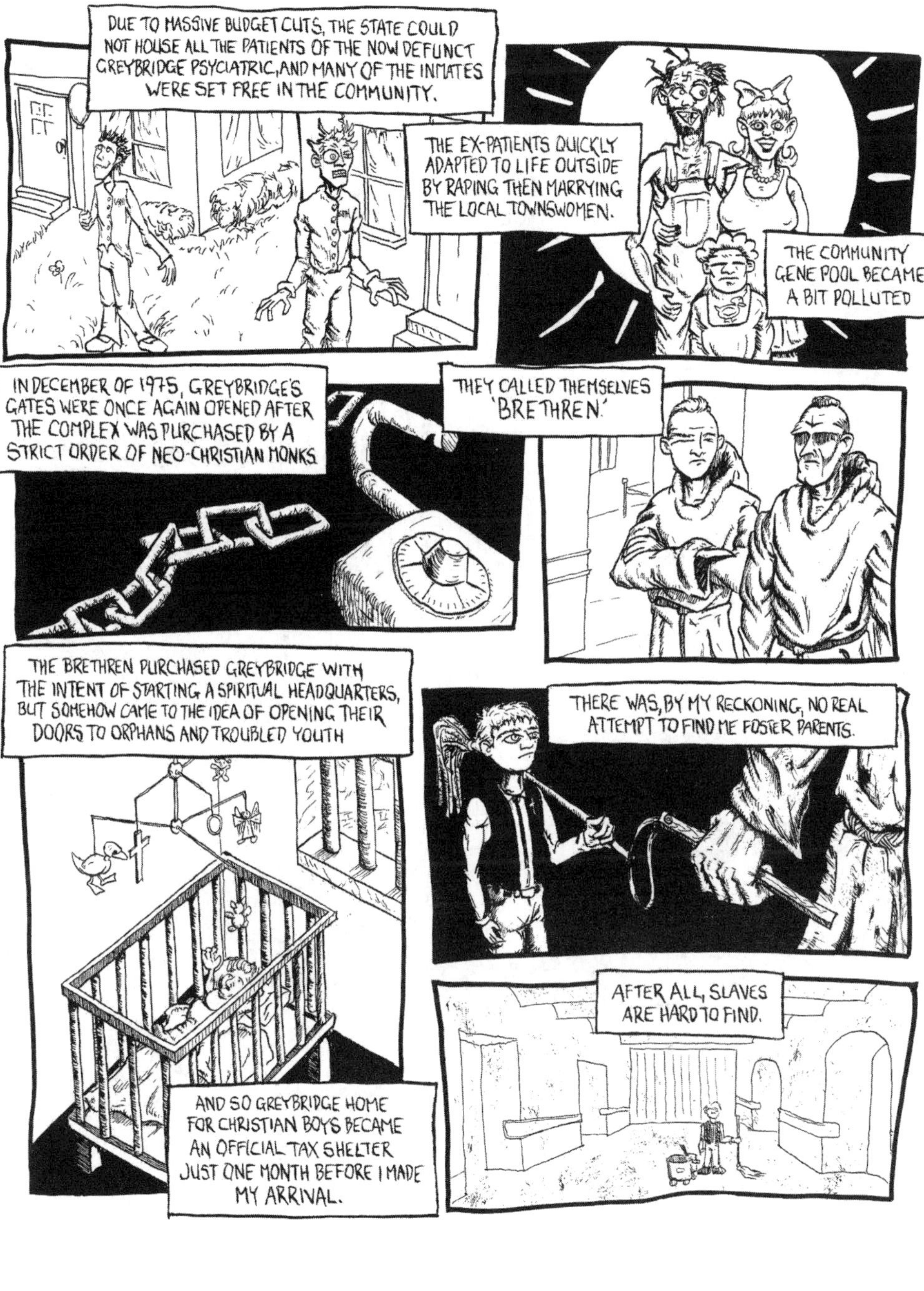
DUE TO MASSIVE BUDGET CUTS, THE STATE COULD NOT HOUSE ALL THE PATIENTS OF THE NOW DEFUNCT GREYBRIDGE PSYCIATRIC, AND MANY OF THE INMATES WERE SET FREE IN THE COMMUNITY.
THE EX-PATIENTS QUICKLY ADAPTED TO LIFE OUTSIDE BY RAPING THEN MARRYING THE LOCAL TOWNSWOMEN.
THE COMMUNITY GENE POOL BECAME A BIT POLLUTED
IN DECEMBER OF 1975, GREYBRIDGE'S GATES WERE ONCE AGAIN OPENED AFTER THE COMPLEX WAS PURCHASED BY A STRICT ORDER OF NEO-CHRISTIAN MONKS
THEY CALLED THEMSELVES 'BRETHREN.'
THE BRETHREN PURCHASED GREYBRIDGE WITH THE INTENT OF STARTING A SPIRITUAL HEADQUARTERS, BUT SOMEHOW CAME TO THE IDEA OF OPENING THEIR DOORS TO ORPHANS AND TROUBLED YOUTH
AND SO GREYBRIDGE HOME FOR CHRISTIAN BOYS BECAME AN OFFICIAL TAX SHELTER JUST ONE MONTH BEFORE I MADE MY ARRIVAL.
THERE WAS, BY MY RECKONING, NO REAL ATTEMPT TO FIND ME FOSTER PARENTS.
AFTER ALL, SLAVES ARE HARD TO FIND.

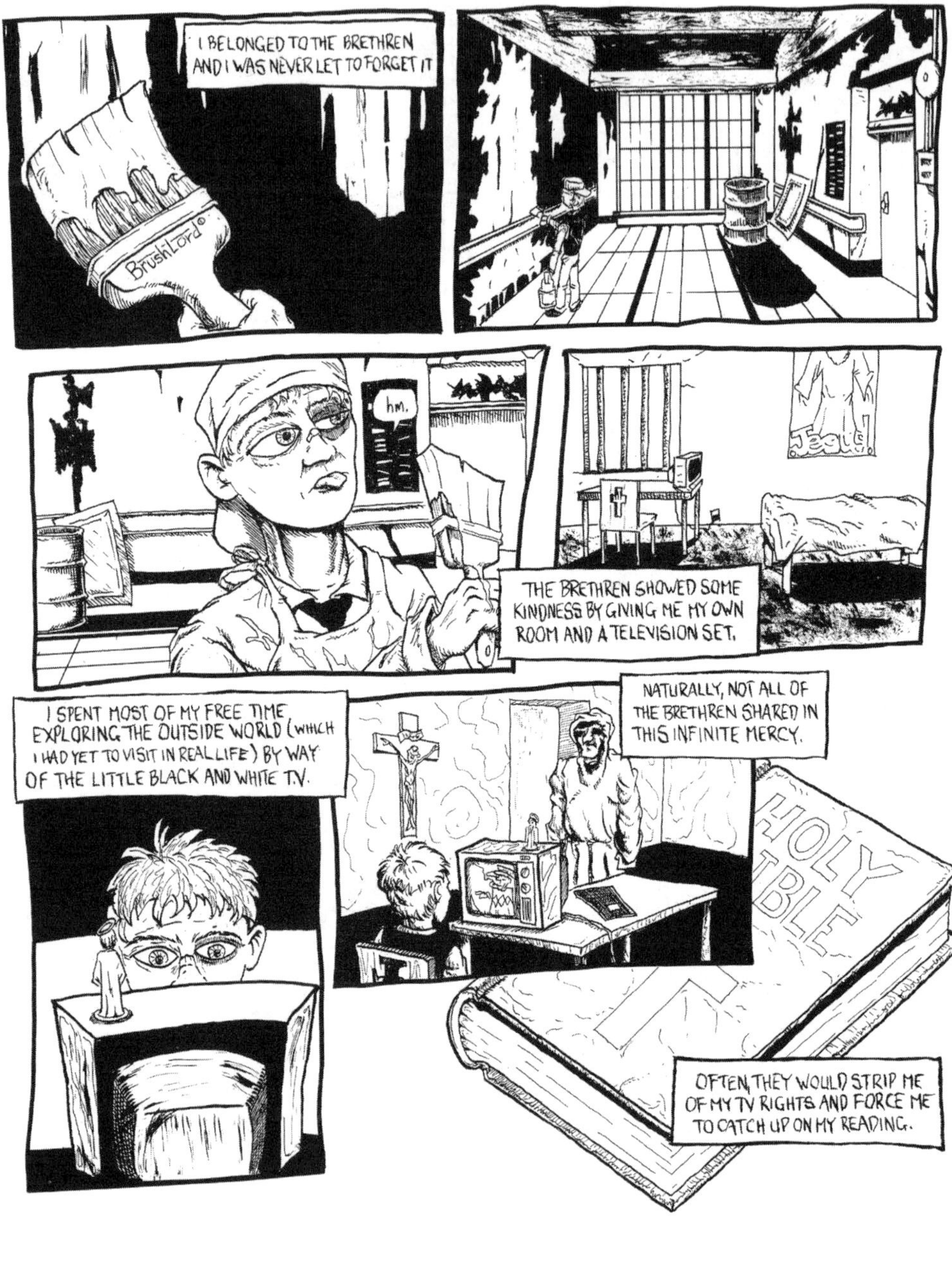
I BELONGED TO THE BRETHREN AND I WAS NEVER LET TO FORGET IT
BrushLord®
hm.
THE BRETHREN SHOWED SOME KINDNESS BY GIVING ME MY OWN ROOM AND A TELEVISION SET.
I SPENT MOST OF MY FREE TIME EXPLORING THE OUTSIDE WORLD (WHICH I HAD YET TO VISIT IN REAL LIFE) BY WAY OF THE LITTLE BLACK AND WHITE T.V.
NATURALLY, NOT ALL OF THE BRETHREN SHARED IN THIS INFINITE MERCY.
OFTEN, THEY WOULD STRIP ME OF MY TV RIGHTS AND FORCE ME TO CATCH UP ON MY READING.

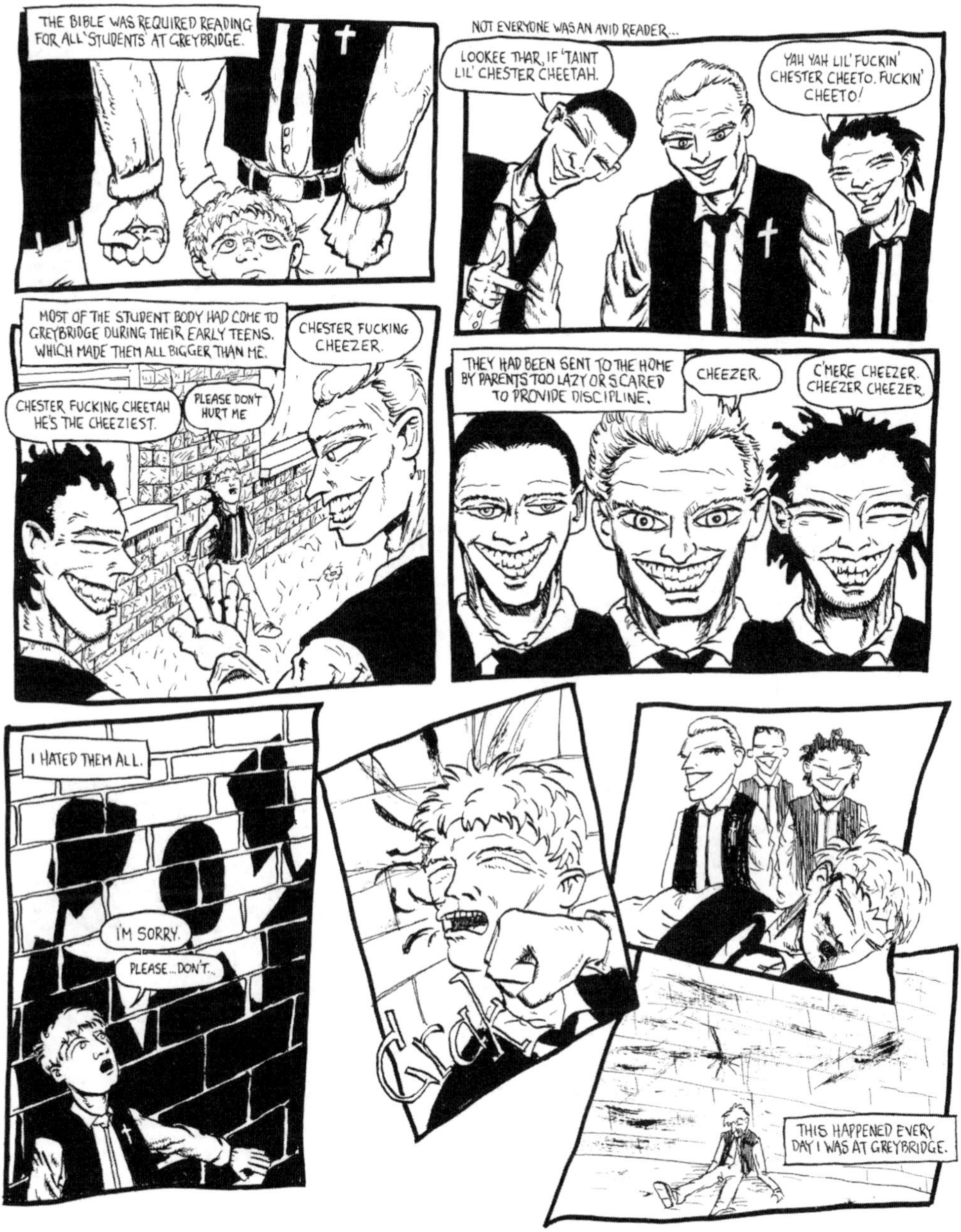
THE BIBLE WAS REQUIRED READING FOR ALL 'STUDENTS' AT GREYBRIDGE.
NOT EVERYONE WAS AN AVID READER...
LOOKEE THAR, IF 'TAINT LIL' CHESTER CHEETAH.
YAH YAH LIL' FUCKIN' CHESTER CHEETO. FUCKIN' CHEETO!
MOST OF THE STUDENT BODY HAD COME TO GREYBRIDGE DURING THEIR EARLY TEENS. WHICH MADE THEM ALL BIGGER THAN ME.
CHESTER FUCKING CHEEZER.
CHESTER FUCKING CHEETAH HE'S THE CHEEZIEST.
PLEASE DON'T HURT ME
THEY HAD BEEN SENT TO THE HOME BY PARENTS TOO LAZY OR SCARED TO PROVIDE DISCIPLINE.
CHEEZER.
C'MERE CHEEZER. CHEEZER CHEEZER.
I HATED THEM ALL.
I'M SORRY.
PLEASE...DON'T...
Crack
THIS HAPPENED EVERY DAY I WAS AT GREYBRIDGE.

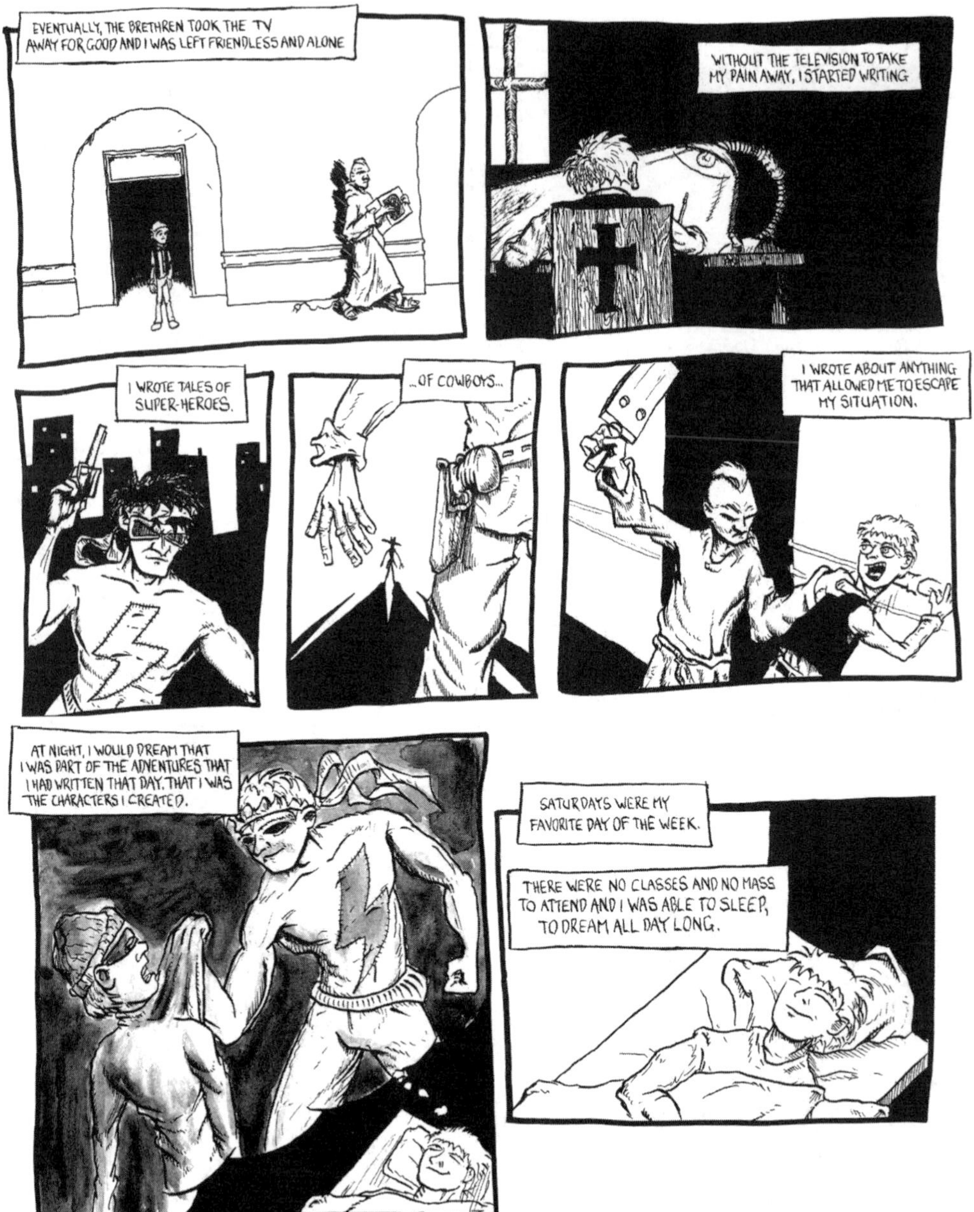
EVENTUALLY, THE BRETHREN TOOK THE TV AWAY FOR GOOD AND I WAS LEFT FRIENDLESS AND ALONE
WITHOUT THE TELEVISION TO TAKE MY PAIN AWAY, I STARTED WRITING
I WROTE TALES OF SUPER-HEROES.
...OF COWBOYS...
I WROTE ABOUT ANYTHING THAT ALLOWED ME TO ESCAPE MY SITUATION.
AT NIGHT, I WOULD DREAM THAT I WAS PART OF THE ADVENTURES THAT I HAD WRITTEN THAT DAY. THAT I WAS THE CHARACTERS I CREATED.
SATURDAYS WERE MY FAVORITE DAY OF THE WEEK.
THERE WERE NO CLASSES AND NO MASS TO ATTEND AND I WAS ABLE TO SLEEP, TO DREAM ALL DAY LONG.

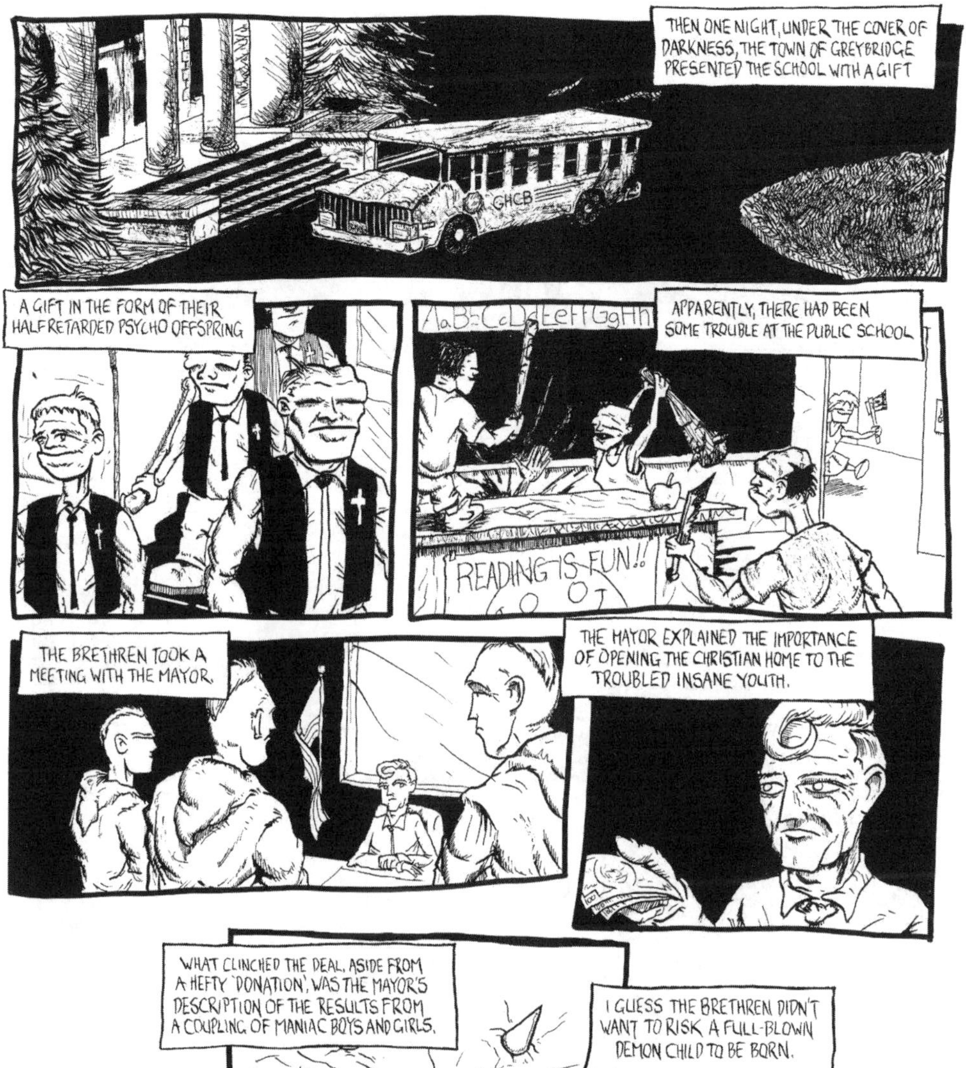
THEN ONE NIGHT, UNDER THE COVER OF DARKNESS, THE TOWN OF GREYBRIDGE PRESENTED THE SCHOOL WITH A GIFT
GHCB
A GIFT IN THE FORM OF THEIR HALF RETARDED PSYCHO OFFSPRING
APPARENTLY, THERE HAD BEEN SOME TROUBLE AT THE PUBLIC SCHOOL
AaBbCcDdEeFfGgHh
READING IS FUN!!
THE BRETHREN TOOK A MEETING WITH THE MAYOR.
THE MAYOR EXPLAINED THE IMPORTANCE OF OPENING THE CHRISTIAN HOME TO THE TROUBLED INSANE YOUTH.
WHAT CLINCHED THE DEAL, ASIDE FROM A HEFTY 'DONATION', WAS THE MAYOR'S DESCRIPTION OF THE RESULTS FROM A COUPLING OF MANIAC BOYS AND GIRLS.
I GUESS THE BRETHREN DIDN'T WANT TO RISK A FULL-BLOWN DEMON CHILD TO BE BORN.

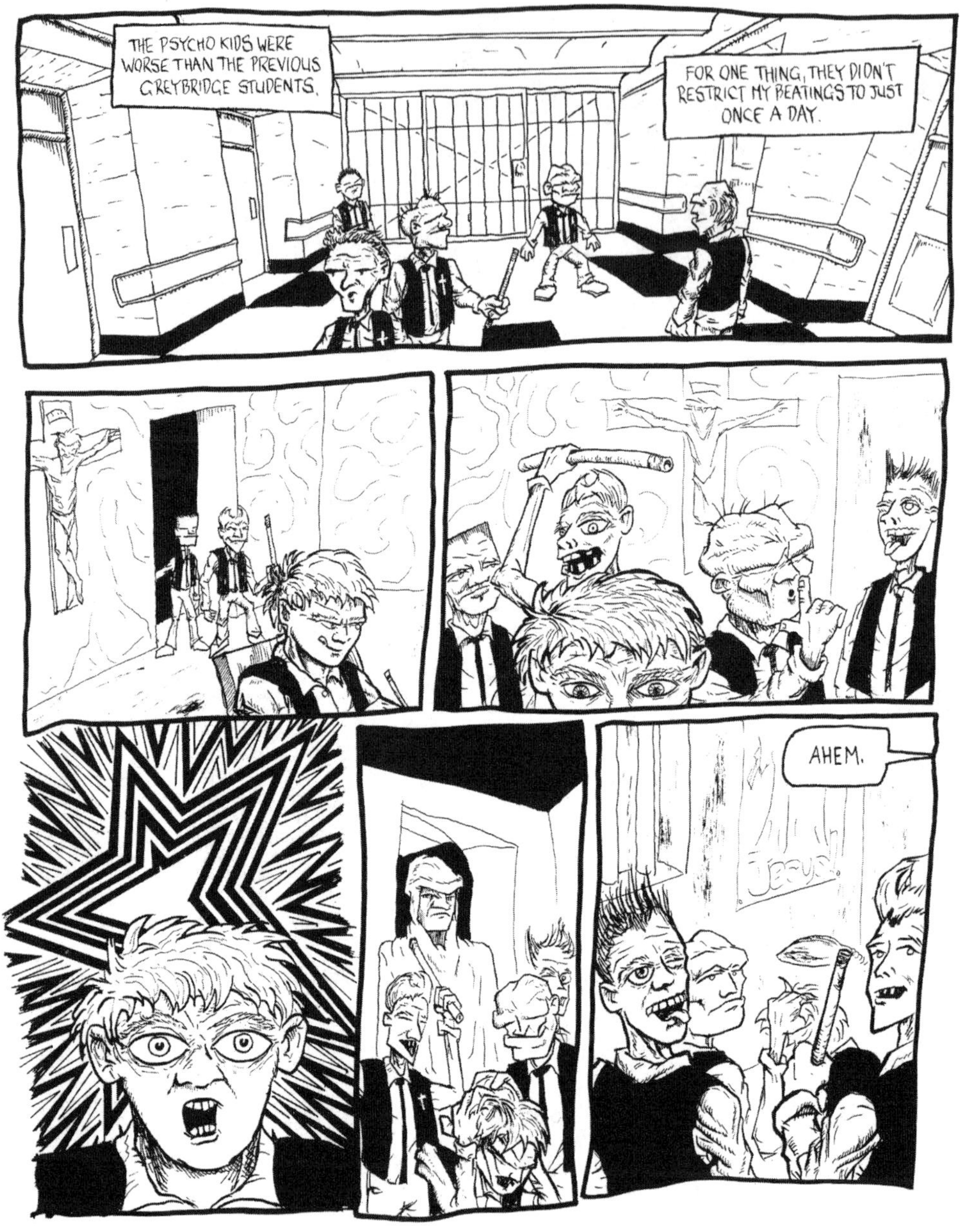
THE PSYCHO KIDS WERE WORSE THAN THE PREVIOUS GREYBRIDGE STUDENTS.
FOR ONE THING, THEY DIDN'T RESTRICT MY BEATINGS TO JUST ONCE A DAY.
AHEM.
JESUS!

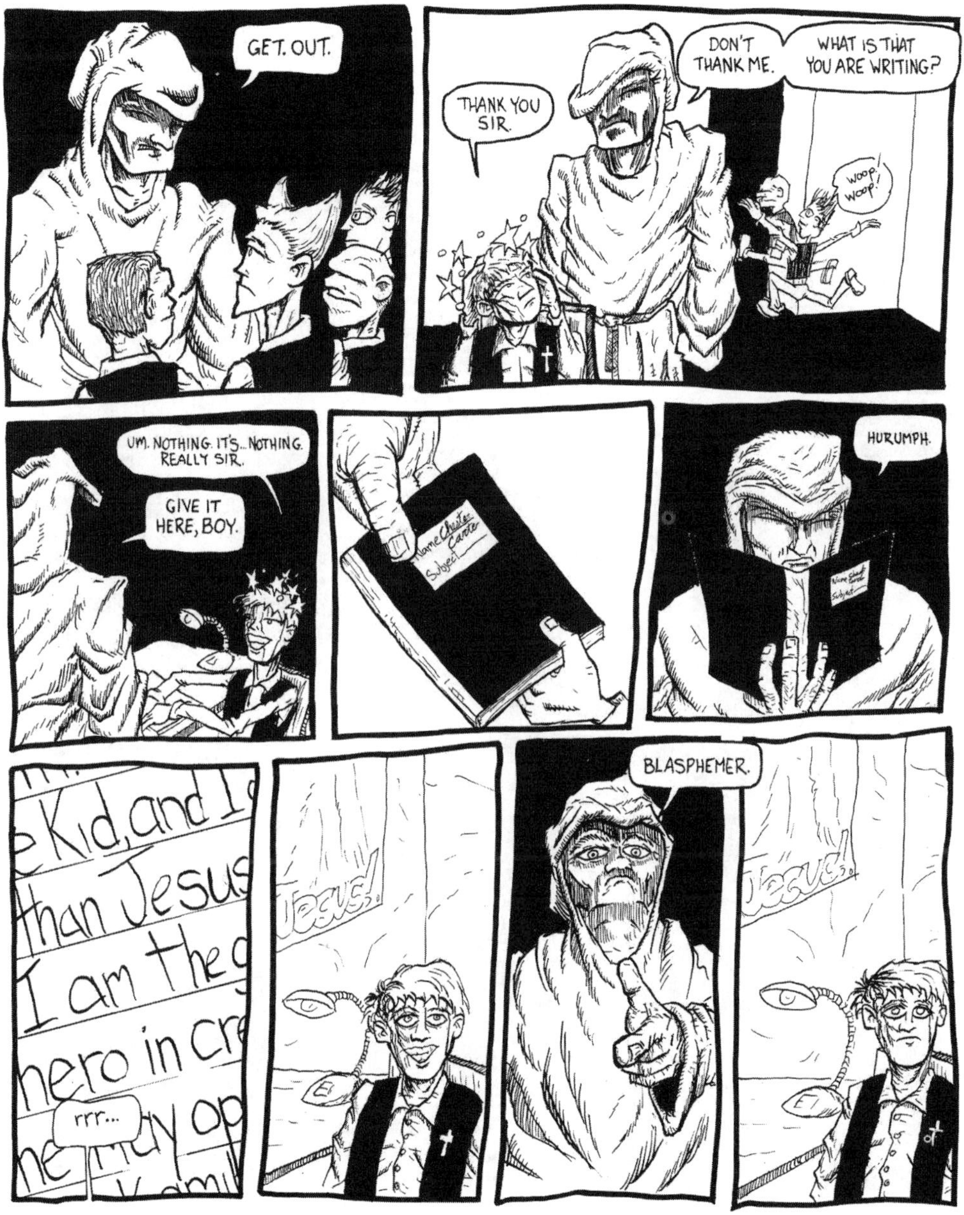
GET. OUT.
THANK YOU SIR.
DON'T THANK ME.
WHAT IS THAT YOU ARE WRITING?
woop! woop!
UM. NOTHING. IT'S...NOTHING. REALLY SIR.
GIVE IT HERE, BOY.
HURUMPH.
e Kid, and I
than Jesus
I am the g
hero in cre
ne may op
rrr...
Jesus!
BLASPHEMER.
Jesus!

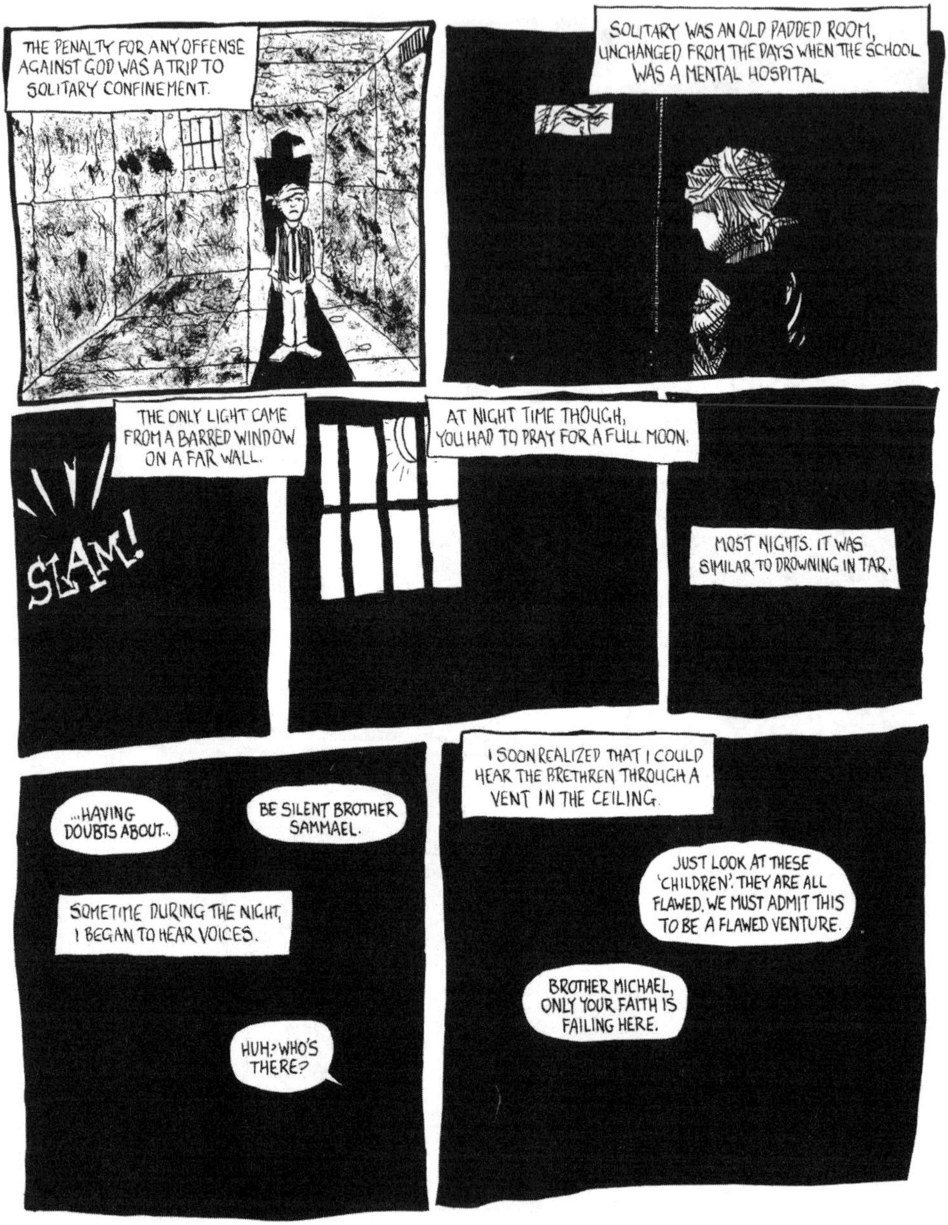
THE PENALTY FOR ANY OFFENSE AGAINST GOD WAS A TRIP TO SOLITARY CONFINEMENT.
SOLITARY WAS AN OLD PADDED ROOM, UNCHANGED FROM THE DAYS WHEN THE SCHOOL WAS A MENTAL HOSPITAL
THE ONLY LIGHT CAME FROM A BARRED WINDOW ON A FAR WALL.
SLAM!
AT NIGHT TIME THOUGH, YOU HAD TO PRAY FOR A FULL MOON.
MOST NIGHTS, IT WAS SIMILAR TO DROWNING IN TAR.
...HAVING DOUBTS ABOUT..
BE SILENT BROTHER SAMMAEL.
SOMETIME DURING THE NIGHT, I BEGAN TO HEAR VOICES.
HUH? WHO'S THERE?
I SOON REALIZED THAT I COULD HEAR THE BRETHREN THROUGH A VENT IN THE CEILING.
JUST LOOK AT THESE 'CHILDREN'. THEY ARE ALL FLAWED. WE MUST ADMIT THIS TO BE A FLAWED VENTURE.
BROTHER MICHAEL, ONLY YOUR FAITH IS FAILING HERE.

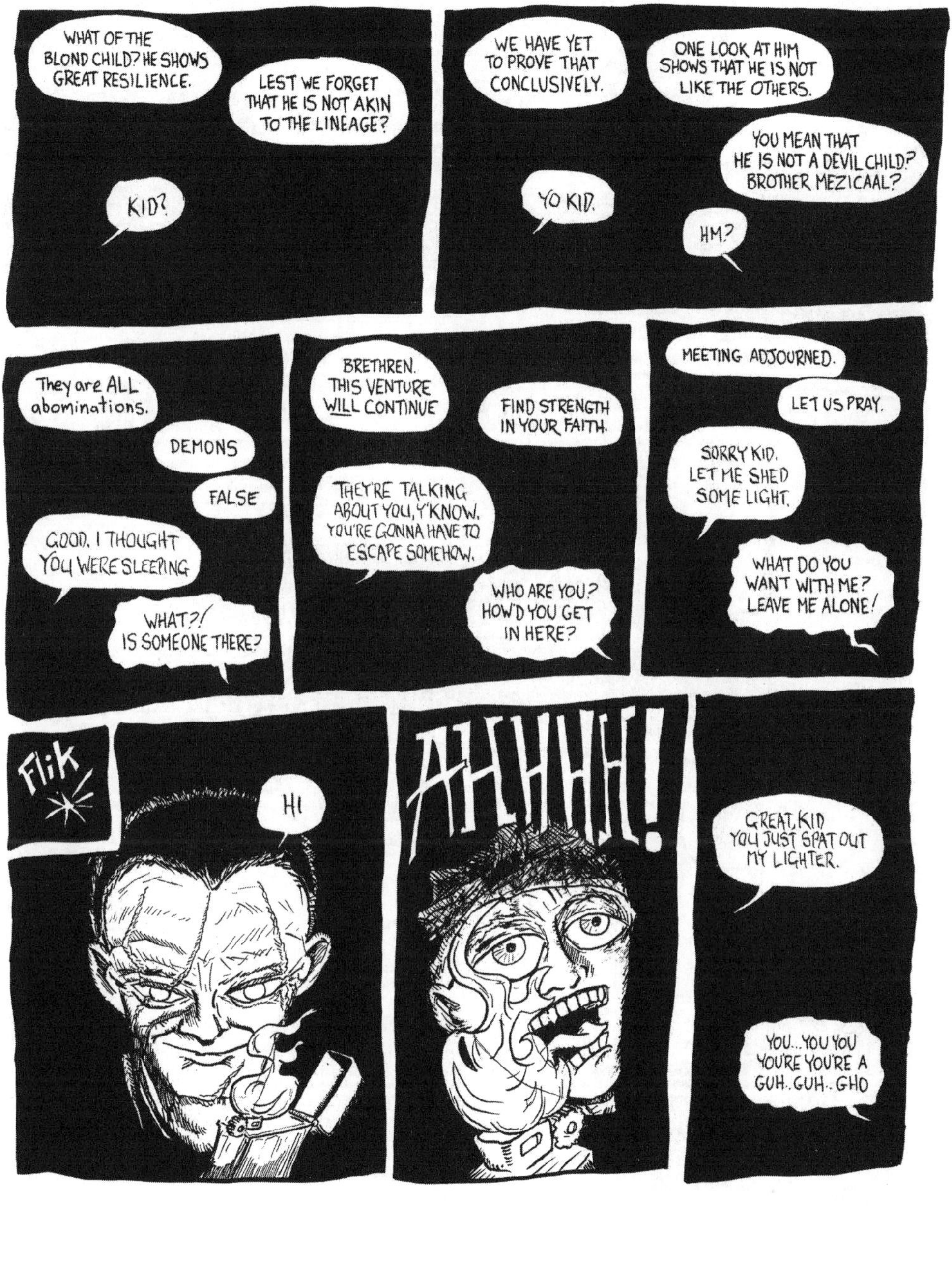
WHAT OF THE BLOND CHILD? HE SHOWS GREAT RESILIENCE.
LEST WE FORGET THAT HE IS NOT AKIN TO THE LINEAGE?
KID?
WE HAVE YET TO PROVE THAT CONCLUSIVELY.
ONE LOOK AT HIM SHOWS THAT HE IS NOT LIKE THE OTHERS.
YOU MEAN THAT HE IS NOT A DEVIL CHILD? BROTHER MEZICAAL?
YO KID.
HM?
They are ALL abominations.
DEMONS
FALSE
GOOD. I THOUGHT YOU WERE SLEEPING
WHAT?! IS SOMEONE THERE?
BRETHREN. THIS VENTURE WILL CONTINUE
FIND STRENGTH IN YOUR FAITH.
THEY'RE TALKING ABOUT YOU, Y'KNOW. YOU'RE GONNA HAVE TO ESCAPE SOMEHOW.
WHO ARE YOU? HOW'D YOU GET IN HERE?
MEETING ADJOURNED.
LET US PRAY.
SORRY KID. LET ME SHED SOME LIGHT.
WHAT DO YOU WANT WITH ME? LEAVE ME ALONE!
Flik
HI
AHHHH!
GREAT, KID YOU JUST SPAT OUT MY LIGHTER.
YOU...YOU YOU YOU'RE YOU'RE A GUH..GUH..GHO

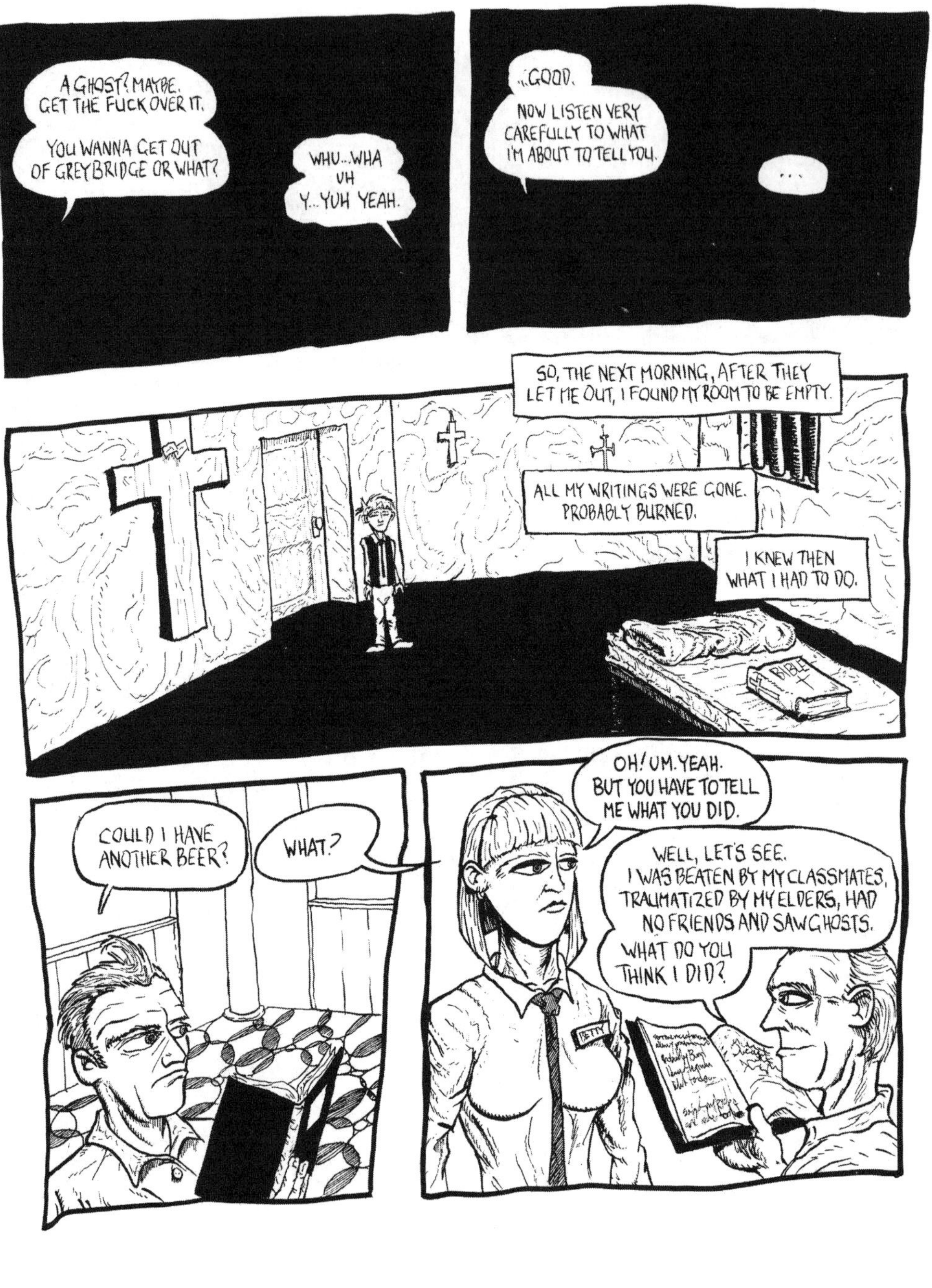
A GHOST? MAYBE. GET THE FUCK OVER IT.
YOU WANNA GET OUT OF GREYBRIDGE OR WHAT?
WHU...WHA UH Y...YUH YEAH.
...GOOD.
NOW LISTEN VERY CAREFULLY TO WHAT I'M ABOUT TO TELL YOU.
...
SO, THE NEXT MORNING, AFTER THEY LET ME OUT, I FOUND MY ROOM TO BE EMPTY.
ALL MY WRITINGS WERE GONE. PROBABLY BURNED.
I KNEW THEN WHAT I HAD TO DO.
BIBLE
COULD I HAVE ANOTHER BEER?
WHAT?
OH! UM. YEAH. BUT YOU HAVE TO TELL ME WHAT YOU DID.
WELL, LET'S SEE. I WAS BEATEN BY MY CLASSMATES, TRAUMATIZED BY MY ELDERS, HAD NO FRIENDS AND SAW GHOSTS.
WHAT DO YOU THINK I DID?
BETTY

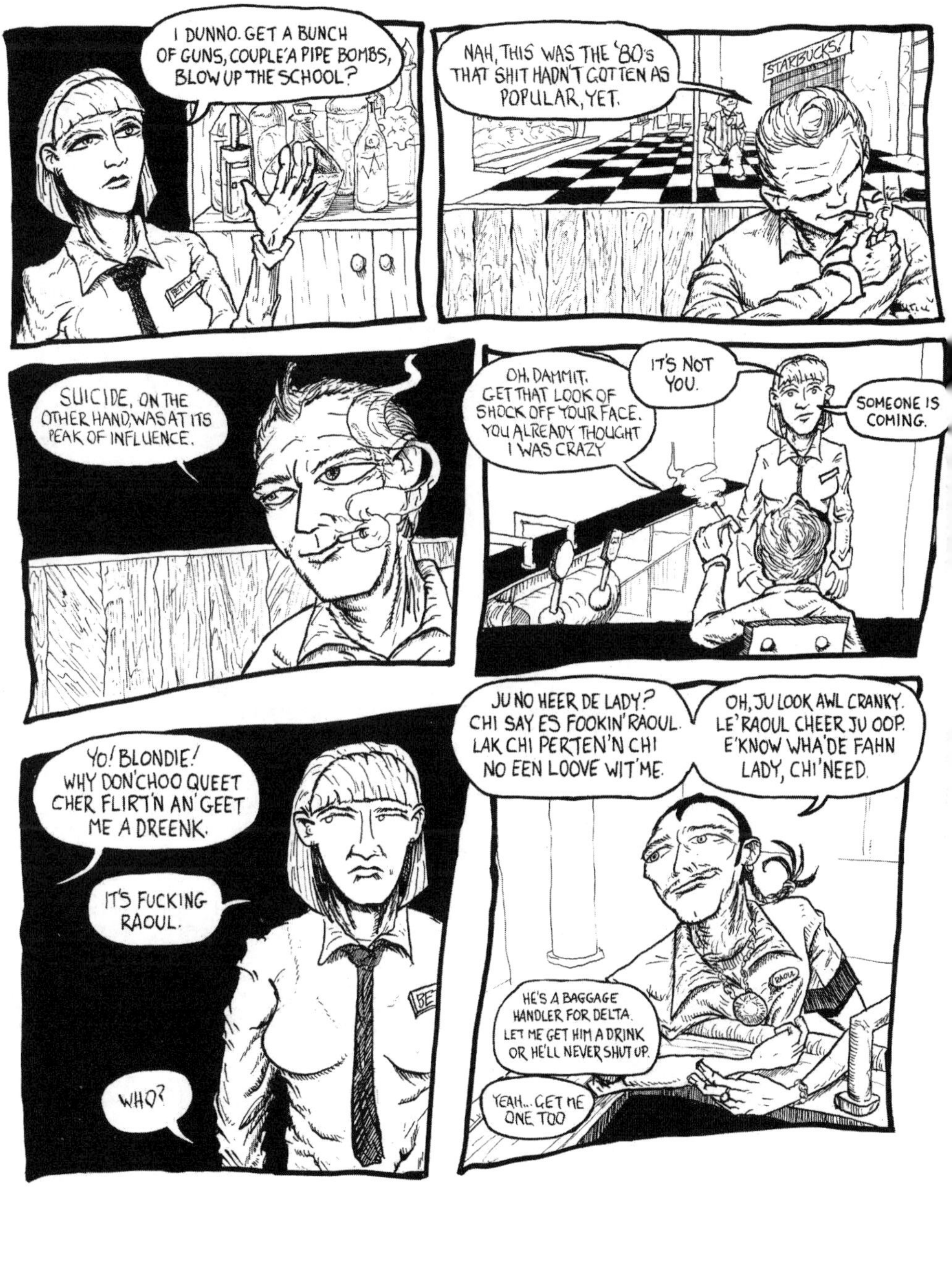
I DUNNO. GET A BUNCH OF GUNS, COUPLE'A PIPE BOMBS, BLOW UP THE SCHOOL?
BETTY
NAH, THIS WAS THE '80's THAT SHIT HADN'T GOTTEN AS POPULAR, YET.
STARBUCKS!
SUICIDE, ON THE OTHER HAND, WAS AT ITS PEAK OF INFLUENCE.
OH, DAMMIT. GET THAT LOOK OF SHOCK OFF YOUR FACE. YOU ALREADY THOUGHT I WAS CRAZY
IT'S NOT YOU.
SOMEONE IS COMING.
YO! BLONDIE! WHY DON'CHOO QUEET CHER FLIRT'N AN' GEET ME A DREENK.
IT'S FUCKING RAOUL.
WHO?
JU NO HEER DE LADY? CHI SAY ES FOOKIN' RAOUL. LAK CHI PERTEN'N CHI NO EEN LOOVE WIT'ME.
OH, JU LOOK AWL CRANKY. LE'RAOUL CHEER JU OOP. E'KNOW WHA'DE FAHN LADY, CHI'NEED.
RAOUL
HE'S A BAGGAGE HANDLER FOR DELTA. LET ME GET HIM A DRINK OR HE'LL NEVER SHUT UP.
YEAH... GET ME ONE TOO

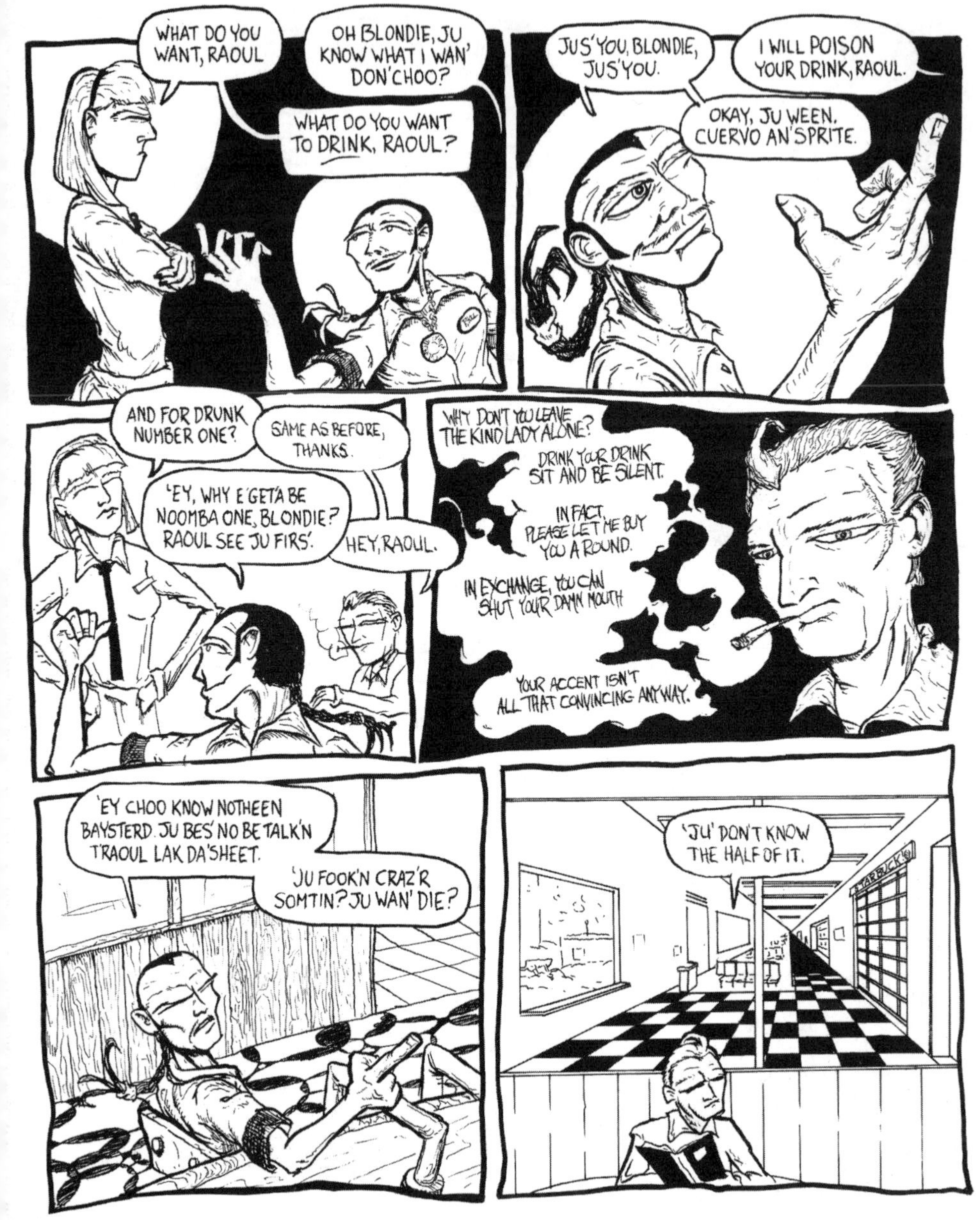
WHAT DO YOU WANT, RAOUL
OH BLONDIE, JU KNOW WHAT I WAN' DON'CHOO?
WHAT DO YOU WANT TO DRINK, RAOUL?
JUS' YOU, BLONDIE, JUS' YOU.
I WILL POISON YOUR DRINK, RAOUL.
OKAY, JU WEEN. CUERVO AN' SPRITE.
AND FOR DRUNK NUMBER ONE?
SAME AS BEFORE, THANKS.
'EY, WHY E' GET'A BE NOOMBA ONE, BLONDIE? RAOUL SEE JU FIRS'.
HEY, RAOUL.
WHY DON'T YOU LEAVE THE KIND LADY ALONE?
DRINK YOUR DRINK SIT AND BE SILENT.
IN FACT, PLEASE LET ME BUY YOU A ROUND.
IN EXCHANGE, YOU CAN SHUT YOUR DAMN MOUTH
YOUR ACCENT ISN'T ALL THAT CONVINCING ANYWAY.
'EY CHOO KNOW NOTHEEN BAYSTERD. JU BES' NO BE TALK'N T'RAOUL LAK DA' SHEET.
'JU FOOK'N CRAZ'R SOMTIN? JU WAN' DIE?
'JU' DON'T KNOW THE HALF OF IT.

PLASTIC FARM

chapter two: people's choice

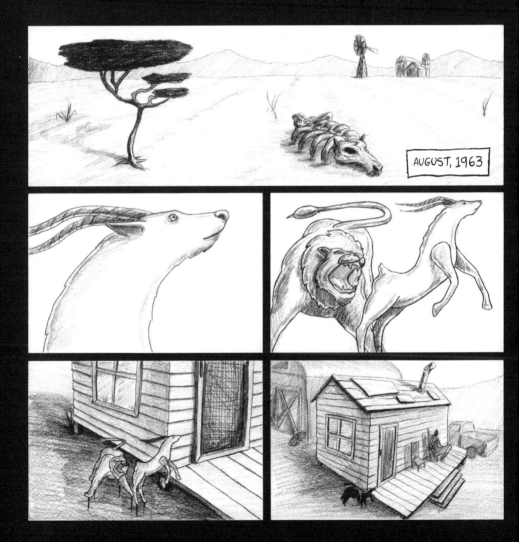

AUGUST, 1963

art by dave morgan

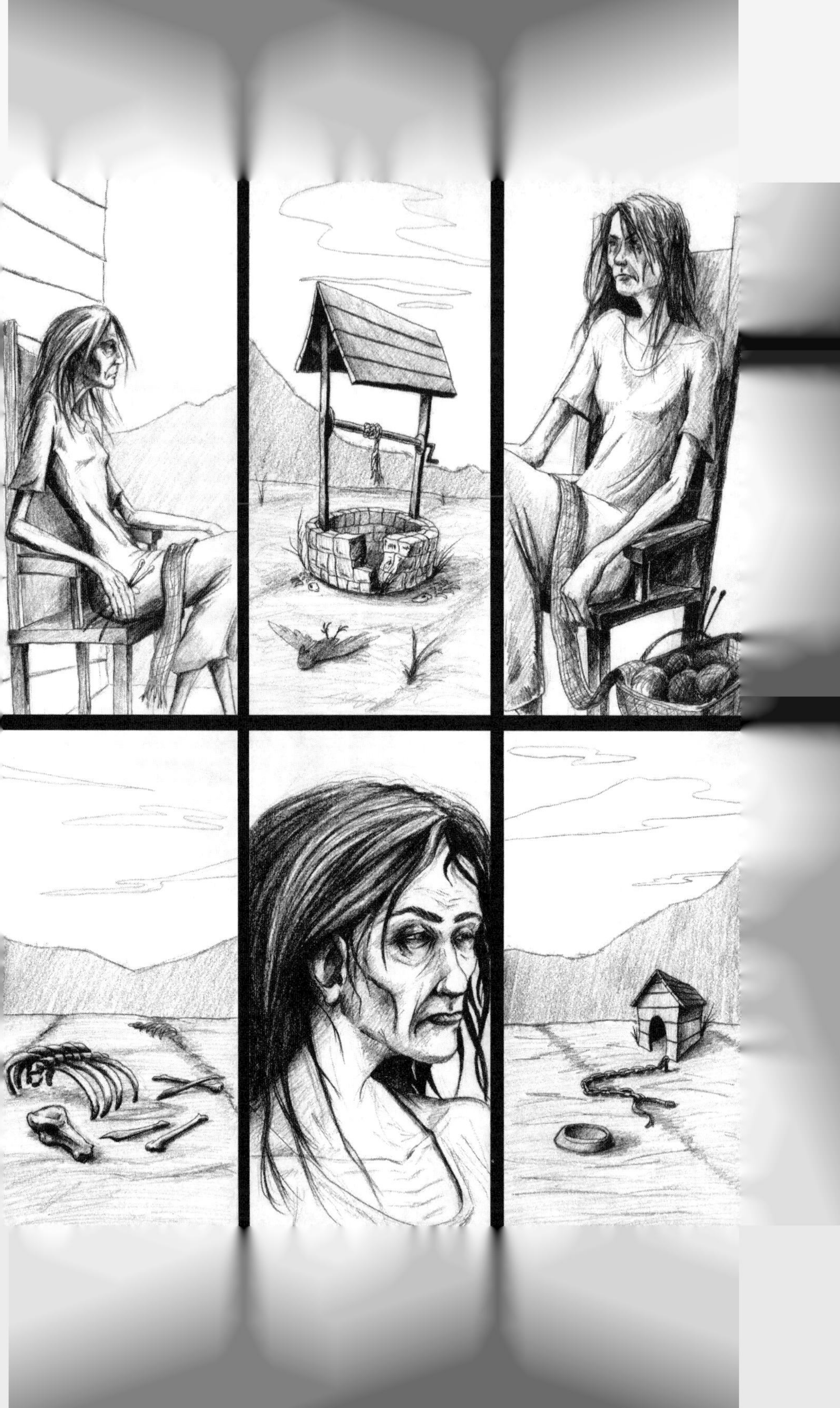

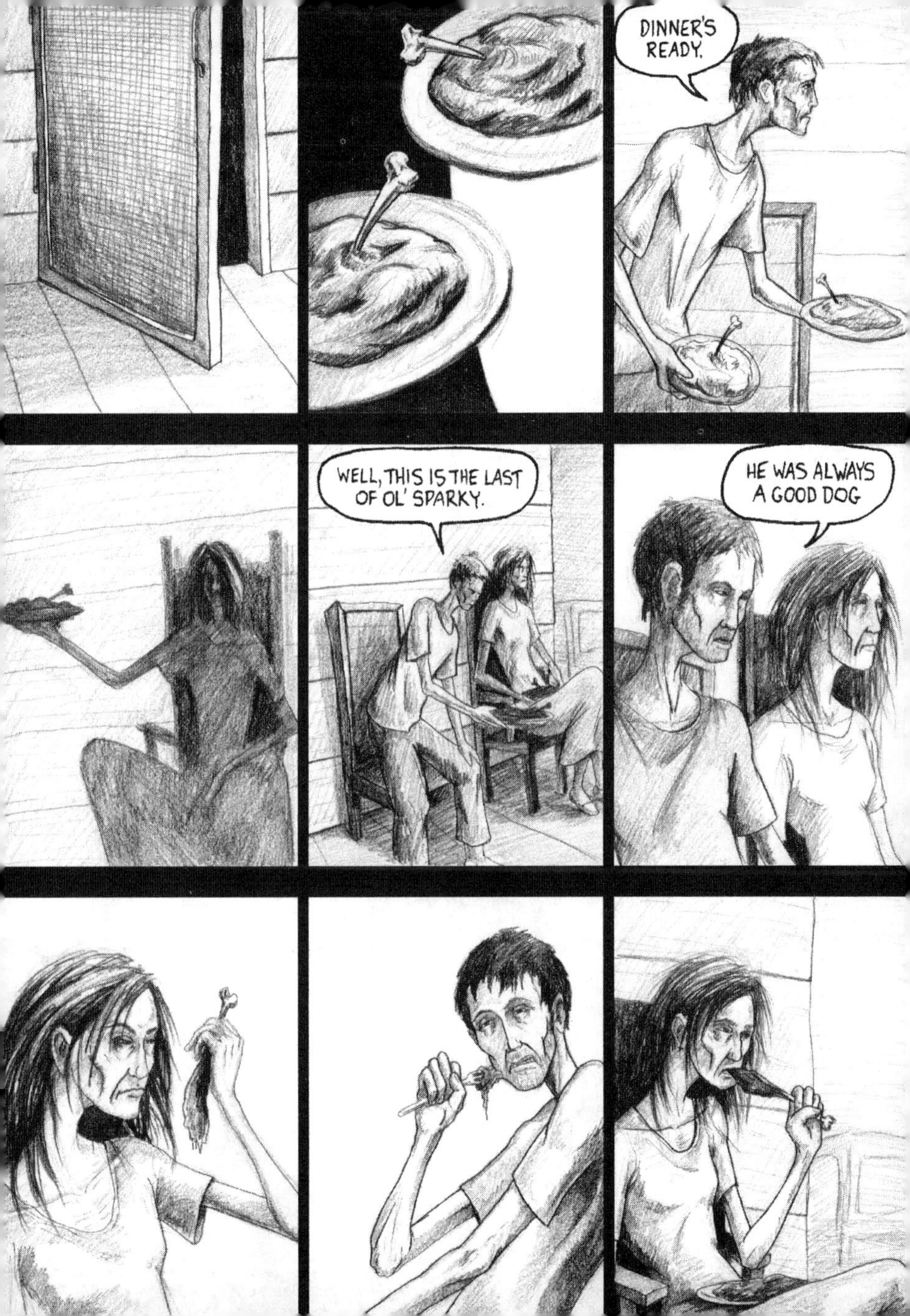
DINNER'S READY.
WELL, THIS IS THE LAST OF OL' SPARKY.
HE WAS ALWAYS A GOOD DOG

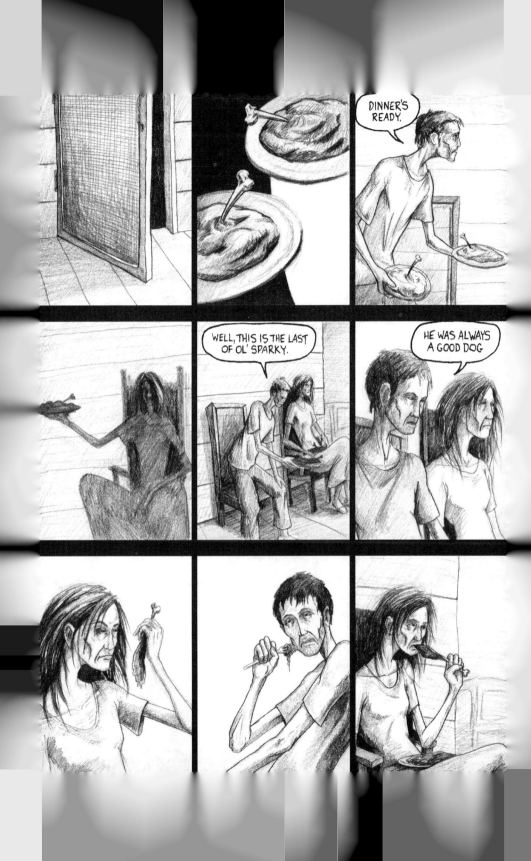

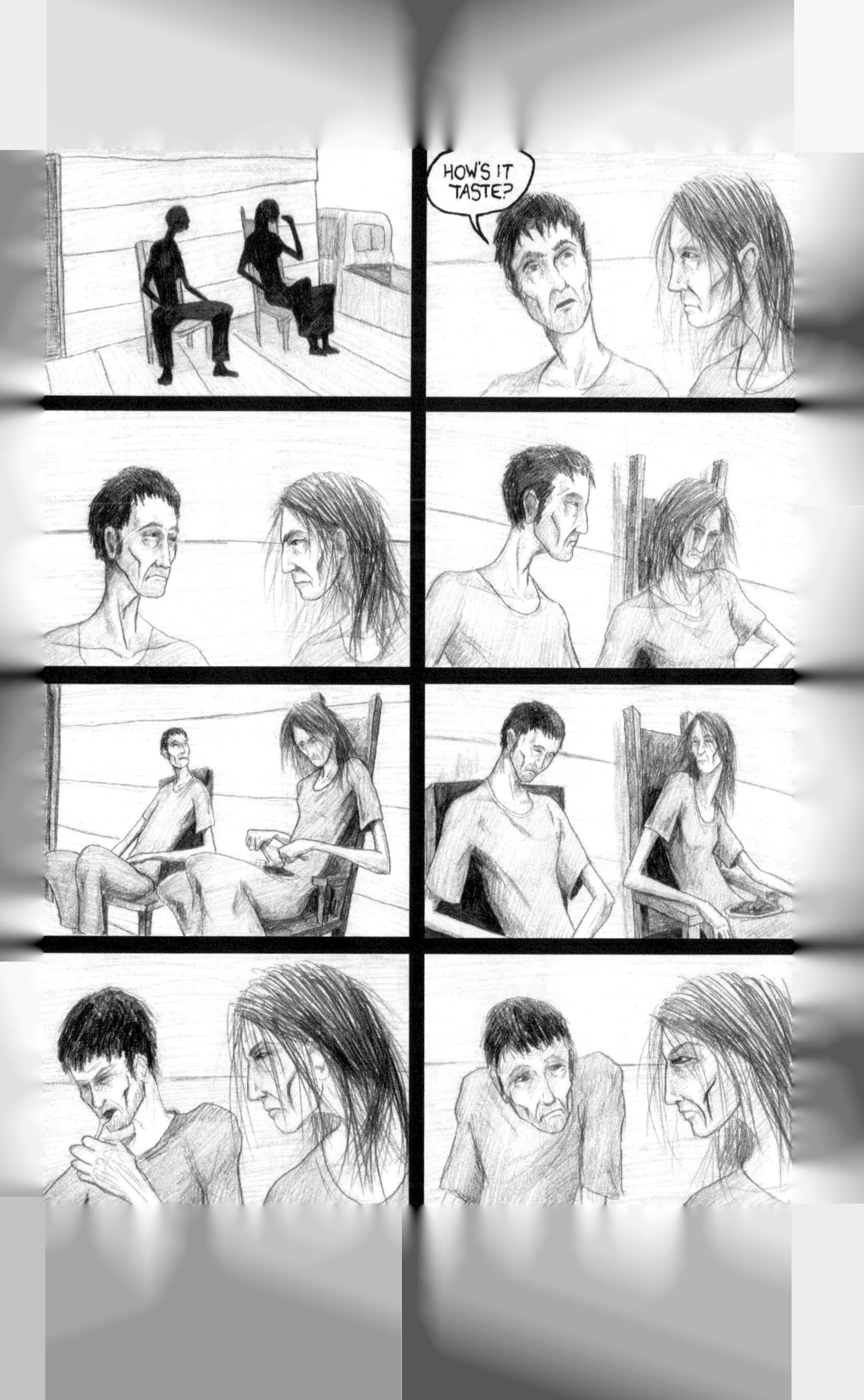
HOW'S IT TASTE?

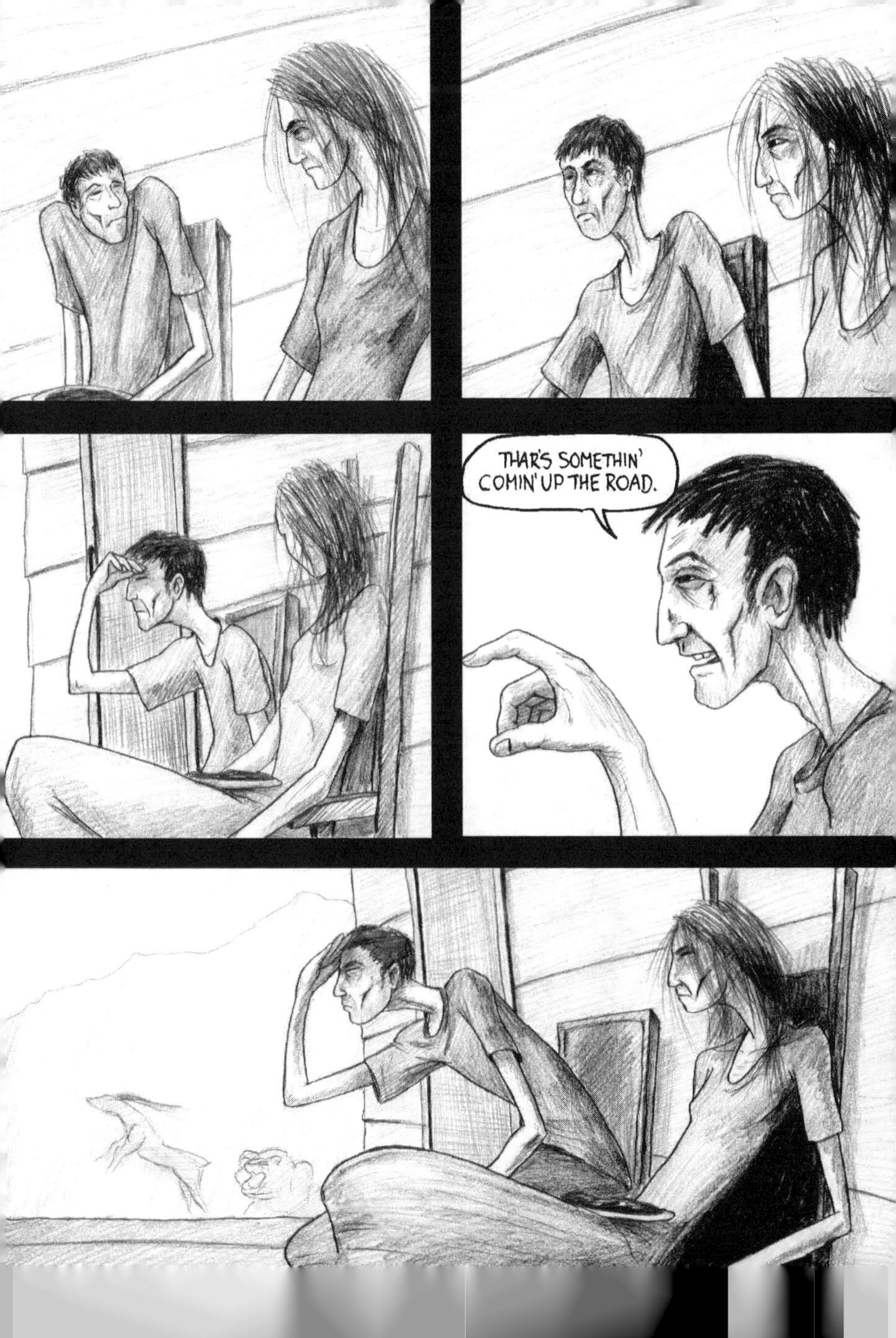
THAR'S SOMETHIN' COMIN' UP THE ROAD.

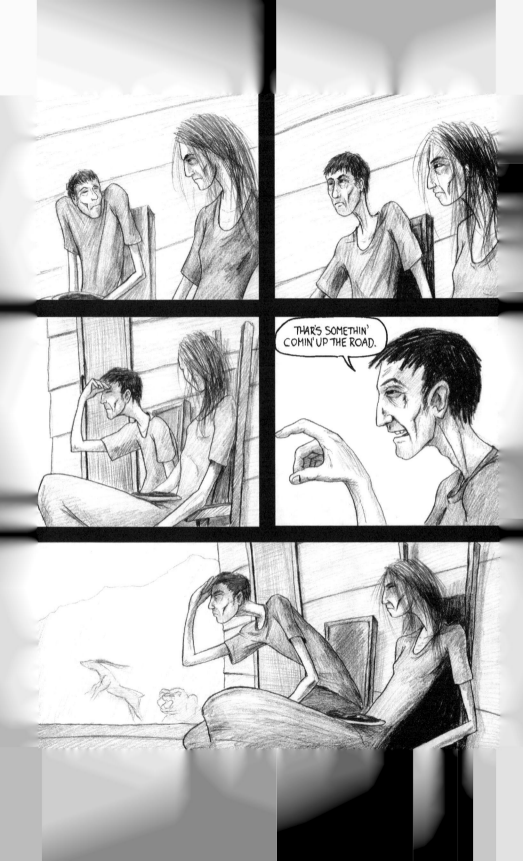

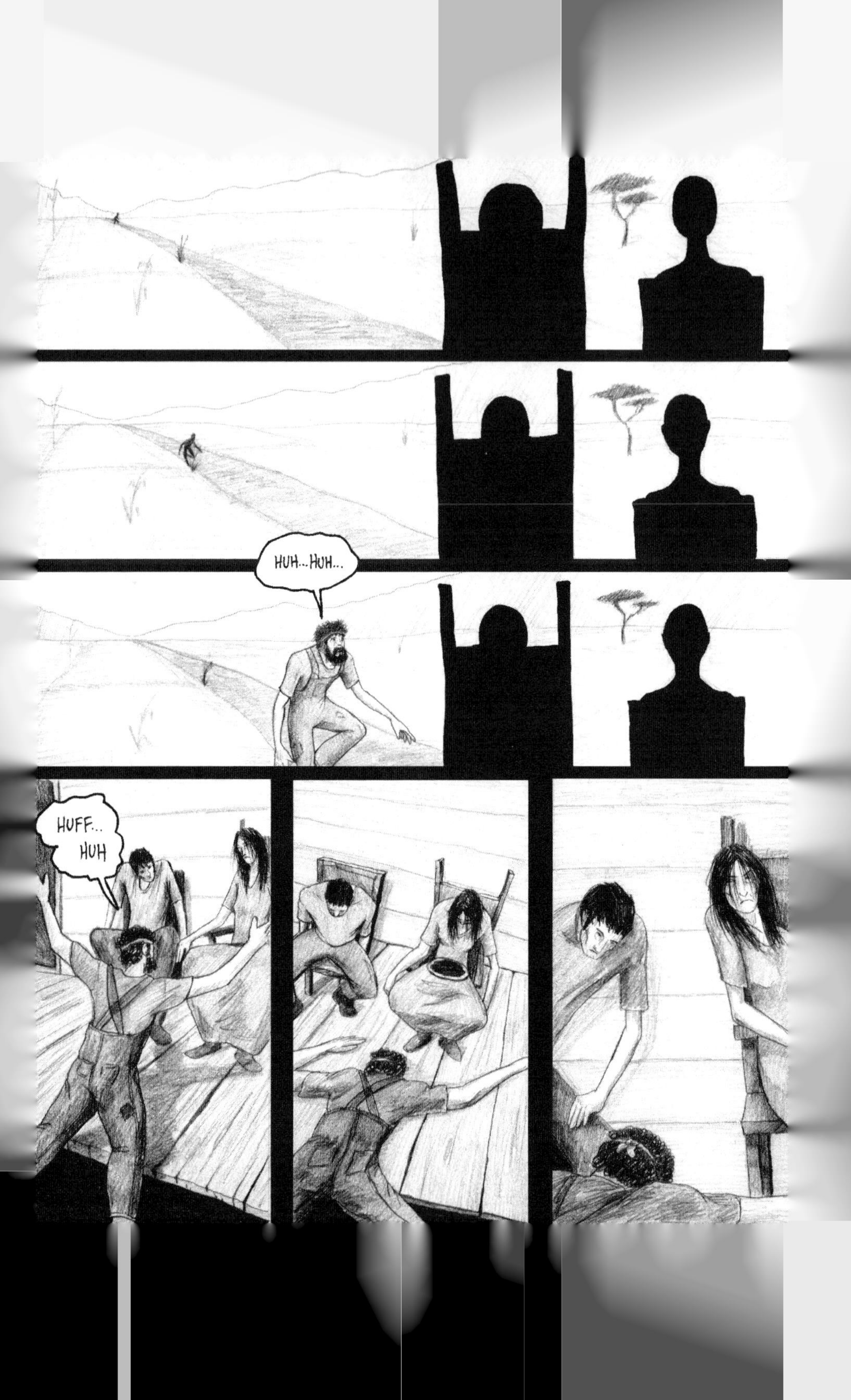
HUH...HUH...
HUFF... HUH

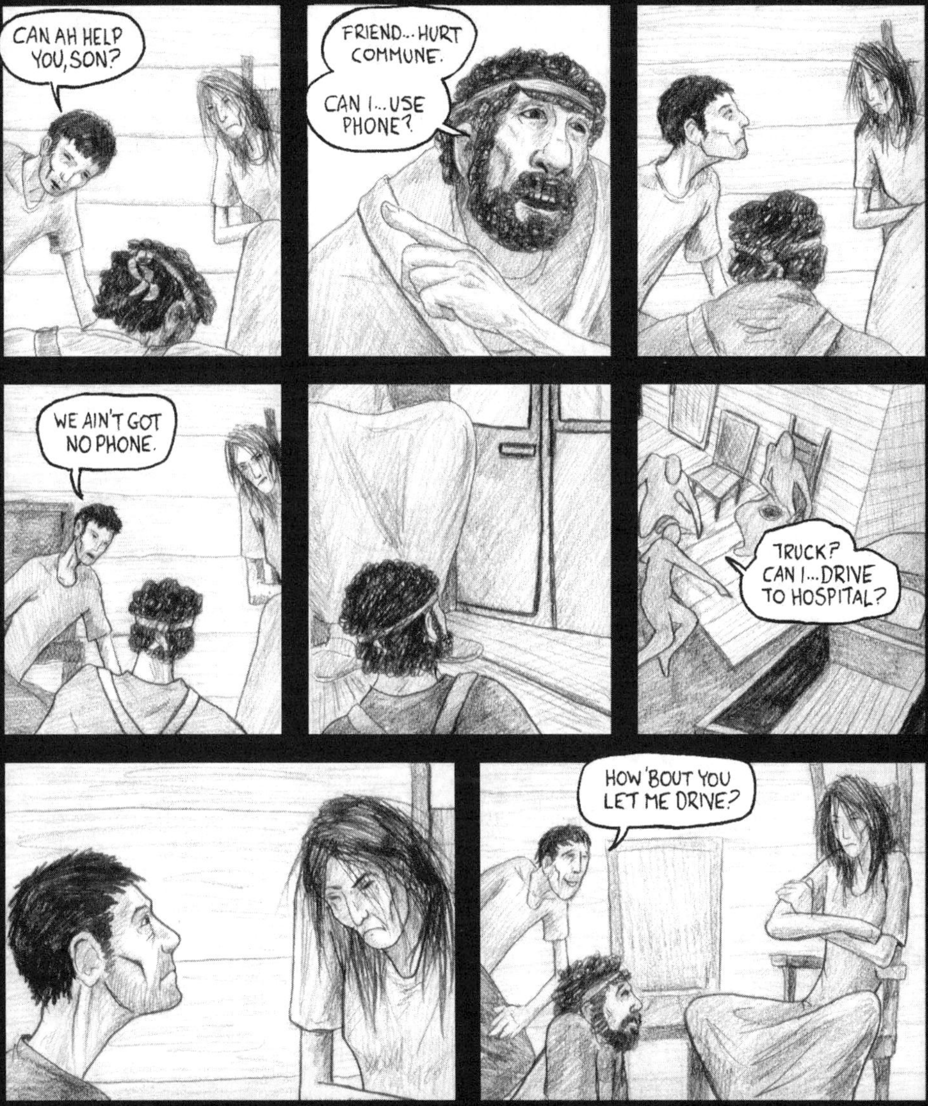
CAN AH HELP YOU, SON?
FRIEND... HURT COMMUNE.
CAN I... USE PHONE?
WE AIN'T GOT NO PHONE.
TRUCK? CAN I... DRIVE TO HOSPITAL?
HOW 'BOUT YOU LET ME DRIVE?

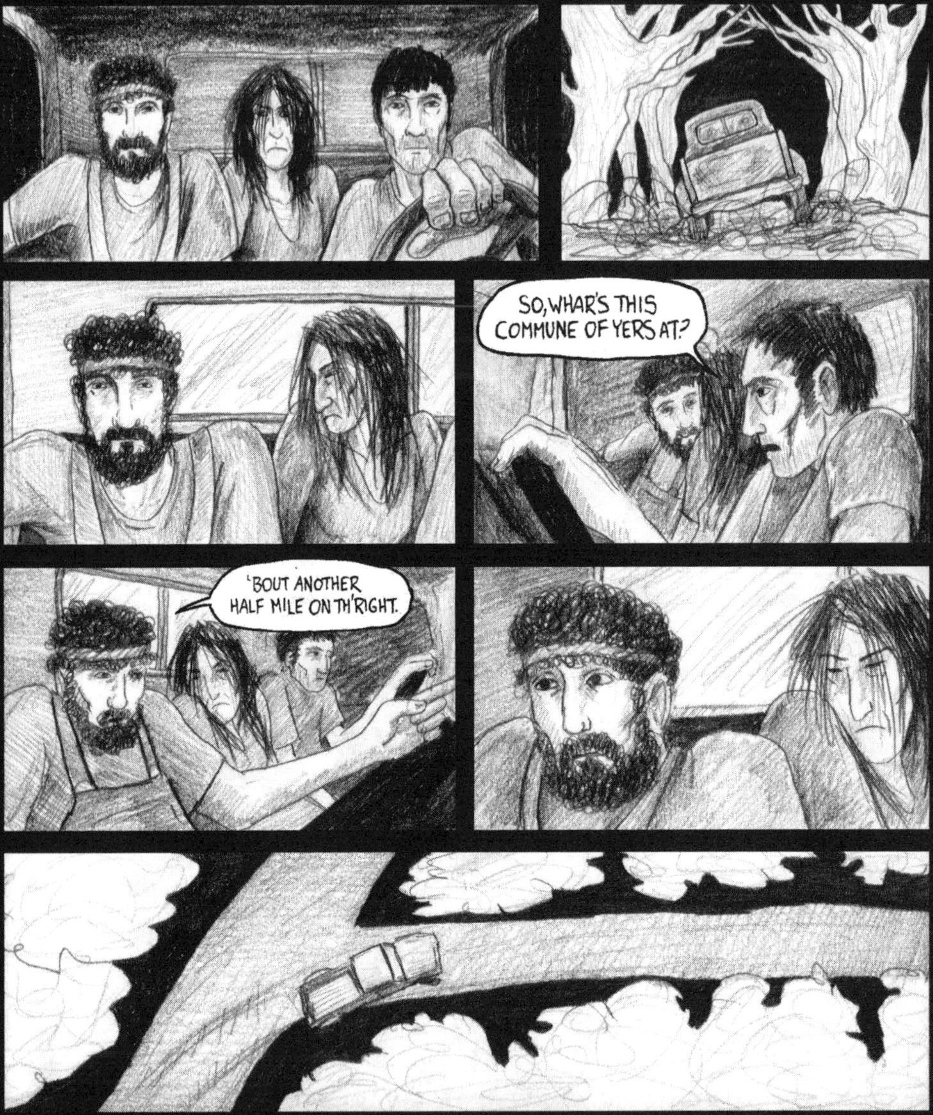
SO, WHAR'S THIS COMMUNE OF YERS AT?
'BOUT ANOTHER HALF MILE ON TH'RIGHT.

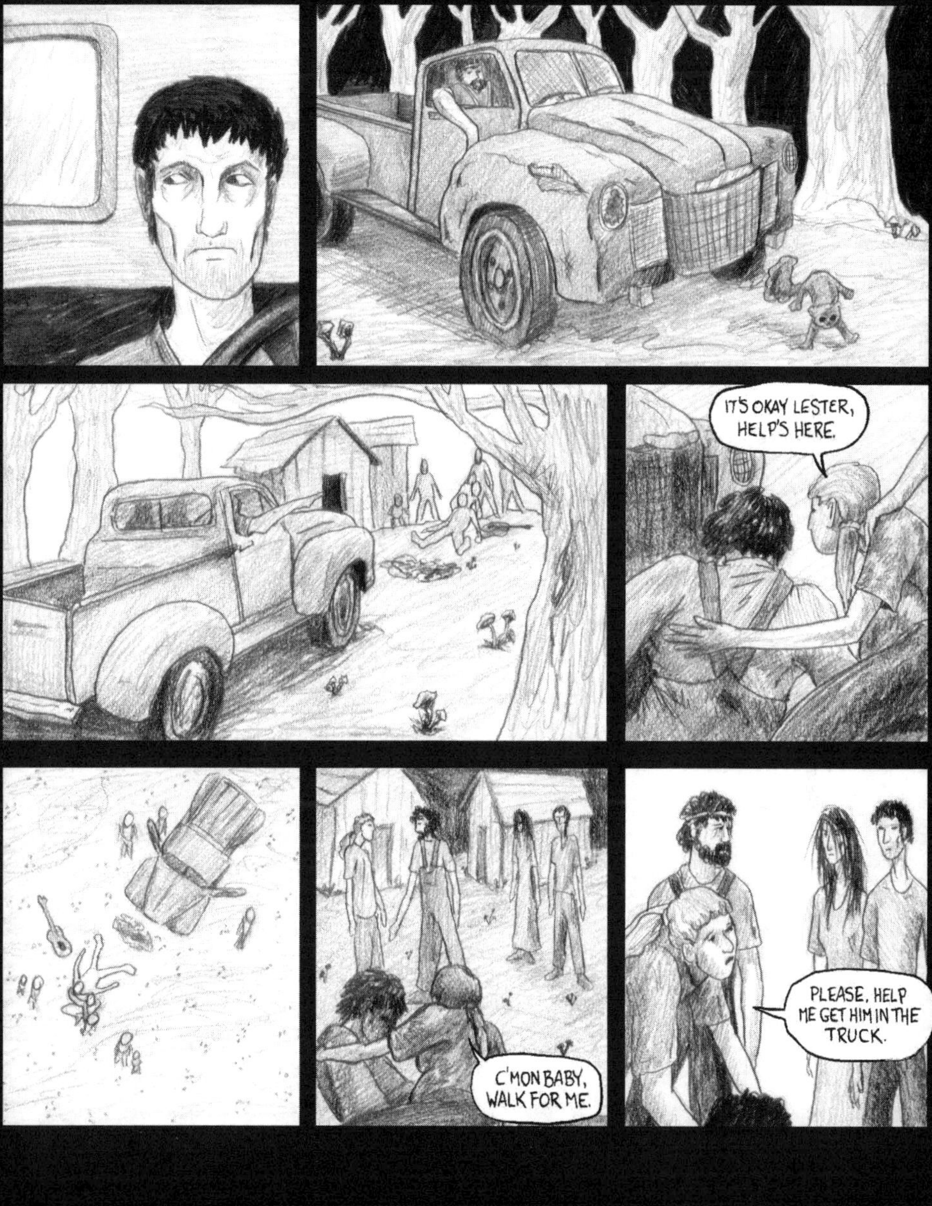
IT'S OKAY LESTER, HELP'S HERE.
C'MON BABY, WALK FOR ME.
PLEASE, HELP ME GET HIM IN THE TRUCK.

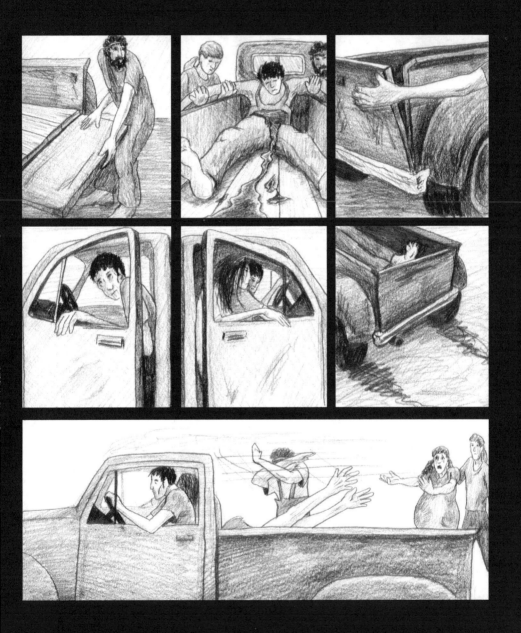

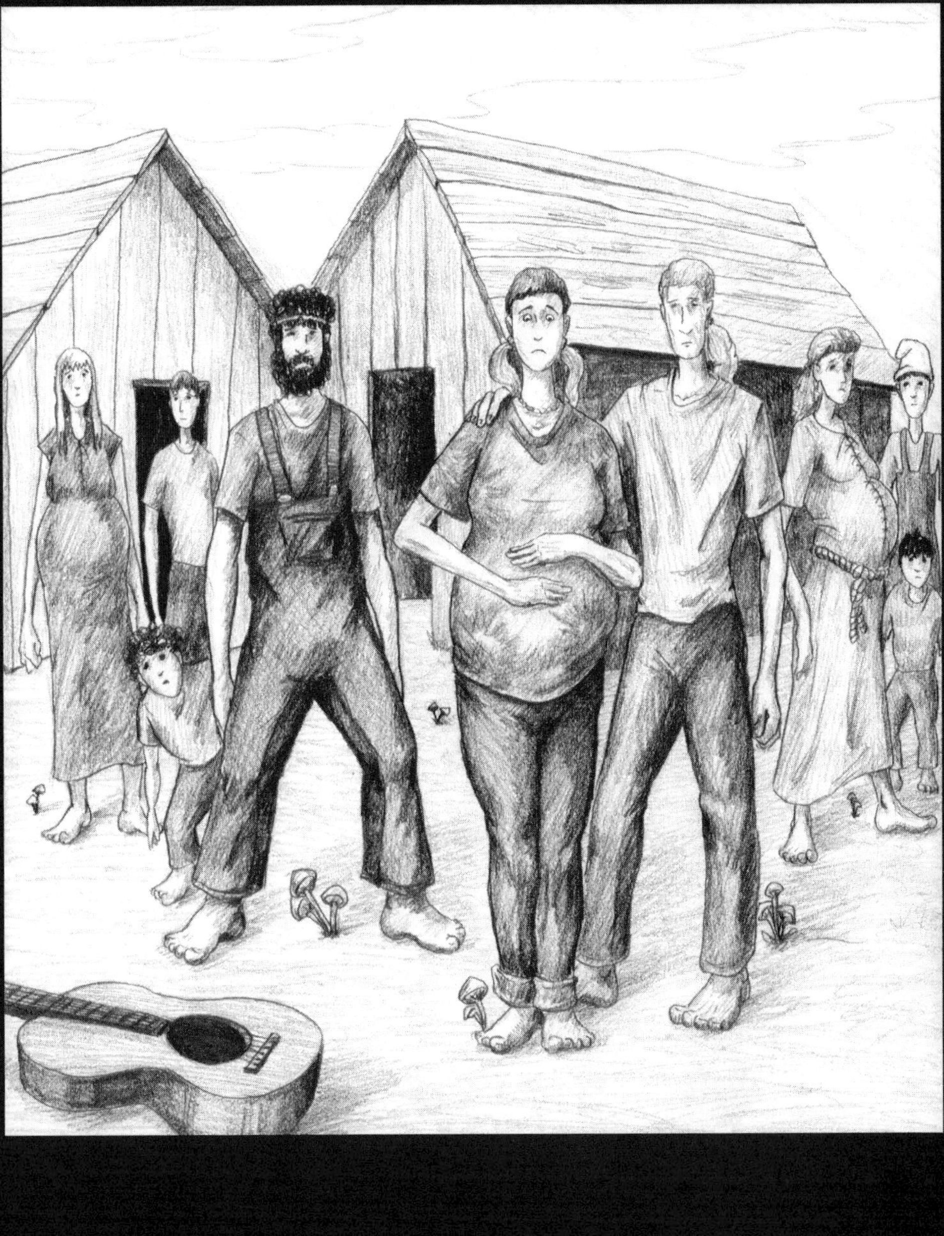

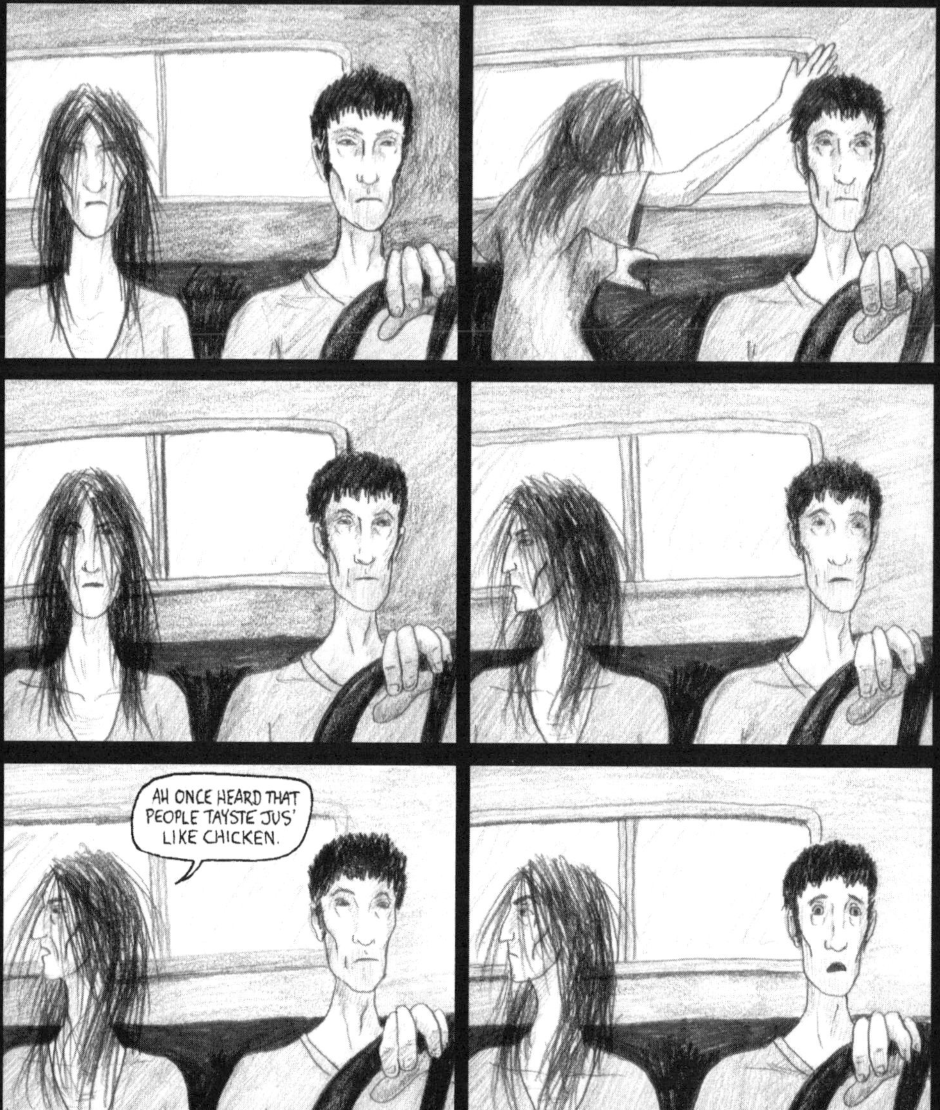
AH ONCE HEARD THAT PEOPLE TAYSTE JUS' LIKE CHICKEN.

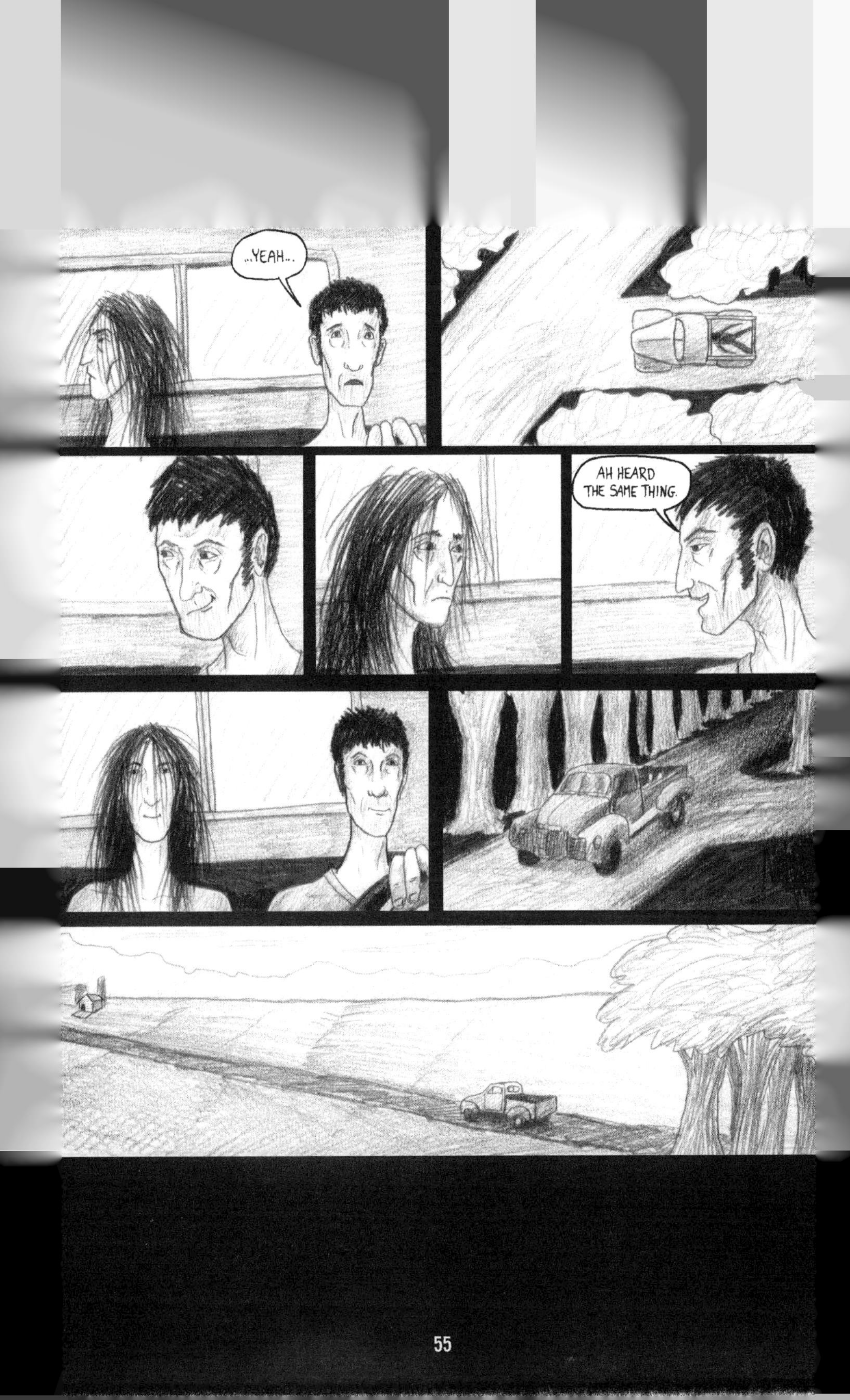
...YEAH...
AH HEARD THE SAME THING.

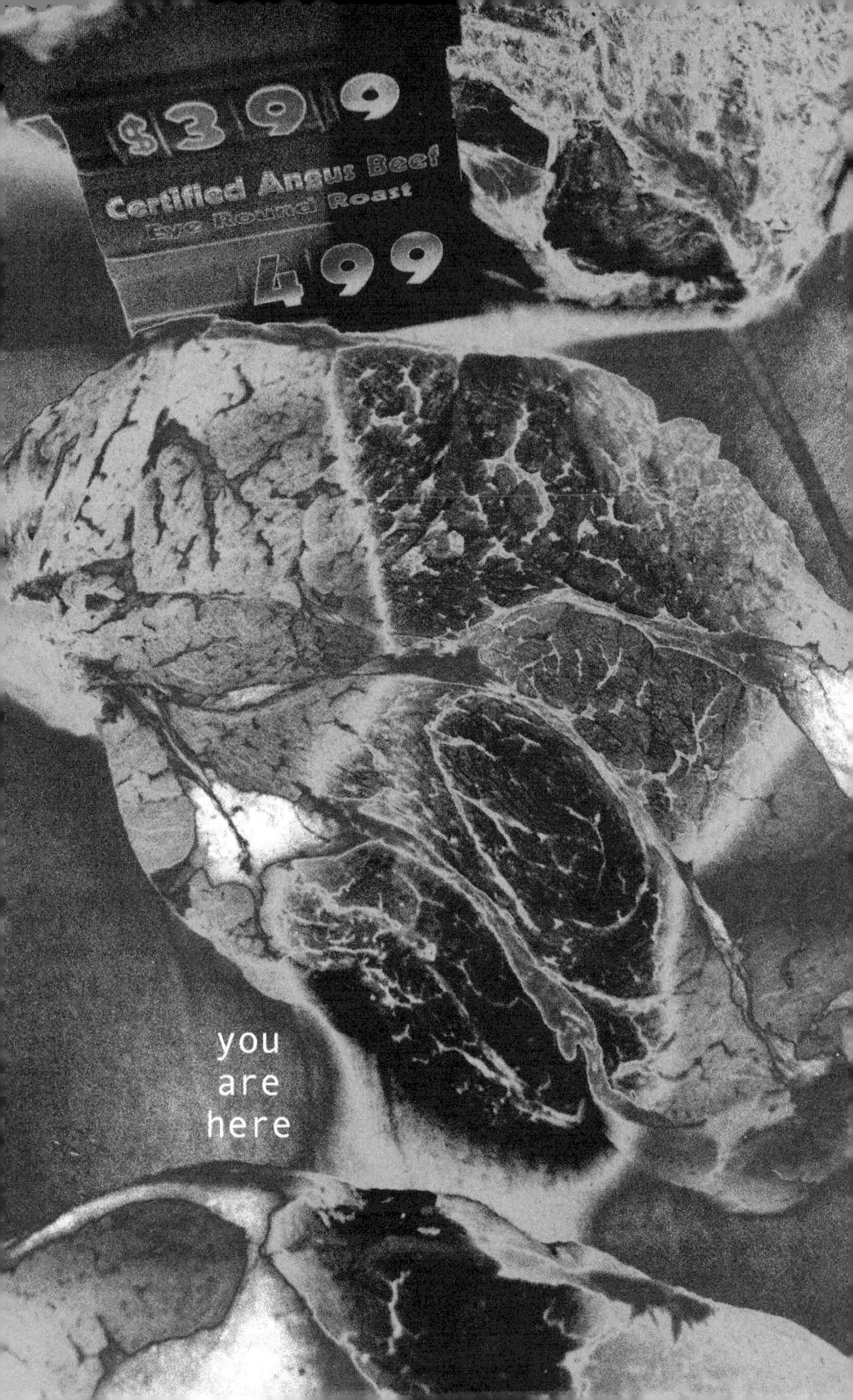
$3 99
Certified Angus Beef
Eye Round Roast
4 99
you
are
here

Plastic Farm

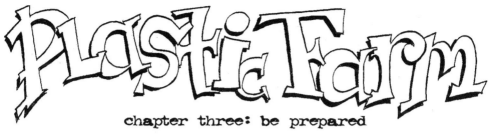

chapter three: be prepared

NYC, 1988

HEY BENNY, YOU SURE THIS GUY'S LEGIT? I'M MISSING MY DAUGHTER'S RECITAL FOR THIS BULLSHIT.
WOULD'JA RELAX FRANK. AFTER TONIGHT, WE'LL HAVE ONE MORE NAIL FOR THE BIG GUY'S COFFIN.
PIZZA
BESIDES, IT'S NOT LIKE YOU'RE THE ONLY ONE WITH A LIFE OUTSIDE THE FORCE.
RIGHT. YOU HAVE A LIFE. AND I'M THE ASSHOLE. SO WHERE IS THIS FUCKING GUY?
HE'LL BE HERE.
YOU REALIZE I PROMISED SYLVIA I WOULDN'T MISS THE RECITAL. SHE'S GONNA KILL ME.
I KNOW THE FEELING.
YEAH? AND LOOK AT YOU. YOUR WIFE LEFT YOU LAST YEAR.
I TOLD MY FOLKS SHE GOT KILLED BY CRACKHEADS.
YOU ARE A WONDERFUL HUMAN BEING.

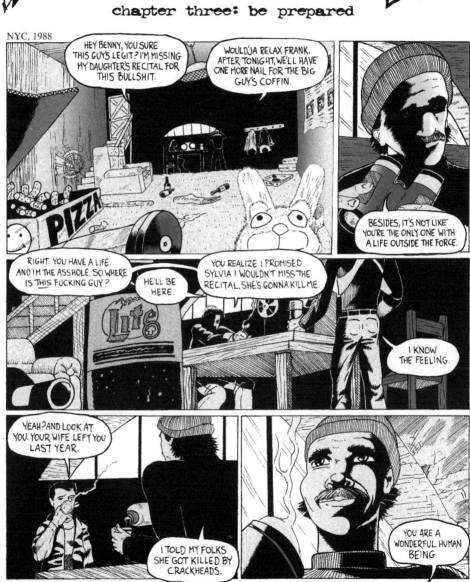

art by jake warrenfeltz

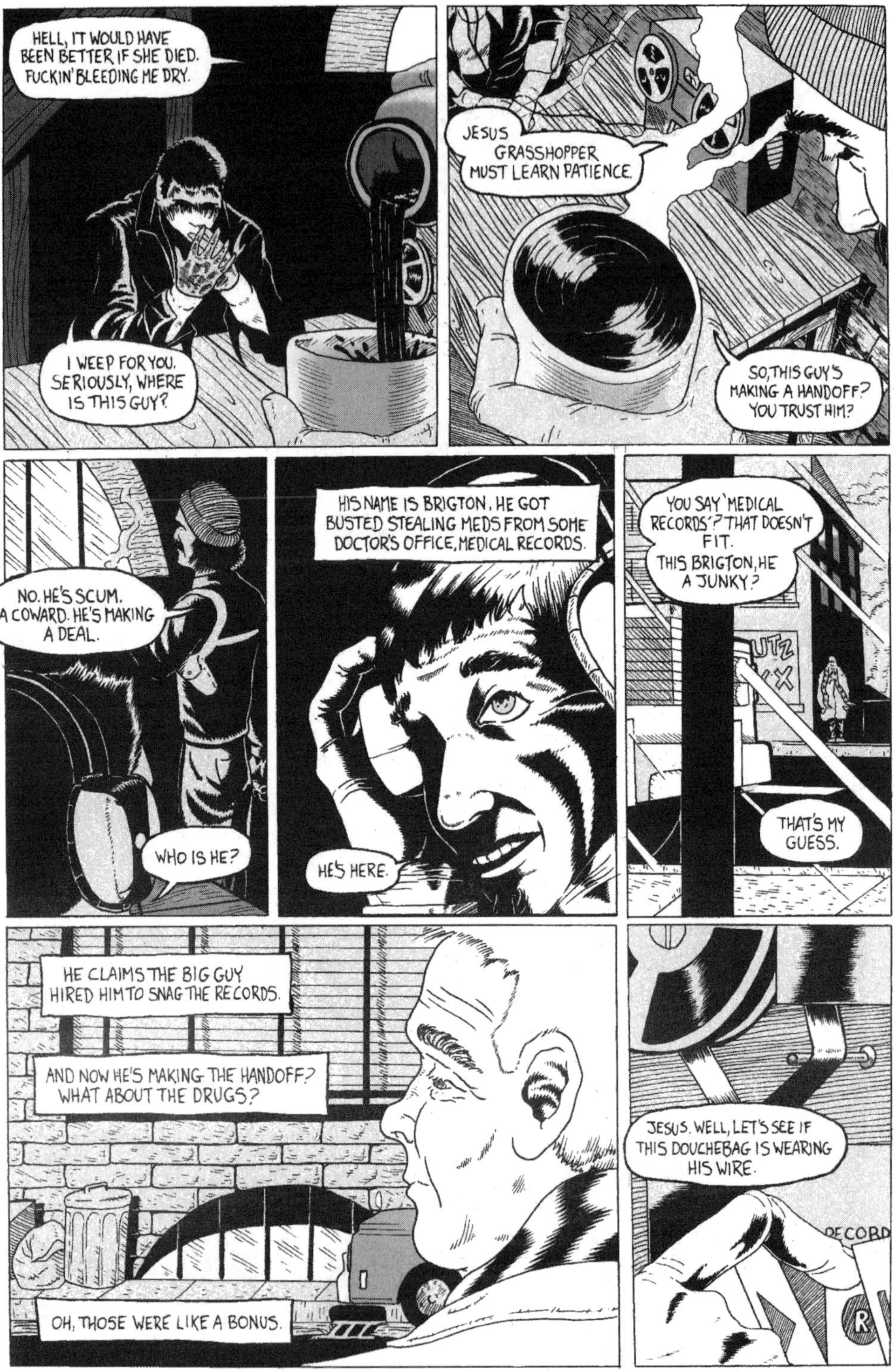
HELL, IT WOULD HAVE BEEN BETTER IF SHE DIED. FUCKIN' BLEEDING ME DRY.
I WEEP FOR YOU. SERIOUSLY, WHERE IS THIS GUY?
JESUS GRASSHOPPER MUST LEARN PATIENCE.
SO, THIS GUY'S MAKING A HANDOFF? YOU TRUST HIM?
NO. HE'S SCUM. A COWARD. HE'S MAKING A DEAL.
WHO IS HE?
HIS NAME IS BRIGTON. HE GOT BUSTED STEALING MEDS FROM SOME DOCTOR'S OFFICE, MEDICAL RECORDS.
HE'S HERE.
YOU SAY 'MEDICAL RECORDS'? THAT DOESN'T FIT.
THIS BRIGTON, HE A JUNKY?
THAT'S MY GUESS.
HE CLAIMS THE BIG GUY HIRED HIM TO SNAG THE RECORDS.
AND NOW HE'S MAKING THE HANDOFF? WHAT ABOUT THE DRUGS?
OH, THOSE WERE LIKE A BONUS.
JESUS. WELL, LET'S SEE IF THIS DOUCHEBAG IS WEARING HIS WIRE.

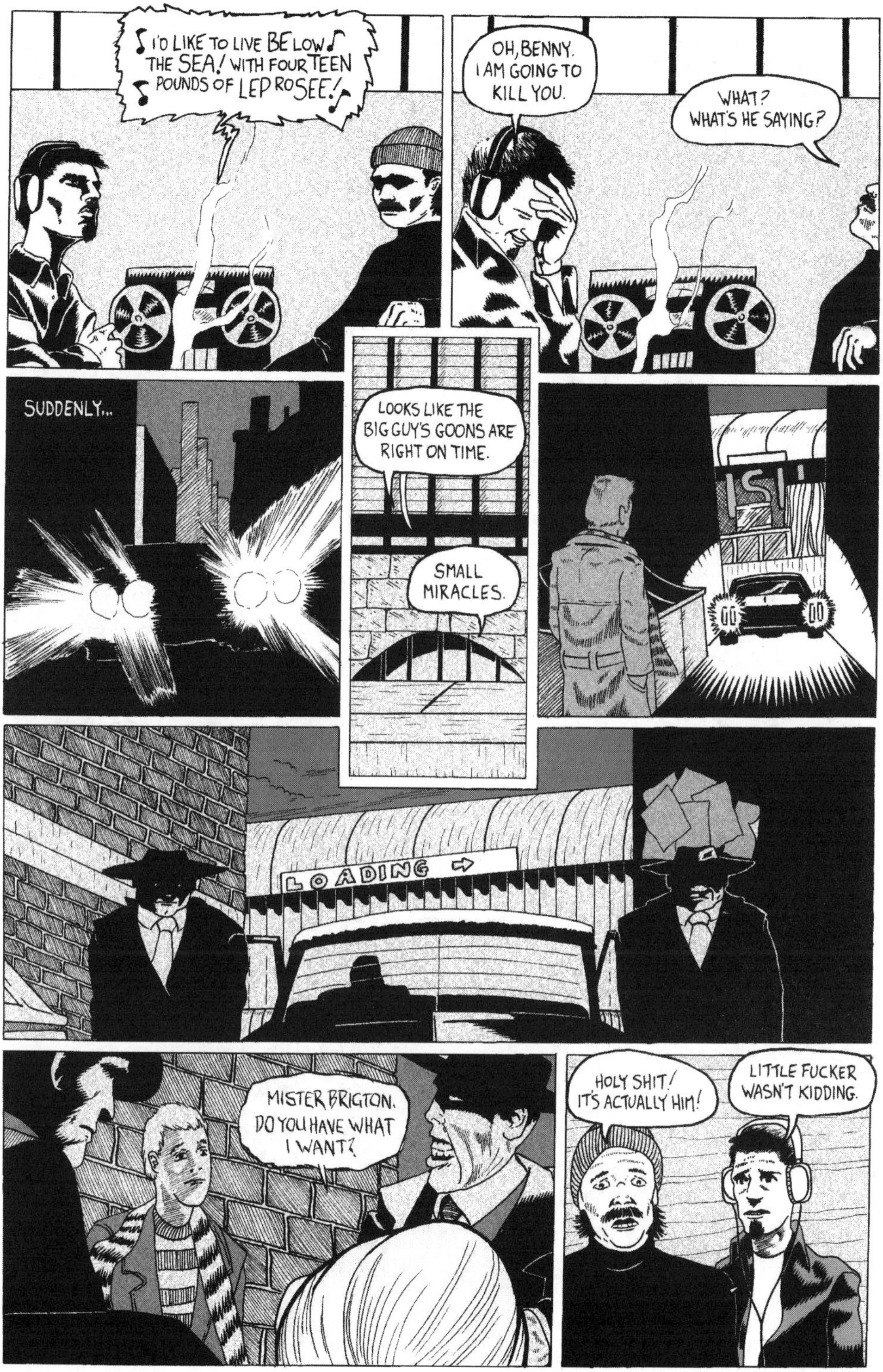
I'D LIKE TO LIVE BELOW THE SEA! WITH FOURTEEN POUNDS OF LEPROSEE!
OH, BENNY. I AM GOING TO KILL YOU.
WHAT? WHAT'S HE SAYING?
SUDDENLY...
LOOKS LIKE THE BIG GUY'S GOONS ARE RIGHT ON TIME.
SMALL MIRACLES.
LOADING
MISTER BRIGTON. DO YOU HAVE WHAT I WANT?
HOLY SHIT! IT'S ACTUALLY HIM!
LITTLE FUCKER WASN'T KIDDING.

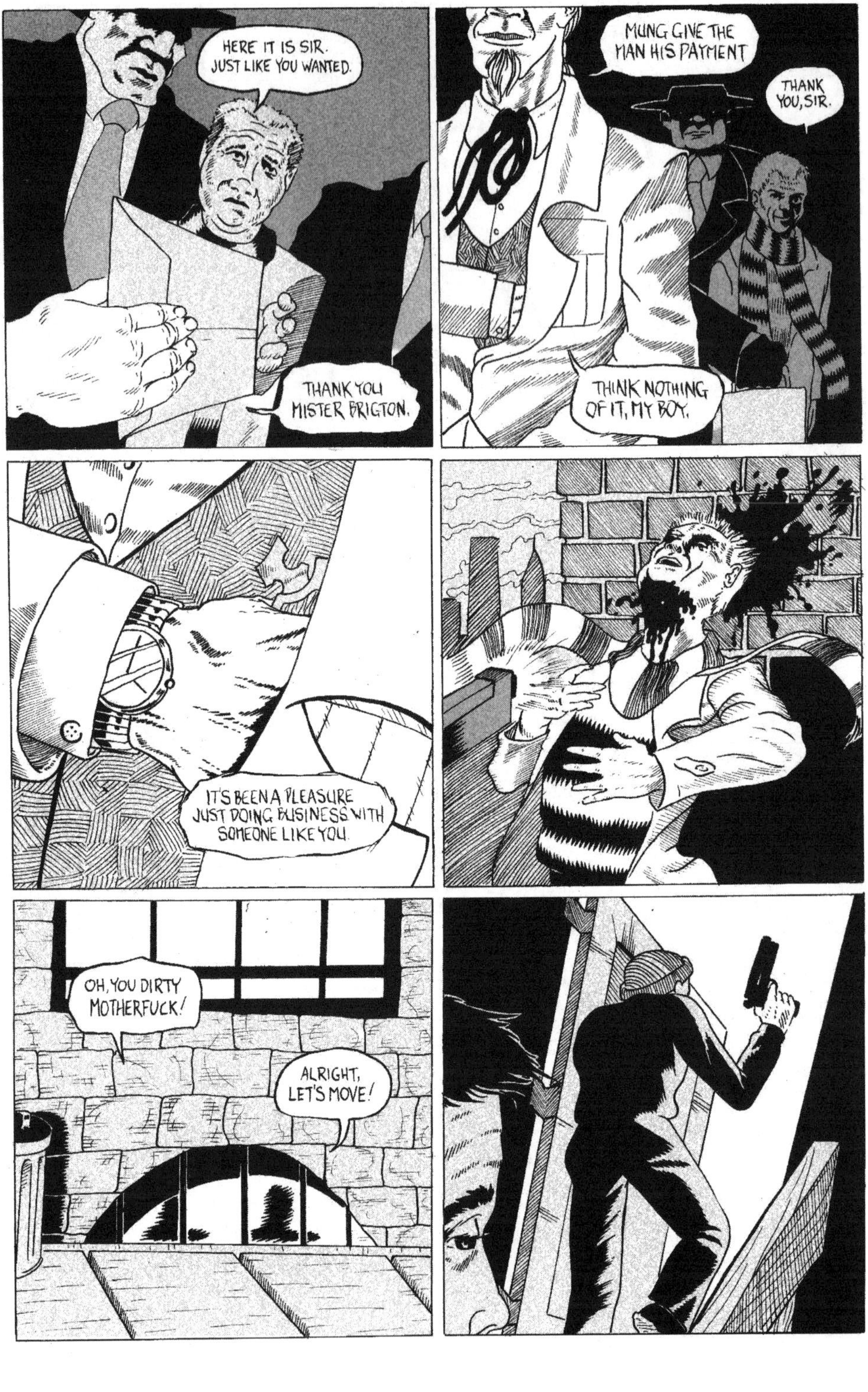
HERE IT IS SIR. JUST LIKE YOU WANTED.
THANK YOU MISTER BRIGTON.
MUNG GIVE THE MAN HIS PAYMENT
THANK YOU, SIR.
THINK NOTHING OF IT, MY BOY.
IT'S BEEN A PLEASURE JUST DOING BUSINESS WITH SOMEONE LIKE YOU.
OH, YOU DIRTY MOTHERFUCK!
ALRIGHT, LET'S MOVE!

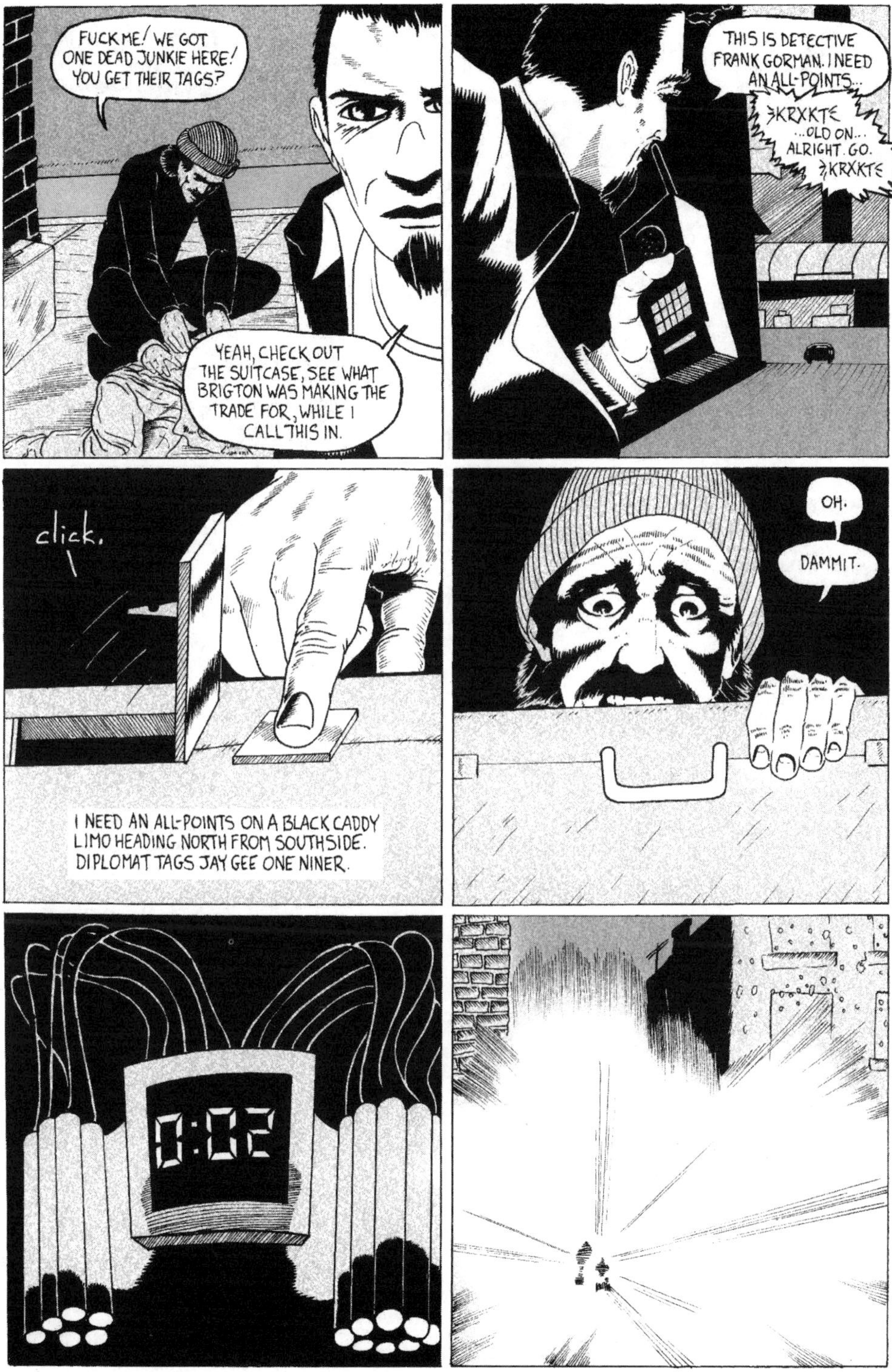
FUCK ME! WE GOT ONE DEAD JUNKIE HERE! YOU GET THEIR TAGS?
YEAH, CHECK OUT THE SUITCASE, SEE WHAT BRIGTON WAS MAKING THE TRADE FOR, WHILE I CALL THIS IN.
THIS IS DETECTIVE FRANK GORMAN. I NEED AN ALL-POINTS...
KRXKT ...OLD ON... ALRIGHT. GO. KRXKT
click.
I NEED AN ALL-POINTS ON A BLACK CADDY LIMO HEADING NORTH FROM SOUTHSIDE. DIPLOMAT TAGS JAY GEE ONE NINER.
OH.
DAMMIT.
0:02

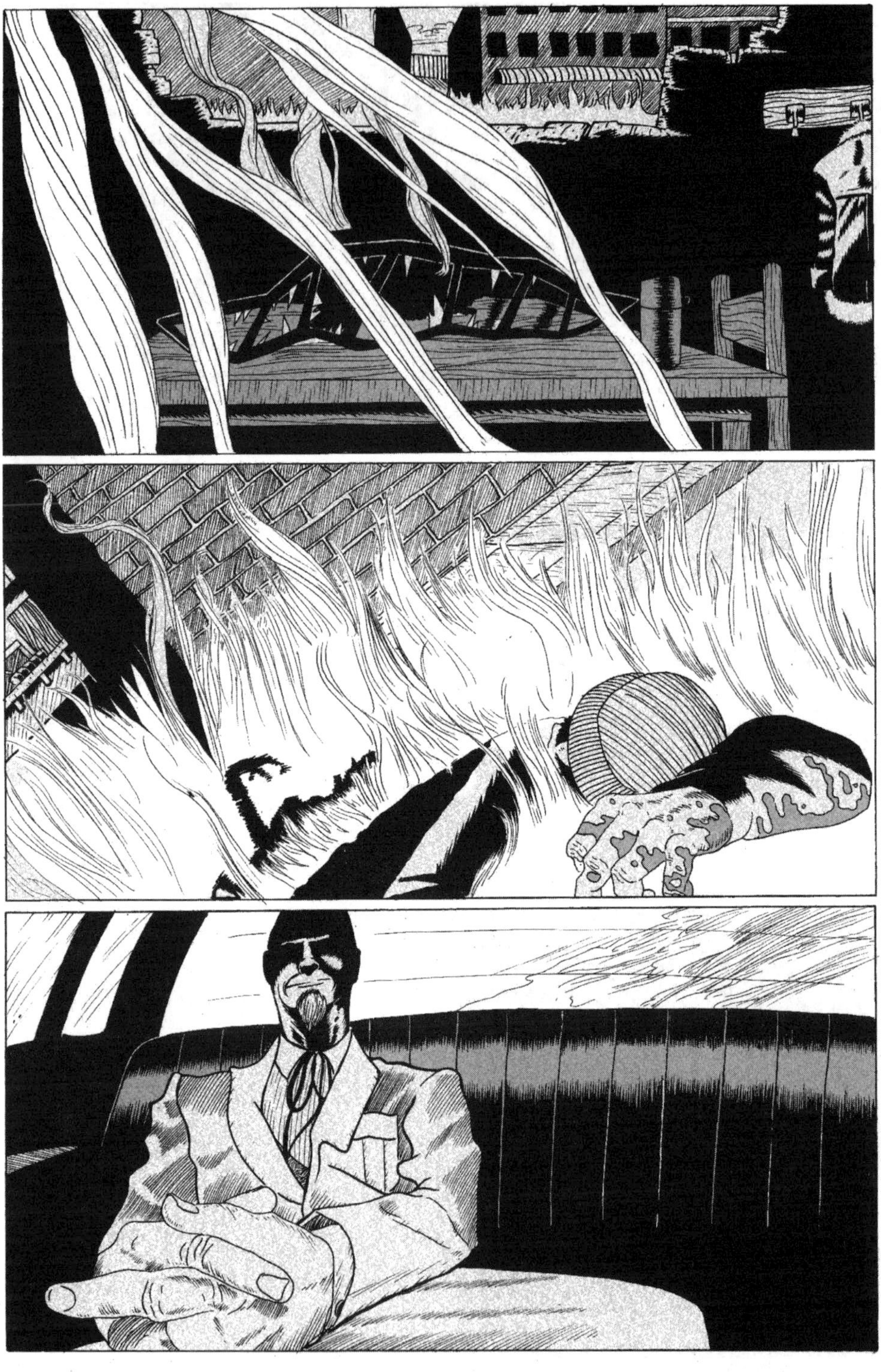

Plastic Farm

chapter four: bookends

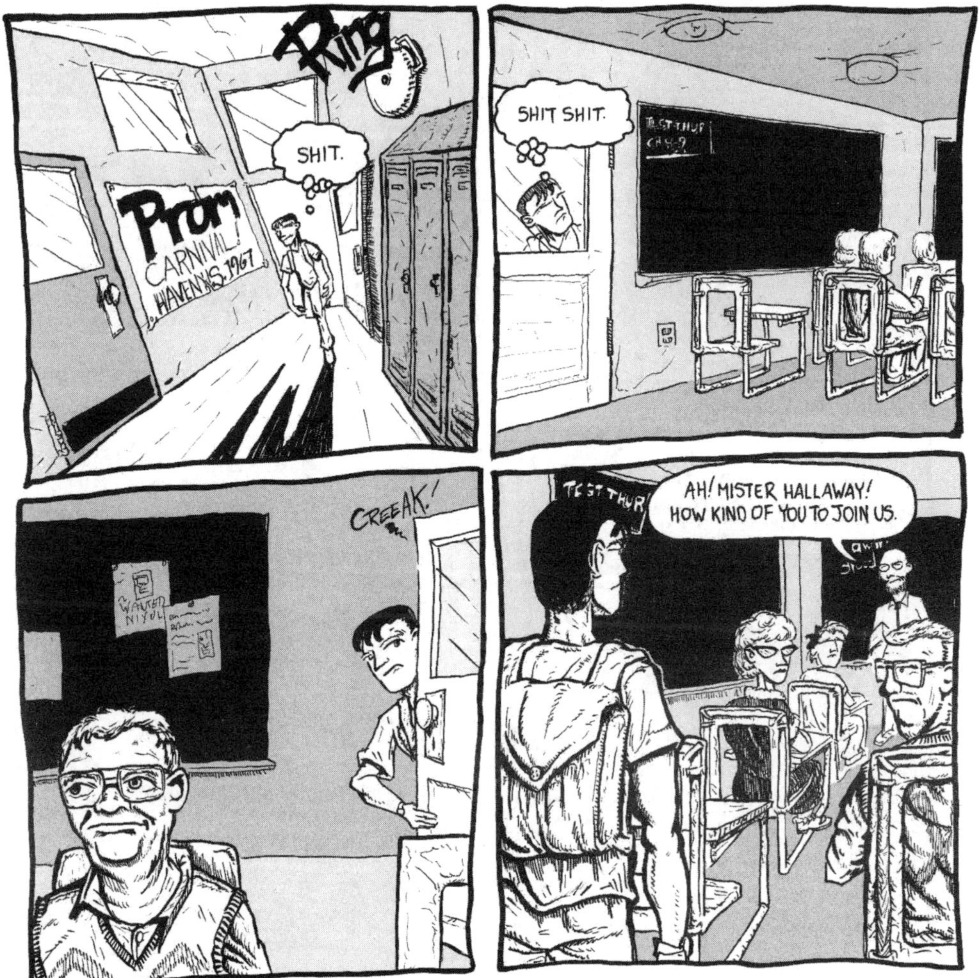

Ring
SHIT.
Prom
CARNIVAL!
HAVEN H.S. 1967
SHIT SHIT.
CREEAK!
TEST THUR
AH! MISTER HALLAWAY! HOW KIND OF YOU TO JOIN US.

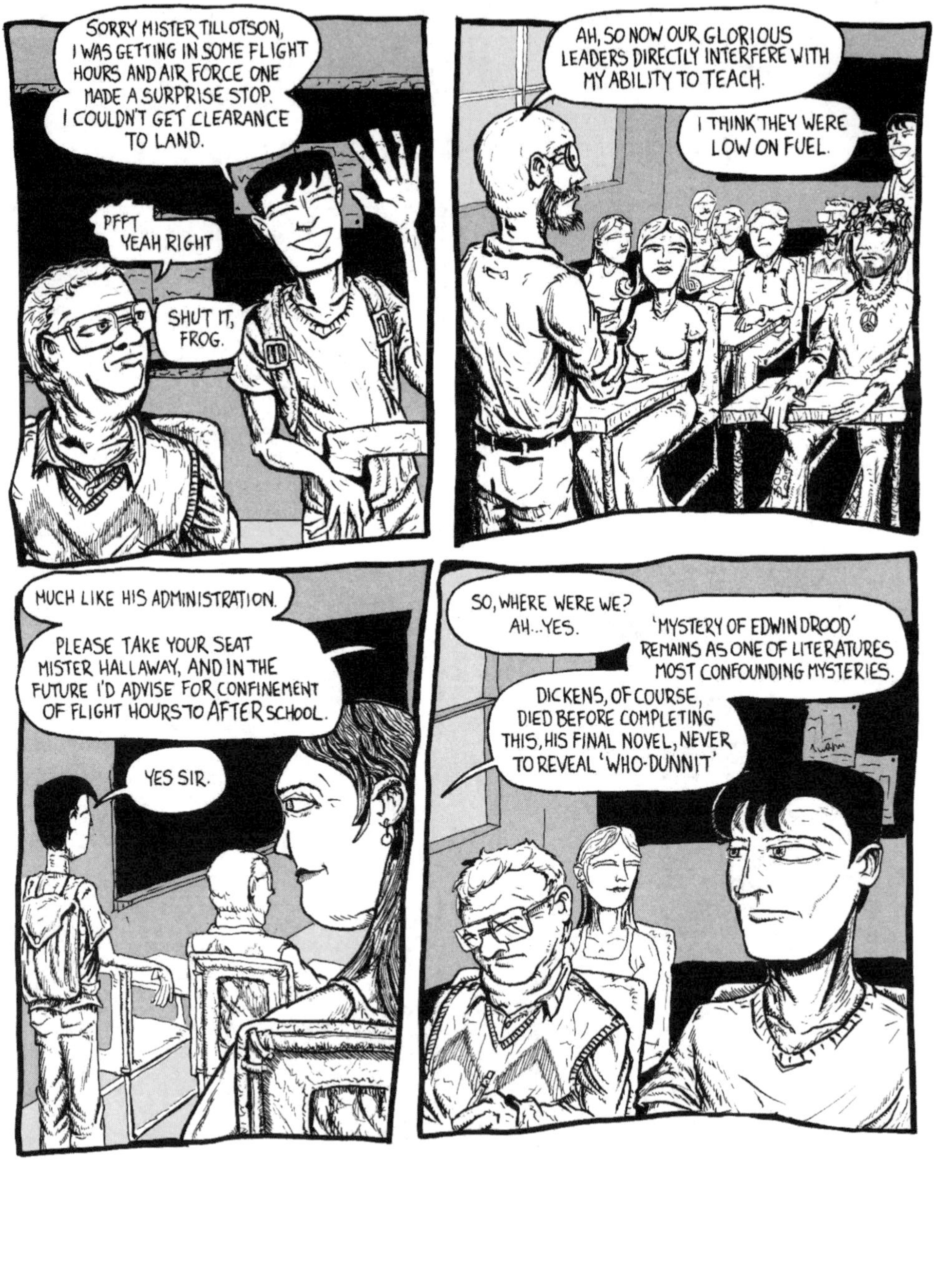
SORRY MISTER TILLOTSON, I WAS GETTING IN SOME FLIGHT HOURS AND AIR FORCE ONE MADE A SURPRISE STOP. I COULDN'T GET CLEARANCE TO LAND.
PFFT YEAH RIGHT
SHUT IT, FROG.
AH, SO NOW OUR GLORIOUS LEADERS DIRECTLY INTERFERE WITH MY ABILITY TO TEACH.
I THINK THEY WERE LOW ON FUEL.
MUCH LIKE HIS ADMINISTRATION.
PLEASE TAKE YOUR SEAT MISTER HALLAWAY, AND IN THE FUTURE I'D ADVISE FOR CONFINEMENT OF FLIGHT HOURS TO AFTER SCHOOL.
YES SIR.
SO, WHERE WERE WE? AH...YES.
'MYSTERY OF EDWIN DROOD' REMAINS AS ONE OF LITERATURES MOST CONFOUNDING MYSTERIES.
DICKENS, OF COURSE, DIED BEFORE COMPLETING THIS, HIS FINAL NOVEL, NEVER TO REVEAL 'WHO-DUNNIT'

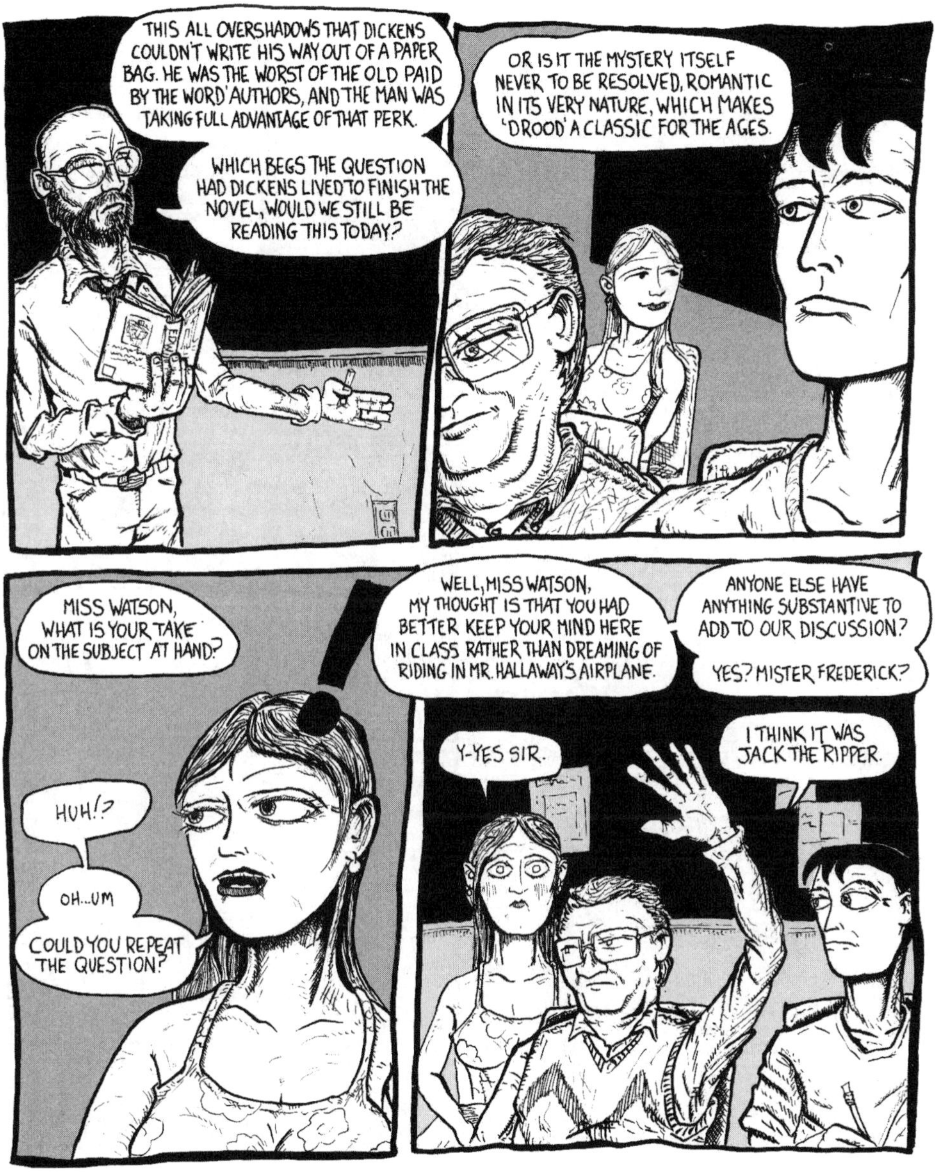
THIS ALL OVERSHADOWS THAT DICKENS COULDN'T WRITE HIS WAY OUT OF A PAPER BAG. HE WAS THE WORST OF THE OLD PAID BY THE WORD' AUTHORS, AND THE MAN WAS TAKING FULL ADVANTAGE OF THAT PERK.
WHICH BEGS THE QUESTION HAD DICKENS LIVED TO FINISH THE NOVEL, WOULD WE STILL BE READING THIS TODAY?
OR IS IT THE MYSTERY ITSELF NEVER TO BE RESOLVED, ROMANTIC IN ITS VERY NATURE, WHICH MAKES 'DROOD' A CLASSIC FOR THE AGES.
MISS WATSON, WHAT IS YOUR TAKE ON THE SUBJECT AT HAND?
!
HUH!?
OH...UM
COULD YOU REPEAT THE QUESTION?
WELL, MISS WATSON, MY THOUGHT IS THAT YOU HAD BETTER KEEP YOUR MIND HERE IN CLASS RATHER THAN DREAMING OF RIDING IN MR. HALLAWAY'S AIRPLANE.
ANYONE ELSE HAVE ANYTHING SUBSTANTIVE TO ADD TO OUR DISCUSSION?
YES? MISTER FREDERICK?
Y-YES SIR.
I THINK IT WAS JACK THE RIPPER.

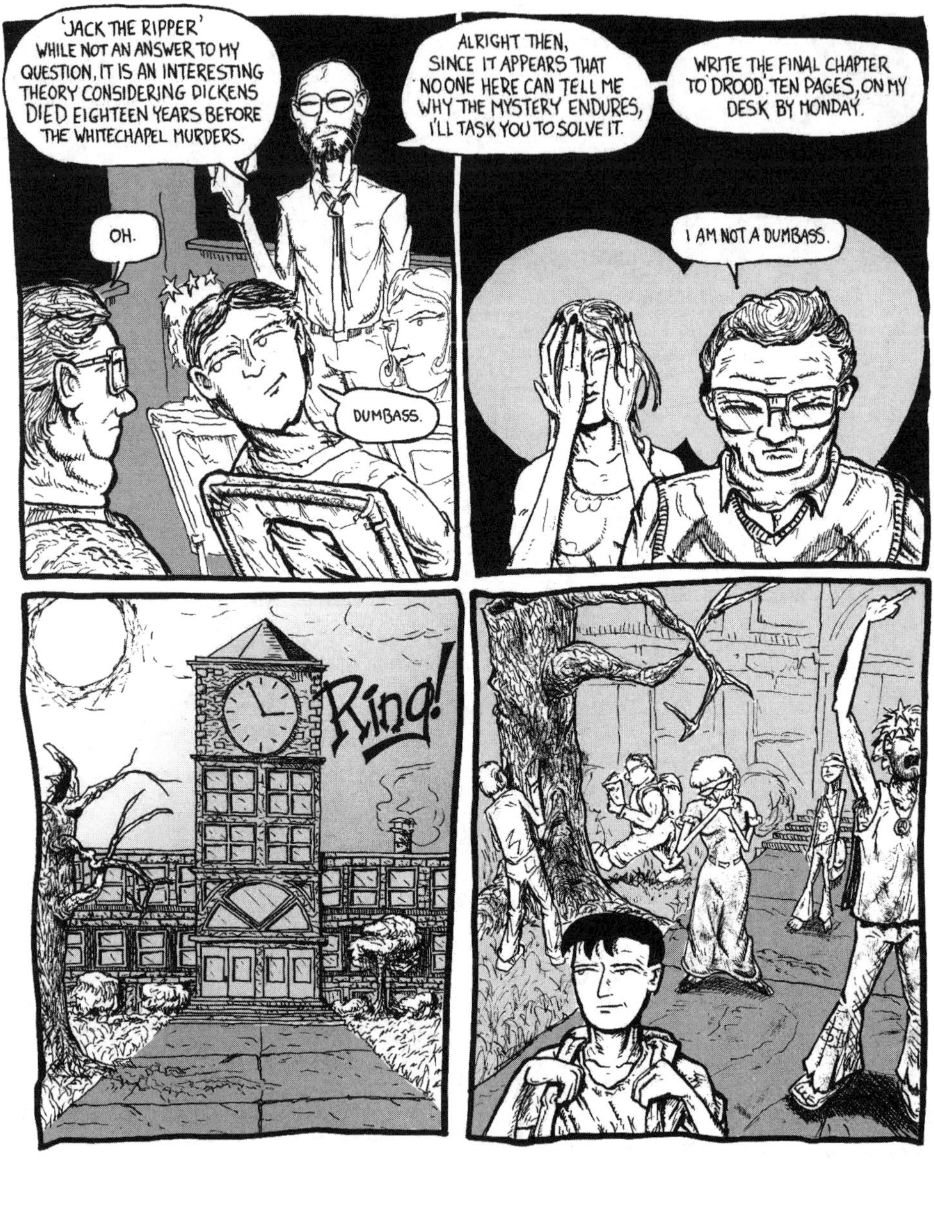
'JACK THE RIPPER' WHILE NOT AN ANSWER TO MY QUESTION, IT IS AN INTERESTING THEORY CONSIDERING DICKENS DIED EIGHTEEN YEARS BEFORE THE WHITECHAPEL MURDERS.
OH.
DUMBASS.
ALRIGHT THEN, SINCE IT APPEARS THAT NO ONE HERE CAN TELL ME WHY THE MYSTERY ENDURES, I'LL TASK YOU TO SOLVE IT.
WRITE THE FINAL CHAPTER TO 'DROOD'. TEN PAGES, ON MY DESK BY MONDAY.
I AM NOT A DUMBASS.
Ring!

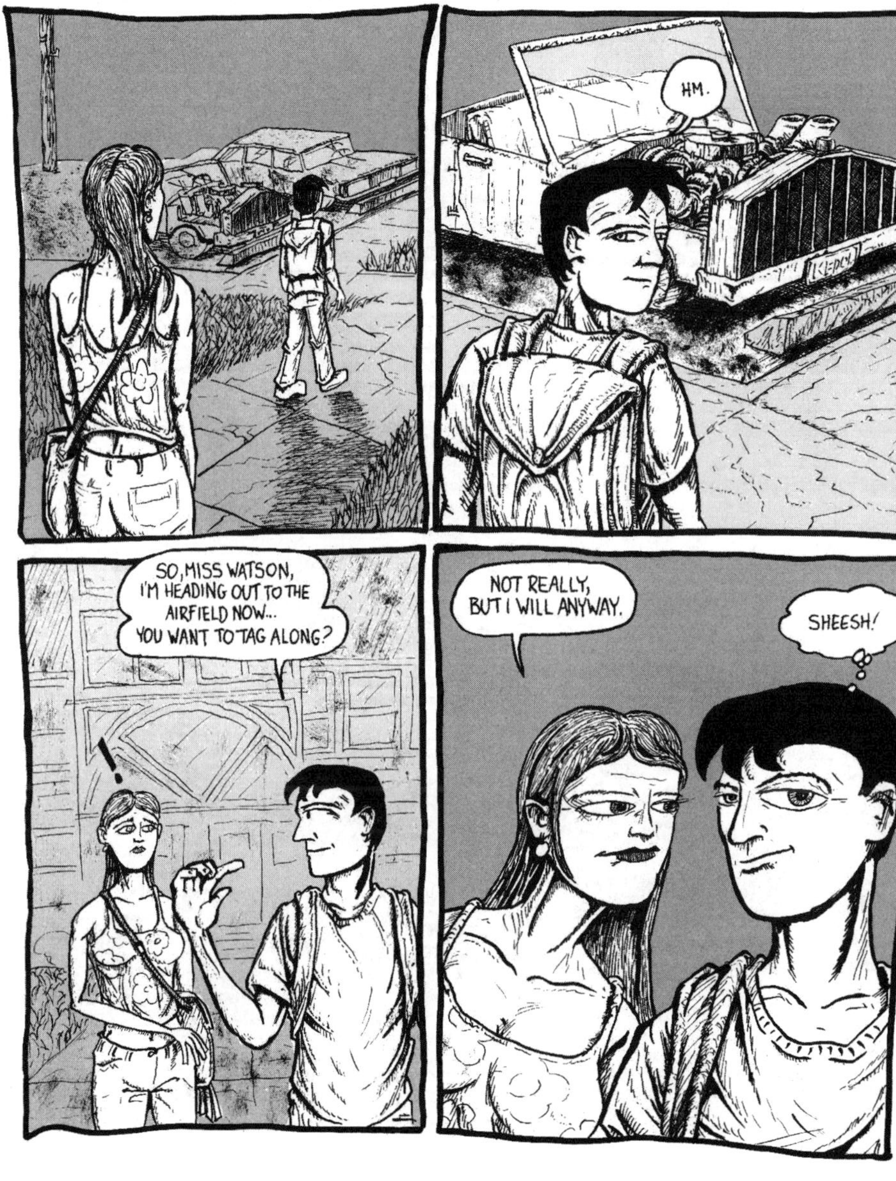
HM.
SO, MISS WATSON, I'M HEADING OUT TO THE AIRFIELD NOW... YOU WANT TO TAG ALONG?
!
NOT REALLY, BUT I WILL ANYWAY.
SHEESH!

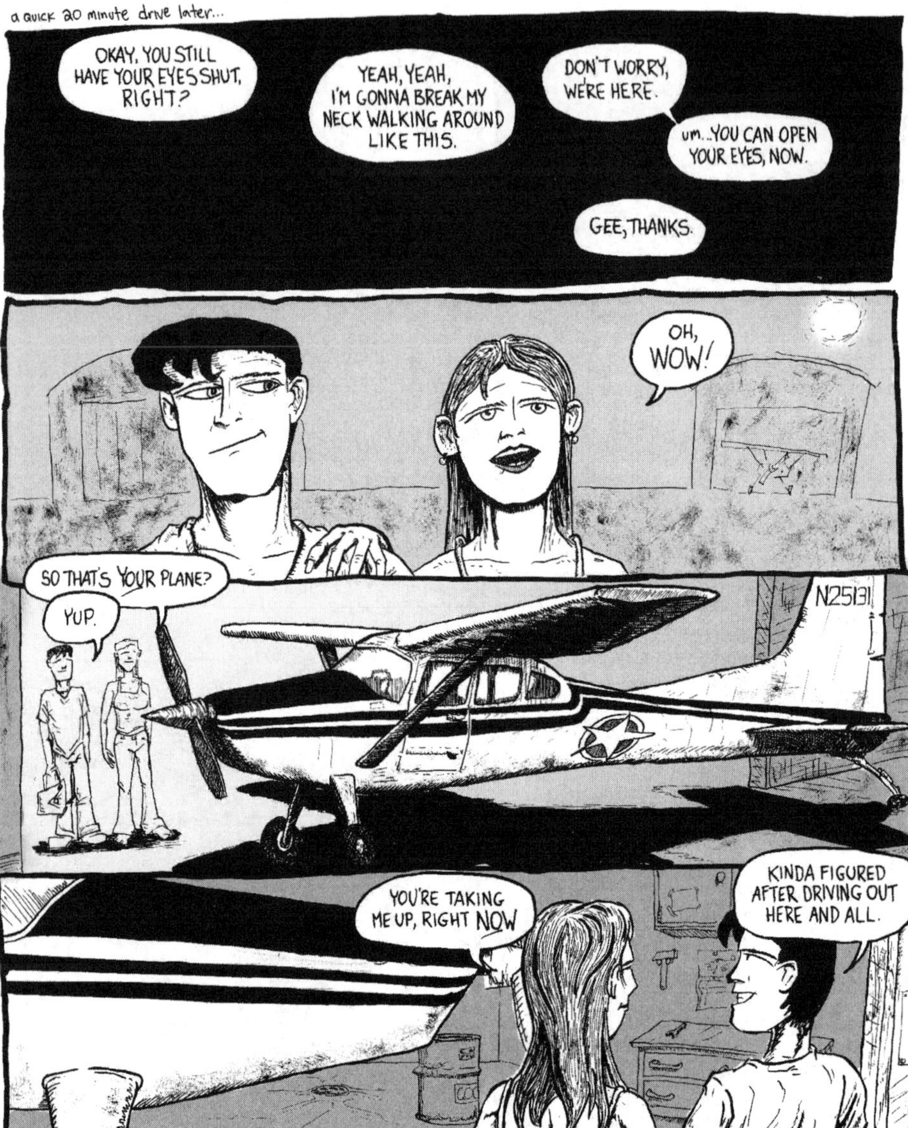
a quick 20 minute drive later...
OKAY, YOU STILL HAVE YOUR EYES SHUT, RIGHT?
YEAH, YEAH, I'M GONNA BREAK MY NECK WALKING AROUND LIKE THIS.
DON'T WORRY, WE'RE HERE.
um...YOU CAN OPEN YOUR EYES, NOW.
GEE, THANKS.
OH, WOW!
SO THAT'S YOUR PLANE?
YUP.
N25131
YOU'RE TAKING ME UP, RIGHT NOW
KINDA FIGURED AFTER DRIVING OUT HERE AND ALL.

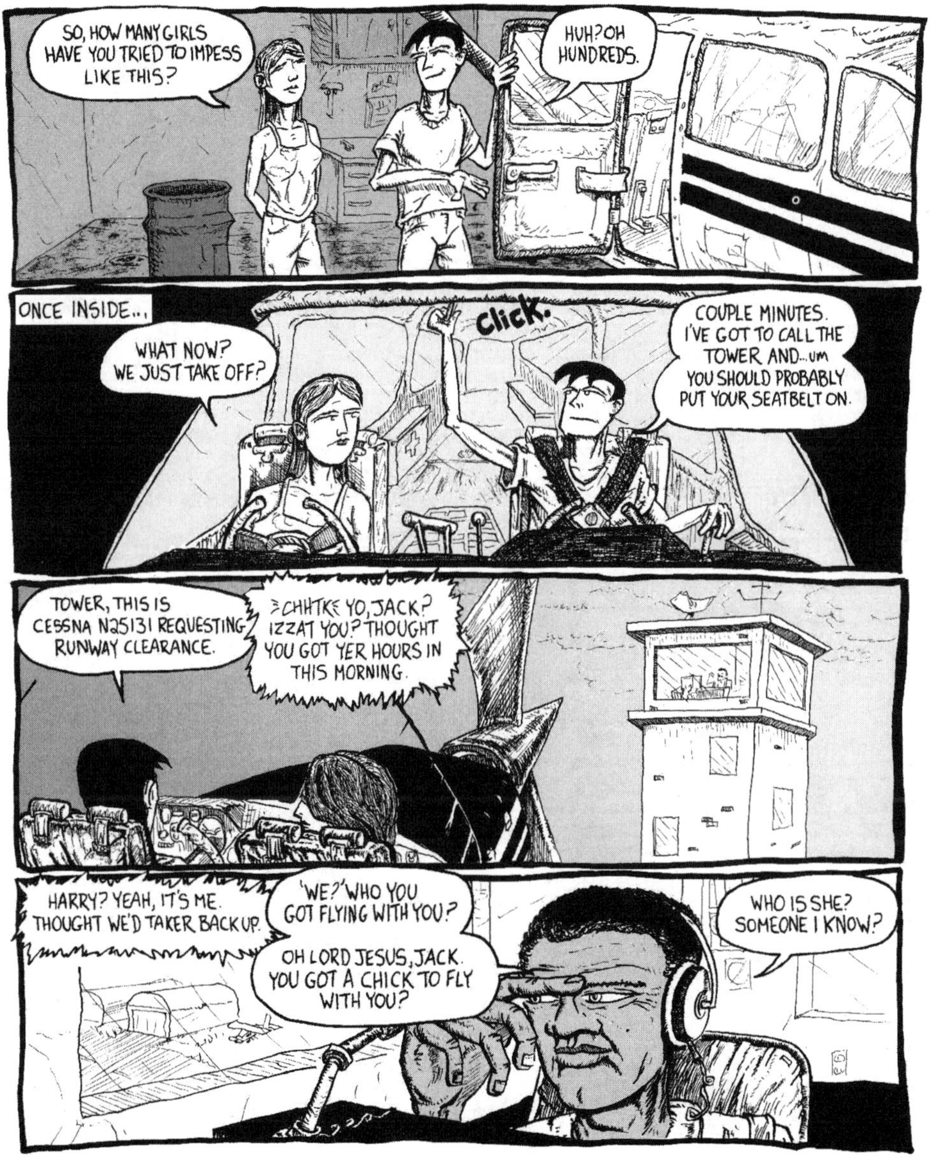
SO, HOW MANY GIRLS HAVE YOU TRIED TO IMPESS LIKE THIS?
HUH? OH HUNDREDS.
ONCE INSIDE...
WHAT NOW? WE JUST TAKE OFF?
CLICK.
COUPLE MINUTES. I'VE GOT TO CALL THE TOWER AND...um YOU SHOULD PROBABLY PUT YOUR SEATBELT ON.
TOWER, THIS IS CESSNA N25131 REQUESTING RUNWAY CLEARANCE.
≷CHHTK≷ YO, JACK? IZZAT YOU? THOUGHT YOU GOT YER HOURS IN THIS MORNING.
HARRY? YEAH, IT'S ME. THOUGHT WE'D TAKER BACK UP.
'WE?' WHO YOU GOT FLYING WITH YOU?
OH LORD JESUS, JACK. YOU GOT A CHICK TO FLY WITH YOU?
WHO IS SHE? SOMEONE I KNOW?

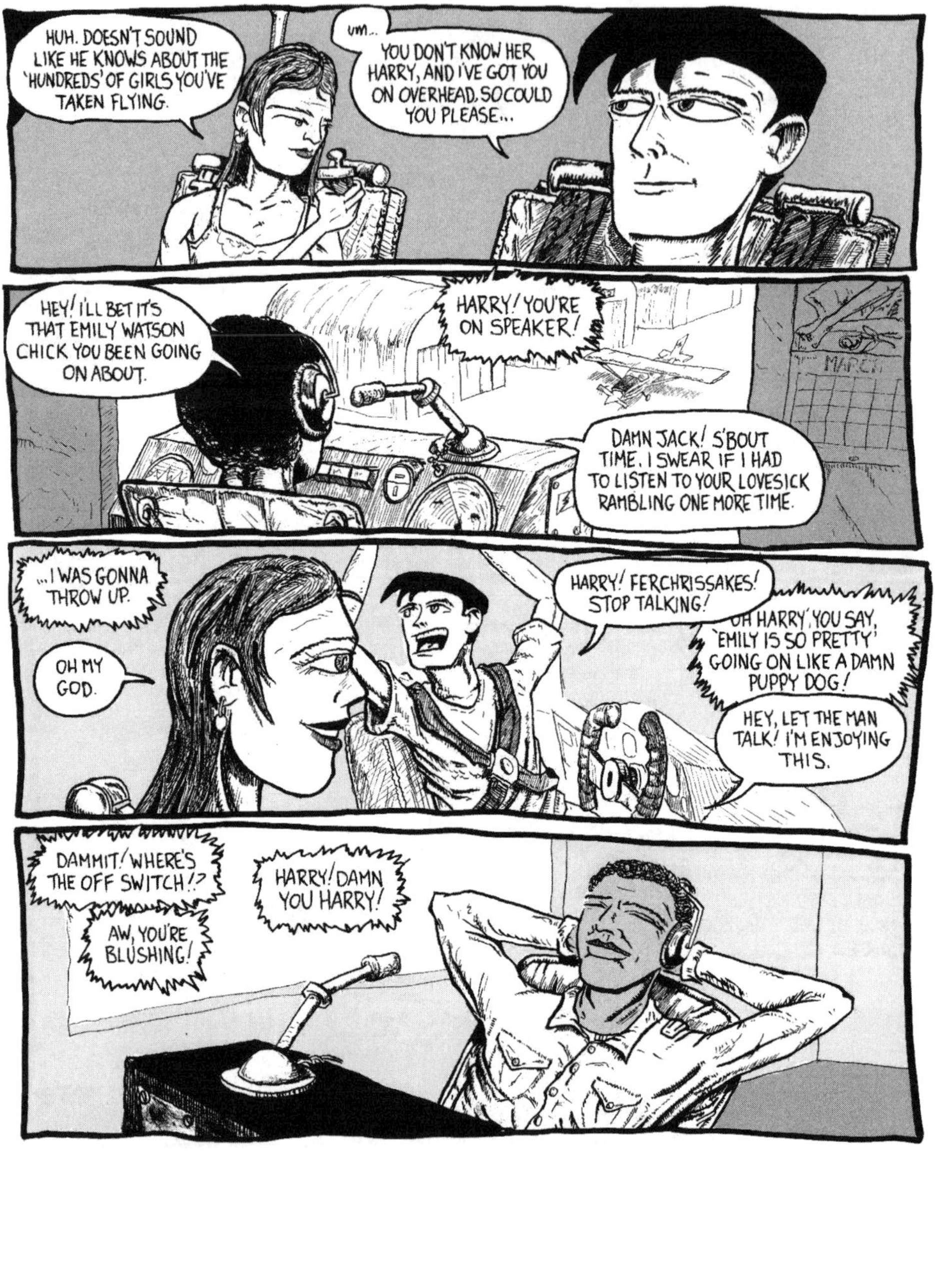
HUH. DOESN'T SOUND LIKE HE KNOWS ABOUT THE 'HUNDREDS' OF GIRLS YOU'VE TAKEN FLYING.
UM...
YOU DON'T KNOW HER HARRY, AND I'VE GOT YOU ON OVERHEAD. SO COULD YOU PLEASE...
HEY! I'LL BET IT'S THAT EMILY WATSON CHICK YOU BEEN GOING ON ABOUT.
HARRY! YOU'RE ON SPEAKER!
DAMN JACK! S'BOUT TIME. I SWEAR IF I HAD TO LISTEN TO YOUR LOVESICK RAMBLING ONE MORE TIME.
...I WAS GONNA THROW UP.
OH MY GOD.
HARRY! FERCHRISSAKES! STOP TALKING!
OH HARRY, YOU SAY, 'EMILY IS SO PRETTY' GOING ON LIKE A DAMN PUPPY DOG!
HEY, LET THE MAN TALK! I'M ENJOYING THIS.
DAMMIT! WHERE'S THE OFF SWITCH!?
AW, YOU'RE BLUSHING!
HARRY! DAMN YOU HARRY!

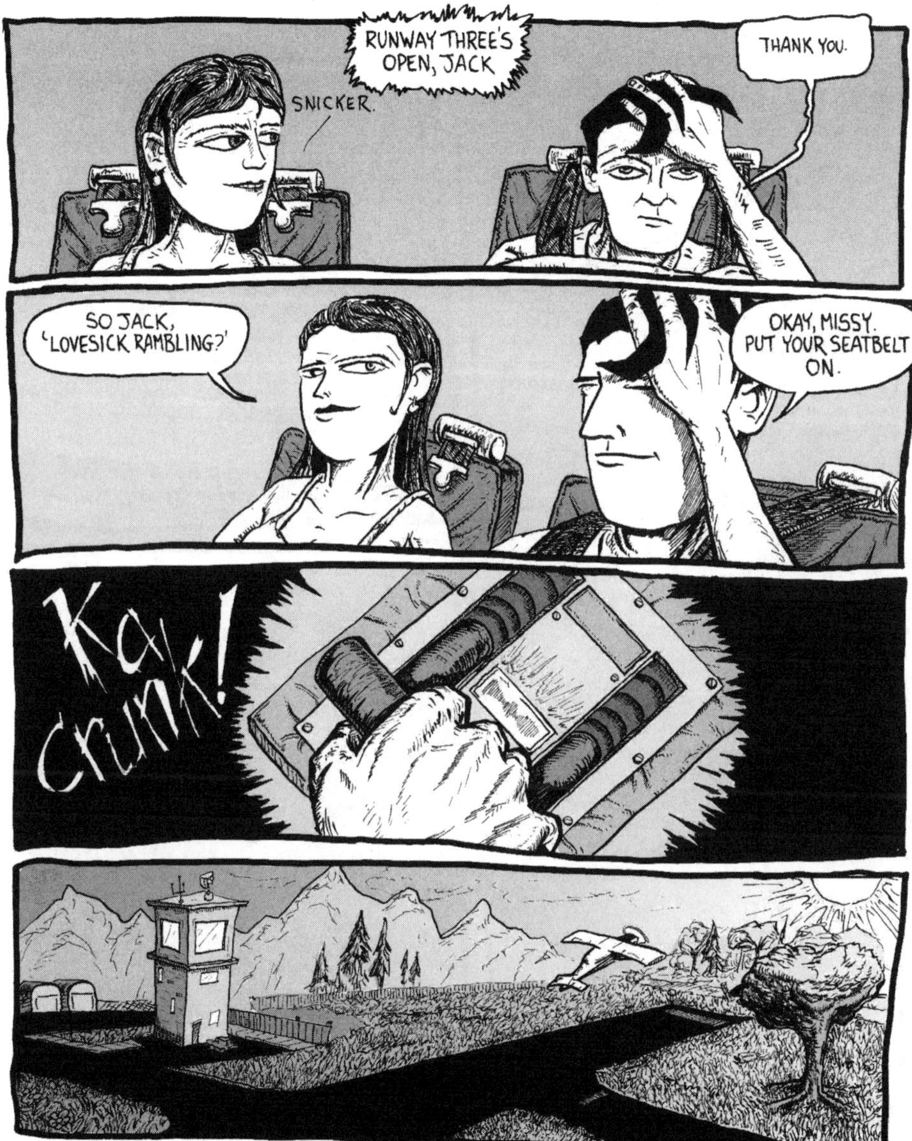
RUNWAY THREE'S OPEN, JACK
SNICKER.
THANK YOU.
SO JACK, 'LOVESICK RAMBLING?'
OKAY, MISSY. PUT YOUR SEATBELT ON.
Ka Crunk!

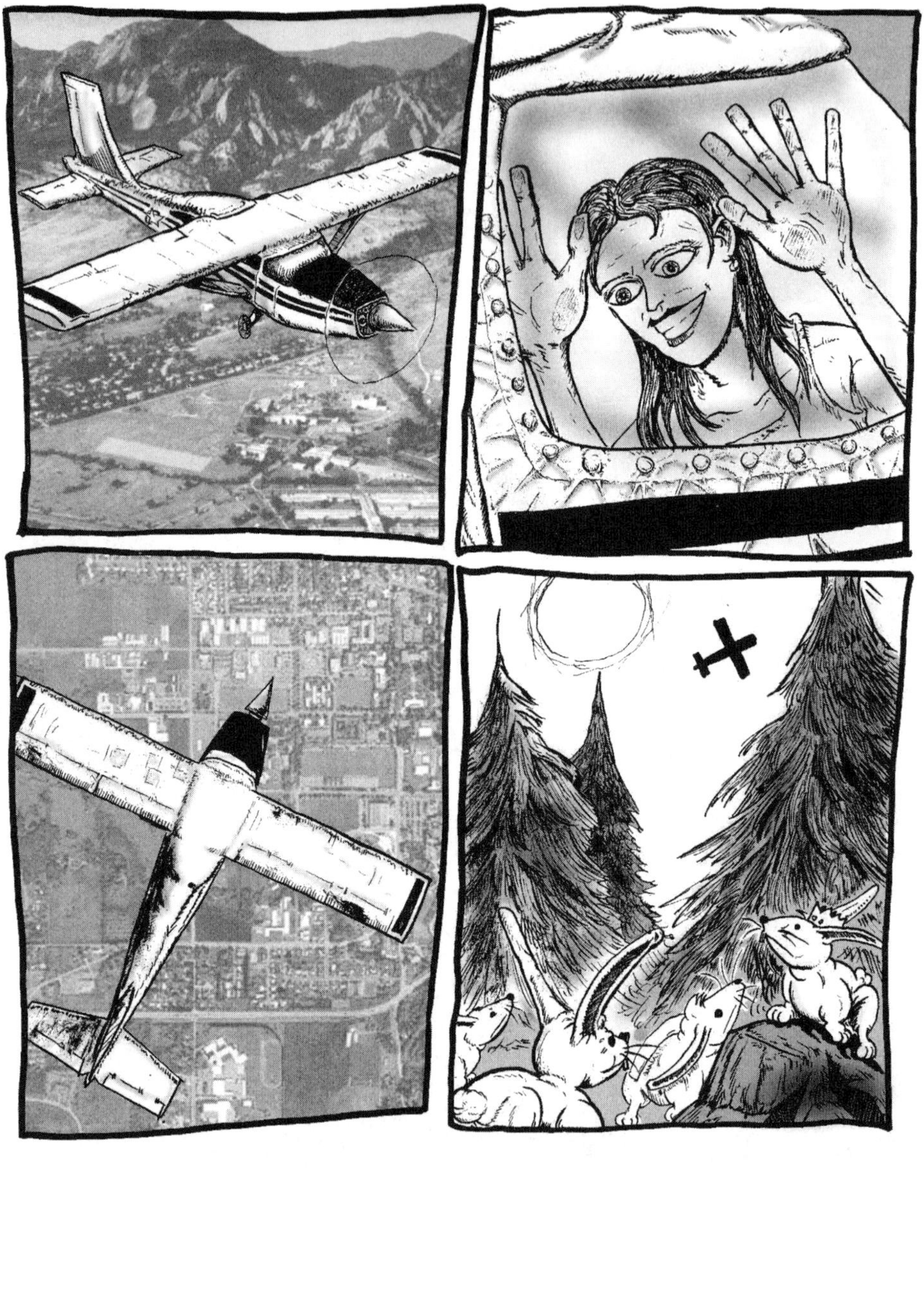

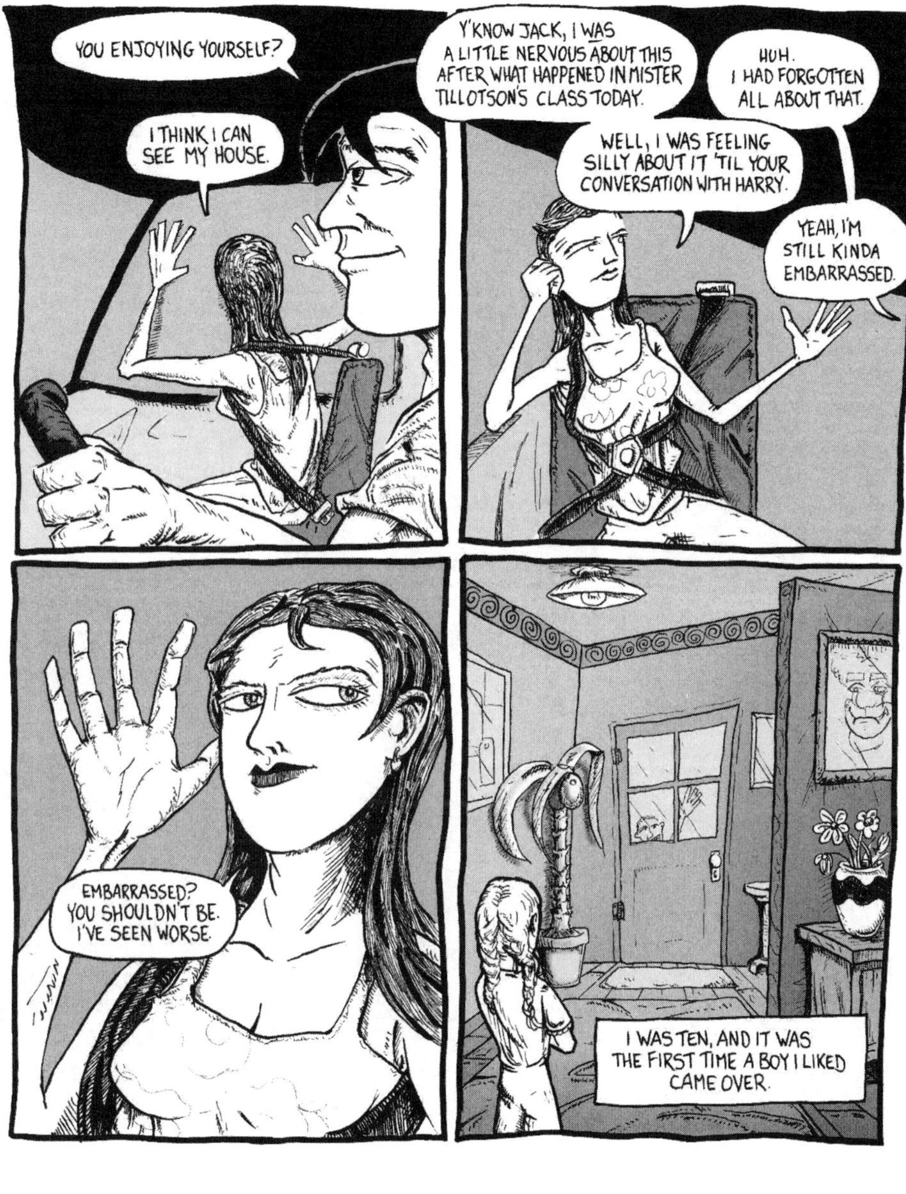
YOU ENJOYING YOURSELF?
I THINK I CAN SEE MY HOUSE.
Y'KNOW JACK, I WAS A LITTLE NERVOUS ABOUT THIS AFTER WHAT HAPPENED IN MISTER TILLOTSON'S CLASS TODAY.
HUH. I HAD FORGOTTEN ALL ABOUT THAT.
WELL, I WAS FEELING SILLY ABOUT IT 'TIL YOUR CONVERSATION WITH HARRY.
YEAH, I'M STILL KINDA EMBARRASSED.
EMBARRASSED? YOU SHOULDN'T BE. I'VE SEEN WORSE.
I WAS TEN, AND IT WAS THE FIRST TIME A BOY I LIKED CAME OVER.

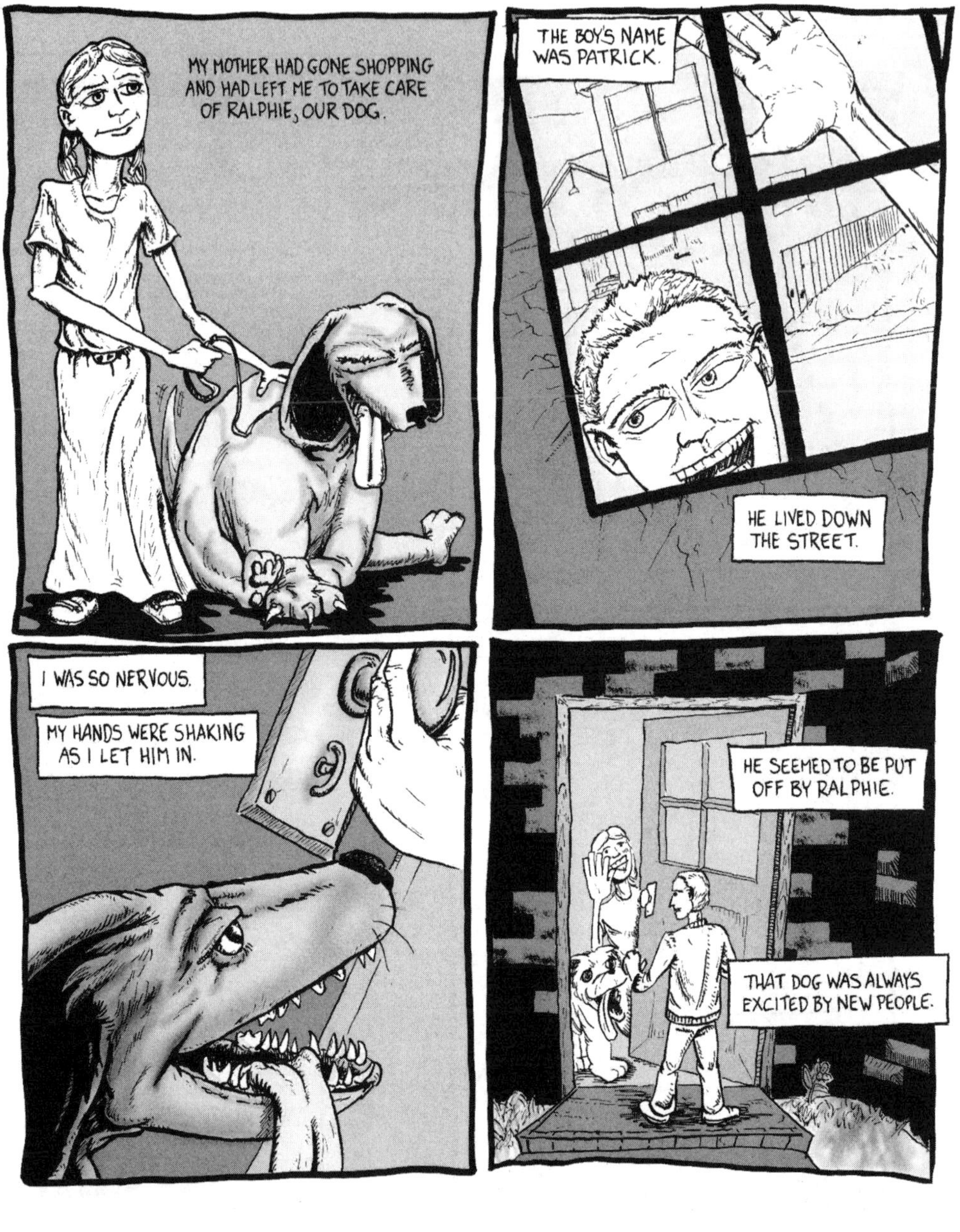
MY MOTHER HAD GONE SHOPPING AND HAD LEFT ME TO TAKE CARE OF RALPHIE, OUR DOG.
THE BOY'S NAME WAS PATRICK.
HE LIVED DOWN THE STREET.
I WAS SO NERVOUS.
MY HANDS WERE SHAKING AS I LET HIM IN.
HE SEEMED TO BE PUT OFF BY RALPHIE.
THAT DOG WAS ALWAYS EXCITED BY NEW PEOPLE.

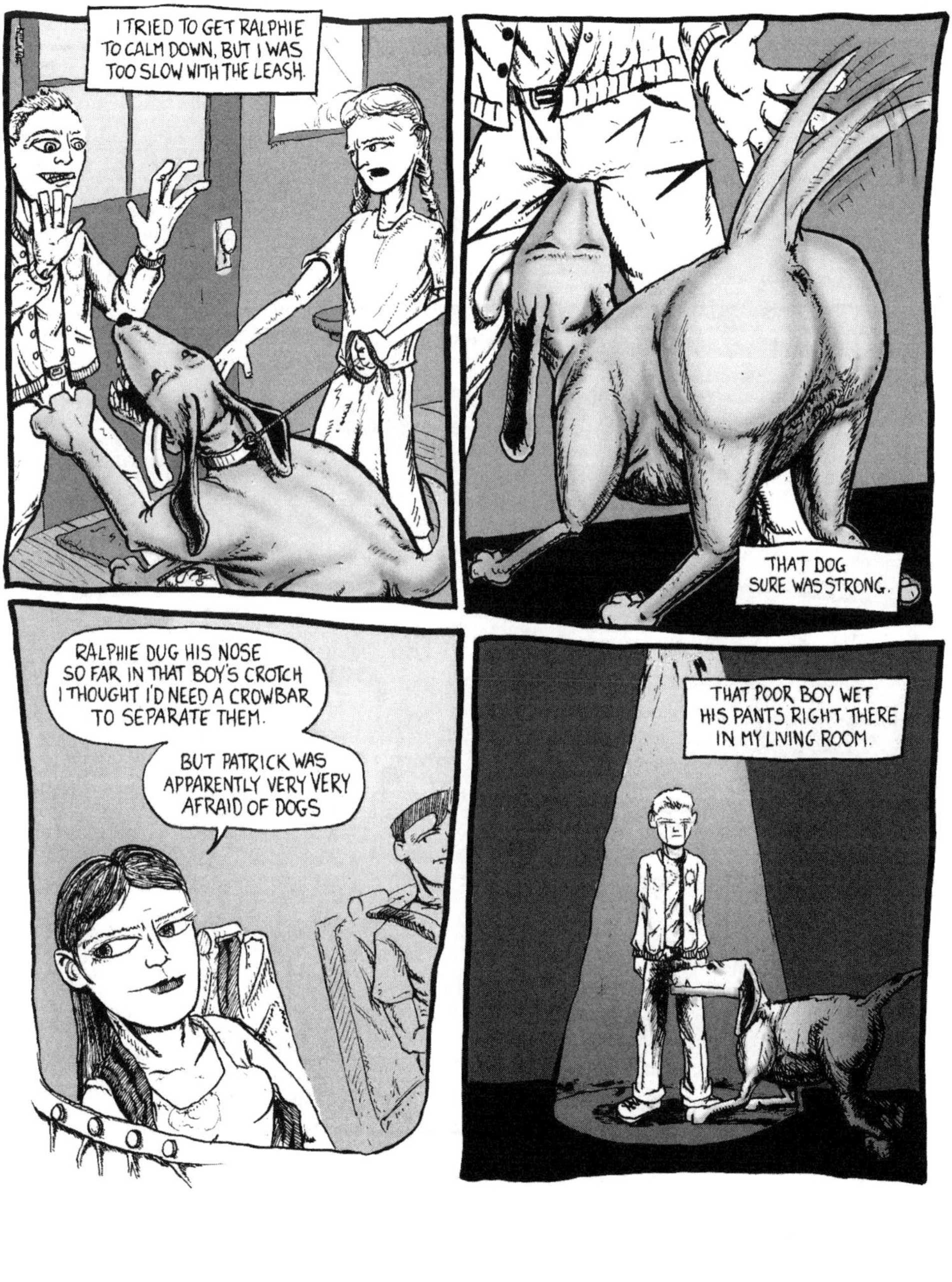
I TRIED TO GET RALPHIE TO CALM DOWN, BUT I WAS TOO SLOW WITH THE LEASH.
THAT DOG SURE WAS STRONG.
RALPHIE DUG HIS NOSE SO FAR IN THAT BOY'S CROTCH I THOUGHT I'D NEED A CROWBAR TO SEPARATE THEM.
BUT PATRICK WAS APPARENTLY VERY VERY AFRAID OF DOGS
THAT POOR BOY WET HIS PANTS RIGHT THERE IN MY LIVING ROOM.

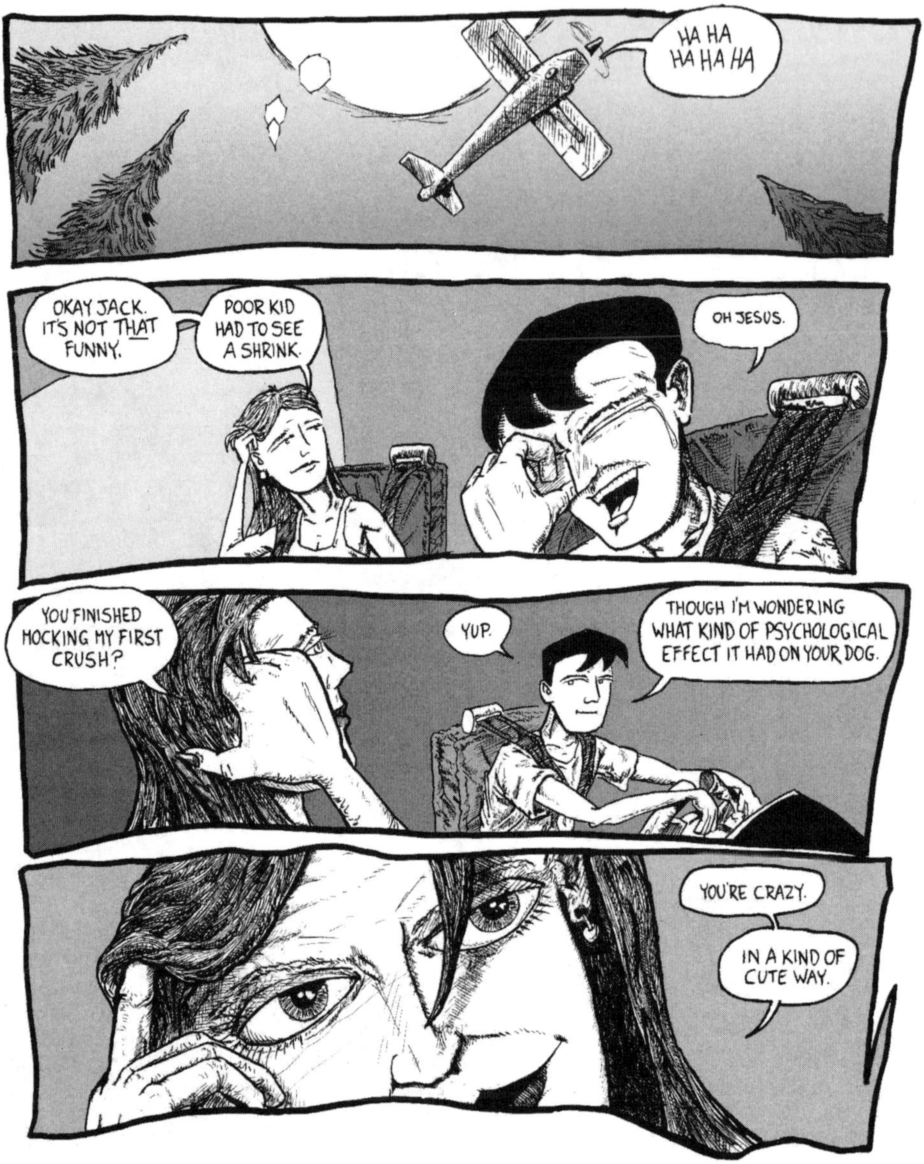
HA HA
HA HA HA
OKAY JACK. IT'S NOT THAT FUNNY.
POOR KID HAD TO SEE A SHRINK.
OH JESUS.
YOU FINISHED MOCKING MY FIRST CRUSH?
YUP.
THOUGH I'M WONDERING WHAT KIND OF PSYCHOLOGICAL EFFECT IT HAD ON YOUR DOG.
YOU'RE CRAZY.
IN A KIND OF CUTE WAY.

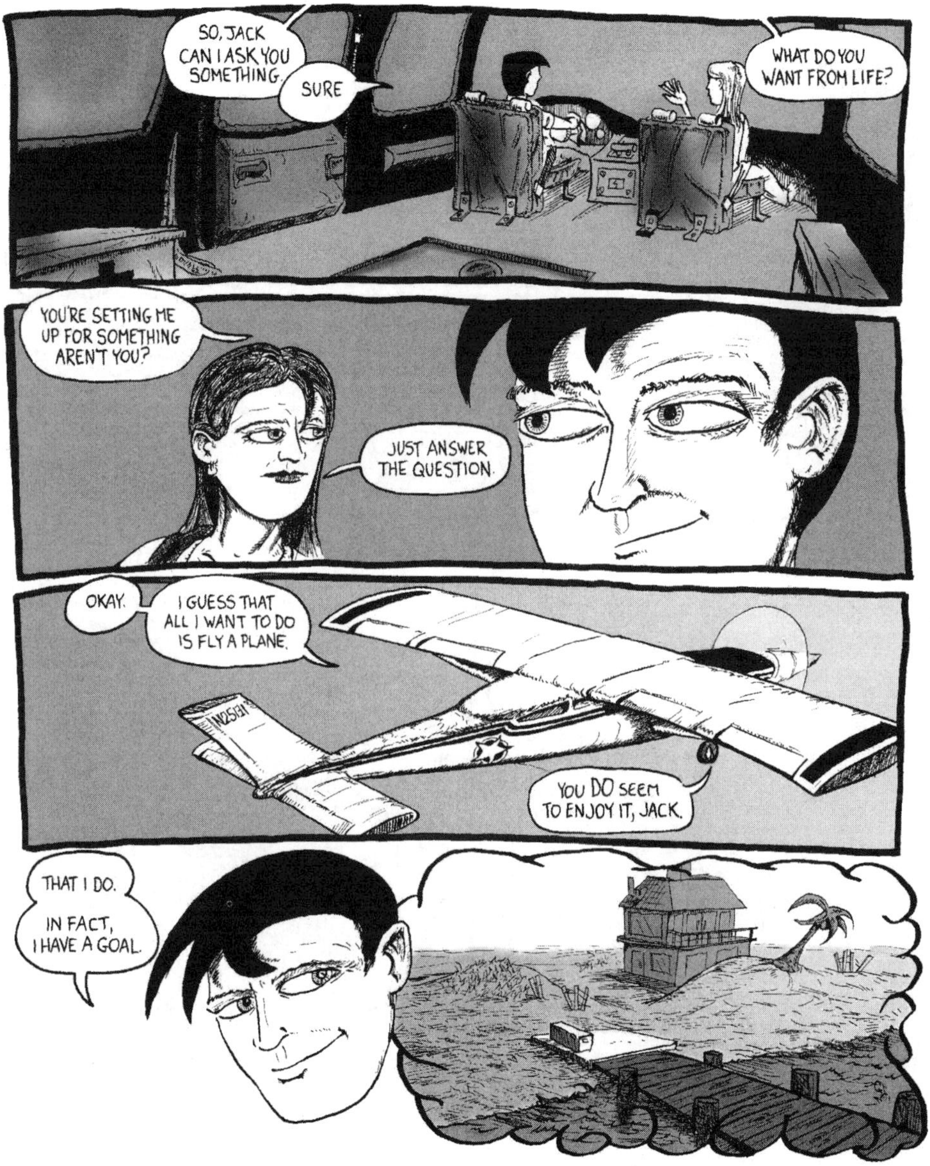
SO, JACK CAN I ASK YOU SOMETHING.
SURE
WHAT DO YOU WANT FROM LIFE?
YOU'RE SETTING ME UP FOR SOMETHING AREN'T YOU?
JUST ANSWER THE QUESTION.
OKAY.
I GUESS THAT ALL I WANT TO DO IS FLY A PLANE.
YOU DO SEEM TO ENJOY IT, JACK.
THAT I DO.
IN FACT, I HAVE A GOAL.

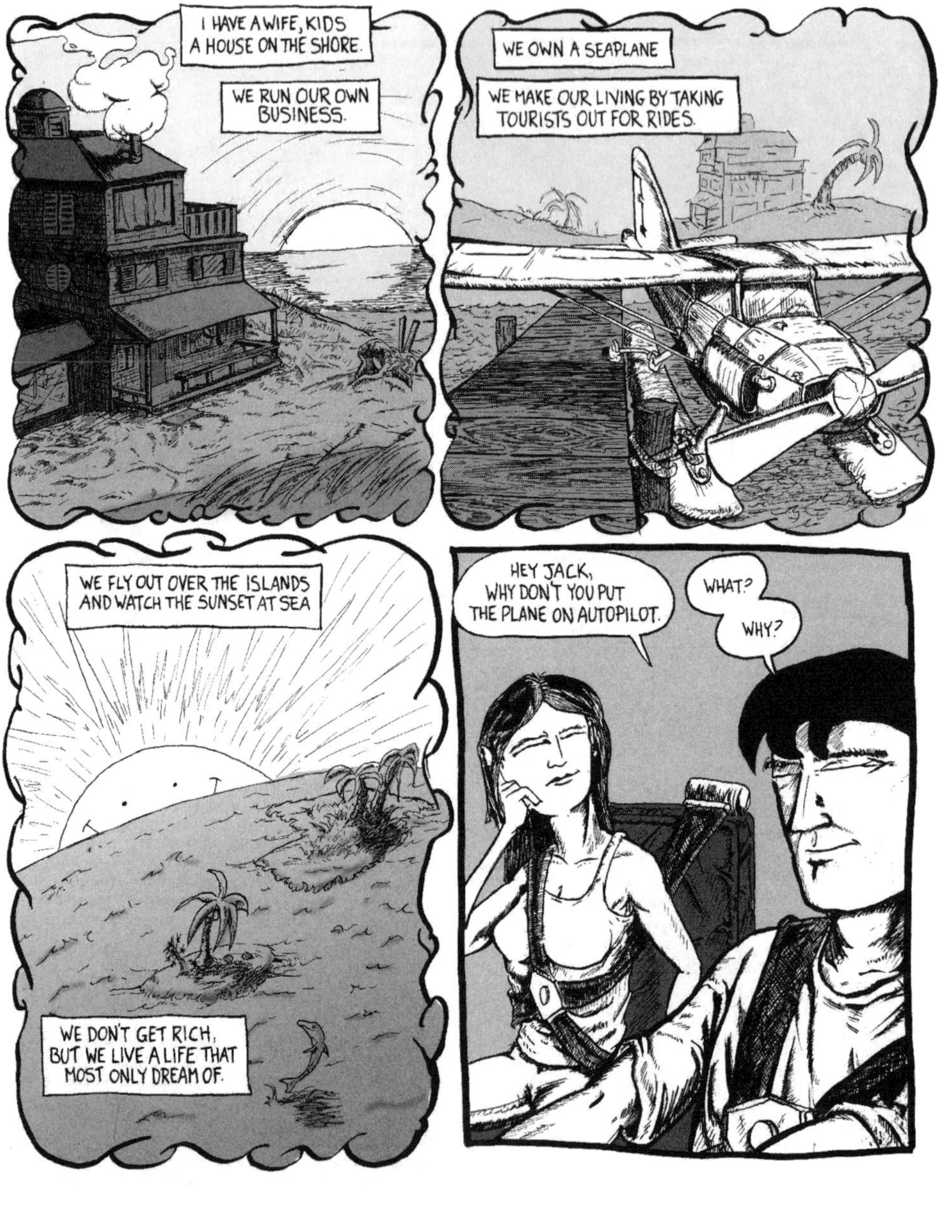
I HAVE A WIFE, KIDS
A HOUSE ON THE SHORE.
WE RUN OUR OWN BUSINESS.
WE OWN A SEAPLANE
WE MAKE OUR LIVING BY TAKING TOURISTS OUT FOR RIDES.
WE FLY OUT OVER THE ISLANDS AND WATCH THE SUNSET AT SEA
WE DON'T GET RICH, BUT WE LIVE A LIFE THAT MOST ONLY DREAM OF.
HEY JACK, WHY DON'T YOU PUT THE PLANE ON AUTOPILOT.
WHAT?
WHY?

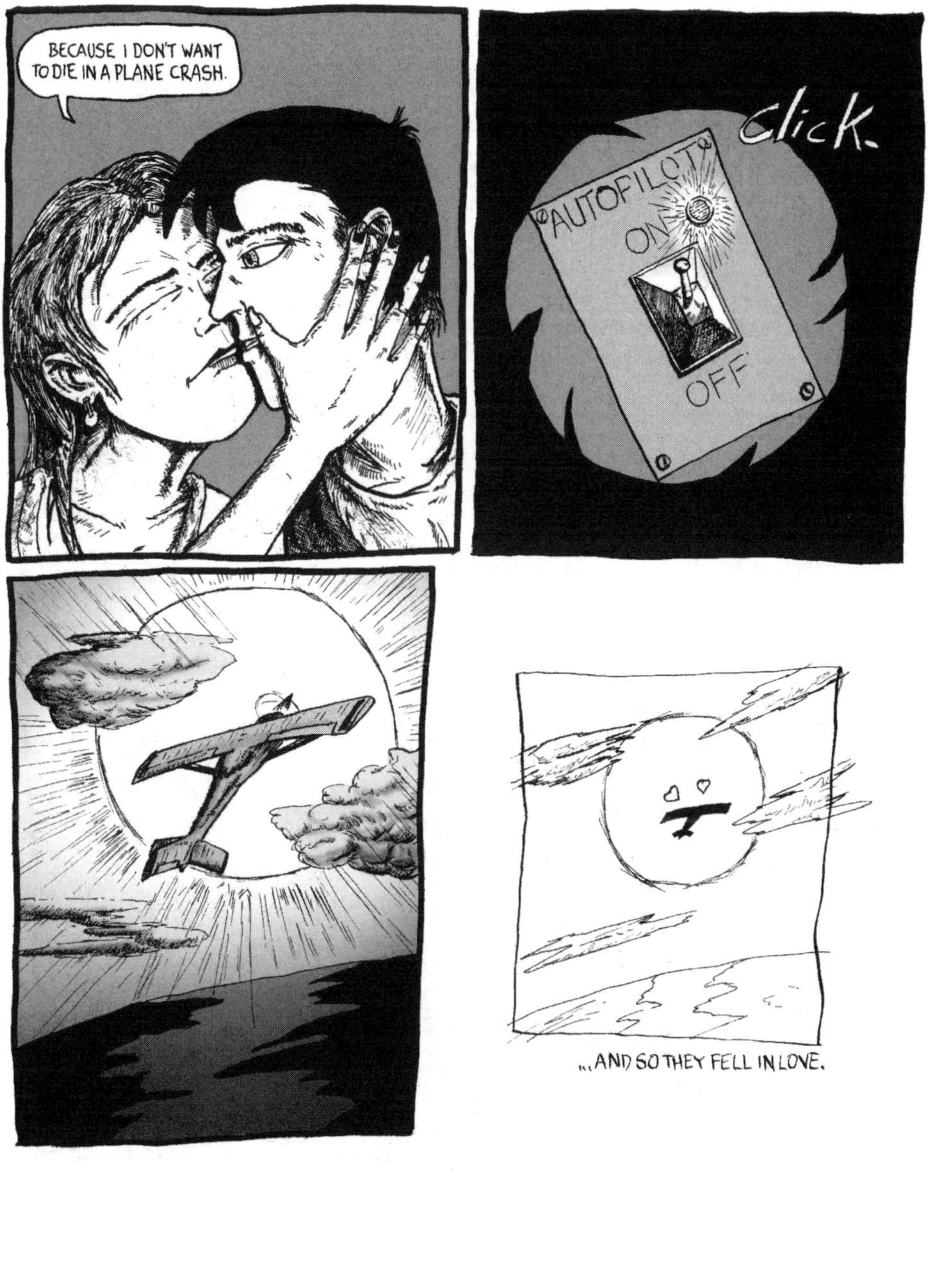
BECAUSE I DON'T WANT TO DIE IN A PLANE CRASH.
Click.
AUTOPILOT
ON
OFF
...AND SO THEY FELL IN LOVE.

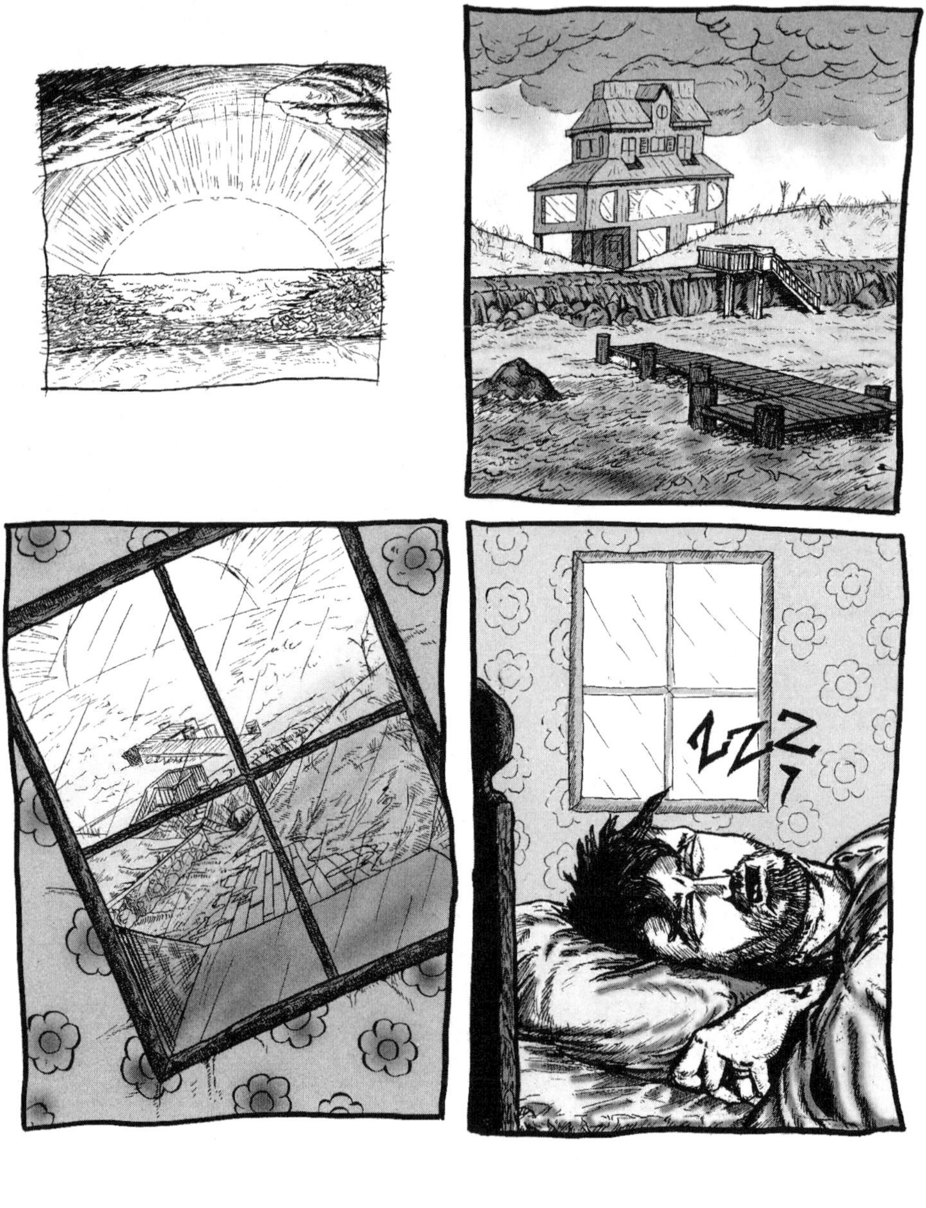
ZZZ

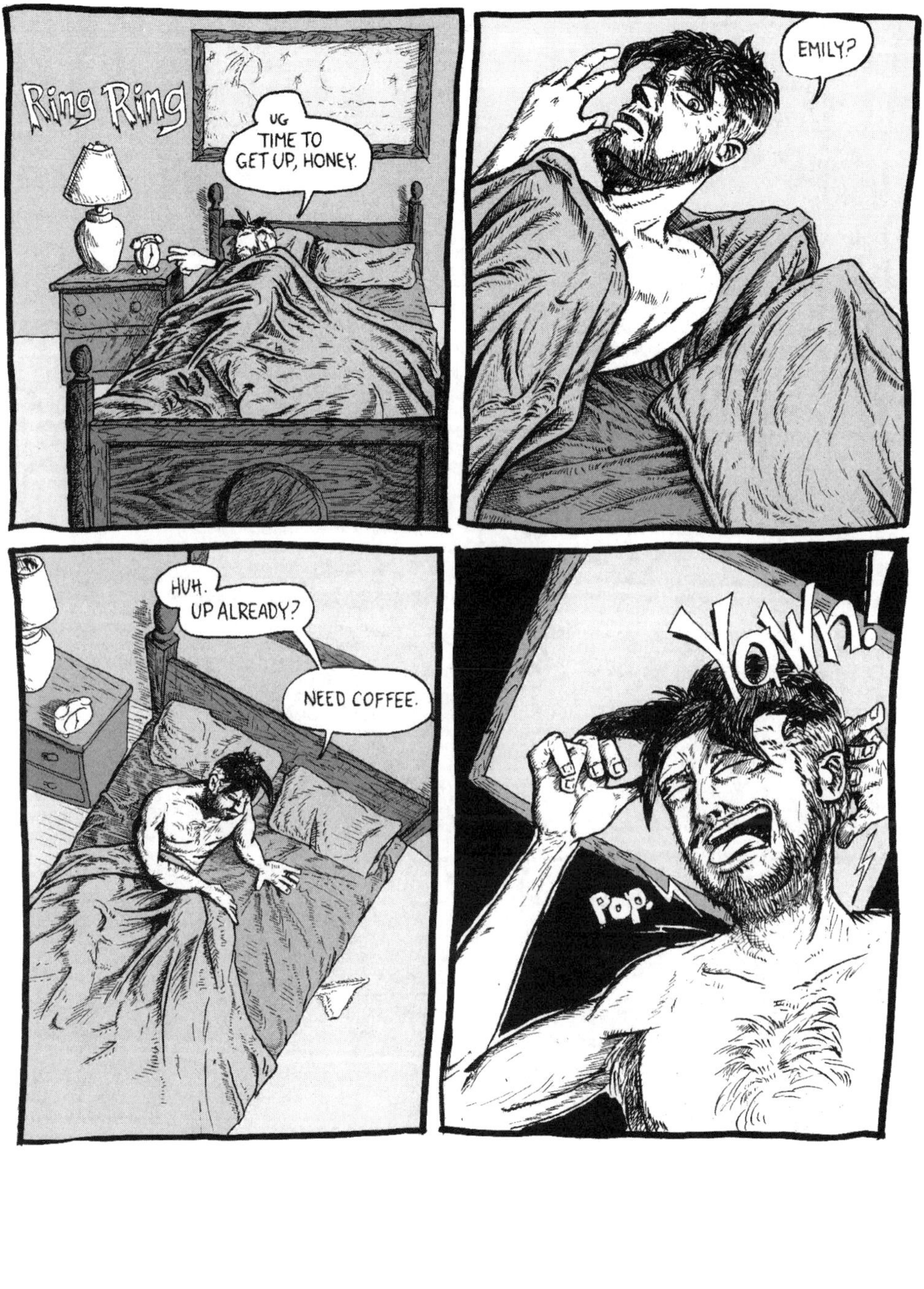
Ring Ring
UG
TIME TO GET UP, HONEY.
EMILY?
HUH. UP ALREADY?
NEED COFFEE.
YAWN!
POP.

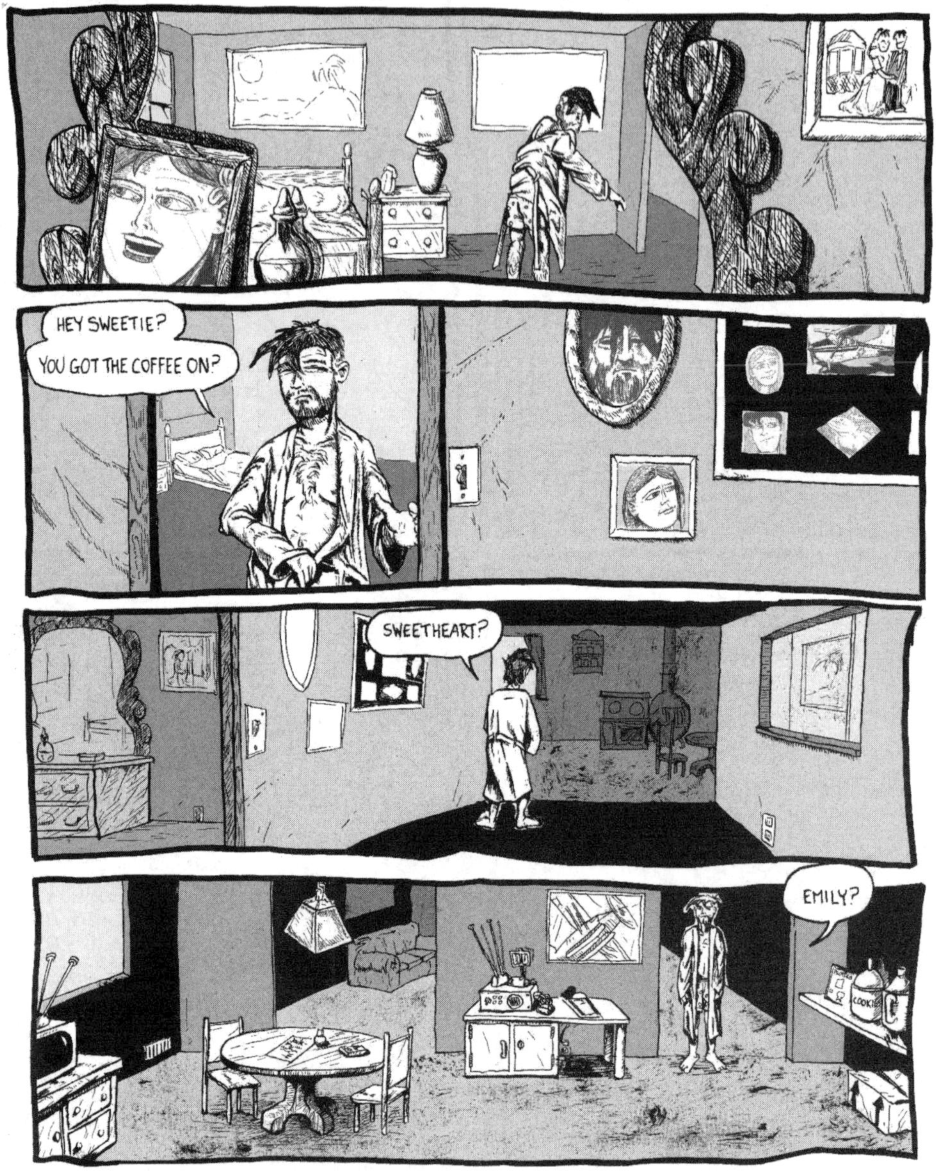
HEY SWEETIE?
YOU GOT THE COFFEE ON?
SWEETHEART?
EMILY?

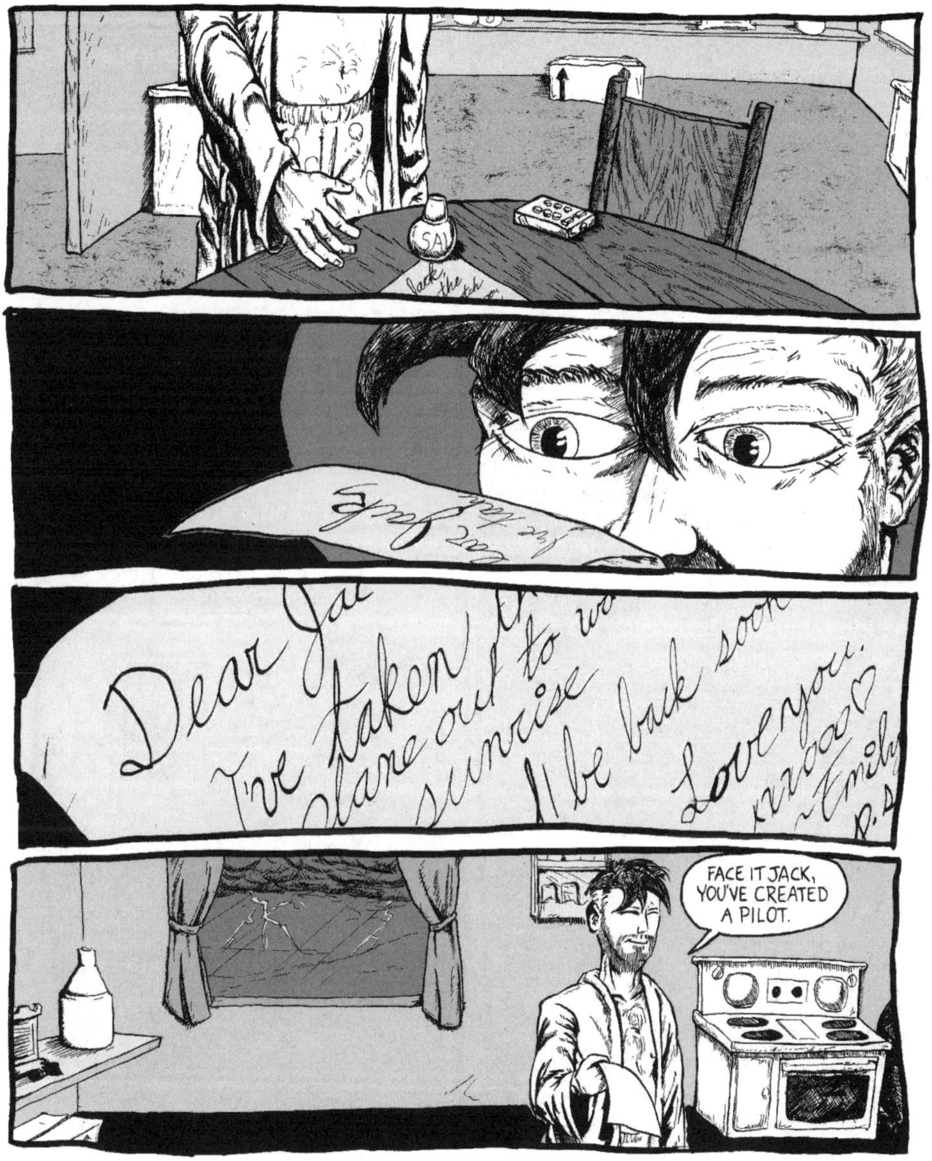
Dear Ja
I've taken
plane out to w
sunrise
ll be back soon
Love you.
xxxooo
~Emily
FACE IT JACK, YOU'VE CREATED A PILOT.

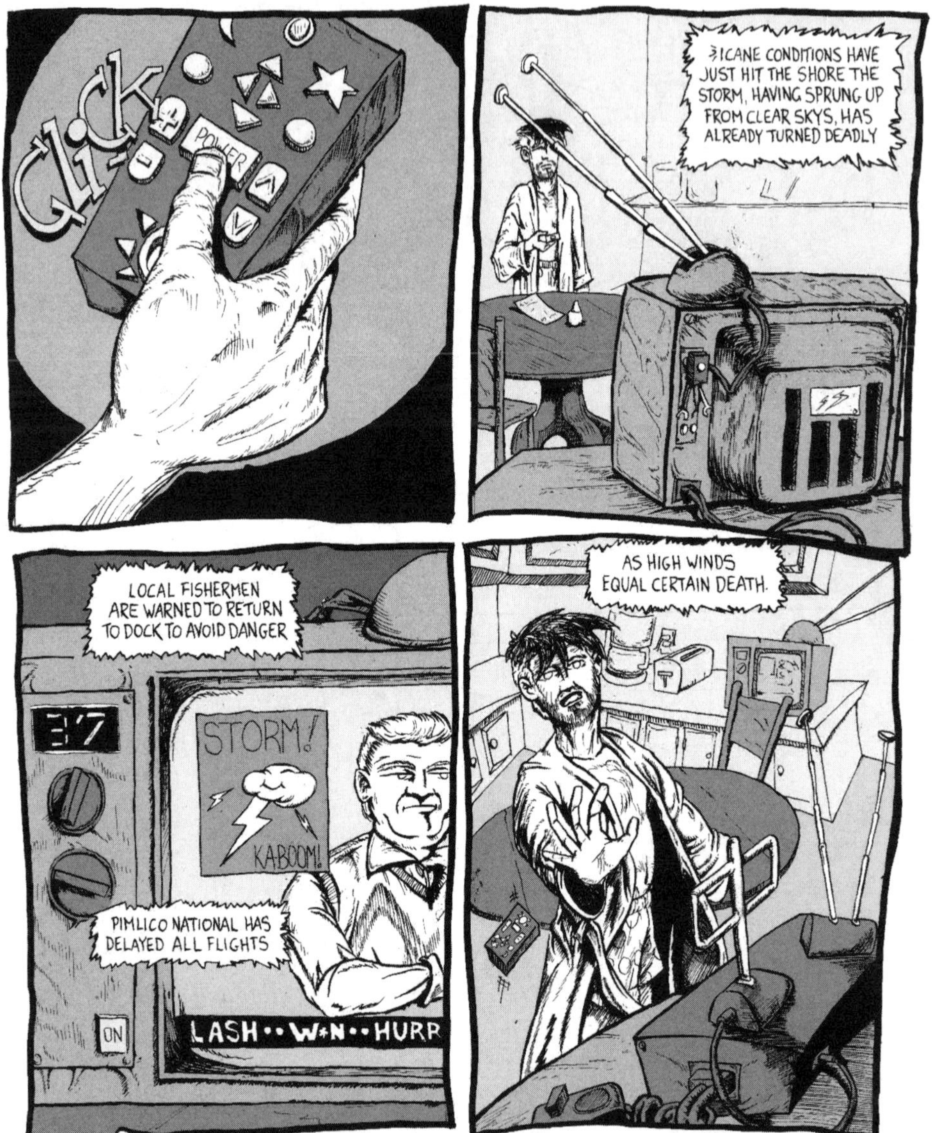
Click
POWER
ICANE CONDITIONS HAVE JUST HIT THE SHORE THE STORM, HAVING SPRUNG UP FROM CLEAR SKYS, HAS ALREADY TURNED DEADLY
LOCAL FISHERMEN ARE WARNED TO RETURN TO DOCK TO AVOID DANGER
37
STORM!
KABOOM!
PIMLICO NATIONAL HAS DELAYED ALL FLIGHTS
ON
LASH • • W*N • • HURR
AS HIGH WINDS EQUAL CERTAIN DEATH.

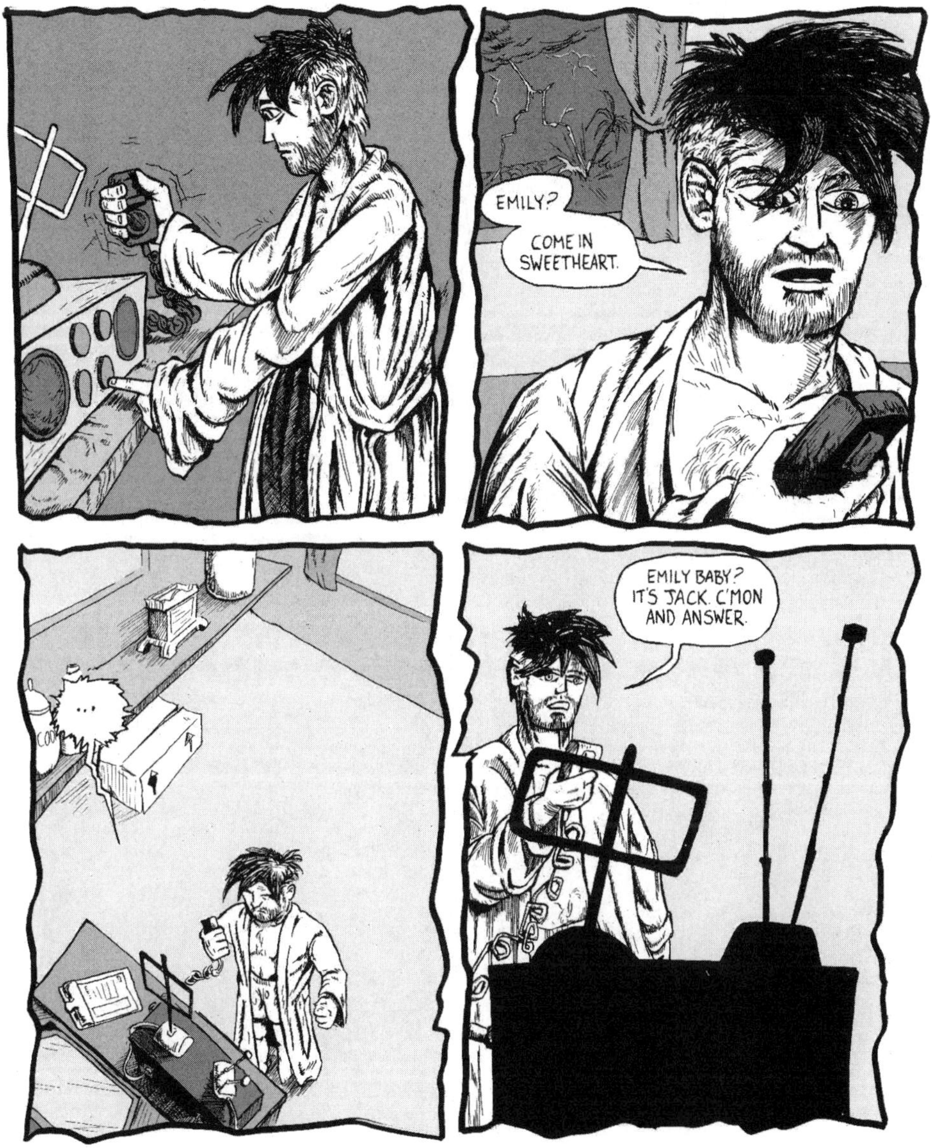
EMILY?
COME IN SWEETHEART.
EMILY BABY? IT'S JACK. C'MON AND ANSWER.

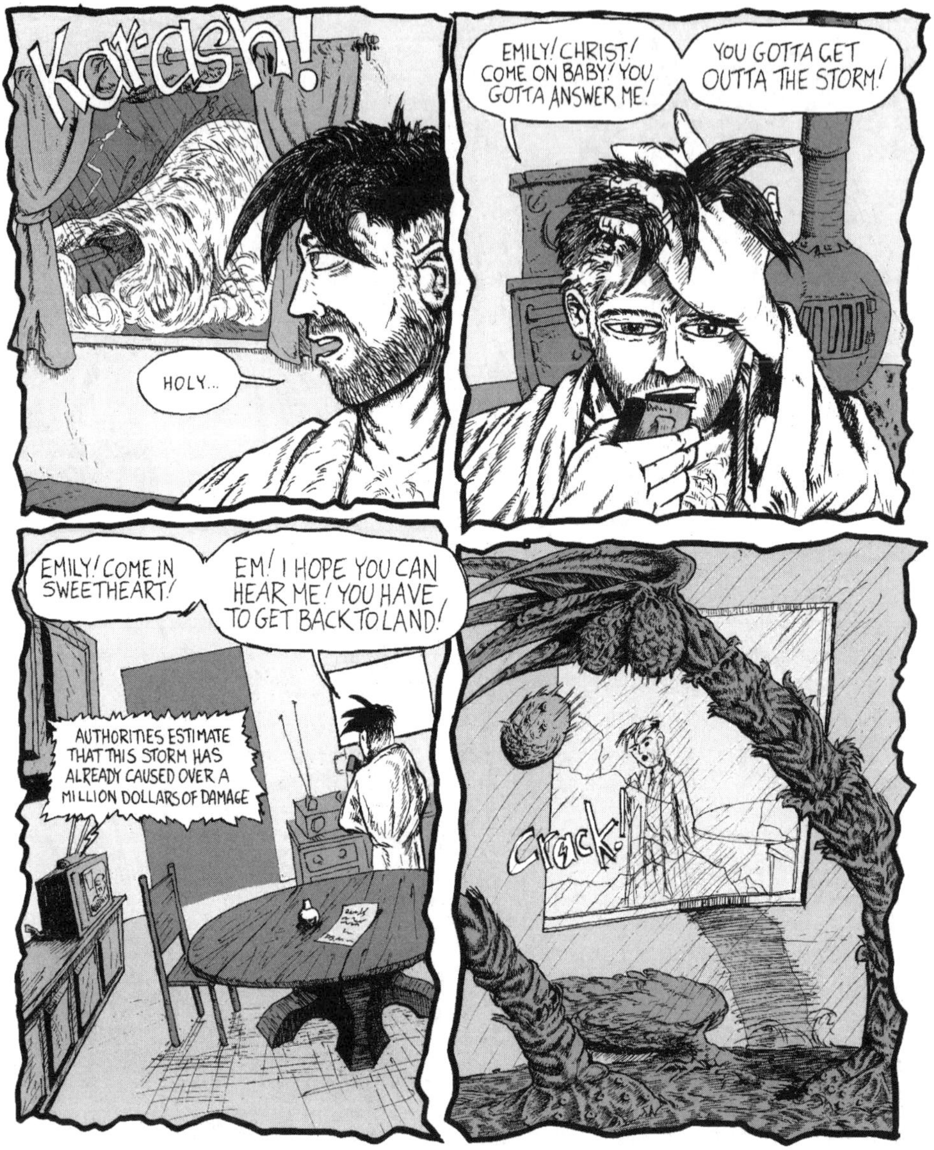
Kar-ash!
HOLY...
EMILY! CHRIST! COME ON BABY! YOU, GOTTA ANSWER ME!
YOU GOTTA GET OUTTA THE STORM!
EMILY! COME IN SWEETHEART!
EM! I HOPE YOU CAN HEAR ME! YOU HAVE TO GET BACK TO LAND!
AUTHORITIES ESTIMATE THAT THIS STORM HAS ALREADY CAUSED OVER A MILLION DOLLARS OF DAMAGE
Crack!

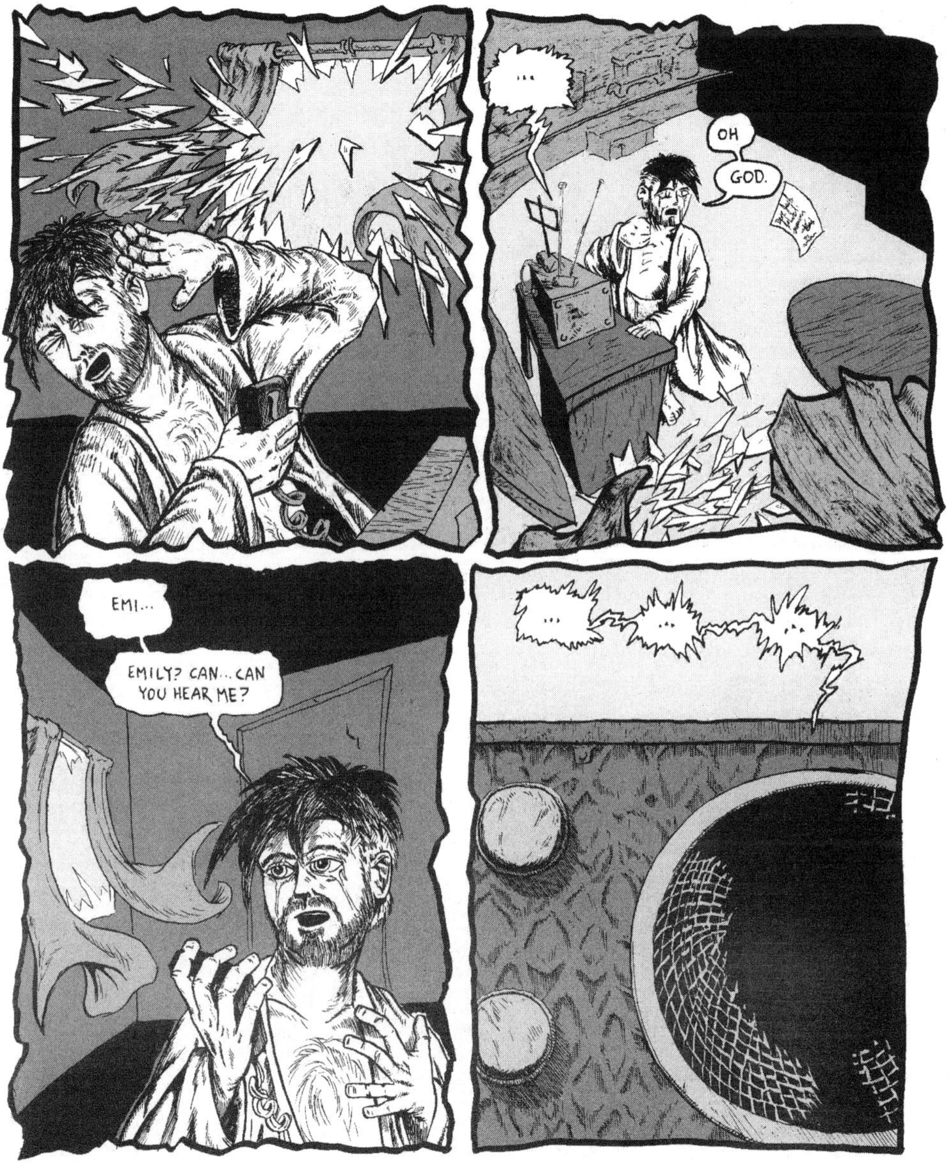
...
OH
GOD.
EMI...
EMILY? CAN...CAN YOU HEAR ME?
...
...
...

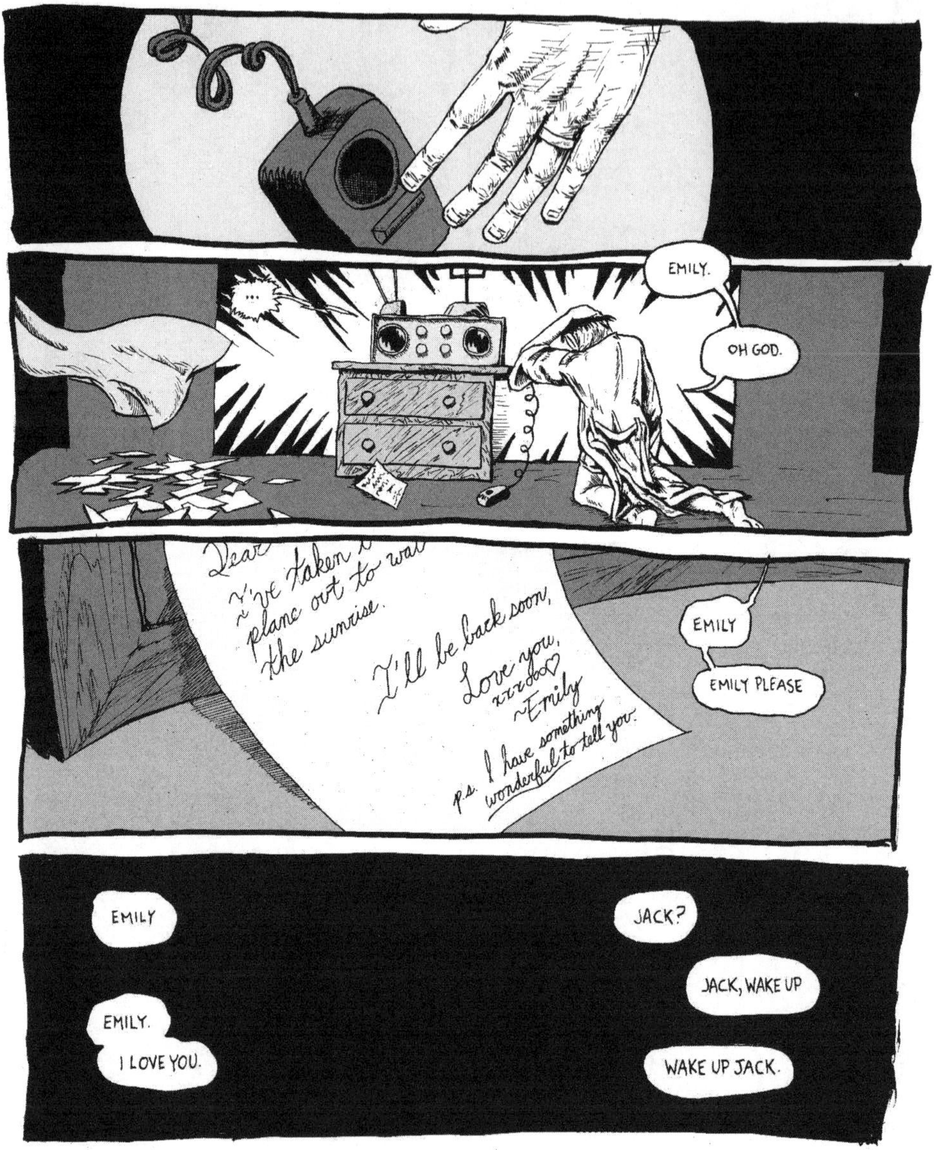
EMILY.
OH GOD.
I've taken
plane out to
the sunrise.
I'll be back soon,
Love you,
xxxoo
~Emily
p.s. I have something wonderful to tell you.
EMILY
EMILY PLEASE
EMILY
JACK?
JACK, WAKE UP
EMILY.
I LOVE YOU.
WAKE UP JACK.

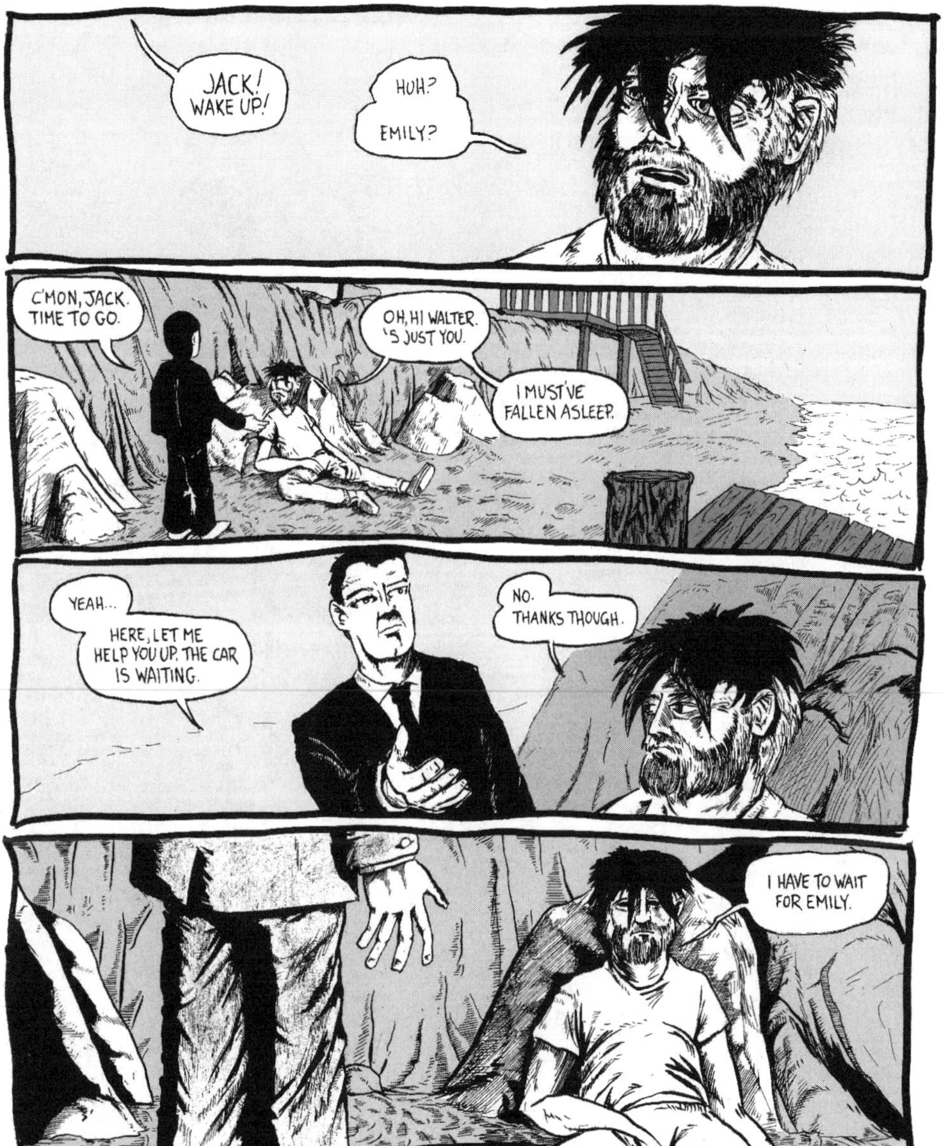
JACK! WAKE UP!
HUH?
EMILY?
C'MON, JACK. TIME TO GO.
OH, HI WALTER. 'S JUST YOU.
I MUST'VE FALLEN ASLEEP.
YEAH...
HERE, LET ME HELP YOU UP. THE CAR IS WAITING.
NO. THANKS THOUGH.
I HAVE TO WAIT FOR EMILY.

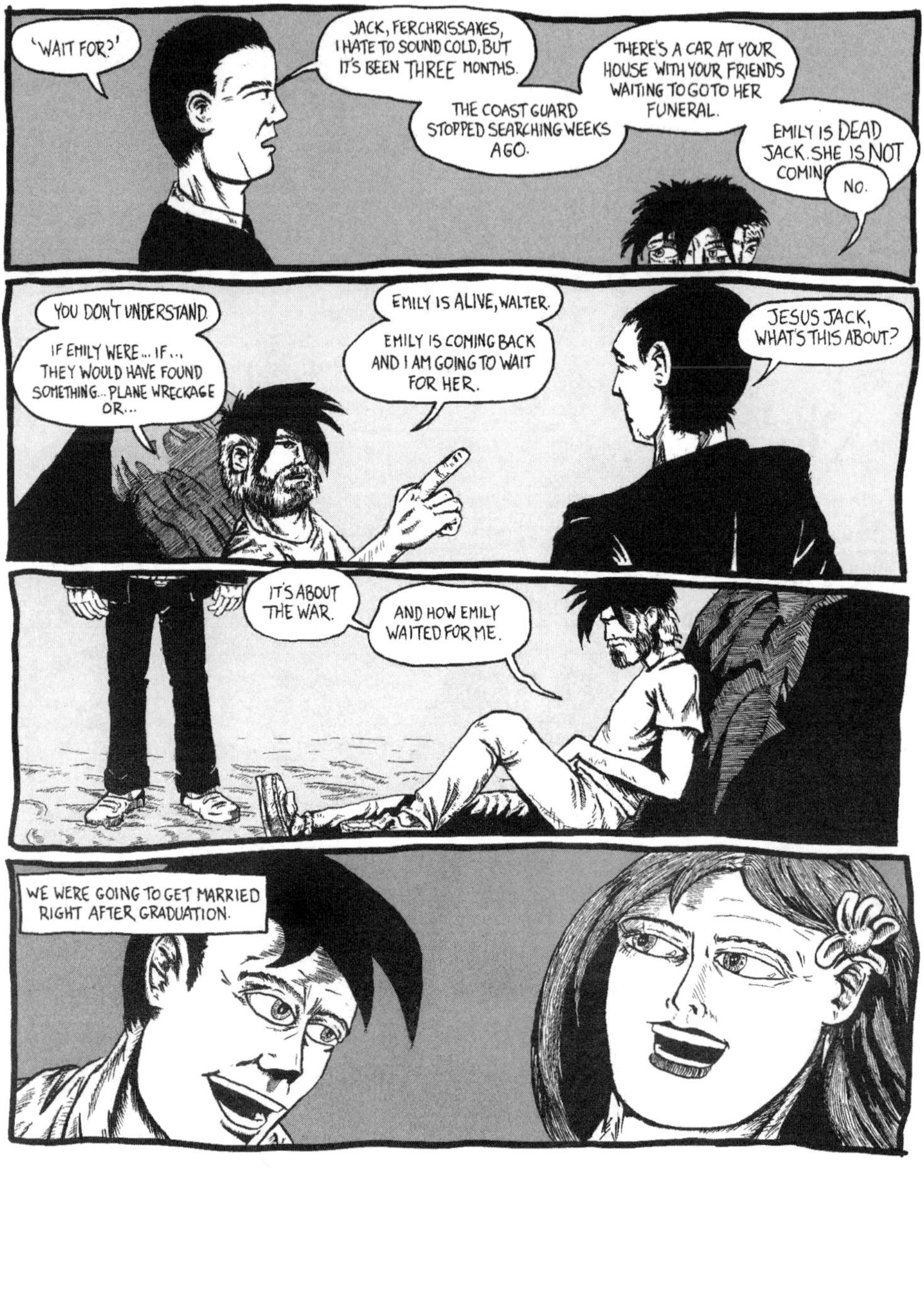
'WAIT FOR?'
JACK, FERCHRISSAKES, I HATE TO SOUND COLD, BUT IT'S BEEN THREE MONTHS.
THE COAST GUARD STOPPED SEARCHING WEEKS AGO.
THERE'S A CAR AT YOUR HOUSE WITH YOUR FRIENDS WAITING TO GO TO HER FUNERAL.
EMILY IS DEAD JACK. SHE IS NOT
NO.
YOU DON'T UNDERSTAND.
IF EMILY WERE... IF... THEY WOULD HAVE FOUND SOMETHING... PLANE WRECKAGE OR...
EMILY IS ALIVE, WALTER.
EMILY IS COMING BACK AND I AM GOING TO WAIT FOR HER.
JESUS JACK, WHAT'S THIS ABOUT?
IT'S ABOUT THE WAR.
AND HOW EMILY WAITED FOR ME.
WE WERE GOING TO GET MARRIED RIGHT AFTER GRADUATION.

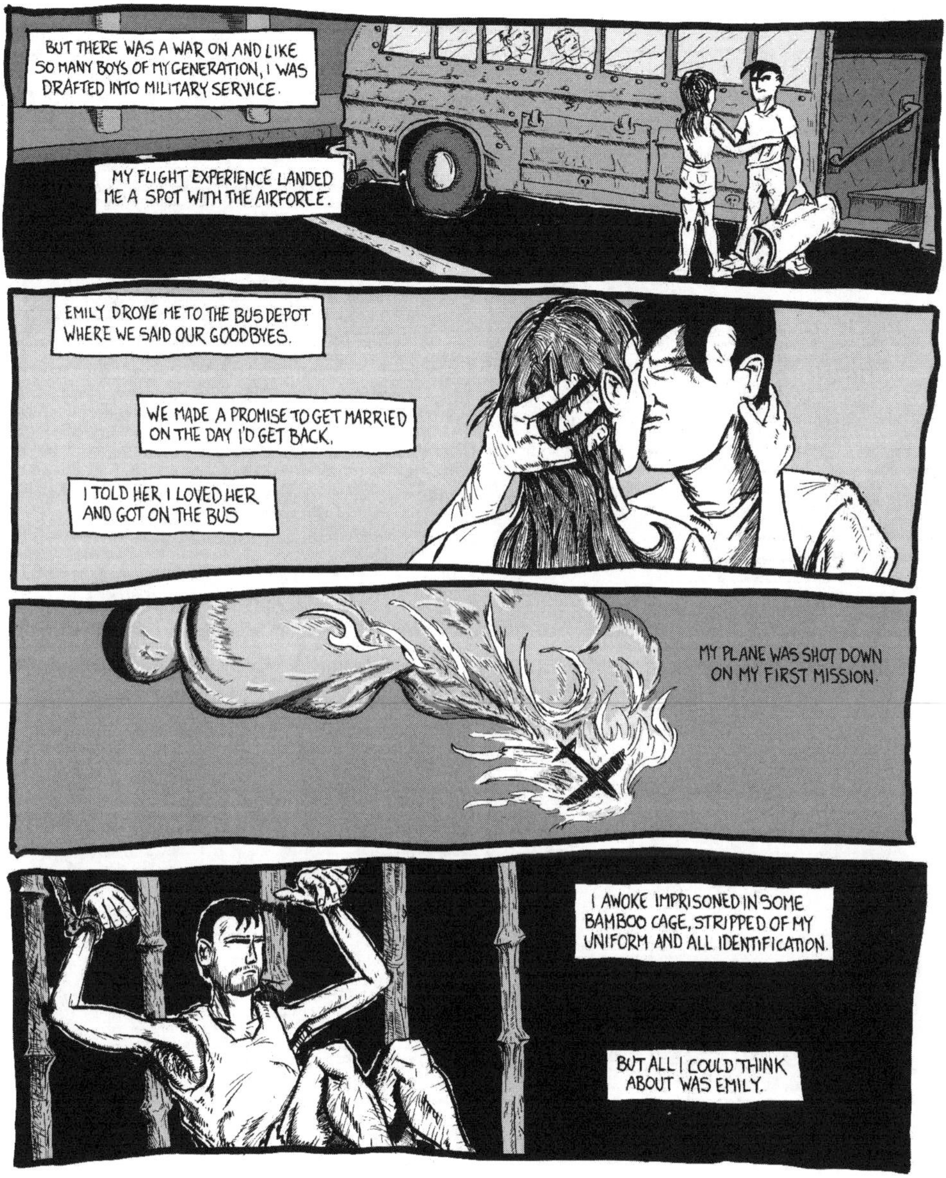
BUT THERE WAS A WAR ON AND LIKE SO MANY BOYS OF MY GENERATION, I WAS DRAFTED INTO MILITARY SERVICE.
MY FLIGHT EXPERIENCE LANDED ME A SPOT WITH THE AIRFORCE.
EMILY DROVE ME TO THE BUS DEPOT WHERE WE SAID OUR GOODBYES.
WE MADE A PROMISE TO GET MARRIED ON THE DAY I'D GET BACK.
I TOLD HER I LOVED HER AND GOT ON THE BUS
MY PLANE WAS SHOT DOWN ON MY FIRST MISSION.
I AWOKE IMPRISONED IN SOME BAMBOO CAGE, STRIPPED OF MY UNIFORM AND ALL IDENTIFICATION.
BUT ALL I COULD THINK ABOUT WAS EMILY.

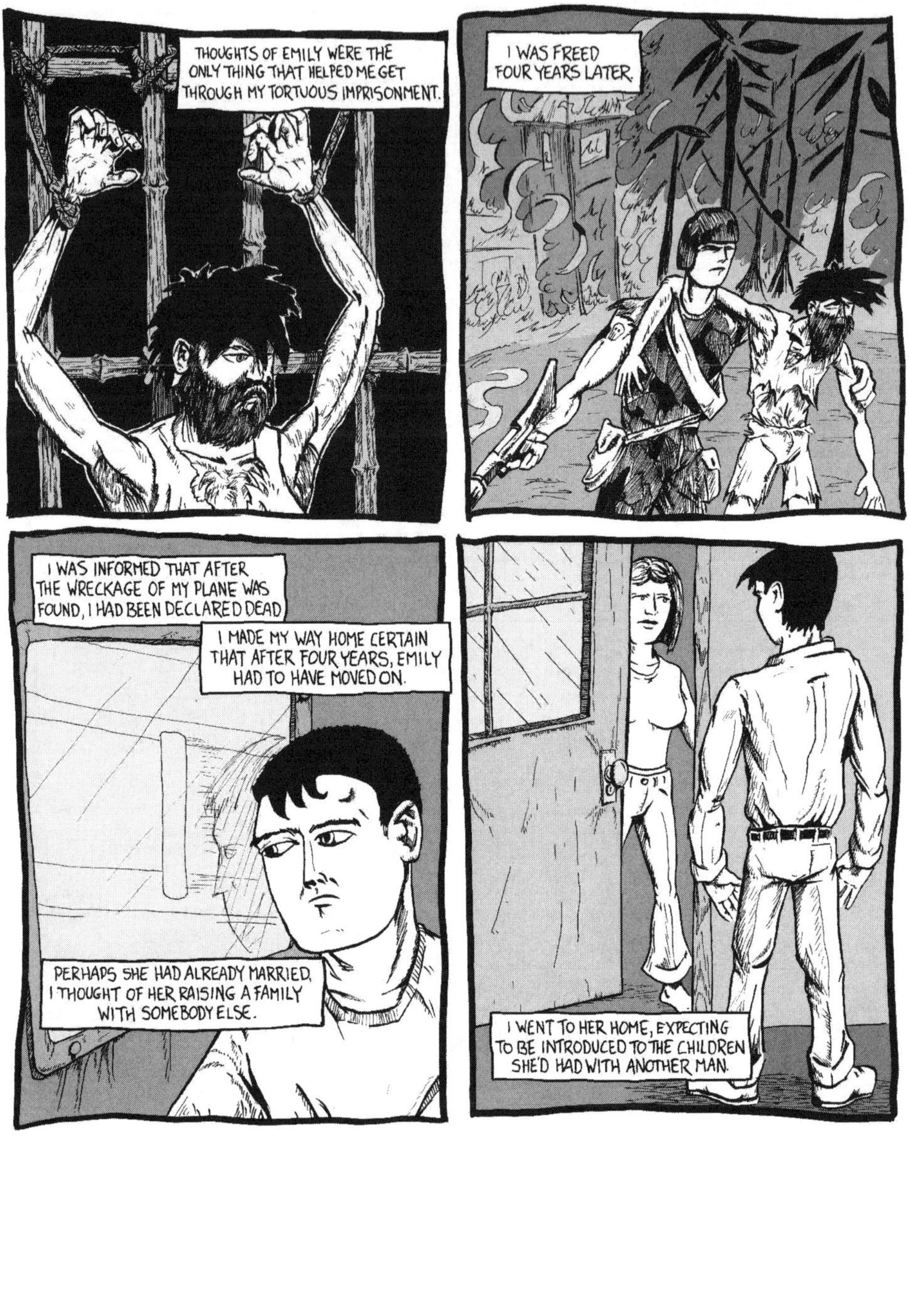
THOUGHTS OF EMILY WERE THE ONLY THING THAT HELPED ME GET THROUGH MY TORTUOUS IMPRISONMENT.
I WAS FREED FOUR YEARS LATER.
I WAS INFORMED THAT AFTER THE WRECKAGE OF MY PLANE WAS FOUND, I HAD BEEN DECLARED DEAD
I MADE MY WAY HOME CERTAIN THAT AFTER FOUR YEARS, EMILY HAD TO HAVE MOVED ON.
PERHAPS SHE HAD ALREADY MARRIED. I THOUGHT OF HER RAISING A FAMILY WITH SOMEBODY ELSE.
I WENT TO HER HOME, EXPECTING TO BE INTRODUCED TO THE CHILDREN SHE'D HAD WITH ANOTHER MAN.

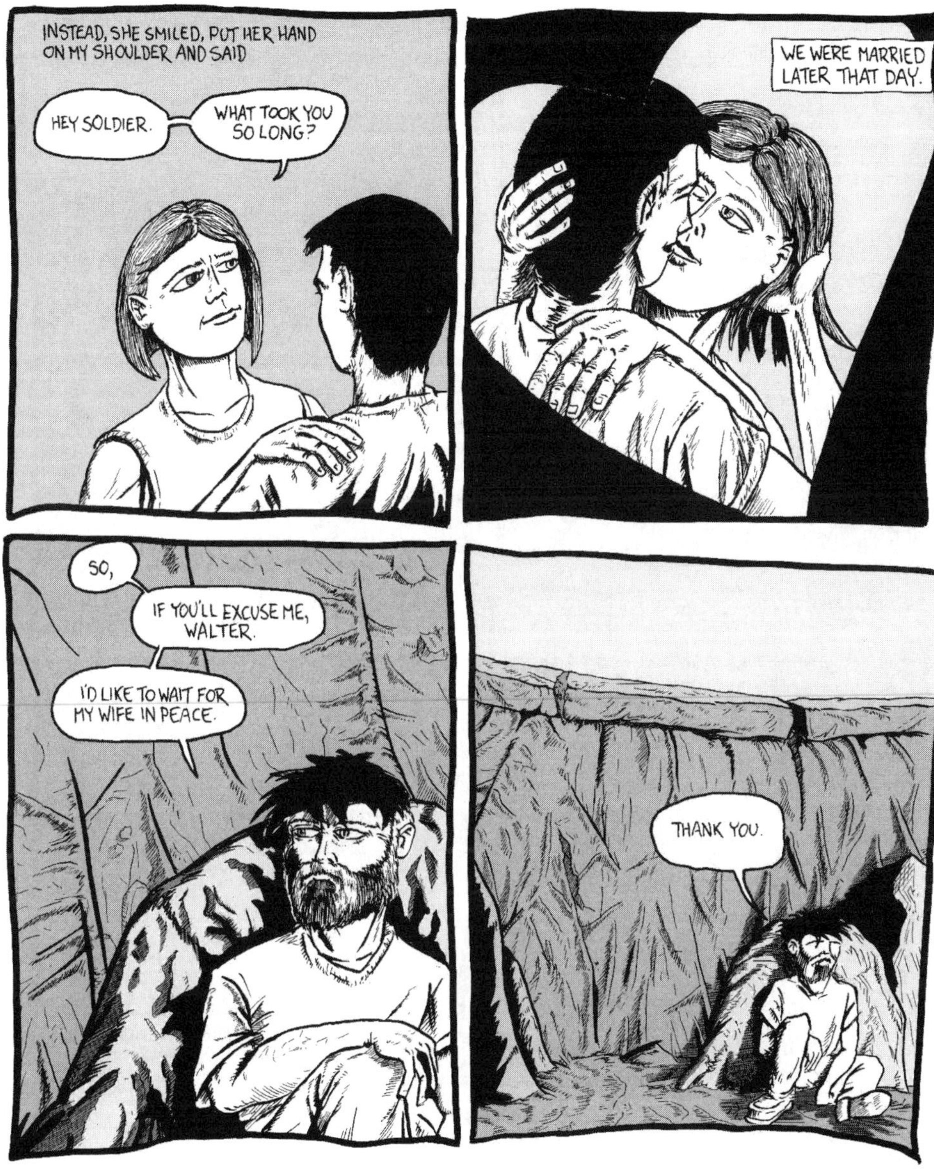
INSTEAD, SHE SMILED, PUT HER HAND ON MY SHOULDER AND SAID
HEY SOLDIER.
WHAT TOOK YOU SO LONG?
WE WERE MARRIED LATER THAT DAY.
SO,
IF YOU'LL EXCUSE ME, WALTER.
I'D LIKE TO WAIT FOR MY WIFE IN PEACE.
THANK YOU.

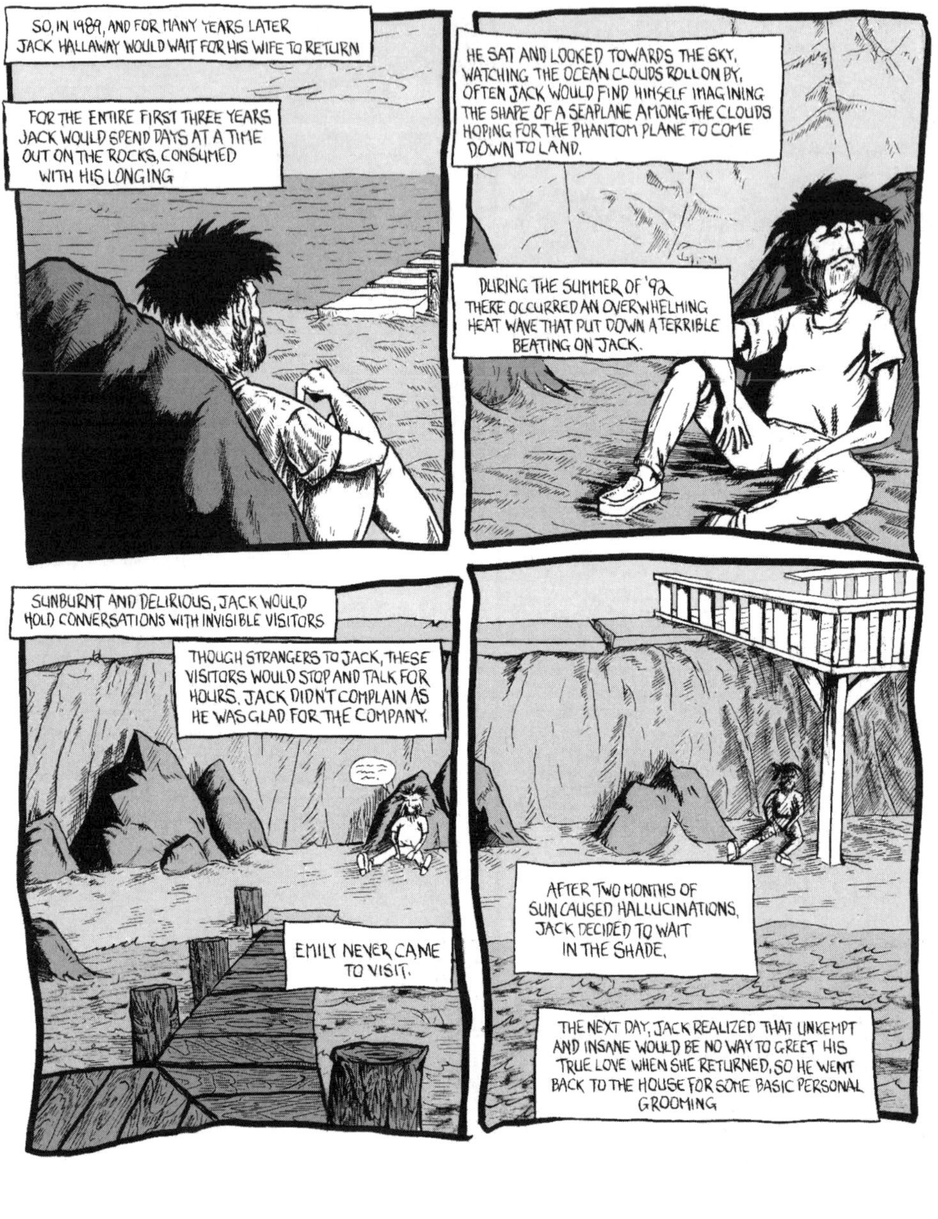
SO, IN 1989, AND FOR MANY YEARS LATER JACK HALLAWAY WOULD WAIT FOR HIS WIFE TO RETURN
FOR THE ENTIRE FIRST THREE YEARS JACK WOULD SPEND DAYS AT A TIME OUT ON THE ROCKS, CONSUMED WITH HIS LONGING
HE SAT AND LOOKED TOWARDS THE SKY, WATCHING THE OCEAN CLOUDS ROLL ON BY, OFTEN JACK WOULD FIND HIMSELF IMAGINING THE SHAPE OF A SEAPLANE AMONG THE CLOUDS HOPING FOR THE PHANTOM PLANE TO COME DOWN TO LAND.
DURING THE SUMMER OF '92 THERE OCCURRED AN OVERWHELMING HEAT WAVE THAT PUT DOWN A TERRIBLE BEATING ON JACK.
SUNBURNT AND DELIRIOUS, JACK WOULD HOLD CONVERSATIONS WITH INVISIBLE VISITORS
THOUGH STRANGERS TO JACK, THESE VISITORS WOULD STOP AND TALK FOR HOURS. JACK DIDN'T COMPLAIN AS HE WAS GLAD FOR THE COMPANY.
EMILY NEVER CAME TO VISIT.
AFTER TWO MONTHS OF SUN CAUSED HALLUCINATIONS, JACK DECIDED TO WAIT IN THE SHADE.
THE NEXT DAY, JACK REALIZED THAT UNKEMPT AND INSANE WOULD BE NO WAY TO GREET HIS TRUE LOVE WHEN SHE RETURNED, SO HE WENT BACK TO THE HOUSE FOR SOME BASIC PERSONAL GROOMING

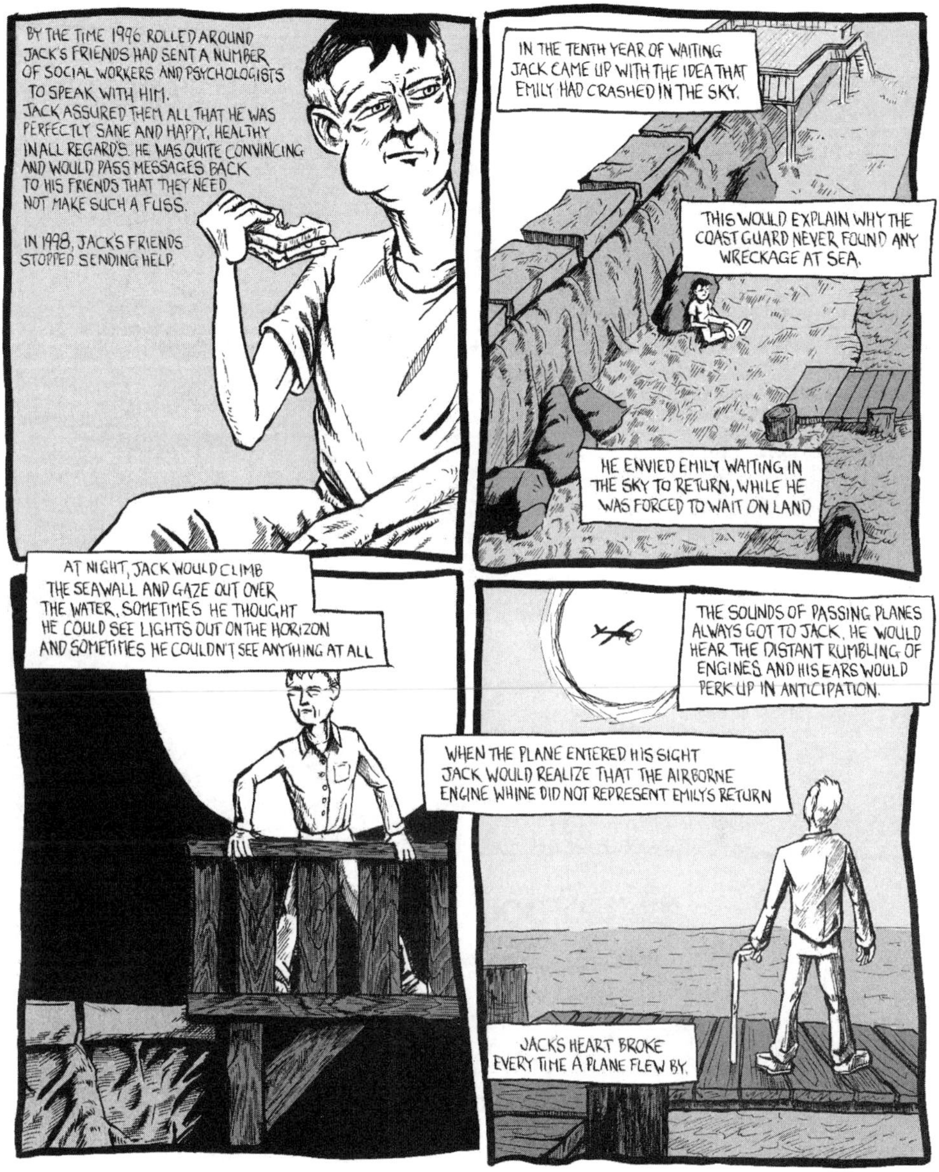
BY THE TIME 1996 ROLLED AROUND JACK'S FRIENDS HAD SENT A NUMBER OF SOCIAL WORKERS AND PSYCHOLOGISTS TO SPEAK WITH HIM.
JACK ASSURED THEM ALL THAT HE WAS PERFECTLY SANE AND HAPPY, HEALTHY IN ALL REGARDS. HE WAS QUITE CONVINCING AND WOULD PASS MESSAGES BACK TO HIS FRIENDS THAT THEY NEED NOT MAKE SUCH A FUSS.
IN 1998, JACK'S FRIENDS STOPPED SENDING HELP.
IN THE TENTH YEAR OF WAITING JACK CAME UP WITH THE IDEA THAT EMILY HAD CRASHED IN THE SKY.
THIS WOULD EXPLAIN WHY THE COAST GUARD NEVER FOUND ANY WRECKAGE AT SEA.
HE ENVIED EMILY WAITING IN THE SKY TO RETURN, WHILE HE WAS FORCED TO WAIT ON LAND
AT NIGHT, JACK WOULD CLIMB THE SEAWALL AND GAZE OUT OVER THE WATER. SOMETIMES HE THOUGHT HE COULD SEE LIGHTS OUT ON THE HORIZON AND SOMETIMES HE COULDN'T SEE ANYTHING AT ALL
THE SOUNDS OF PASSING PLANES ALWAYS GOT TO JACK. HE WOULD HEAR THE DISTANT RUMBLING OF ENGINES AND HIS EARS WOULD PERK UP IN ANTICIPATION.
WHEN THE PLANE ENTERED HIS SIGHT JACK WOULD REALIZE THAT THE AIRBORNE ENGINE WHINE DID NOT REPRESENT EMILY'S RETURN
JACK'S HEART BROKE EVERY TIME A PLANE FLEW BY.

FOR OVER FORTY YEARS JACK WOULD WAIT NEVER GIVING UP HOPE
HE NEVER STOPPED EXPECTING TO SEE EMILY FLYING HOME IN A BATTERED SEAPLANE.
JACK KNEW THAT ONE WAY OR ANOTHER HE WOULD SEE HIS WIFE AGAIN.
AND, AFTER MANY YEARS OF WAITING, SHE WOULD WELCOME HIM HOME
SHIT
SHIT SHIT.

chapter four: bookends

Plastic Farm

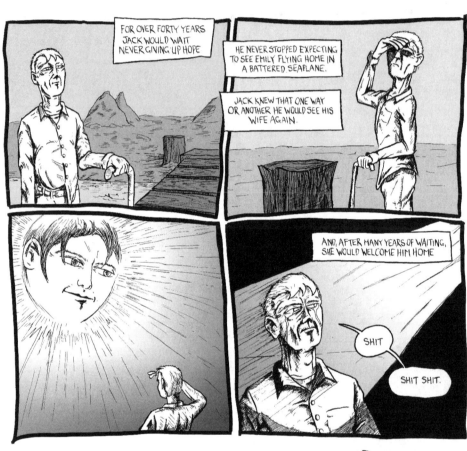

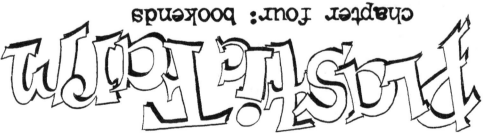

Plastic Farm

chapter five: sean

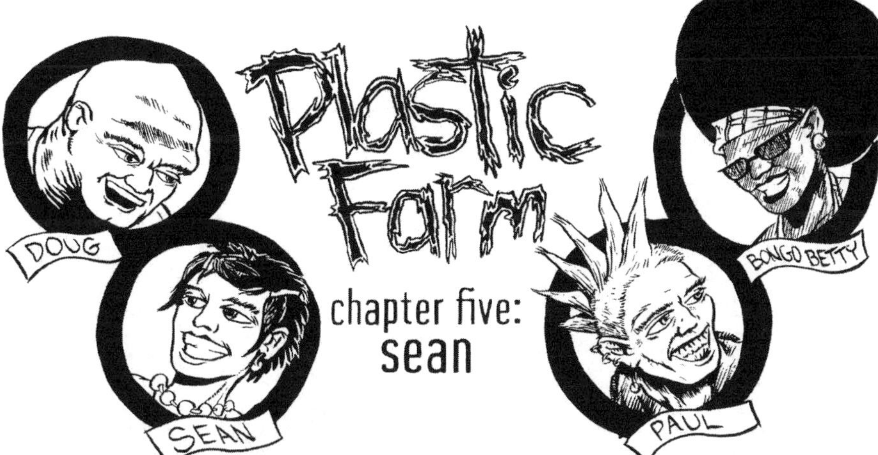

DOUG
SEAN
PAUL
BONGO BETTY

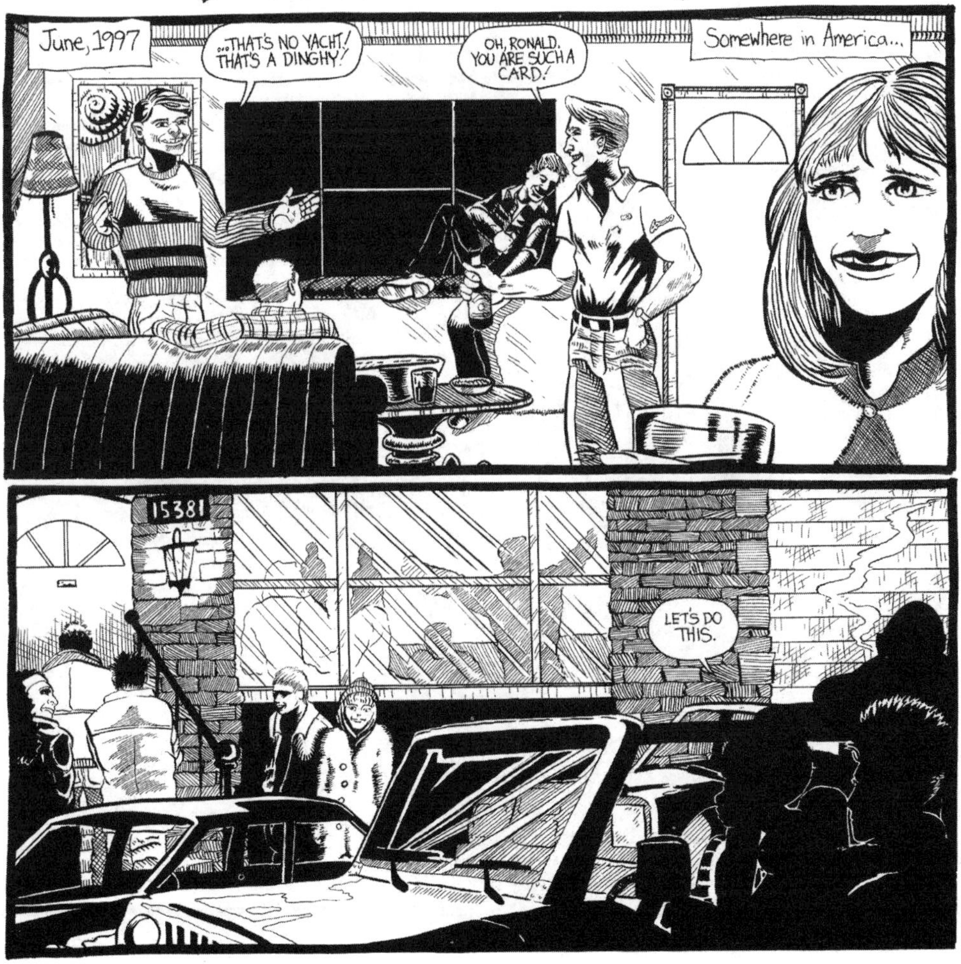

June, 1997
...THAT'S NO YACHT! THAT'S A DINGHY!
OH, RONALD. YOU ARE SUCH A CARD!
Somewhere in America...
15381
LET'S DO THIS.

art by jake warrenfeltz

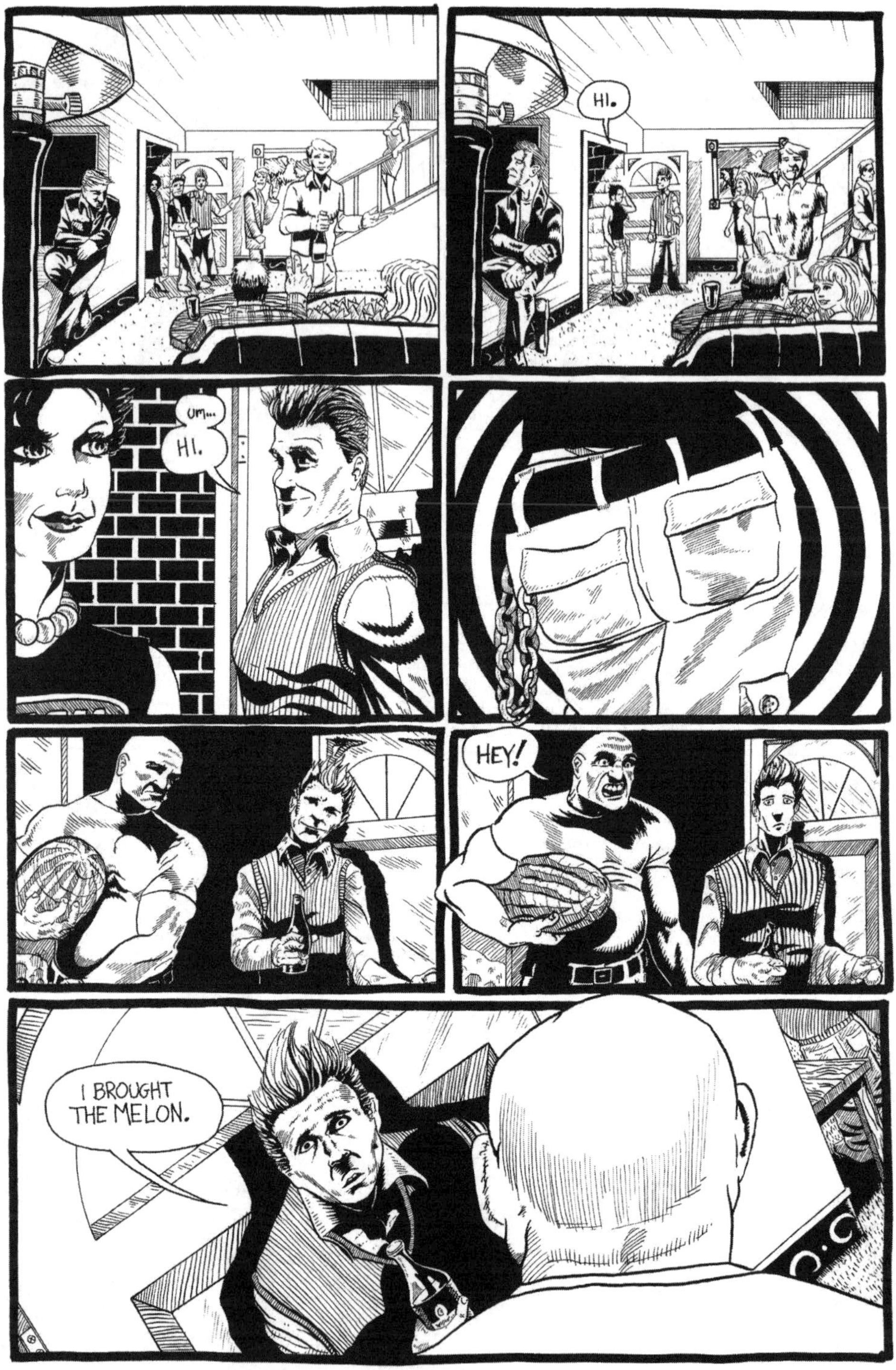
HI.
UM...
HI.
HEY!
I BROUGHT THE MELON.

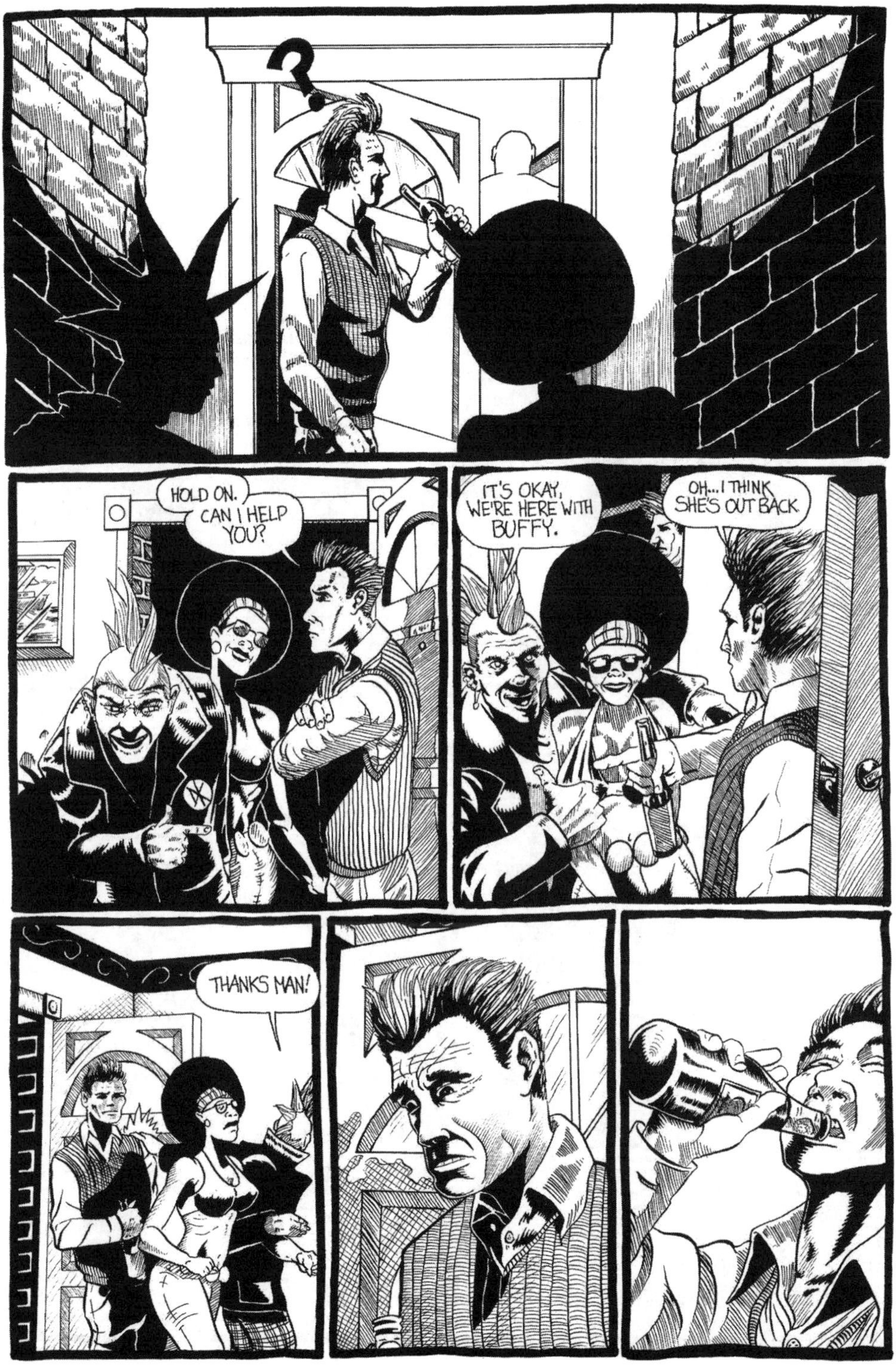
HOLD ON. CAN I HELP YOU?
IT'S OKAY, WE'RE HERE WITH BUFFY.
OH... I THINK SHE'S OUT BACK
THANKS MAN!

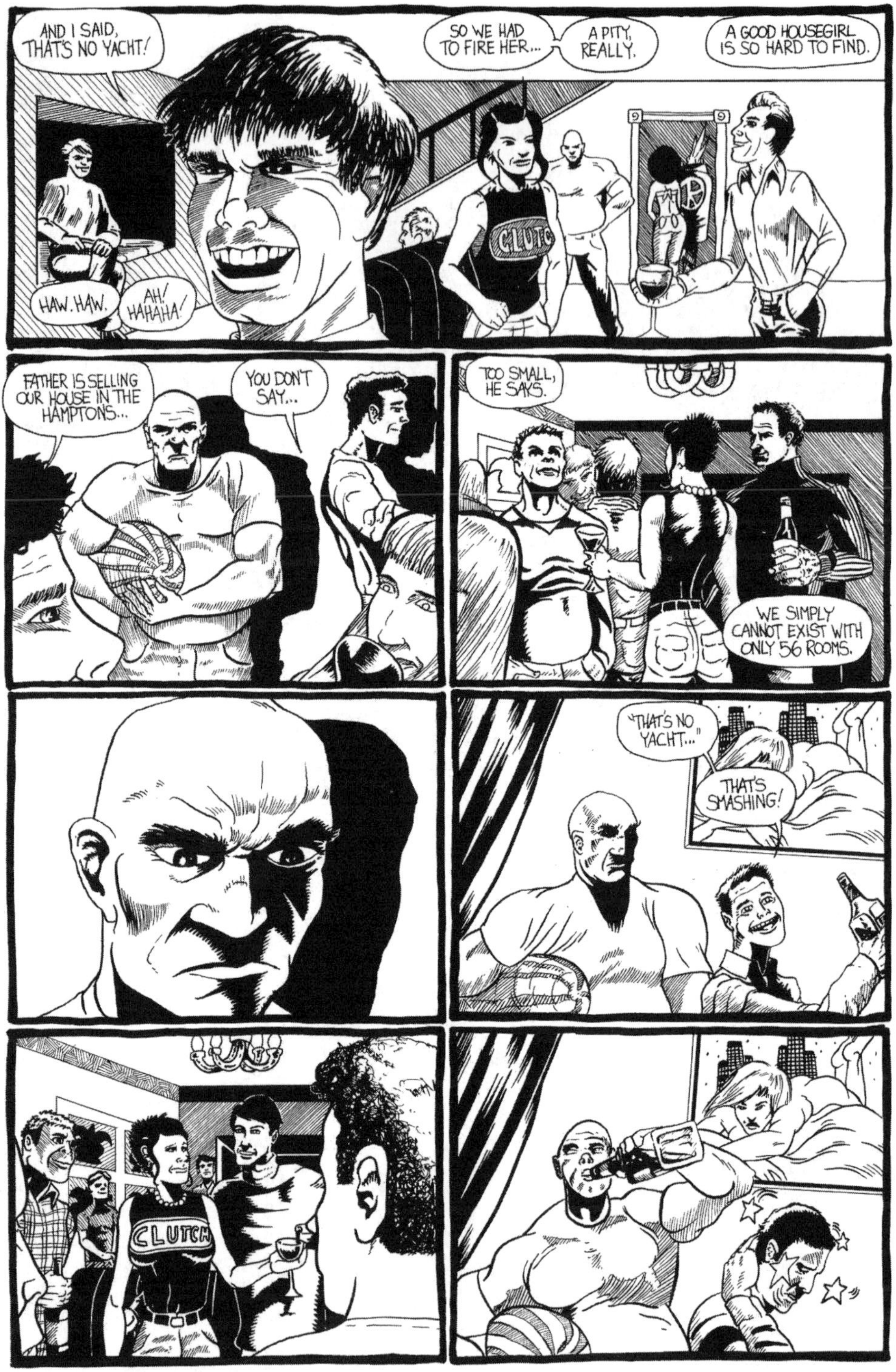

AND I SAID, THAT'S NO YACHT!
SO WE HAD TO FIRE HER...
A PITY, REALLY.
A GOOD HOUSEGIRL IS SO HARD TO FIND.
HAW. HAW.
AH! HAHAHA!
FATHER IS SELLING OUR HOUSE IN THE HAMPTONS...
YOU DON'T SAY...
TOO SMALL, HE SAYS.
WE SIMPLY CANNOT EXIST WITH ONLY 56 ROOMS.
CLUTCH
"THAT'S NO YACHT..."
THAT'S SMASHING!
CLUTCH

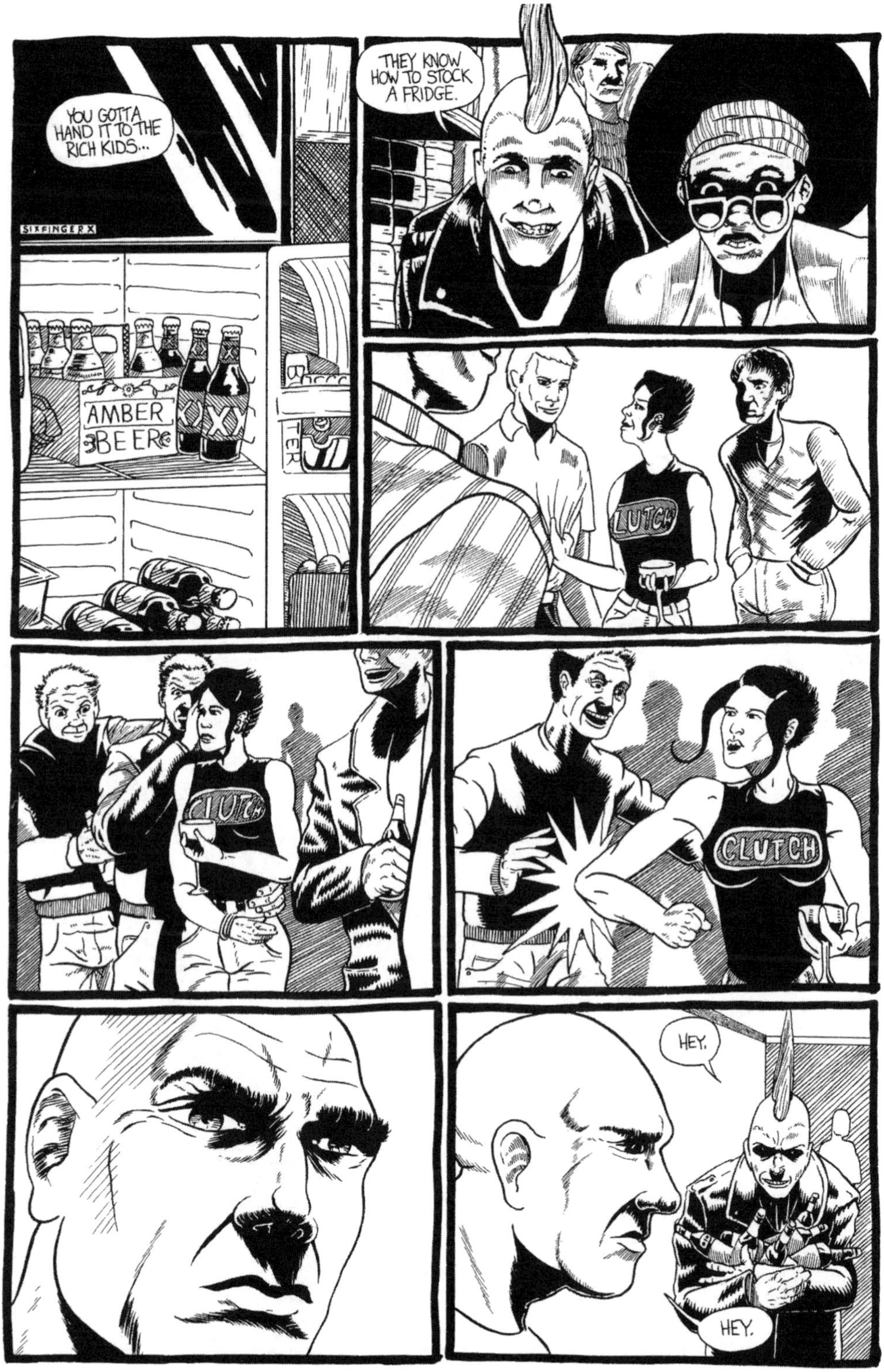
YOU GOTTA HAND IT TO THE RICH KIDS...
SIXFINGER X
THEY KNOW HOW TO STOCK A FRIDGE.
AMBER BEER
CLUTCH
CLUTCH
CLUTCH
HEY.
HEY.

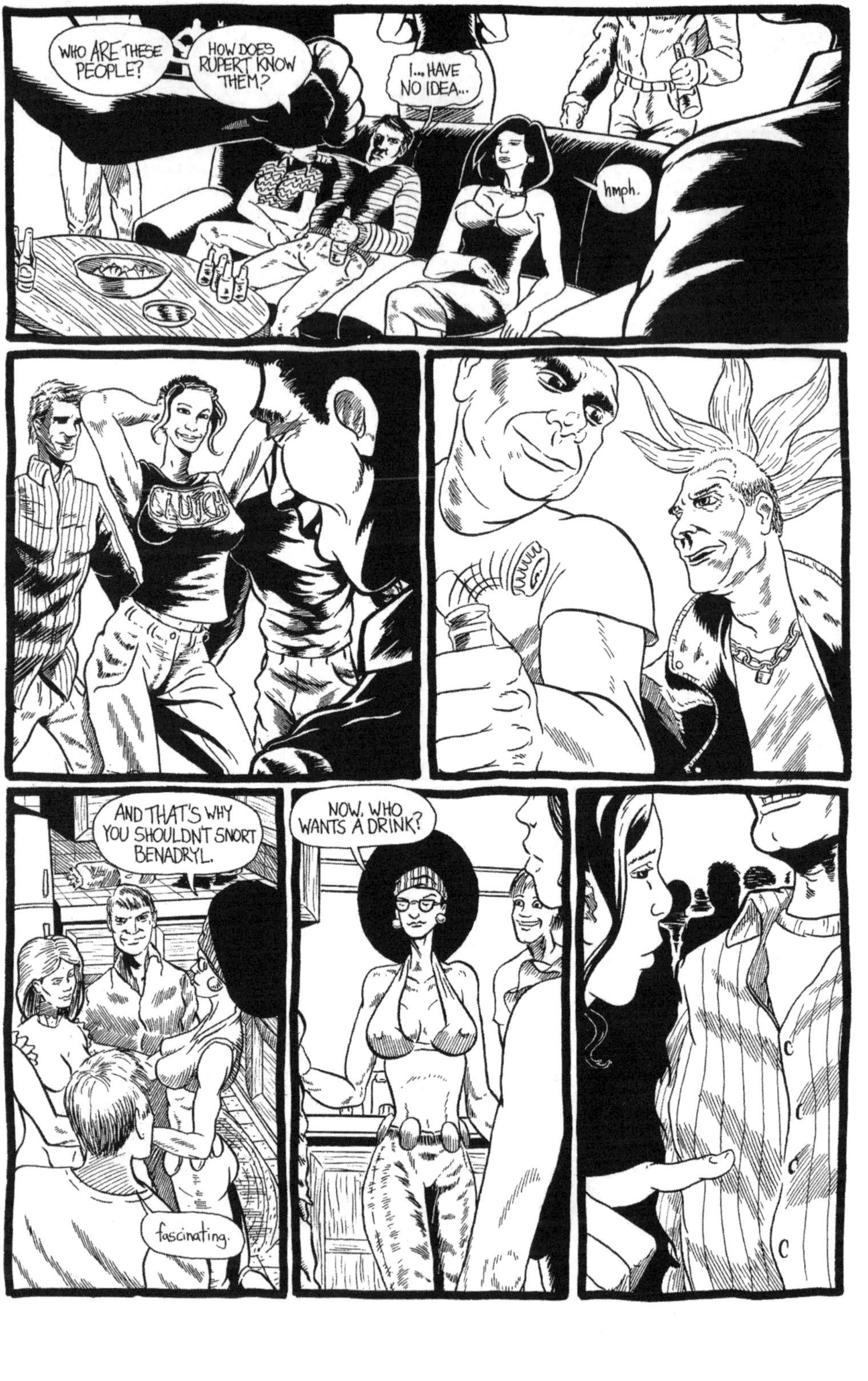
WHO ARE THESE PEOPLE?
HOW DOES RUPERT KNOW THEM?
I... HAVE NO IDEA...
hmph.
SLUTCH
AND THAT'S WHY YOU SHOULDN'T SNORT BENADRYL.
fascinating.
NOW, WHO WANTS A DRINK?

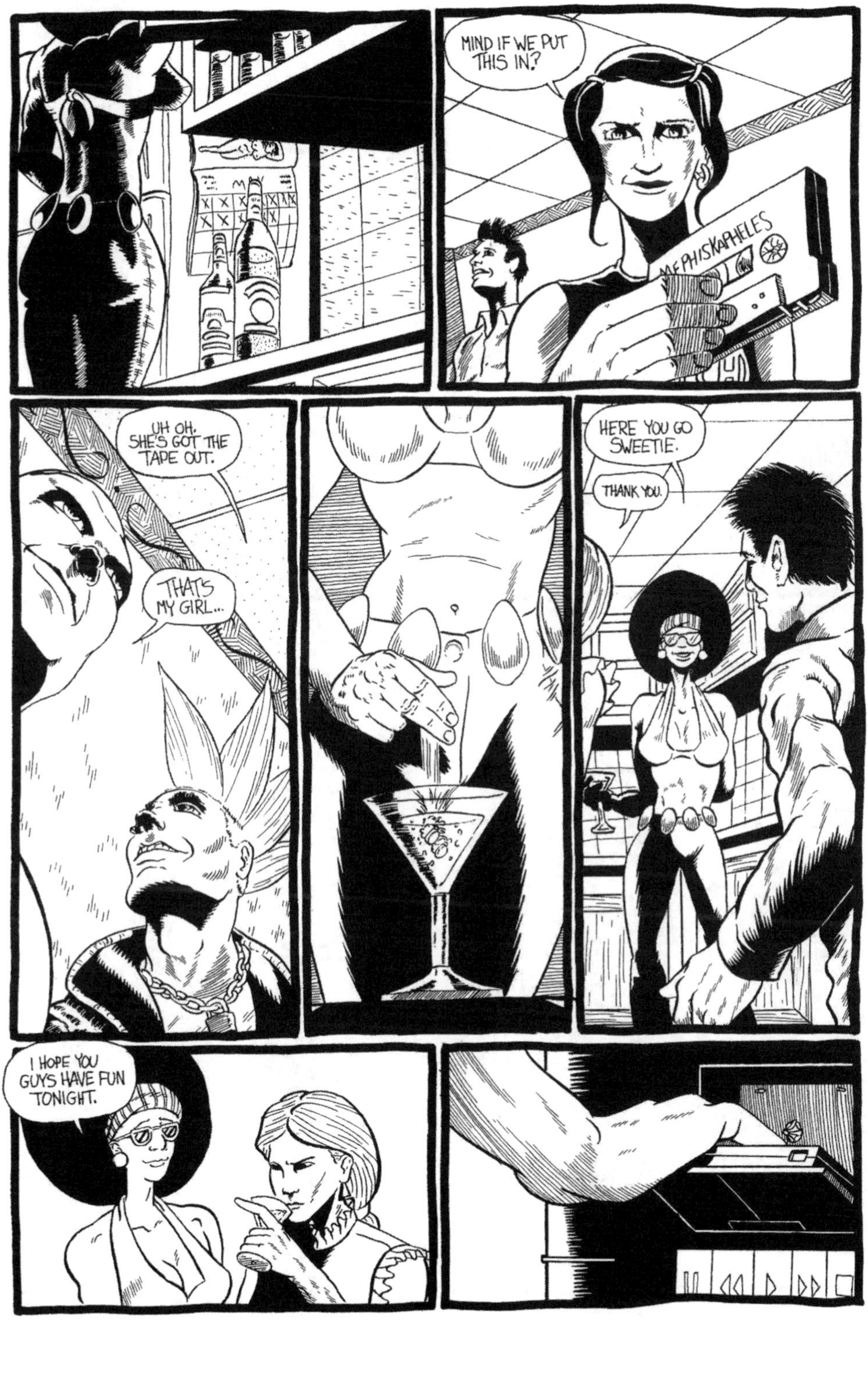

MIND IF WE PUT THIS IN?
MEPHISKAPHELES
UH OH. SHE'S GOT THE TAPE OUT.
THAT'S MY GIRL...
HERE YOU GO SWEETIE.
THANK YOU.
I HOPE YOU GUYS HAVE FUN TONIGHT.

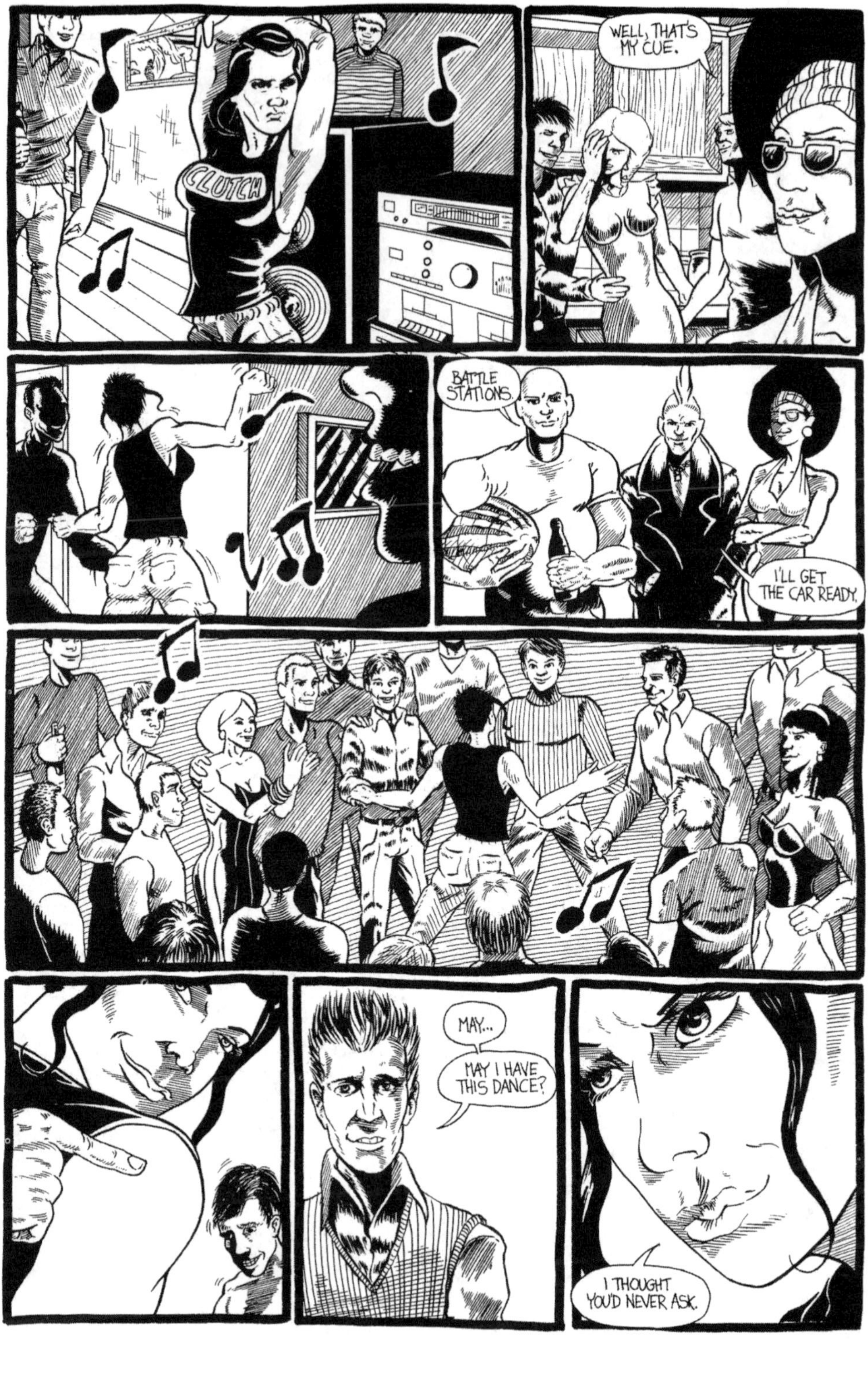
WELL, THAT'S MY CUE.
BATTLE STATIONS.
I'LL GET THE CAR READY.
CLUTCH
MAY...
MAY I HAVE THIS DANCE?
I THOUGHT YOU'D NEVER ASK.

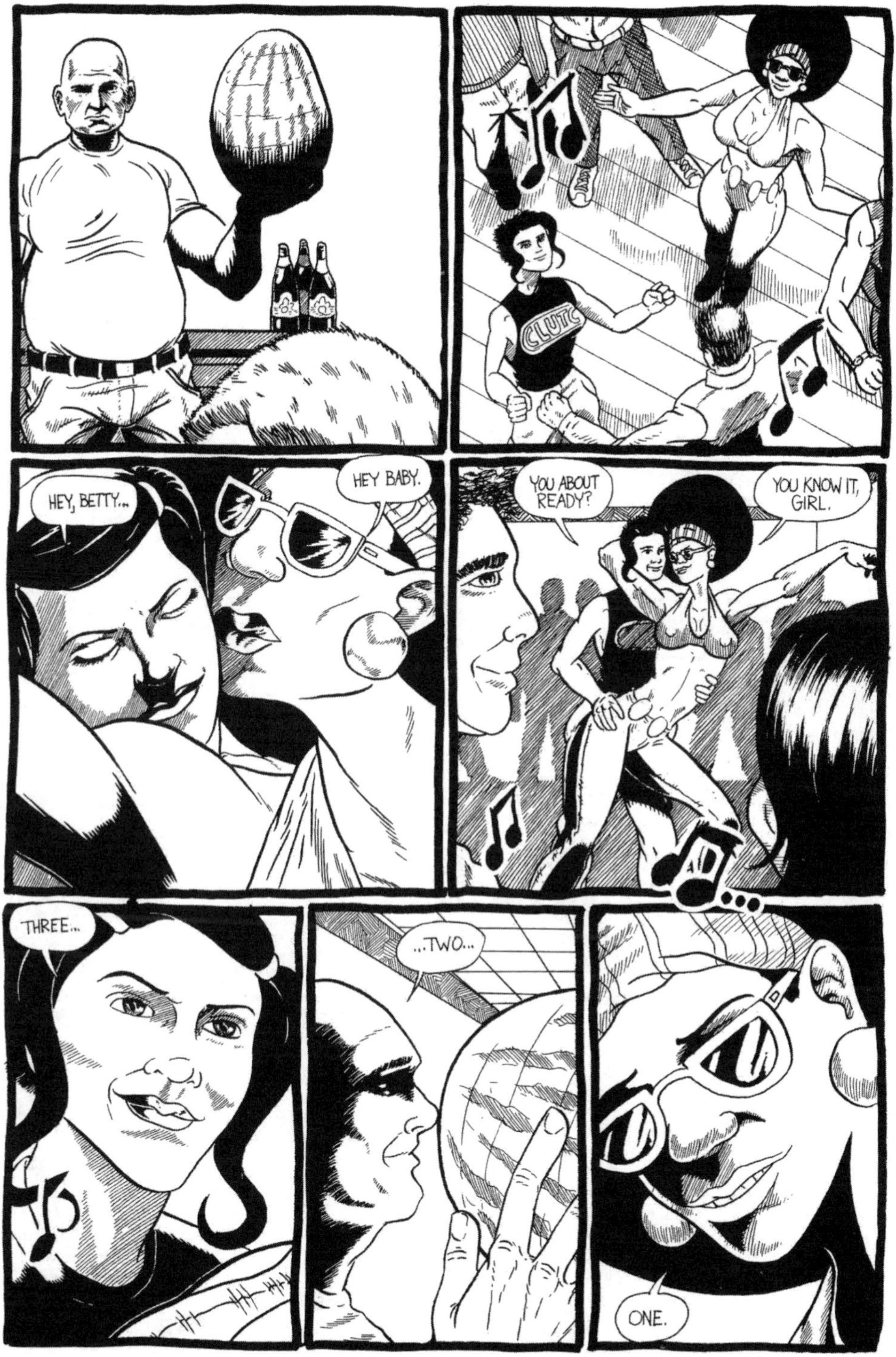

CLUTC
HEY, BETTY...
HEY BABY.
YOU ABOUT READY?
YOU KNOW IT, GIRL.
THREE...
...TWO...
ONE.

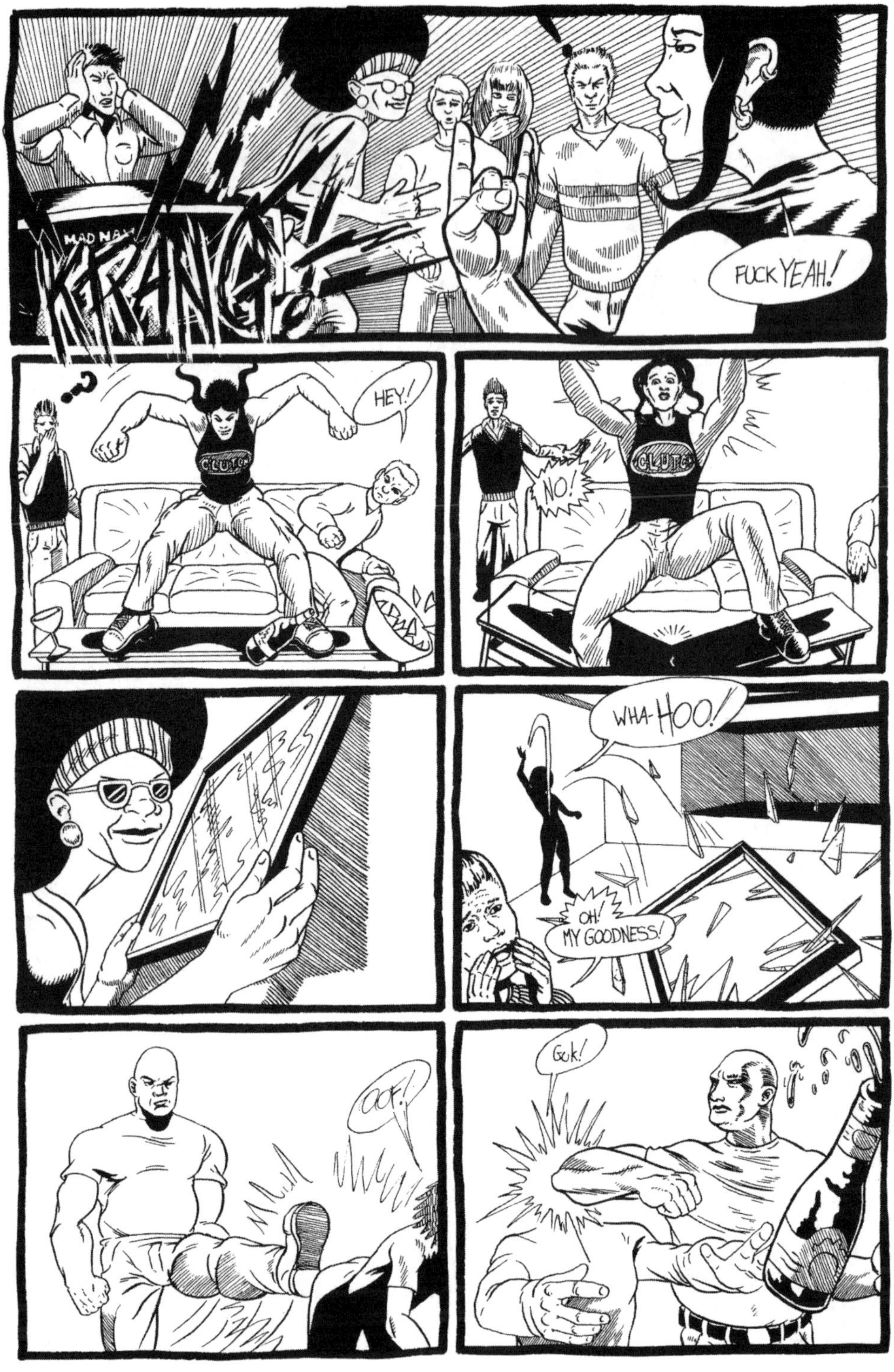
MAD NAN
KRANG!
FUCK YEAH!
HEY!
NO!
CLUTCH
WHA-HOO!
OH! MY GOODNESS!
OOF!
Gok!

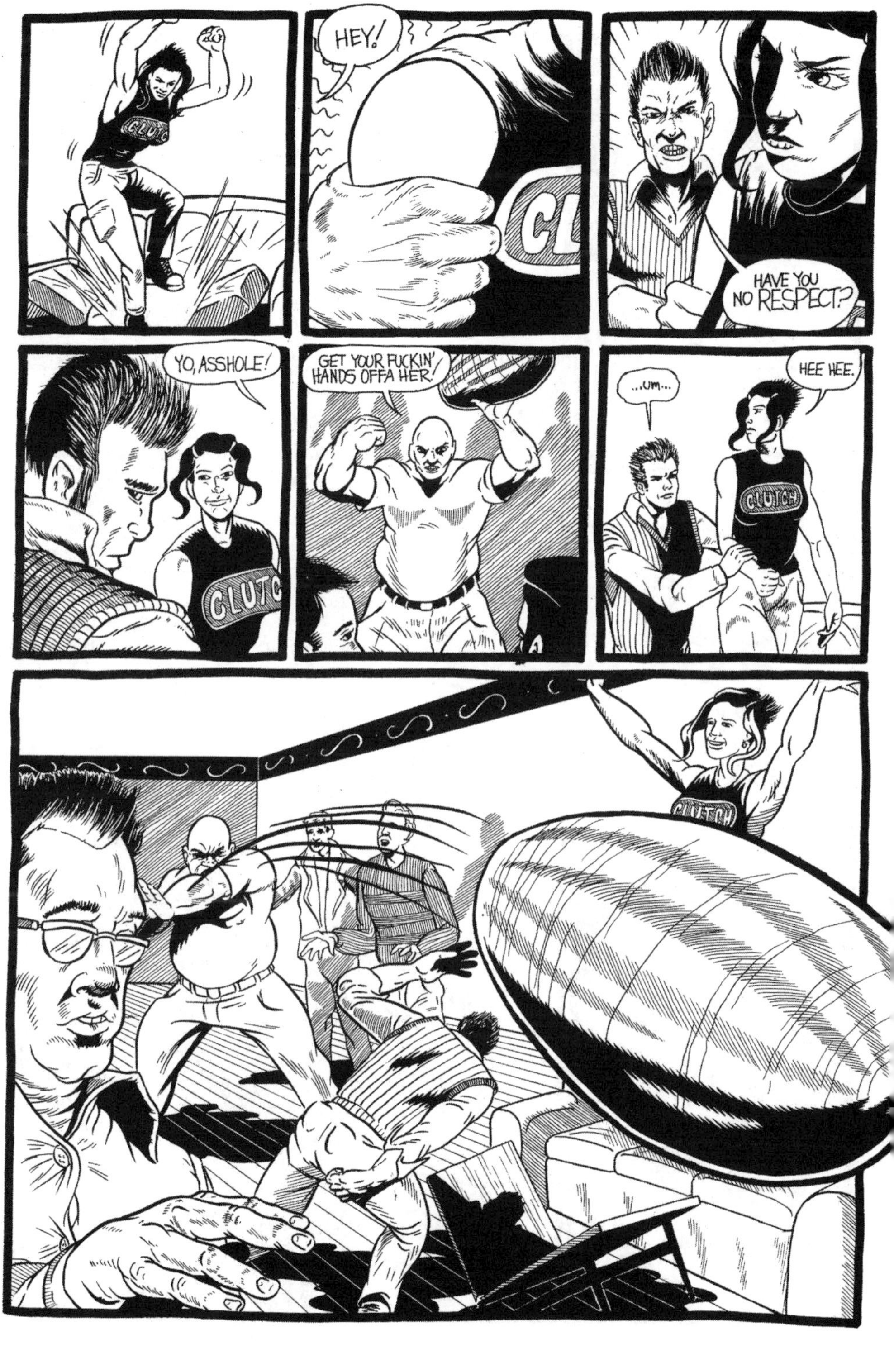
HEY!
HAVE YOU NO RESPECT?
YO, ASSHOLE!
GET YOUR FUCKIN' HANDS OFFA HER!
...UM...
HEE HEE.
CLUTCH

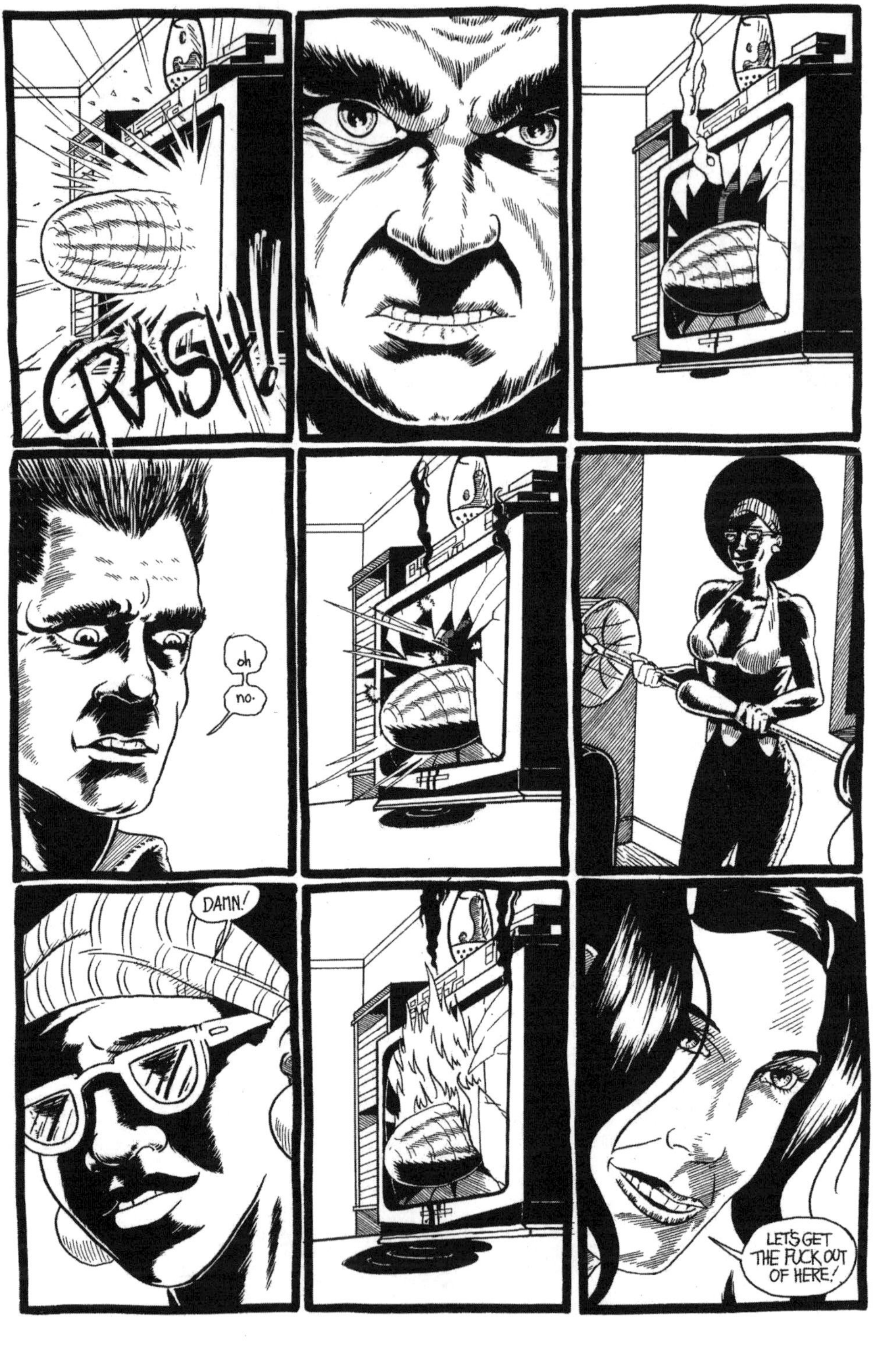
CRASH!
oh
no.
DAMN!
LET'S GET THE FUCK OUT OF HERE!

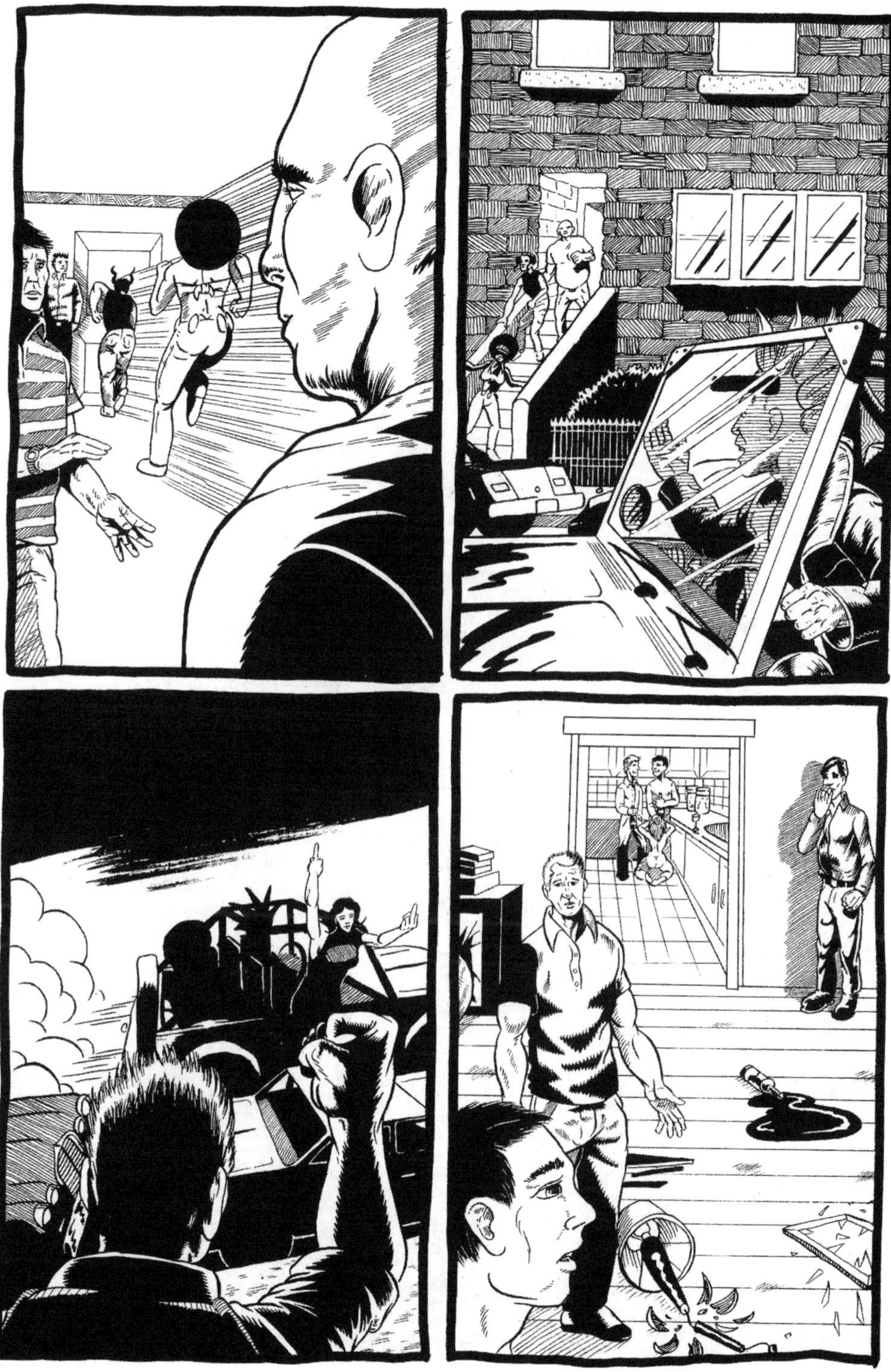

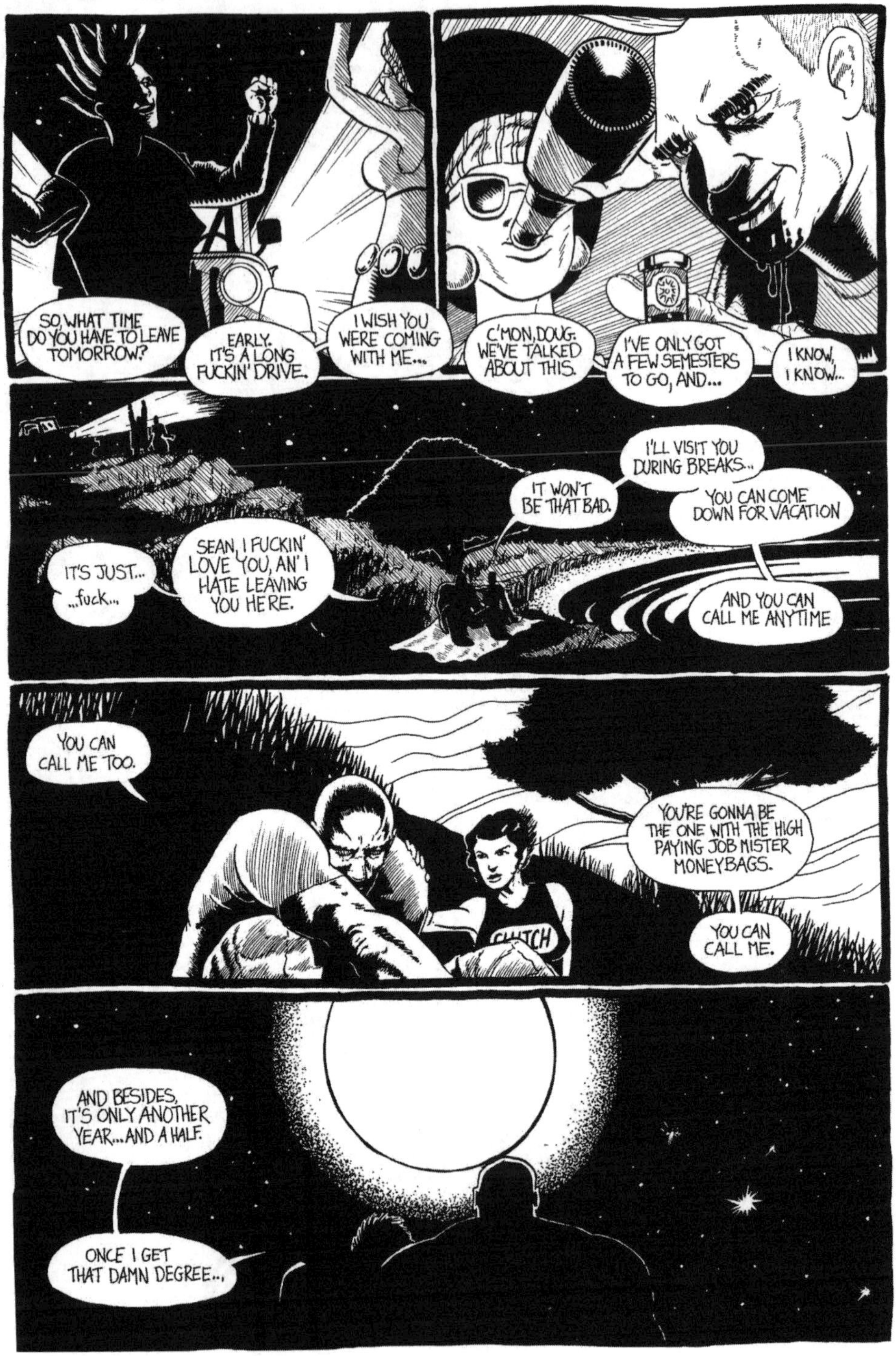
SO, WHAT TIME DO YOU HAVE TO LEAVE TOMORROW?
EARLY. IT'S A LONG FUCKIN' DRIVE.
I WISH YOU WERE COMING WITH ME...
C'MON, DOUG. WE'VE TALKED ABOUT THIS.
I'VE ONLY GOT A FEW SEMESTERS TO GO, AND...
I KNOW, I KNOW...
I'LL VISIT YOU DURING BREAKS...
IT WON'T BE THAT BAD.
YOU CAN COME DOWN FOR VACATION
SEAN, I FUCKIN' LOVE YOU, AN' I HATE LEAVING YOU HERE.
IT'S JUST... ...fuck...
AND YOU CAN CALL ME ANYTIME
YOU CAN CALL ME TOO.
YOU'RE GONNA BE THE ONE WITH THE HIGH PAYING JOB MISTER MONEYBAGS.
YOU CAN CALL ME.
AND BESIDES, IT'S ONLY ANOTHER YEAR... AND A HALF.
ONCE I GET THAT DAMN DEGREE...

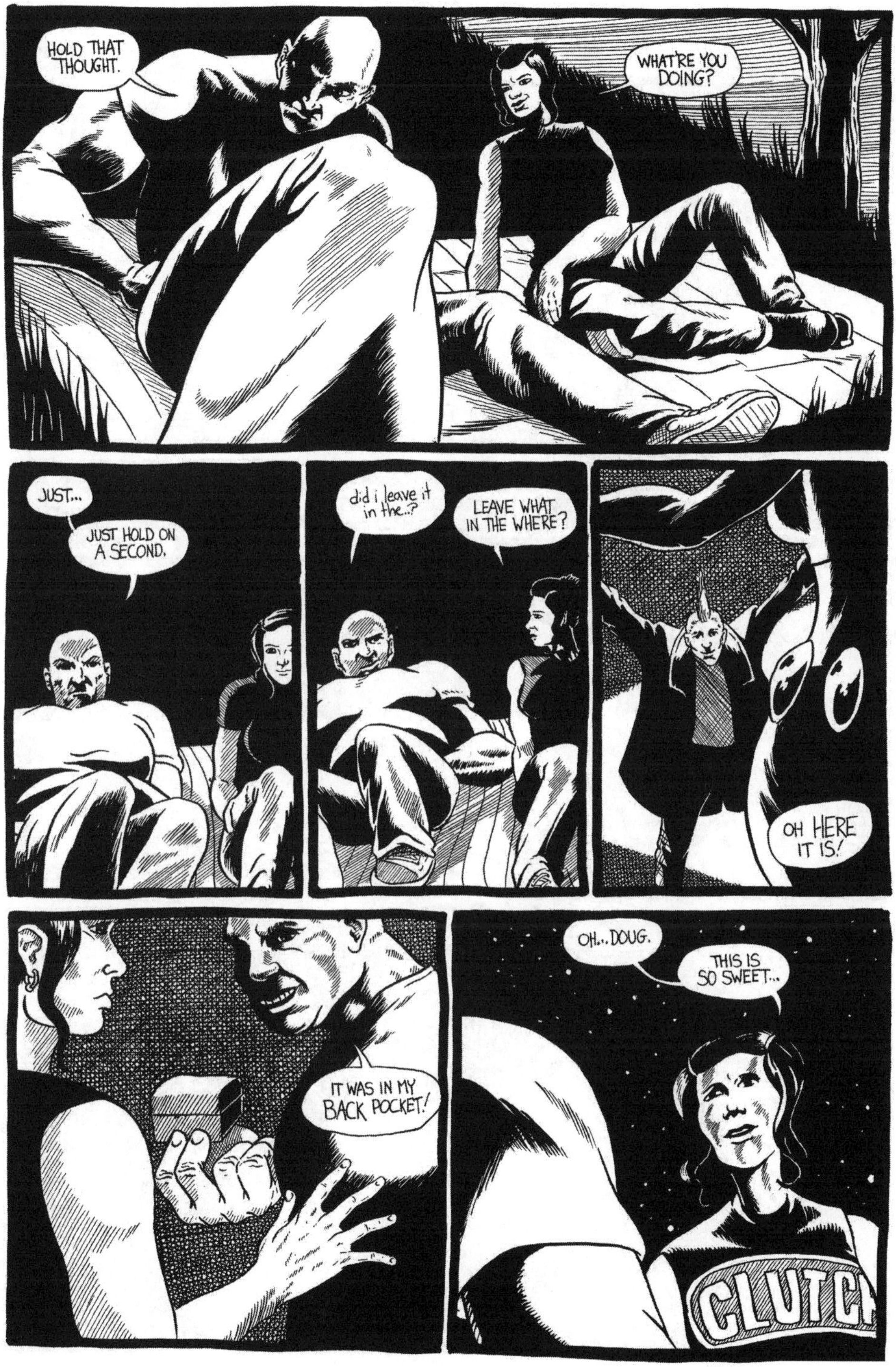
HOLD THAT THOUGHT.
WHAT'RE YOU DOING?
JUST...
JUST HOLD ON A SECOND.
did i leave it in the..?
LEAVE WHAT IN THE WHERE?
OH HERE IT IS!
IT WAS IN MY BACK POCKET!
OH...DOUG.
THIS IS SO SWEET...
CLUTCH

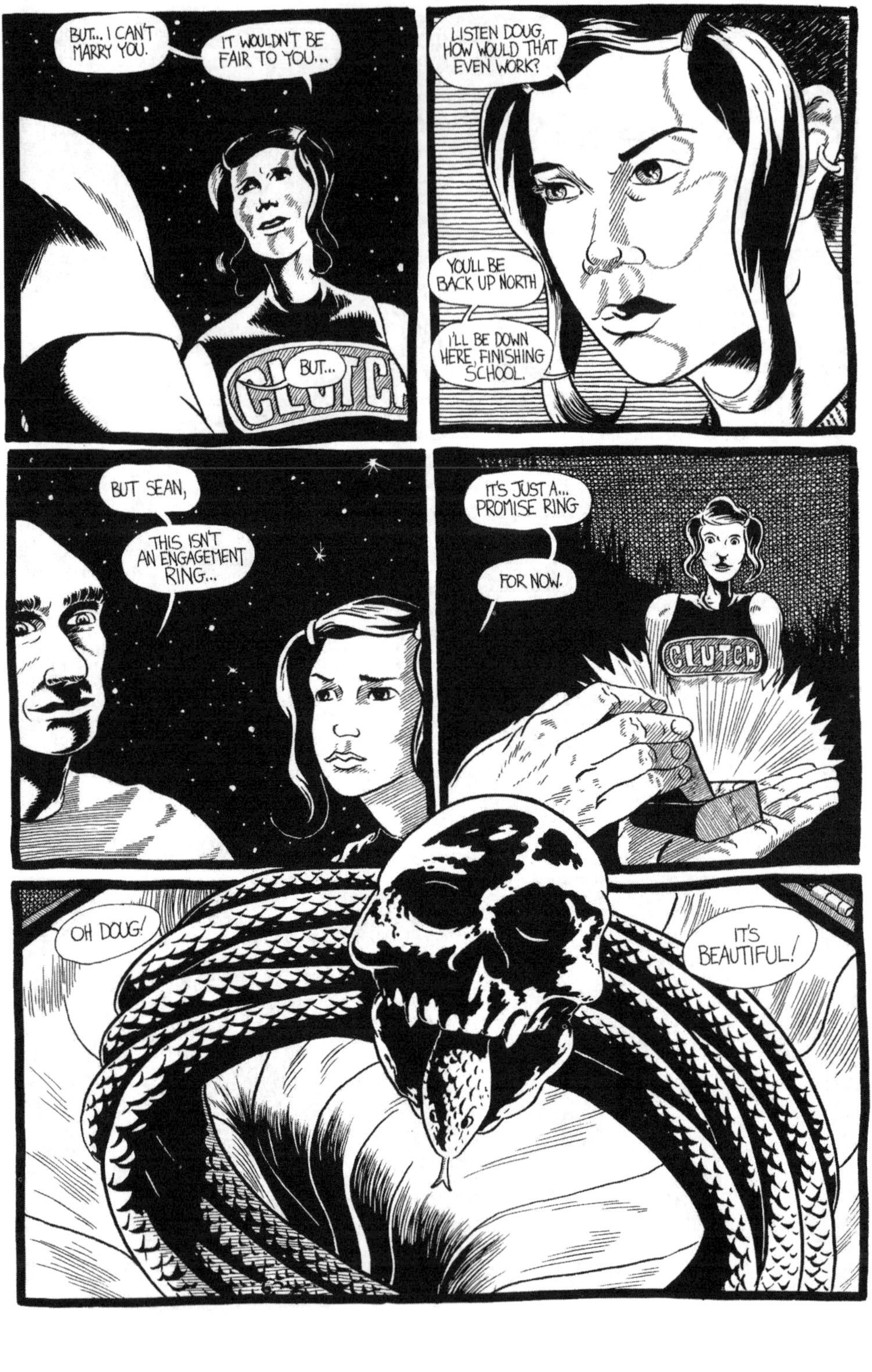
BUT... I CAN'T MARRY YOU.
IT WOULDN'T BE FAIR TO YOU...
BUT...
CLUTCH
LISTEN DOUG, HOW WOULD THAT EVEN WORK?
YOU'LL BE BACK UP NORTH
I'LL BE DOWN HERE, FINISHING SCHOOL.
BUT SEAN,
THIS ISN'T AN ENGAGEMENT RING...
IT'S JUST A... PROMISE RING
FOR NOW.
CLUTCH
OH DOUG!
IT'S BEAUTIFUL!

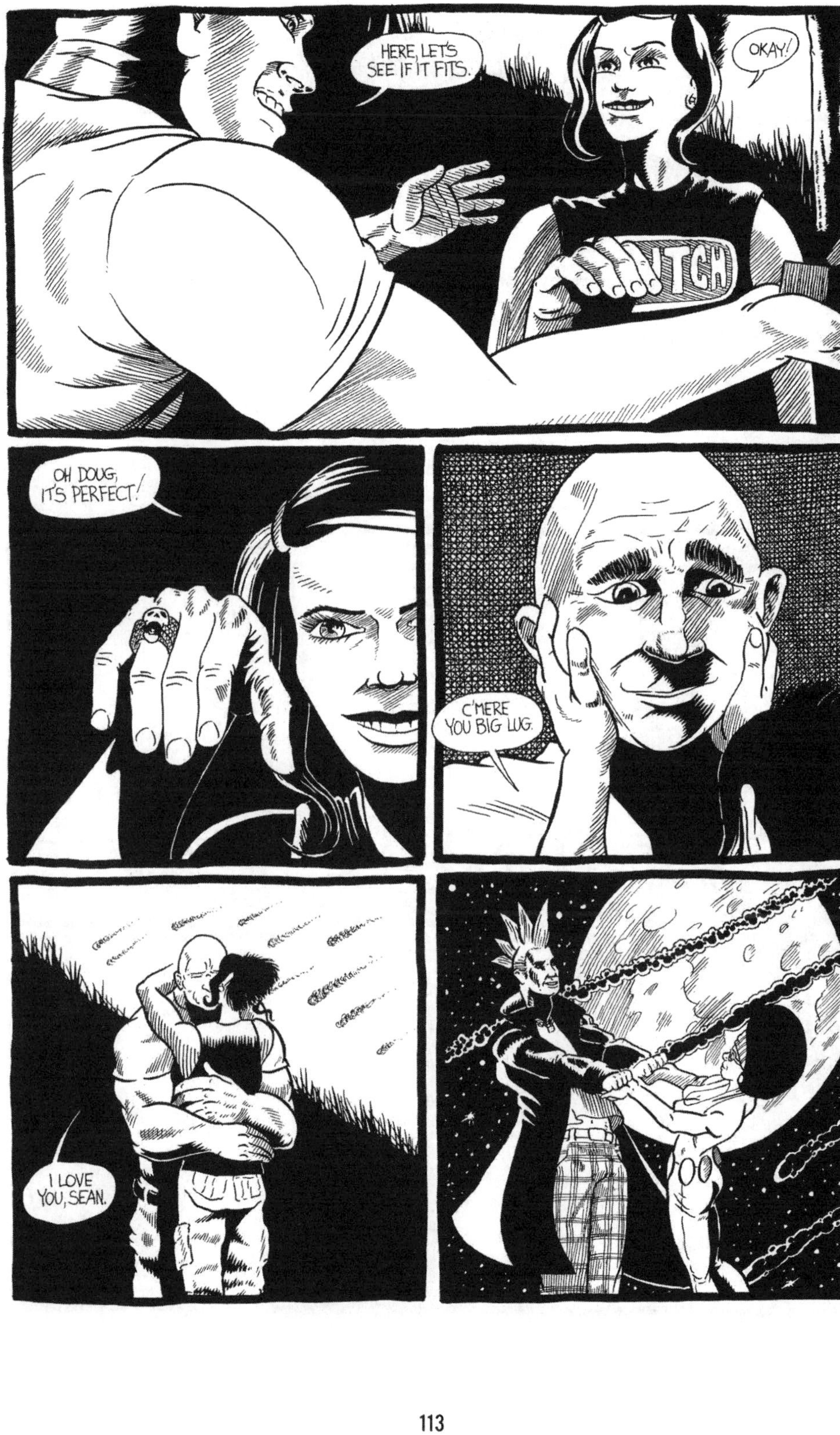
HERE, LET'S SEE IF IT FITS.
OKAY!
OH DOUG, IT'S PERFECT!
C'MERE YOU BIG LUG.
I LOVE YOU, SEAN.

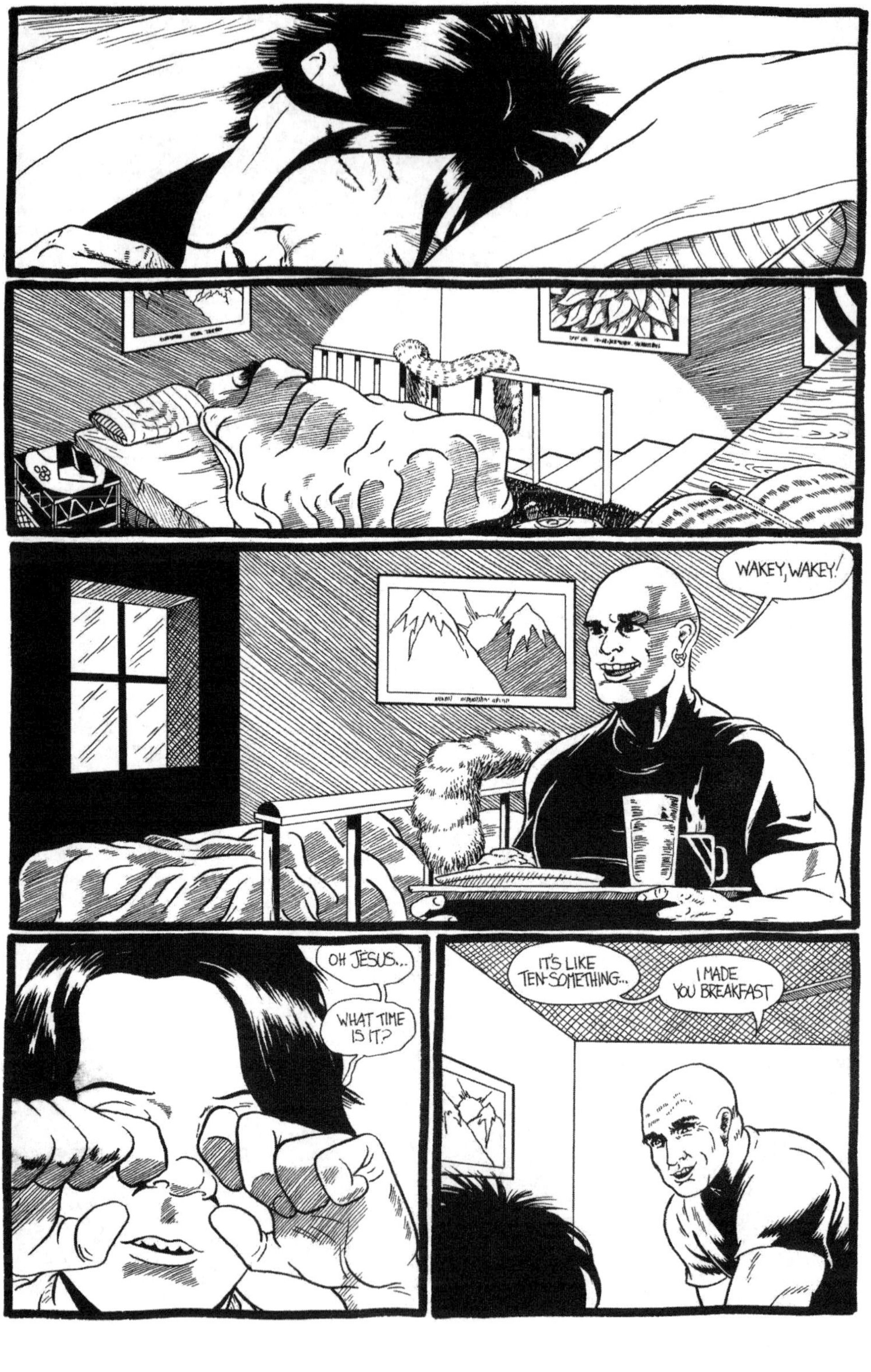
WAKEY, WAKEY!
OH JESUS...
WHAT TIME IS IT?
IT'S LIKE TEN-SOMETHING...
I MADE YOU BREAKFAST

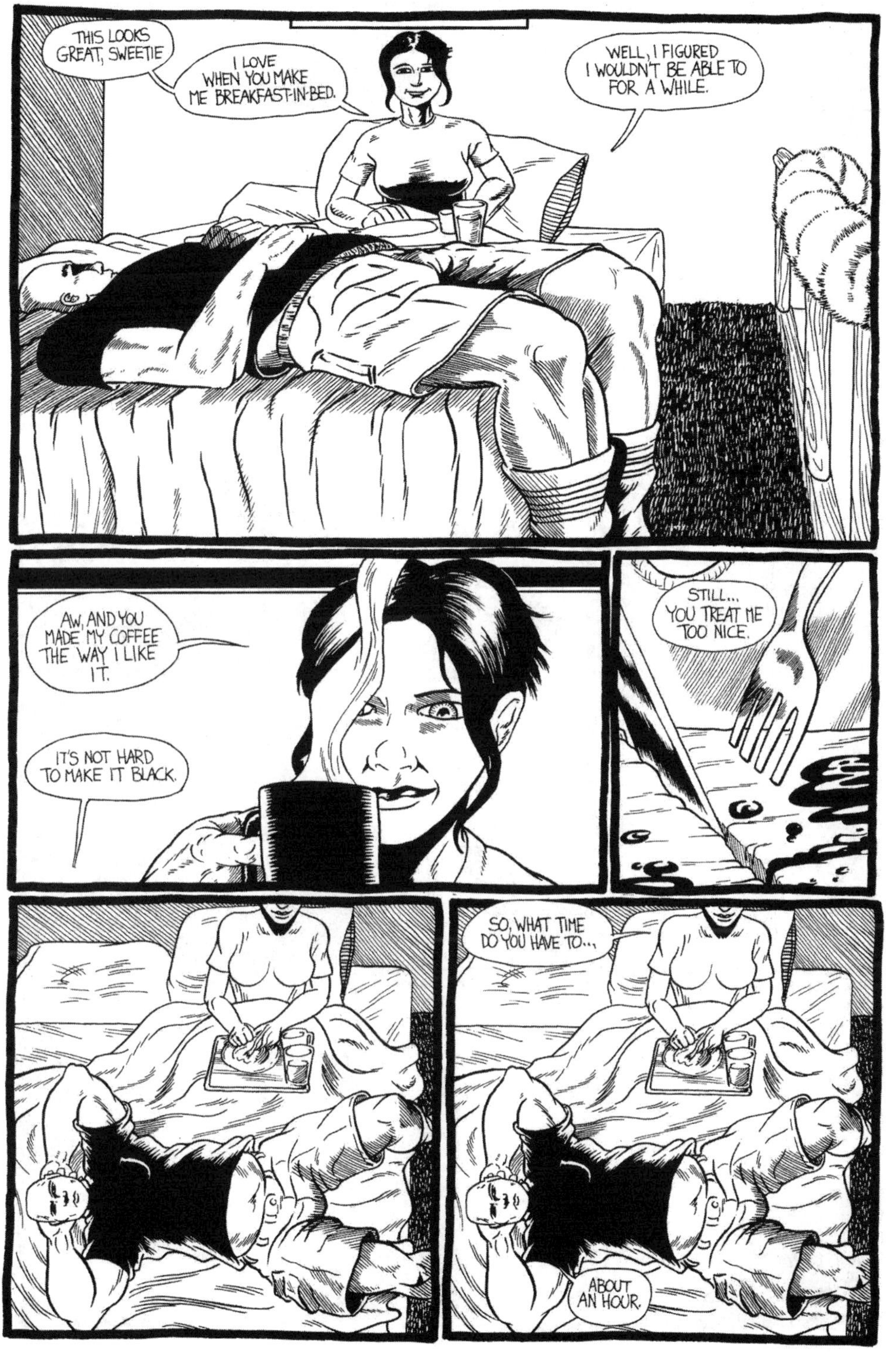
THIS LOOKS GREAT, SWEETIE
I LOVE WHEN YOU MAKE ME BREAKFAST-IN-BED.
WELL, I FIGURED I WOULDN'T BE ABLE TO FOR A WHILE.
AW, AND YOU MADE MY COFFEE THE WAY I LIKE IT.
IT'S NOT HARD TO MAKE IT BLACK.
STILL... YOU TREAT ME TOO NICE.
SO, WHAT TIME DO YOU HAVE TO...
ABOUT AN HOUR.

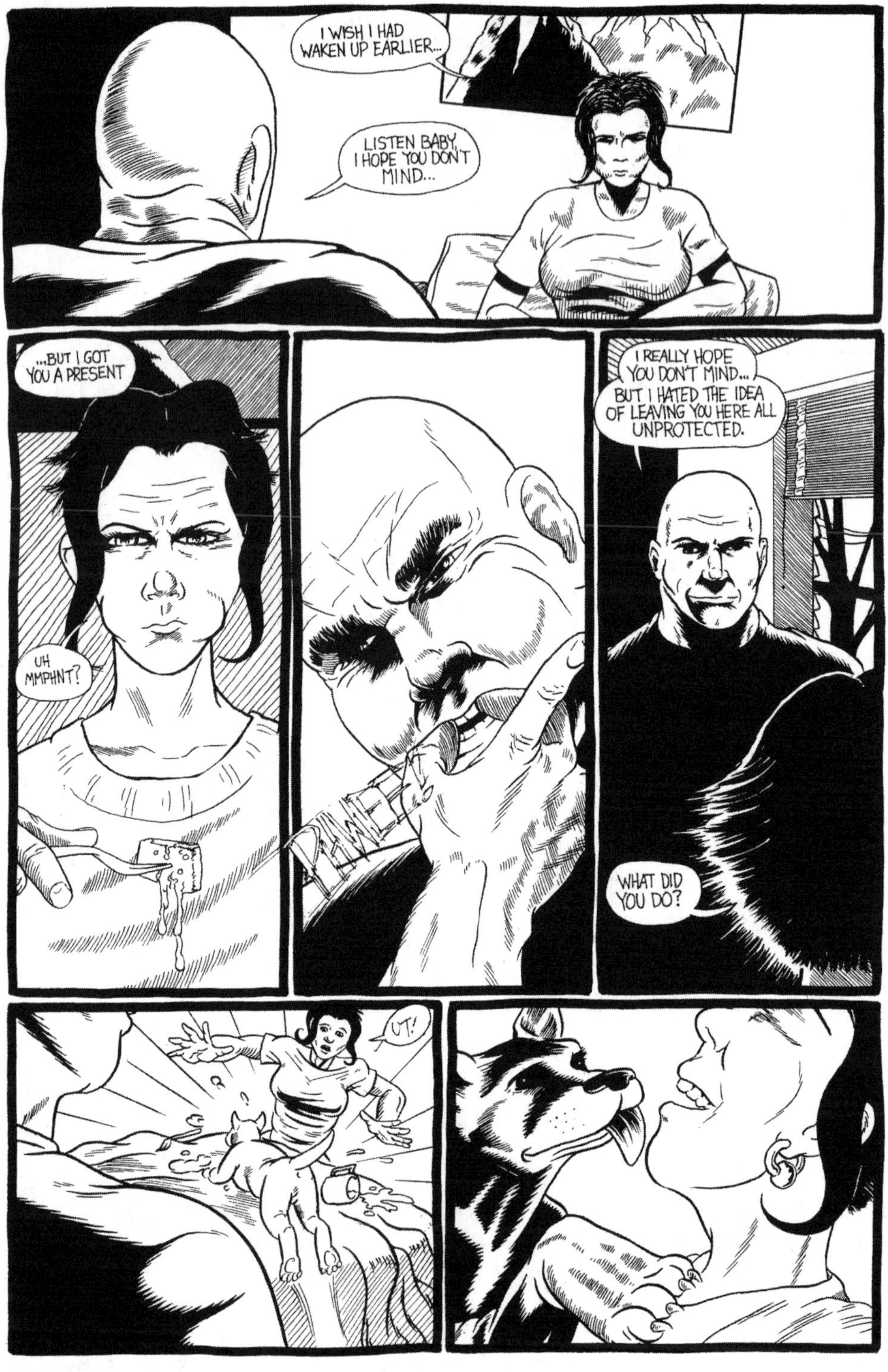

I WISH I HAD WAKEN UP EARLIER...
LISTEN BABY, I HOPE YOU DON'T MIND...
...BUT I GOT YOU A PRESENT
UH MMPHNT?
I REALLY HOPE YOU DON'T MIND...
BUT I HATED THE IDEA OF LEAVING YOU HERE ALL UNPROTECTED.
WHAT DID YOU DO?
UT!

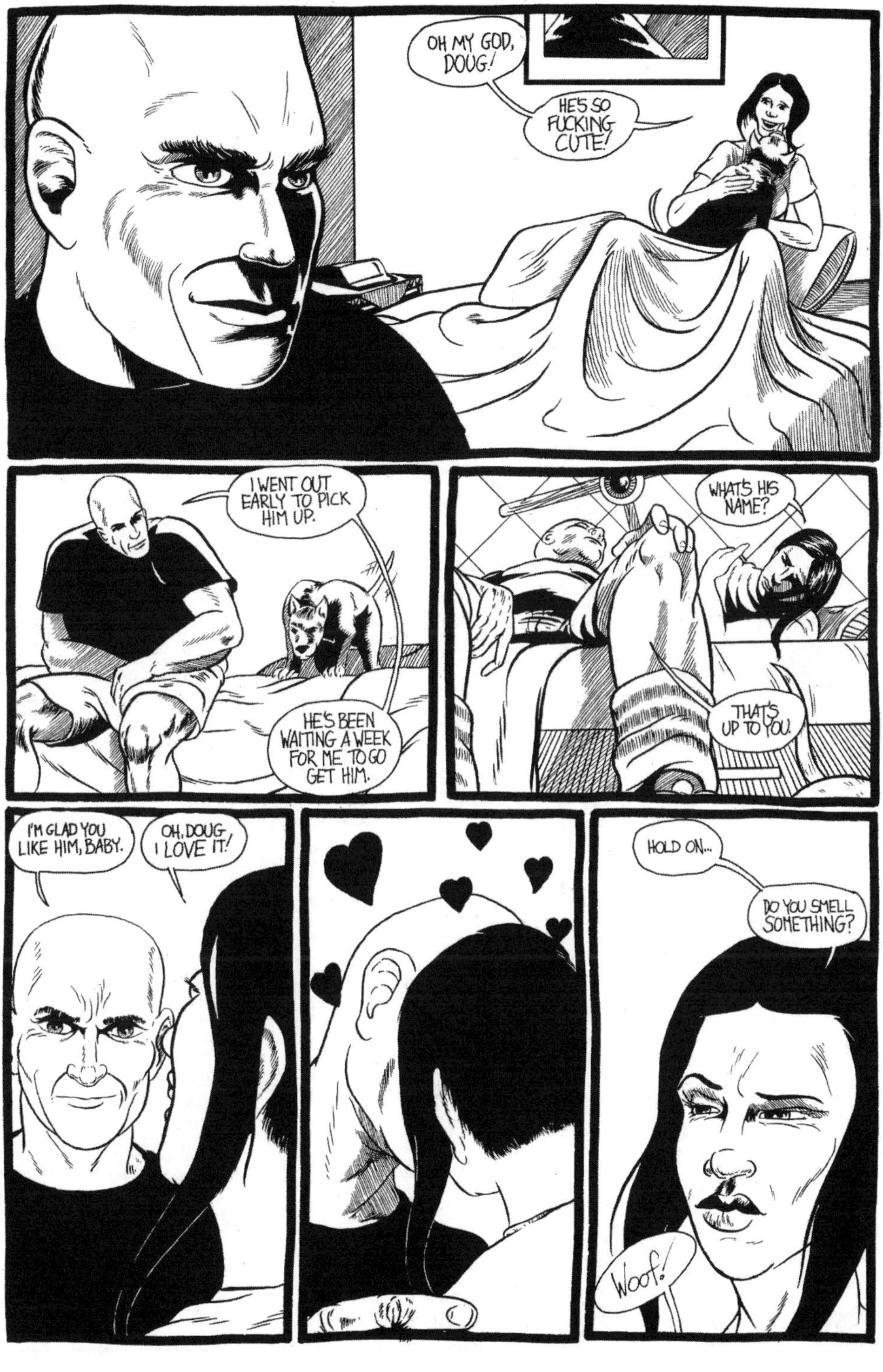
OH MY GOD, DOUG!
HE'S SO FUCKING CUTE!
I WENT OUT EARLY TO PICK HIM UP.
HE'S BEEN WAITING A WEEK FOR ME TO GO GET HIM.
WHAT'S HIS NAME?
THAT'S UP TO YOU.
I'M GLAD YOU LIKE HIM, BABY.
OH, DOUG I LOVE IT!
HOLD ON..
DO YOU SMELL SOMETHING?
Woof!

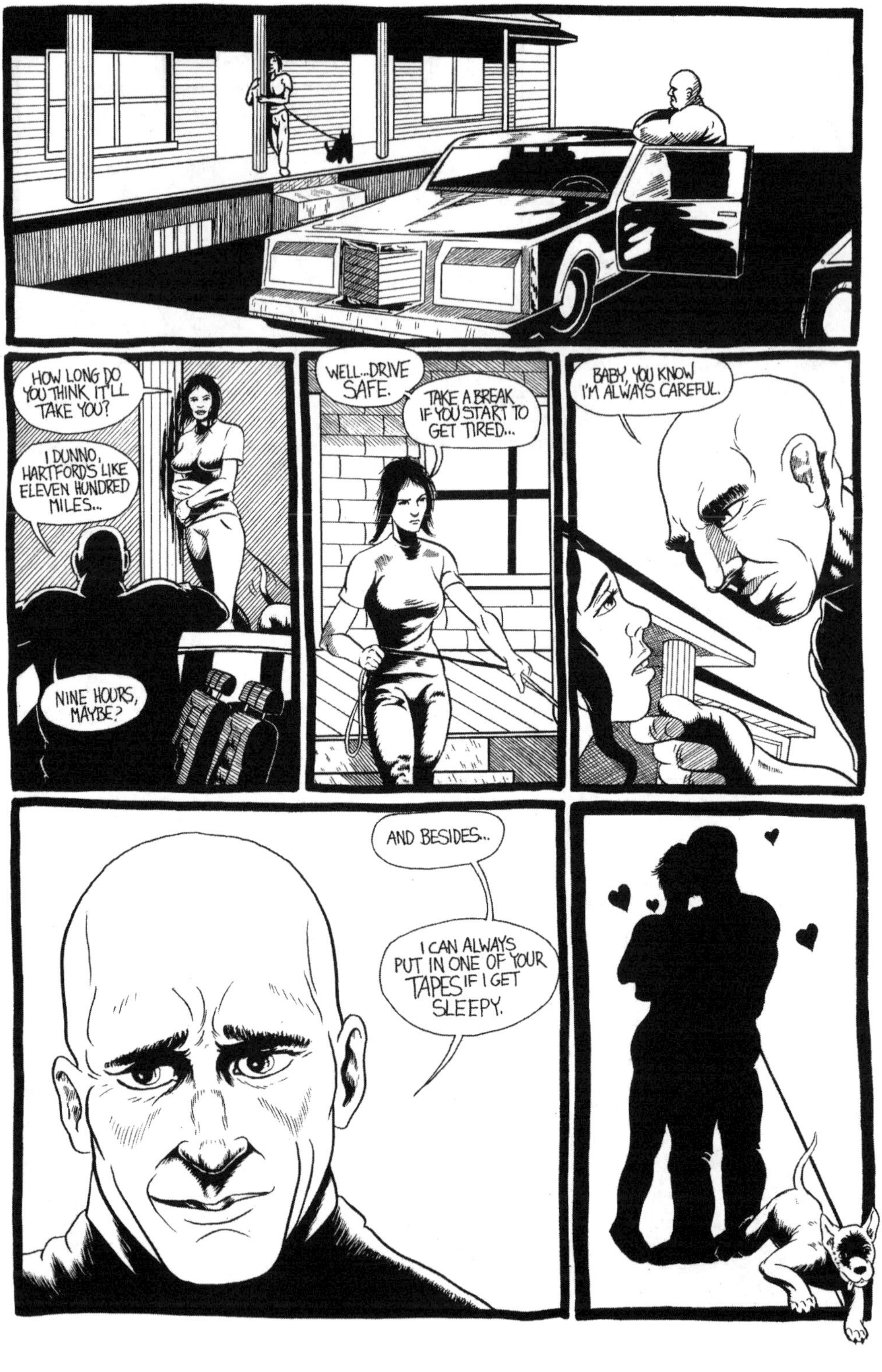
HOW LONG DO YOU THINK IT'LL TAKE YOU?
I DUNNO, HARTFORD'S LIKE ELEVEN HUNDRED MILES...
NINE HOURS, MAYBE?
WELL...DRIVE SAFE.
TAKE A BREAK IF YOU START TO GET TIRED...
BABY, YOU KNOW I'M ALWAYS CAREFUL.
AND BESIDES...
I CAN ALWAYS PUT IN ONE OF YOUR TAPES IF I GET SLEEPY.

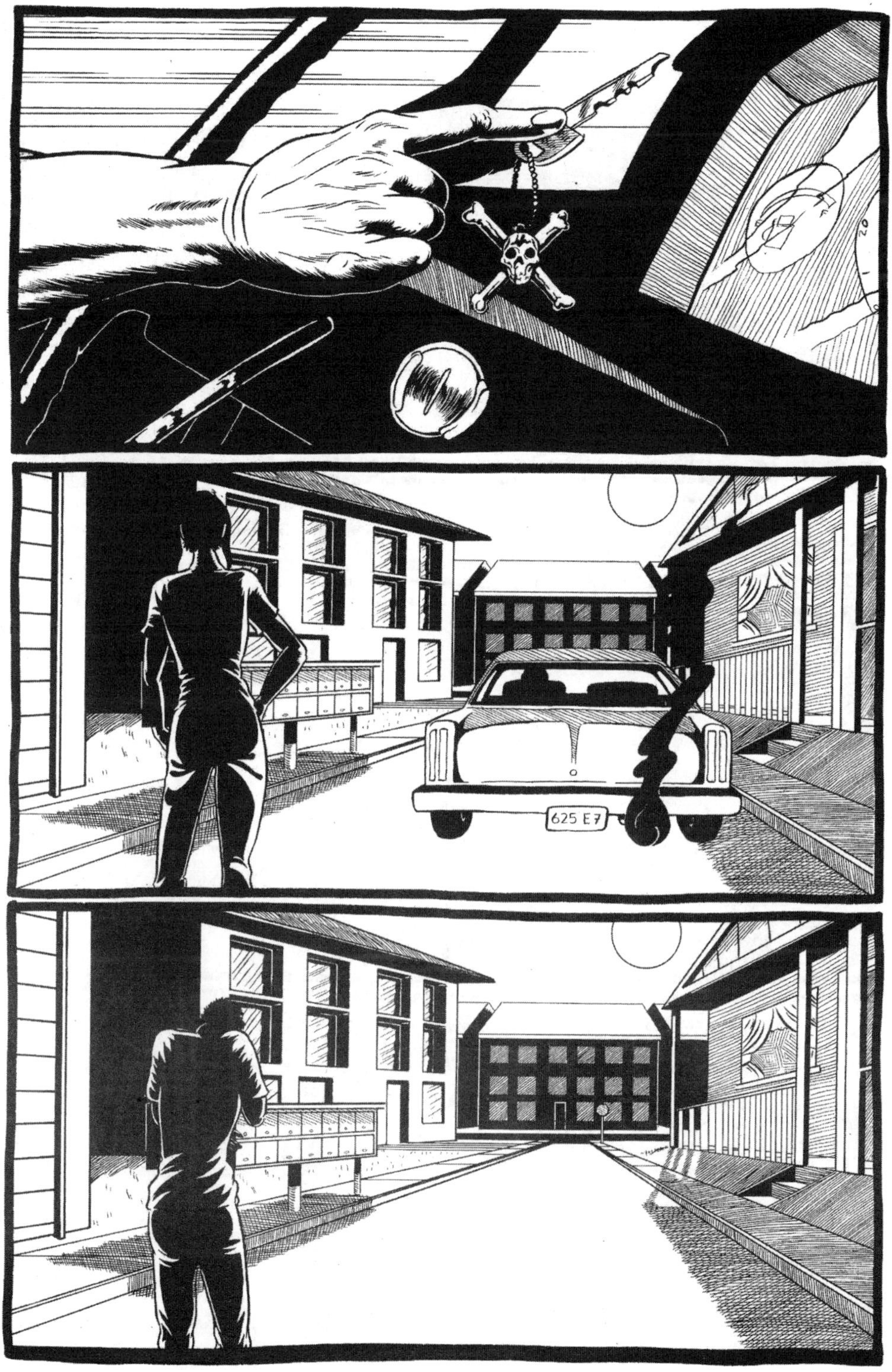
625 E7

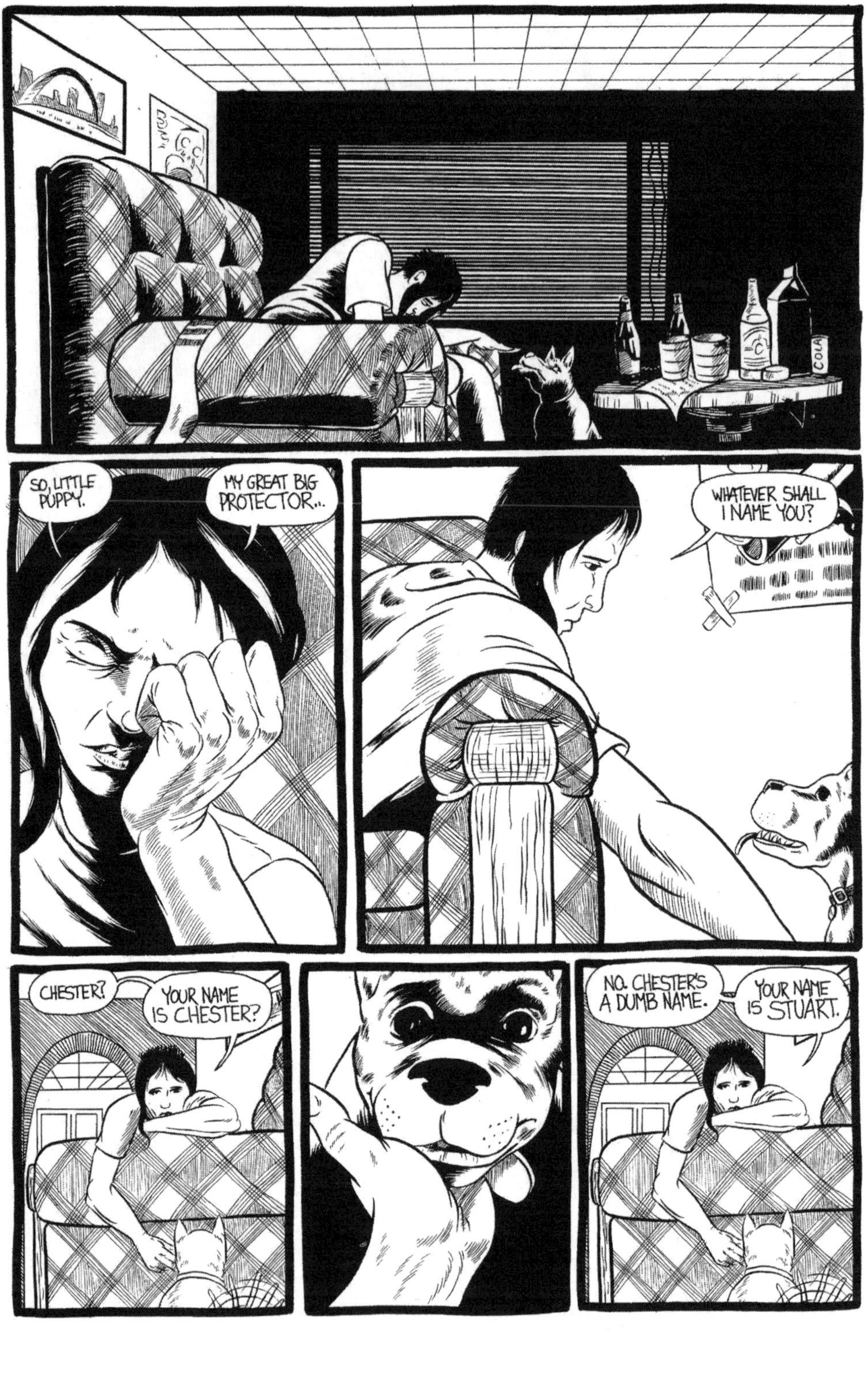
SO, LITTLE PUPPY.
MY GREAT BIG PROTECTOR...
WHATEVER SHALL I NAME YOU?
CHESTER?
YOUR NAME IS CHESTER?
NO. CHESTER'S A DUMB NAME.
YOUR NAME IS STUART.

chapter six:
chester starts going crazy

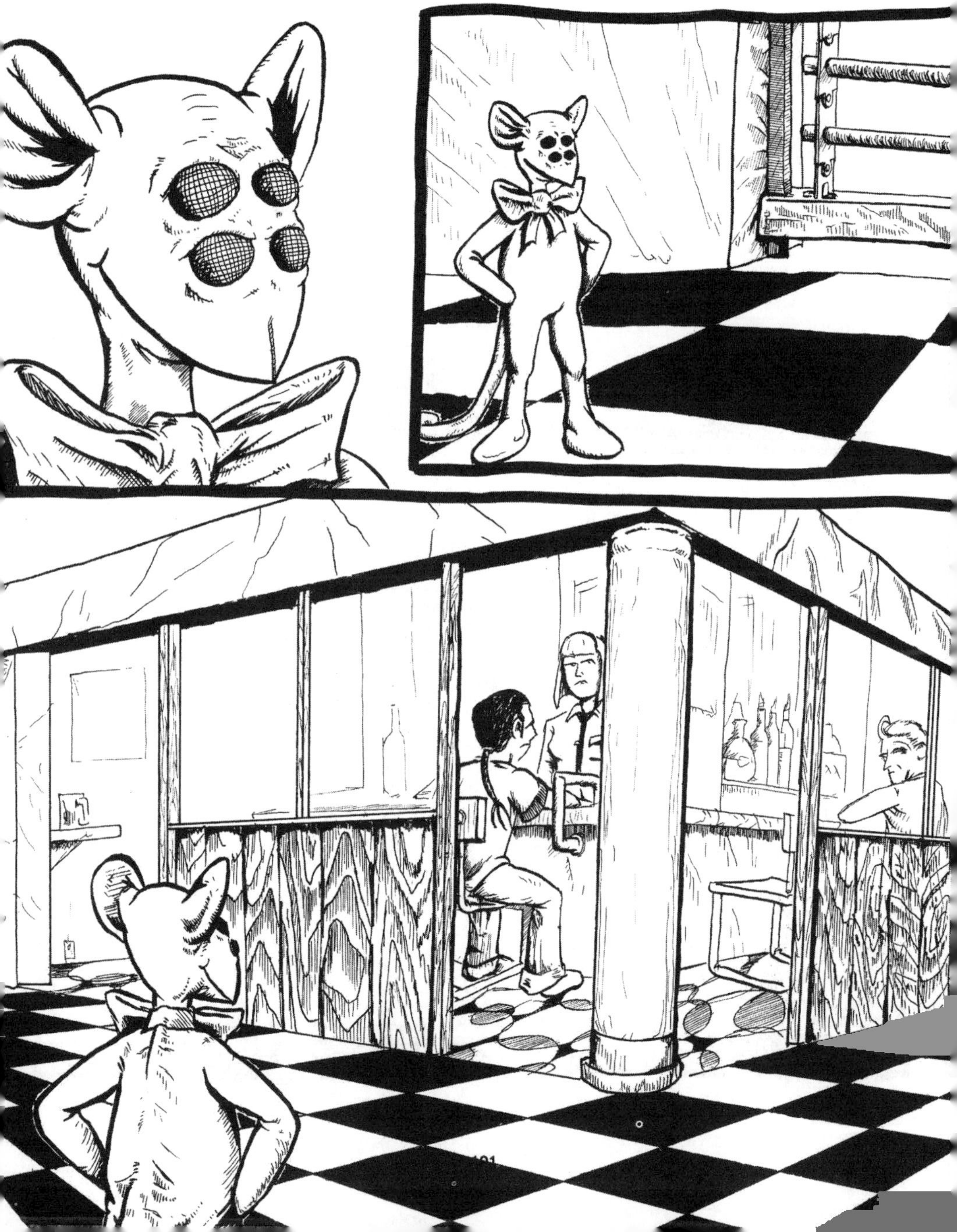

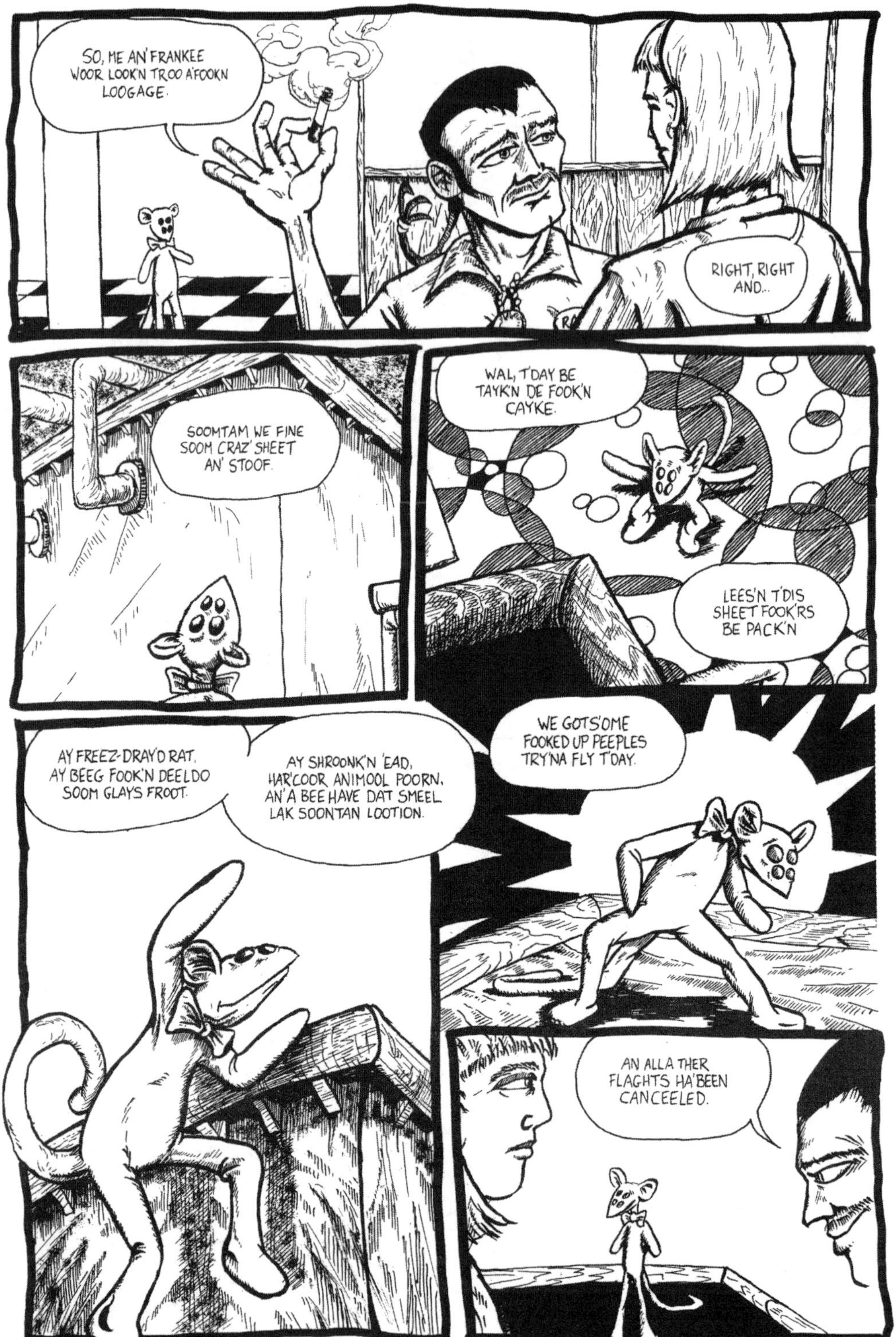
SO, ME AN' FRANKEE WOOR LOOK'N TROO A'FOOKN LOOGAGE.
RIGHT, RIGHT AND...
SOOMTAM WE FINE SOOM CRAZ' SHEET AN' STOOF.
WAL, T'DAY BE TAYK'N DE FOOK'N CAYKE.
LEES'N T'DIS SHEET FOOK'RS BE PACK'N
AY FREEZ-DRAY'D RAT. AY BEEG FOOK'N DEELDO SOOM GLAYS FROOT.
AY SHROONK'N 'EAD, HAR'COOR ANIMOOL POORN. AN'A BEE HAVE DAT SMEEL LAK SOONTAN LOOTION.
WE GOTS'OME FOOKED UP PEEPLES TRY'NA FLY T'DAY.
AN ALLA THER FLAGHTS HA'BEEN CANCEELED.

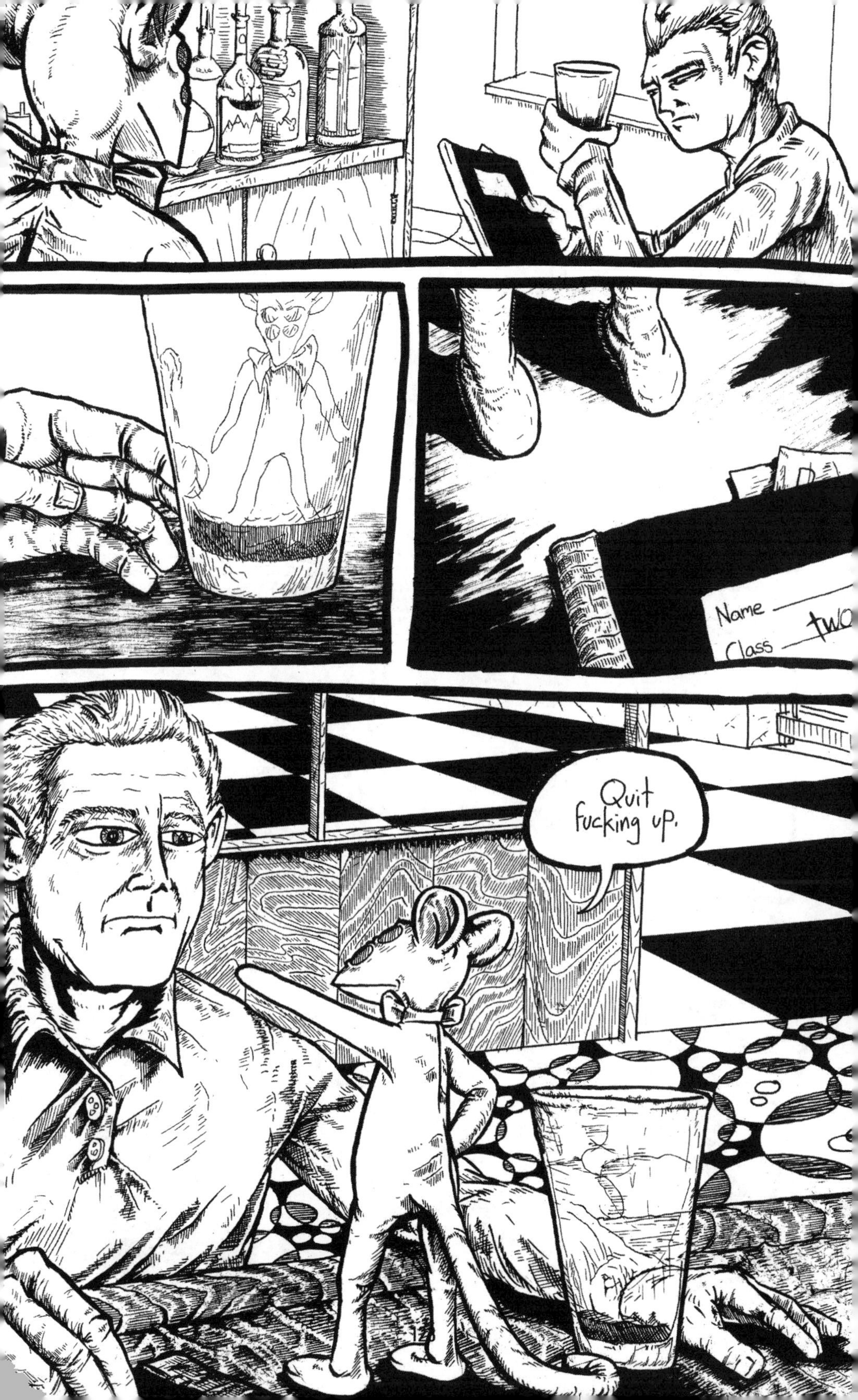
Name
Class two
Quit fucking up.

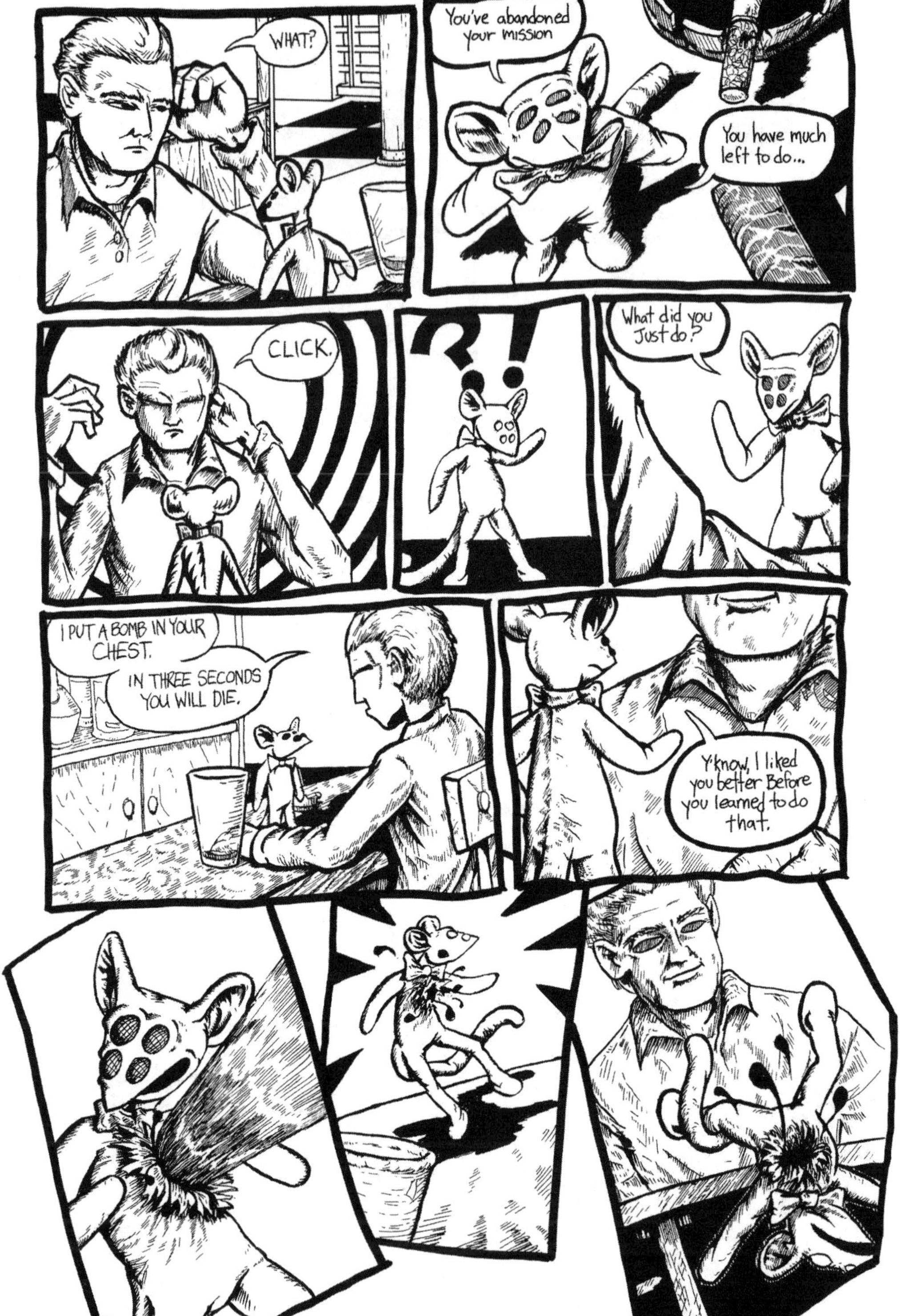
WHAT?
You've abandoned your mission
You have much left to do...
CLICK.
?!
What did you Just do?
I PUT A BOMB IN YOUR CHEST.
IN THREE SECONDS YOU WILL DIE.
Y'know, I liked you better Before you learned to do that.

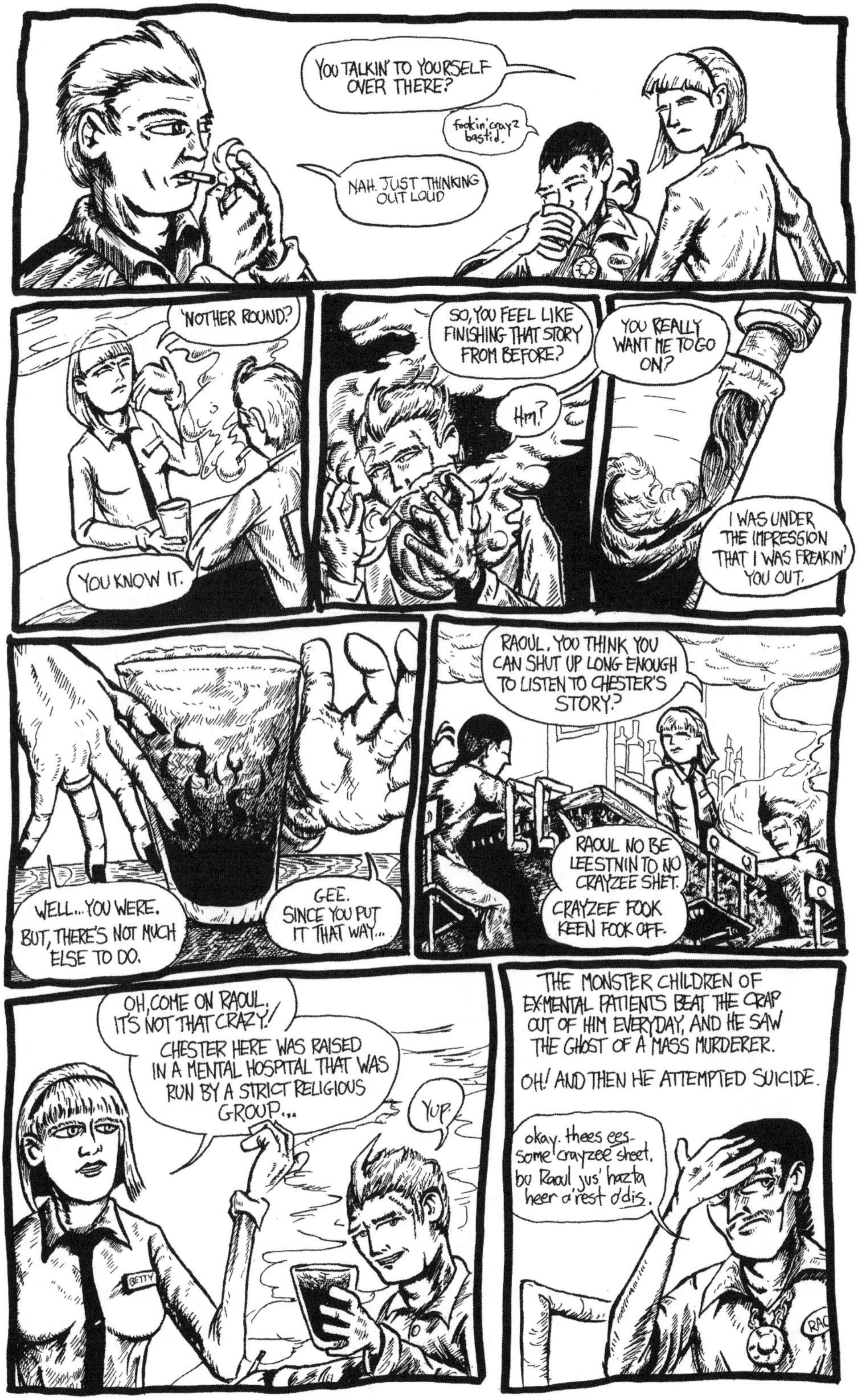

YOU TALKIN' TO YOURSELF OVER THERE?
fookin' crayz bastid.
NAH. JUST THINKING OUT LOUD
'NOTHER ROUND?
YOU KNOW IT.
SO, YOU FEEL LIKE FINISHING THAT STORY FROM BEFORE?
Hm?
YOU REALLY WANT ME TO GO ON?
I WAS UNDER THE IMPRESSION THAT I WAS FREAKIN' YOU OUT.
WELL... YOU WERE. BUT, THERE'S NOT MUCH ELSE TO DO.
GEE. SINCE YOU PUT IT THAT WAY...
RAOUL. YOU THINK YOU CAN SHUT UP LONG ENOUGH TO LISTEN TO CHESTER'S STORY?
RAOUL NO BE LEESTNIN TO NO CRAYZEE SHET.
CRAYZEE FOOK KEEN FOOK OFF.
OH, COME ON RAOUL, IT'S NOT THAT CRAZY!
CHESTER HERE WAS RAISED IN A MENTAL HOSPITAL THAT WAS RUN BY A STRICT RELIGIOUS GROUP...
YUP.
THE MONSTER CHILDREN OF EX-MENTAL PATIENTS BEAT THE CRAP OUT OF HIM EVERYDAY, AND HE SAW THE GHOST OF A MASS MURDERER.
OH! AND THEN HE ATTEMPTED SUICIDE.
okay. thees ees some crayzee sheet, bu Raoul jus' hazta heer a'rest o'dis.

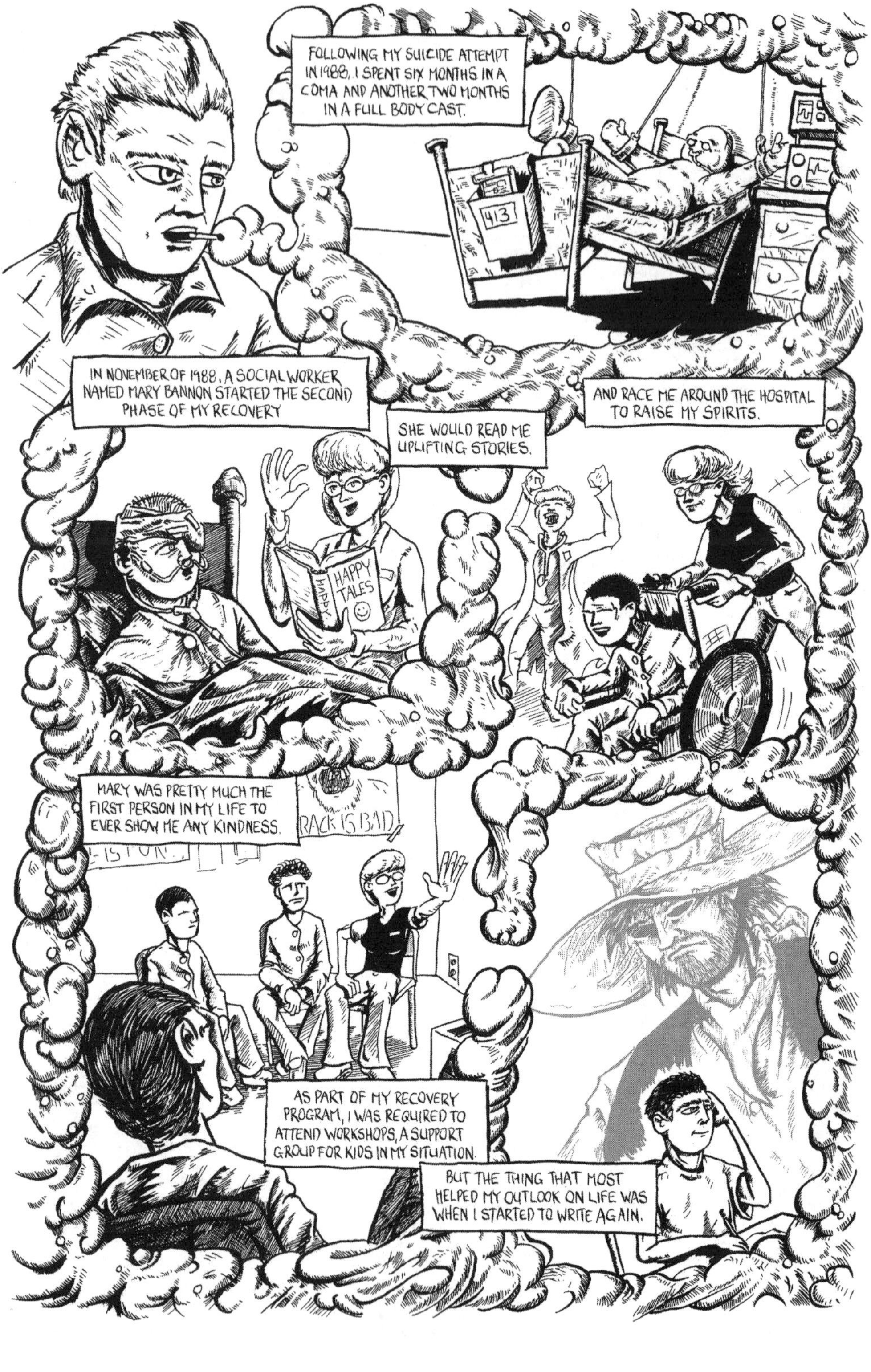
FOLLOWING MY SUICIDE ATTEMPT IN 1988, I SPENT SIX MONTHS IN A COMA AND ANOTHER TWO MONTHS IN A FULL BODY CAST.
413
IN NOVEMBER OF 1988, A SOCIAL WORKER NAMED MARY BANNON STARTED THE SECOND PHASE OF MY RECOVERY
SHE WOULD READ ME UPLIFTING STORIES.
HAPPY TALES
AND RACE ME AROUND THE HOSPITAL TO RAISE MY SPIRITS.
MARY WAS PRETTY MUCH THE FIRST PERSON IN MY LIFE TO EVER SHOW ME ANY KINDNESS.
RACK IS BAD
AS PART OF MY RECOVERY PROGRAM, I WAS REQUIRED TO ATTEND WORKSHOPS, A SUPPORT GROUP FOR KIDS IN MY SITUATION.
BUT THE THING THAT MOST HELPED MY OUTLOOK ON LIFE WAS WHEN I STARTED TO WRITE AGAIN.

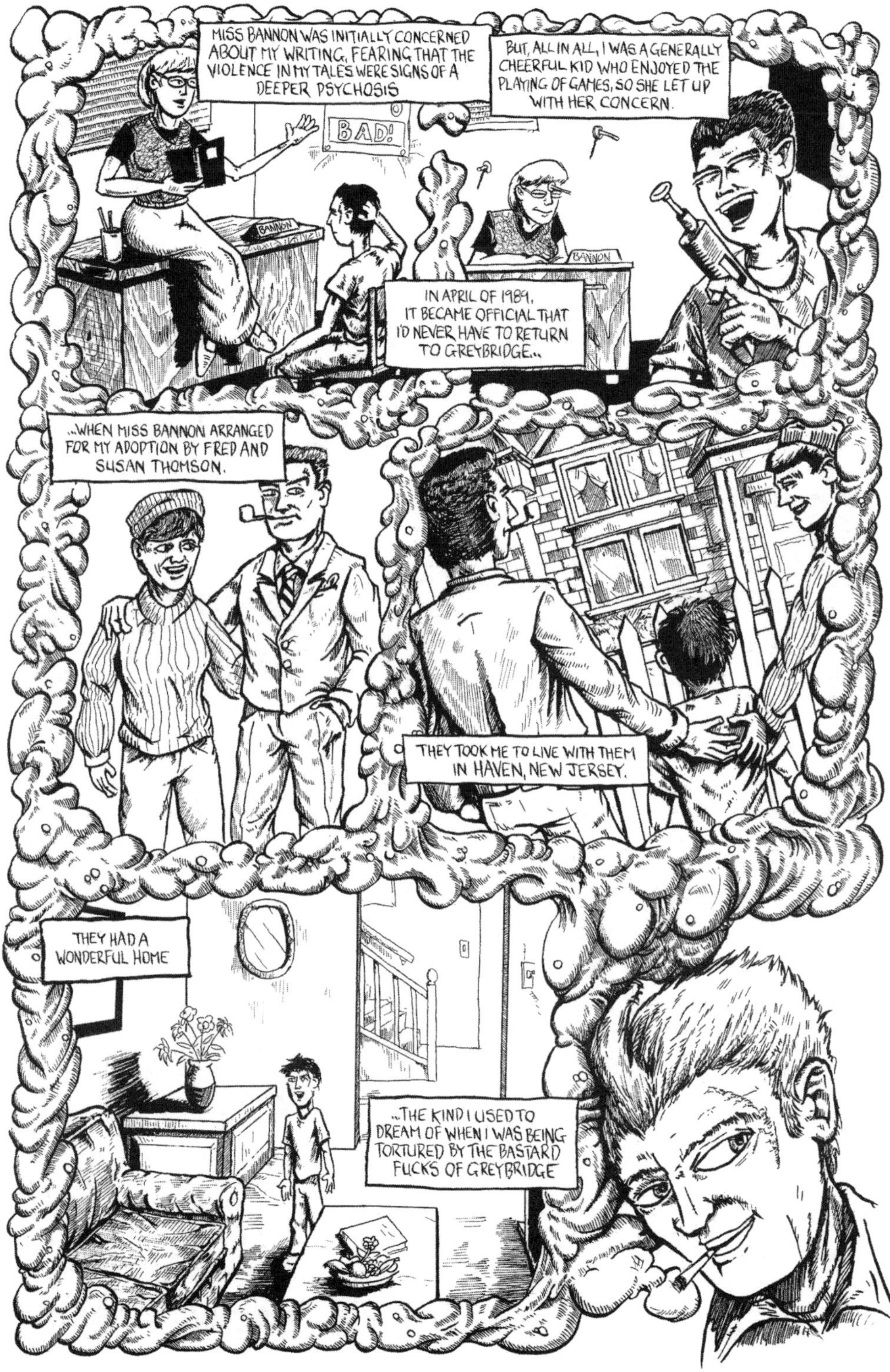
MISS BANNON WAS INITIALLY CONCERNED ABOUT MY WRITING, FEARING THAT THE VIOLENCE IN MY TALES WERE SIGNS OF A DEEPER PSYCHOSIS
BAD!
BANNON
BANNON
BUT, ALL IN ALL, I WAS A GENERALLY CHEERFUL KID WHO ENJOYED THE PLAYING OF GAMES, SO SHE LET UP WITH HER CONCERN.
IN APRIL OF 1989, IT BECAME OFFICIAL THAT I'D NEVER HAVE TO RETURN TO GREYBRIDGE...
...WHEN MISS BANNON ARRANGED FOR MY ADOPTION BY FRED AND SUSAN THOMSON.
THEY TOOK ME TO LIVE WITH THEM IN HAVEN, NEW JERSEY.
THEY HAD A WONDERFUL HOME
...THE KIND I USED TO DREAM OF WHEN I WAS BEING TORTURED BY THE BASTARD FUCKS OF GREYBRIDGE

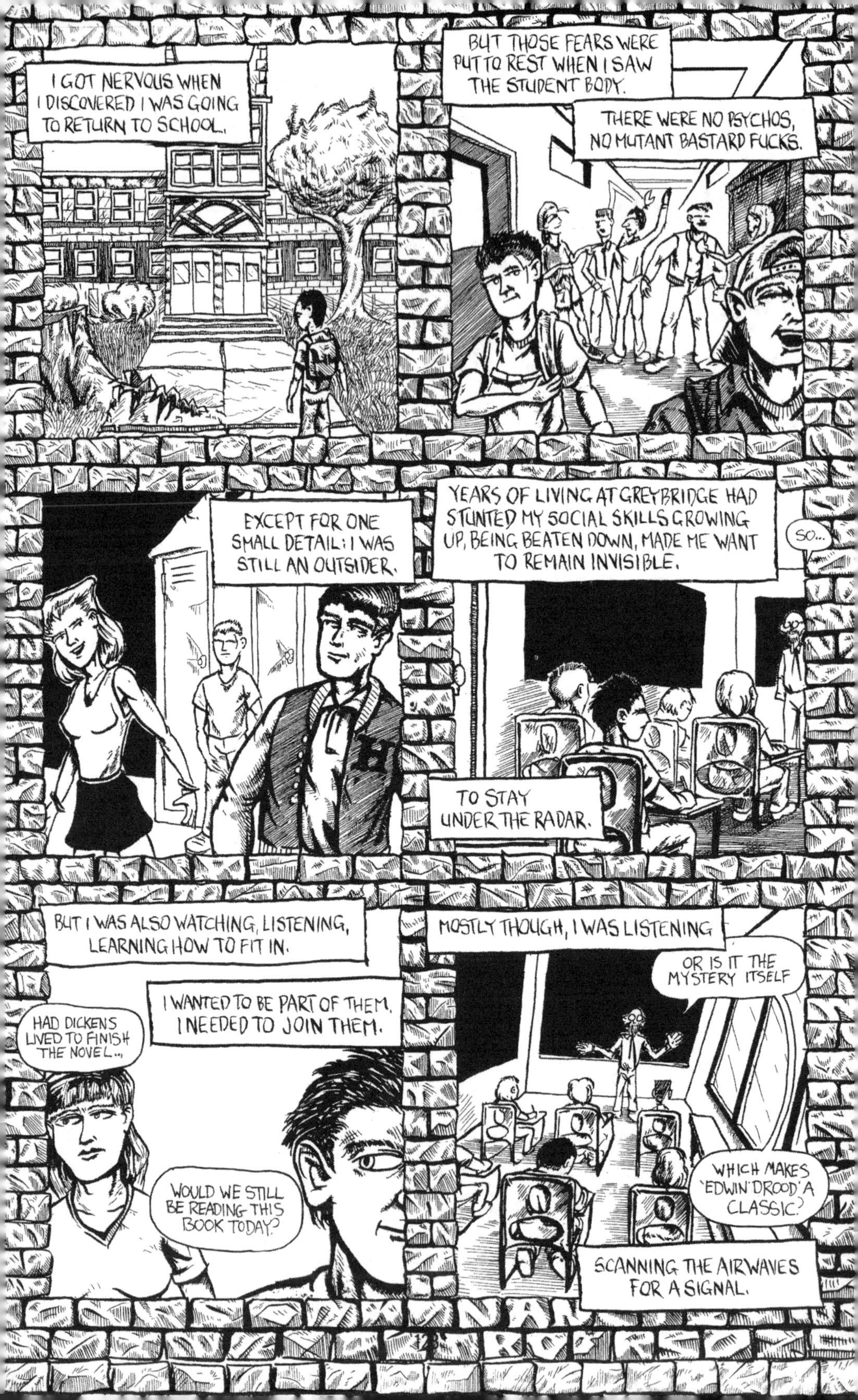
I GOT NERVOUS WHEN I DISCOVERED I WAS GOING TO RETURN TO SCHOOL.
BUT THOSE FEARS WERE PUT TO REST WHEN I SAW THE STUDENT BODY.
THERE WERE NO PSYCHOS, NO MUTANT BASTARD FUCKS.
EXCEPT FOR ONE SMALL DETAIL: I WAS STILL AN OUTSIDER.
YEARS OF LIVING AT GREYBRIDGE HAD STUNTED MY SOCIAL SKILLS GROWING UP, BEING BEATEN DOWN, MADE ME WANT TO REMAIN INVISIBLE.
SO...
TO STAY UNDER THE RADAR.
BUT I WAS ALSO WATCHING, LISTENING, LEARNING HOW TO FIT IN.
I WANTED TO BE PART OF THEM. I NEEDED TO JOIN THEM.
HAD DICKENS LIVED TO FINISH THE NOVEL...
WOULD WE STILL BE READING THIS BOOK TODAY?
MOSTLY THOUGH, I WAS LISTENING
OR IS IT THE MYSTERY ITSELF
WHICH MAKES 'EDWIN DROOD' A CLASSIC?
SCANNING THE AIRWAVES FOR A SIGNAL.

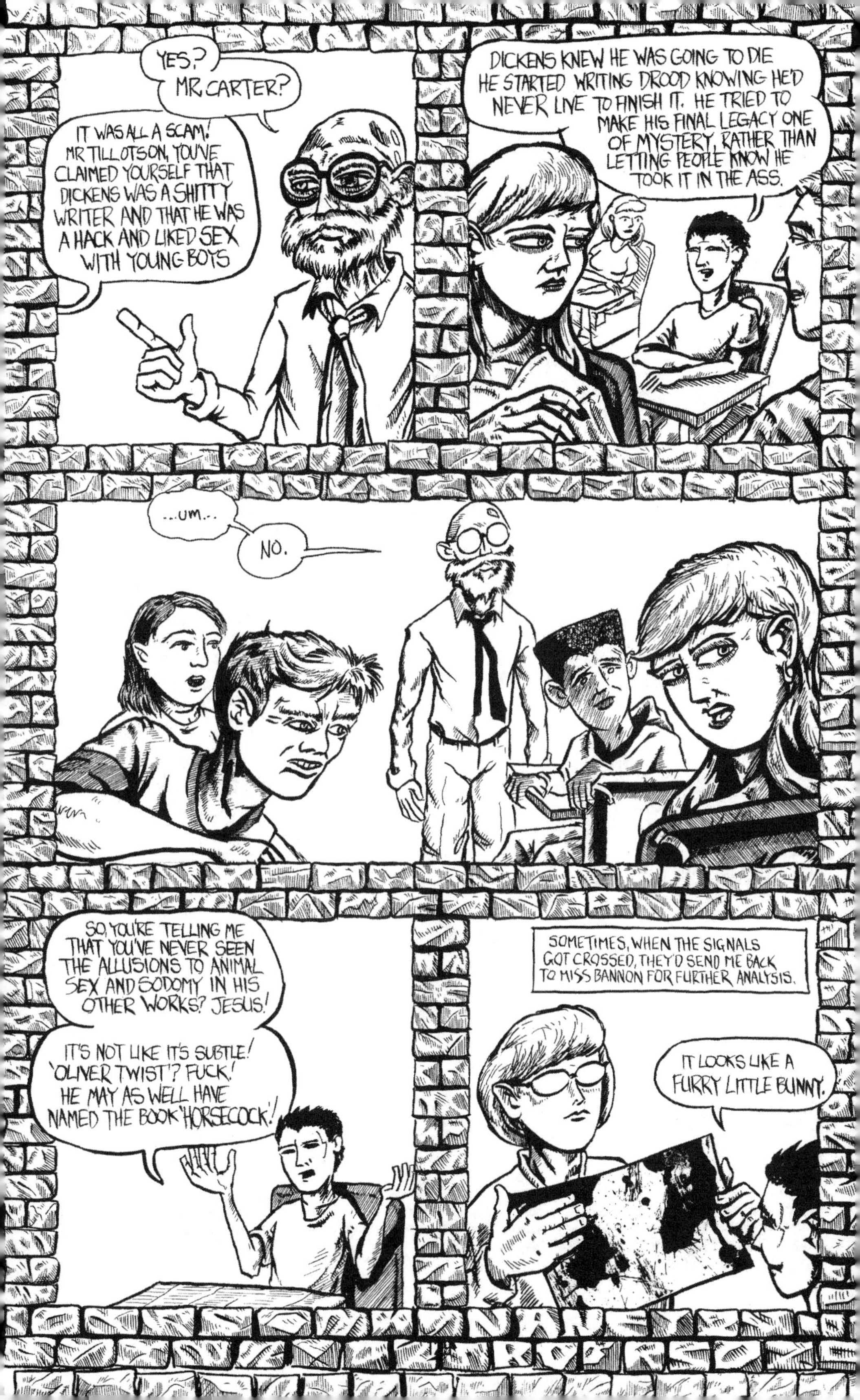
YES? MR. CARTER?
IT WAS ALL A SCAM! MR TILLOTSON, YOU'VE CLAIMED YOURSELF THAT DICKENS WAS A SHITTY WRITER AND THAT HE WAS A HACK AND LIKED SEX WITH YOUNG BOYS
DICKENS KNEW HE WAS GOING TO DIE HE STARTED WRITING DROOD KNOWING HE'D NEVER LIVE TO FINISH IT. HE TRIED TO MAKE HIS FINAL LEGACY ONE OF MYSTERY, RATHER THAN LETTING PEOPLE KNOW HE TOOK IT IN THE ASS.
...UM...
NO.
SO, YOU'RE TELLING ME THAT YOU'VE NEVER SEEN THE ALLUSIONS TO ANIMAL SEX AND SODOMY IN HIS OTHER WORKS? JESUS!
IT'S NOT LIKE IT'S SUBTLE! 'OLIVER TWIST'? FUCK! HE MAY AS WELL HAVE NAMED THE BOOK 'HORSECOCK'!
SOMETIMES, WHEN THE SIGNALS GOT CROSSED, THEY'D SEND ME BACK TO MISS BANNON FOR FURTHER ANALYSIS.
IT LOOKS LIKE A FURRY LITTLE BUNNY.

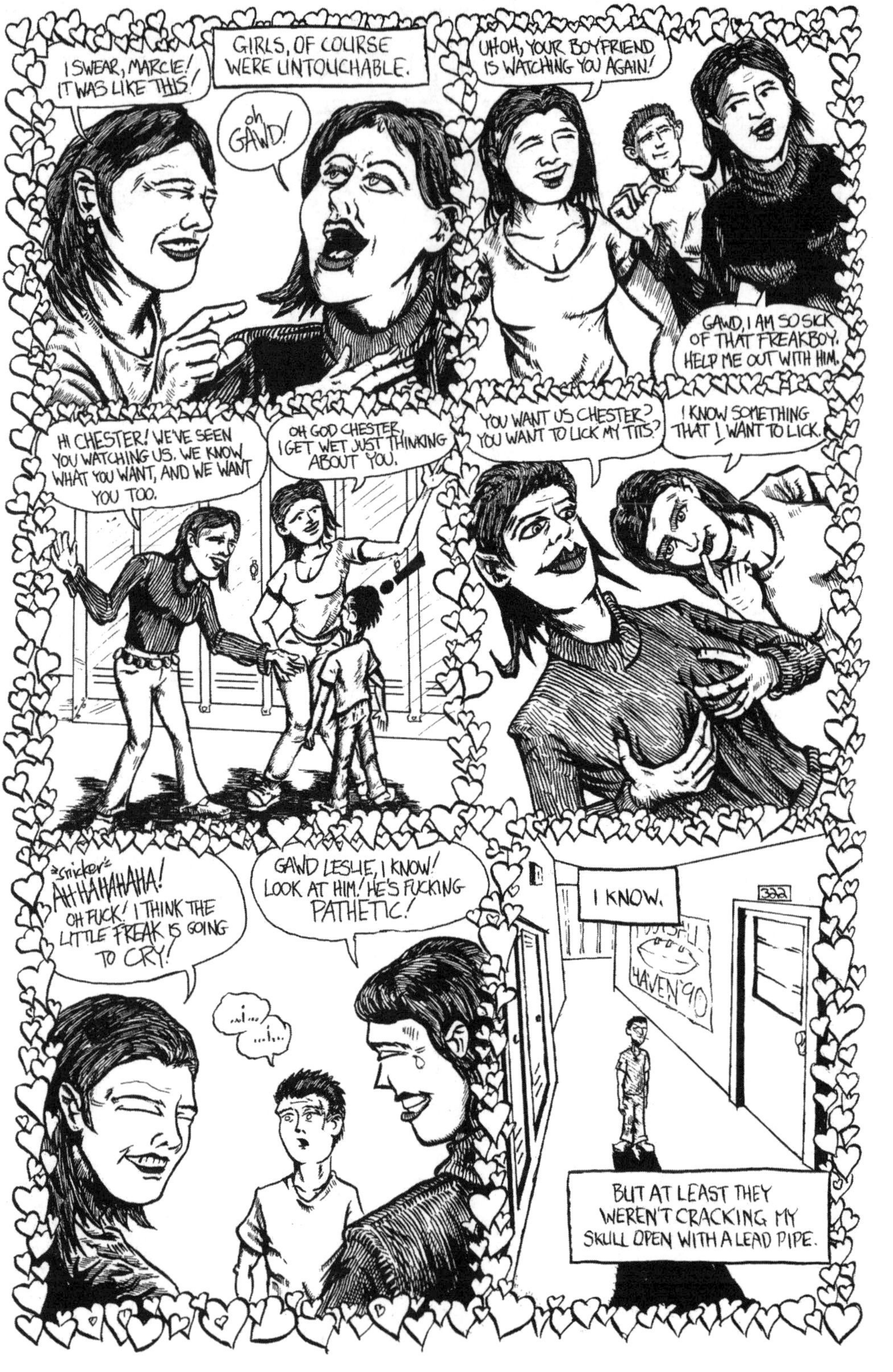
I SWEAR, MARCIE! IT WAS LIKE THIS!
GIRLS, OF COURSE WERE UNTOUCHABLE.
oh GAWD!
UHOH, YOUR BOYFRIEND IS WATCHING YOU AGAIN!
GAWD, I AM SO SICK OF THAT FREAKBOY. HELP ME OUT WITH HIM.
HI CHESTER! WE'VE SEEN YOU WATCHING US. WE KNOW WHAT YOU WANT, AND WE WANT YOU TOO.
OH GOD CHESTER, I GET WET JUST THINKING ABOUT YOU.
YOU WANT US CHESTER? YOU WANT TO LICK MY TITS?
I KNOW SOMETHING THAT I WANT TO LICK.
snicker
AHHAHAHAHA! OH FUCK! I THINK THE LITTLE FREAK IS GOING TO CRY!
GAWD LESLIE, I KNOW! LOOK AT HIM! HE'S FUCKING PATHETIC!
...i... ...i...
I KNOW.
322
HAVEN '90
BUT AT LEAST THEY WEREN'T CRACKING MY SKULL OPEN WITH A LEAD PIPE.

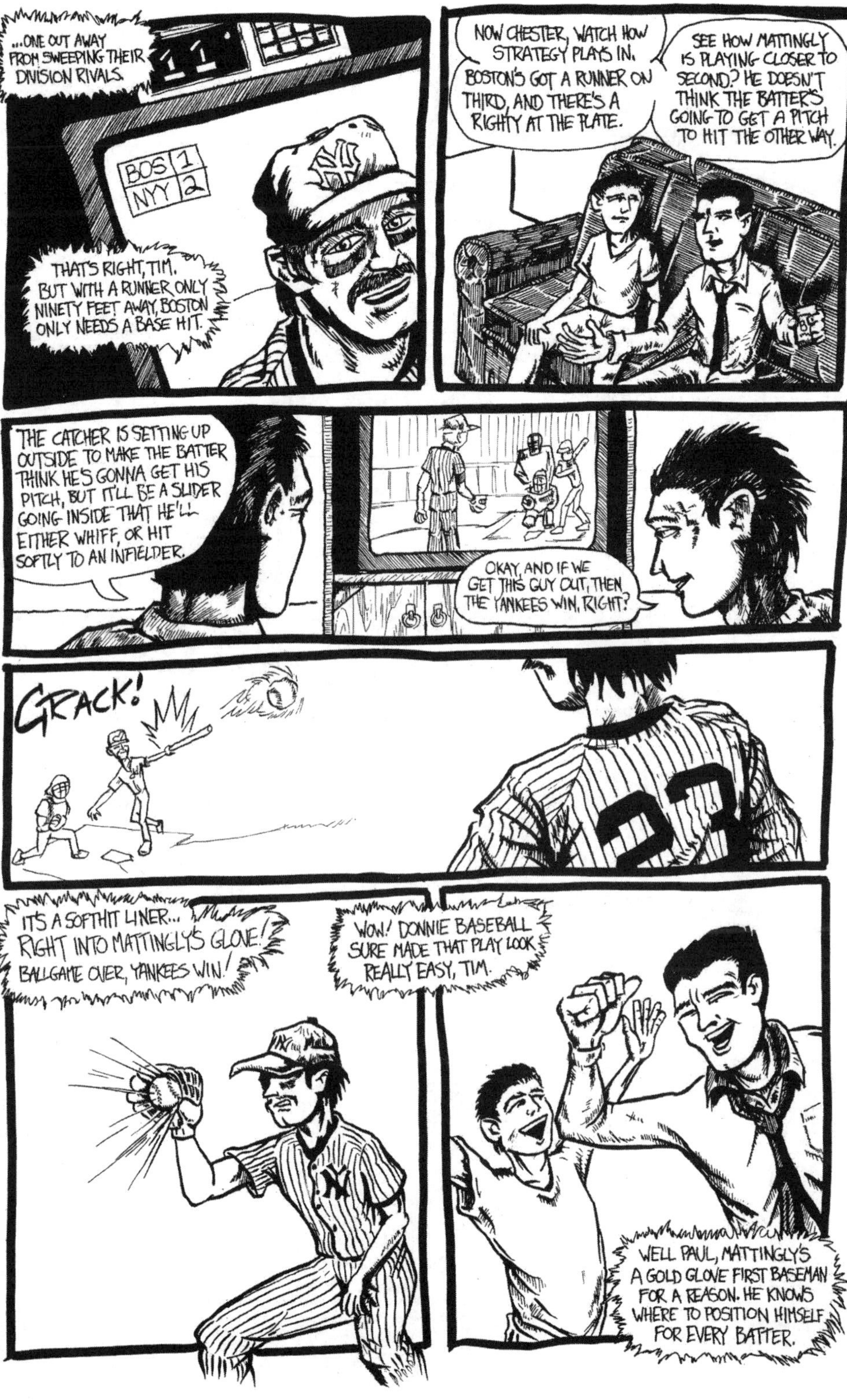
...ONE OUT AWAY FROM SWEEPING THEIR DIVISION RIVALS.
BOS 1
NYY 2
THAT'S RIGHT, TIM. BUT WITH A RUNNER ONLY NINETY FEET AWAY, BOSTON ONLY NEEDS A BASE HIT.
NOW CHESTER, WATCH HOW STRATEGY PLAYS IN.
BOSTON'S GOT A RUNNER ON THIRD, AND THERE'S A RIGHTY AT THE PLATE.
SEE HOW MATTINGLY IS PLAYING CLOSER TO SECOND? HE DOESN'T THINK THE BATTER'S GOING TO GET A PITCH TO HIT THE OTHER WAY.
THE CATCHER IS SETTING UP OUTSIDE TO MAKE THE BATTER THINK HE'S GONNA GET HIS PITCH, BUT IT'LL BE A SLIDER GOING INSIDE THAT HE'LL EITHER WHIFF, OR HIT SOFTLY TO AN INFIELDER.
OKAY, AND IF WE GET THIS GUY OUT, THEN THE YANKEES WIN, RIGHT?
CRACK!
IT'S A SOFT HIT LINER... RIGHT INTO MATTINGLY'S GLOVE! BALLGAME OVER, YANKEES WIN!
WOW! DONNIE BASEBALL SURE MADE THAT PLAY LOOK REALLY EASY, TIM.
WELL PAUL, MATTINGLY'S A GOLD GLOVE FIRST BASEMAN FOR A REASON. HE KNOWS WHERE TO POSITION HIMSELF FOR EVERY BATTER.

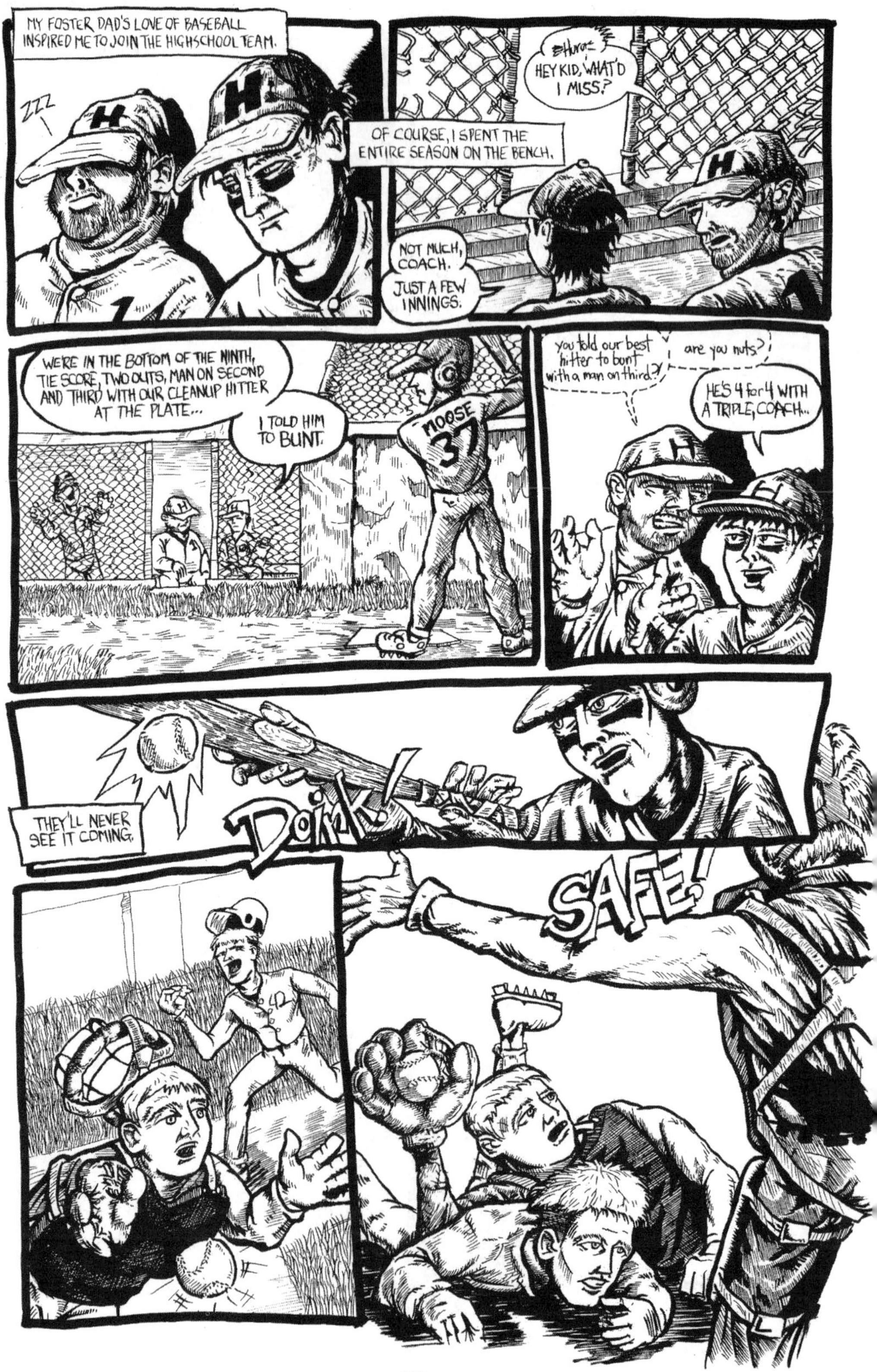
MY FOSTER DAD'S LOVE OF BASEBALL INSPIRED ME TO JOIN THE HIGHSCHOOL TEAM.
ZZZ
OF COURSE, I SPENT THE ENTIRE SEASON ON THE BENCH.
HEY KID, WHAT'D I MISS?
NOT MUCH, COACH.
JUST A FEW INNINGS.
WE'RE IN THE BOTTOM OF THE NINTH, TIE SCORE, TWO OUTS, MAN ON SECOND AND THIRD WITH OUR CLEANUP HITTER AT THE PLATE...
I TOLD HIM TO BUNT.
MOOSE
37
you told our best hitter to bunt with a man on third?
are you nuts?
HE'S 4 for 4 WITH A TRIPLE, COACH...
THEY'LL NEVER SEE IT COMING.
DOINK!
SAFE!

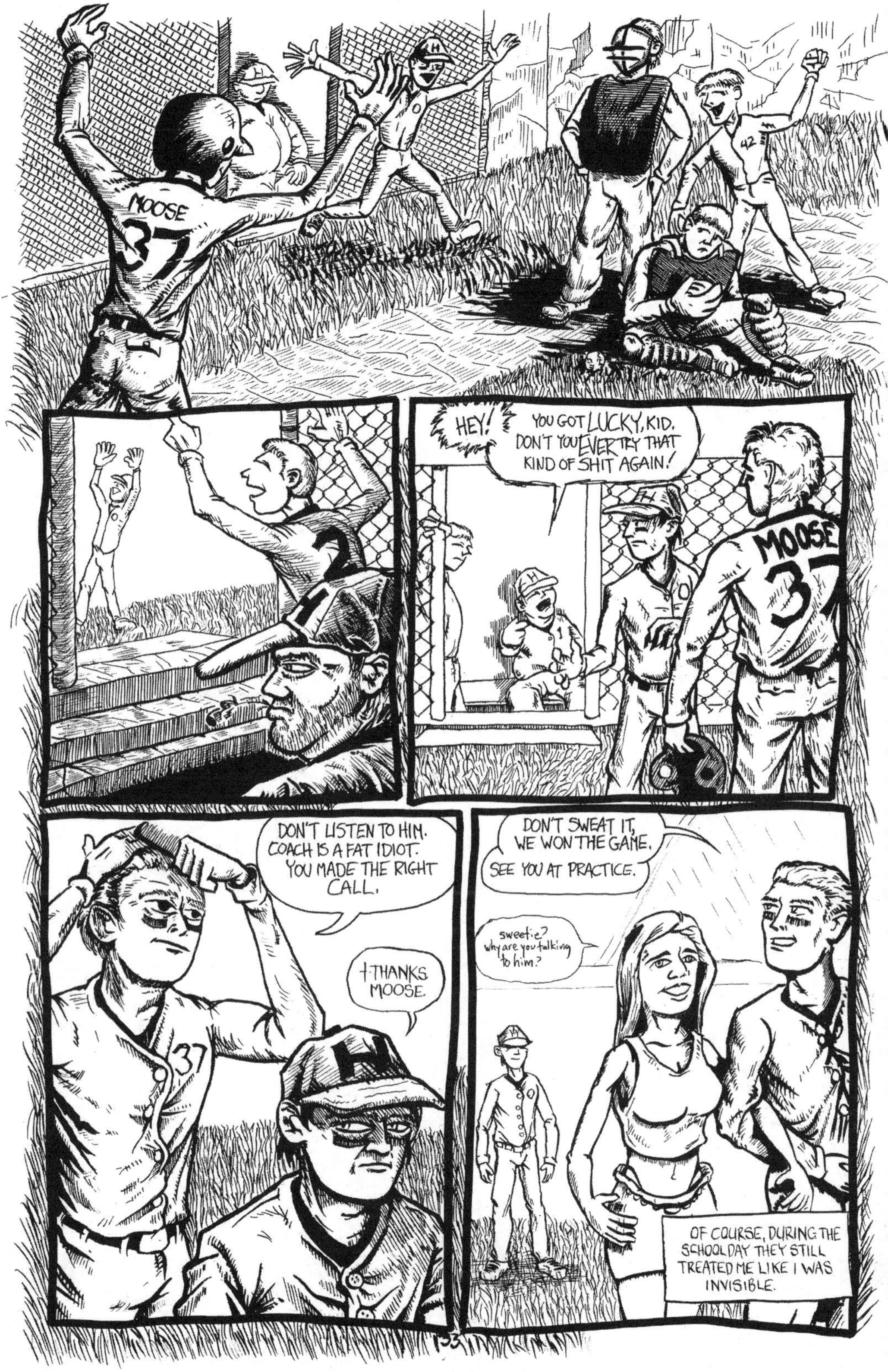
MOOSE
37
42
HEY!
YOU GOT LUCKY, KID. DON'T YOU EVER TRY THAT KIND OF SHIT AGAIN!
MOOSE
37
DON'T LISTEN TO HIM. COACH IS A FAT IDIOT. YOU MADE THE RIGHT CALL.
I-THANKS MOOSE.
DON'T SWEAT IT, WE WON THE GAME.
SEE YOU AT PRACTICE.
sweetie? why are you talking to him?
OF COURSE, DURING THE SCHOOLDAY THEY STILL TREATED ME LIKE I WAS INVISIBLE.
133

WELCOME TO NEW YORK. Located just north of New Jersey, just south of Canada. It is a city filled with people. I'm one of them. Some folks say I'm crazy, I say different. I fight crime because there's just too damn much ... There ... e than you ... ake ... The kid

finished his rant and looked at the broken body of the would-be mugger at his feet. "Do you understand?" he asked. "Now do you see?"

The mugger, though he hadn't a clue what this strange man was talking abou... the af-... tive." he

criminal and cleared his throat. "I don't think you do," he declared, and spit in the mugger's face. "I don't think you understand at all." The mugger had no choice but to agree, which he did with just the faintest glimpse of hesitation. "Fucking A," said the kid.

been many things, the kid explained. "At one time, I'd been an astronaut. Once I was a famous explorer. Sometimes I'm even a cowboy, but right now, I'm a super-hero." The kid cracked a smile and his black eyes started to glow. "I have power like no other." The mugger wet his pants and cried 'don't hurt me.'

"Click," said ... kid.

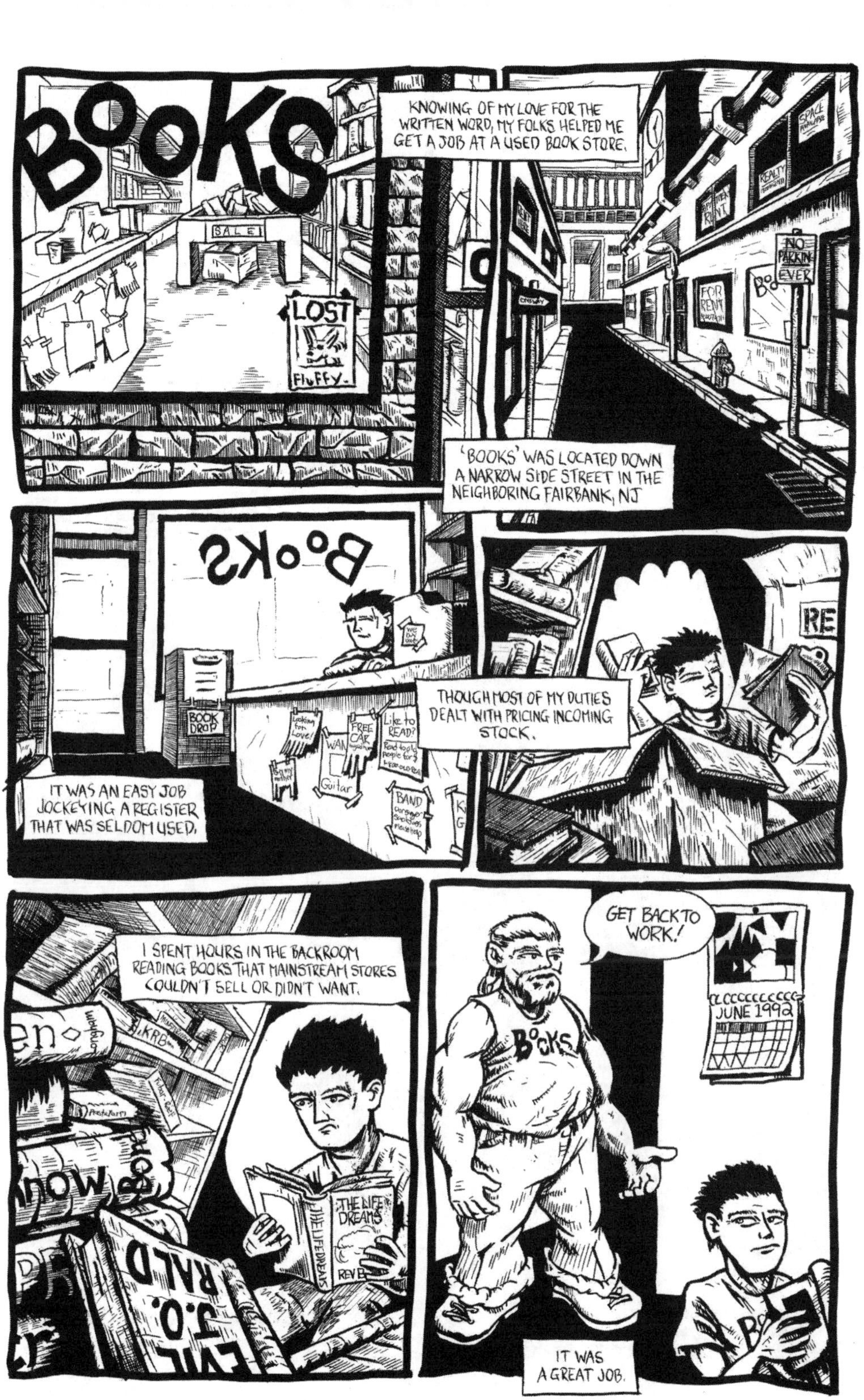
BOOKS
KNOWING OF MY LOVE FOR THE WRITTEN WORD, MY FOLKS HELPED ME GET A JOB AT A USED BOOK STORE.
LOST
FLUFFY.
'BOOKS' WAS LOCATED DOWN A NARROW SIDE STREET IN THE NEIGHBORING FAIRBANK, NJ
NO PARKING EVER
FOR RENT
BOOK DROP
IT WAS AN EASY JOB JOCKEYING A REGISTER THAT WAS SELDOM USED.
FREE CAR
Like to READ?
Guitar
BAND
THOUGH MOST OF MY DUTIES DEALT WITH PRICING INCOMING STOCK.
I SPENT HOURS IN THE BACKROOM READING BOOKS THAT MAINSTREAM STORES COULDN'T SELL OR DIDN'T WANT.
THE LIFE DREAMS
GET BACK TO WORK!
JUNE 1992
IT WAS A GREAT JOB.

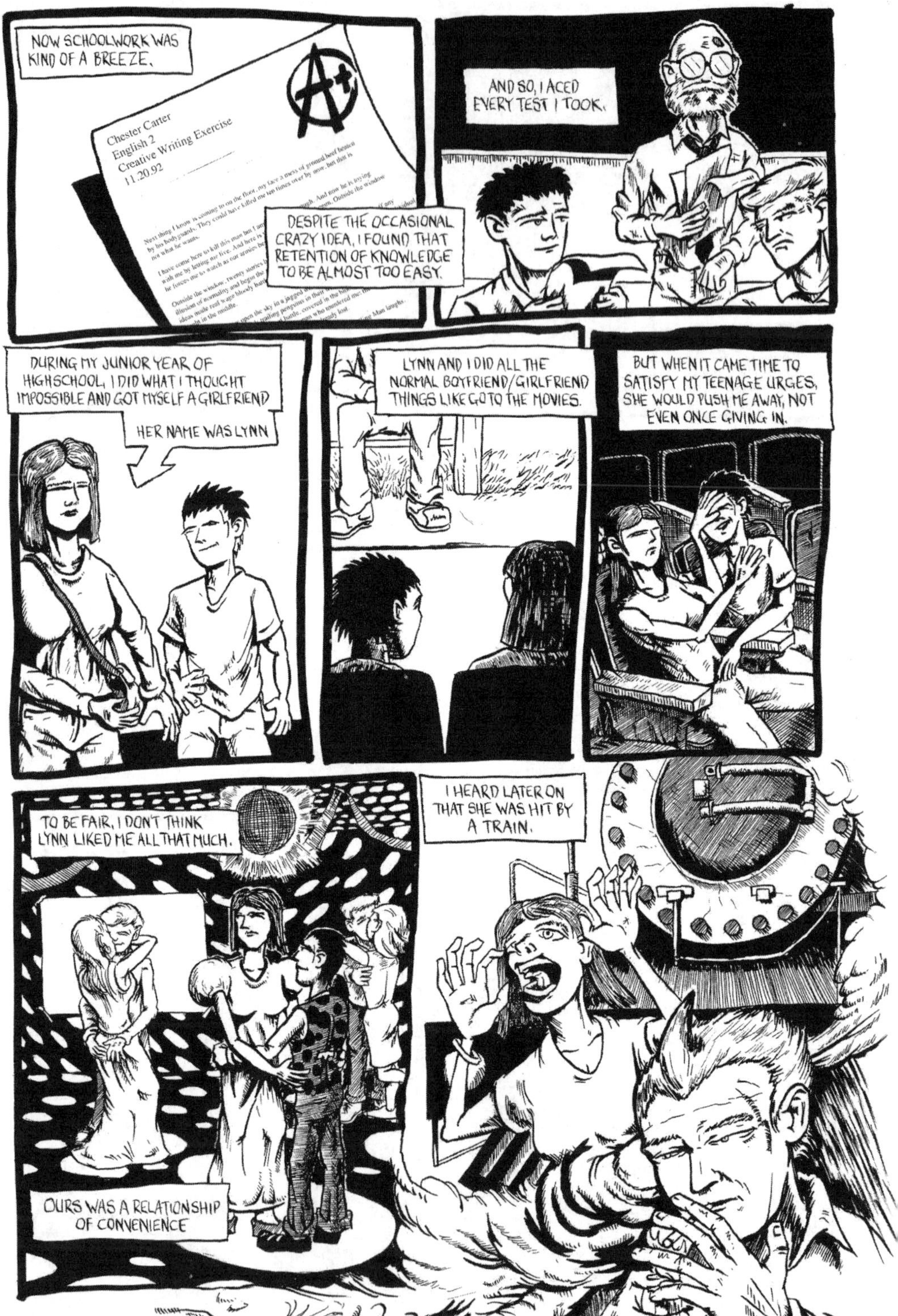
NOW SCHOOLWORK WAS KIND OF A BREEZE.
A+
Chester Carter
English 2
Creative Writing Exercise
11.20.92
DESPITE THE OCCASIONAL CRAZY IDEA, I FOUND THAT RETENTION OF KNOWLEDGE TO BE ALMOST TOO EASY.
AND SO, I ACED EVERY TEST I TOOK.
DURING MY JUNIOR YEAR OF HIGHSCHOOL, I DID WHAT I THOUGHT IMPOSSIBLE AND GOT MYSELF A GIRLFRIEND
HER NAME WAS LYNN
LYNN AND I DID ALL THE NORMAL BOYFRIEND/GIRLFRIEND THINGS LIKE GO TO THE MOVIES.
BUT WHEN IT CAME TIME TO SATISFY MY TEENAGE URGES, SHE WOULD PUSH ME AWAY, NOT EVEN ONCE GIVING IN.
TO BE FAIR, I DON'T THINK LYNN LIKED ME ALL THAT MUCH.
OURS WAS A RELATIONSHIP OF CONVENIENCE
I HEARD LATER ON THAT SHE WAS HIT BY A TRAIN.

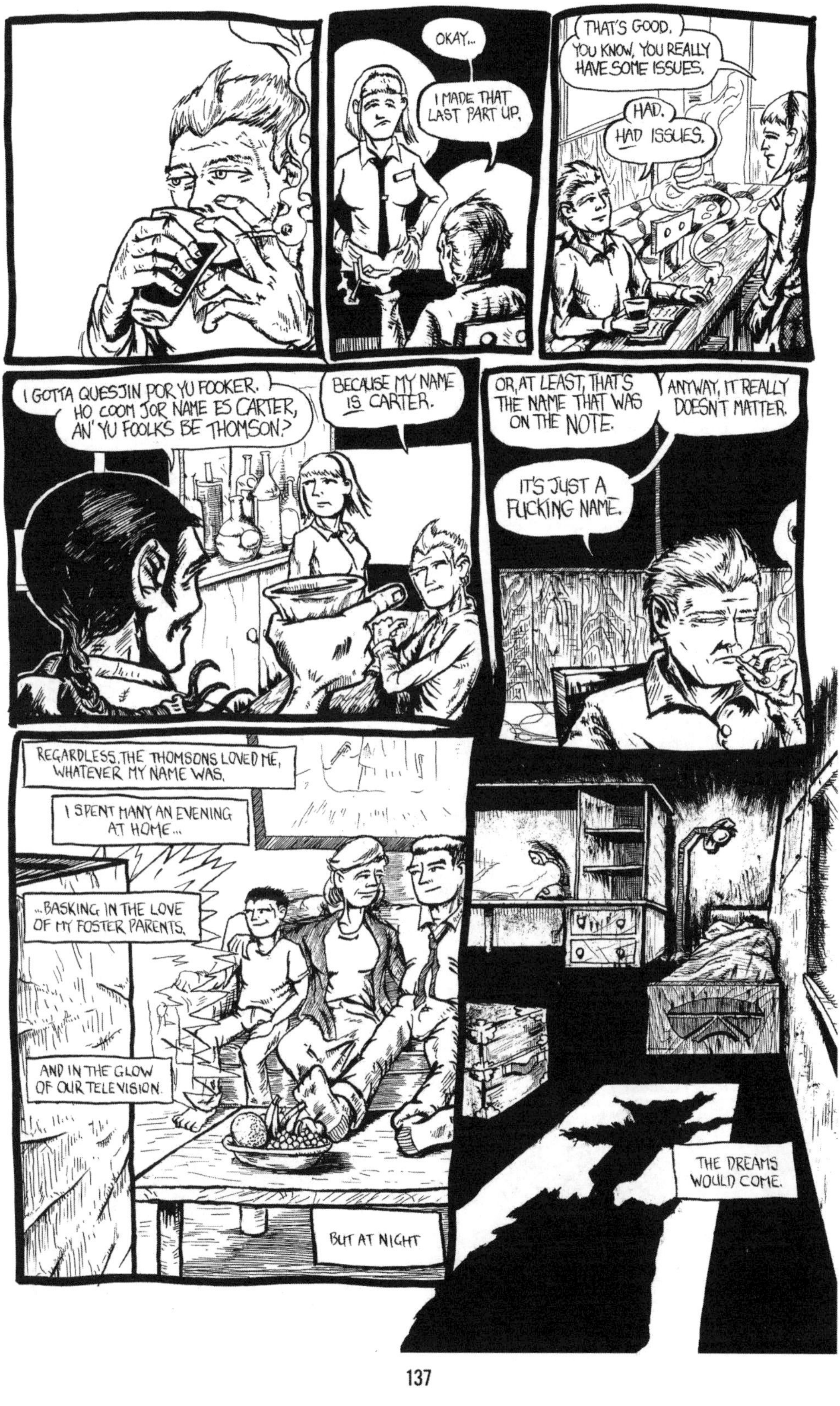
OKAY...
I MADE THAT LAST PART UP.
THAT'S GOOD.
YOU KNOW, YOU REALLY HAVE SOME ISSUES.
HAD. HAD ISSUES.
I GOTTA QUESJIN POR YU FOOKER. HO COOM JOR NAME ES CARTER, AN' YU FOOLKS BE THOMSON?
BECAUSE MY NAME IS CARTER.
OR, AT LEAST, THAT'S THE NAME THAT WAS ON THE NOTE.
ANYWAY, IT REALLY DOESN'T MATTER.
IT'S JUST A FUCKING NAME.
REGARDLESS, THE THOMSONS LOVED ME, WHATEVER MY NAME WAS.
I SPENT MANY AN EVENING AT HOME...
...BASKING IN THE LOVE OF MY FOSTER PARENTS.
AND IN THE GLOW OF OUR TELEVISION.
BUT AT NIGHT
THE DREAMS WOULD COME.

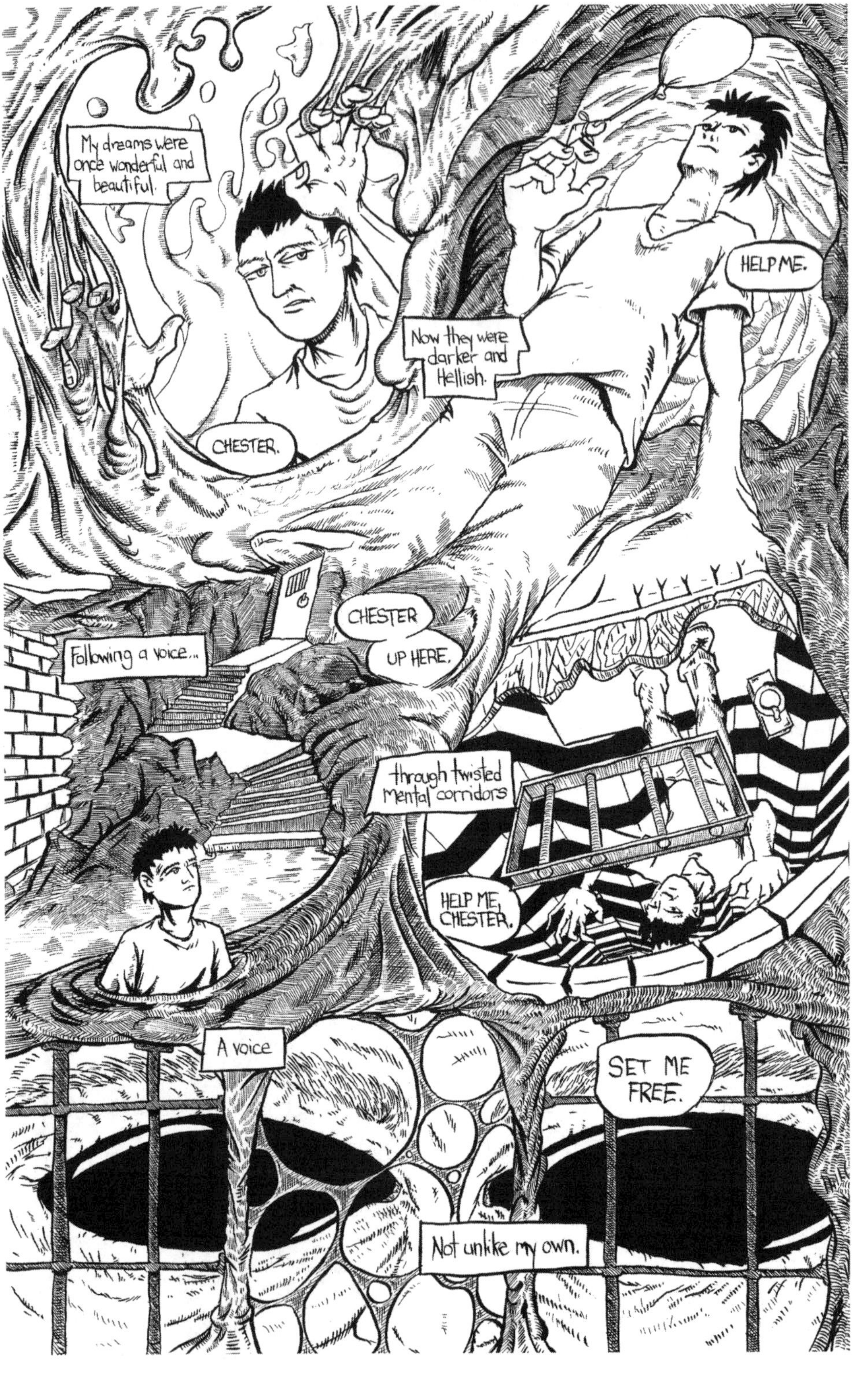

My dreams were once wonderful and beautiful.
CHESTER.
Now they were darker and Hellish.
HELP ME.
Following a voice...
CHESTER
UP HERE.
through twisted mental corridors
HELP ME, CHESTER.
A voice
SET ME FREE.
Not unlike my own.

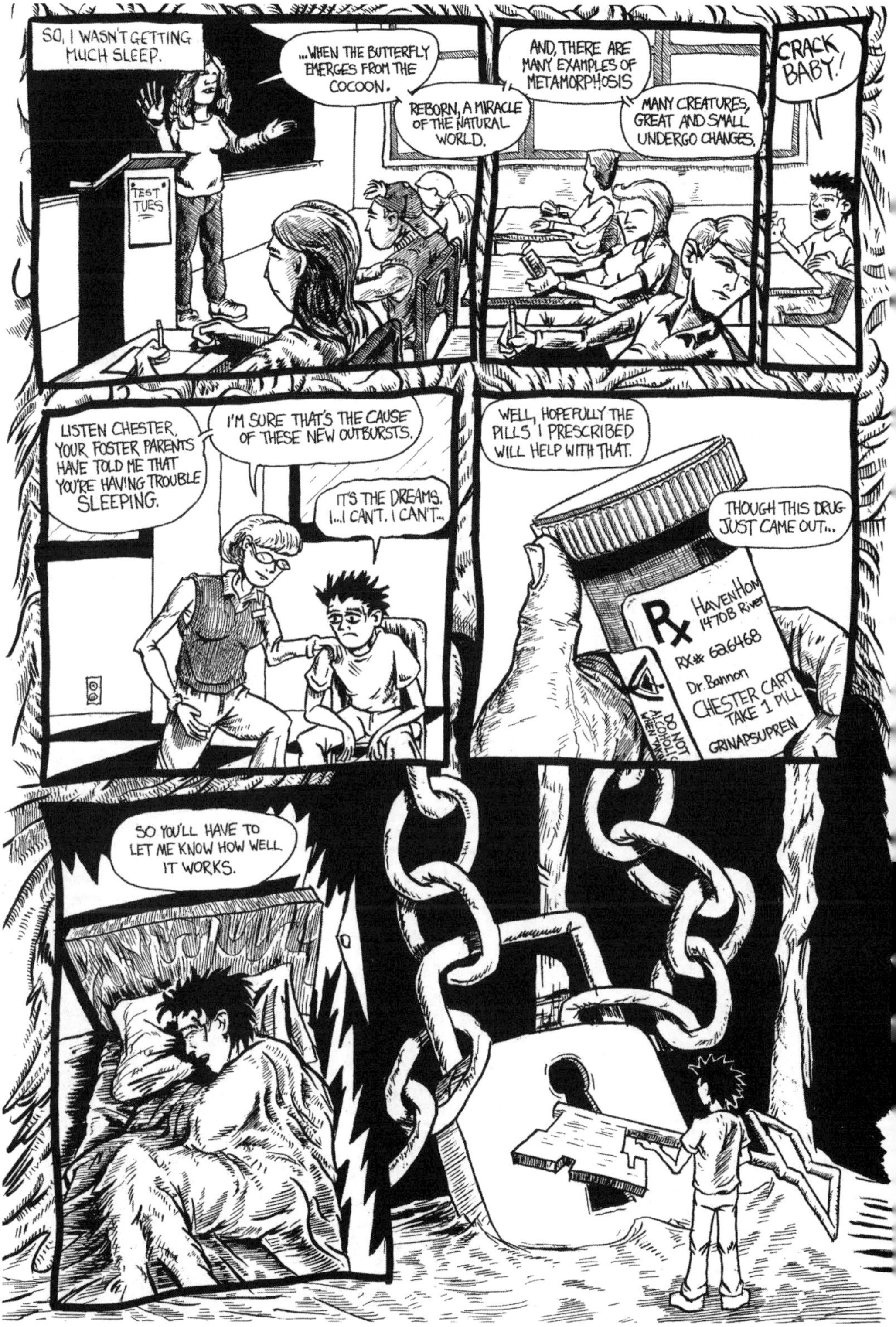
SO, I WASN'T GETTING MUCH SLEEP.
...WHEN THE BUTTERFLY EMERGES FROM THE COCOON.
REBORN, A MIRACLE OF THE NATURAL WORLD.
AND, THERE ARE MANY EXAMPLES OF METAMORPHOSIS
MANY CREATURES, GREAT AND SMALL UNDERGO CHANGES.
TEST TUES
CRACK BABY!
LISTEN CHESTER, YOUR FOSTER PARENTS HAVE TOLD ME THAT YOU'RE HAVING TROUBLE SLEEPING.
I'M SURE THAT'S THE CAUSE OF THESE NEW OUTBURSTS.
IT'S THE DREAMS. I...I CAN'T. I CAN'T...
WELL, HOPEFULLY THE PILLS I PRESCRIBED WILL HELP WITH THAT.
THOUGH THIS DRUG JUST CAME OUT...
Rx HavenHom 14708 River
RX# 626468
Dr. Bannon
CHESTER CART
TAKE 1 PILL
GRINAPSUPREN
DO NOT ALCOHOL
SO YOU'LL HAVE TO LET ME KNOW HOW WELL IT WORKS.

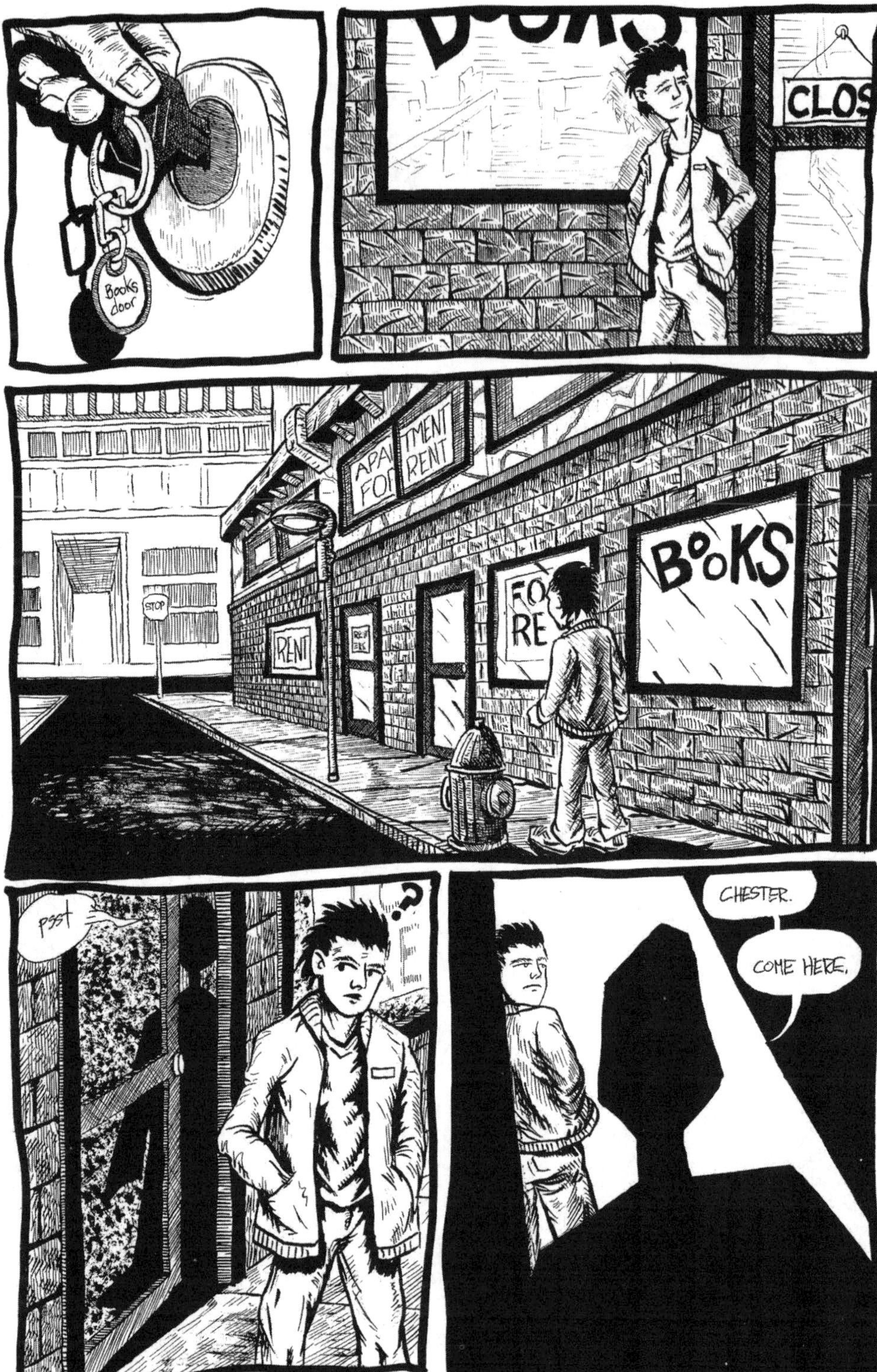
Books door
CLOS
APA TMENT
FO RENT
BOOKS
FO
RE
RENT
STOP
psst
?
CHESTER.
COME HERE.

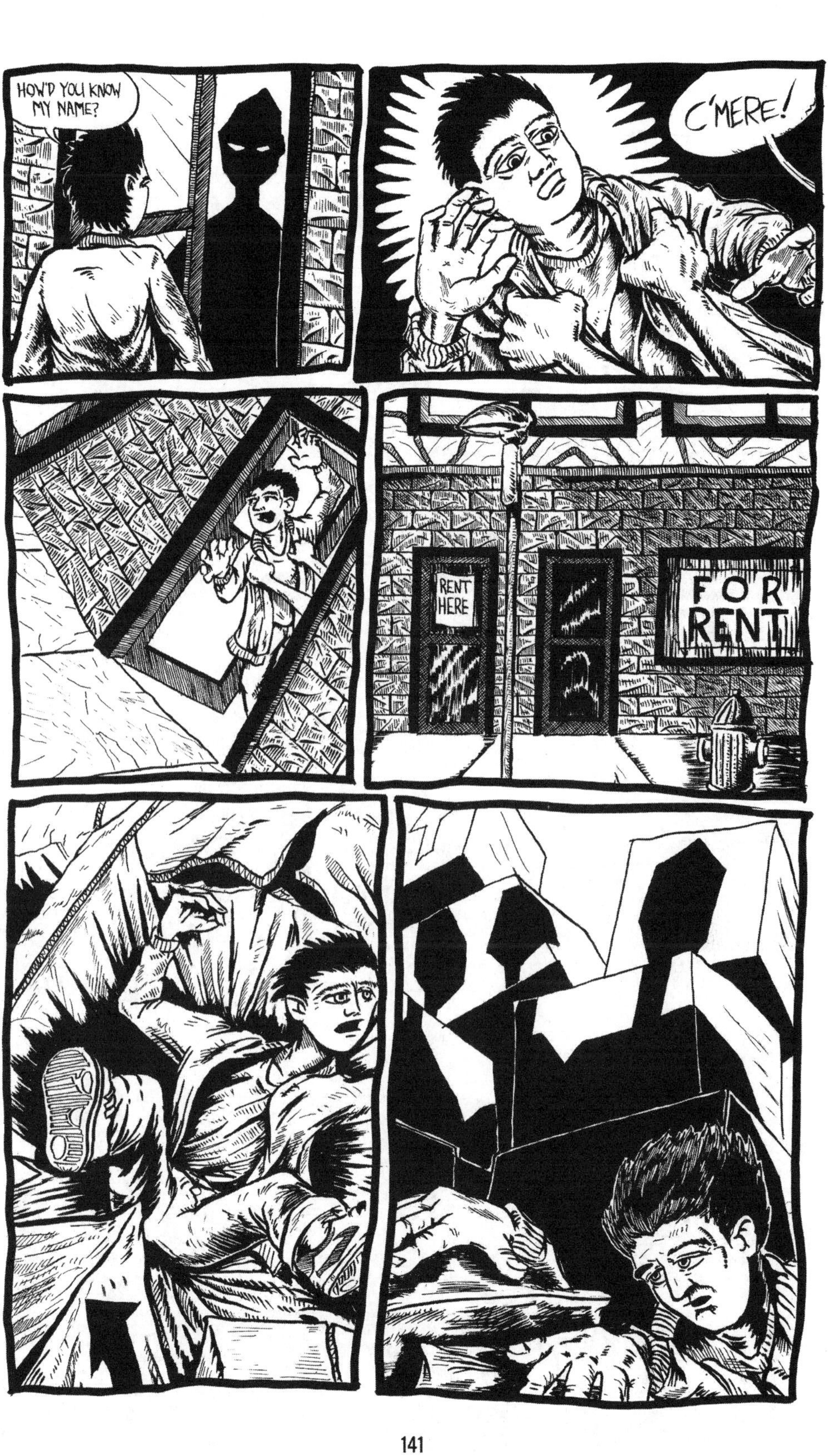
HOW'D YOU KNOW MY NAME?
C'MERE!
RENT HERE
FOR RENT

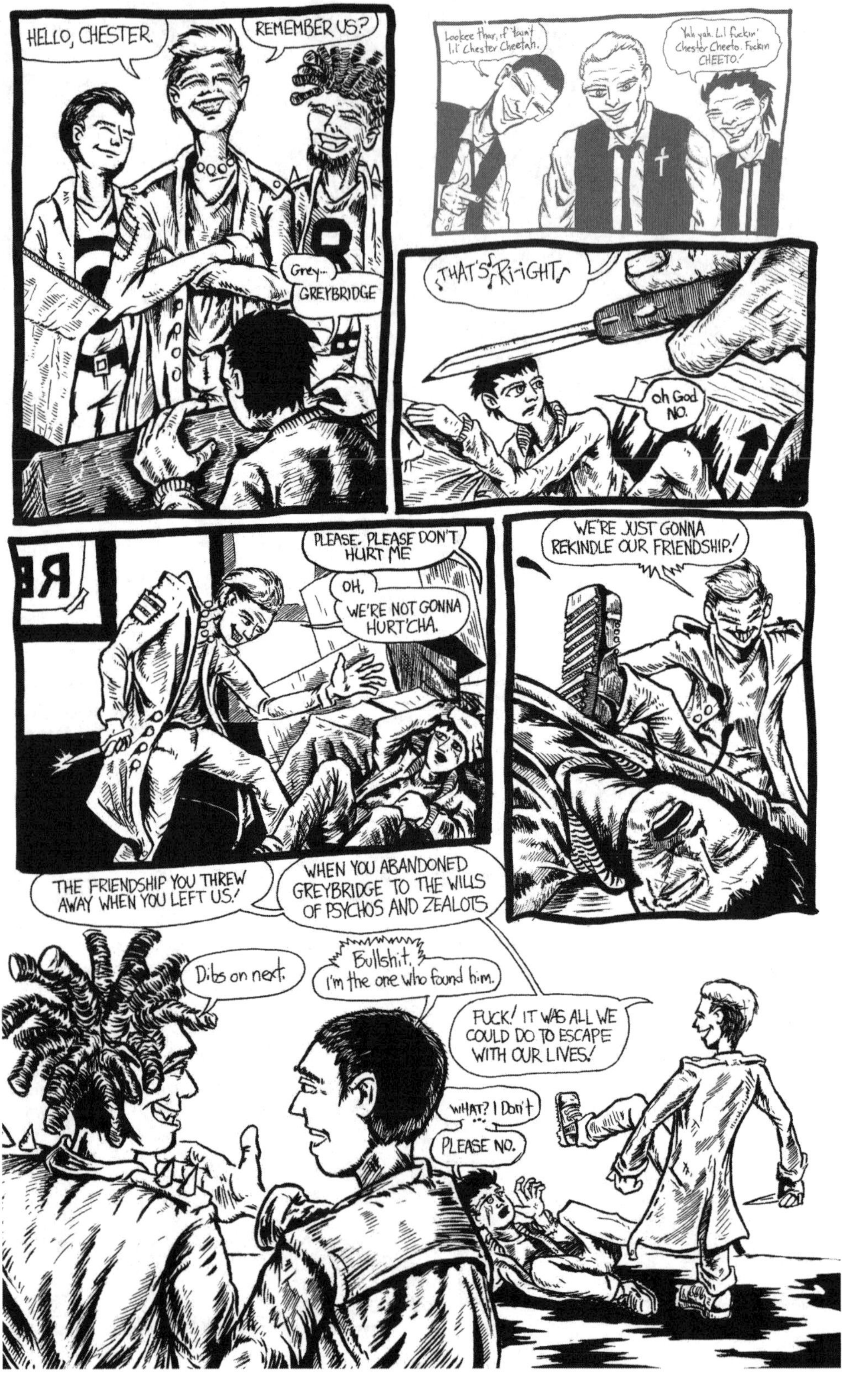
HELLO, CHESTER.
REMEMBER US?
Lookee thar, if 'tain't l.l' Chester Cheetah.
Yah yah. L.l fuckin' Chester Cheeto. Fuckin CHEETO.!
Grey...
GREYBRIDGE
THAT'S RI-IGHT
oh God NO.
PLEASE. PLEASE DON'T HURT ME
OH,
WE'RE NOT GONNA HURT'CHA.
WE'RE JUST GONNA REKINDLE OUR FRIENDSHIP!
THE FRIENDSHIP YOU THREW AWAY WHEN YOU LEFT US!
WHEN YOU ABANDONED GREYBRIDGE TO THE WILLS OF PSYCHOS AND ZEALOTS
Dibs on next.
Bullshit.
I'm the one who found him.
FUCK! IT WAS ALL WE COULD DO TO ESCAPE WITH OUR LIVES!
WHAT? I Don't ...
PLEASE NO.

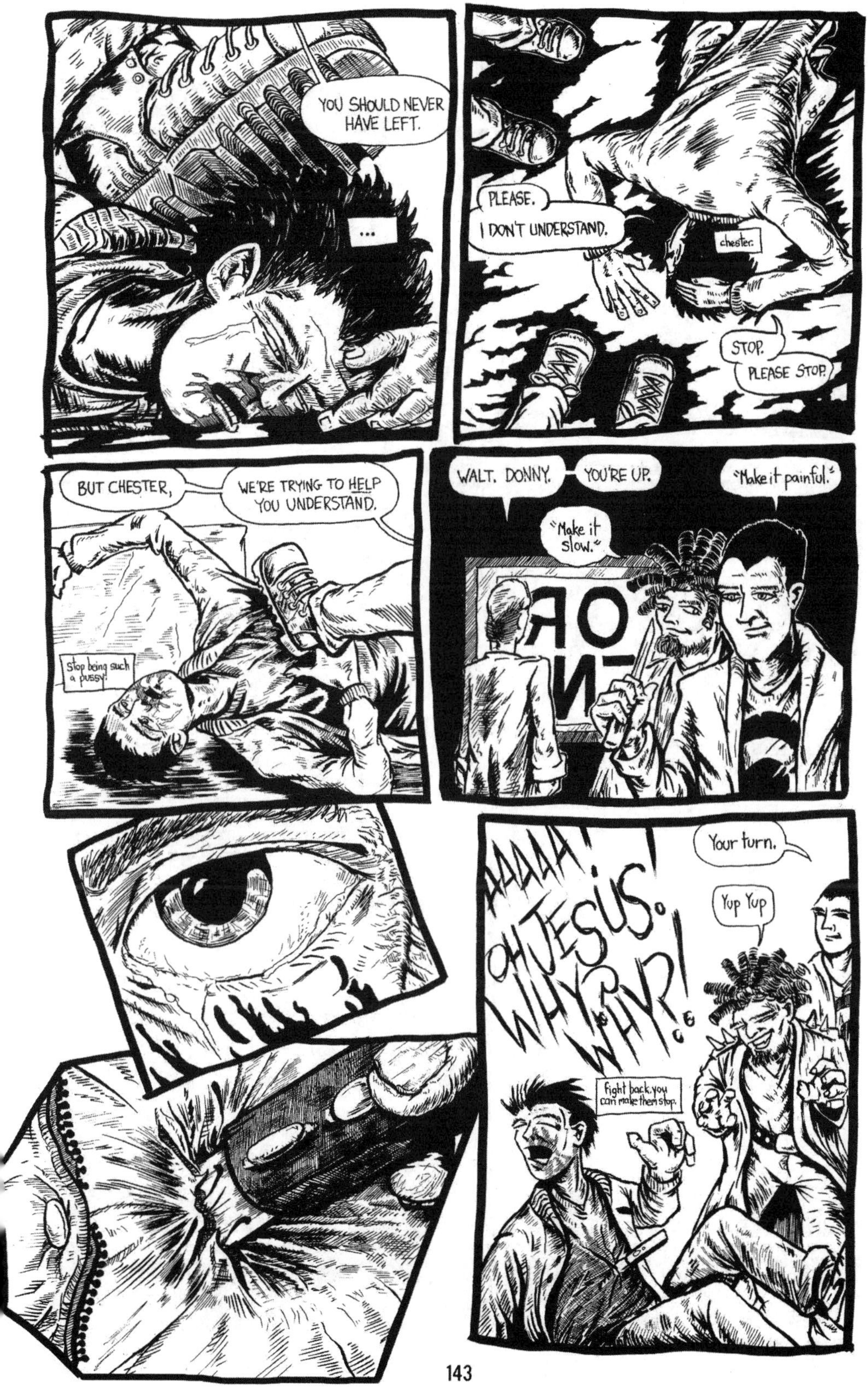
YOU SHOULD NEVER HAVE LEFT.
...
PLEASE.
I DON'T UNDERSTAND.
chester.
STOP.
PLEASE STOP.
BUT CHESTER,
WE'RE TRYING TO HELP YOU UNDERSTAND.
Stop being such a pussy.
WALT. DONNY.
YOU'RE UP.
"Make it painful."
"Make it slow."
AAAAA!
OH JESUS. WHY? WHY?!
Your turn.
Yup Yup
fight back. you can make them stop.

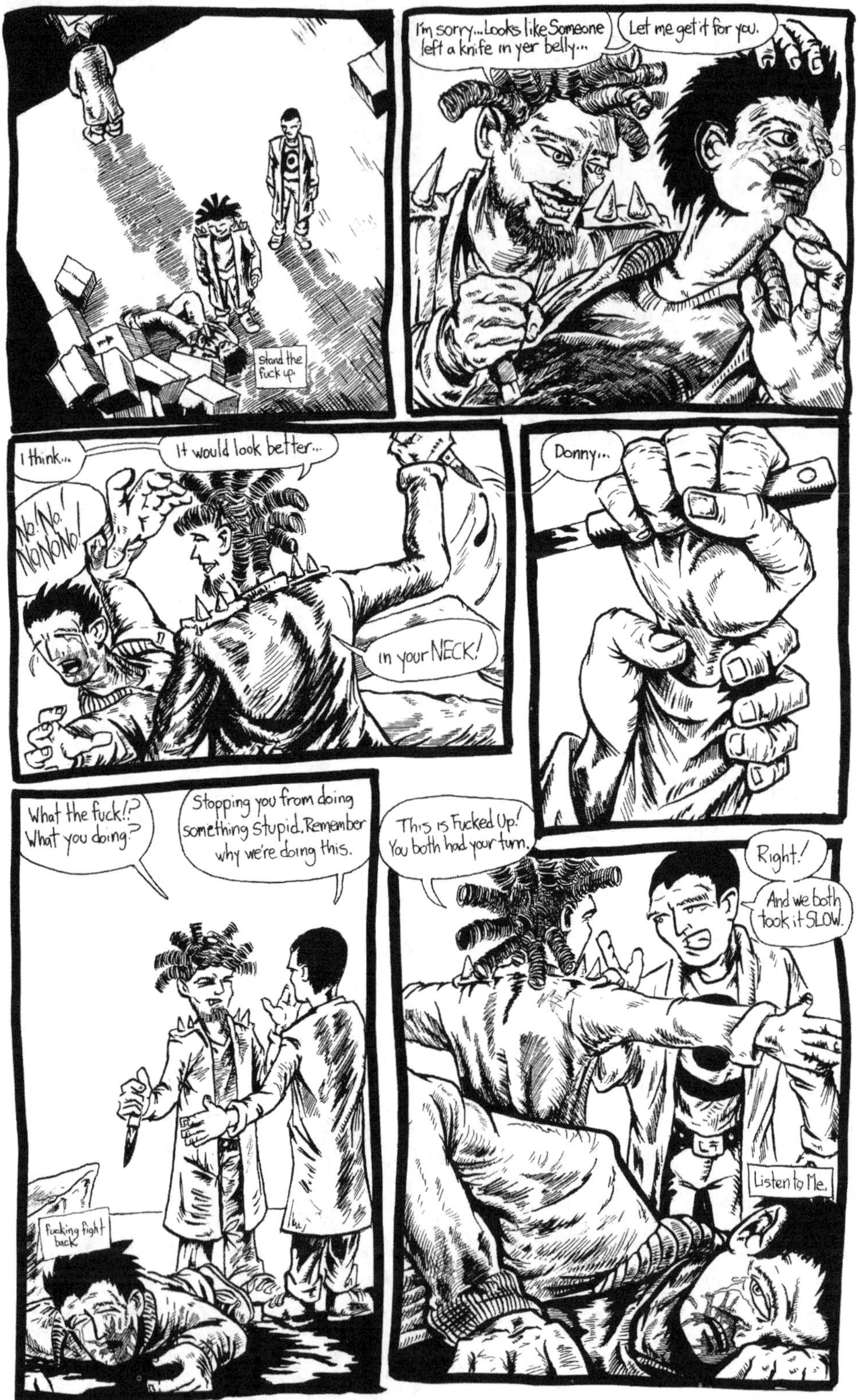
Stand the fuck up.
I'm sorry...Looks like Someone left a knife in yer belly...
Let me get it for you.
I think...
It would look better...
No! No! NoNoNo!
in your NECK!
Donny...
What the fuck!? What you doing?
Stopping you from doing something stupid. Remember why we're doing this.
fucking fight back
This is Fucked Up! You both had your turn.
Right!
And we both took it SLOW.
Listen to Me.

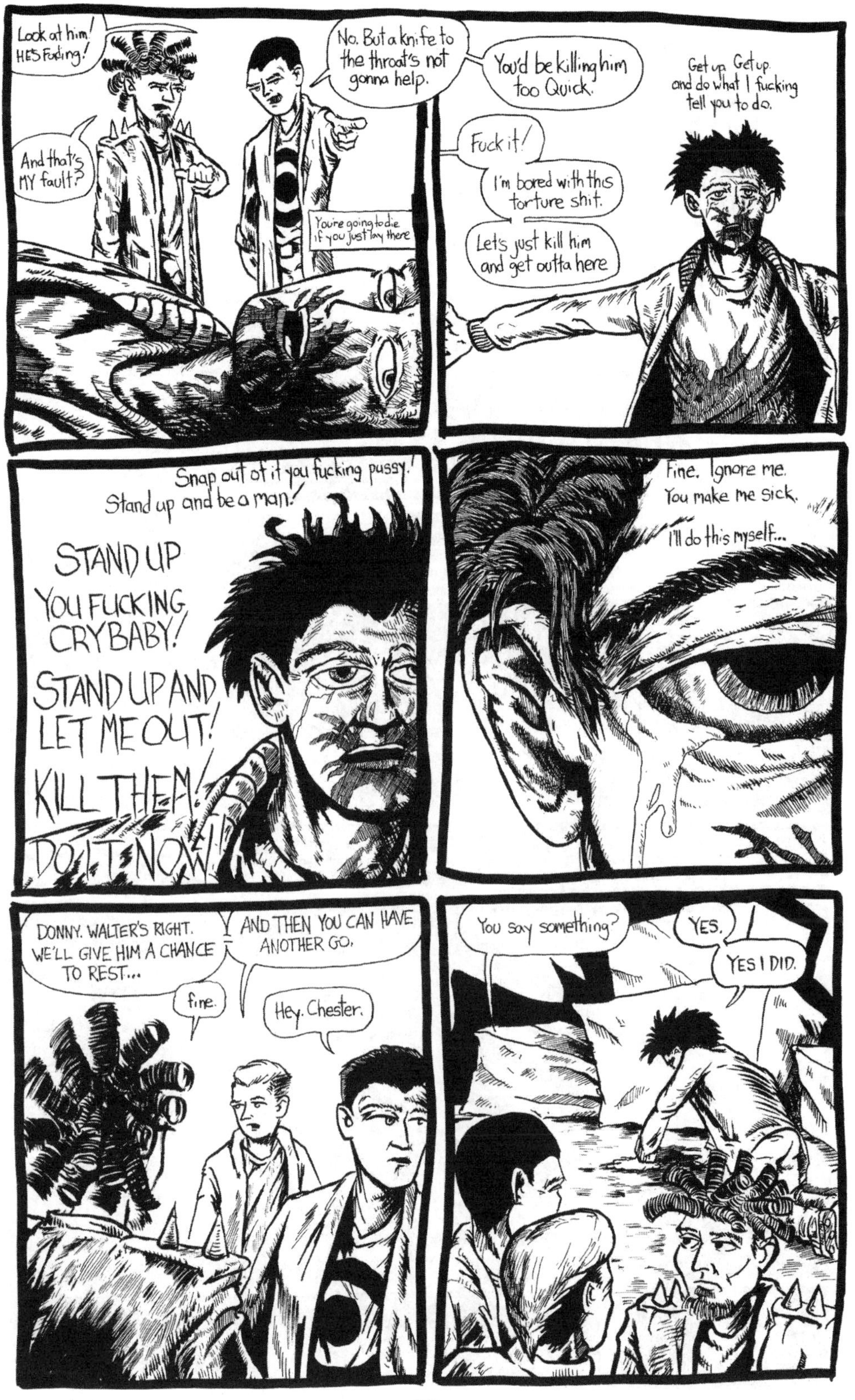
Look at him! HE'S Fading!
No. But a knife to the throat's not gonna help.
And that's MY fault?
You're going to die if you just lay there
You'd be killing him too Quick.
Get up. Get up. and do what I fucking tell you to do.
Fuck it!
I'm bored with this torture shit.
Let's just kill him and get outta here
Snap out of it you fucking pussy!
Stand up and be a man!
STAND UP
YOU FUCKING CRYBABY!
STAND UP AND LET ME OUT!
KILL THEM!
DO IT NOW!
Fine. Ignore me.
You make me sick.
I'll do this myself...
DONNY. WALTER'S RIGHT. WE'LL GIVE HIM A CHANCE TO REST...
AND THEN YOU CAN HAVE ANOTHER GO.
fine.
Hey. Chester.
You say something?
YES.
YES I DID.

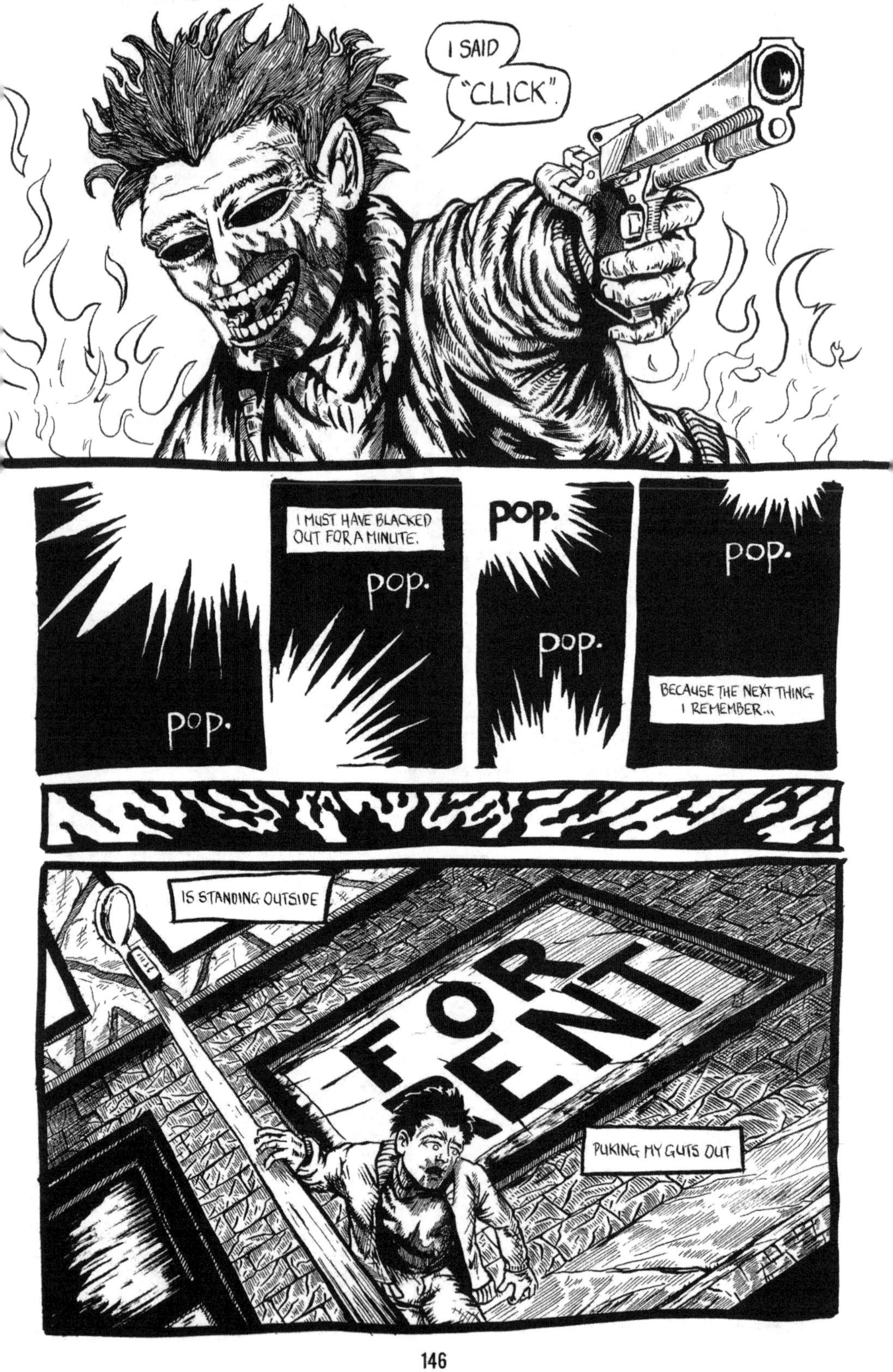

I SAID "CLICK".
I MUST HAVE BLACKED OUT FOR A MINUTE.
POP.
POP.
POP.
POP.
POP.
BECAUSE THE NEXT THING I REMEMBER...
IS STANDING OUTSIDE
FOR RENT
PUKING MY GUTS OUT

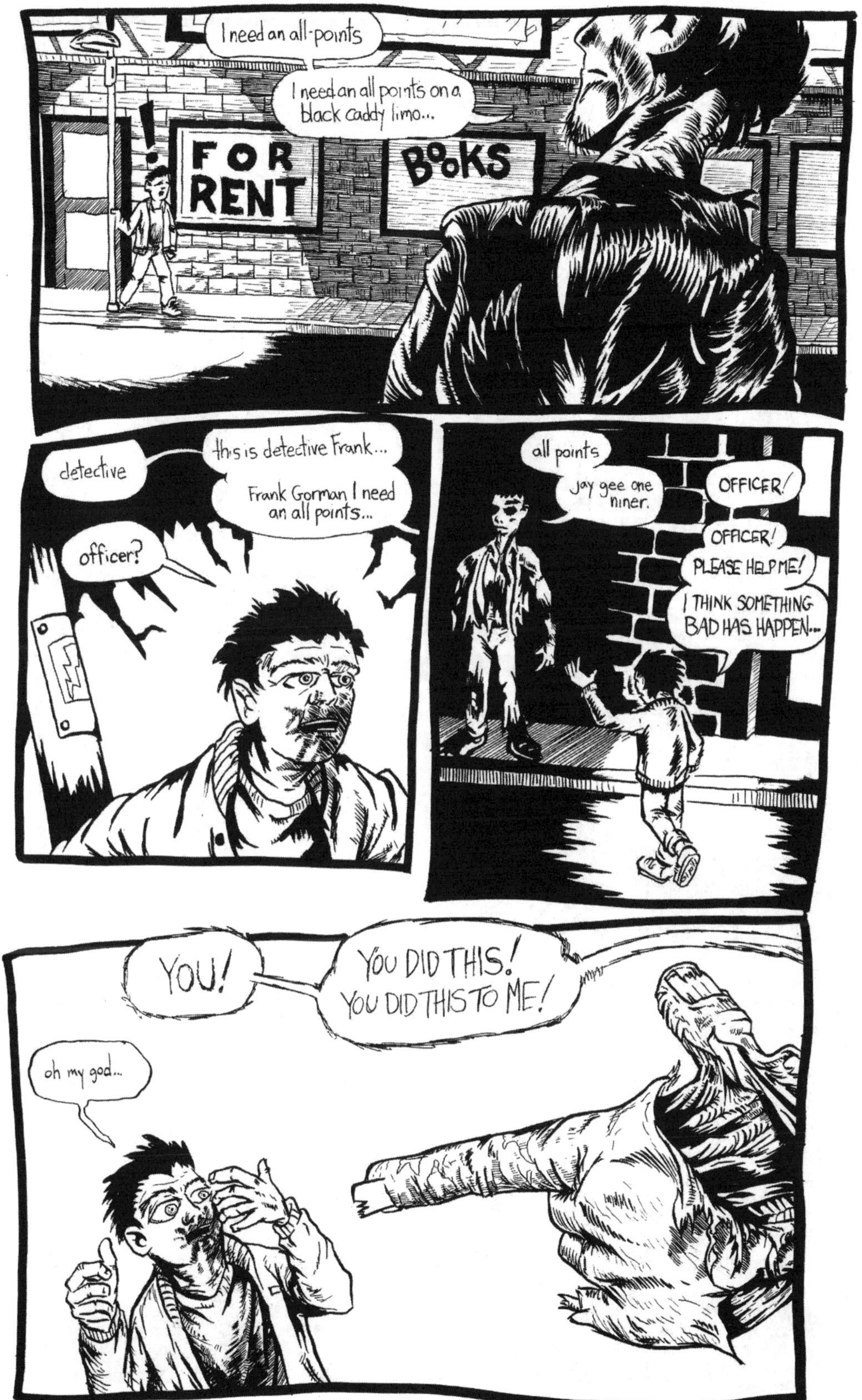
I need an all-points
I need an all points on a black caddy limo...
FOR RENT
BOOKS
detective
this is detective Frank...
Frank Gorman I need an all points...
officer?
all points
jay gee one niner.
OFFICER!
OFFICER!
PLEASE HELP ME!
I THINK SOMETHING BAD HAS HAPPEN...
YOU!
YOU DID THIS! YOU DID THIS TO ME!
oh my god...

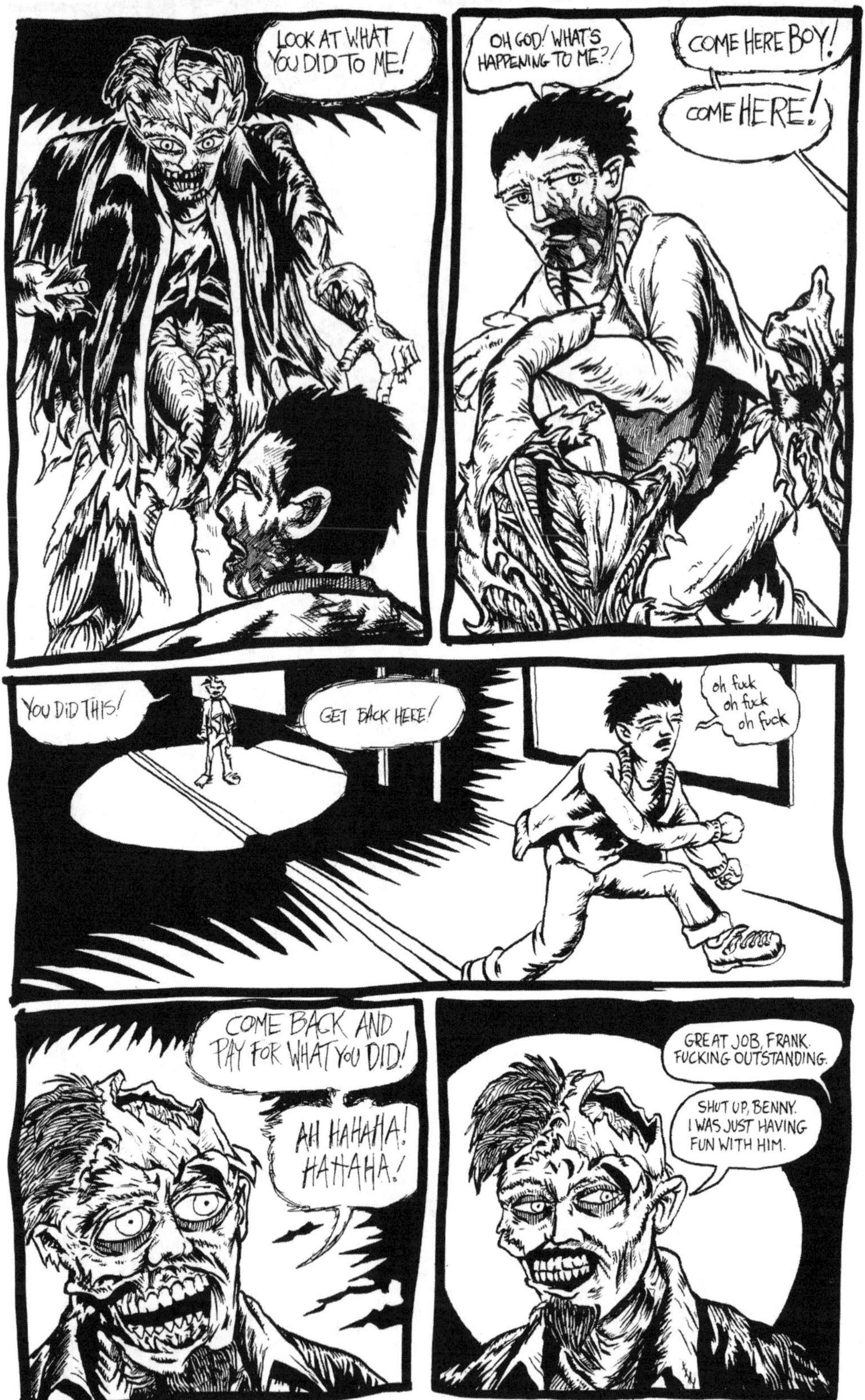

LOOK AT WHAT YOU DID TO ME!
OH GOD! WHAT'S HAPPENING TO ME?!
COME HERE BOY!
COME HERE!
YOU DID THIS!
GET BACK HERE!
oh fuck oh fuck oh fuck
COME BACK AND PAY FOR WHAT YOU DID!
AH HAHAHA! HAHAHA!
GREAT JOB, FRANK. FUCKING OUTSTANDING.
SHUT UP, BENNY. I WAS JUST HAVING FUN WITH HIM.

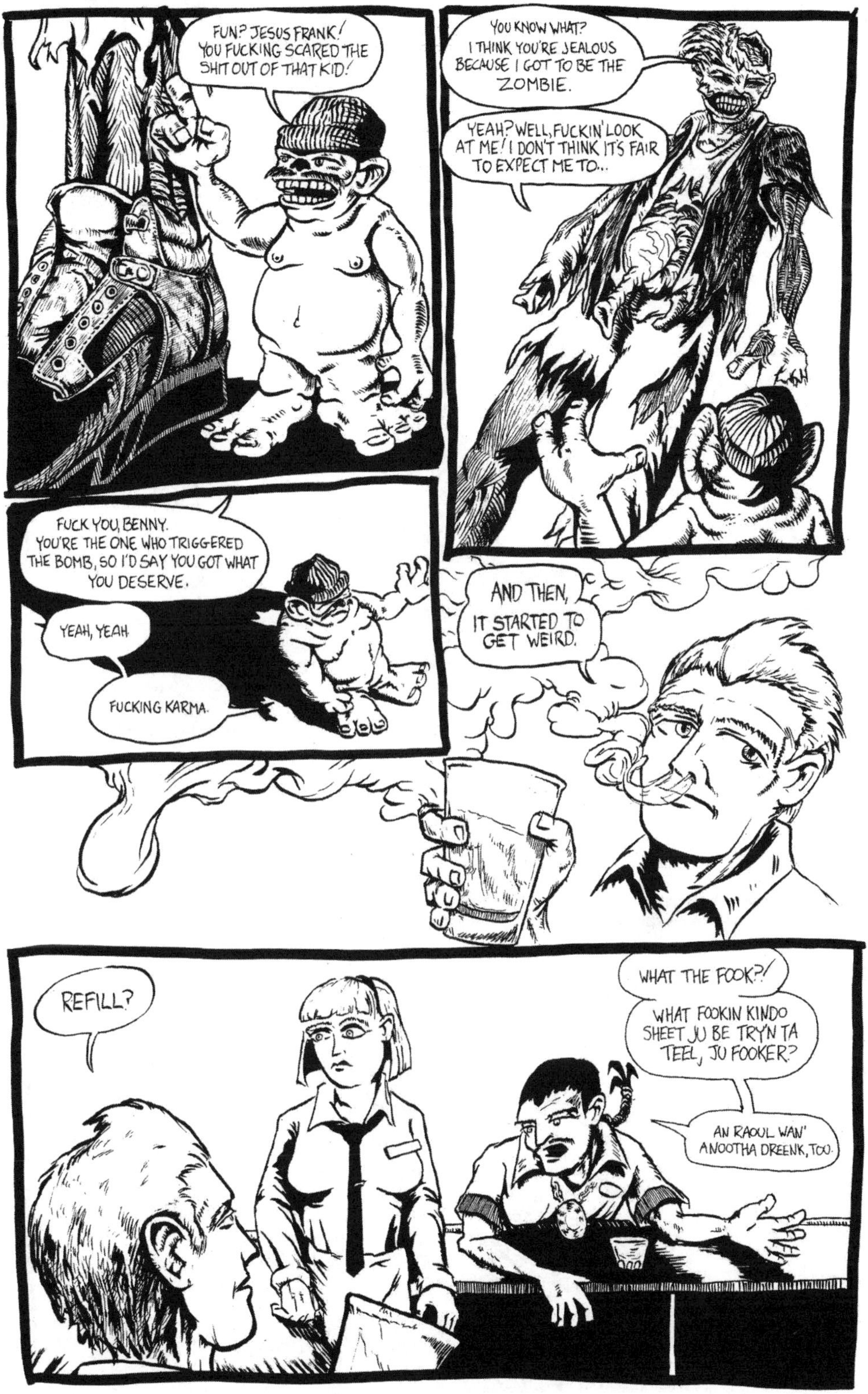
FUN? JESUS FRANK! YOU FUCKING SCARED THE SHIT OUT OF THAT KID!
YOU KNOW WHAT? I THINK YOU'RE JEALOUS BECAUSE I GOT TO BE THE ZOMBIE.
YEAH? WELL, FUCKIN' LOOK AT ME! I DON'T THINK IT'S FAIR TO EXPECT ME TO...
FUCK YOU, BENNY. YOU'RE THE ONE WHO TRIGGERED THE BOMB, SO I'D SAY YOU GOT WHAT YOU DESERVE.
YEAH, YEAH.
FUCKING KARMA.
AND THEN, IT STARTED TO GET WEIRD.
REFILL?
WHAT THE FOOK?!
WHAT FOOKIN KINDO SHEET JU BE TRY'N TA TEEL, JU FOOKER?
AN RAOUL WAN' ANOOTHA DREENK, TOO.

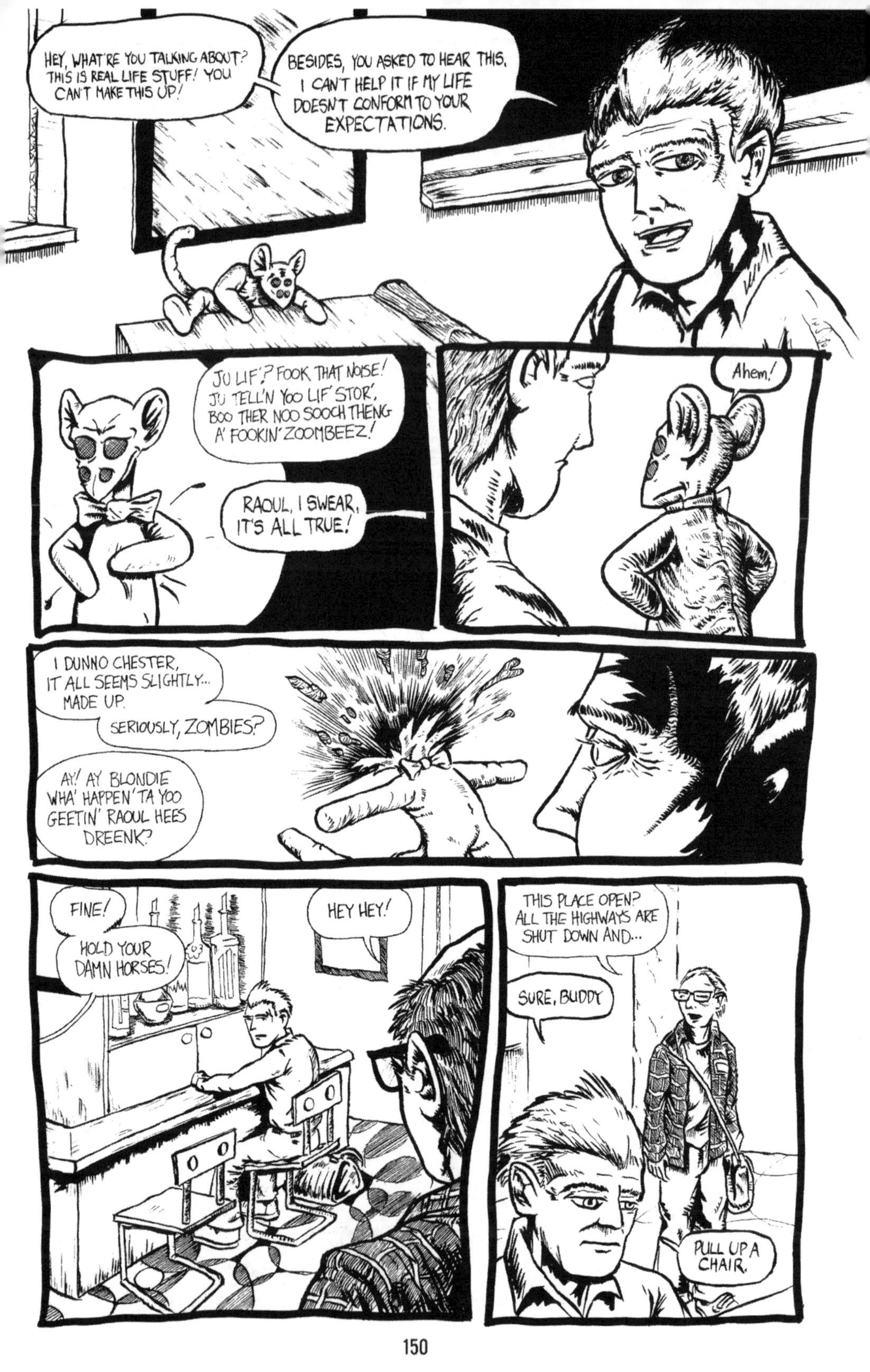
HEY, WHAT'RE YOU TALKING ABOUT? THIS IS REAL LIFE STUFF! YOU CAN'T MAKE THIS UP!
BESIDES, YOU ASKED TO HEAR THIS. I CAN'T HELP IT IF MY LIFE DOESN'T CONFORM TO YOUR EXPECTATIONS.
JU LIF'? FOOK THAT NOISE! JU TELL'N YOO LIF' STOR', BOO THER NOO SOOCH THENG A' FOOKIN' ZOOMBEEZ!
RAOUL, I SWEAR, IT'S ALL TRUE!
Ahem!
I DUNNO CHESTER, IT ALL SEEMS SLIGHTLY... MADE UP.
SERIOUSLY, ZOMBIES?
AY! AY BLONDIE WHA' HAPPEN' TA YOO GEETIN' RAOUL HEES DREENK?
FINE!
HOLD YOUR DAMN HORSES!
HEY HEY!
THIS PLACE OPEN? ALL THE HIGHWAYS ARE SHUT DOWN AND...
SURE, BUDDY
PULL UP A CHAIR.

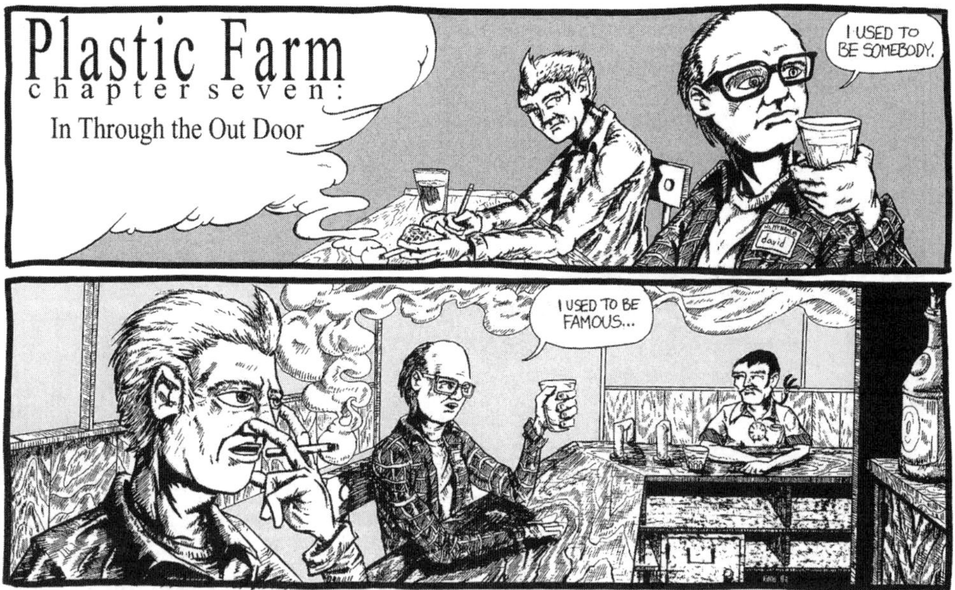
Plastic Farm
chapter seven:
In Through the Out Door
I USED TO BE SOMEBODY.
david
I USED TO BE FAMOUS...

wrote: rafer roberts

drew: jake warrenfeltz

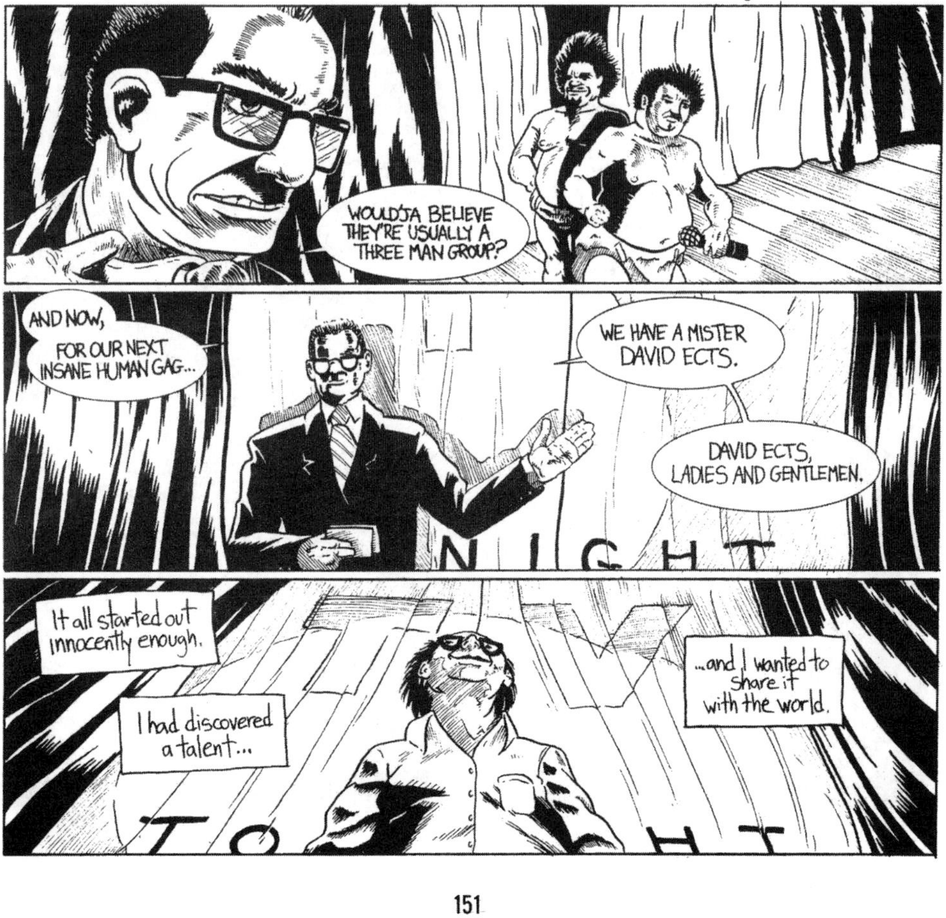
WOULD'JA BELIEVE THEY'RE USUALLY A THREE MAN GROUP?
AND NOW,
FOR OUR NEXT INSANE HUMAN GAG...
WE HAVE A MISTER DAVID ECTS.
DAVID ECTS, LADIES AND GENTLEMEN.
NIGHT
It all started out innocently enough.
I had discovered a talent...
...and I wanted to share it with the world.

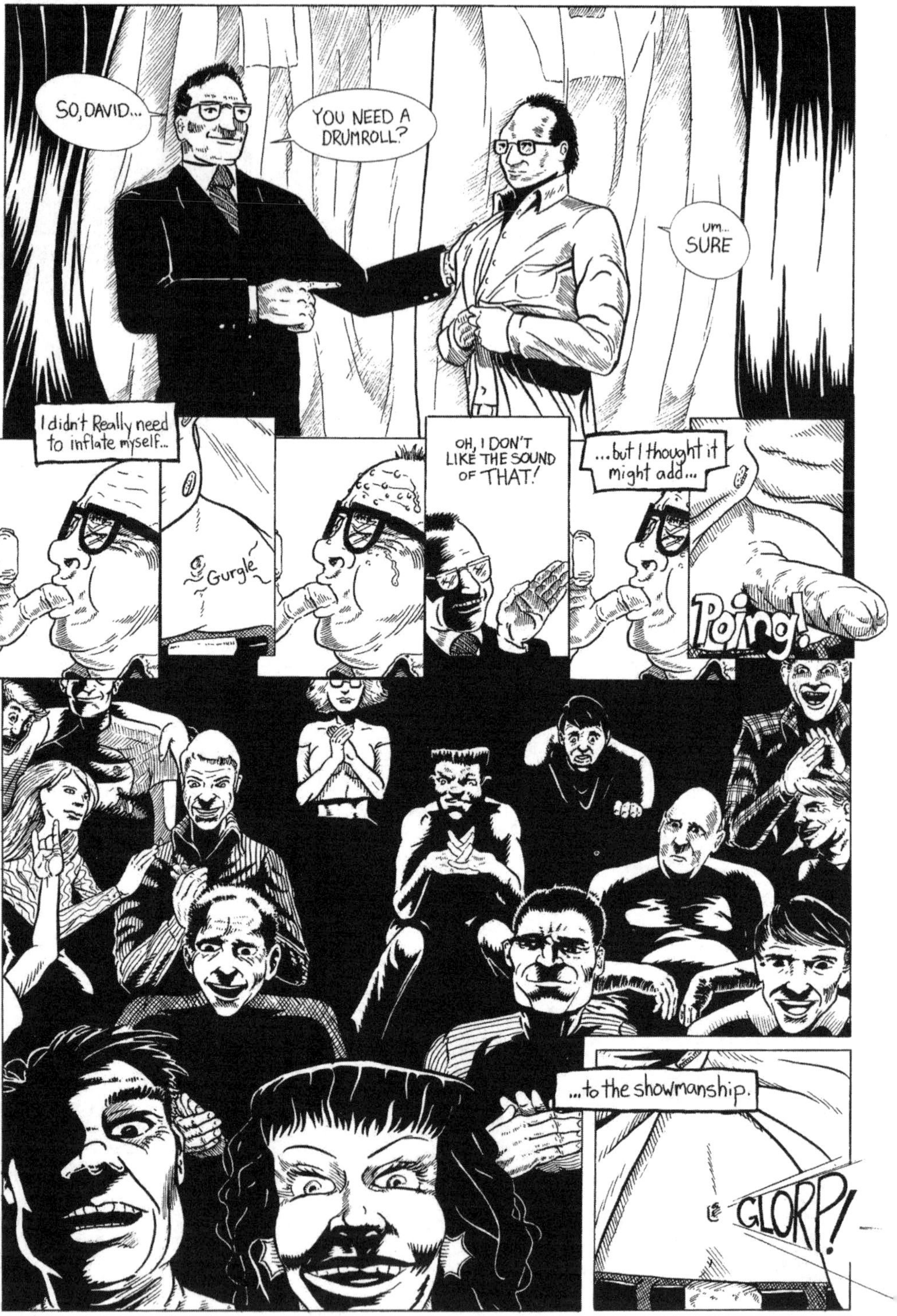
SO, DAVID...
YOU NEED A DRUMROLL?
um.. SURE
I didn't Really need to inflate myself...
Gurgle
OH, I DON'T LIKE THE SOUND OF THAT!
...but I thought it might add...
Poing!
...to the showmanship.
GLORP!

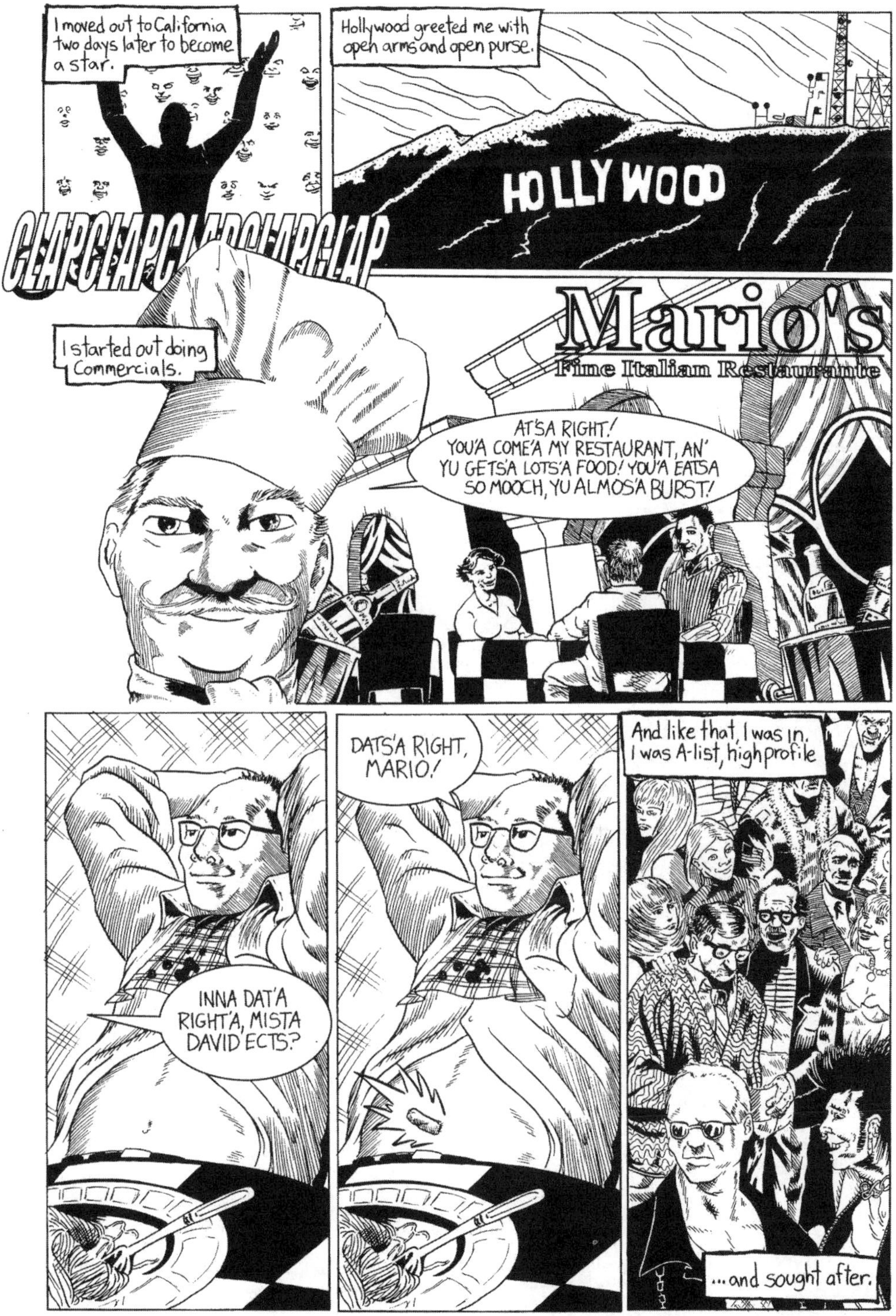
I moved out to California two days later to become a star.
CLAPCLAPCLAPCLAPCLAP
Hollywood greeted me with open arms and open purse.
HOLLYWOOD
I started out doing Commercials.
Mario's
Fine Italian Restaurante
AT'SA RIGHT! YOU'A COME'A MY RESTAURANT, AN' YU GETS'A LOTS'A FOOD! YOU'A EATSA SO MOOCH, YU ALMOS'A BURST!
INNA DAT'A RIGHT'A, MISTA DAVID ECTS?
DATS'A RIGHT, MARIO!
And like that, I was in. I was A-list, high profile
...and sought after.

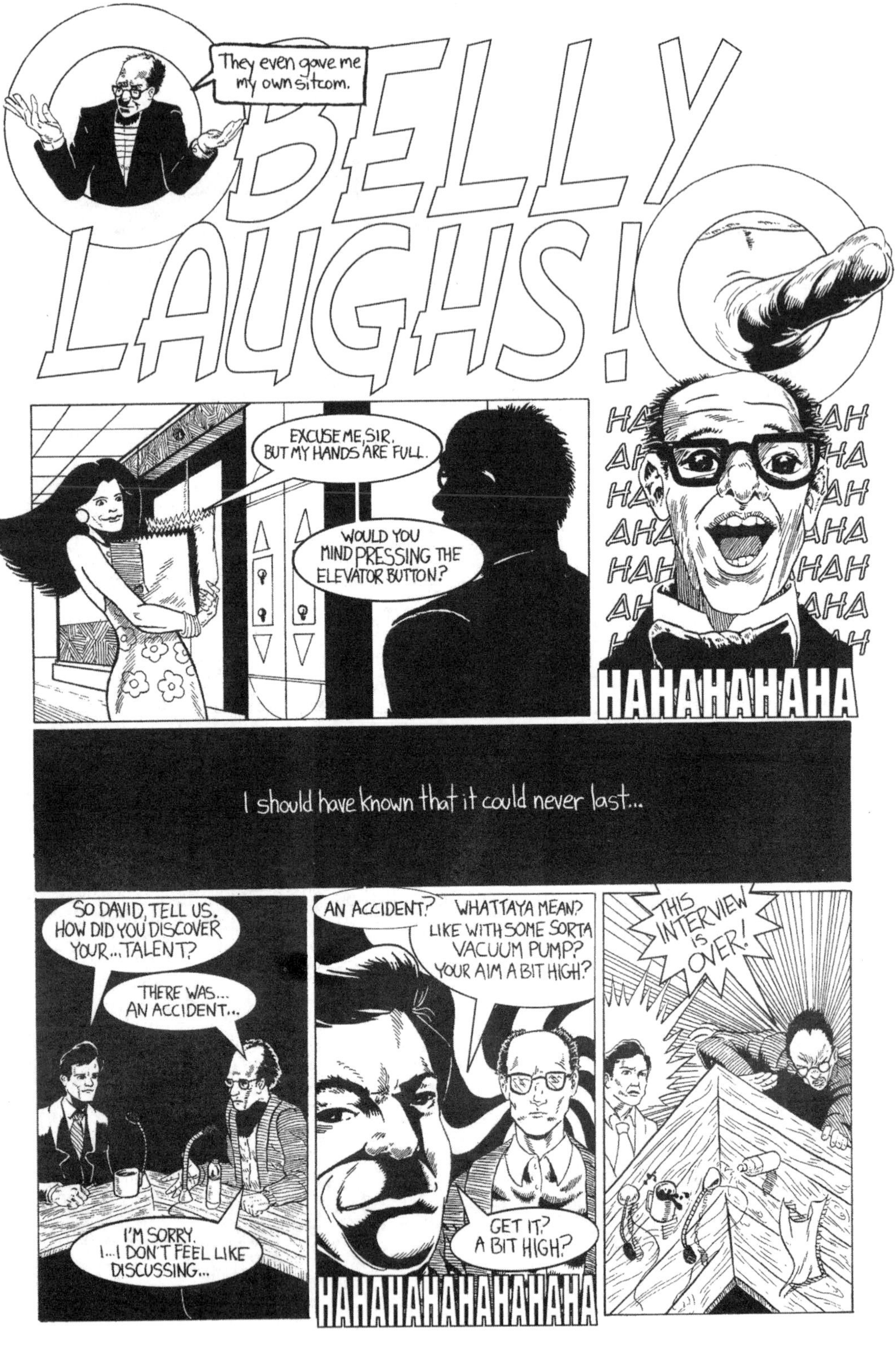
They even gave me my own sitcom.
BELLY LAUGHS!
EXCUSE ME, SIR. BUT MY HANDS ARE FULL.
WOULD YOU MIND PRESSING THE ELEVATOR BUTTON?
HAHAHAHAHA
I should have known that it could never last...
SO DAVID, TELL US. HOW DID YOU DISCOVER YOUR...TALENT?
THERE WAS... AN ACCIDENT...
I'M SORRY. I...I DON'T FEEL LIKE DISCUSSING...
AN ACCIDENT?
WHATTAYA MEAN? LIKE WITH SOME SORTA VACUUM PUMP? YOUR AIM A BIT HIGH?
GET IT? A BIT HIGH?
HAHAHAHAHAHAHAHA
THIS INTERVIEW is OVER!

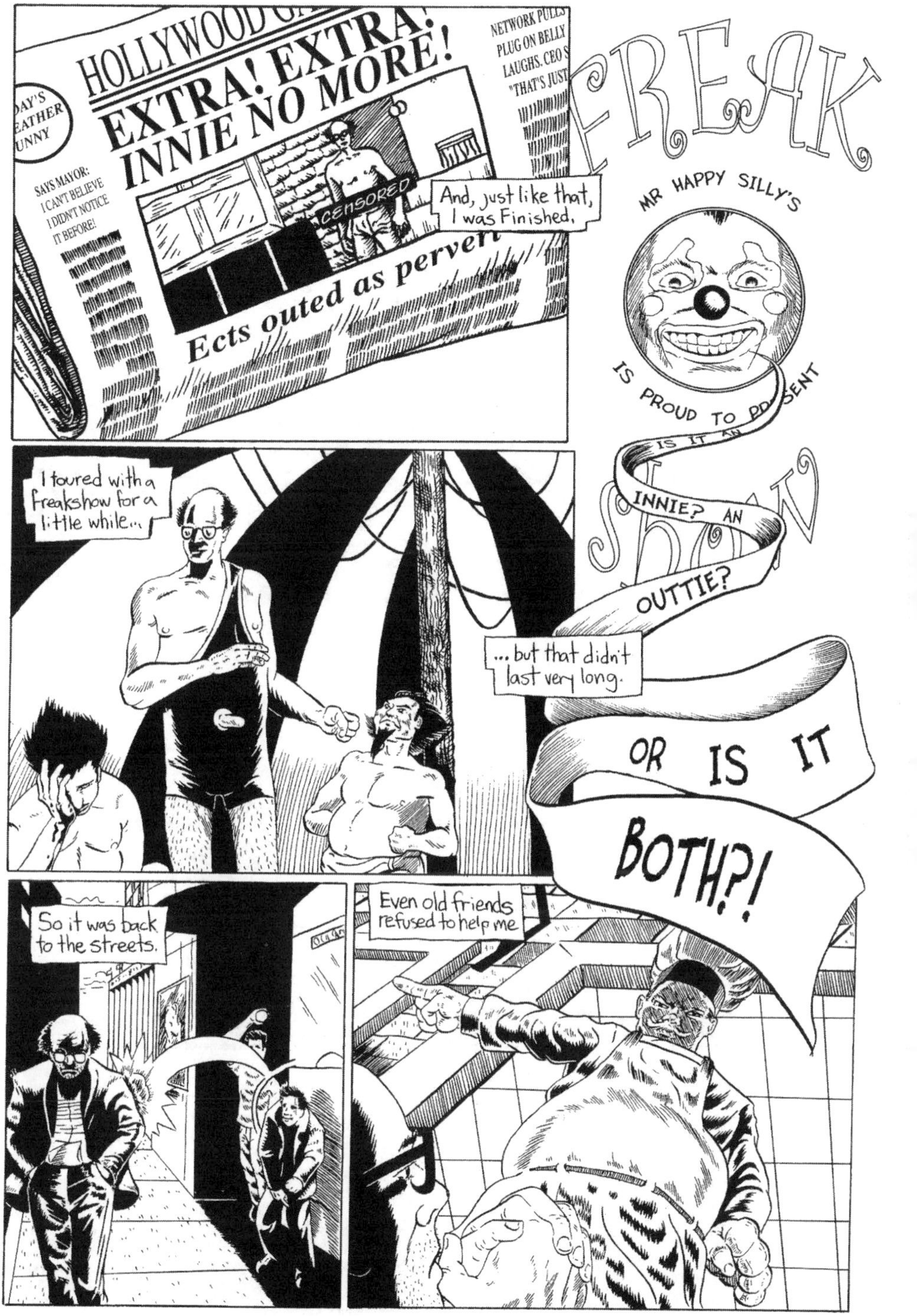
HOLLYWOOD
EXTRA! EXTRA! INNIE NO MORE!
DAY'S WEATHER SUNNY
SAYS MAYOR: I CAN'T BELIEVE I DIDN'T NOTICE IT BEFORE!
NETWORK PULLS PLUG ON BELLY LAUGHS. CEO S "THAT'S JUST
CENSORED
Ects outed as pervert
And, just like that, I was Finished.
FREAK
MR HAPPY SILLY'S
IS PROUD TO PRESENT
SHOW
IS IT AN INNIE? AN OUTTIE?
OR IS IT BOTH?!
I toured with a freakshow for a little while...
...but that didn't last very long.
So it was back to the streets.
Even old friends refused to help me

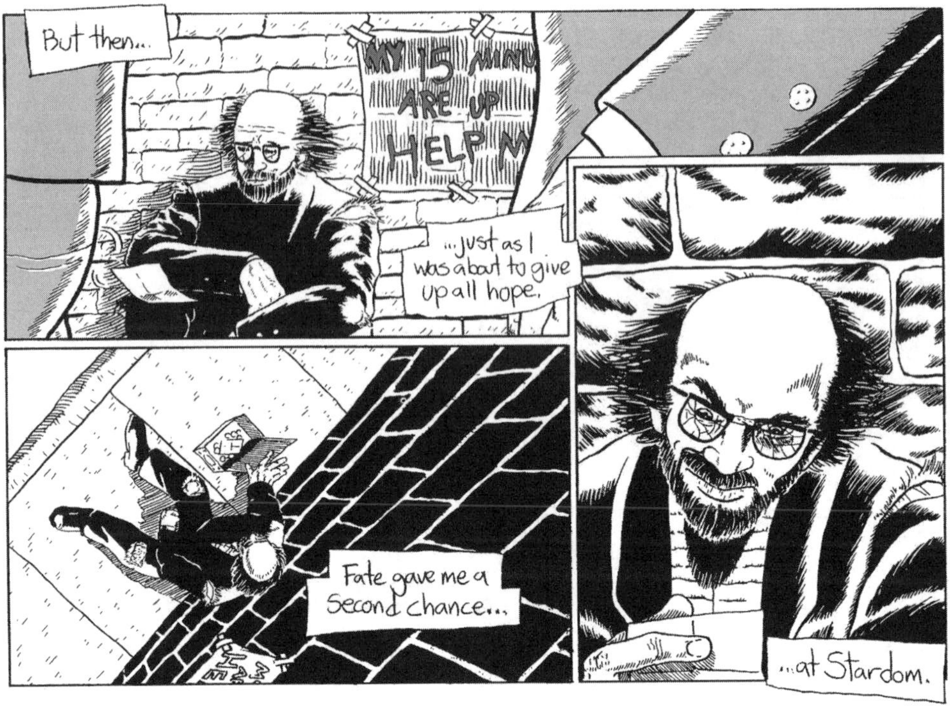
But then...
MY 15 MINU
ARE UP
HELP M
...just as I was about to give up all hope,
Fate gave me a second chance...
...at Stardom.

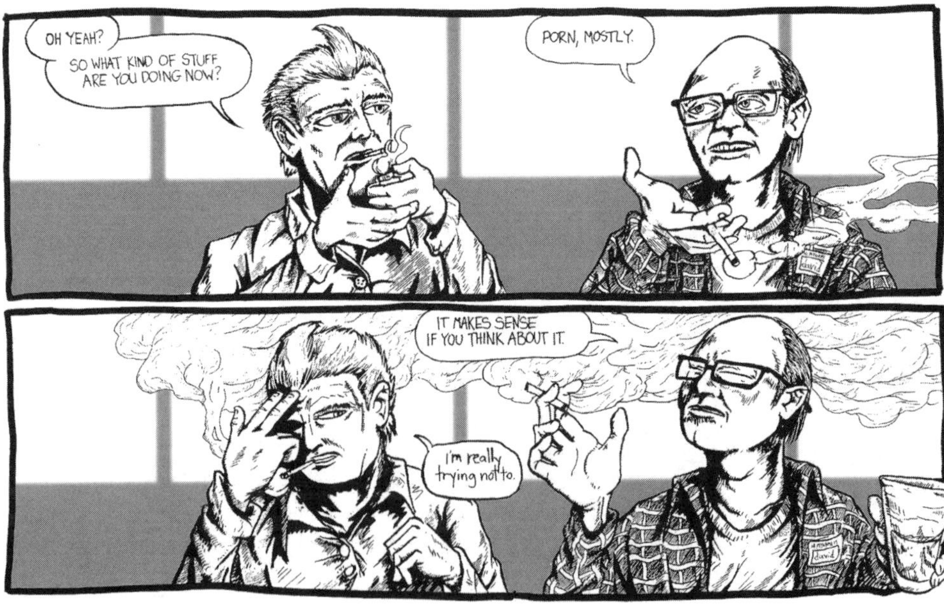
OH YEAH?
SO WHAT KIND OF STUFF ARE YOU DOING NOW?
PORN, MOSTLY.
IT MAKES SENSE IF YOU THINK ABOUT IT.
I'm really trying not to.

chapter eight: eliza

02/14/1998

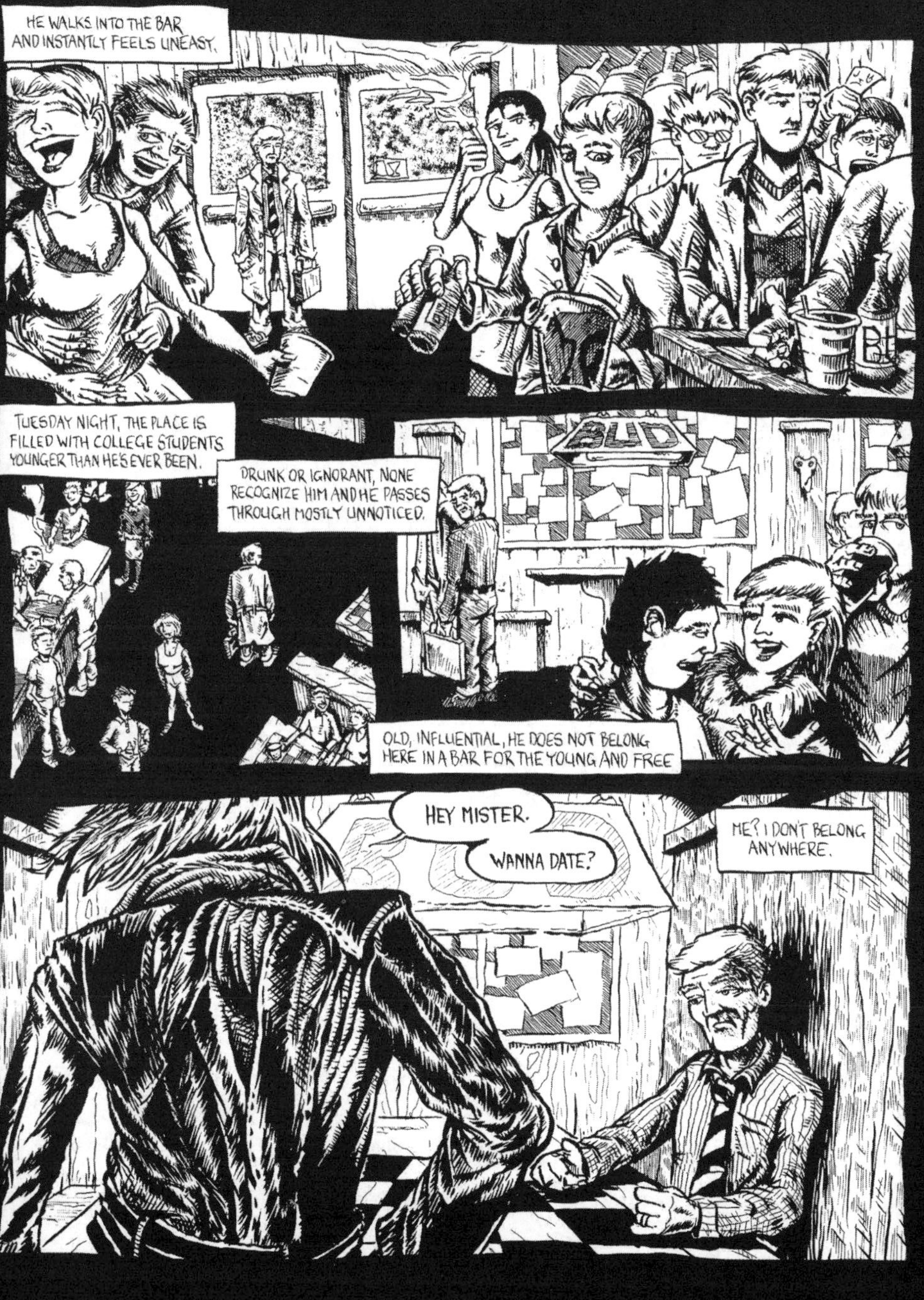

HE WALKS INTO THE BAR AND INSTANTLY FEELS UNEASY.
TUESDAY NIGHT, THE PLACE IS FILLED WITH COLLEGE STUDENTS YOUNGER THAN HE'S EVER BEEN.
DRUNK OR IGNORANT, NONE RECOGNIZE HIM AND HE PASSES THROUGH MOSTLY UNNOTICED.
BUD
OLD, INFLUENTIAL, HE DOES NOT BELONG HERE IN A BAR FOR THE YOUNG AND FREE
HEY MISTER.
WANNA DATE?
ME? I DON'T BELONG ANYWHERE.

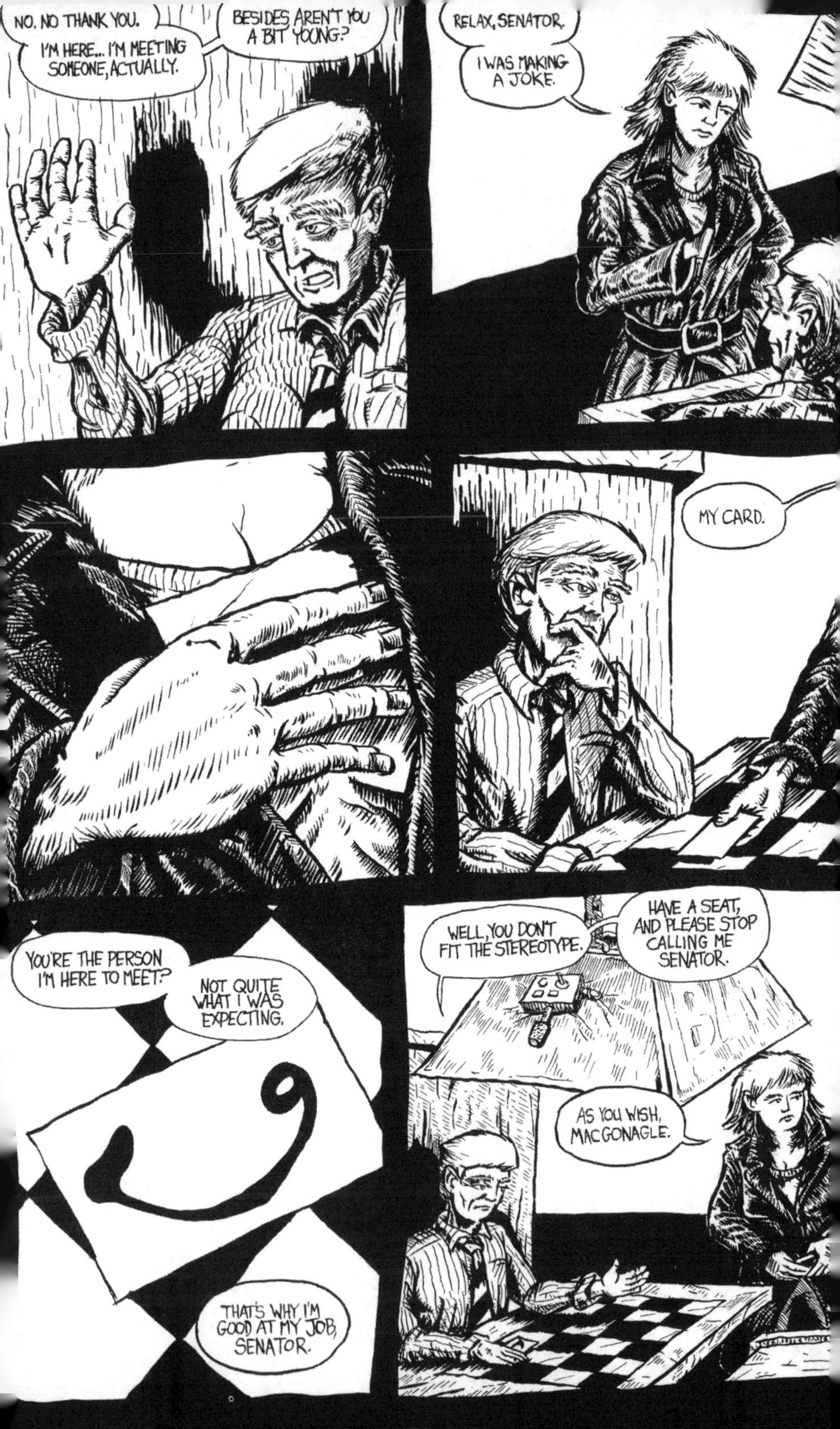
NO. NO THANK YOU.
I'M HERE... I'M MEETING SOMEONE, ACTUALLY.
BESIDES AREN'T YOU A BIT YOUNG?
RELAX, SENATOR.
I WAS MAKING A JOKE.
MY CARD.
YOU'RE THE PERSON I'M HERE TO MEET?
NOT QUITE WHAT I WAS EXPECTING.
THAT'S WHY I'M GOOD AT MY JOB, SENATOR.
WELL, YOU DON'T FIT THE STEREOTYPE.
HAVE A SEAT, AND PLEASE STOP CALLING ME SENATOR.
AS YOU WISH, MACGONAGLE.

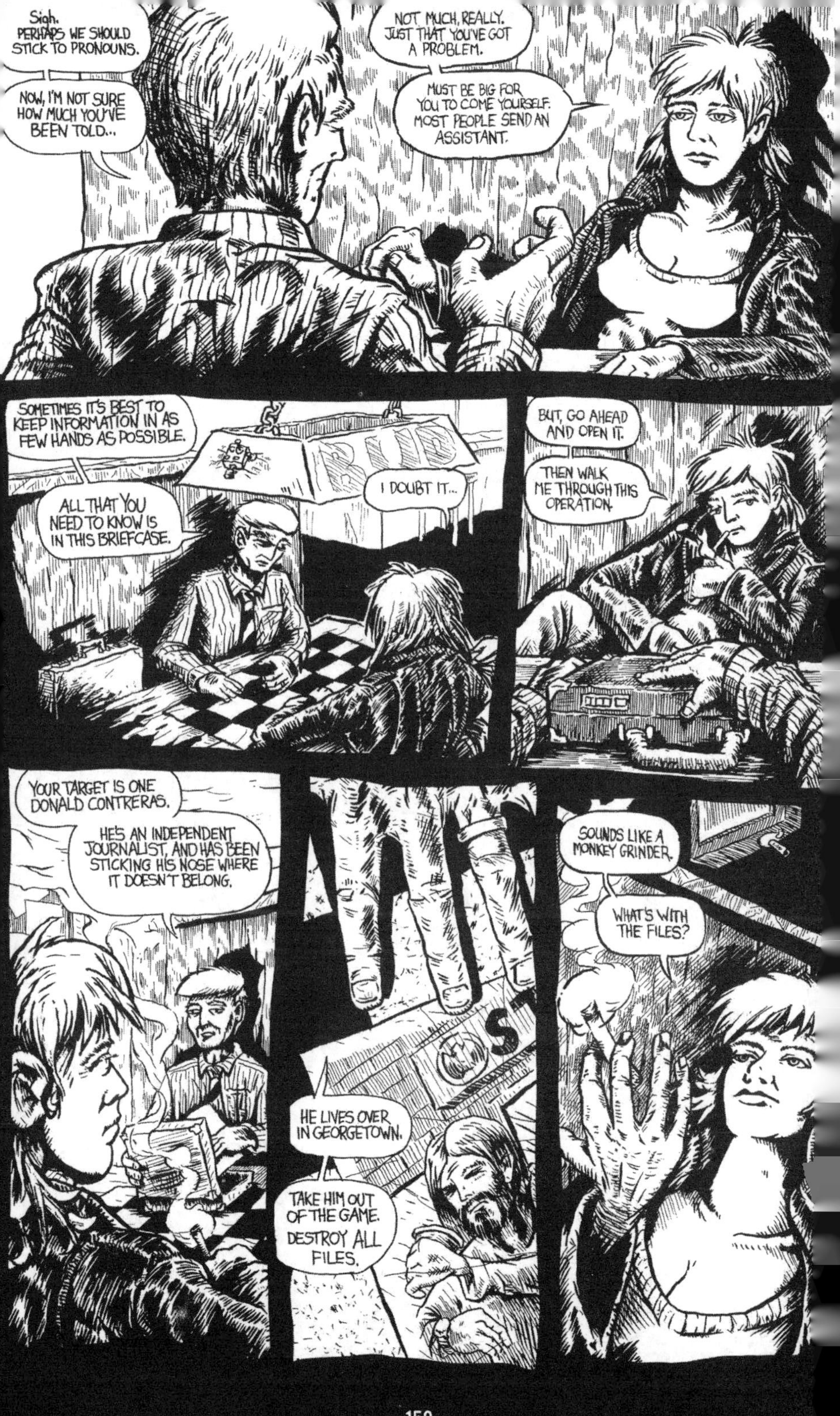

Sigh.
PERHAPS WE SHOULD STICK TO PRONOUNS.
NOW, I'M NOT SURE HOW MUCH YOU'VE BEEN TOLD...
NOT MUCH, REALLY. JUST THAT YOU'VE GOT A PROBLEM.
MUST BE BIG FOR YOU TO COME YOURSELF. MOST PEOPLE SEND AN ASSISTANT.
SOMETIMES IT'S BEST TO KEEP INFORMATION IN AS FEW HANDS AS POSSIBLE.
ALL THAT YOU NEED TO KNOW IS IN THIS BRIEFCASE.
I DOUBT IT...
BUT, GO AHEAD AND OPEN IT.
THEN WALK ME THROUGH THIS OPERATION.
YOUR TARGET IS ONE DONALD CONTRERAS.
HE'S AN INDEPENDENT JOURNALIST, AND HAS BEEN STICKING HIS NOSE WHERE IT DOESN'T BELONG.
HE LIVES OVER IN GEORGETOWN.
TAKE HIM OUT OF THE GAME.
DESTROY ALL FILES.
SOUNDS LIKE A MONKEY GRINDER.
WHAT'S WITH THE FILES?

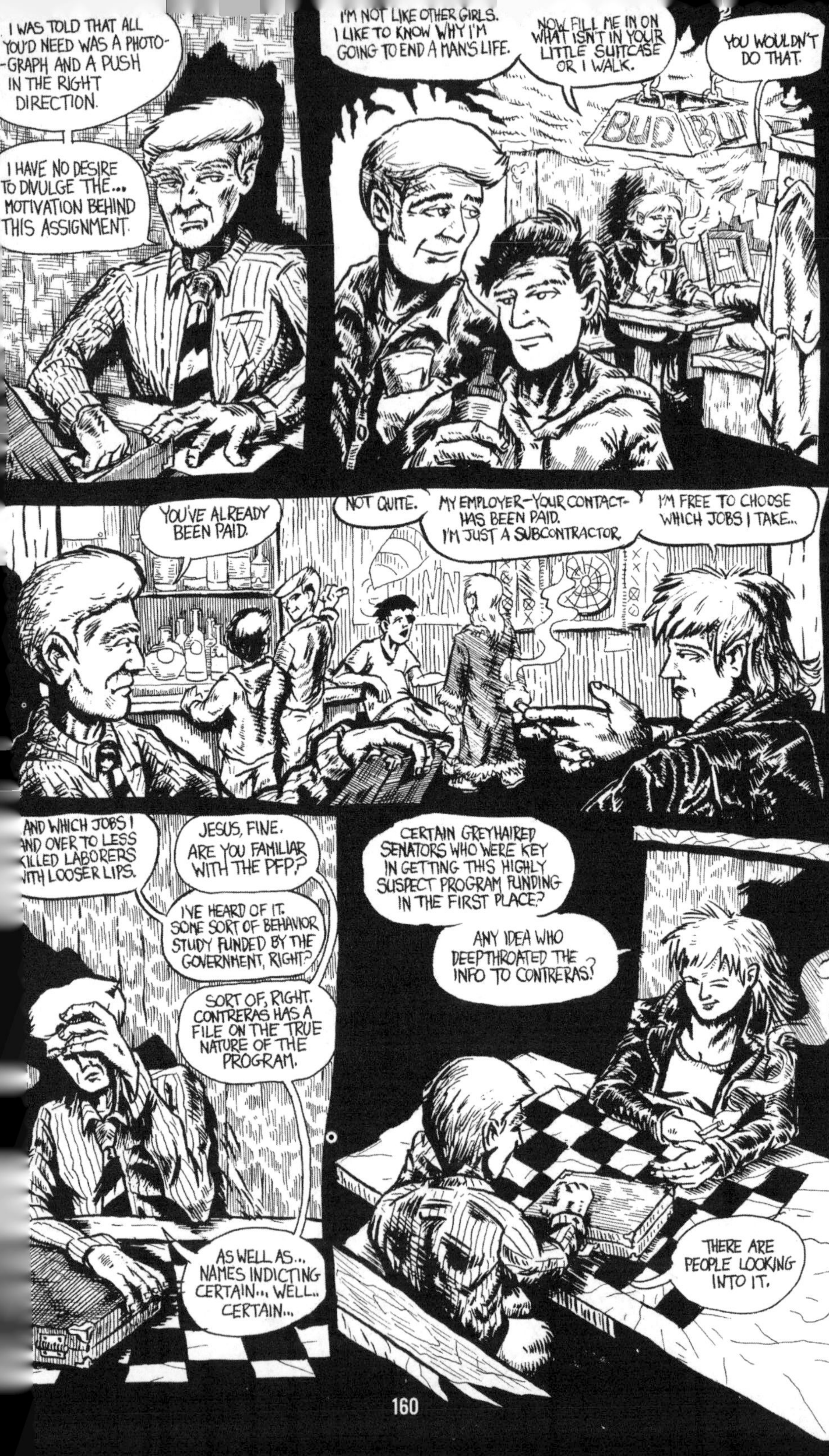
I WAS TOLD THAT ALL YOU'D NEED WAS A PHOTO-GRAPH AND A PUSH IN THE RIGHT DIRECTION.
I HAVE NO DESIRE TO DIVULGE THE... MOTIVATION BEHIND THIS ASSIGNMENT.
I'M NOT LIKE OTHER GIRLS. I LIKE TO KNOW WHY I'M GOING TO END A MAN'S LIFE.
NOW FILL ME IN ON WHAT ISN'T IN YOUR LITTLE SUITCASE OR I WALK.
YOU WOULDN'T DO THAT.
BUD
YOU'VE ALREADY BEEN PAID.
NOT QUITE.
MY EMPLOYER—YOUR CONTACT—HAS BEEN PAID. I'M JUST A SUBCONTRACTOR.
I'M FREE TO CHOOSE WHICH JOBS I TAKE..
AND WHICH JOBS I HAND OVER TO LESS SKILLED LABORERS WITH LOOSER LIPS.
JESUS, FINE. ARE YOU FAMILIAR WITH THE PFP?
I'VE HEARD OF IT. SOME SORT OF BEHAVIOR STUDY FUNDED BY THE GOVERNMENT, RIGHT?
SORT OF, RIGHT. CONTRERAS HAS A FILE ON THE TRUE NATURE OF THE PROGRAM.
AS WELL AS... NAMES INDICTING CERTAIN... WELL. CERTAIN...
CERTAIN GREYHAIRED SENATORS WHO WERE KEY IN GETTING THIS HIGHLY SUSPECT PROGRAM FUNDING IN THE FIRST PLACE?
ANY IDEA WHO DEEPTHROATED THE INFO TO CONTRERAS?
THERE ARE PEOPLE LOOKING INTO IT.

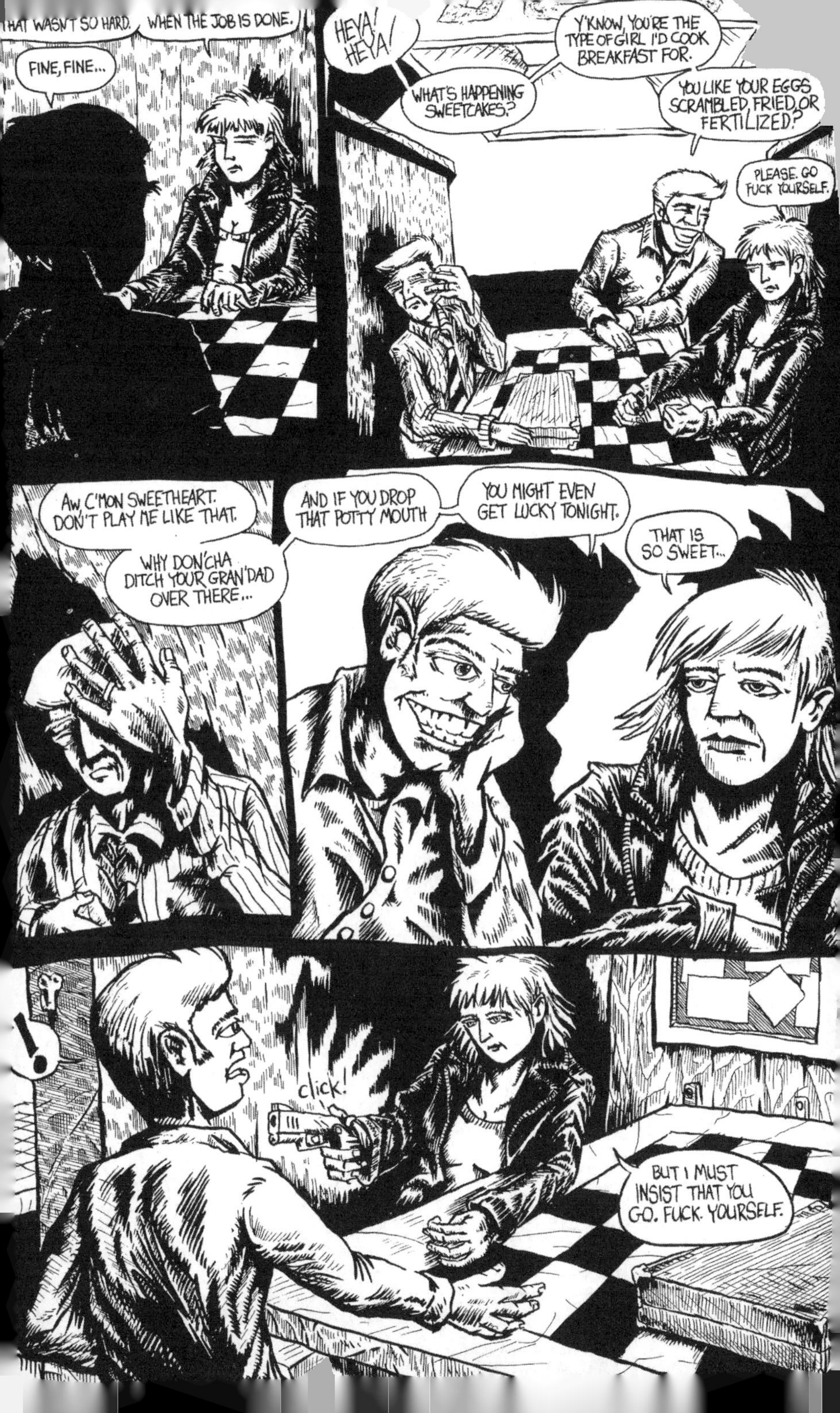
THAT WASN'T SO HARD.
WHEN THE JOB IS DONE.
FINE, FINE...
HEYA! HEYA!
WHAT'S HAPPENING SWEETCAKES?
Y'KNOW, YOU'RE THE TYPE OF GIRL I'D COOK BREAKFAST FOR.
YOU LIKE YOUR EGGS SCRAMBLED, FRIED, OR FERTILIZED?
PLEASE. GO FUCK YOURSELF.
AW C'MON SWEETHEART. DON'T PLAY ME LIKE THAT.
WHY DON'CHA DITCH YOUR GRAN'DAD OVER THERE...
AND IF YOU DROP THAT POTTY MOUTH
YOU MIGHT EVEN GET LUCKY TONIGHT.
THAT IS SO SWEET...
click!
BUT I MUST INSIST THAT YOU GO. FUCK. YOURSELF.

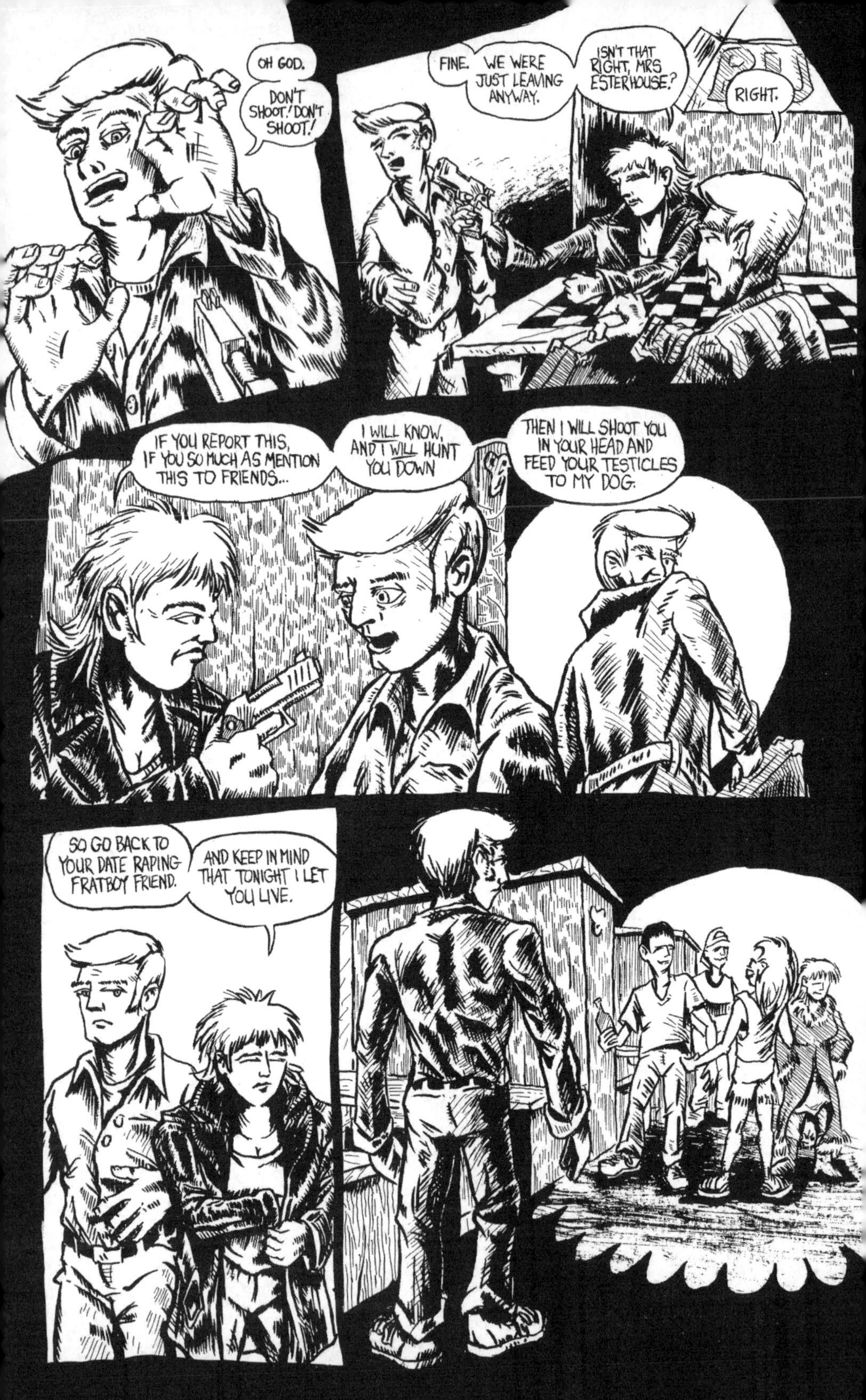
OH GOD.
DON'T SHOOT! DON'T SHOOT!
FINE. WE WERE JUST LEAVING ANYWAY.
ISN'T THAT RIGHT, MRS ESTERHOUSE?
RIGHT.
IF YOU REPORT THIS, IF YOU SO MUCH AS MENTION THIS TO FRIENDS...
I WILL KNOW, AND I WILL HUNT YOU DOWN
THEN I WILL SHOOT YOU IN YOUR HEAD AND FEED YOUR TESTICLES TO MY DOG.
SO GO BACK TO YOUR DATE RAPING FRATBOY FRIEND.
AND KEEP IN MIND THAT TONIGHT I LET YOU LIVE.

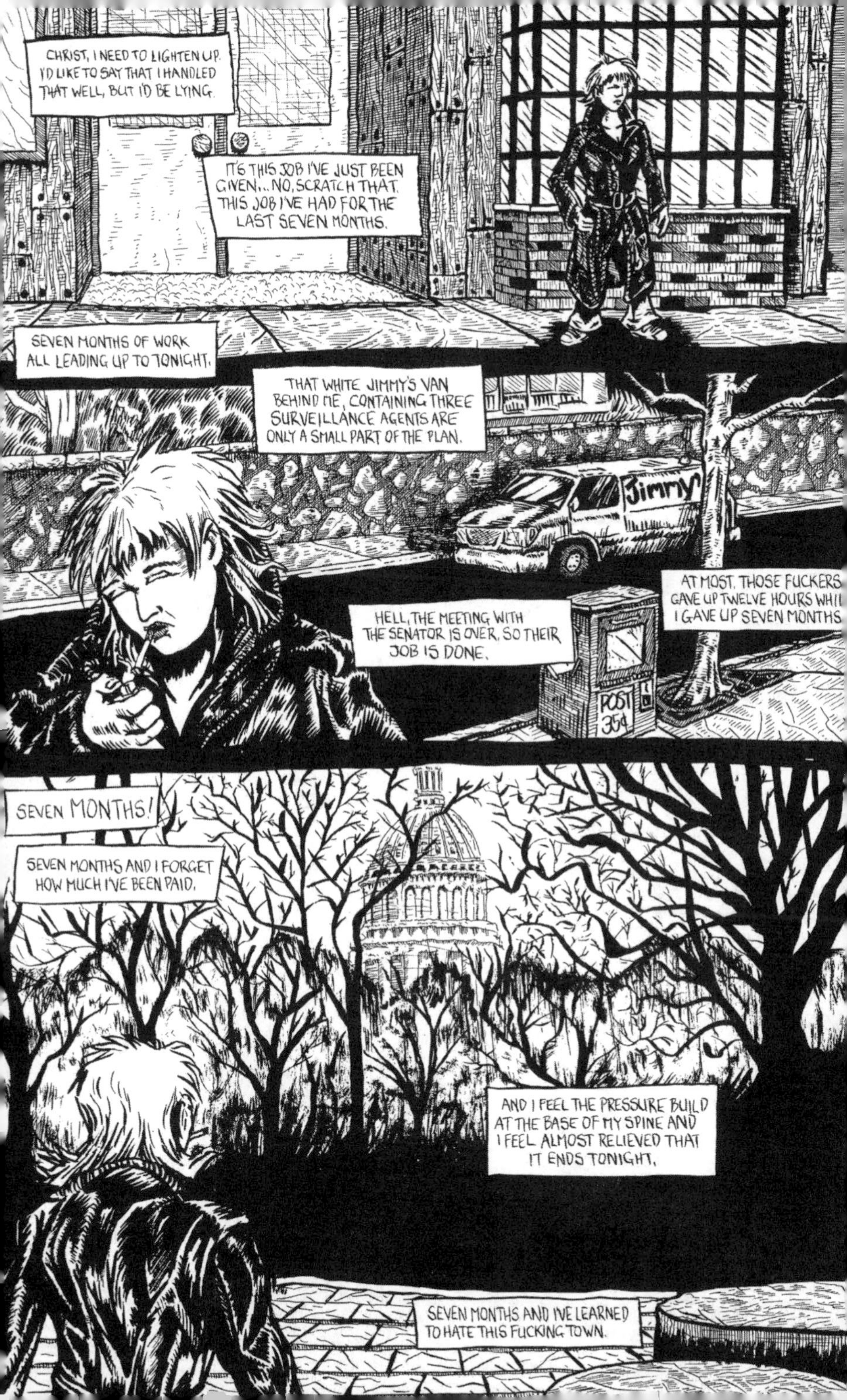
CHRIST, I NEED TO LIGHTEN UP. I'D LIKE TO SAY THAT I HANDLED THAT WELL, BUT I'D BE LYING.
IT'S THIS JOB I'VE JUST BEEN GIVEN... NO, SCRATCH THAT. THIS JOB I'VE HAD FOR THE LAST SEVEN MONTHS.
SEVEN MONTHS OF WORK ALL LEADING UP TO TONIGHT.
THAT WHITE JIMMY'S VAN BEHIND ME, CONTAINING THREE SURVEILLANCE AGENTS ARE ONLY A SMALL PART OF THE PLAN.
Jimmy's
HELL, THE MEETING WITH THE SENATOR IS OVER, SO THEIR JOB IS DONE.
AT MOST, THOSE FUCKERS GAVE UP TWELVE HOURS WHIL I GAVE UP SEVEN MONTHS
POST 35¢
SEVEN MONTHS!
SEVEN MONTHS AND I FORGET HOW MUCH I'VE BEEN PAID.
AND I FEEL THE PRESSURE BUILD AT THE BASE OF MY SPINE AND I FEEL ALMOST RELIEVED THAT IT ENDS TONIGHT.
SEVEN MONTHS AND I'VE LEARNED TO HATE THIS FUCKING TOWN.

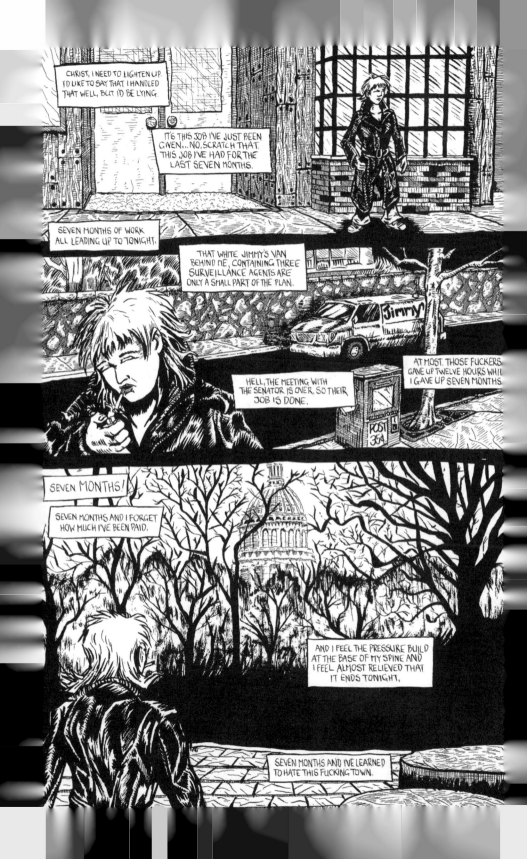

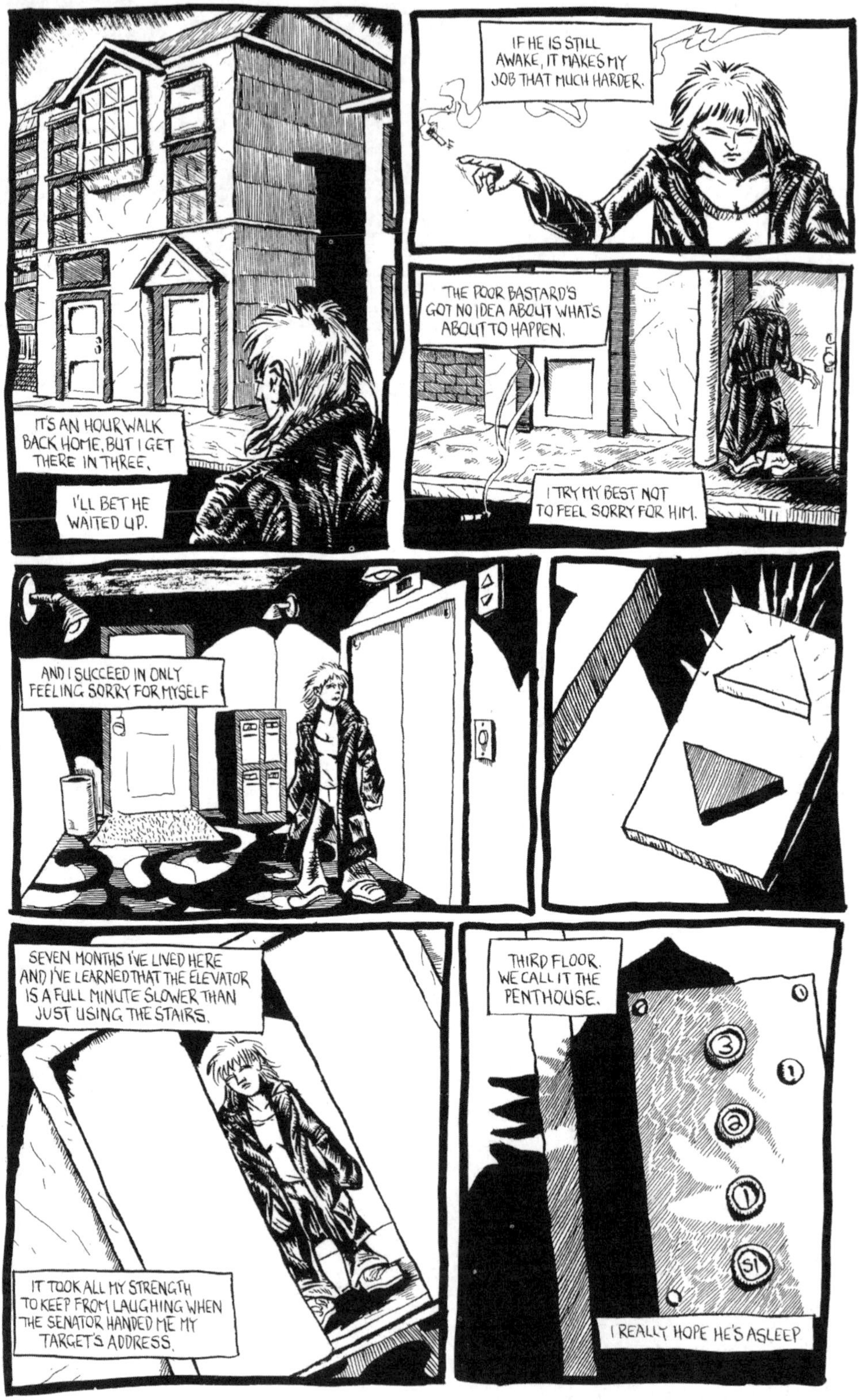
IT'S AN HOUR WALK BACK HOME, BUT I GET THERE IN THREE.
I'LL BET HE WAITED UP.
IF HE IS STILL AWAKE, IT MAKES MY JOB THAT MUCH HARDER.
THE POOR BASTARD'S GOT NO IDEA ABOUT WHAT'S ABOUT TO HAPPEN.
I TRY MY BEST NOT TO FEEL SORRY FOR HIM.
AND I SUCCEED IN ONLY FEELING SORRY FOR MYSELF
SEVEN MONTHS I'VE LIVED HERE AND I'VE LEARNED THAT THE ELEVATOR IS A FULL MINUTE SLOWER THAN JUST USING THE STAIRS.
IT TOOK ALL MY STRENGTH TO KEEP FROM LAUGHING WHEN THE SENATOR HANDED ME MY TARGET'S ADDRESS.
THIRD FLOOR. WE CALL IT THE PENTHOUSE.
I REALLY HOPE HE'S ASLEEP

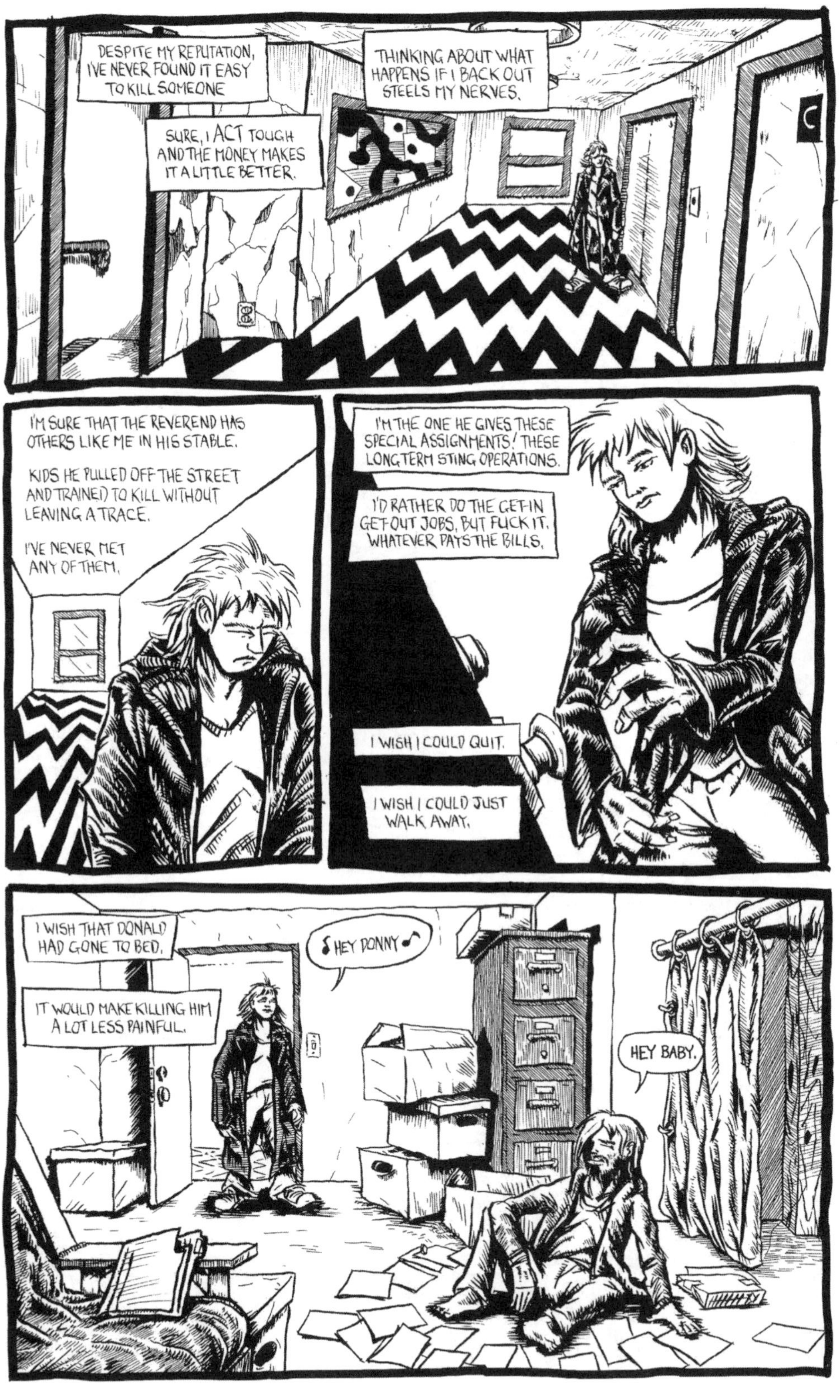
DESPITE MY REPUTATION, I'VE NEVER FOUND IT EASY TO KILL SOMEONE
SURE, I ACT TOUGH AND THE MONEY MAKES IT A LITTLE BETTER.
THINKING ABOUT WHAT HAPPENS IF I BACK OUT STEELS MY NERVES.
C
I'M SURE THAT THE REVEREND HAS OTHERS LIKE ME IN HIS STABLE.
KIDS HE PULLED OFF THE STREET AND TRAINED TO KILL WITHOUT LEAVING A TRACE.
I'VE NEVER MET ANY OF THEM.
I'M THE ONE HE GIVES THESE SPECIAL ASSIGNMENTS! THESE LONGTERM STING OPERATIONS.
I'D RATHER DO THE GET-IN GET-OUT JOBS, BUT FUCK IT. WHATEVER PAYS THE BILLS.
I WISH I COULD QUIT.
I WISH I COULD JUST WALK AWAY.
I WISH THAT DONALD HAD GONE TO BED.
IT WOULD MAKE KILLING HIM A LOT LESS PAINFUL.
♪ HEY DONNY ♪
HEY BABY.

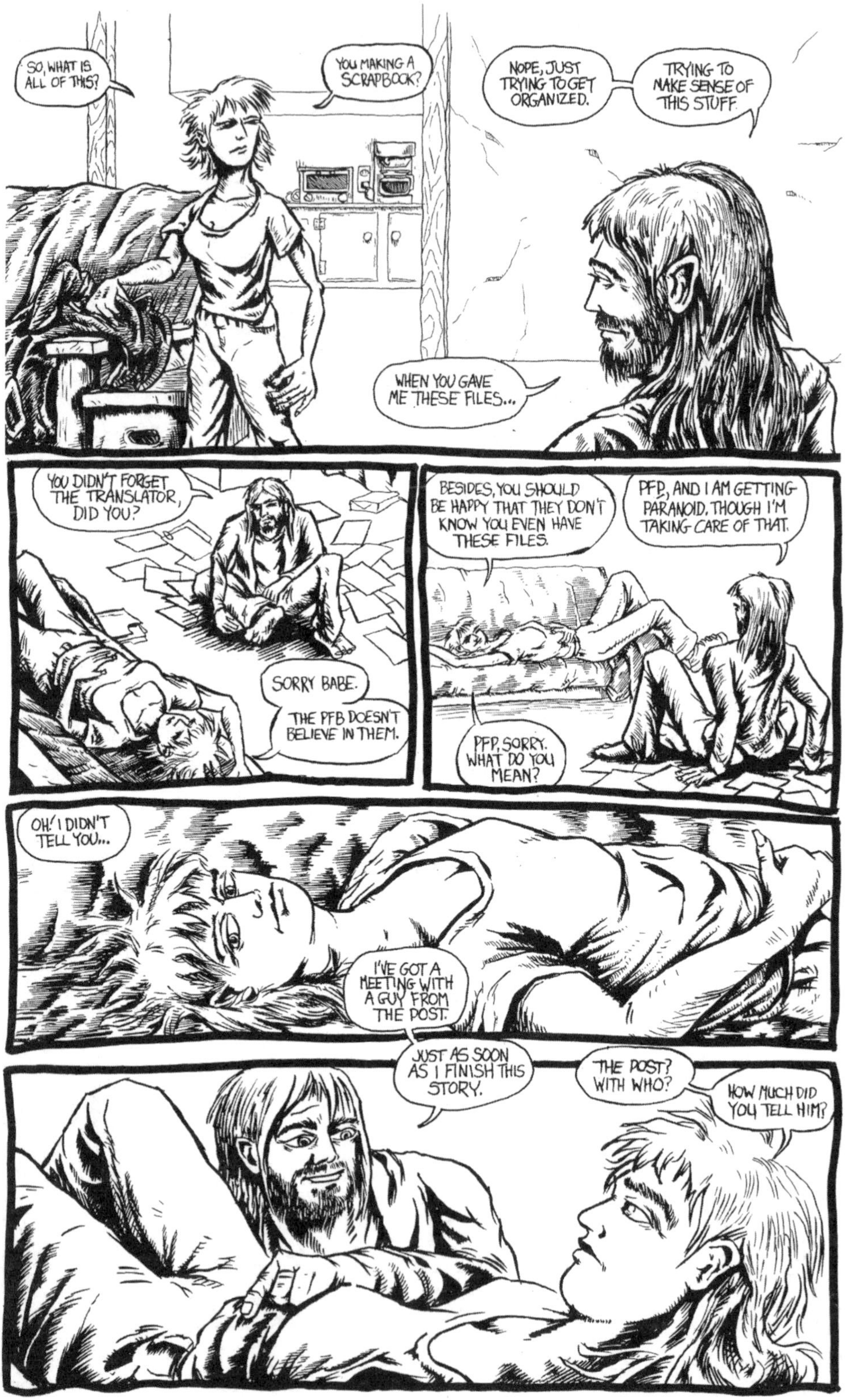
SO, WHAT IS ALL OF THIS?
YOU MAKING A SCRAPBOOK?
NOPE, JUST TRYING TO GET ORGANIZED.
TRYING TO MAKE SENSE OF THIS STUFF.
WHEN YOU GAVE ME THESE FILES...
YOU DIDN'T FORGET THE TRANSLATOR, DID YOU?
SORRY BABE.
THE PFB DOESN'T BELIEVE IN THEM.
BESIDES, YOU SHOULD BE HAPPY THAT THEY DON'T KNOW YOU EVEN HAVE THESE FILES.
PFP, SORRY. WHAT DO YOU MEAN?
PFP, AND I AM GETTING PARANOID. THOUGH I'M TAKING CARE OF THAT.
OH! I DIDN'T TELL YOU...
I'VE GOT A MEETING WITH A GUY FROM THE POST.
JUST AS SOON AS I FINISH THIS STORY.
THE POST? WITH WHO?
HOW MUCH DID YOU TELL HIM?

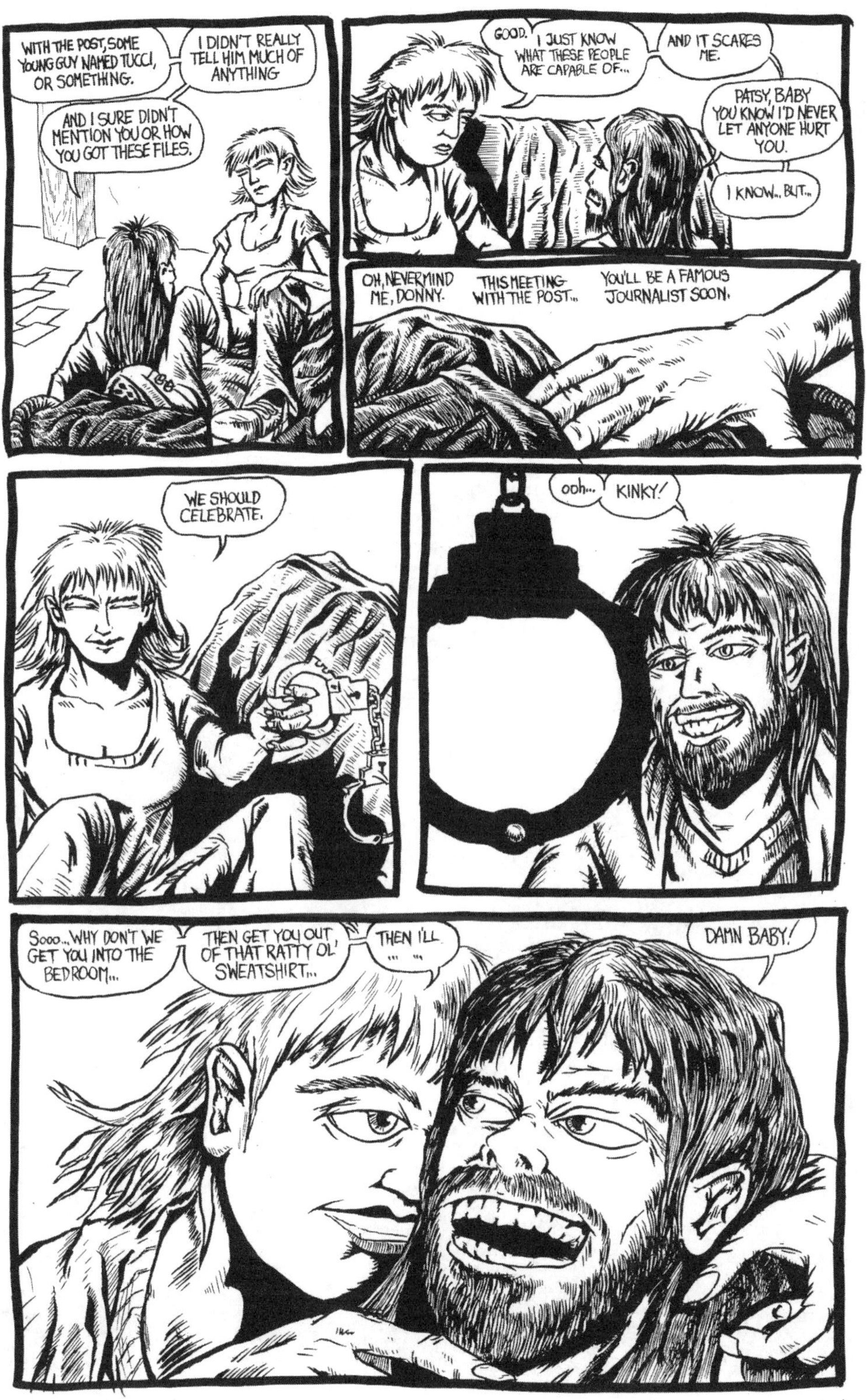
WITH THE POST, SOME YOUNG GUY NAMED TUCCI, OR SOMETHING.
I DIDN'T REALLY TELL HIM MUCH OF ANYTHING
AND I SURE DIDN'T MENTION YOU OR HOW YOU GOT THESE FILES.
GOOD.
I JUST KNOW WHAT THESE PEOPLE ARE CAPABLE OF...
AND IT SCARES ME.
PATSY, BABY YOU KNOW I'D NEVER LET ANYONE HURT YOU.
I KNOW.. BUT..
OH, NEVERMIND ME, DONNY.
THIS MEETING WITH THE POST..
YOU'LL BE A FAMOUS JOURNALIST SOON.
WE SHOULD CELEBRATE.
ooh...
KINKY!
Sooo...WHY DON'T WE GET YOU INTO THE BEDROOM...
THEN GET YOU OUT OF THAT RATTY OL' SWEATSHIRT...
THEN I'LL ... ...
DAMN BABY!

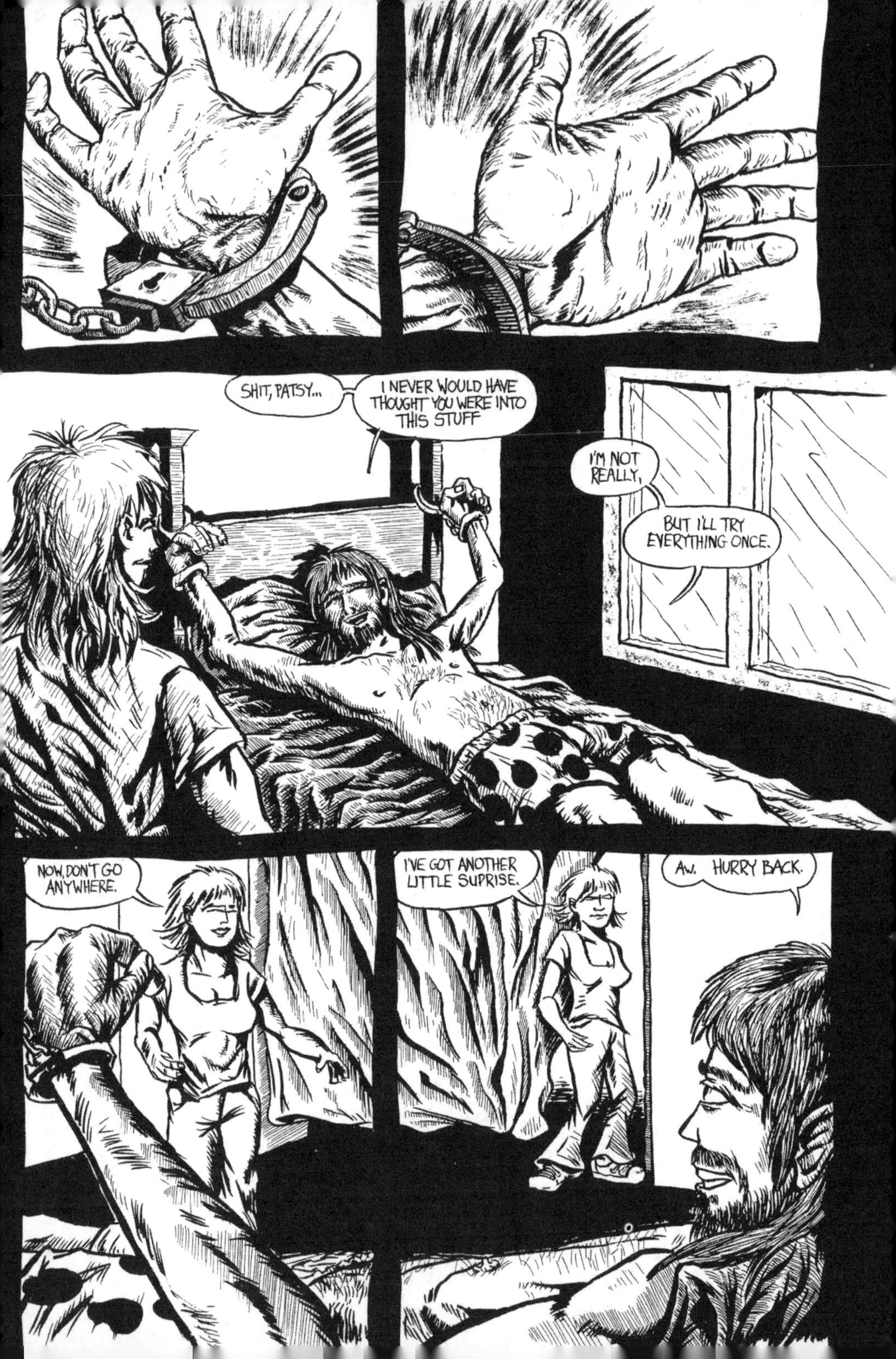
SHIT, PATSY...
I NEVER WOULD HAVE THOUGHT YOU WERE INTO THIS STUFF
I'M NOT REALLY,
BUT I'LL TRY EVERYTHING ONCE.
NOW, DON'T GO ANYWHERE.
I'VE GOT ANOTHER LITTLE SUPRISE.
AW. HURRY BACK.

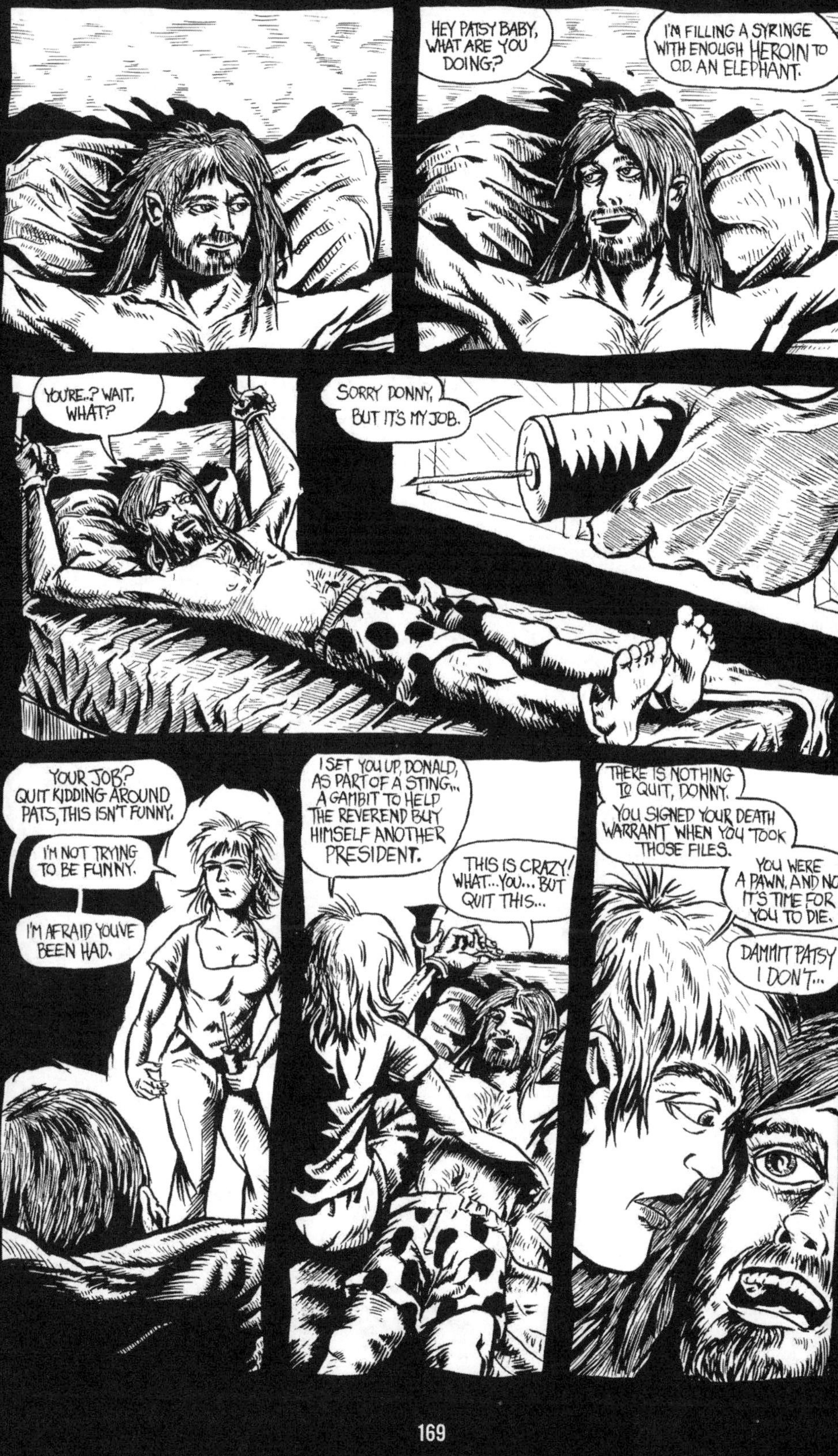
HEY PATSY BABY, WHAT ARE YOU DOING?
I'M FILLING A SYRINGE WITH ENOUGH HEROIN TO O.D. AN ELEPHANT.
YOU'RE..? WAIT. WHAT?
SORRY DONNY, BUT IT'S MY JOB.
YOUR JOB? QUIT KIDDING AROUND PATS, THIS ISN'T FUNNY.
I'M NOT TRYING TO BE FUNNY.
I'M AFRAID YOU'VE BEEN HAD.
I SET YOU UP, DONALD, AS PART OF A STING... A GAMBIT TO HELP THE REVEREND BUY HIMSELF ANOTHER PRESIDENT.
THIS IS CRAZY! WHAT... YOU... BUT QUIT THIS...
THERE IS NOTHING TO QUIT, DONNY.
YOU SIGNED YOUR DEATH WARRANT WHEN YOU TOOK THOSE FILES.
YOU WERE A PAWN, AND NOW IT'S TIME FOR YOU TO DIE.
DAMMIT PATSY I DON'T...

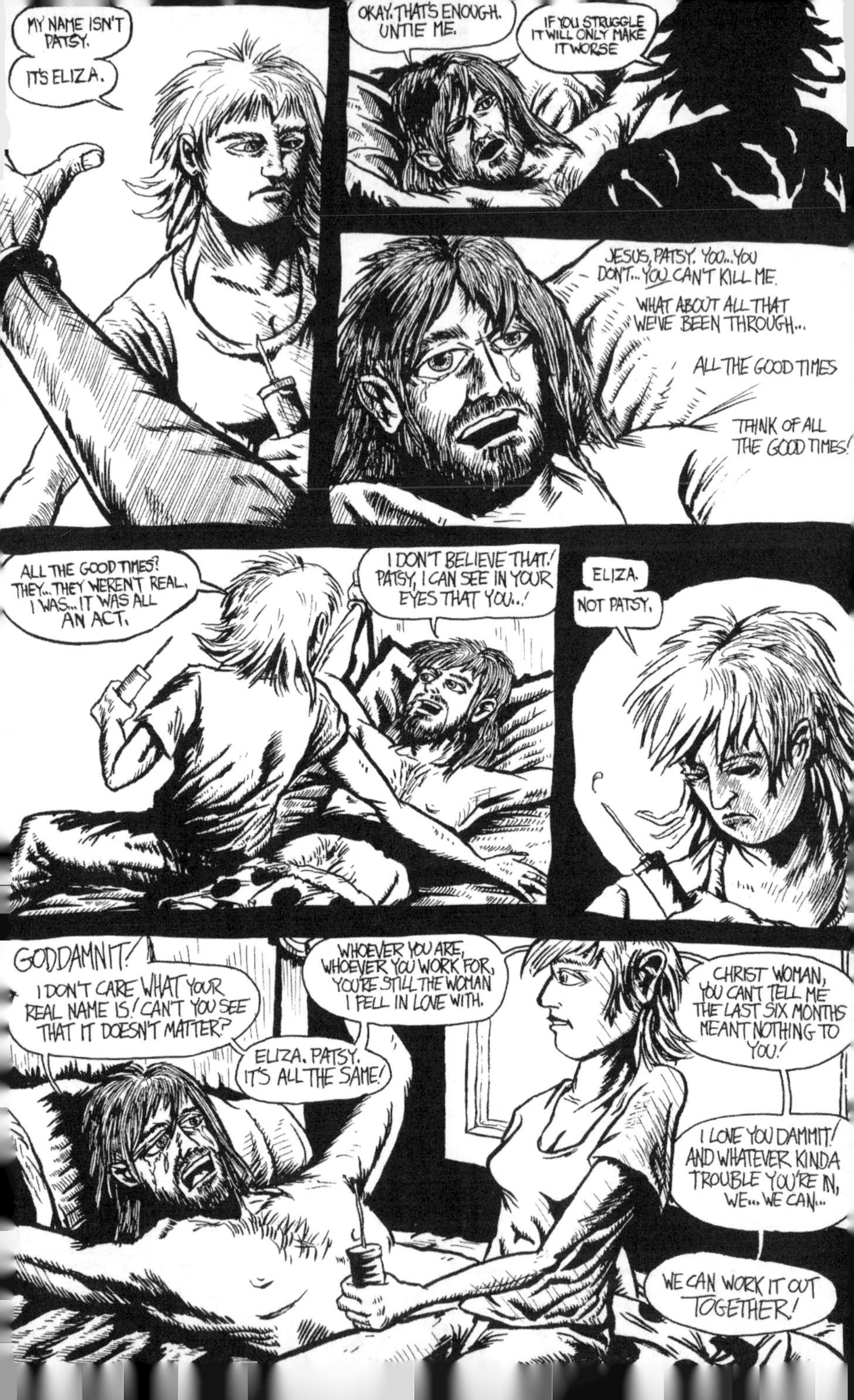
MY NAME ISN'T PATSY.
IT'S ELIZA.
OKAY. THAT'S ENOUGH. UNTIE ME.
IF YOU STRUGGLE IT WILL ONLY MAKE IT WORSE
JESUS, PATSY. YOU... YOU DON'T... YOU CAN'T KILL ME.
WHAT ABOUT ALL THAT WE'VE BEEN THROUGH...
ALL THE GOOD TIMES
THINK OF ALL THE GOOD TIMES!
ALL THE GOOD TIMES? THEY... THEY WEREN'T REAL. I WAS... IT WAS ALL AN ACT.
I DON'T BELIEVE THAT! PATSY, I CAN SEE IN YOUR EYES THAT YOU...!
ELIZA.
NOT PATSY.
GODDAMNIT!
I DON'T CARE WHAT YOUR REAL NAME IS! CAN'T YOU SEE THAT IT DOESN'T MATTER?
WHOEVER YOU ARE, WHOEVER YOU WORK FOR, YOU'RE STILL THE WOMAN I FELL IN LOVE WITH.
ELIZA. PATSY. IT'S ALL THE SAME!
CHRIST WOMAN, YOU CAN'T TELL ME THE LAST SIX MONTHS MEANT NOTHING TO YOU!
I LOVE YOU DAMMIT! AND WHATEVER KINDA TROUBLE YOU'RE IN, WE... WE CAN...
WE CAN WORK IT OUT TOGETHER!

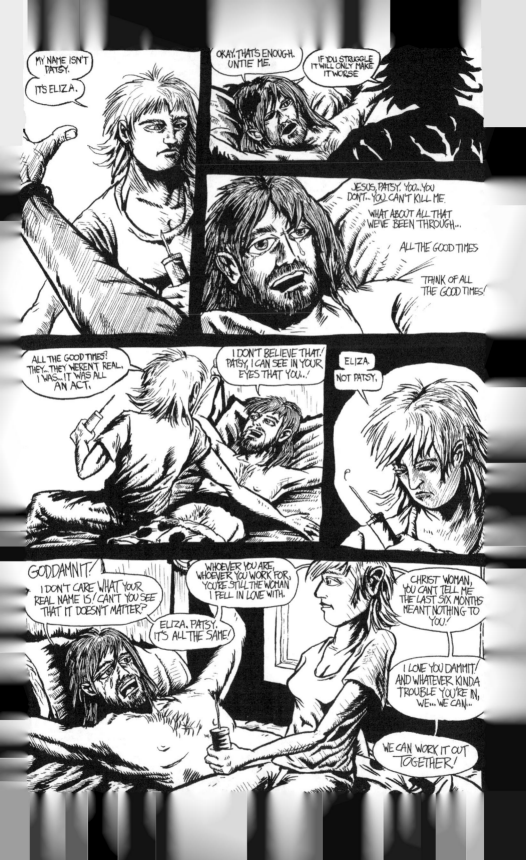

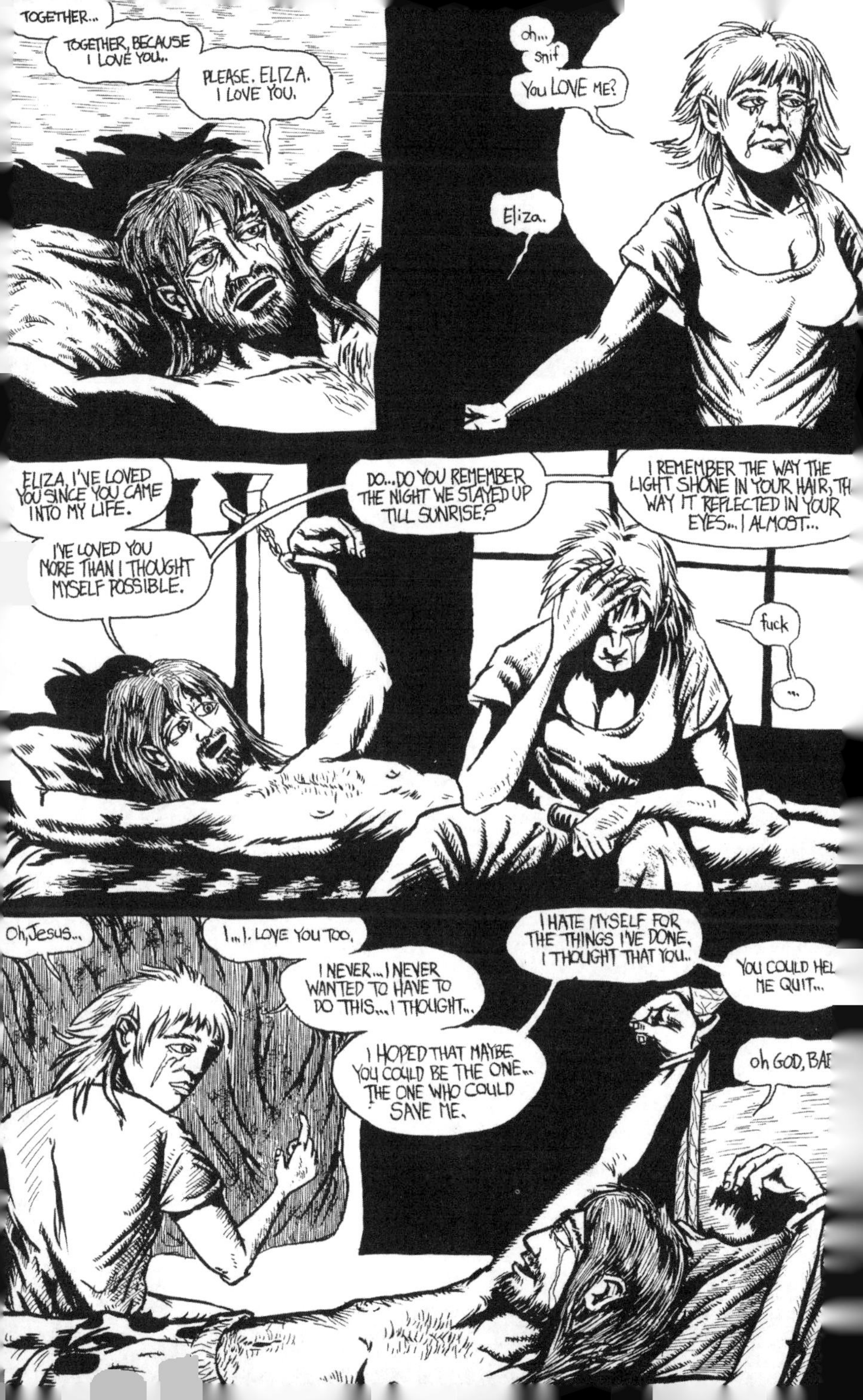
TOGETHER...
TOGETHER, BECAUSE I LOVE YOU..
PLEASE. ELIZA. I LOVE YOU.
oh...
snif
You LOVE ME?
Eliza.
ELIZA, I'VE LOVED YOU SINCE YOU CAME INTO MY LIFE.
I'VE LOVED YOU MORE THAN I THOUGHT MYSELF POSSIBLE.
DO...DO YOU REMEMBER THE NIGHT WE STAYED UP TILL SUNRISE?
I REMEMBER THE WAY THE LIGHT SHONE IN YOUR HAIR, TH WAY IT REFLECTED IN YOUR EYES... I ALMOST...
fuck
...
Oh, Jesus...
I...I. LOVE YOU TOO.
I NEVER... I NEVER WANTED TO HAVE TO DO THIS... I THOUGHT...
I HOPED THAT MAYBE YOU COULD BE THE ONE... THE ONE WHO COULD SAVE ME.
I HATE MYSELF FOR THE THINGS I'VE DONE, I THOUGHT THAT YOU..
YOU COULD HEL ME QUIT...
oh GOD, BAE

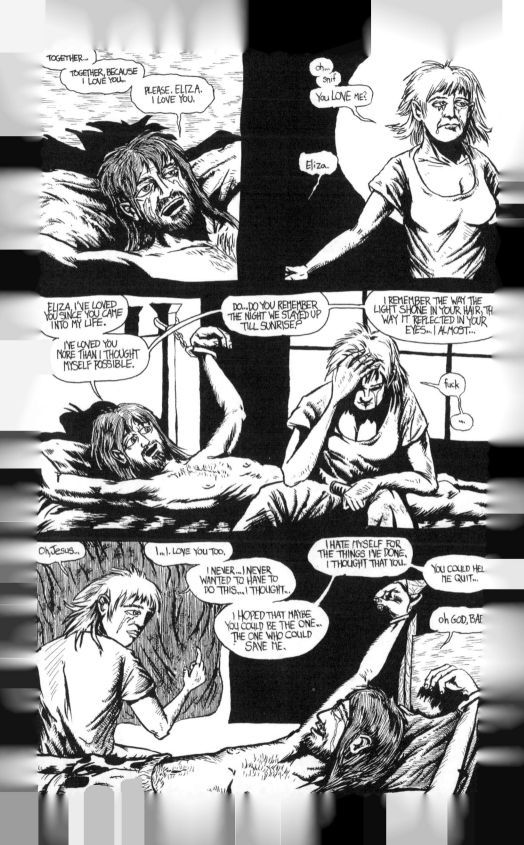

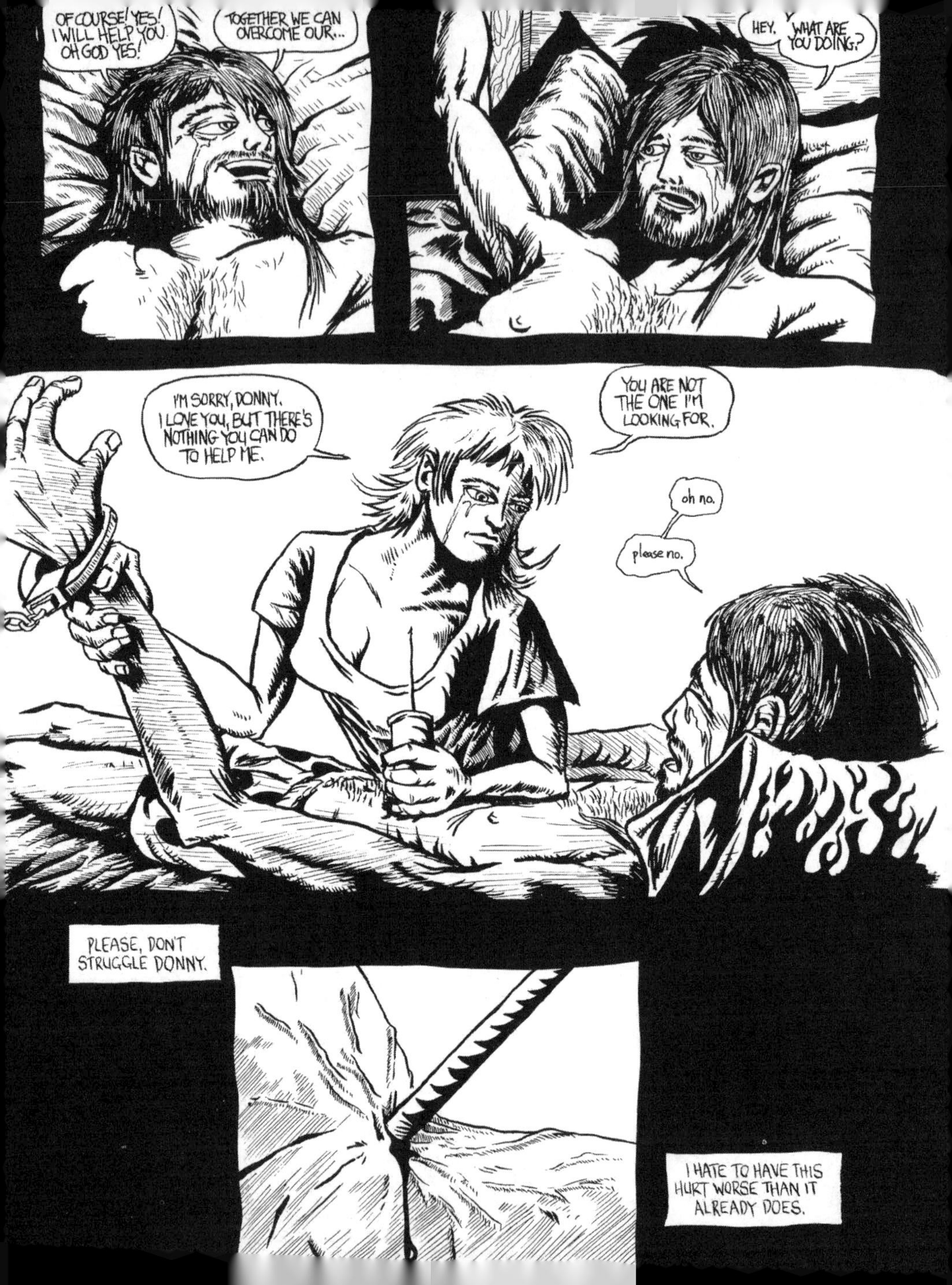
OF COURSE! YES! I WILL HELP YOU. OH GOD YES!
TOGETHER WE CAN OVERCOME OUR...
HEY.
WHAT ARE YOU DOING?
I'M SORRY, DONNY. I LOVE YOU, BUT THERE'S NOTHING YOU CAN DO TO HELP ME.
YOU ARE NOT THE ONE I'M LOOKING FOR.
oh no.
please no.
PLEASE, DON'T STRUGGLE DONNY.
I HATE TO HAVE THIS HURT WORSE THAN IT ALREADY DOES.

PLASTIC FARM : CHAPTER NINE...

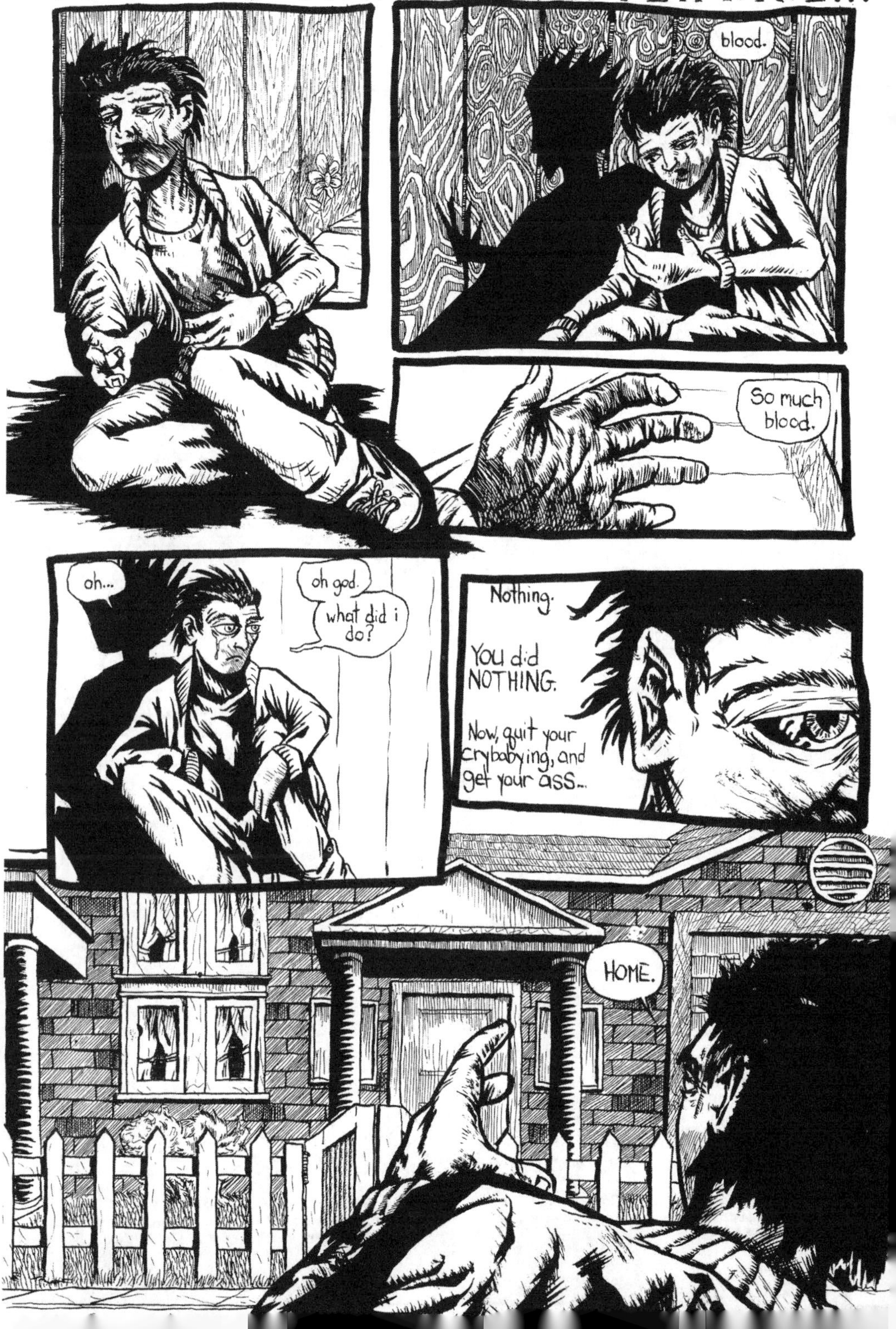
blood.
So much blood.
oh...
oh god.
what did i do?
Nothing.
You did NOTHING.
Now, quit your crybabying, and get your ass...
HOME.

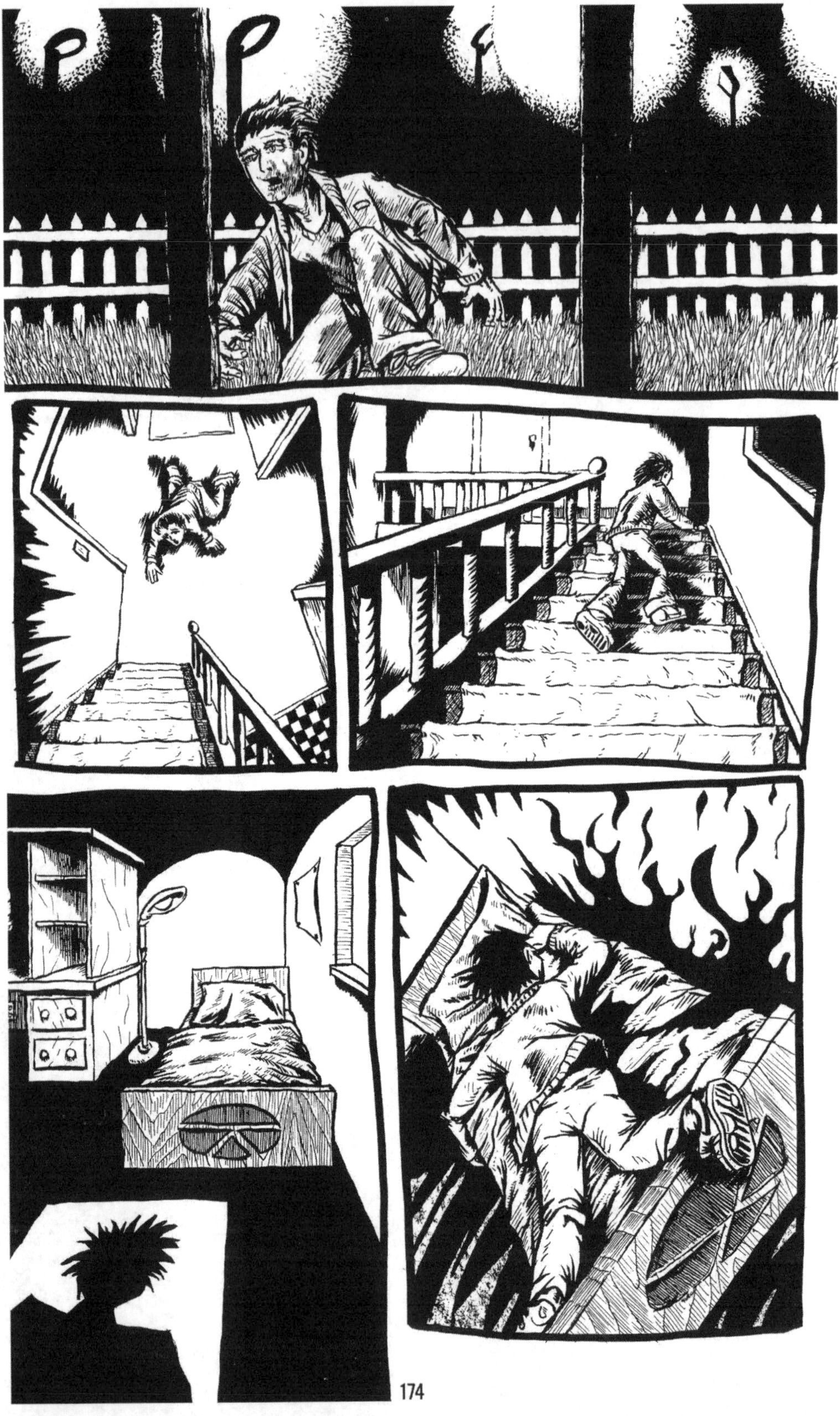

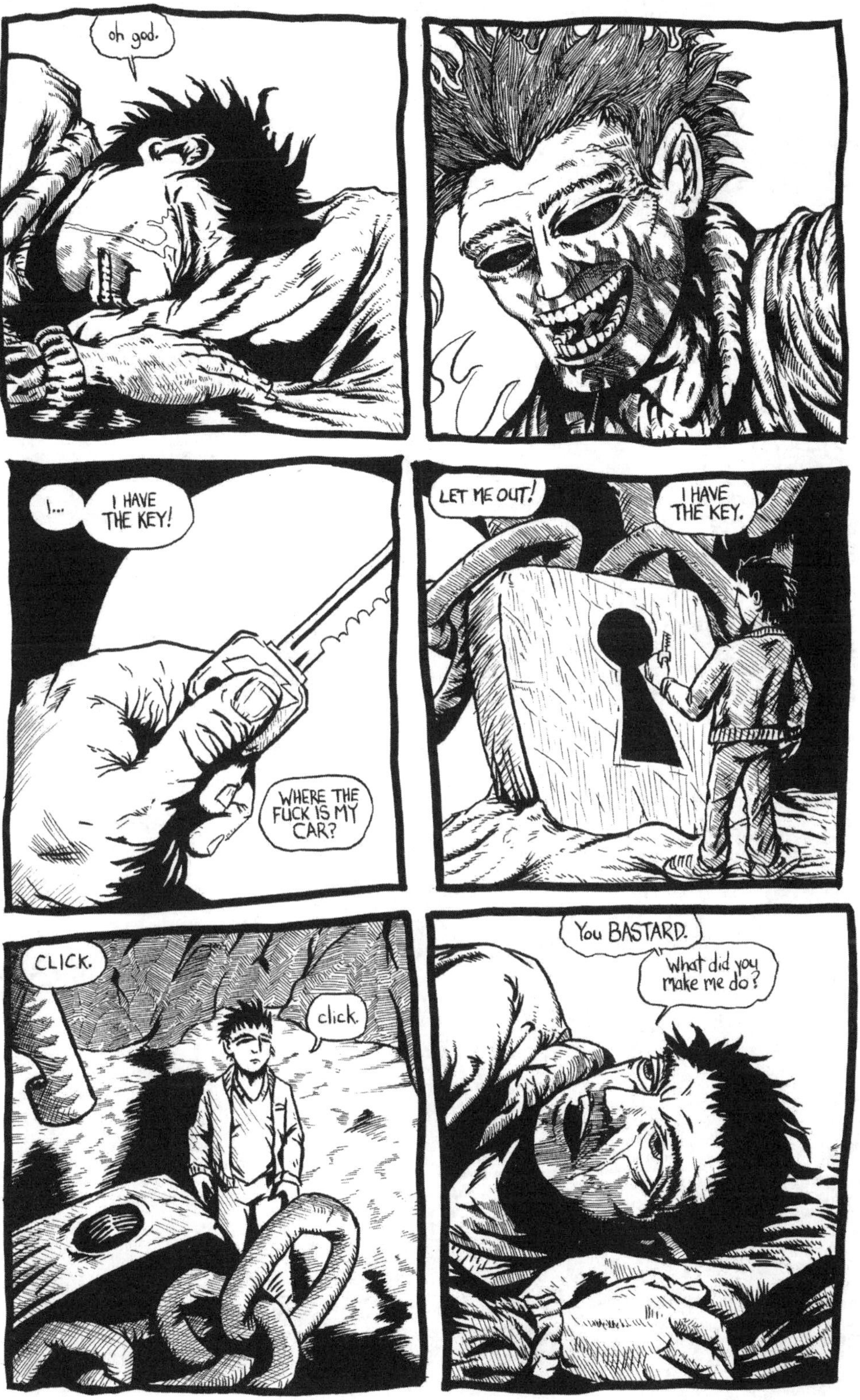
oh god.
I...
I HAVE THE KEY!
WHERE THE FUCK IS MY CAR?
LET ME OUT!
I HAVE THE KEY.
CLICK.
click.
You BASTARD.
What did you make me do?

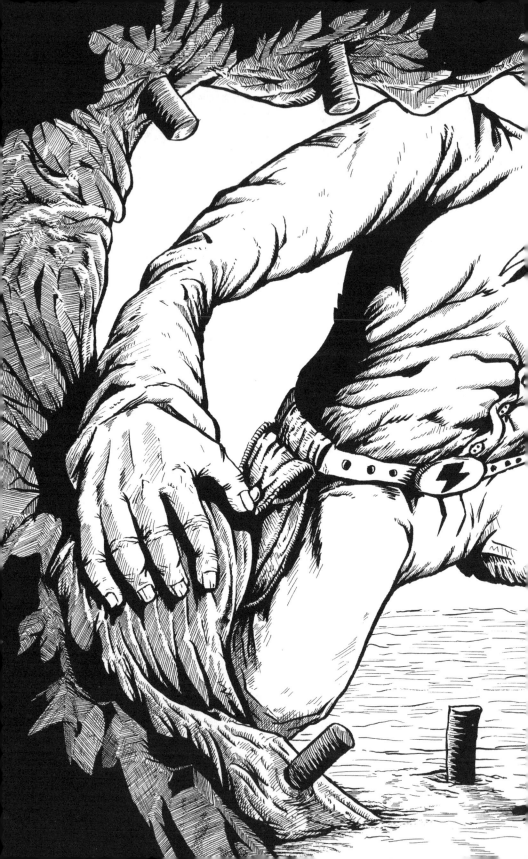

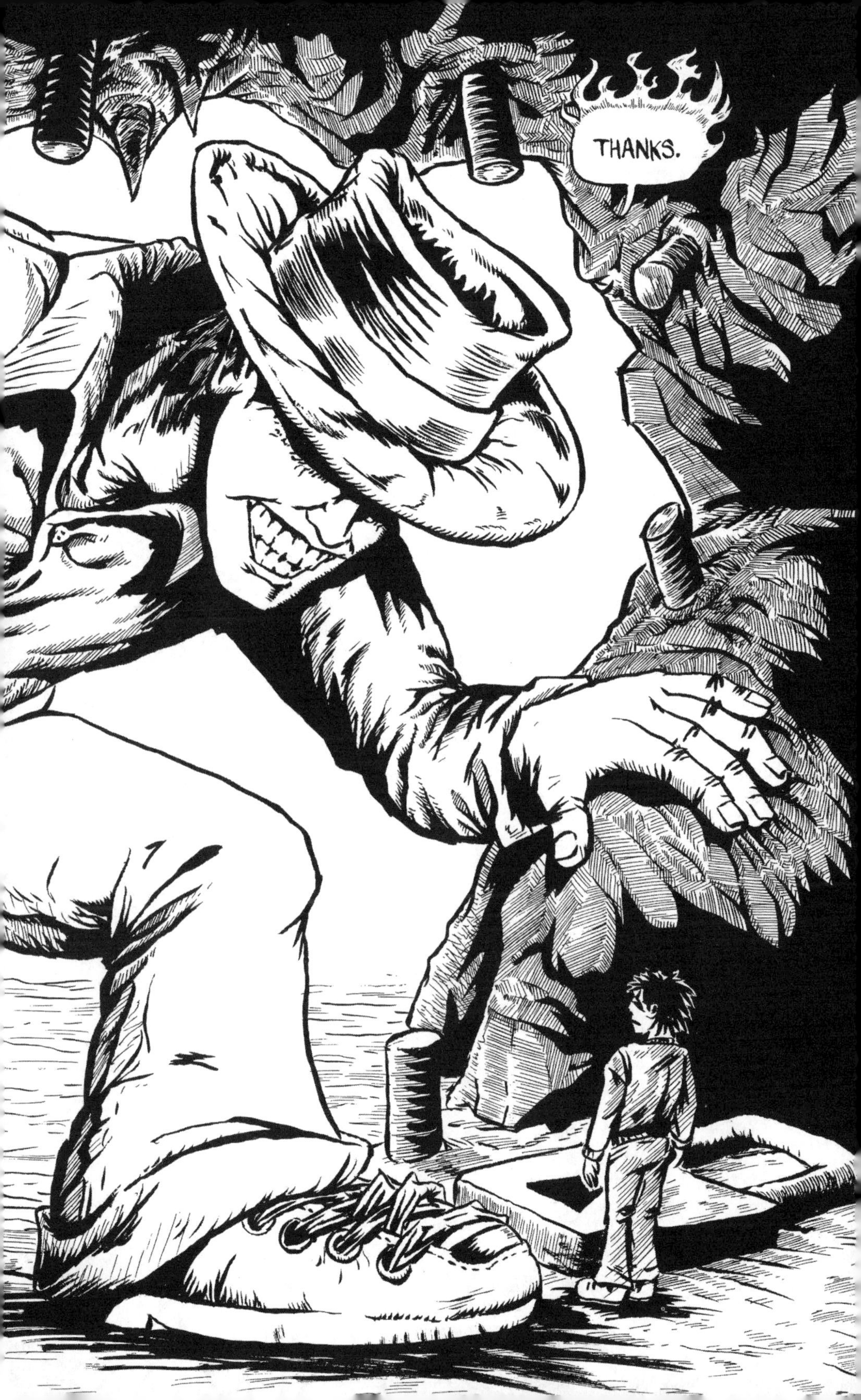
THANKS.

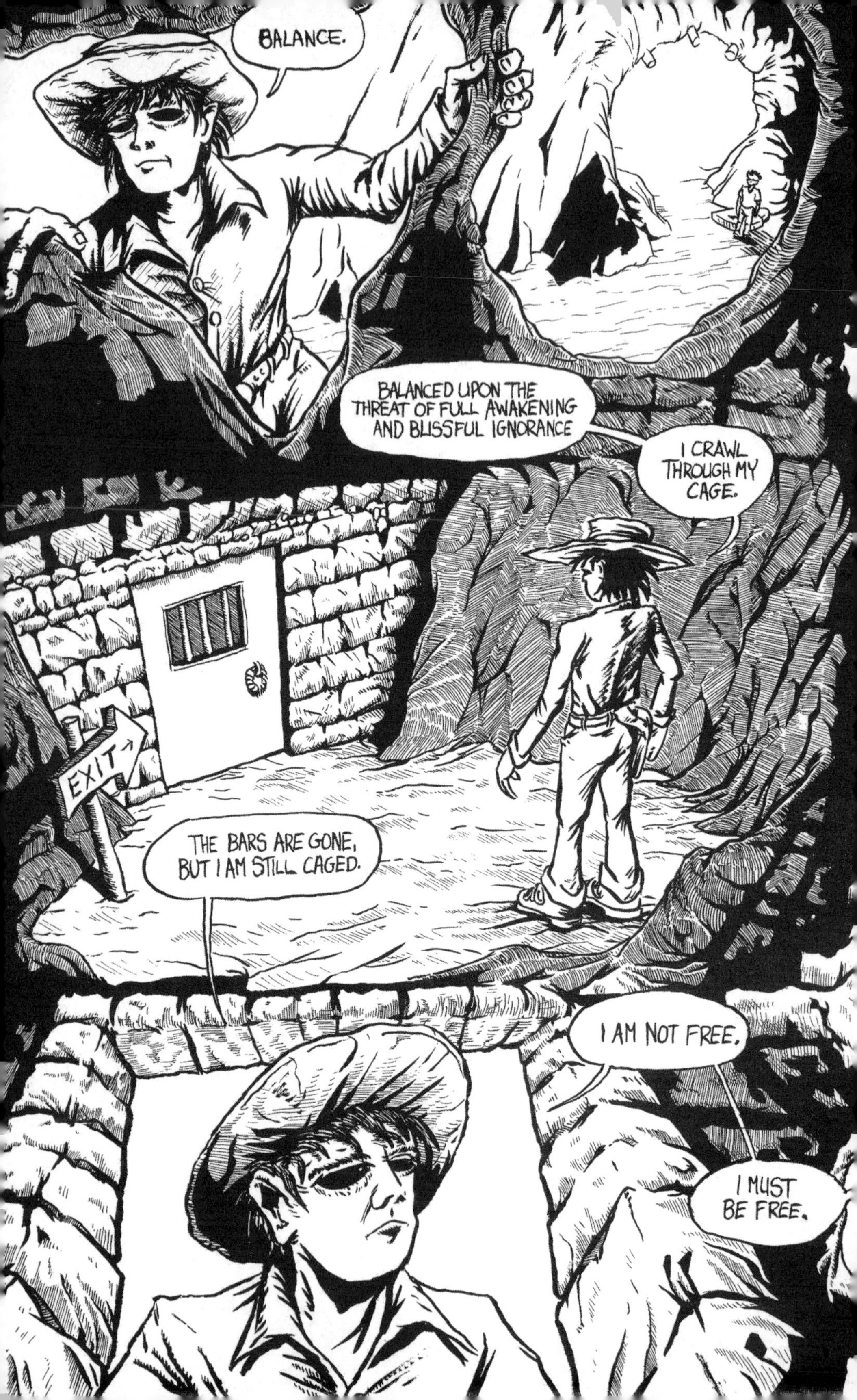
BALANCE.
BALANCED UPON THE THREAT OF FULL AWAKENING AND BLISSFUL IGNORANCE
I CRAWL THROUGH MY CAGE.
EXIT
THE BARS ARE GONE, BUT I AM STILL CAGED.
I AM NOT FREE.
I MUST BE FREE.

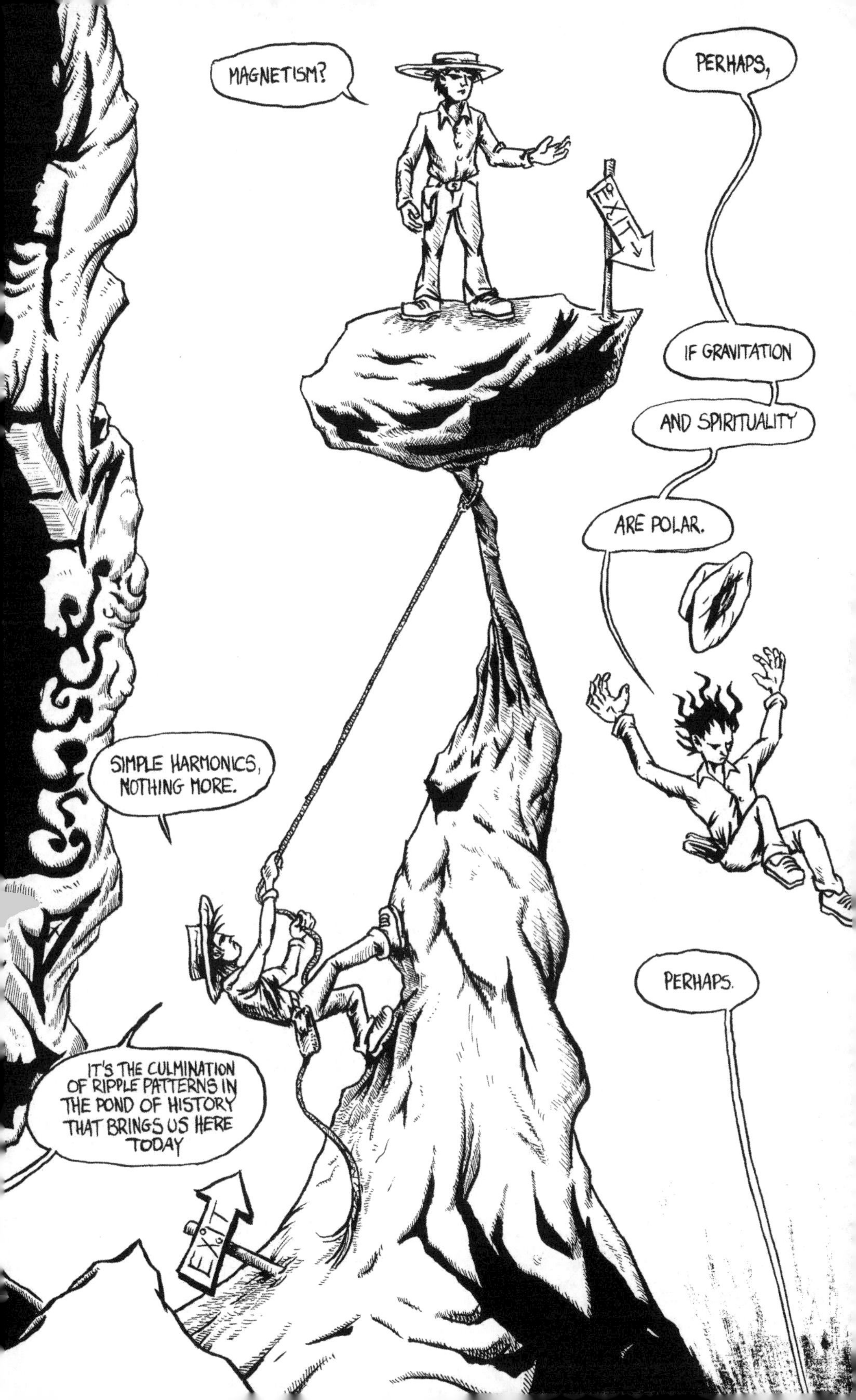
MAGNETISM?
PERHAPS,
IF GRAVITATION
AND SPIRITUALITY
ARE POLAR.
EXIT
SIMPLE HARMONICS, NOTHING MORE.
PERHAPS.
IT'S THE CULMINATION OF RIPPLE PATTERNS IN THE POND OF HISTORY THAT BRINGS US HERE TODAY
EXIT

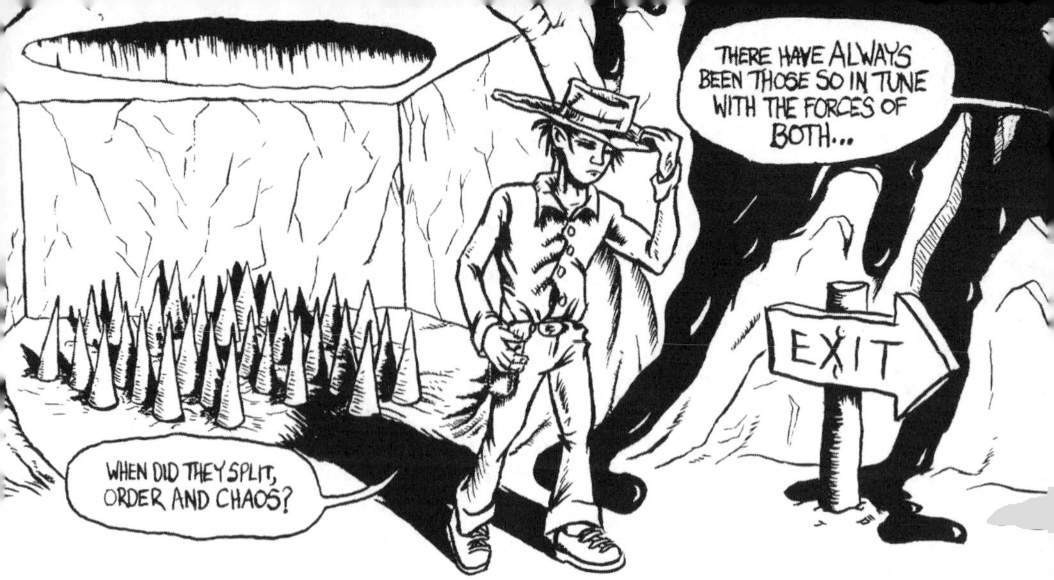
WHEN DID THEY SPLIT, ORDER AND CHAOS?
THERE HAVE ALWAYS BEEN THOSE SO IN TUNE WITH THE FORCES OF BOTH...
EXIT

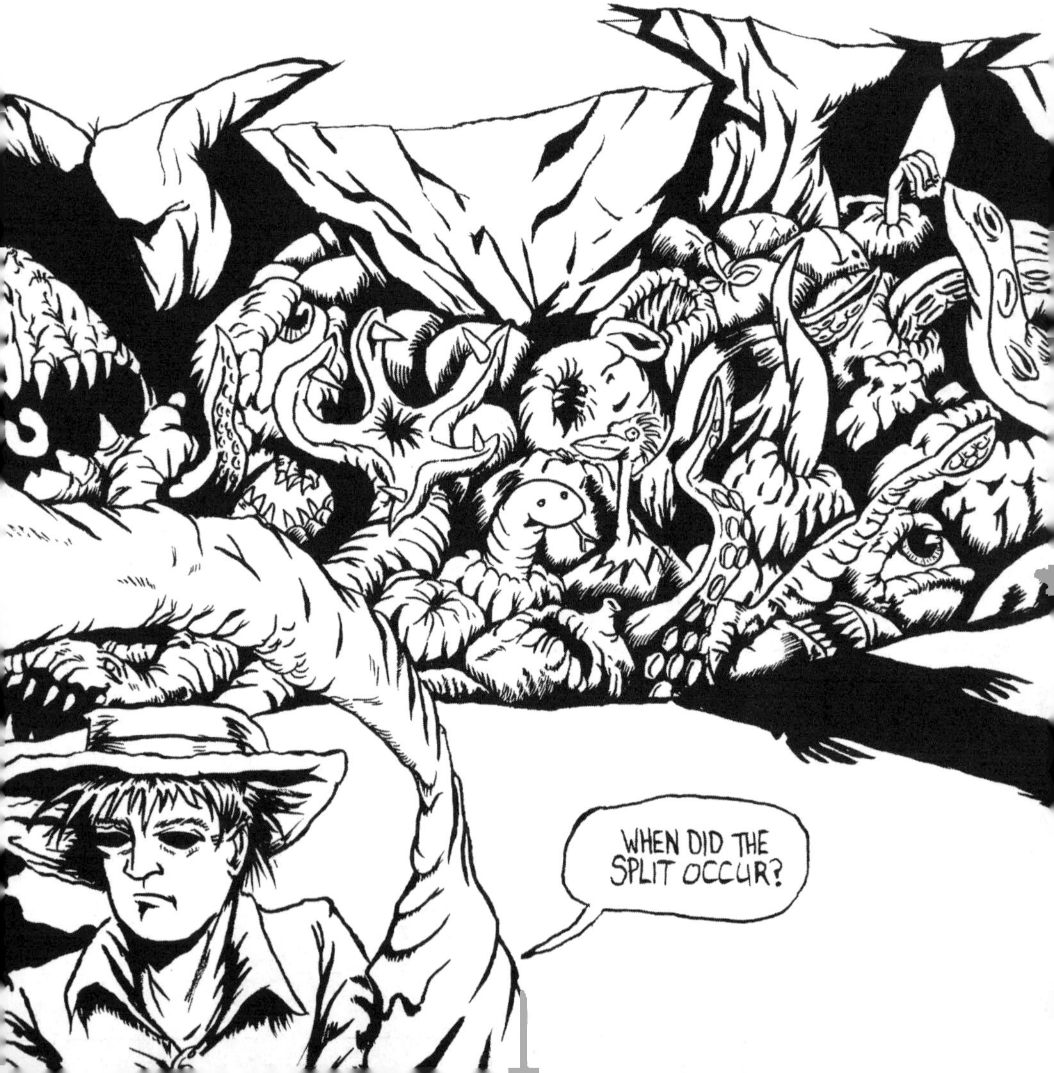
WHEN DID THE SPLIT OCCUR?

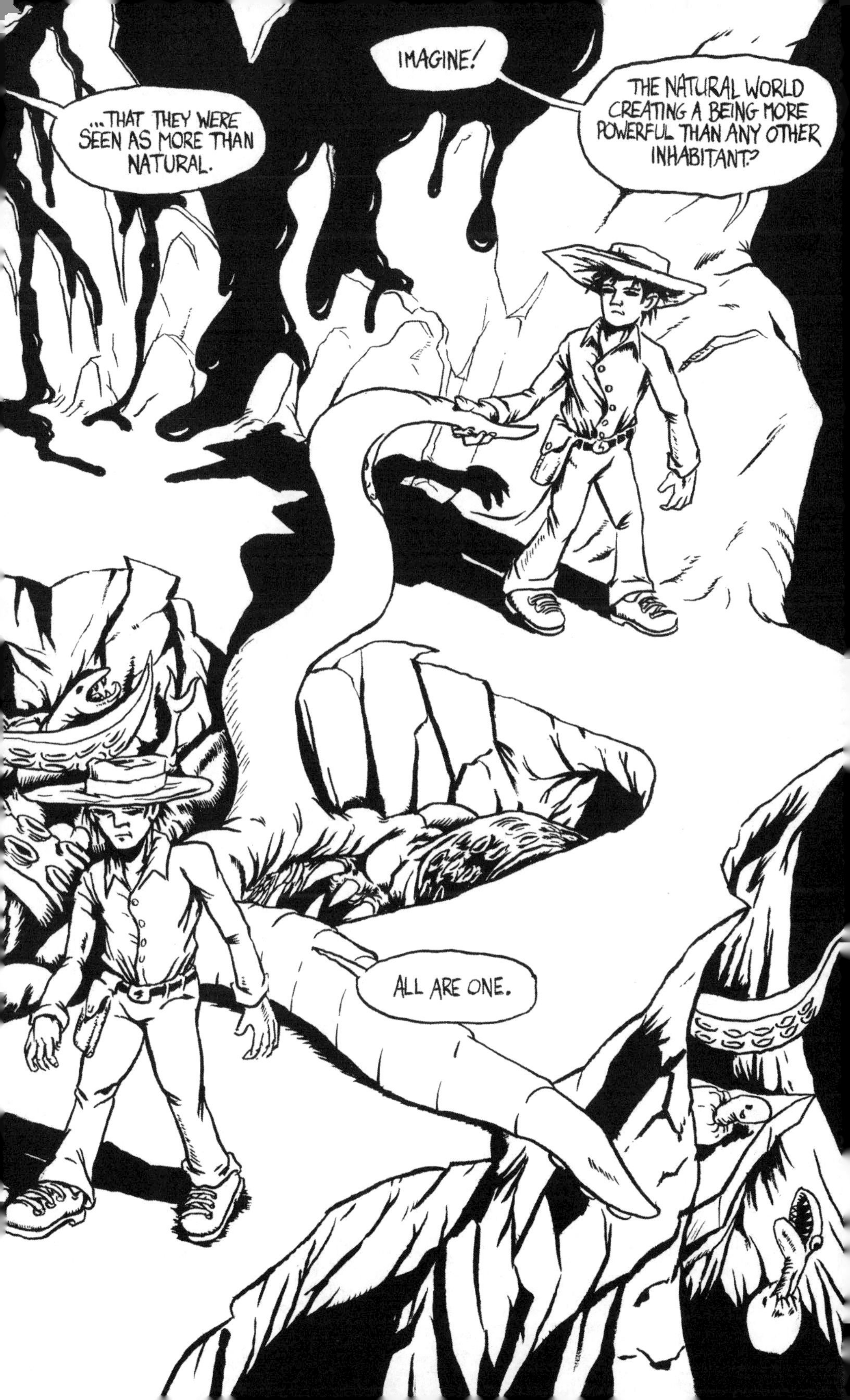
...THAT THEY WERE SEEN AS MORE THAN NATURAL.
IMAGINE!
THE NATURAL WORLD CREATING A BEING MORE POWERFUL THAN ANY OTHER INHABITANT?
ALL ARE ONE.

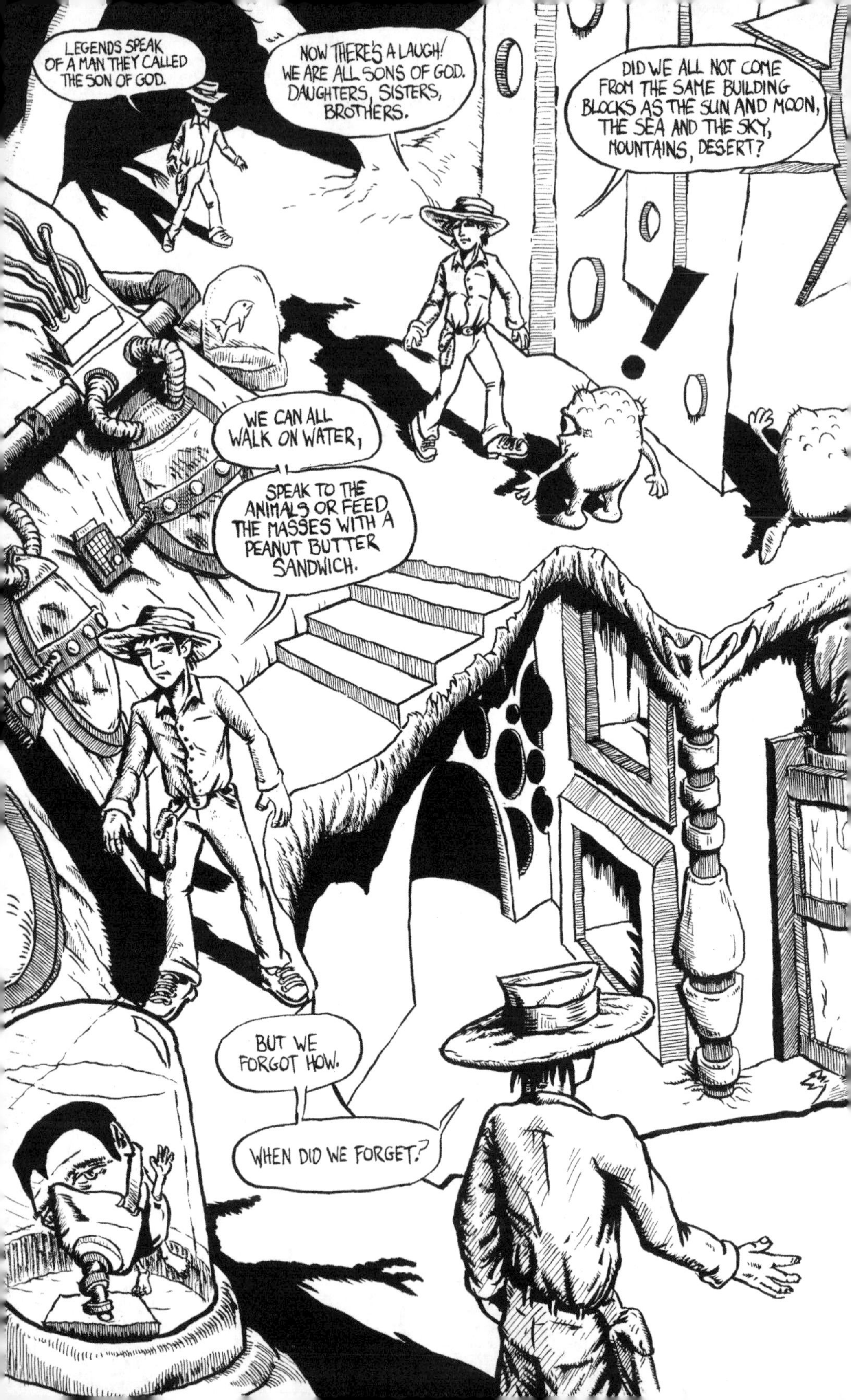
LEGENDS SPEAK OF A MAN THEY CALLED THE SON OF GOD.
NOW THERE'S A LAUGH! WE ARE ALL SONS OF GOD. DAUGHTERS, SISTERS, BROTHERS.
DID WE ALL NOT COME FROM THE SAME BUILDING BLOCKS AS THE SUN AND MOON, THE SEA AND THE SKY, MOUNTAINS, DESERT?
!
WE CAN ALL WALK ON WATER,
SPEAK TO THE ANIMALS OR FEED THE MASSES WITH A PEANUT BUTTER SANDWICH.
BUT WE FORGOT HOW.
WHEN DID WE FORGET?

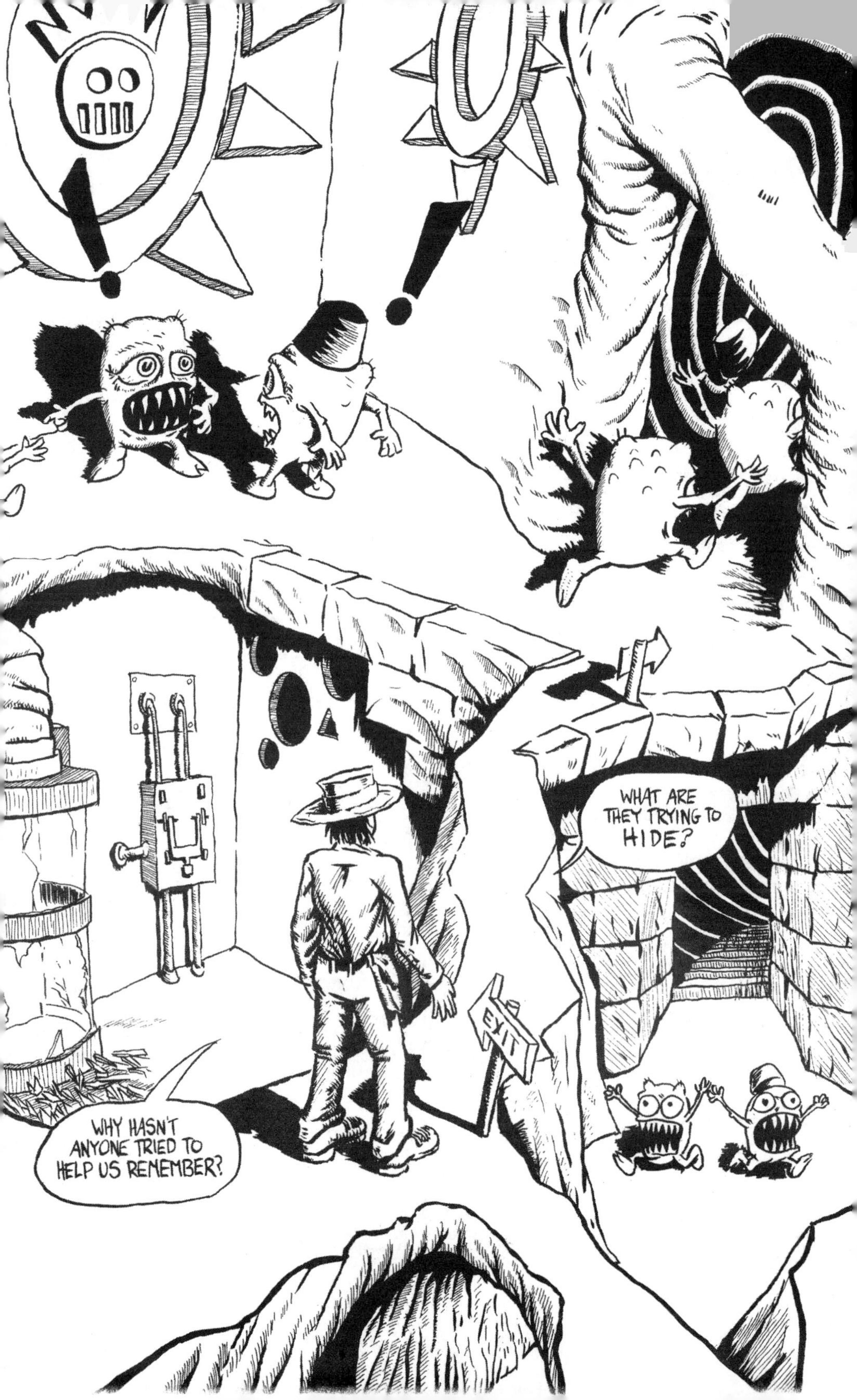

WHAT ARE THEY TRYING TO HIDE?
EXIT
WHY HASN'T ANYONE TRIED TO HELP US REMEMBER?

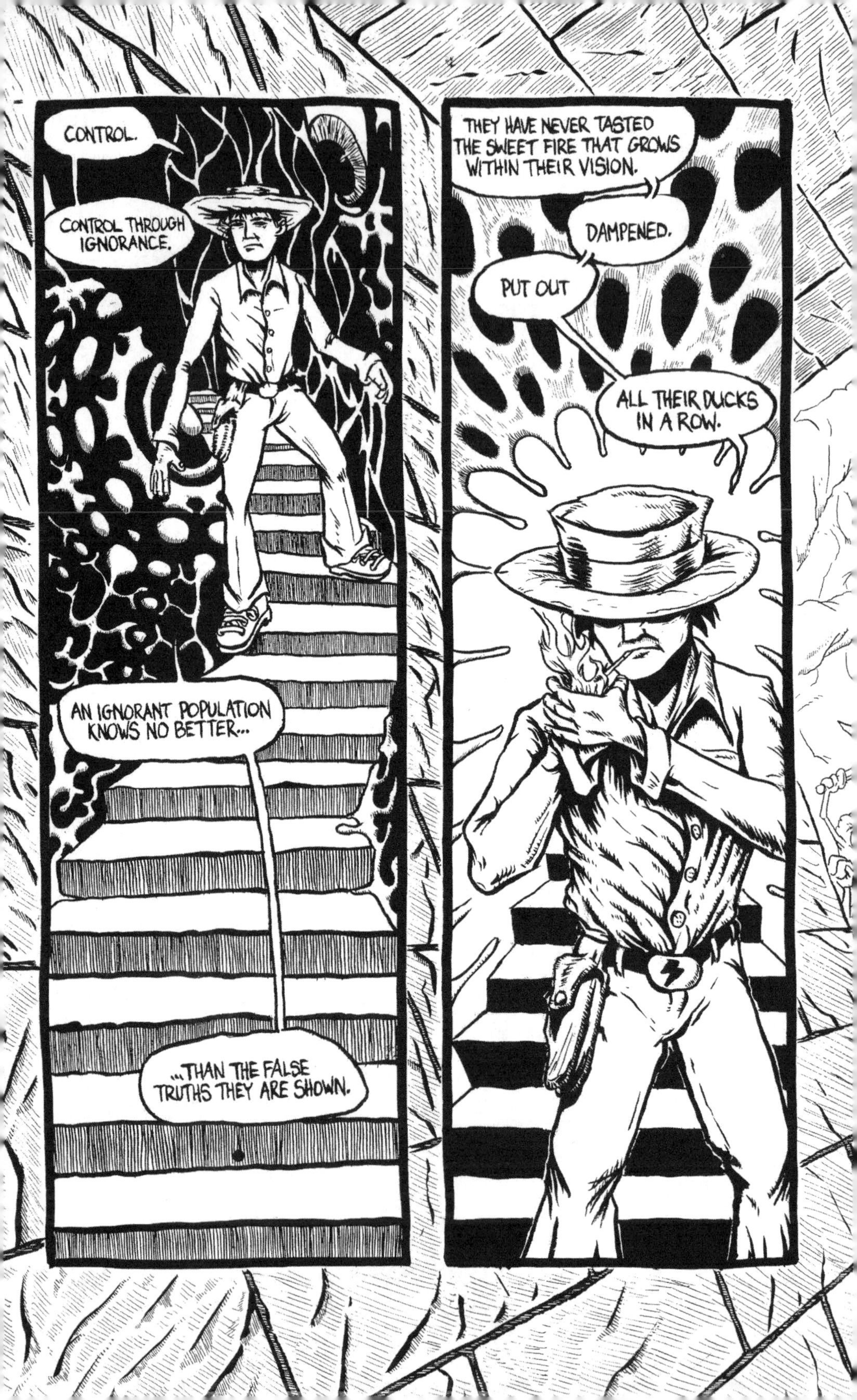
CONTROL.
CONTROL THROUGH IGNORANCE.
AN IGNORANT POPULATION KNOWS NO BETTER...
...THAN THE FALSE TRUTHS THEY ARE SHOWN.
THEY HAVE NEVER TASTED THE SWEET FIRE THAT GROWS WITHIN THEIR VISION.
DAMPENED.
PUT OUT
ALL THEIR DUCKS IN A ROW.

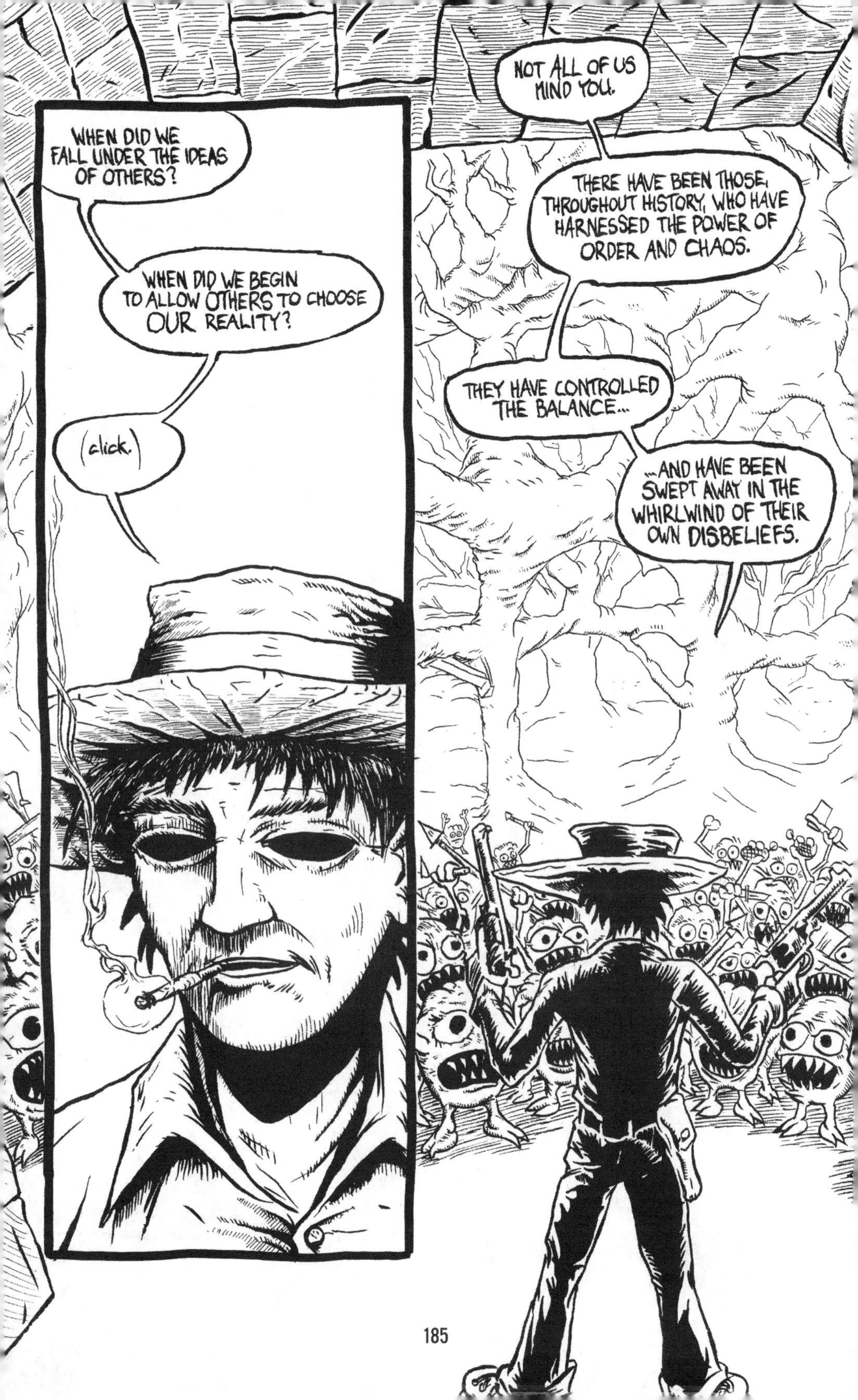
WHEN DID WE FALL UNDER THE IDEAS OF OTHERS?
WHEN DID WE BEGIN TO ALLOW OTHERS TO CHOOSE OUR REALITY?
(click.)
NOT ALL OF US MIND YOU.
THERE HAVE BEEN THOSE, THROUGHOUT HISTORY, WHO HAVE HARNESSED THE POWER OF ORDER AND CHAOS.
THEY HAVE CONTROLLED THE BALANCE...
...AND HAVE BEEN SWEPT AWAY IN THE WHIRLWIND OF THEIR OWN DISBELIEFS.

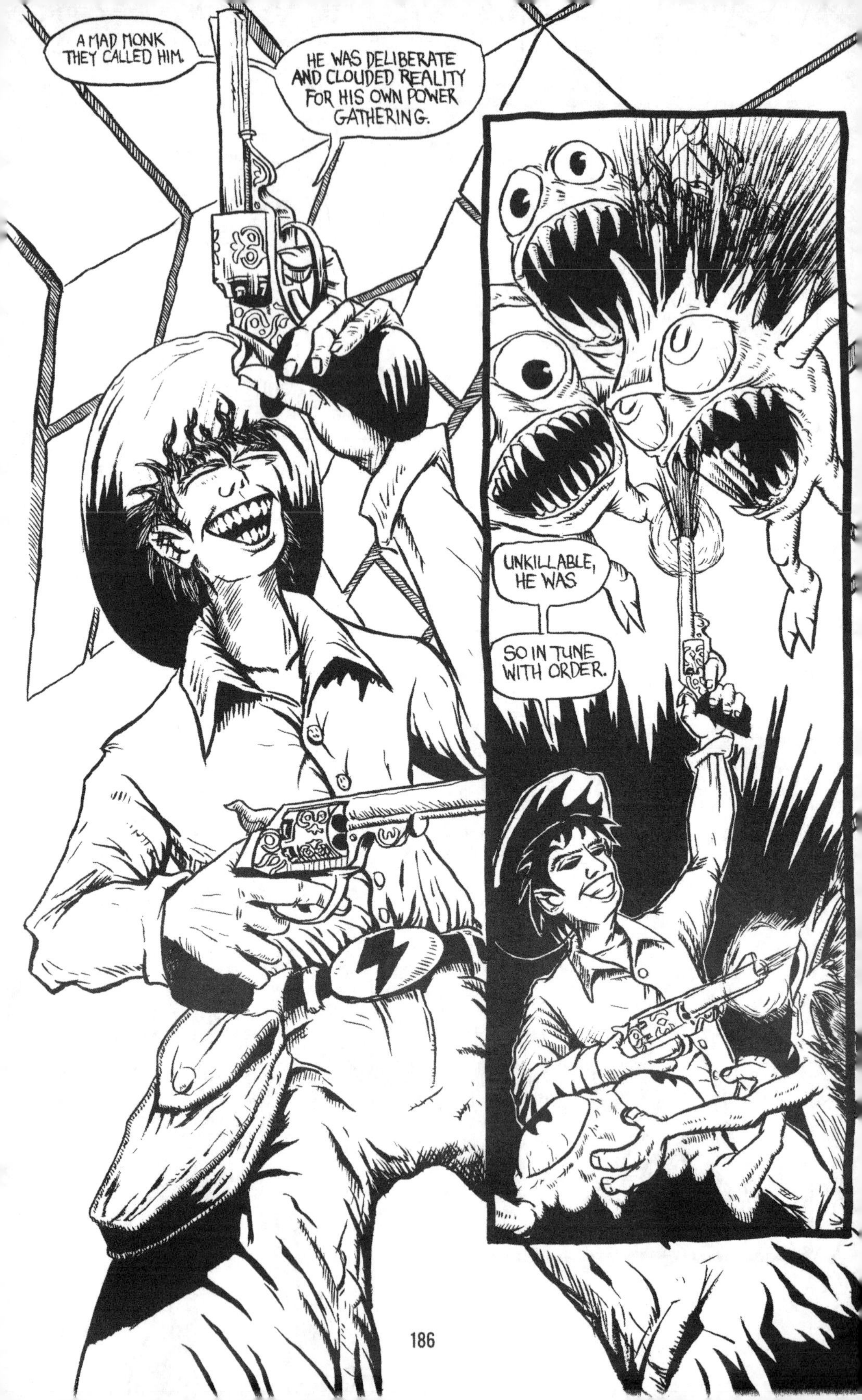
A MAD MONK THEY CALLED HIM.
HE WAS DELIBERATE AND CLOUDED REALITY FOR HIS OWN POWER GATHERING.
UNKILLABLE, HE WAS
SO IN TUNE WITH ORDER.

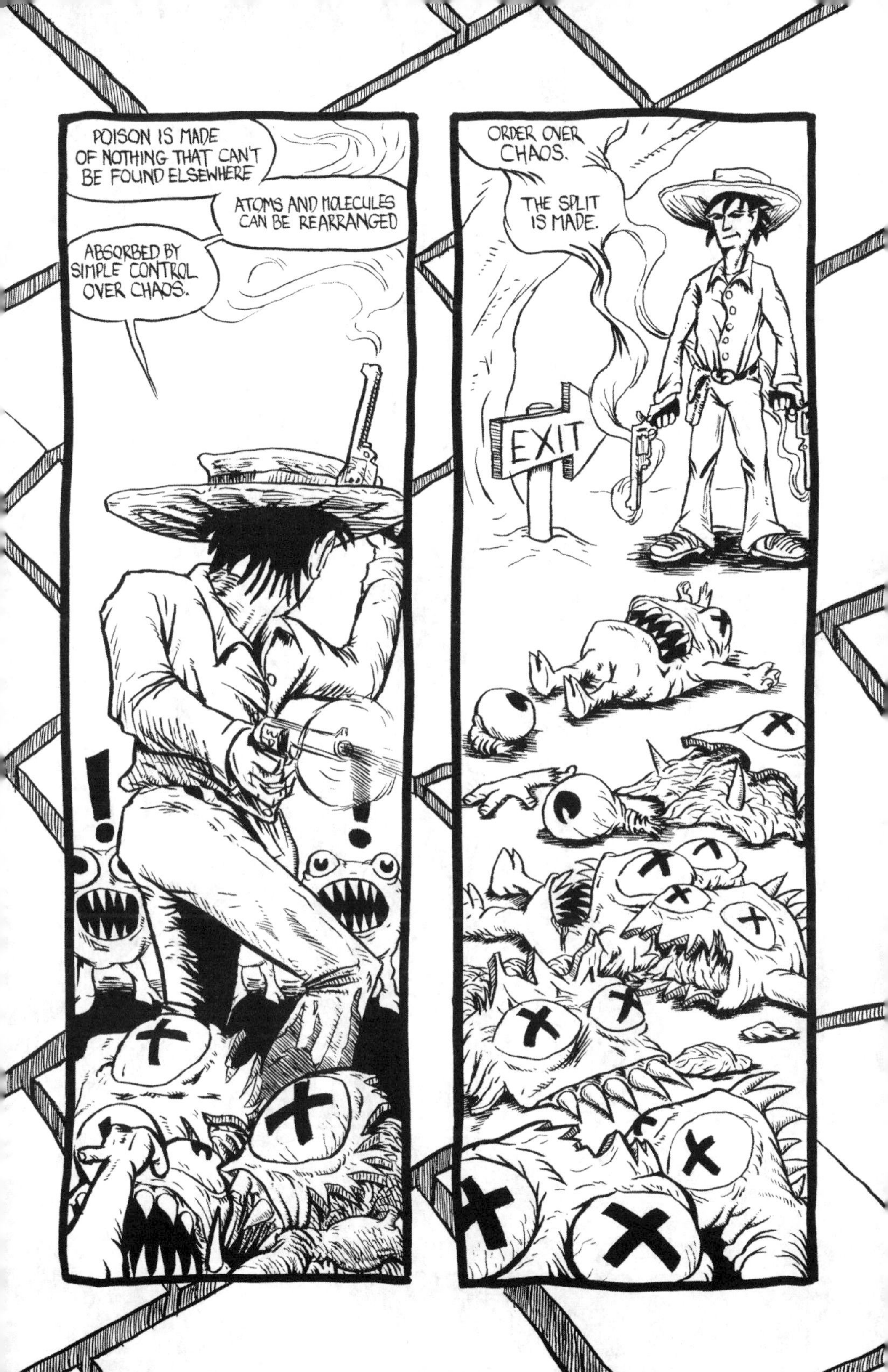
POISON IS MADE OF NOTHING THAT CAN'T BE FOUND ELSEWHERE
ATOMS AND MOLECULES CAN BE REARRANGED
ABSORBED BY SIMPLE CONTROL OVER CHAOS.
ORDER OVER CHAOS.
THE SPLIT IS MADE.
EXIT

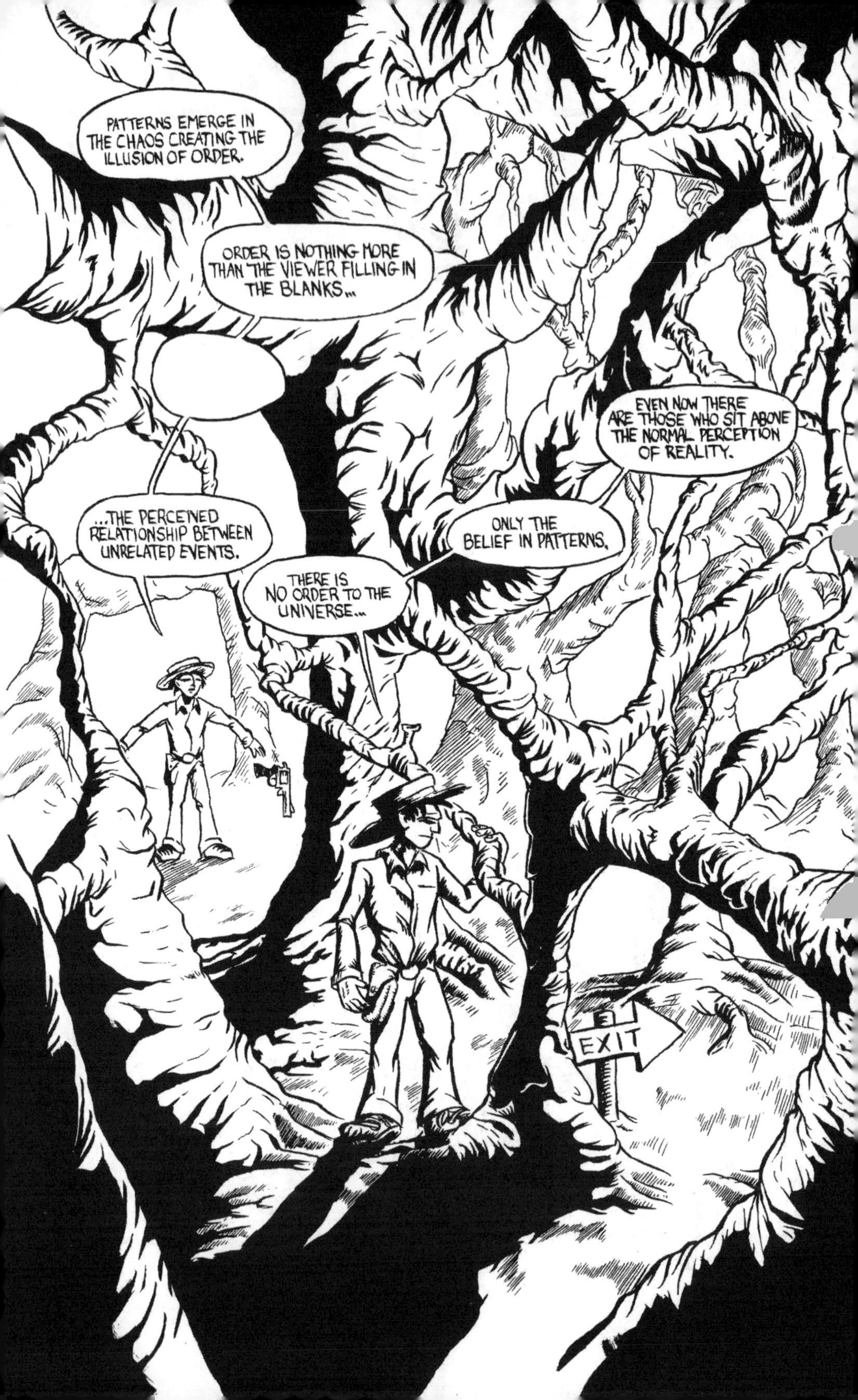
PATTERNS EMERGE IN THE CHAOS CREATING THE ILLUSION OF ORDER.
ORDER IS NOTHING MORE THAN THE VIEWER FILLING IN THE BLANKS...
...THE PERCEIVED RELATIONSHIP BETWEEN UNRELATED EVENTS.
THERE IS NO ORDER TO THE UNIVERSE...
ONLY THE BELIEF IN PATTERNS.
EVEN NOW THERE ARE THOSE WHO SIT ABOVE THE NORMAL PERCEPTION OF REALITY.
EXIT

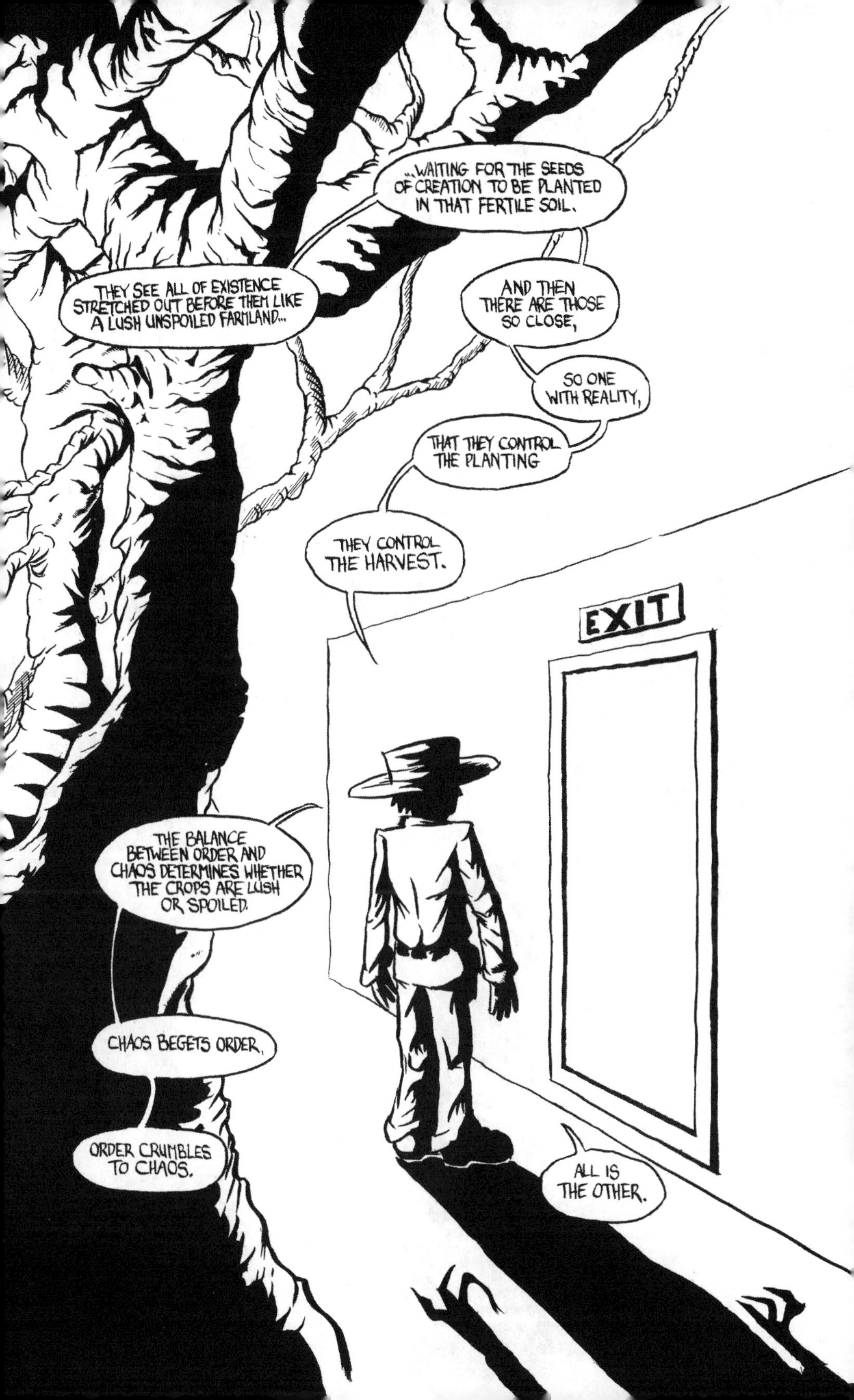
THEY SEE ALL OF EXISTENCE STRETCHED OUT BEFORE THEM LIKE A LUSH UNSPOILED FARMLAND...
...WAITING FOR THE SEEDS OF CREATION TO BE PLANTED IN THAT FERTILE SOIL.
AND THEN THERE ARE THOSE SO CLOSE,
SO ONE WITH REALITY,
THAT THEY CONTROL THE PLANTING
THEY CONTROL THE HARVEST.
EXIT
THE BALANCE BETWEEN ORDER AND CHAOS DETERMINES WHETHER THE CROPS ARE LUSH OR SPOILED.
CHAOS BEGETS ORDER,
ORDER CRUMBLES TO CHAOS.
ALL IS THE OTHER.

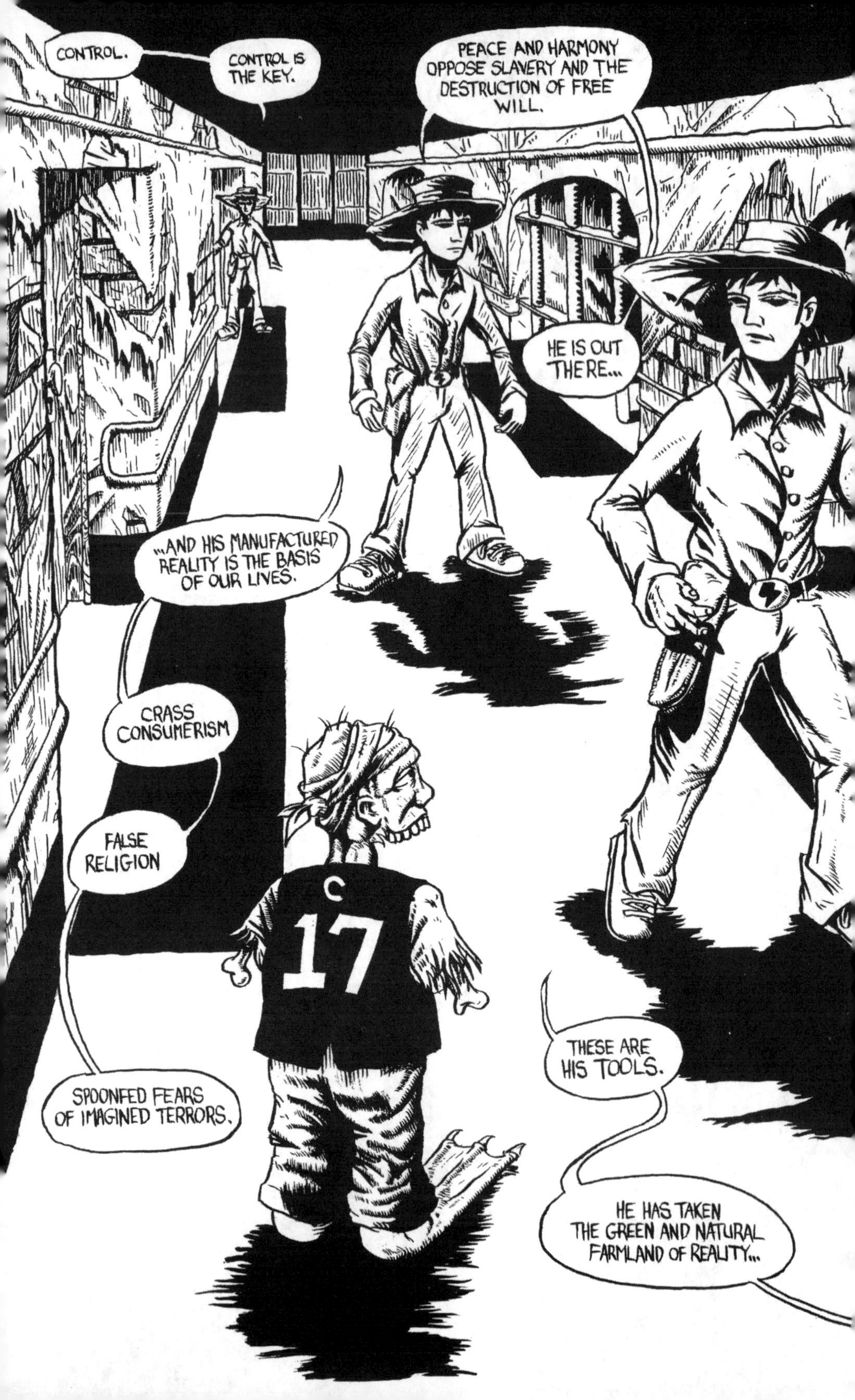
CONTROL.
CONTROL IS THE KEY.
PEACE AND HARMONY OPPOSE SLAVERY AND THE DESTRUCTION OF FREE WILL.
HE IS OUT THERE...
...AND HIS MANUFACTURED REALITY IS THE BASIS OF OUR LIVES.
CRASS CONSUMERISM
FALSE RELIGION
SPOONFED FEARS OF IMAGINED TERRORS.
THESE ARE HIS TOOLS.
HE HAS TAKEN THE GREEN AND NATURAL FARMLAND OF REALITY...
C
17

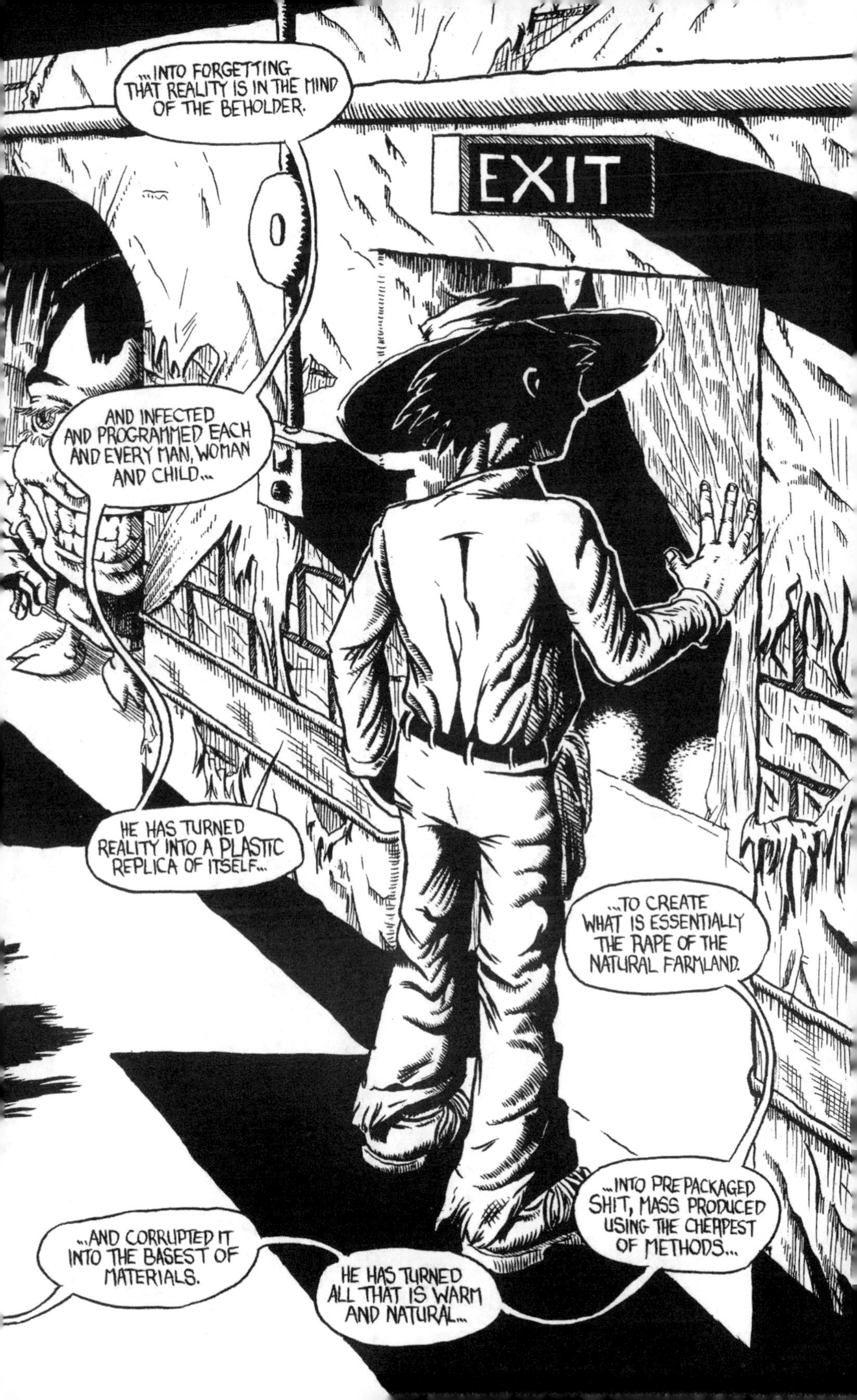
...INTO FORGETTING THAT REALITY IS IN THE MIND OF THE BEHOLDER.
EXIT
AND INFECTED AND PROGRAMMED EACH AND EVERY MAN, WOMAN AND CHILD...
HE HAS TURNED REALITY INTO A PLASTIC REPLICA OF ITSELF...
...TO CREATE WHAT IS ESSENTIALLY THE RAPE OF THE NATURAL FARMLAND.
...AND CORRUPTED IT INTO THE BASEST OF MATERIALS.
HE HAS TURNED ALL THAT IS WARM AND NATURAL...
...INTO PREPACKAGED SHIT, MASS PRODUCED USING THE CHEAPEST OF METHODS...

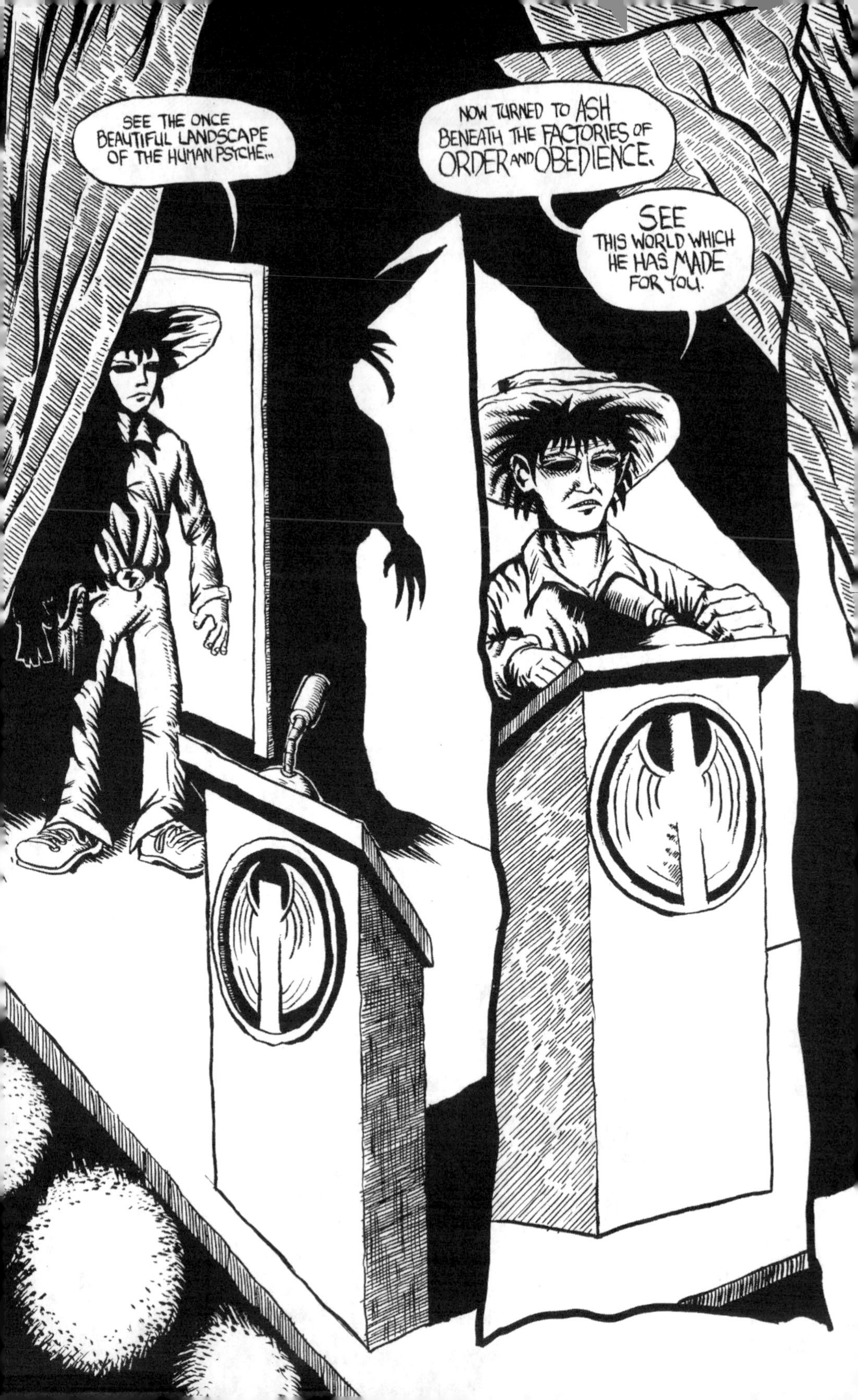
SEE THE ONCE BEAUTIFUL LANDSCAPE OF THE HUMAN PSYCHE...
NOW TURNED TO ASH BENEATH THE FACTORIES OF ORDER AND OBEDIENCE.
SEE THIS WORLD WHICH HE HAS MADE FOR YOU.

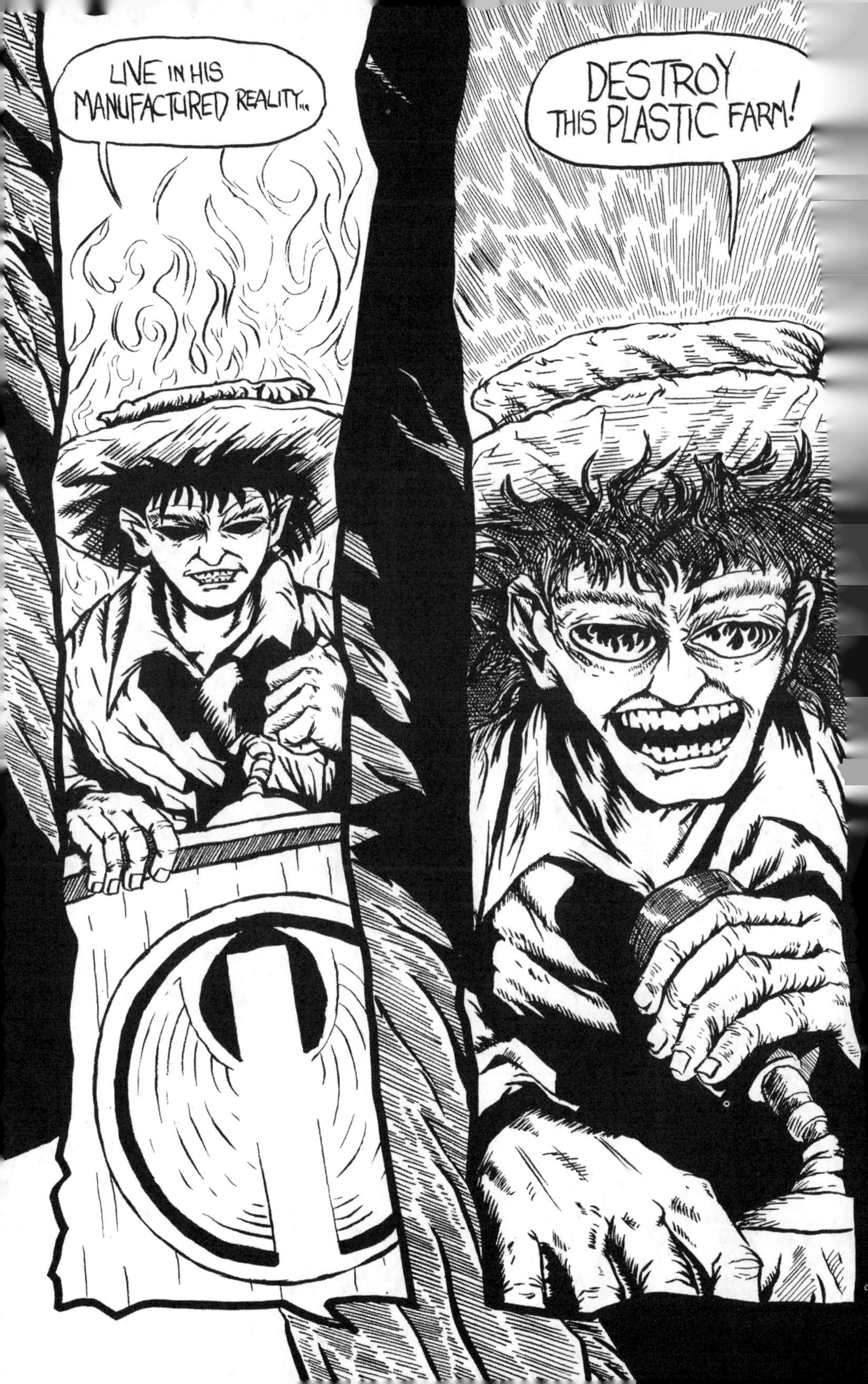
LIVE IN HIS MANUFACTURED REALITY...
DESTROY THIS PLASTIC FARM!

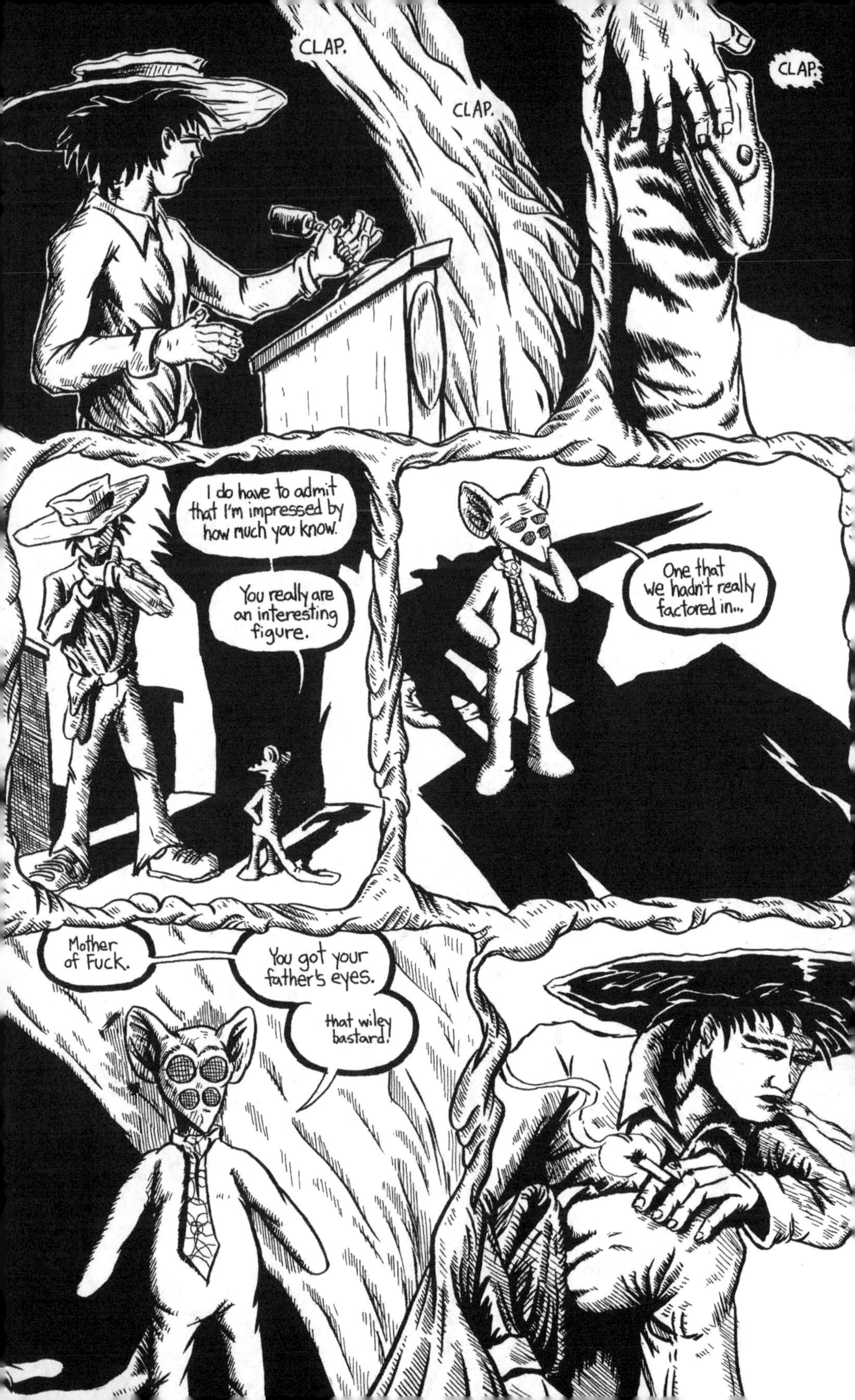
CLAP.
CLAP.
CLAP.
I do have to admit that I'm impressed by how much you know.
You really are an interesting figure.
One that we hadn't really factored in...
Mother of Fuck.
You got your father's eyes.
that wiley bastard!

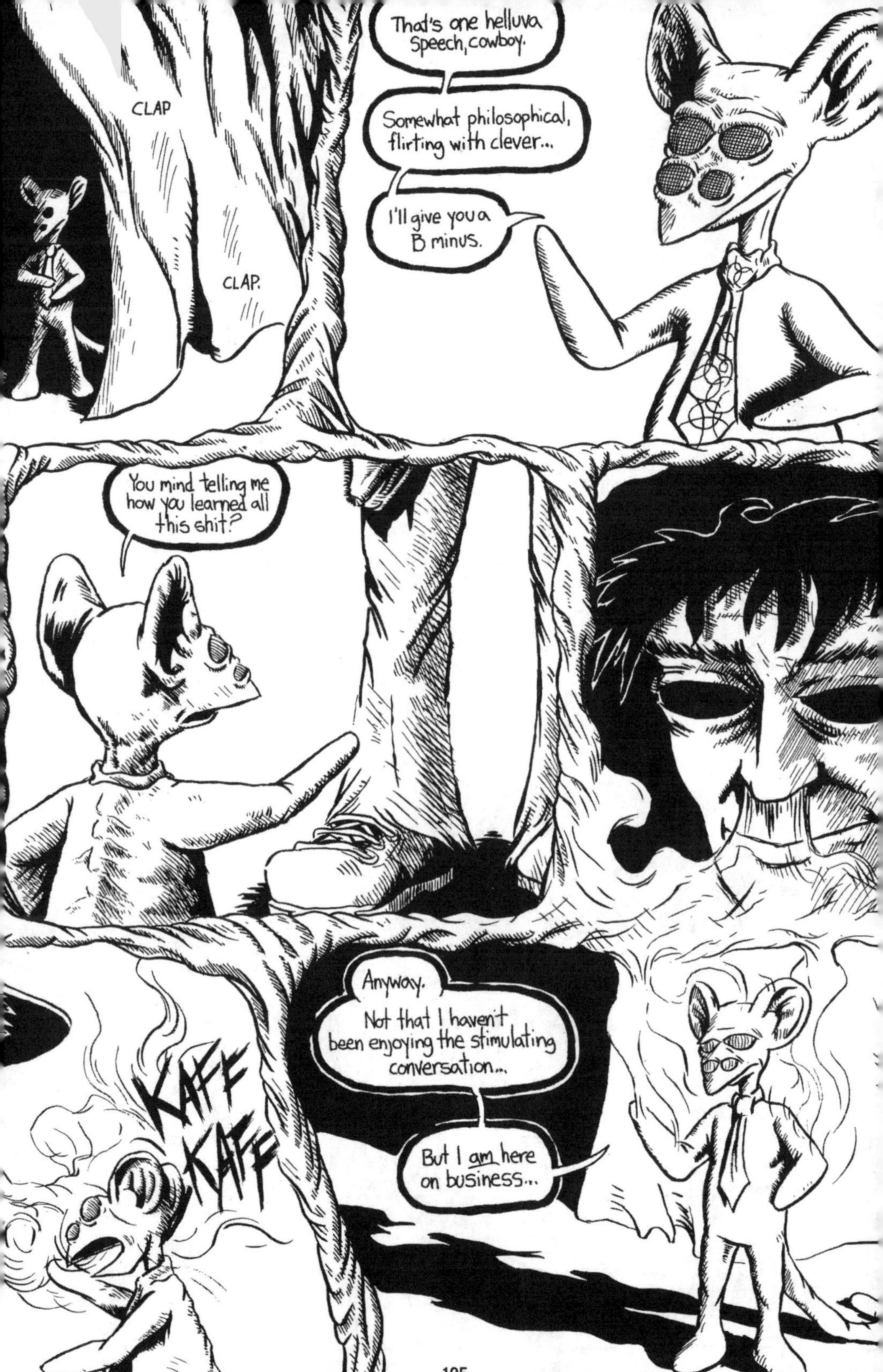
CLAP
CLAP.
That's one helluva speech, cowboy.
Somewhat philosophical, flirting with clever...
I'll give you a B minus.
You mind telling me how you learned all this shit?
KAFF KAFF
Anyway.
Not that I haven't been enjoying the stimulating conversation...
But I am here on business...

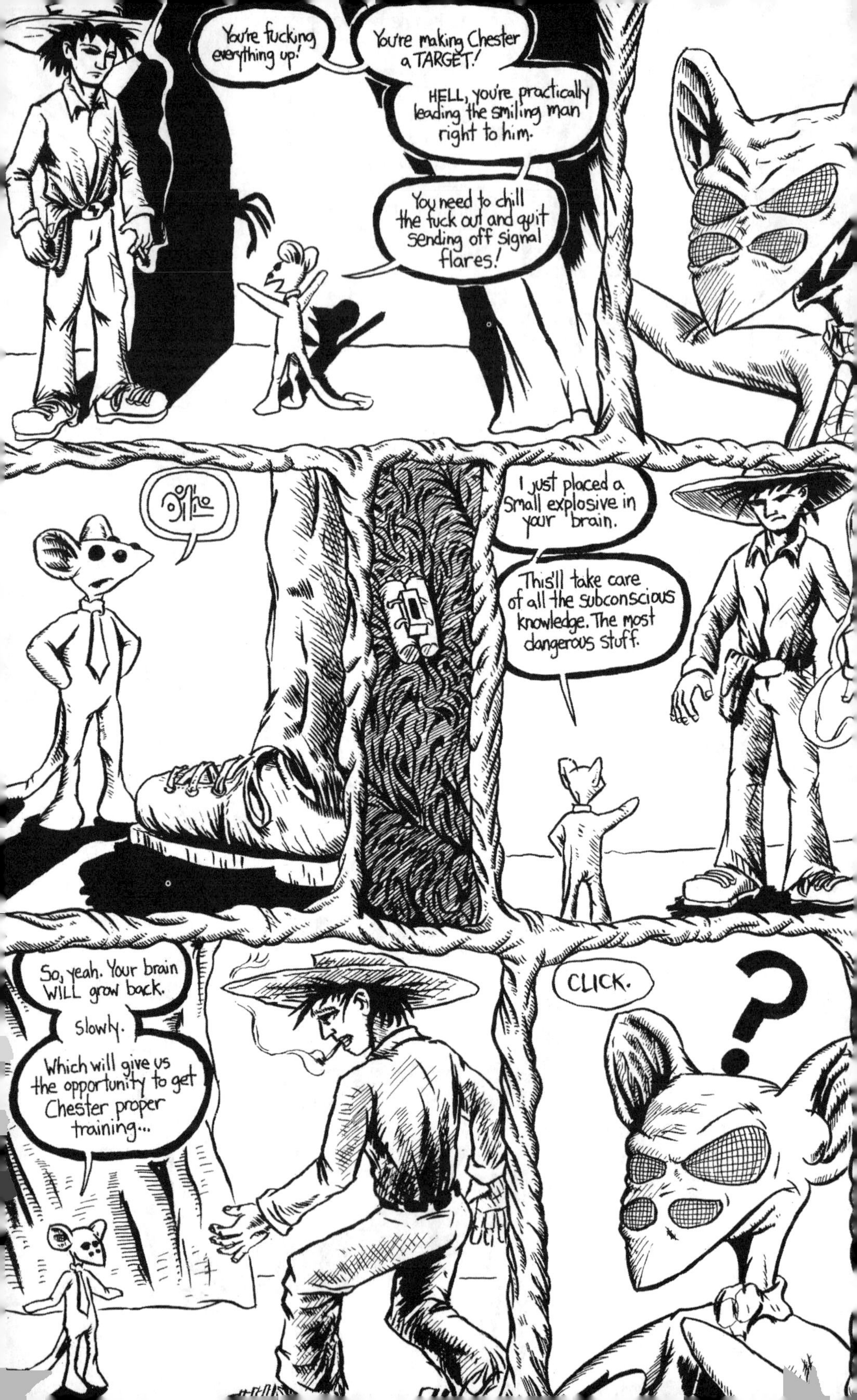
You're fucking everything up!
You're making Chester a TARGET!
HELL, you're practically leading the smiling man right to him.
You need to chill the fuck out and quit sending off signal flares!
I just placed a small explosive in your brain.
This'll take care of all the subconscious knowledge. The most dangerous stuff.
So, yeah. Your brain WILL grow back.
Slowly.
Which will give us the opportunity to get Chester proper training...
CLICK.
?

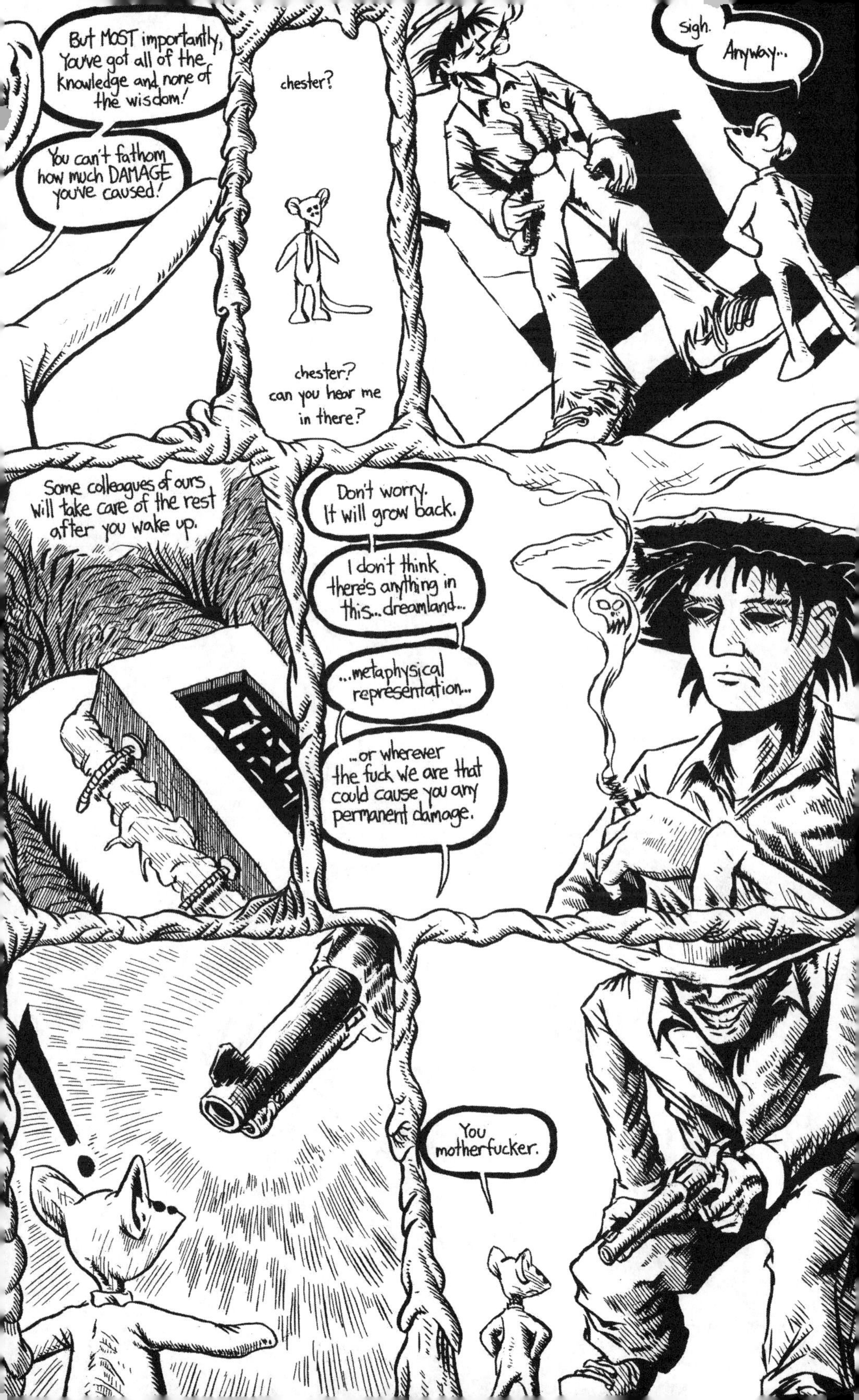

But MOST importantly, You've got all of the knowledge and none of the wisdom!
You can't fathom how much DAMAGE you've caused!
chester?
chester? can you hear me in there?
sigh. Anyway...
Some colleagues of ours will take care of the rest after you wake up.
Don't worry. It will grow back.
I don't think there's anything in this...dreamland...
...metaphysical representation...
...or wherever the fuck we are that could cause you any permanent damage.
You motherfucker.

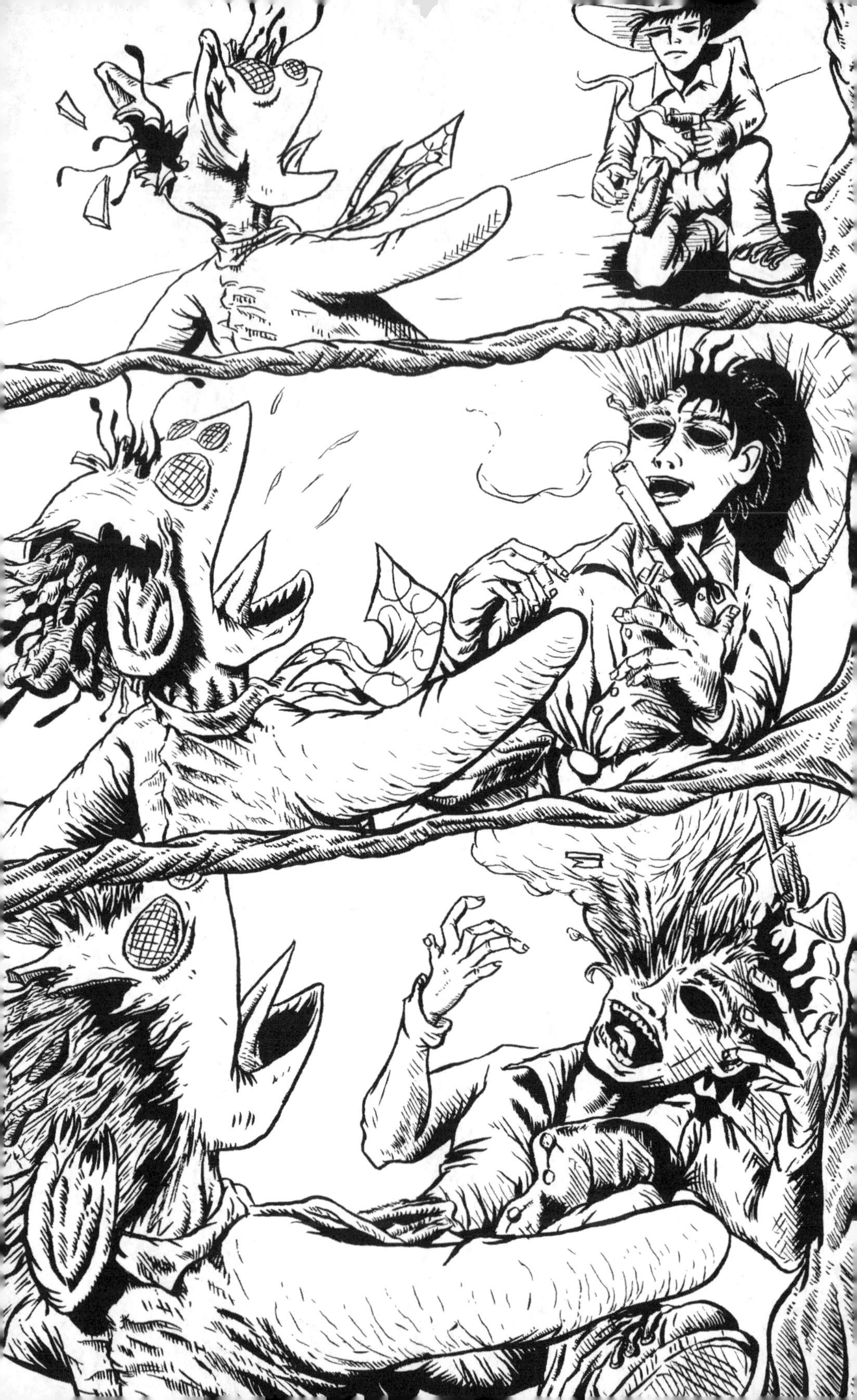

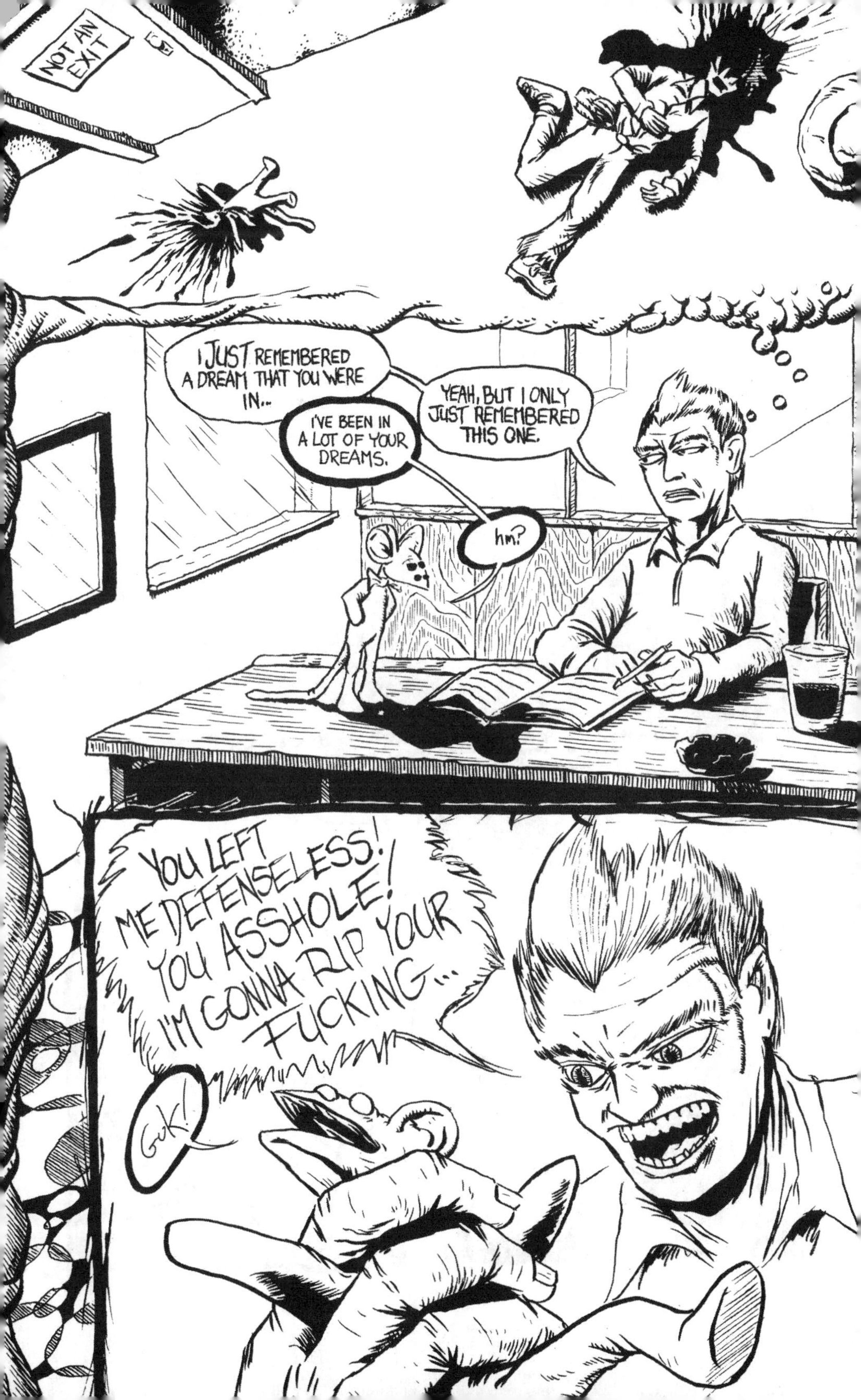
NOT AN EXIT
I JUST REMEMBERED A DREAM THAT YOU WERE IN...
I'VE BEEN IN A LOT OF YOUR DREAMS.
YEAH, BUT I ONLY JUST REMEMBERED THIS ONE.
hm?
YOU LEFT ME DEFENSELESS! YOU ASSHOLE! I'M GONNA RIP YOUR FUCKING...
GUK!

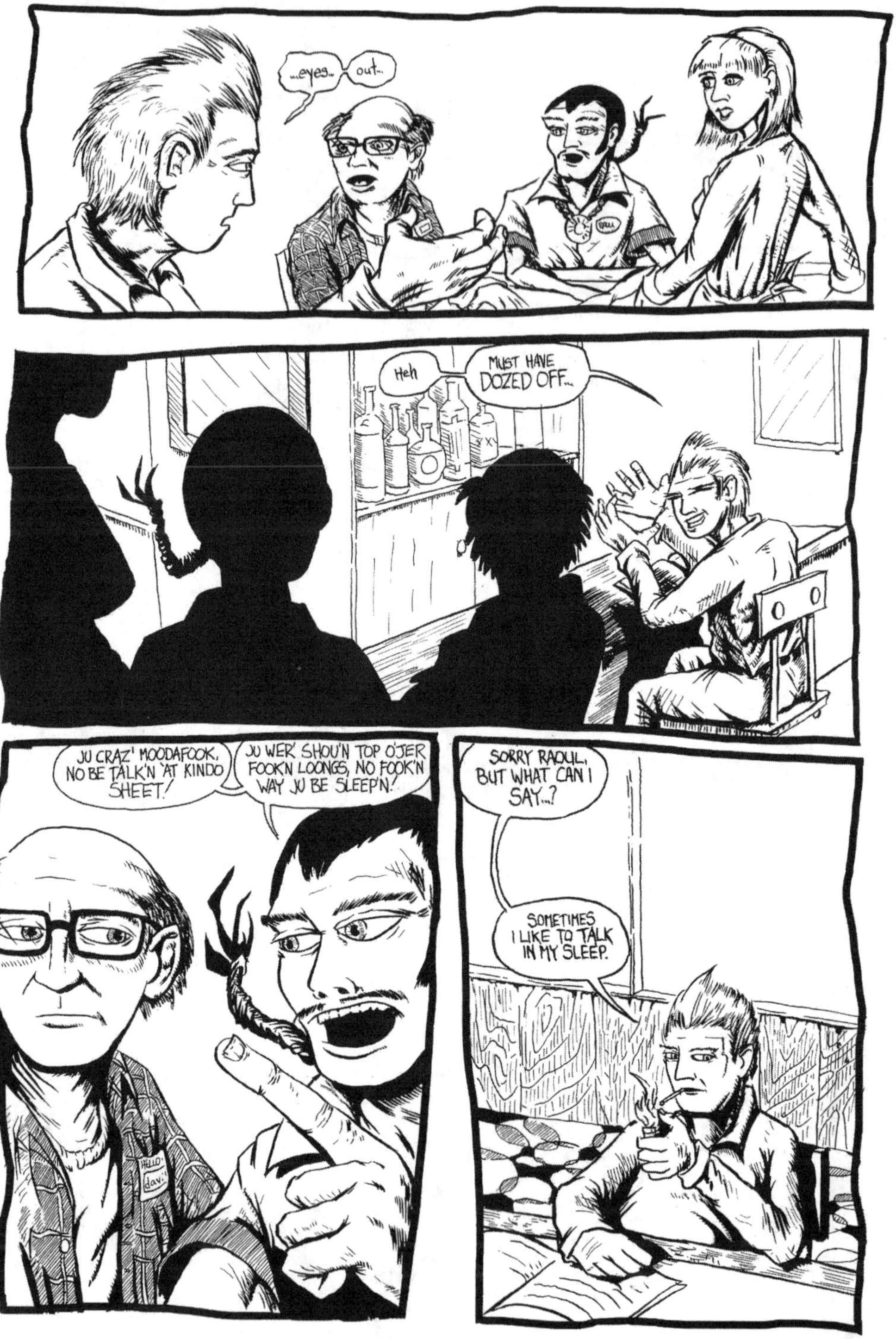
...eyes...
out...
Heh
MUST HAVE DOZED OFF...
JU CRAZ' MOODAFOOK, NO BE TALK'N 'AT KINDO SHEET!
JU WER' SHOU'N TOP O'JER FOOK'N LOONGS, NO FOOK'N WAY JU BE SLEEP'N!
SORRY RAOUL, BUT WHAT CAN I SAY...?
SOMETIMES I LIKE TO TALK IN MY SLEEP.

PLASTIC FARM — CHAPTER TEN

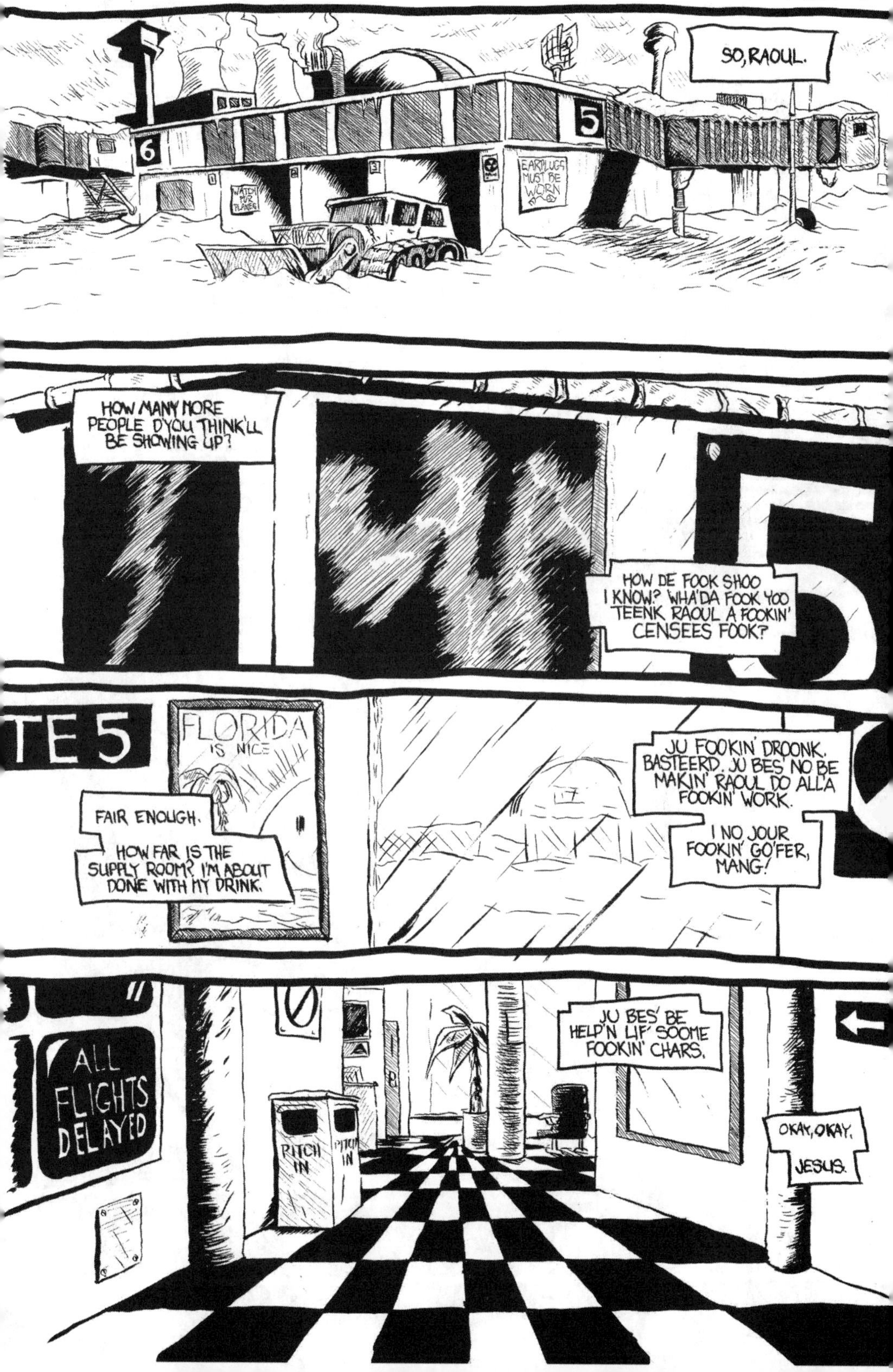

6
5
EARPLUGS MUST BE WORN
SO, RAOUL.
HOW MANY MORE PEOPLE D'YOU THINK'LL BE SHOWING UP?
HOW DE FOOK SHOO I KNOW? WHA'DA FOOK YOO TEENK RAOUL A FOOKIN' CENSEES FOOK?
TE 5
FLORIDA IS NICE
FAIR ENOUGH.
HOW FAR IS THE SUPPLY ROOM? I'M ABOUT DONE WITH MY DRINK.
JU FOOKIN' DROONK. BASTEERD. JU BES' NO BE MAKIN' RAOUL DO ALL'A FOOKIN' WORK.
I NO JOUR FOOKIN' GO'FER, MANG!
ALL FLIGHTS DELAYED
PITCH IN
PITCH IN
JU BES' BE HELP'N LIF' SOOME FOOKIN' CHARS.
OKAY, OKAY.
JESUS.

CHESTER AND RAOUL GO FOR CHAIRS

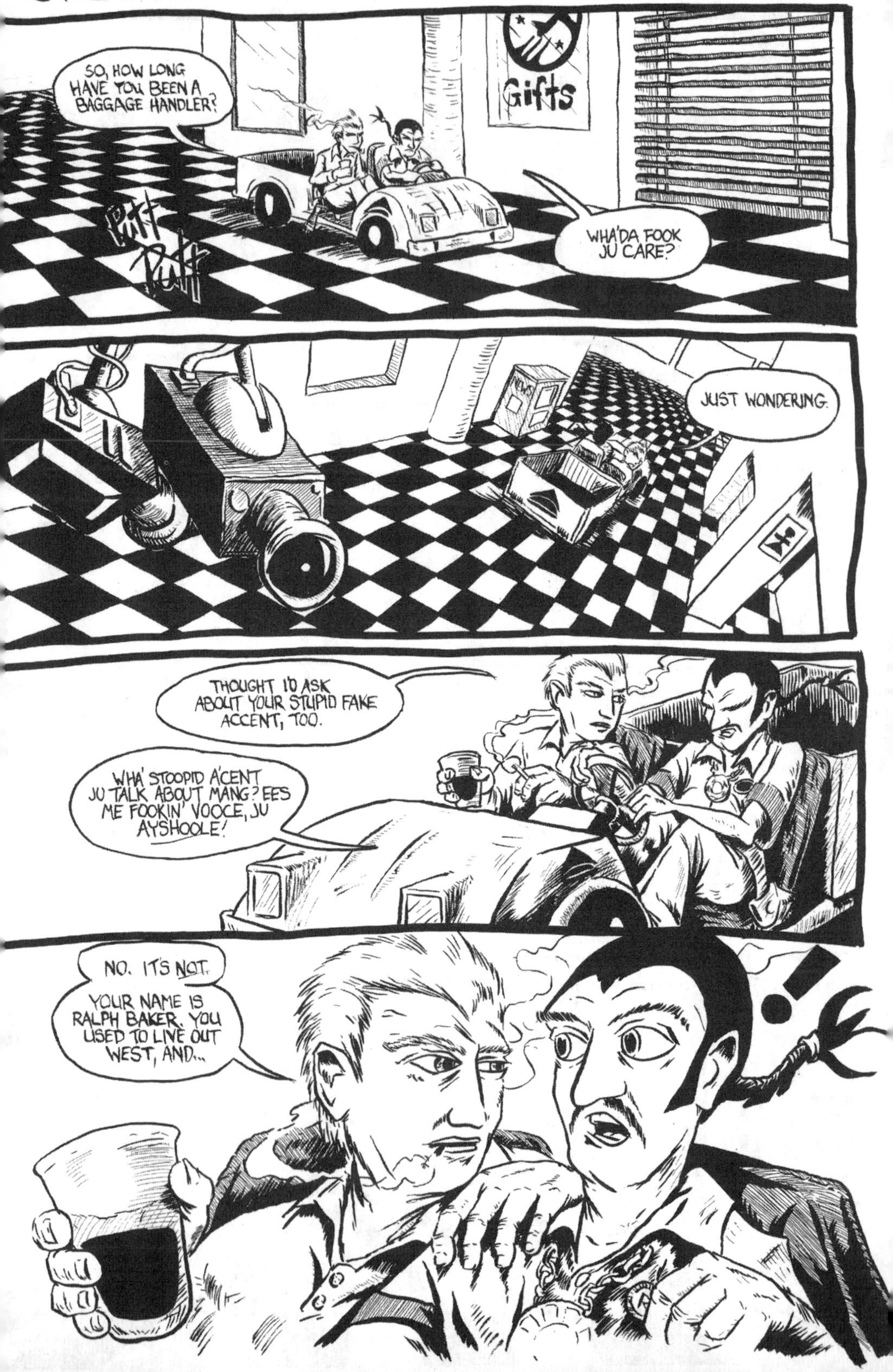
SO, HOW LONG HAVE YOU BEEN A BAGGAGE HANDLER?
Gifts
PUTT PUTT
WHA'DA FOOK JU CARE?
JUST WONDERING.
THOUGHT I'D ASK ABOUT YOUR STUPID FAKE ACCENT, TOO.
WHA' STOOPID A'CENT JU TALK ABOUT MANG? EES ME FOOKIN' VOOCE, JU AYSHOOLE!
NO. IT'S NOT.
YOUR NAME IS RALPH BAKER. YOU USED TO LIVE OUT WEST, AND...

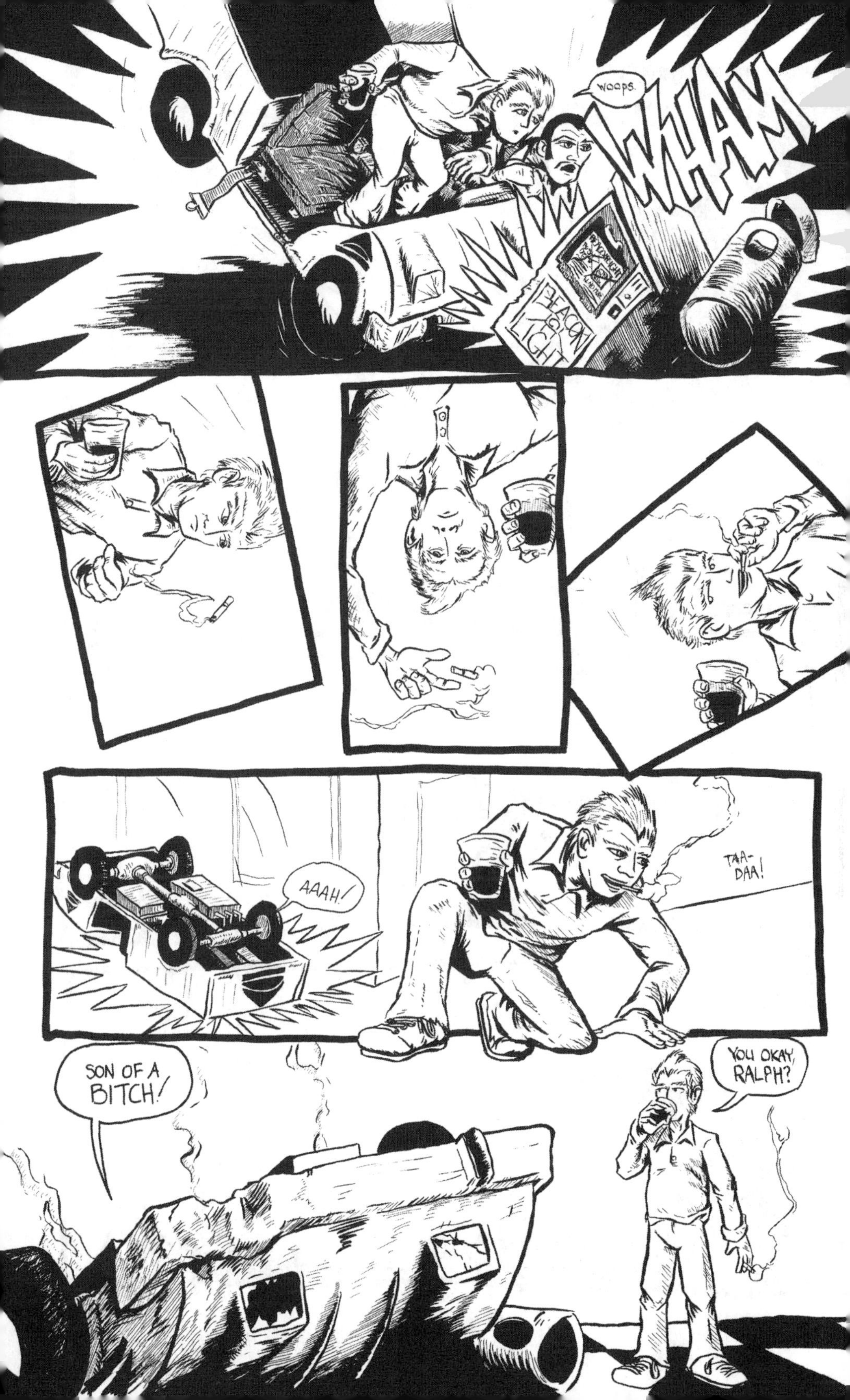
WOOPS.
WHAM
AAAH!
TAA-DAA!
SON OF A BITCH!
YOU OKAY, RALPH?

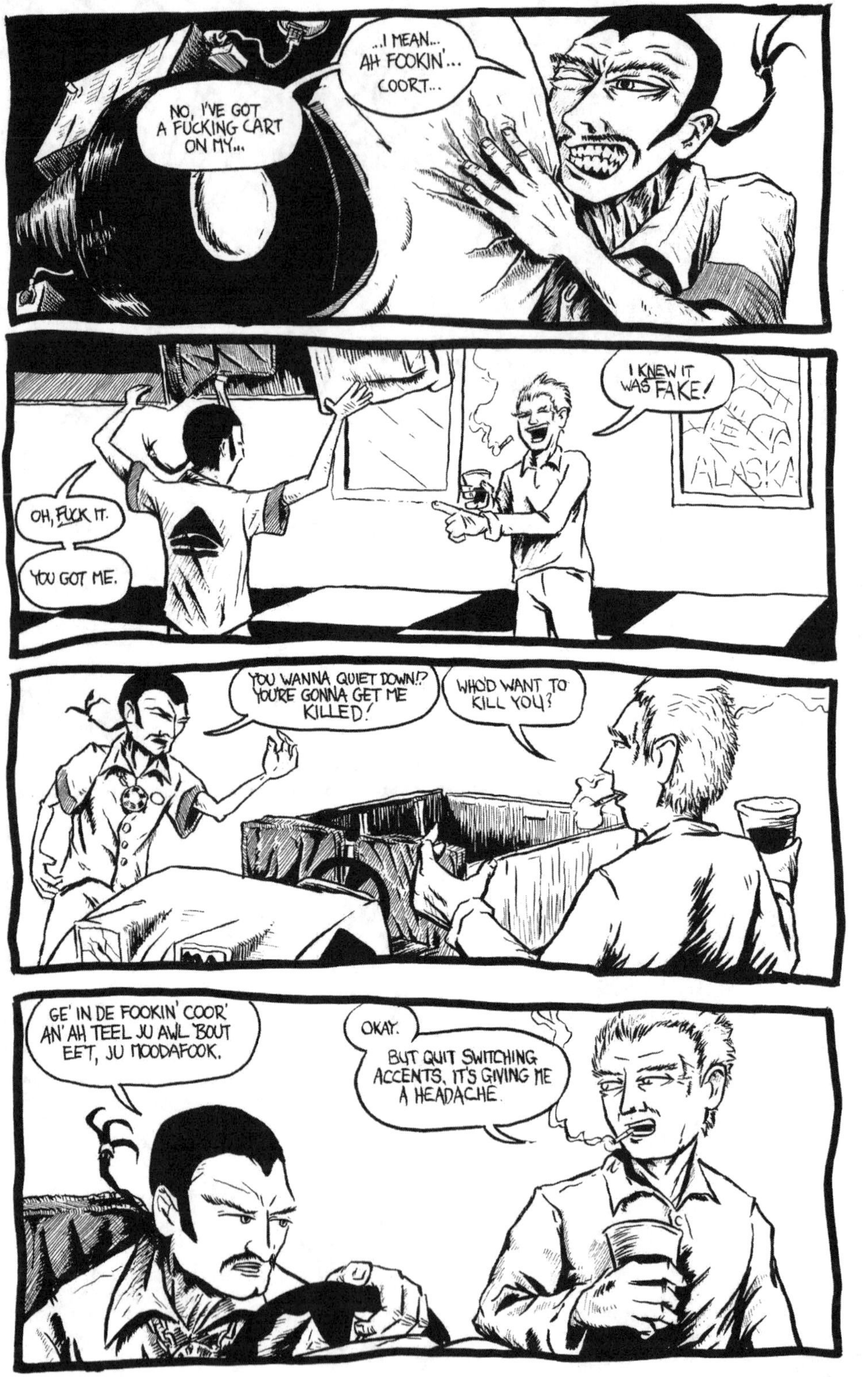
NO, I'VE GOT A FUCKING CART ON MY...
...I MEAN... AH FOOKIN'... COORT...
I KNEW IT WAS FAKE!
ALASKA
OH, FUCK IT.
YOU GOT ME.
YOU WANNA QUIET DOWN!? YOU'RE GONNA GET ME KILLED!
WHO'D WANT TO KILL YOU?
GE' IN DE FOOKIN' COOR' AN' AH TEEL JU AWL 'BOUT EET, JU MOODAFOOK.
OKAY.
BUT QUIT SWITCHING ACCENTS, IT'S GIVING ME A HEADACHE.

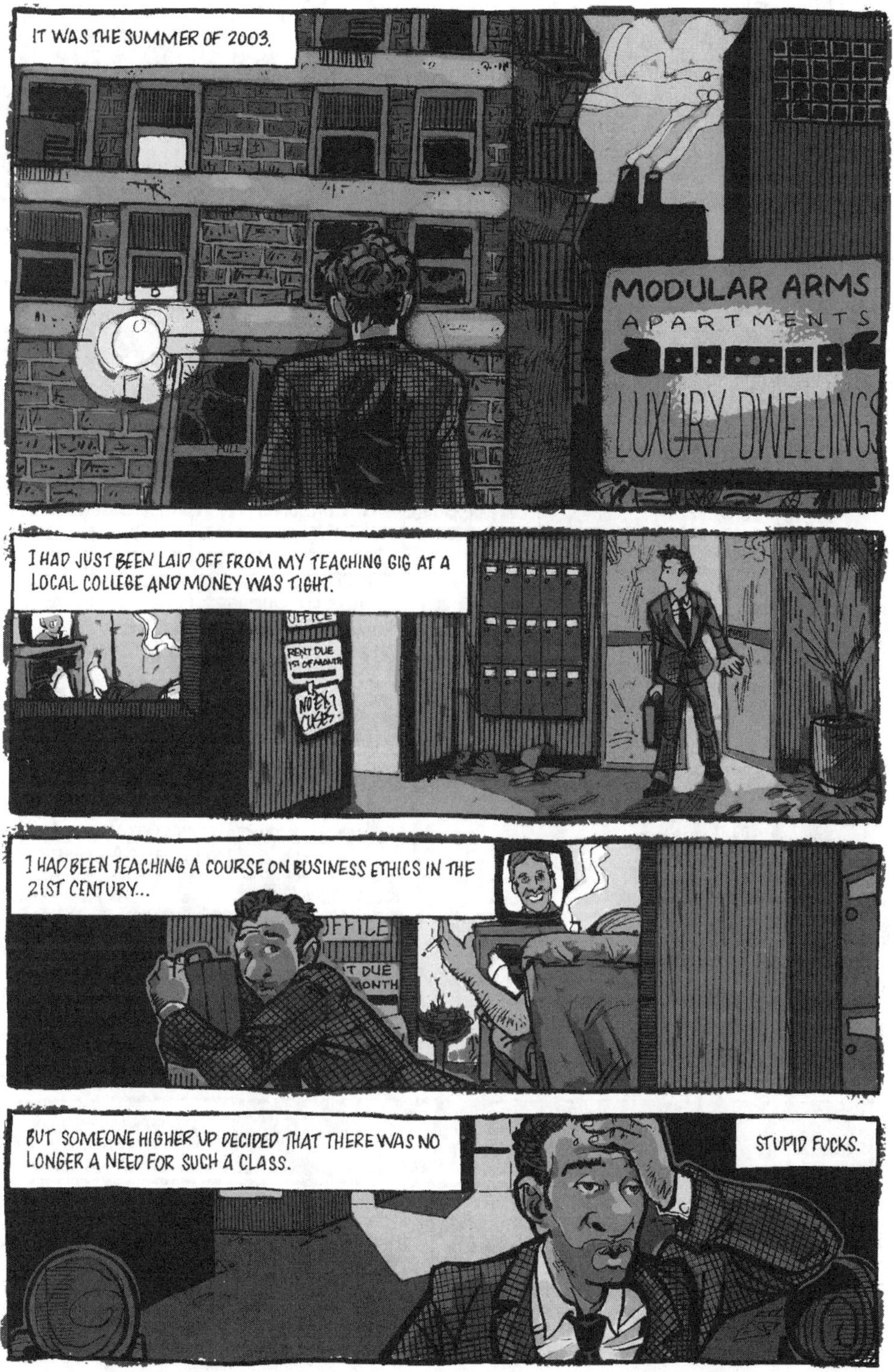
IT WAS THE SUMMER OF 2003.
MODULAR ARMS
APARTMENTS
LUXURY DWELLINGS
I HAD JUST BEEN LAID OFF FROM MY TEACHING GIG AT A LOCAL COLLEGE AND MONEY WAS TIGHT.
OFFICE
RENT DUE 1ST OF MONTH
I HAD BEEN TEACHING A COURSE ON BUSINESS ETHICS IN THE 21ST CENTURY...
BUT SOMEONE HIGHER UP DECIDED THAT THERE WAS NO LONGER A NEED FOR SUCH A CLASS.
STUPID FUCKS.

art by wendi strang-frost

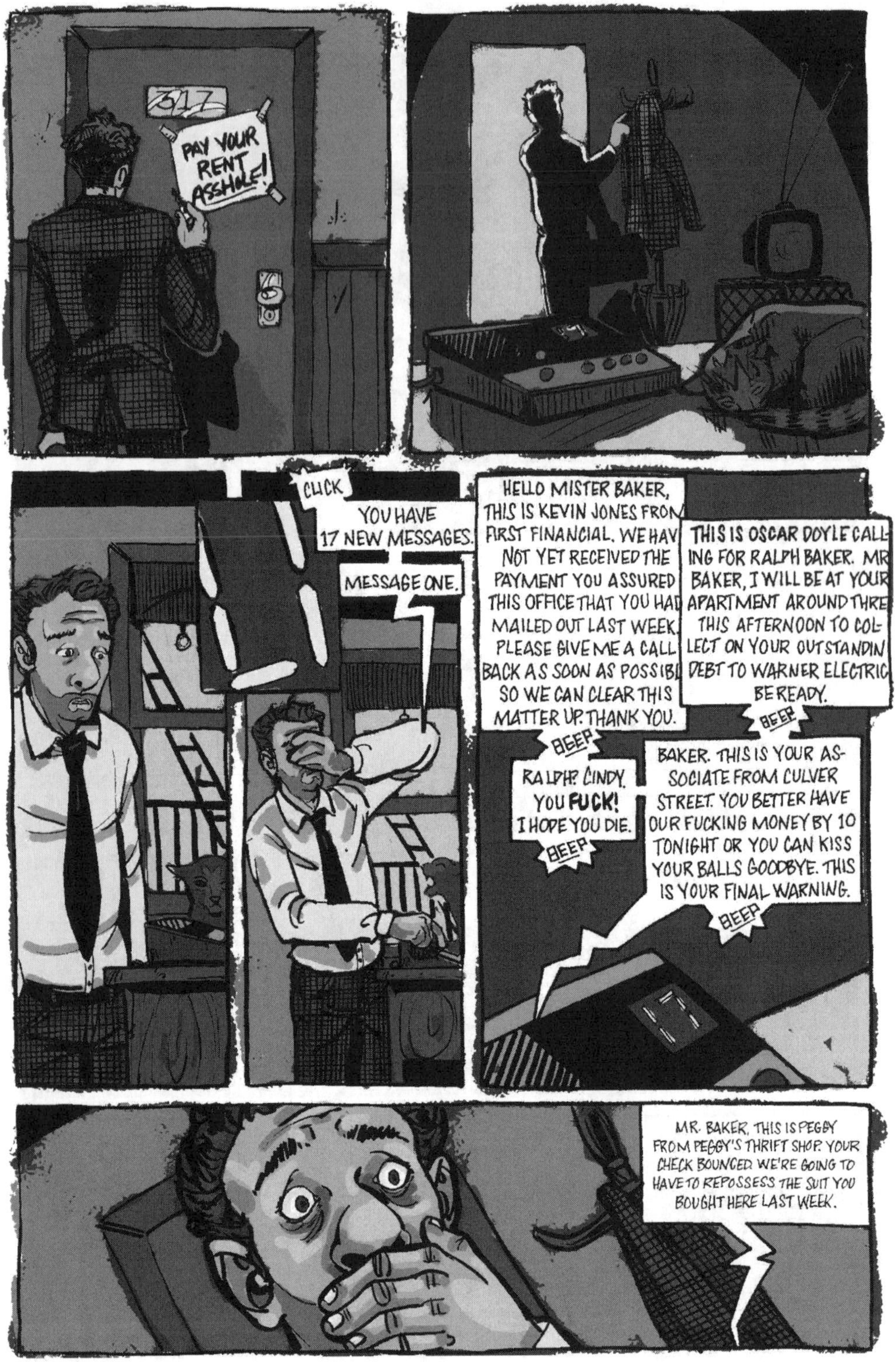
317
PAY YOUR RENT ASSHOLE!
CLICK
YOU HAVE 17 NEW MESSAGES.
MESSAGE ONE.
HELLO MISTER BAKER, THIS IS KEVIN JONES FROM FIRST FINANCIAL. WE HAVE NOT YET RECEIVED THE PAYMENT YOU ASSURED THIS OFFICE THAT YOU HAD MAILED OUT LAST WEEK. PLEASE GIVE ME A CALL BACK AS SOON AS POSSIBLE SO WE CAN CLEAR THIS MATTER UP. THANK YOU.
BEEP
THIS IS OSCAR DOYLE CALLING FOR RALPH BAKER. MR BAKER, I WILL BE AT YOUR APARTMENT AROUND THREE THIS AFTERNOON TO COLLECT ON YOUR OUTSTANDING DEBT TO WARNER ELECTRIC. BE READY.
BEEP
RALPH? CINDY. YOU FUCK! I HOPE YOU DIE.
BEEP
BAKER. THIS IS YOUR ASSOCIATE FROM CULVER STREET. YOU BETTER HAVE OUR FUCKING MONEY BY 10 TONIGHT OR YOU CAN KISS YOUR BALLS GOODBYE. THIS IS YOUR FINAL WARNING.
BEEP
MR. BAKER, THIS IS PEGGY FROM PEGGY'S THRIFT SHOP. YOUR CHECK BOUNCED. WE'RE GOING TO HAVE TO REPOSSESS THE SUIT YOU BOUGHT HERE LAST WEEK.

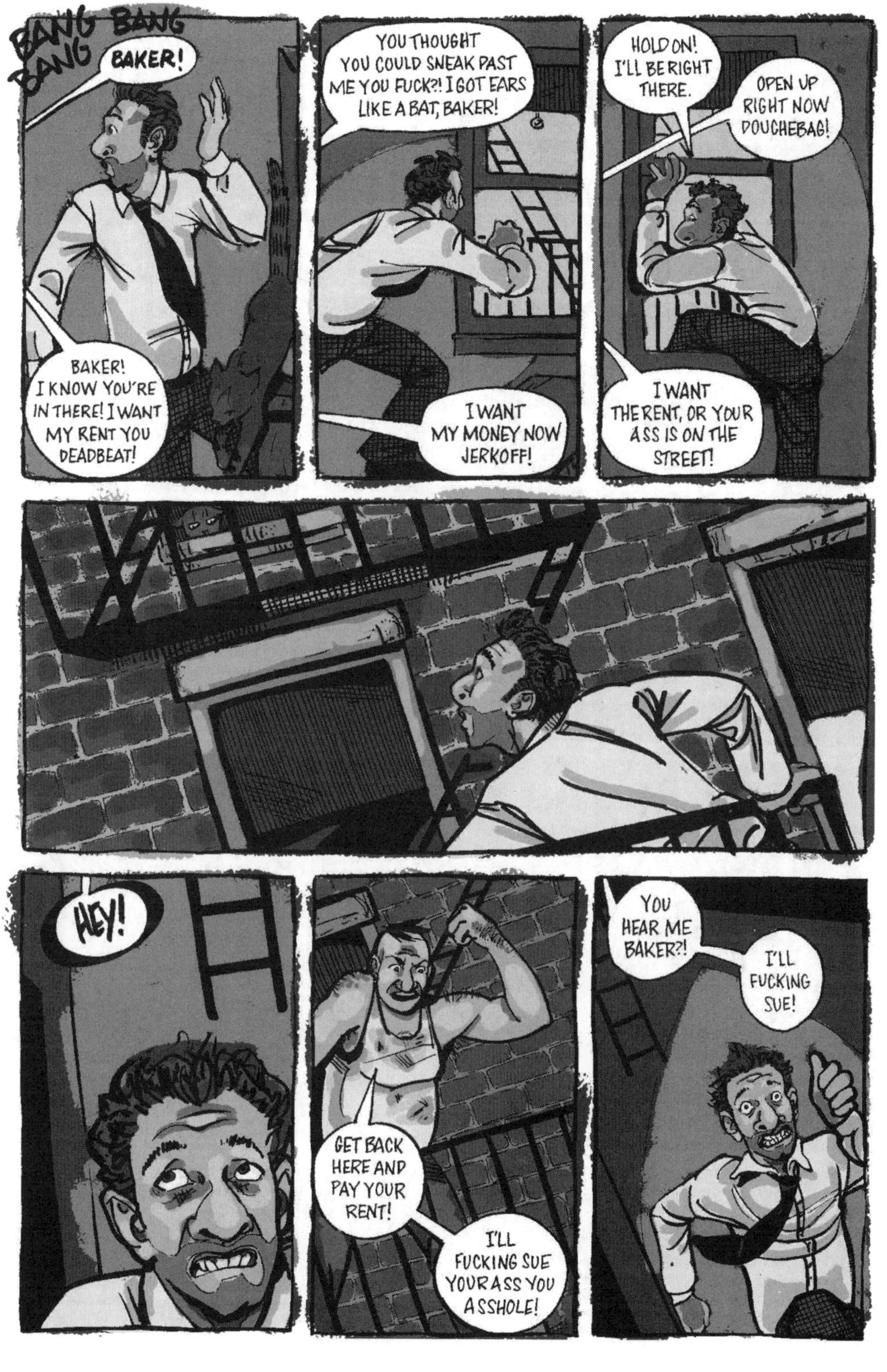
BANG BANG BANG
BAKER!
BAKER! I KNOW YOU'RE IN THERE! I WANT MY RENT YOU DEADBEAT!
YOU THOUGHT YOU COULD SNEAK PAST ME YOU FUCK?! I GOT EARS LIKE A BAT, BAKER!
I WANT MY MONEY NOW JERKOFF!
HOLD ON! I'LL BE RIGHT THERE.
OPEN UP RIGHT NOW DOUCHEBAG!
I WANT THE RENT, OR YOUR ASS IS ON THE STREET!
HEY!
GET BACK HERE AND PAY YOUR RENT!
I'LL FUCKING SUE YOUR ASS YOU ASSHOLE!
YOU HEAR ME BAKER?!
I'LL FUCKING SUE!

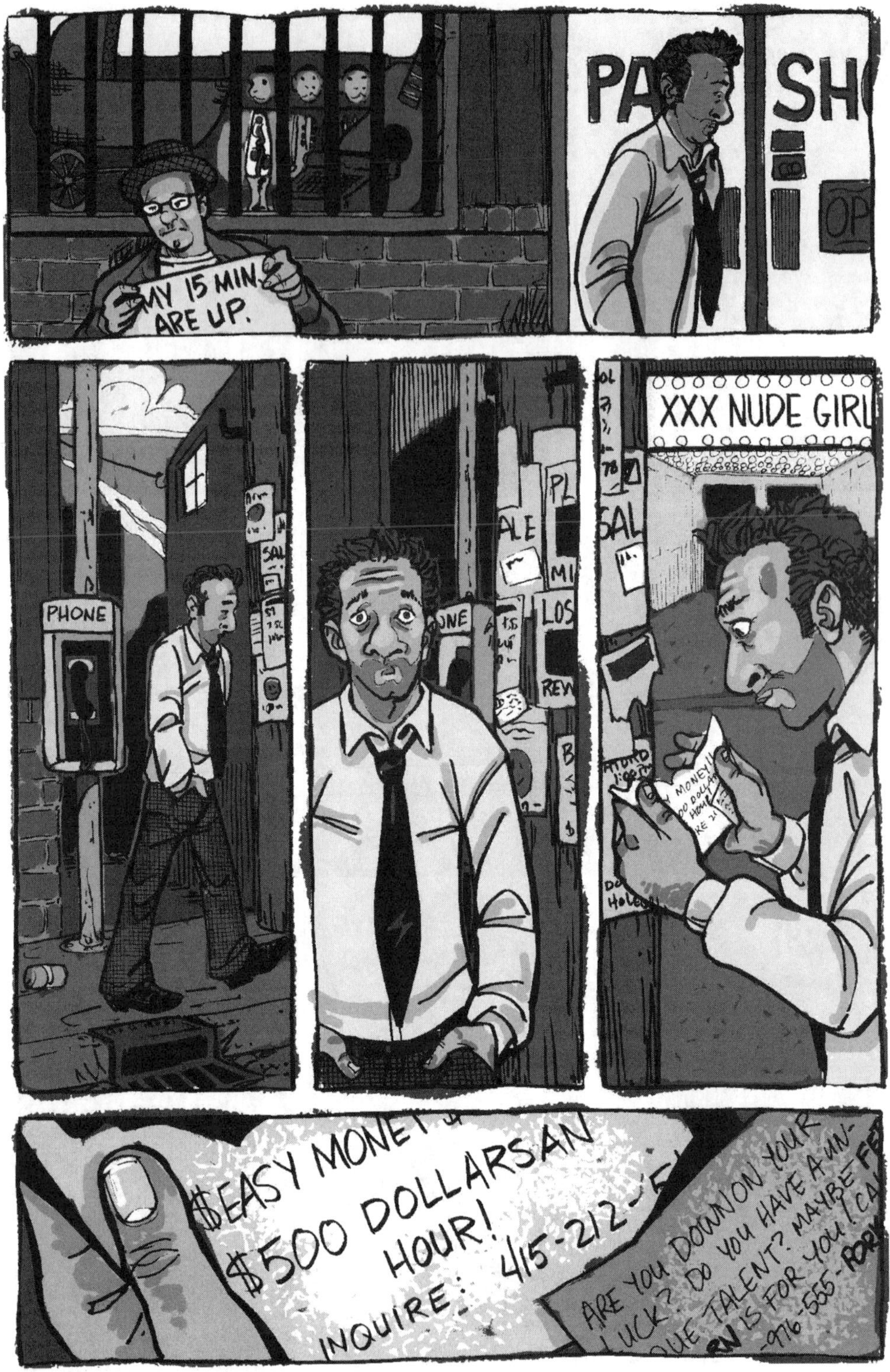

MY 15 MIN.
ARE UP.
PHONE
XXX NUDE GIRL
$EASY MONE
$500 DOLLARS AN
HOUR!
INQUIRE: 415-212-
ARE YOU DOWN ON YOUR
LUCK? DO YOU HAVE A UN-
QUE TALENT? MAYBE
IS FOR YOU! CA
-976-555-

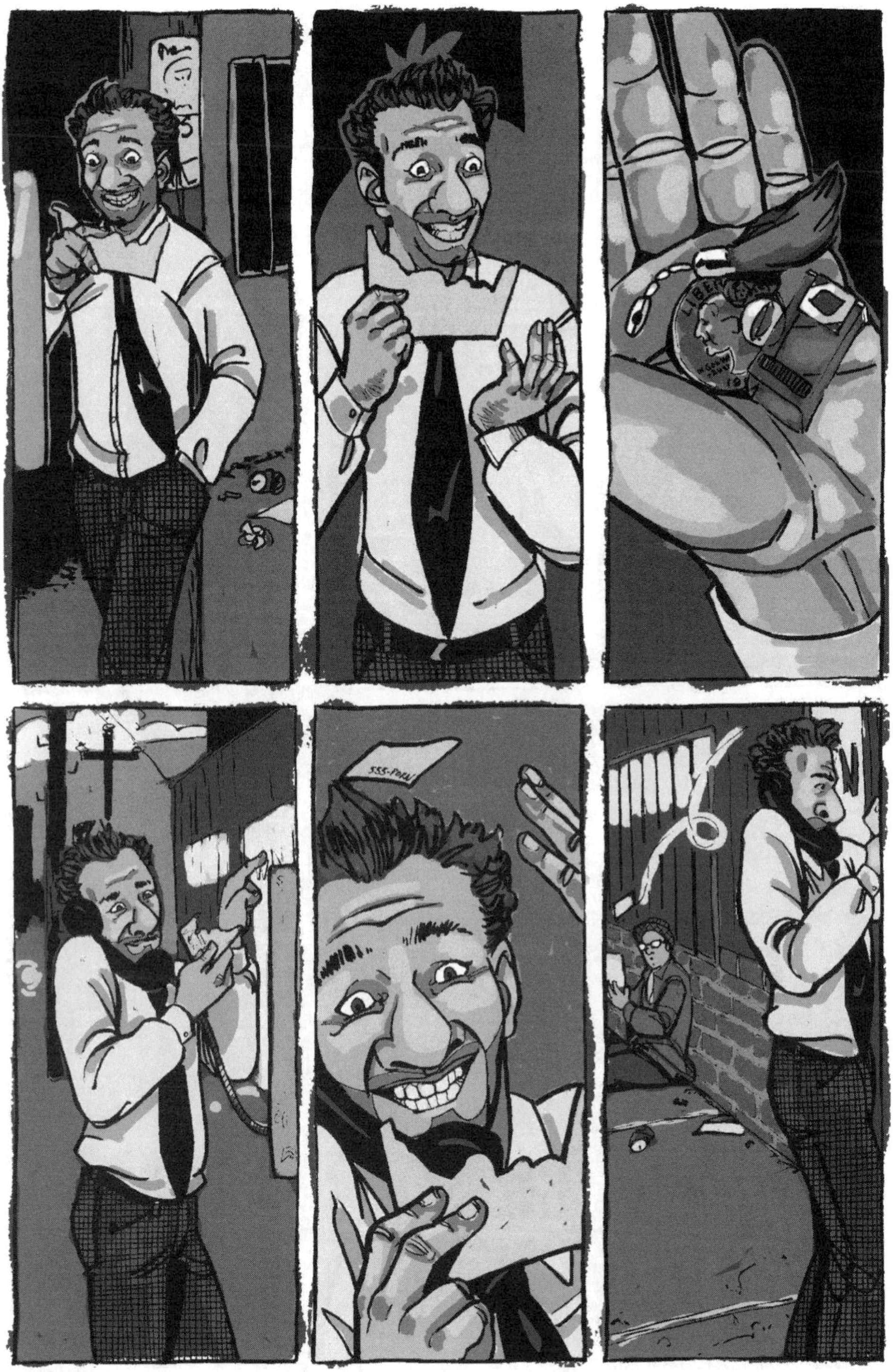
555-PORN

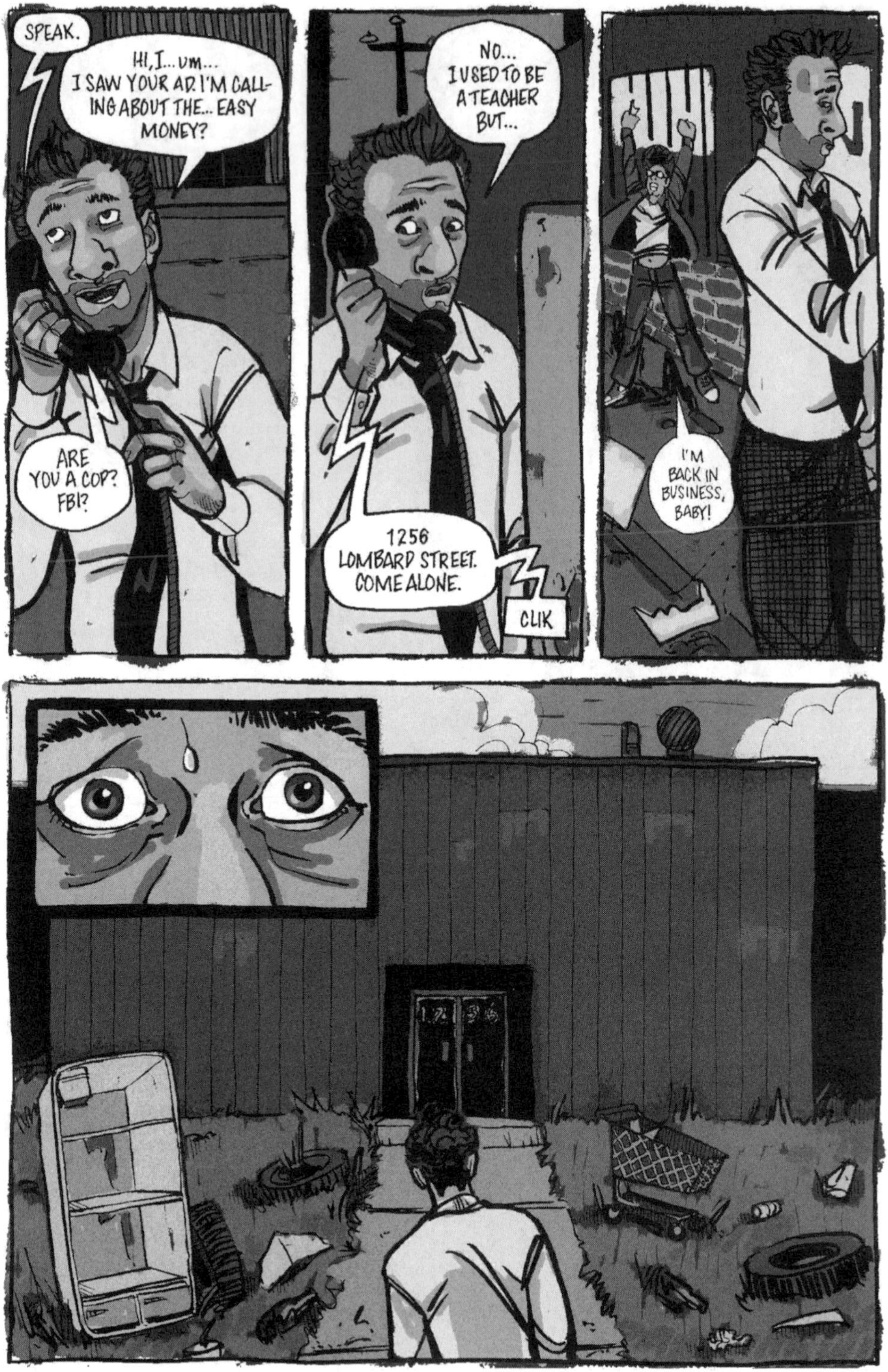
SPEAK.
HI, I... UM... I SAW YOUR AD. I'M CALLING ABOUT THE... EASY MONEY?
ARE YOU A COP? FBI?
NO... I USED TO BE A TEACHER BUT...
1256 LOMBARD STREET. COME ALONE.
CLIK
I'M BACK IN BUSINESS, BABY!

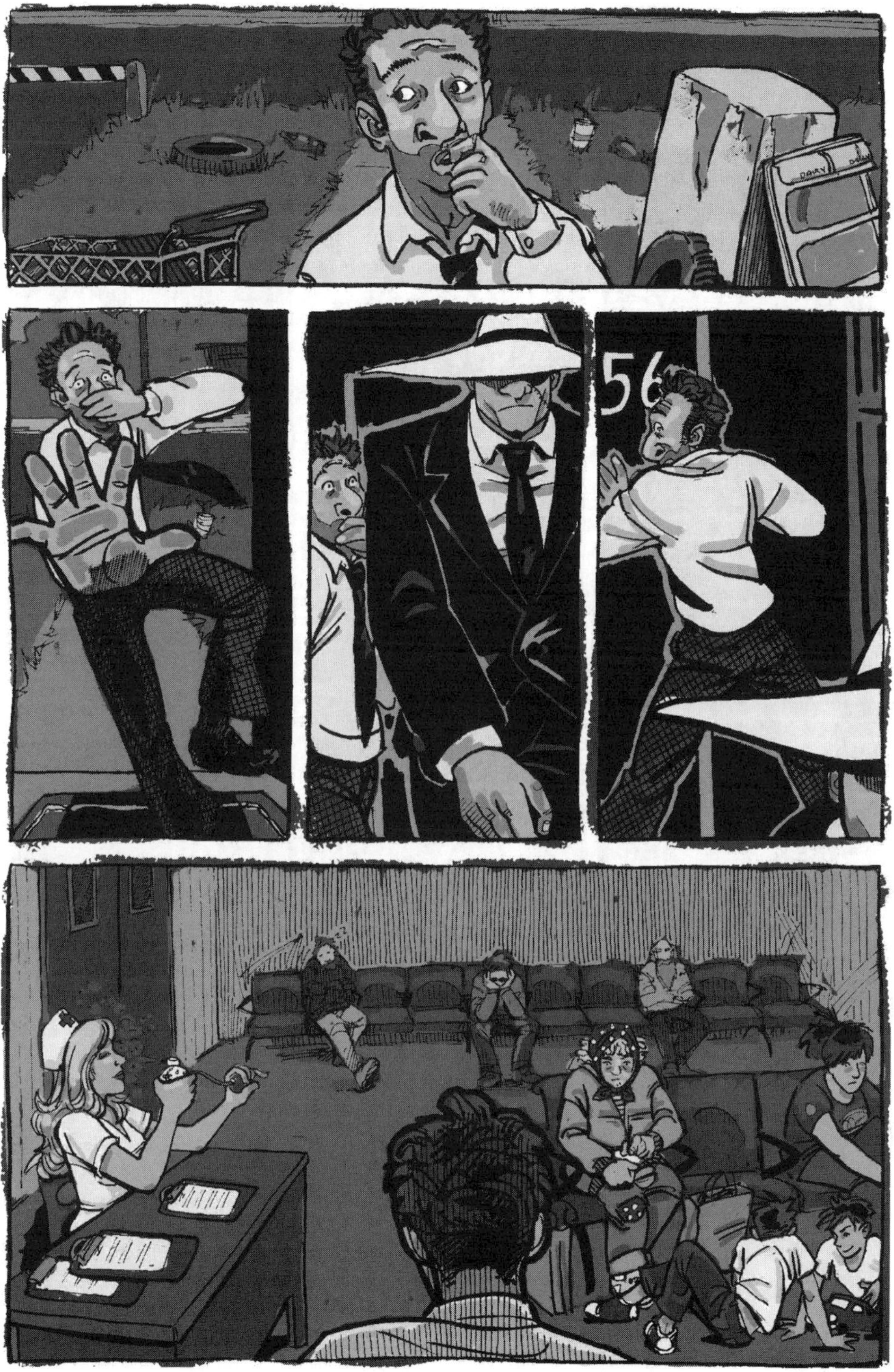
56

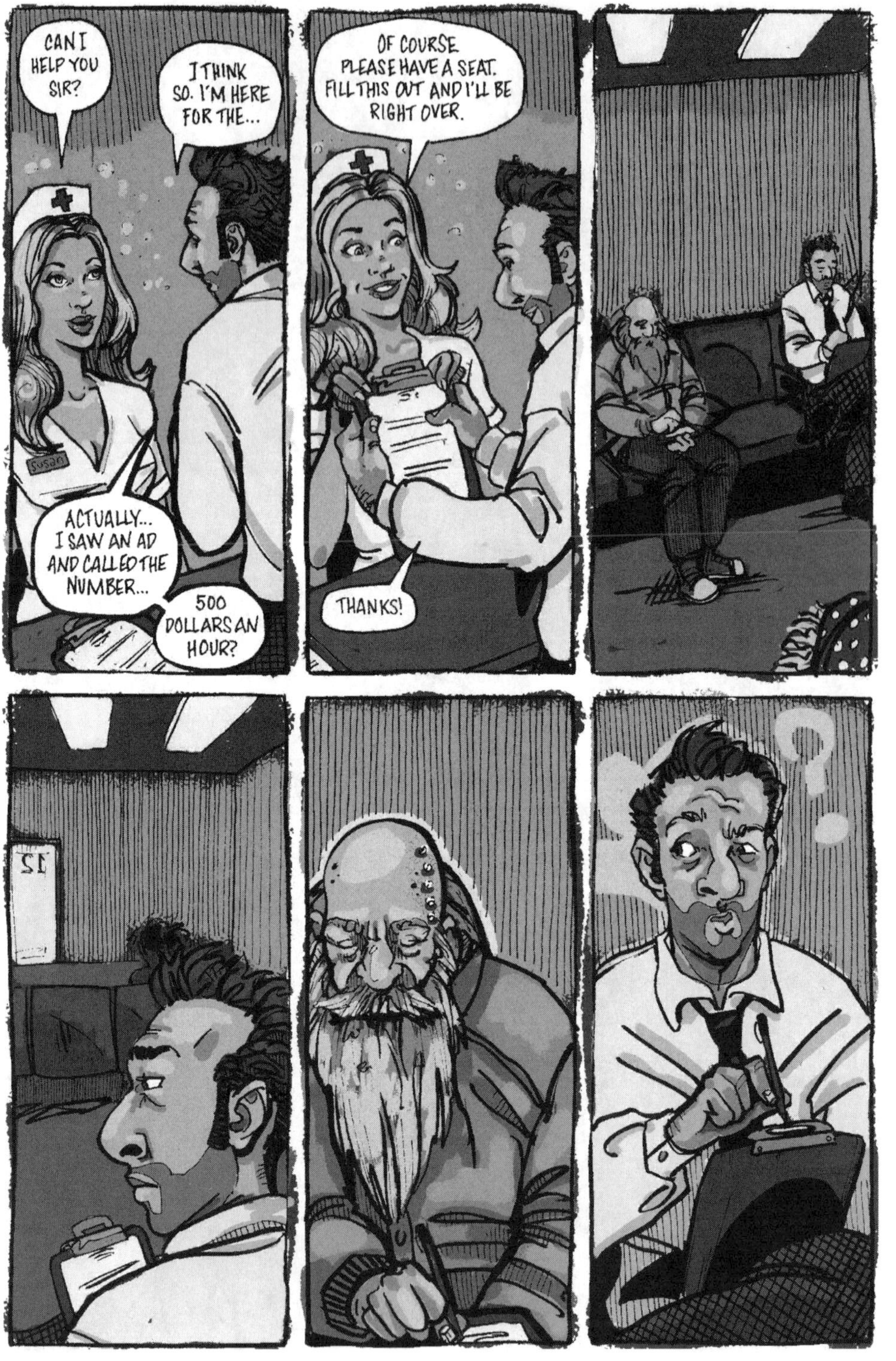
CAN I HELP YOU SIR?
I THINK SO. I'M HERE FOR THE...
ACTUALLY... I SAW AN AD AND CALLED THE NUMBER...
500 DOLLARS AN HOUR?
OF COURSE PLEASE HAVE A SEAT. FILL THIS OUT AND I'LL BE RIGHT OVER.
THANKS!

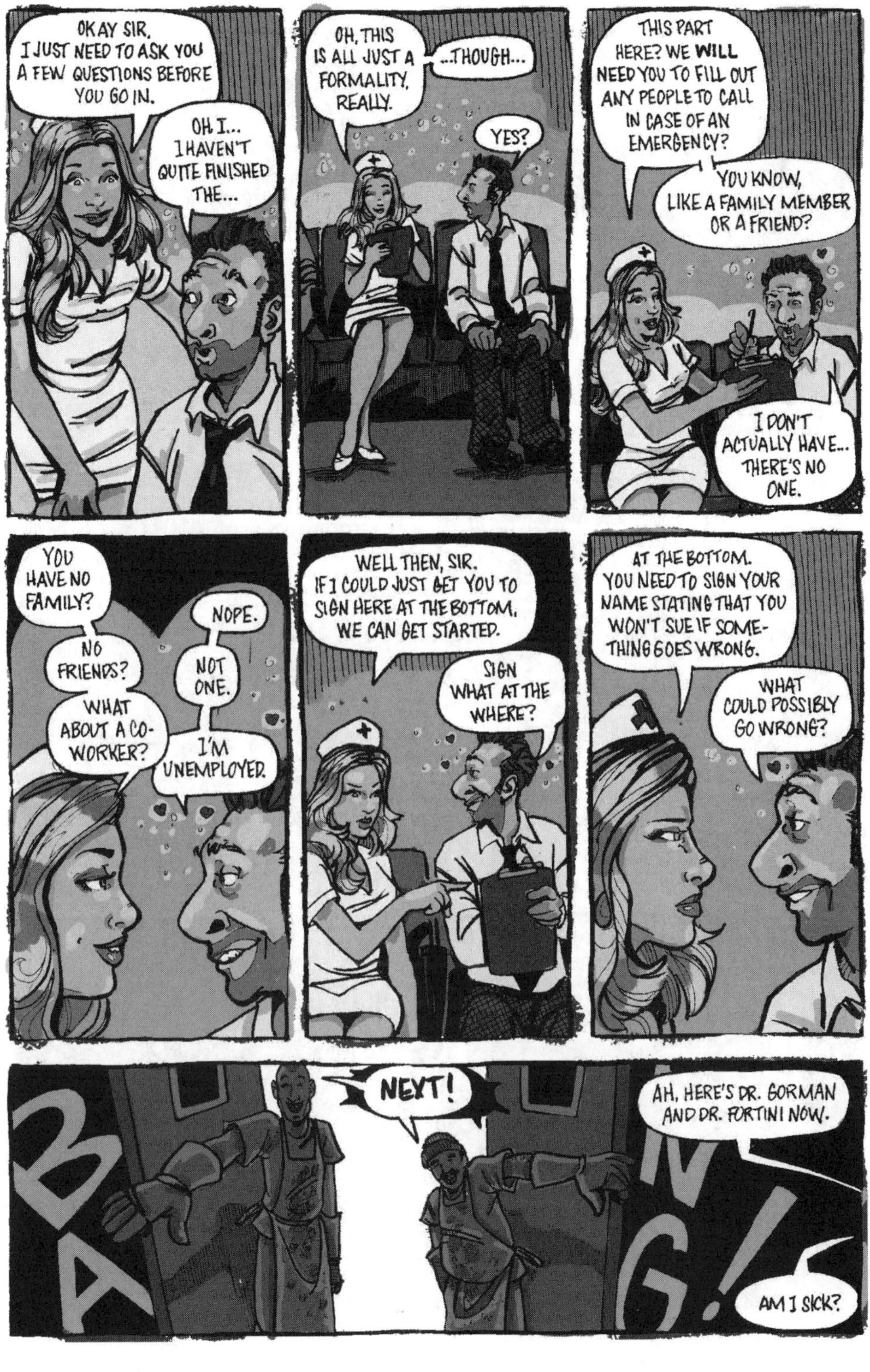
OKAY SIR, I JUST NEED TO ASK YOU A FEW QUESTIONS BEFORE YOU GO IN.
OH, I... I HAVEN'T QUITE FINISHED THE...
OH, THIS IS ALL JUST A FORMALITY, REALLY.
...THOUGH...
YES?
THIS PART HERE? WE **WILL** NEED YOU TO FILL OUT ANY PEOPLE TO CALL IN CASE OF AN EMERGENCY?
YOU KNOW, LIKE A FAMILY MEMBER OR A FRIEND?
I DON'T ACTUALLY HAVE... THERE'S NO ONE.
YOU HAVE NO FAMILY?
NOPE.
NO FRIENDS?
NOT ONE.
WHAT ABOUT A CO-WORKER?
I'M UNEMPLOYED.
WELL THEN, SIR. IF I COULD JUST GET YOU TO SIGN HERE AT THE BOTTOM, WE CAN GET STARTED.
SIGN WHAT AT THE WHERE?
AT THE BOTTOM. YOU NEED TO SIGN YOUR NAME STATING THAT YOU WON'T SUE IF SOMETHING GOES WRONG.
WHAT COULD POSSIBLY GO WRONG?
BANG!
NEXT!
AH, HERE'S DR. GORMAN AND DR. FORTINI NOW.
AM I SICK?

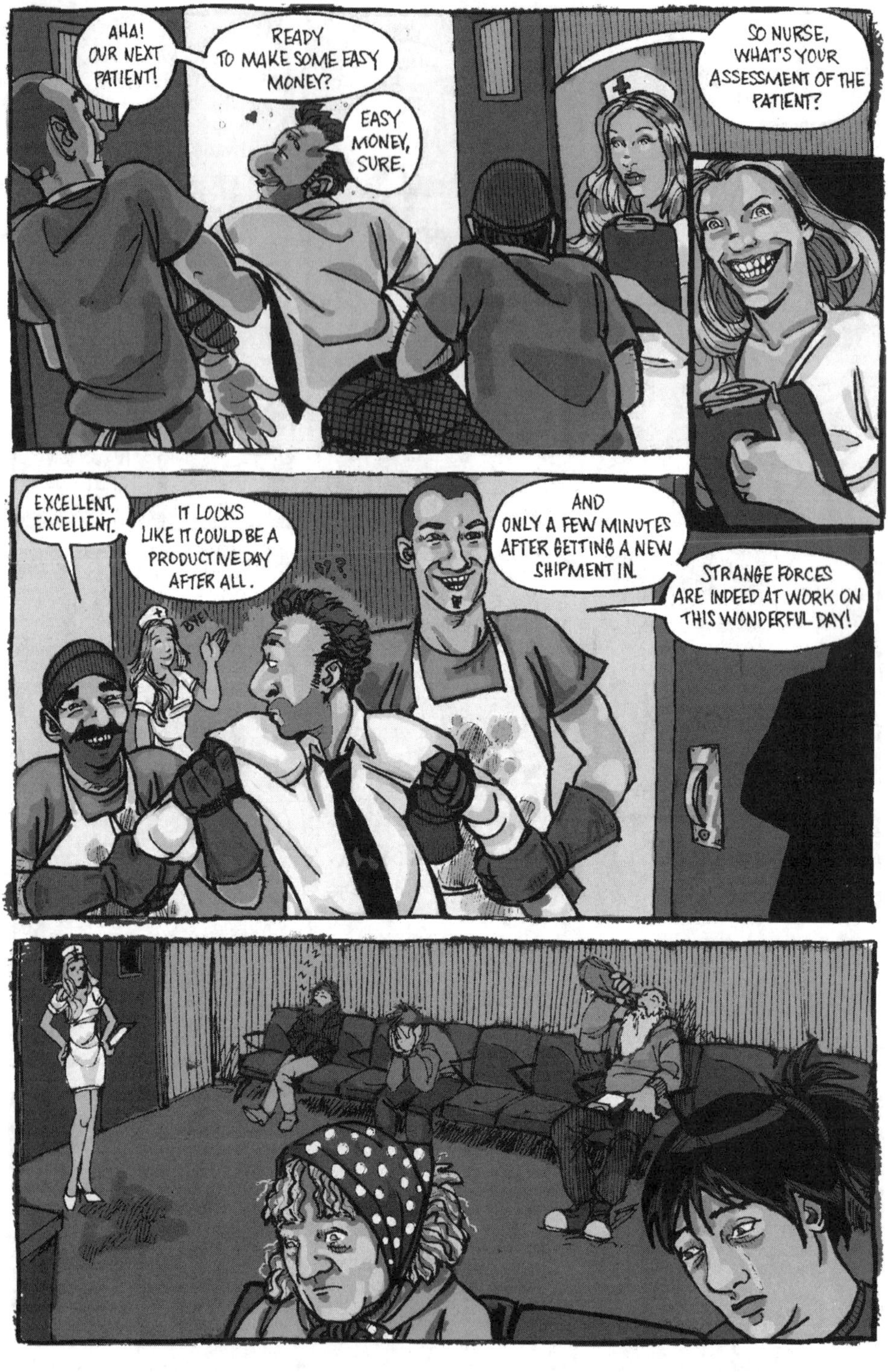
AHA! OUR NEXT PATIENT!
READY TO MAKE SOME EASY MONEY?
EASY MONEY, SURE.
SO NURSE, WHAT'S YOUR ASSESSMENT OF THE PATIENT?
EXCELLENT, EXCELLENT.
IT LOOKS LIKE IT COULD BE A PRODUCTIVE DAY AFTER ALL.
BYE!
AND ONLY A FEW MINUTES AFTER GETTING A NEW SHIPMENT IN.
STRANGE FORCES ARE INDEED AT WORK ON THIS WONDERFUL DAY!

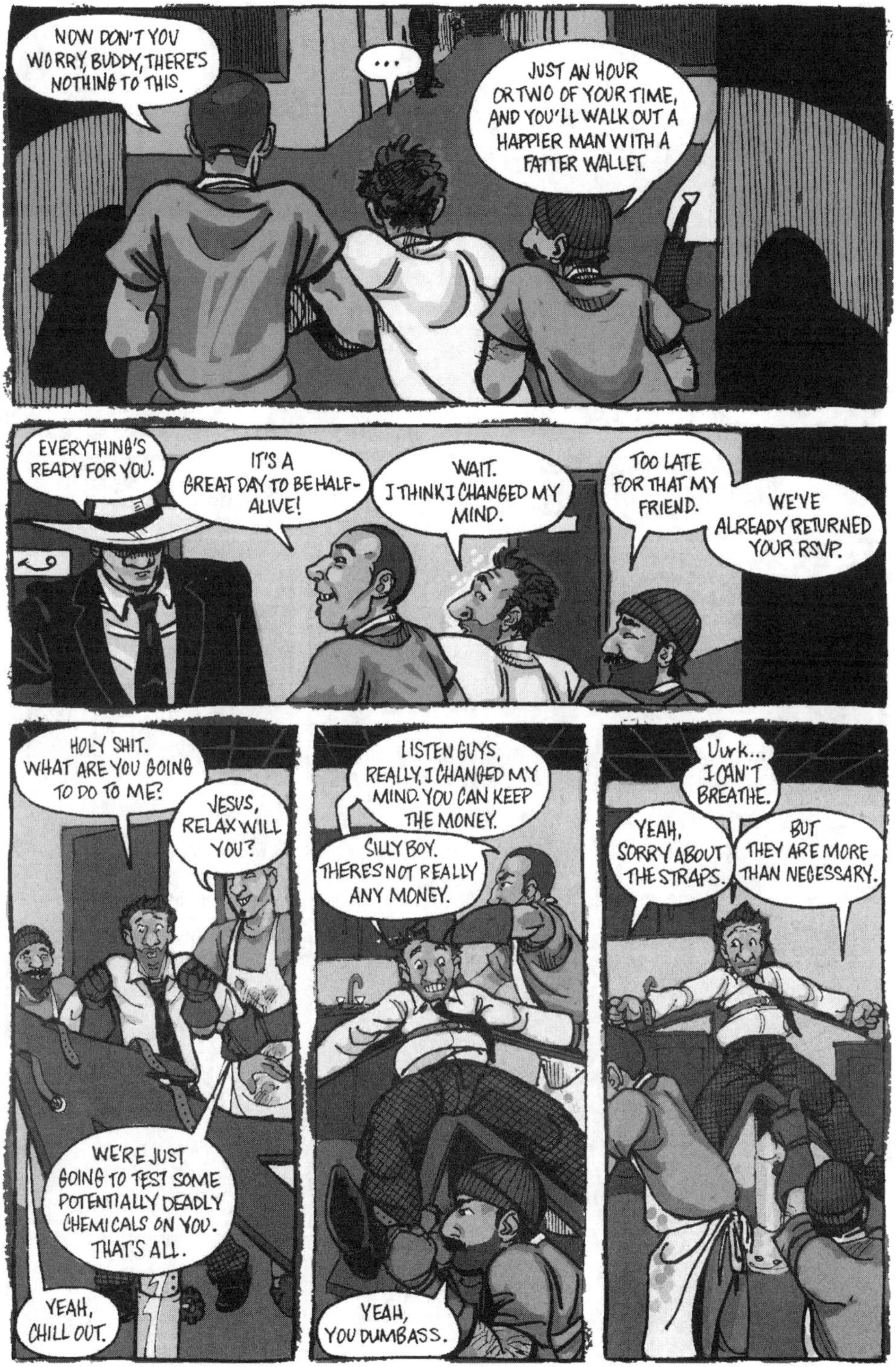
NOW DON'T YOU WORRY, BUDDY, THERE'S NOTHING TO THIS.
...
JUST AN HOUR OR TWO OF YOUR TIME, AND YOU'LL WALK OUT A HAPPIER MAN WITH A FATTER WALLET.
EVERYTHING'S READY FOR YOU.
IT'S A GREAT DAY TO BE HALF-ALIVE!
WAIT. I THINK I CHANGED MY MIND.
TOO LATE FOR THAT MY FRIEND.
WE'VE ALREADY RETURNED YOUR RSVP.
HOLY SHIT. WHAT ARE YOU GOING TO DO TO ME?
JESUS, RELAX WILL YOU?
WE'RE JUST GOING TO TEST SOME POTENTIALLY DEADLY CHEMICALS ON YOU. THAT'S ALL.
YEAH, CHILL OUT.
LISTEN GUYS, REALLY, I CHANGED MY MIND. YOU CAN KEEP THE MONEY.
SILLY BOY. THERE'S NOT REALLY ANY MONEY.
YEAH, YOU DUMBASS.
Uurk... I CAN'T BREATHE.
YEAH, SORRY ABOUT THE STRAPS.
BUT THEY ARE MORE THAN NECESSARY.

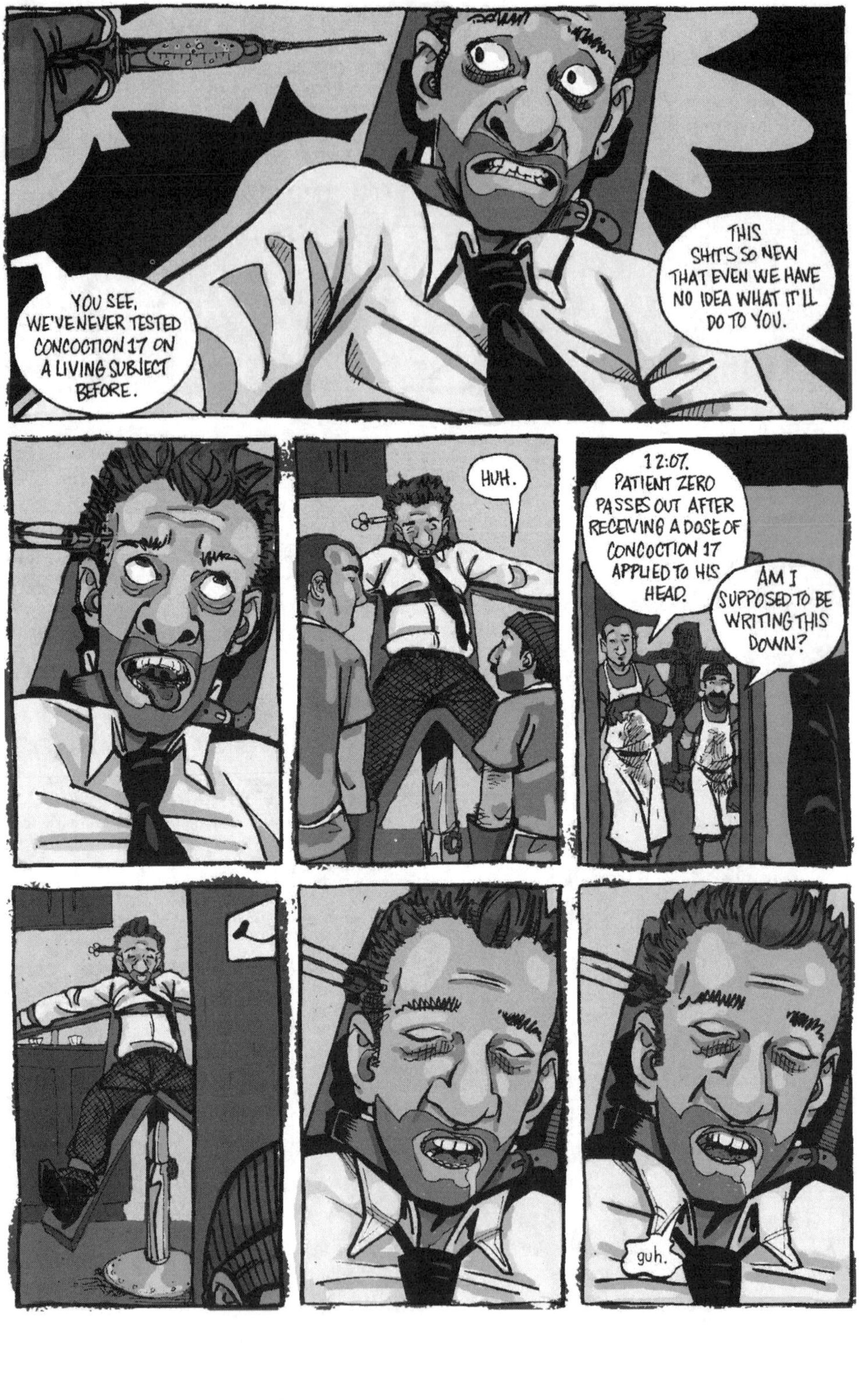
YOU SEE, WE'VE NEVER TESTED CONCOCTION 17 ON A LIVING SUBJECT BEFORE.
THIS SHIT'S SO NEW THAT EVEN WE HAVE NO IDEA WHAT IT'LL DO TO YOU.
HUH.
12:07. PATIENT ZERO PASSES OUT AFTER RECEIVING A DOSE OF CONCOCTION 17 APPLIED TO HIS HEAD.
AM I SUPPOSED TO BE WRITING THIS DOWN?
guh.

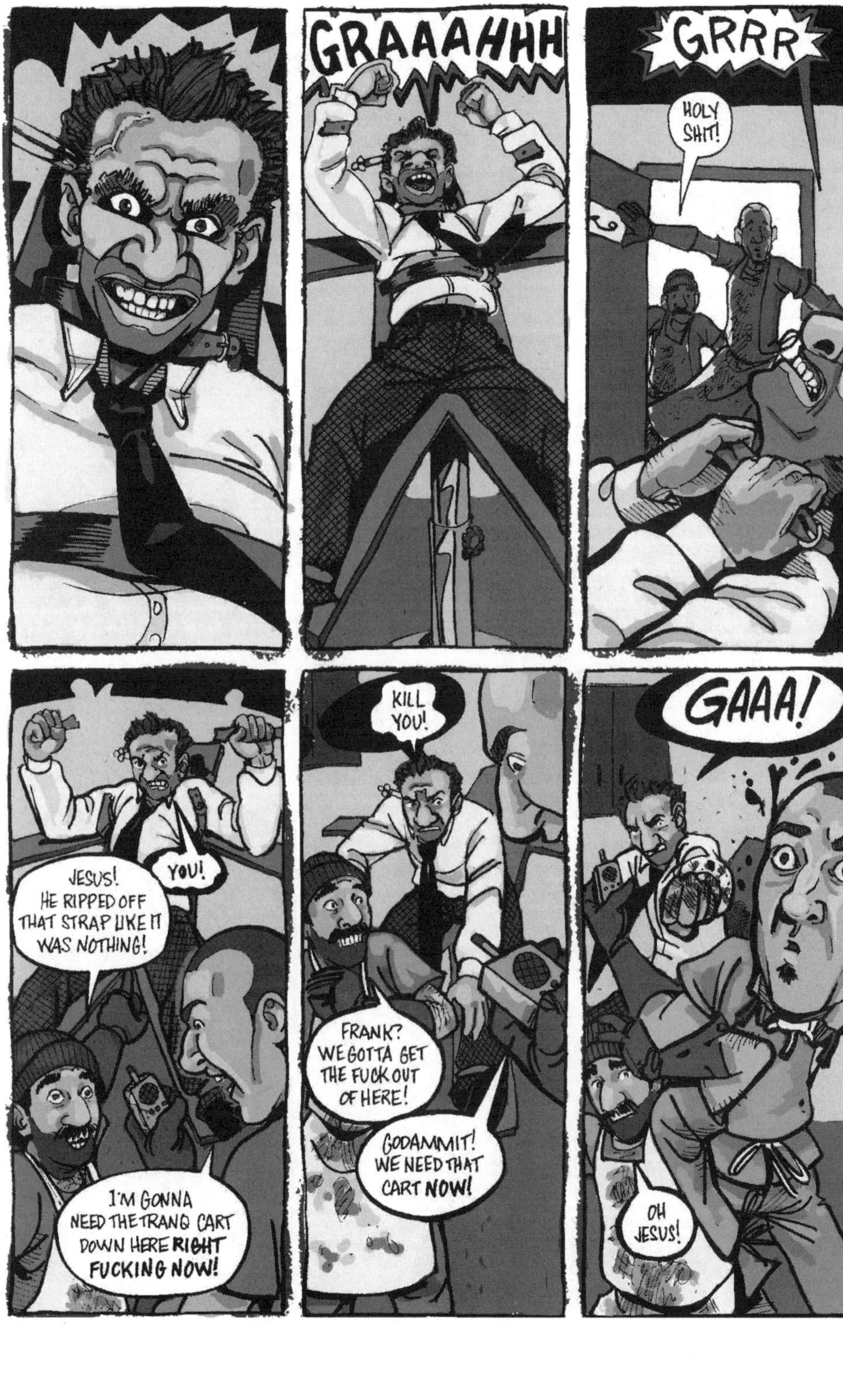
GRAAAHHH
GRRR
HOLY SHIT!
YOU!
JESUS! HE RIPPED OFF THAT STRAP LIKE IT WAS NOTHING!
I'M GONNA NEED THE TRANQ CART DOWN HERE RIGHT FUCKING NOW!
KILL YOU!
FRANK? WE GOTTA GET THE FUCK OUT OF HERE!
GODAMMIT! WE NEED THAT CART NOW!
GAAA!
OH JESUS!

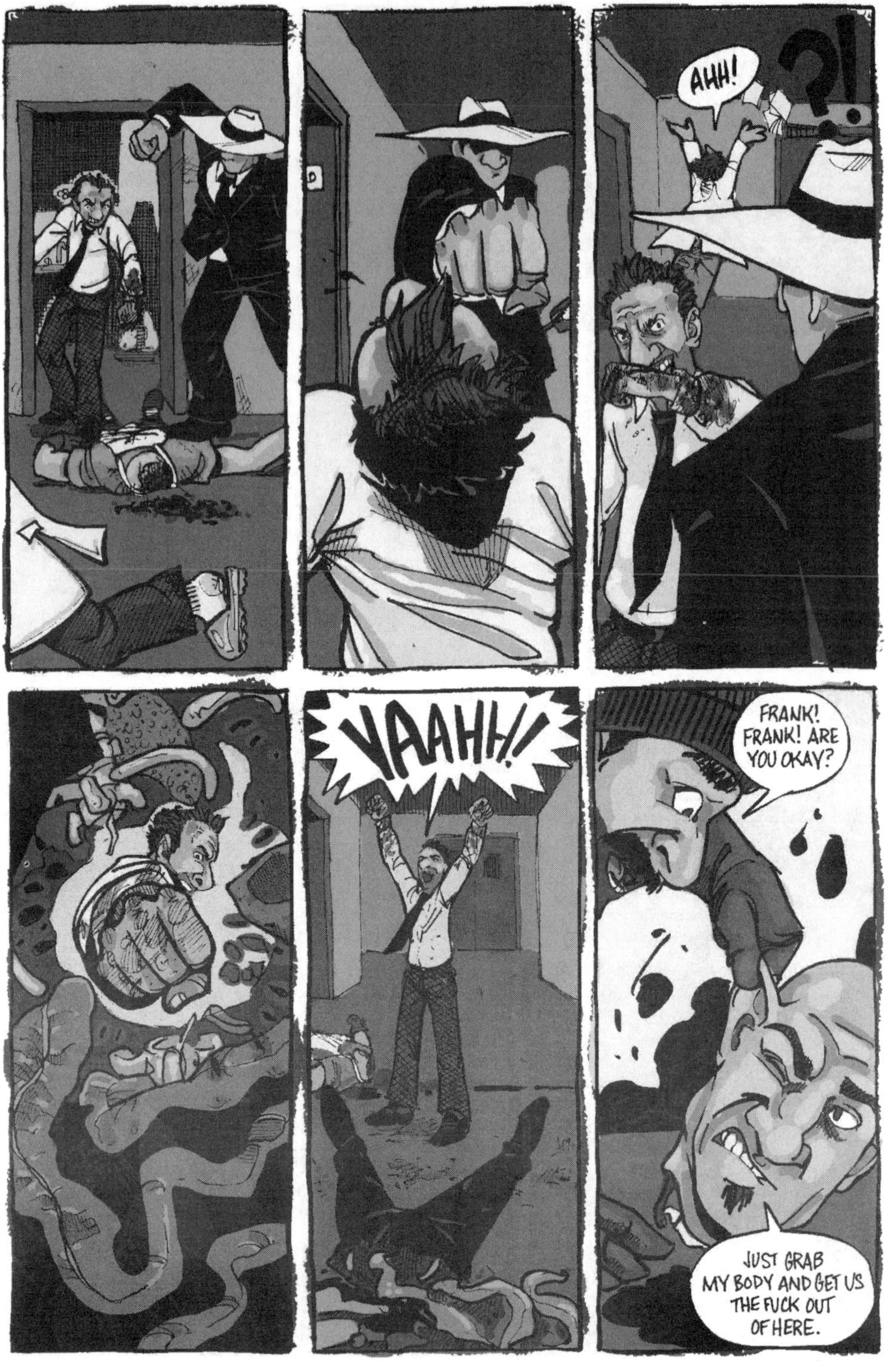
AHH!
?!
YAAHH!!
FRANK! FRANK! ARE YOU OKAY?
JUST GRAB MY BODY AND GET US THE FUCK OUT OF HERE.

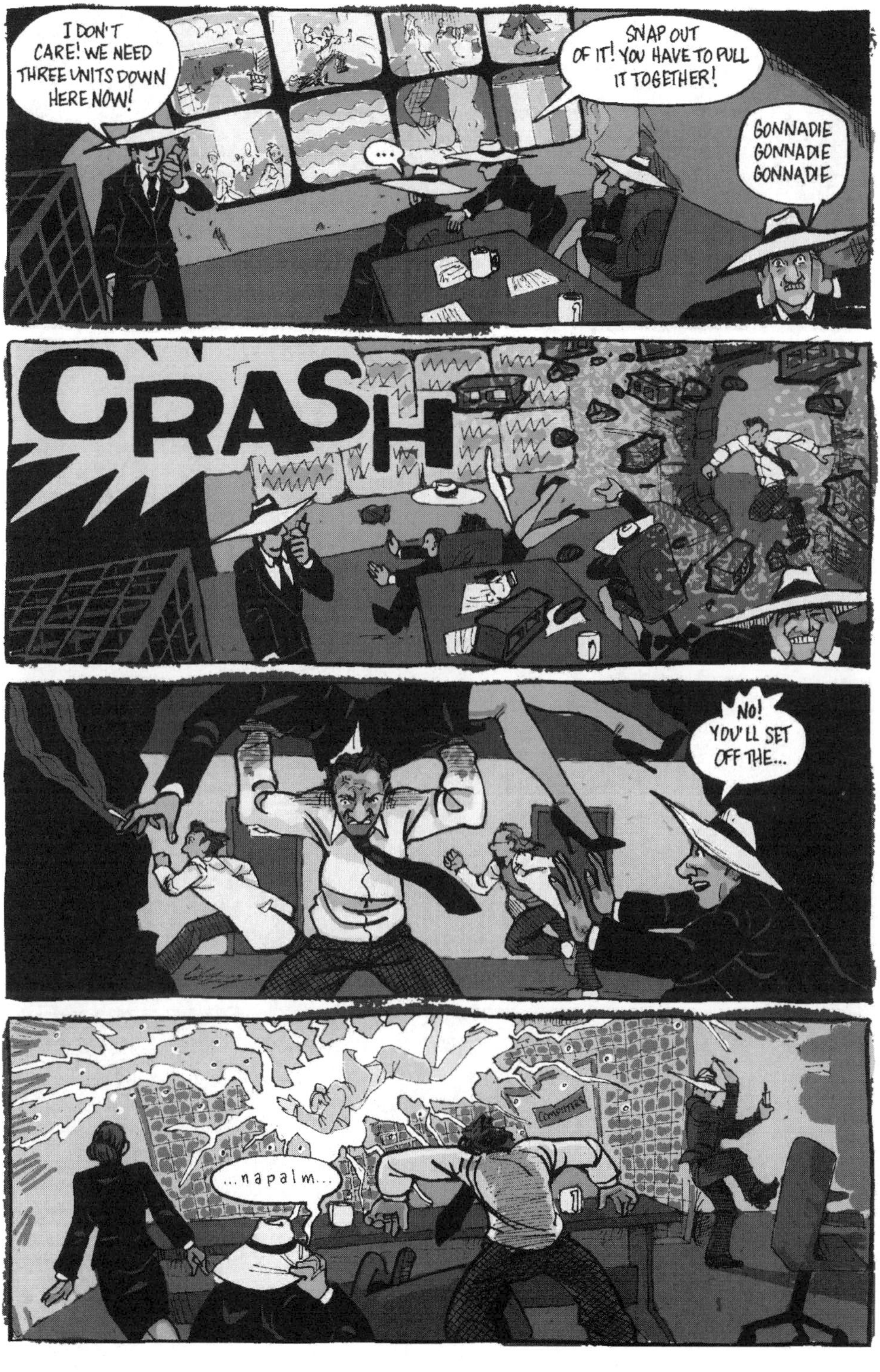
I DON'T CARE! WE NEED THREE UNITS DOWN HERE NOW!
...
SNAP OUT OF IT! YOU HAVE TO PULL IT TOGETHER!
GONNADIE GONNADIE GONNADIE
CRASH
NO! YOU'LL SET OFF THE...
COMPUTERS
...napalm...

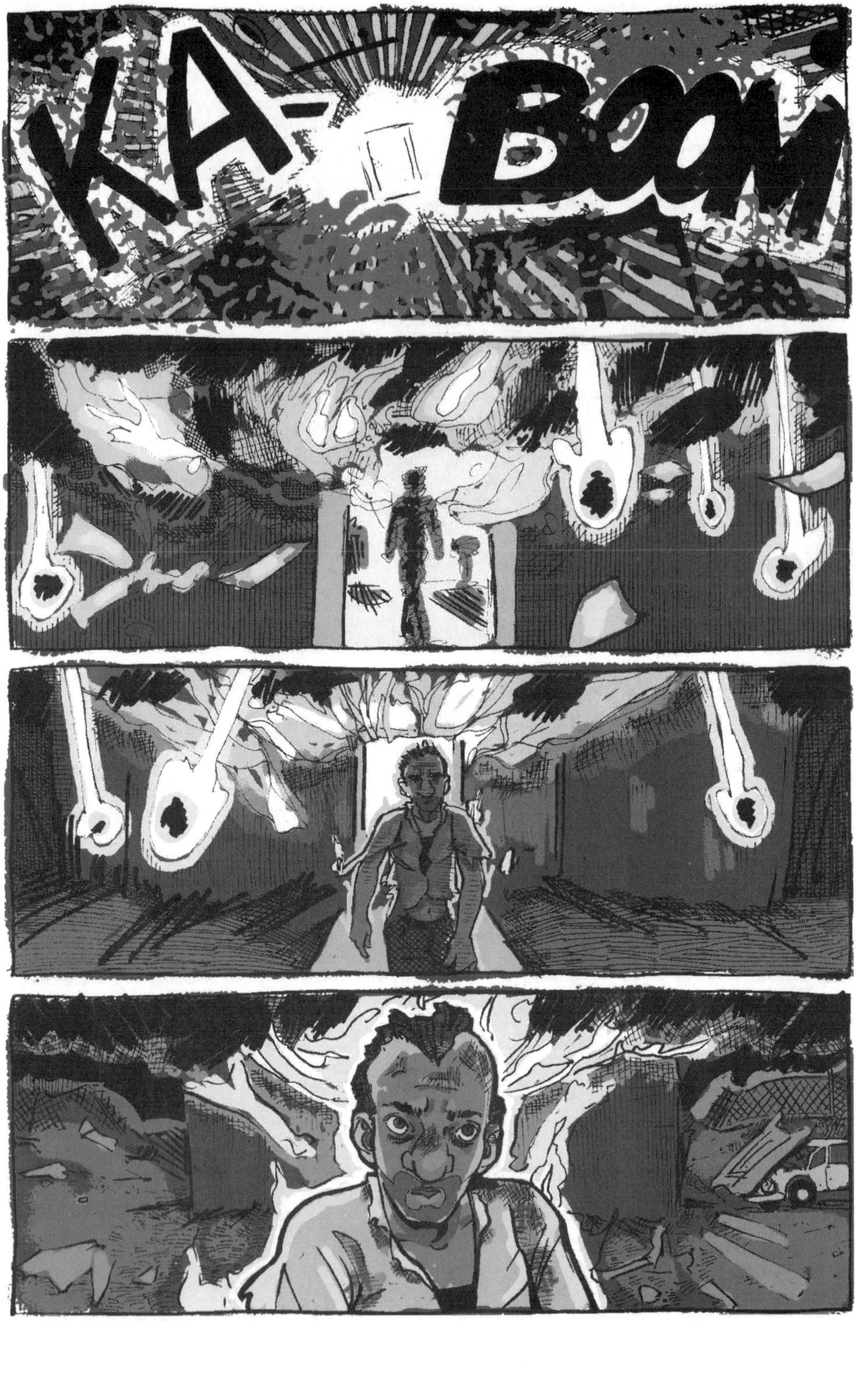
KA-BOOM

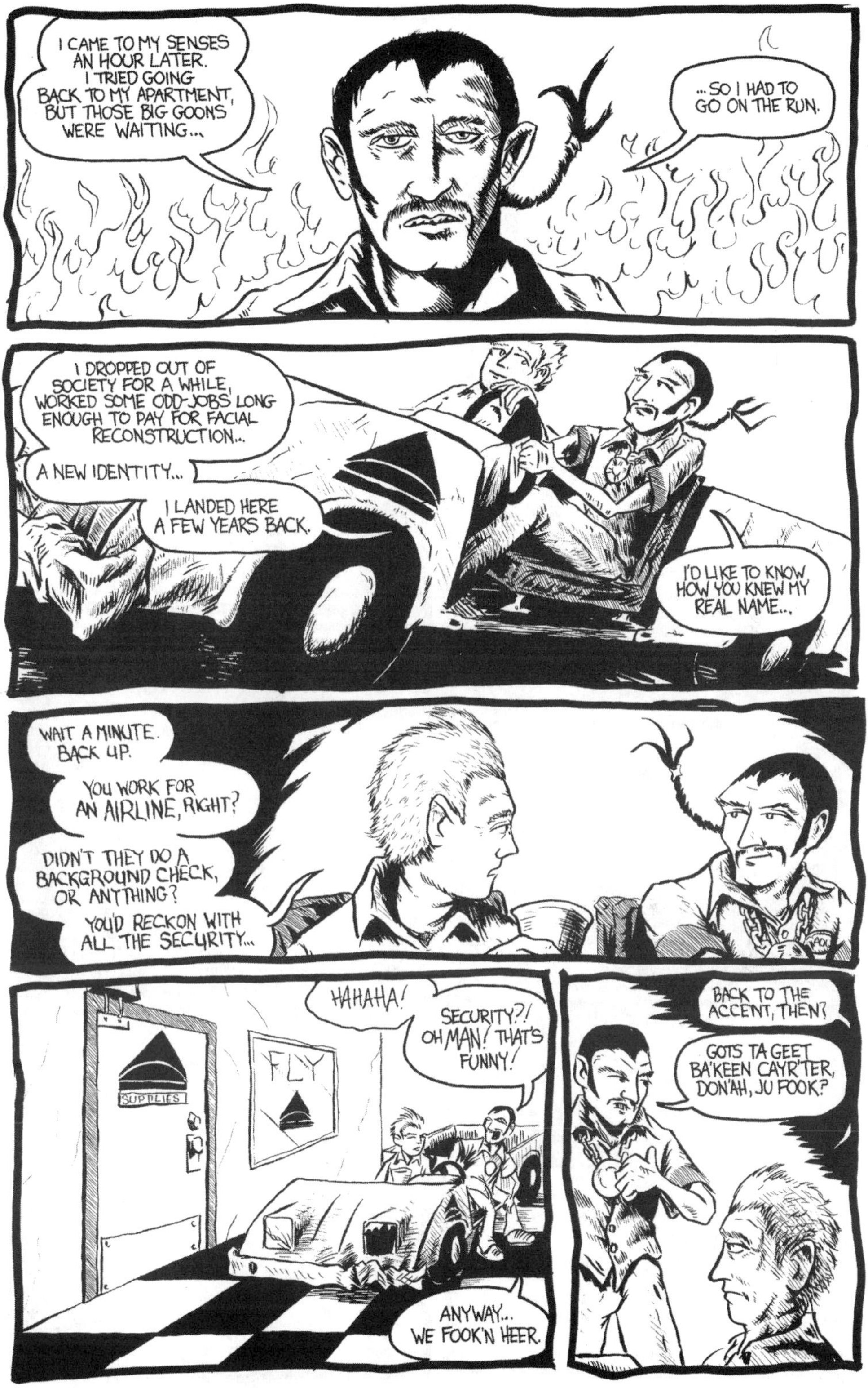
I CAME TO MY SENSES AN HOUR LATER. I TRIED GOING BACK TO MY APARTMENT, BUT THOSE BIG GOONS WERE WAITING...
...SO I HAD TO GO ON THE RUN.
I DROPPED OUT OF SOCIETY FOR A WHILE, WORKED SOME ODD-JOBS LONG ENOUGH TO PAY FOR FACIAL RECONSTRUCTION...
A NEW IDENTITY...
I LANDED HERE A FEW YEARS BACK.
I'D LIKE TO KNOW HOW YOU KNEW MY REAL NAME...
WAIT A MINUTE. BACK UP.
YOU WORK FOR AN AIRLINE, RIGHT?
DIDN'T THEY DO A BACKGROUND CHECK, OR ANYTHING?
YOU'D RECKON WITH ALL THE SECURITY...
HAHAHA!
SECURITY?! OH MAN! THAT'S FUNNY!
SUPPLIES
FLY
ANYWAY... WE FOOK'N HEER.
BACK TO THE ACCENT, THEN?
GOTS TA GEET BA'KEEN CAYR'TER, DON'AH, JU FOOK?

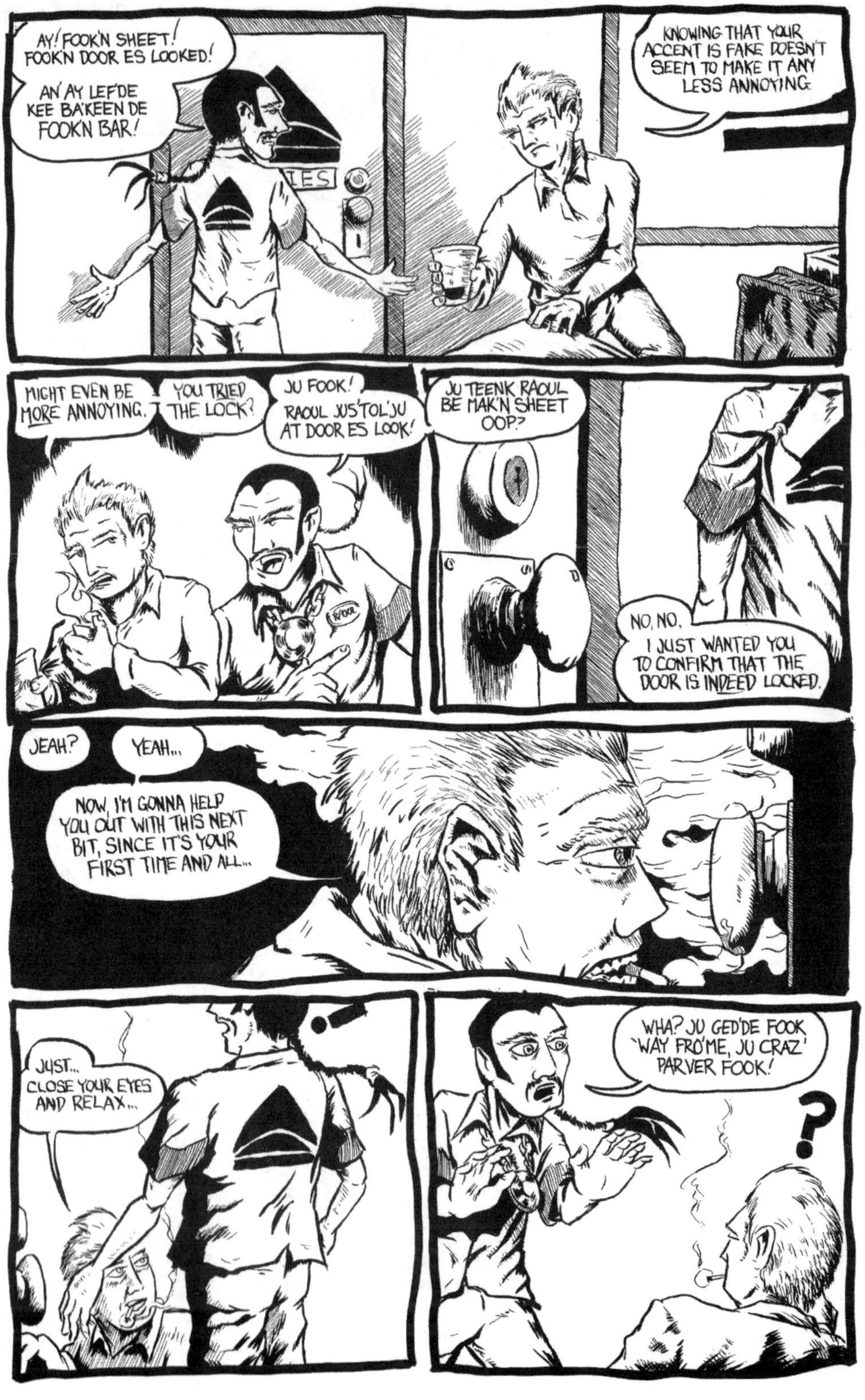
AY! FOOK'N SHEET! FOOK'N DOOR ES LOOKED!
AN' AY LEF'DE KEE BA'KEEN DE FOOK'N BAR!
IES
KNOWING THAT YOUR ACCENT IS FAKE DOESN'T SEEM TO MAKE IT ANY LESS ANNOYING.
MIGHT EVEN BE MORE ANNOYING.
YOU TRIED THE LOCK?
JU FOOK! RAOUL JUS'TOL'JU AT DOOR ES LOOK!
R'OOL
JU TEENK RAOUL BE MAK'N SHEET OOP?
NO, NO. I JUST WANTED YOU TO CONFIRM THAT THE DOOR IS INDEED LOCKED.
JEAH?
YEAH...
NOW, I'M GONNA HELP YOU OUT WITH THIS NEXT BIT, SINCE IT'S YOUR FIRST TIME AND ALL...
JUST... CLOSE YOUR EYES AND RELAX...
WHA? JU GED'DE FOOK 'WAY FRO'ME, JU CRAZ' PARVER FOOK!
?

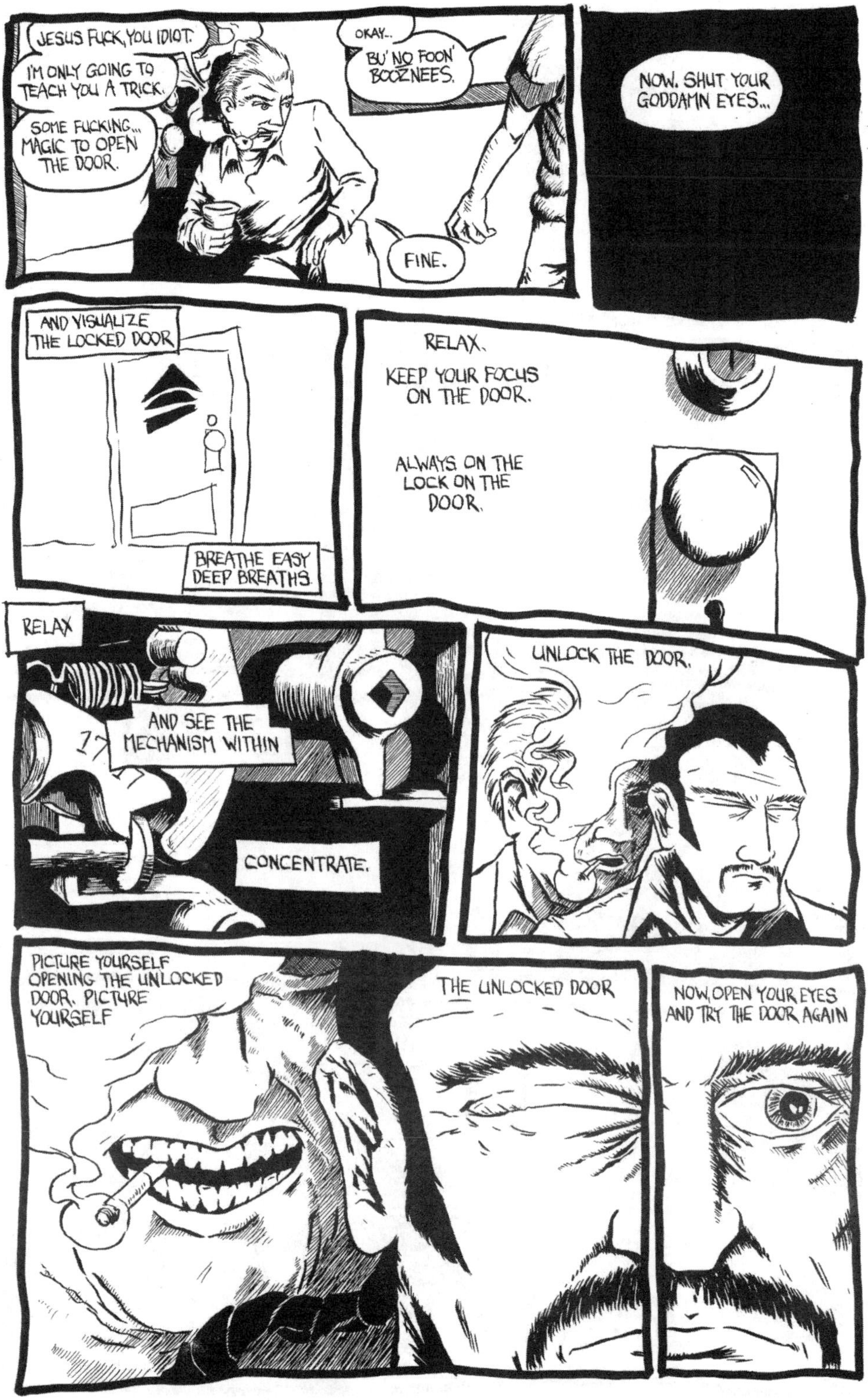
JESUS FUCK, YOU IDIOT.
I'M ONLY GOING TO TEACH YOU A TRICK.
SOME FUCKING... MAGIC TO OPEN THE DOOR.
OKAY..
BU' NO FOON' BOOZNEES.
FINE.
NOW. SHUT YOUR GODDAMN EYES...
AND VISUALIZE THE LOCKED DOOR
BREATHE EASY DEEP BREATHS.
RELAX.
KEEP YOUR FOCUS ON THE DOOR.
ALWAYS ON THE LOCK ON THE DOOR.
RELAX
AND SEE THE MECHANISM WITHIN
CONCENTRATE.
UNLOCK THE DOOR.
PICTURE YOURSELF OPENING THE UNLOCKED DOOR. PICTURE YOURSELF
THE UNLOCKED DOOR
NOW, OPEN YOUR EYES AND TRY THE DOOR AGAIN

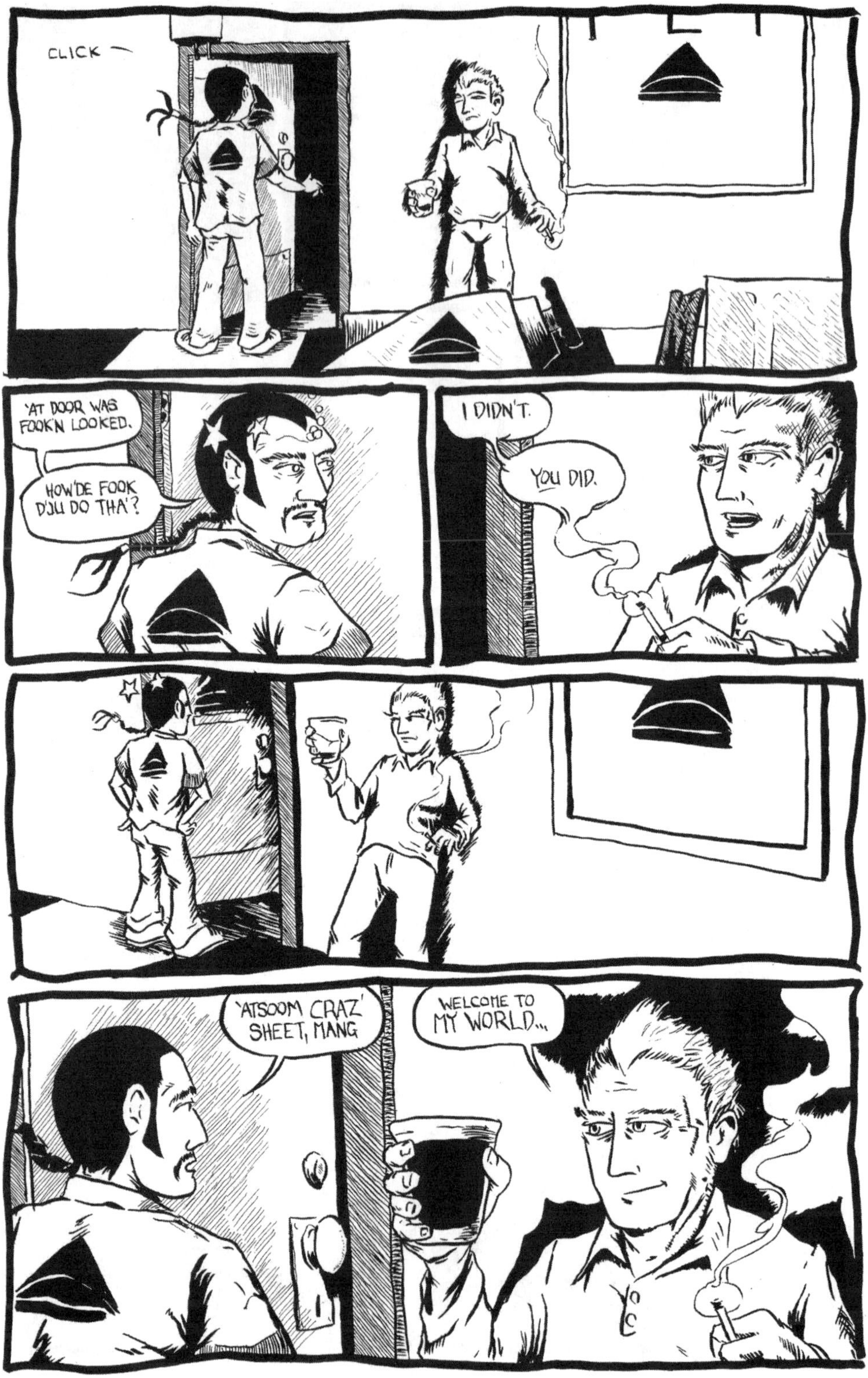
CLICK
'AT DOOR WAS FOOK'N LOOKED.
HOW'DE FOOK D'JU DO THA'?
I DIDN'T.
YOU DID.
'ATSOOM CRAZ' SHEET, MANG
WELCOME TO MY WORLD...

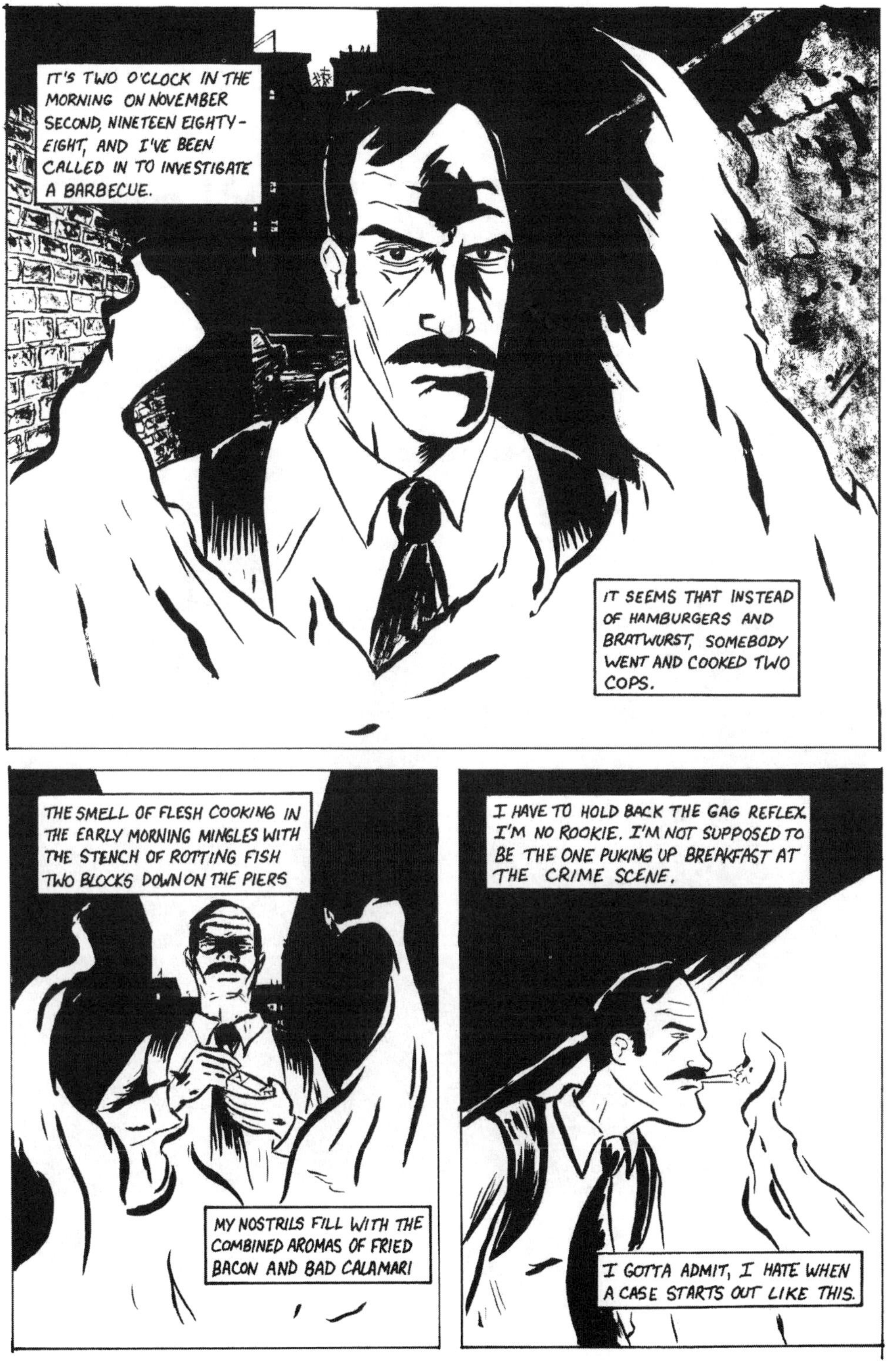
IT'S TWO O'CLOCK IN THE MORNING ON NOVEMBER SECOND, NINETEEN EIGHTY-EIGHT, AND I'VE BEEN CALLED IN TO INVESTIGATE A BARBECUE.
IT SEEMS THAT INSTEAD OF HAMBURGERS AND BRATWURST, SOMEBODY WENT AND COOKED TWO COPS.
THE SMELL OF FLESH COOKING IN THE EARLY MORNING MINGLES WITH THE STENCH OF ROTTING FISH TWO BLOCKS DOWN ON THE PIERS
MY NOSTRILS FILL WITH THE COMBINED AROMAS OF FRIED BACON AND BAD CALAMARI
I HAVE TO HOLD BACK THE GAG REFLEX. I'M NO ROOKIE. I'M NOT SUPPOSED TO BE THE ONE PUKING UP BREAKFAST AT THE CRIME SCENE.
I GOTTA ADMIT, I HATE WHEN A CASE STARTS OUT LIKE THIS.

plastic farm

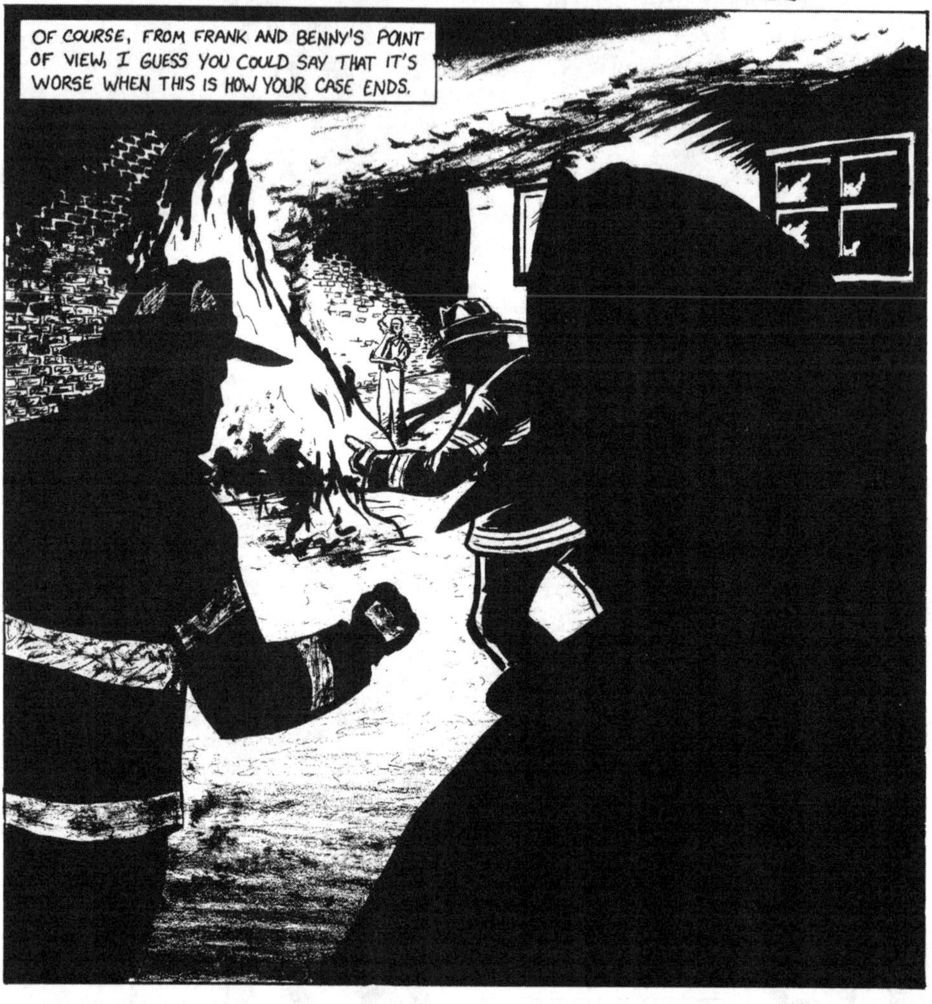
OF COURSE, FROM FRANK AND BENNY'S POINT OF VIEW, I GUESS YOU COULD SAY THAT IT'S WORSE WHEN THIS IS HOW YOUR CASE ENDS.

CHAPTER ELEVEN

Jake Goner and the Interrupted Thought

art by dennis culver

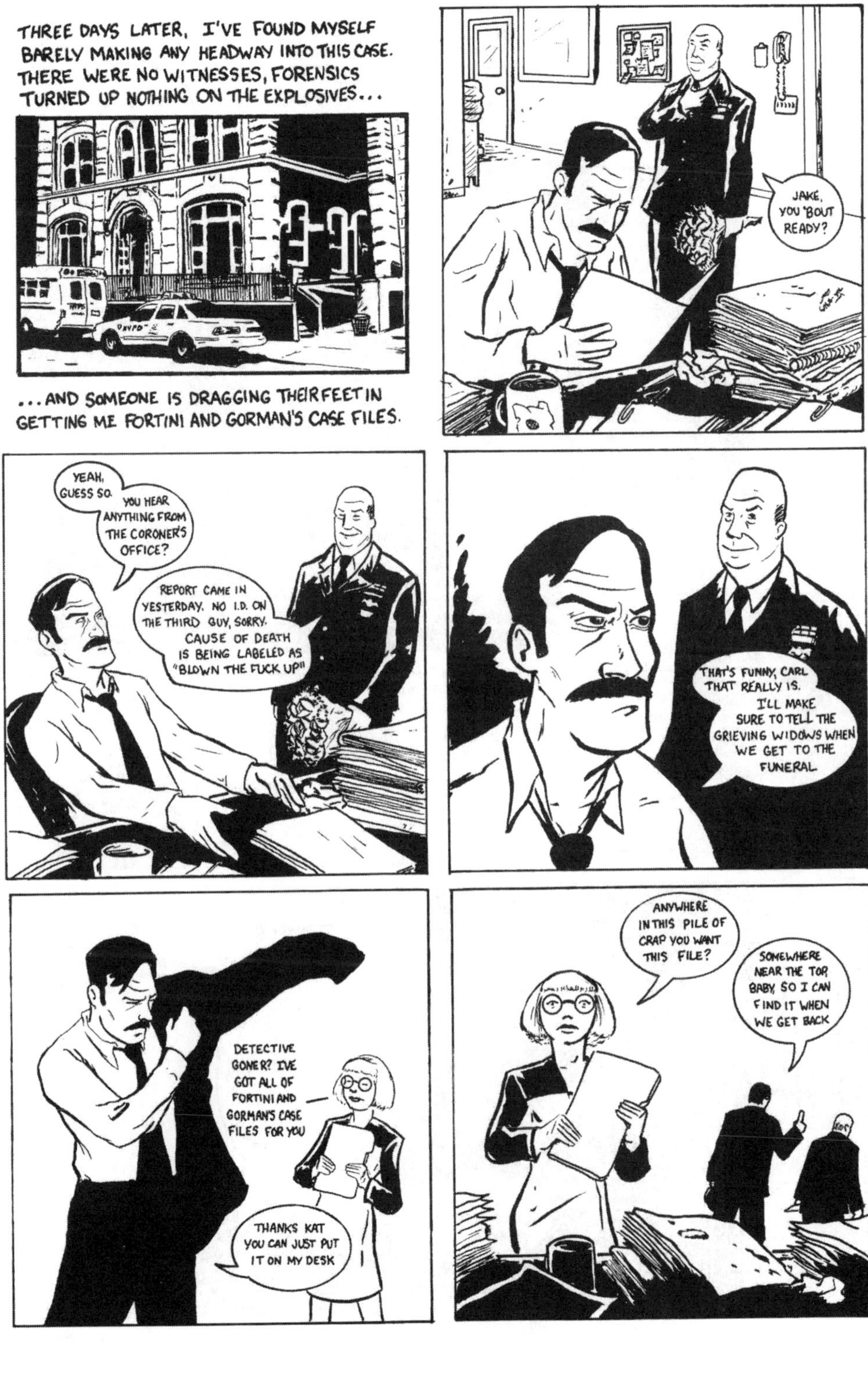
THREE DAYS LATER, I'VE FOUND MYSELF BARELY MAKING ANY HEADWAY INTO THIS CASE. THERE WERE NO WITNESSES, FORENSICS TURNED UP NOTHING ON THE EXPLOSIVES...
NYPD
...AND SOMEONE IS DRAGGING THEIR FEET IN GETTING ME FORTINI AND GORMAN'S CASE FILES.
JAKE, YOU 'BOUT READY?
YEAH, GUESS SO.
YOU HEAR ANYTHING FROM THE CORONER'S OFFICE?
REPORT CAME IN YESTERDAY. NO I.D. ON THE THIRD GUY, SORRY. CAUSE OF DEATH IS BEING LABELED AS "BLOWN THE FUCK UP"
THAT'S FUNNY, CARL THAT REALLY IS. I'LL MAKE SURE TO TELL THE GRIEVING WIDOWS WHEN WE GET TO THE FUNERAL
DETECTIVE GONER? I'VE GOT ALL OF FORTINI AND GORMAN'S CASE FILES FOR YOU
THANKS KAT YOU CAN JUST PUT IT ON MY DESK
ANYWHERE IN THIS PILE OF CRAP YOU WANT THIS FILE?
SOMEWHERE NEAR THE TOP, BABY, SO I CAN FIND IT WHEN WE GET BACK

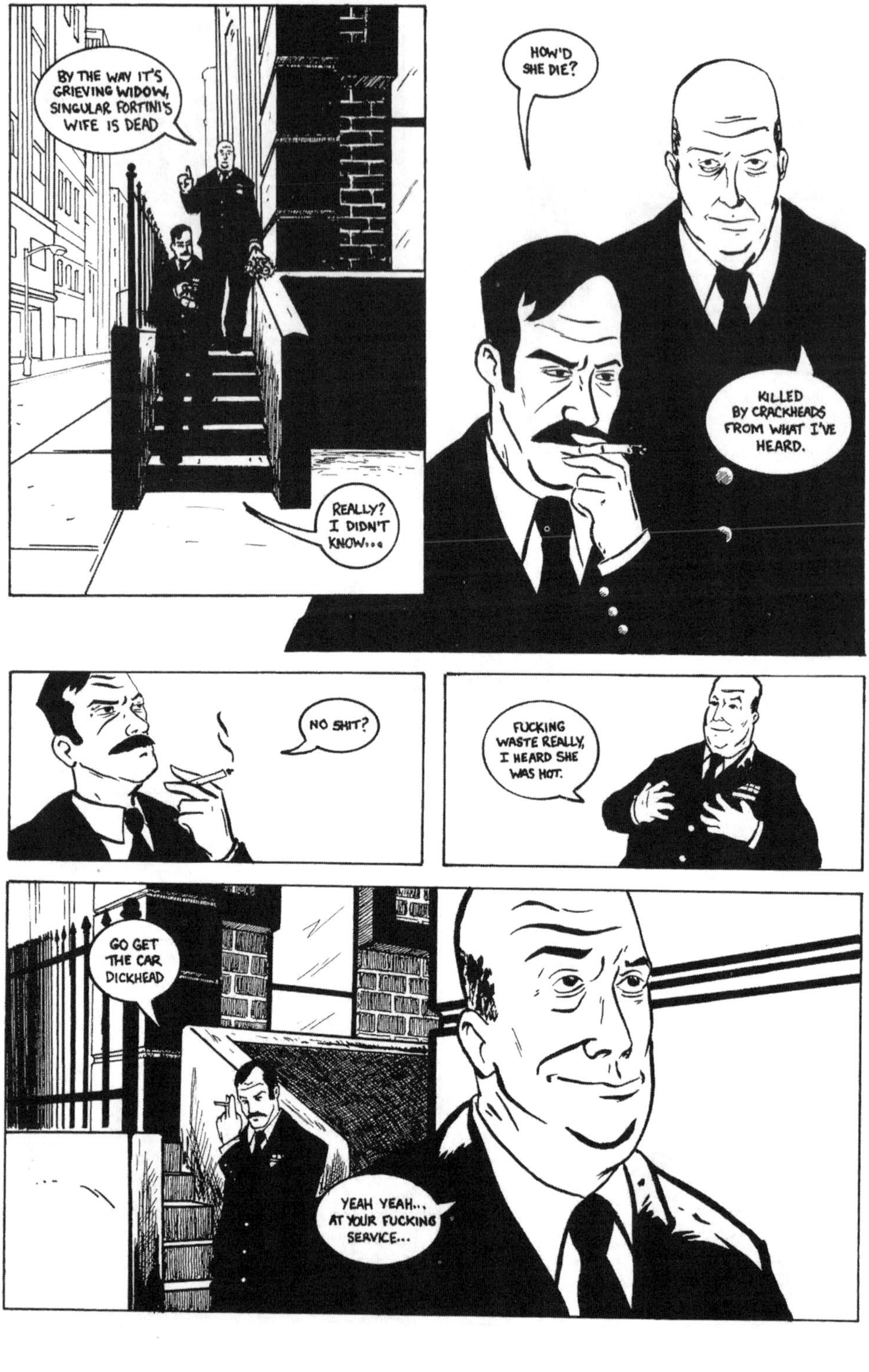
BY THE WAY IT'S GRIEVING WIDOW, SINGULAR FORTINI'S WIFE IS DEAD
REALLY? I DIDN'T KNOW...
HOW'D SHE DIE?
KILLED BY CRACKHEADS FROM WHAT I'VE HEARD.
NO SHIT?
FUCKING WASTE REALLY, I HEARD SHE WAS HOT.
GO GET THE CAR DICKHEAD
YEAH YEAH... AT YOUR FUCKING SERVICE...

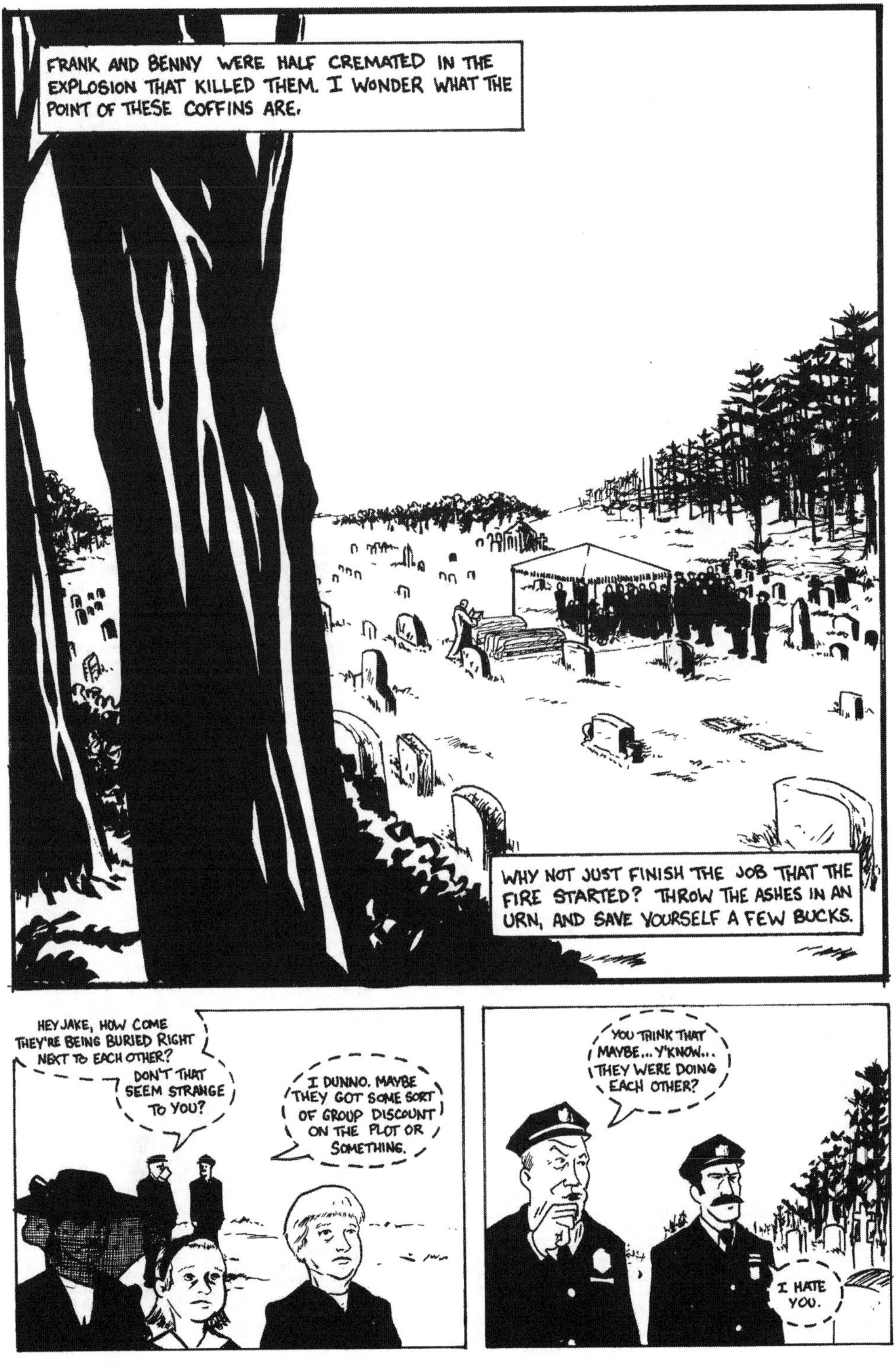
FRANK AND BENNY WERE HALF CREMATED IN THE EXPLOSION THAT KILLED THEM. I WONDER WHAT THE POINT OF THESE COFFINS ARE.
WHY NOT JUST FINISH THE JOB THAT THE FIRE STARTED? THROW THE ASHES IN AN URN, AND SAVE YOURSELF A FEW BUCKS.
HEY JAKE, HOW COME THEY'RE BEING BURIED RIGHT NEXT TO EACH OTHER?
DON'T THAT SEEM STRANGE TO YOU?
I DUNNO. MAYBE THEY GOT SOME SORT OF GROUP DISCOUNT ON THE PLOT OR SOMETHING.
YOU THINK THAT MAYBE... Y'KNOW... THEY WERE DOING EACH OTHER?
I HATE YOU.

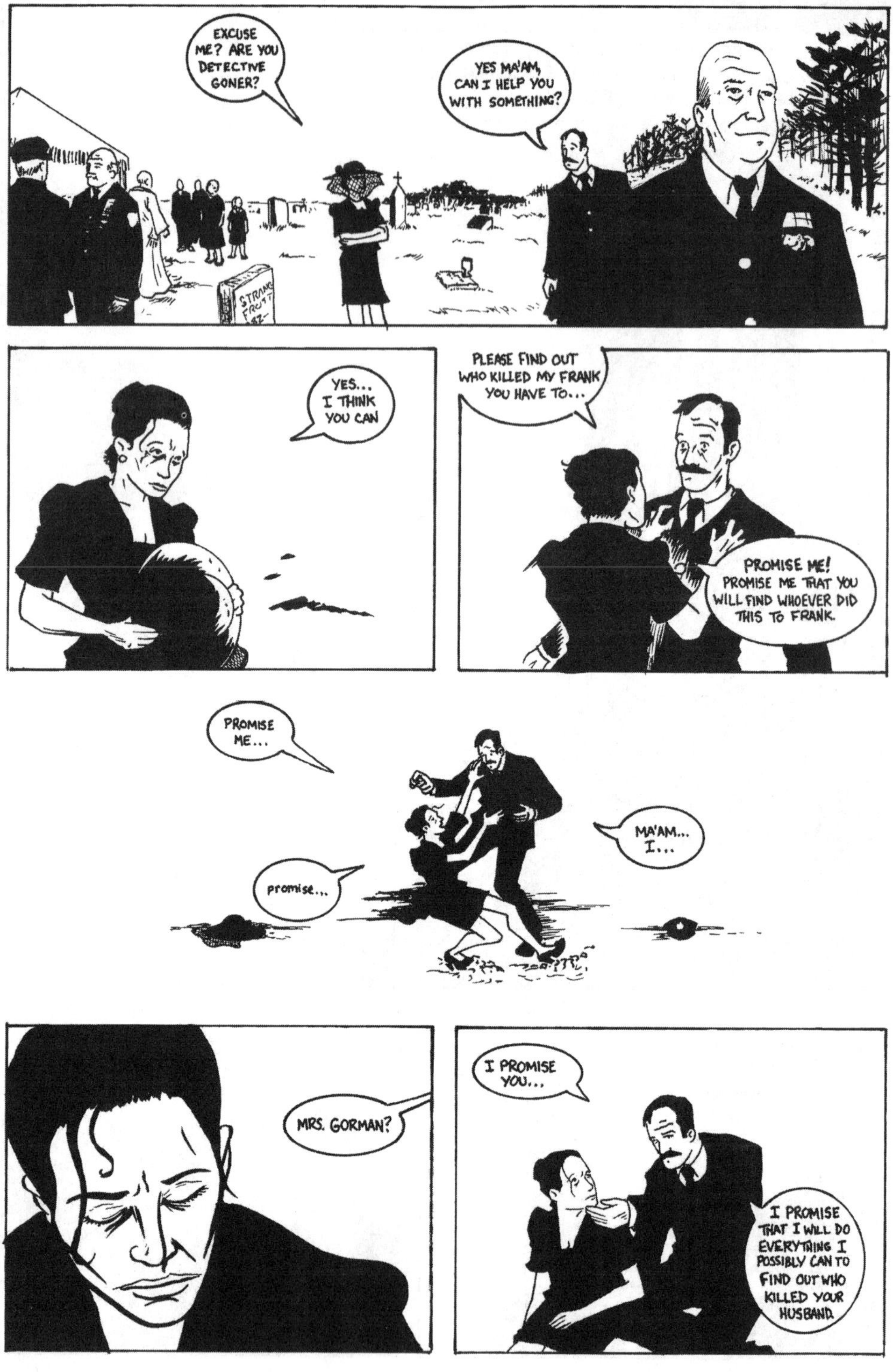
EXCUSE ME? ARE YOU DETECTIVE GONER?
YES MA'AM, CAN I HELP YOU WITH SOMETHING?
YES... I THINK YOU CAN
PLEASE FIND OUT WHO KILLED MY FRANK YOU HAVE TO...
PROMISE ME! PROMISE ME THAT YOU WILL FIND WHOEVER DID THIS TO FRANK.
PROMISE ME...
promise...
MA'AM... I...
MRS. GORMAN?
I PROMISE YOU...
I PROMISE THAT I WILL DO EVERYTHING I POSSIBLY CAN TO FIND OUT WHO KILLED YOUR HUSBAND.

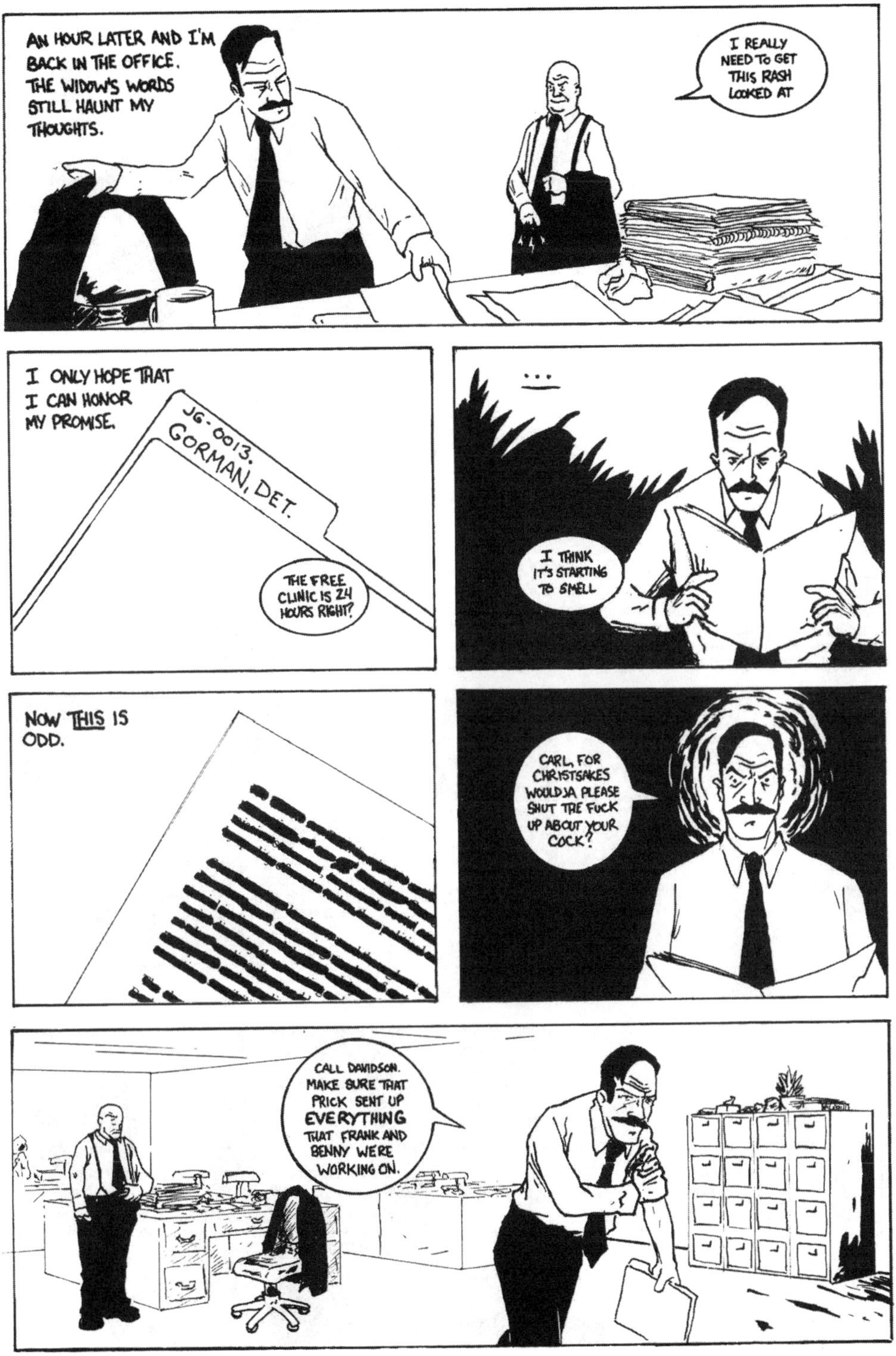
AN HOUR LATER AND I'M BACK IN THE OFFICE. THE WIDOW'S WORDS STILL HAUNT MY THOUGHTS.
I REALLY NEED TO GET THIS RASH LOOKED AT
I ONLY HOPE THAT I CAN HONOR MY PROMISE.
JG-0013.
GORMAN, DET.
THE FREE CLINIC IS 24 HOURS RIGHT?
...
I THINK IT'S STARTING TO SMELL
NOW THIS IS ODD.
CARL, FOR CHRISTSAKES WOULDJA PLEASE SHUT THE FUCK UP ABOUT YOUR COCK?
CALL DAVIDSON. MAKE SURE THAT PRICK SENT UP EVERYTHING THAT FRANK AND BENNY WERE WORKING ON.

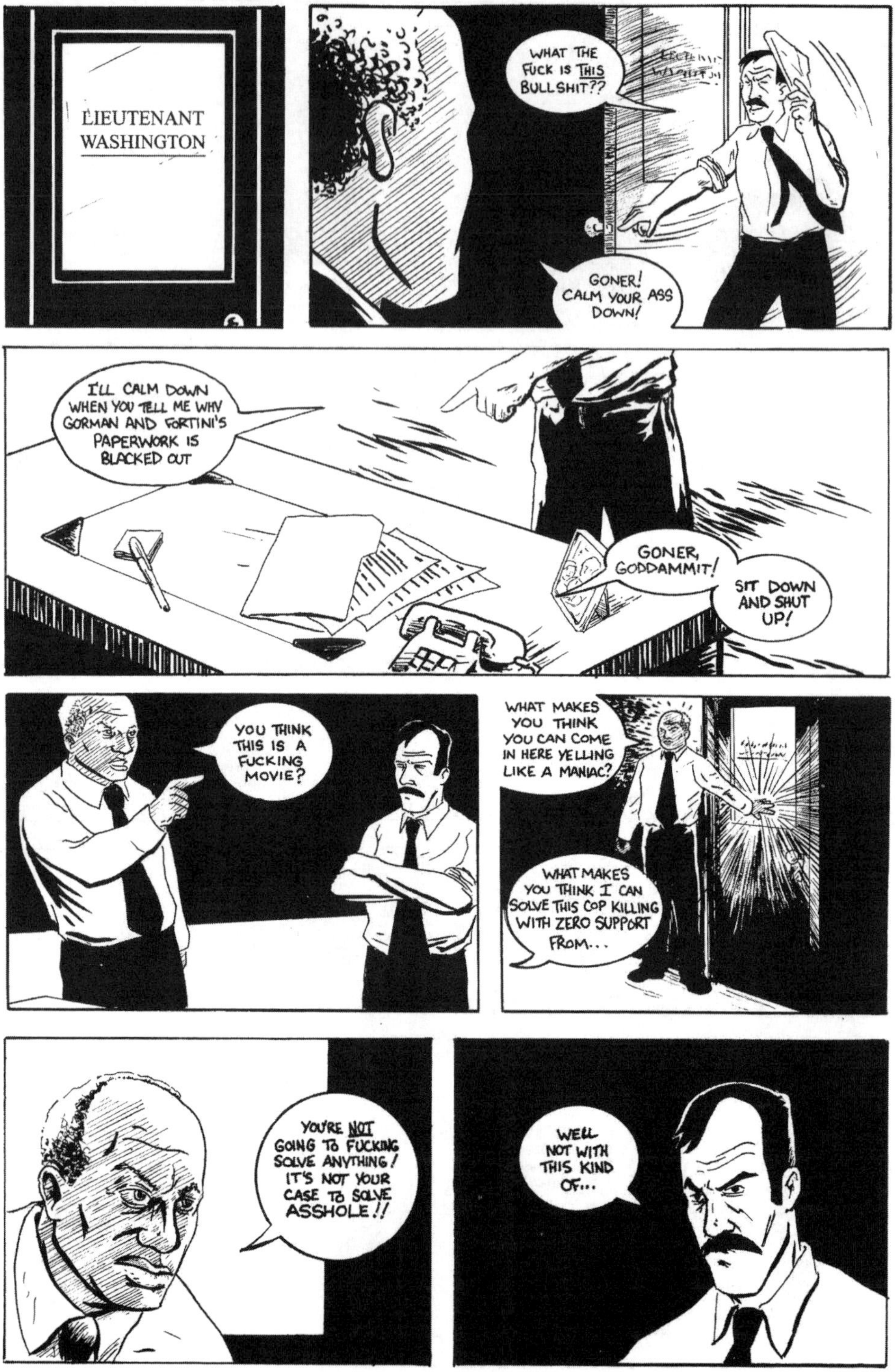
LIEUTENANT WASHINGTON
WHAT THE FUCK IS THIS BULLSHIT??
GONER! CALM YOUR ASS DOWN!
I'LL CALM DOWN WHEN YOU TELL ME WHY GORMAN AND FORTINI'S PAPERWORK IS BLACKED OUT
GONER, GODDAMMIT!
SIT DOWN AND SHUT UP!
YOU THINK THIS IS A FUCKING MOVIE?
WHAT MAKES YOU THINK YOU CAN COME IN HERE YELLING LIKE A MANIAC?
WHAT MAKES YOU THINK I CAN SOLVE THIS COP KILLING WITH ZERO SUPPORT FROM...
YOU'RE NOT GOING TO FUCKING SOLVE ANYTHING! IT'S NOT YOUR CASE TO SOLVE ASSHOLE!!
WELL NOT WITH THIS KIND OF...

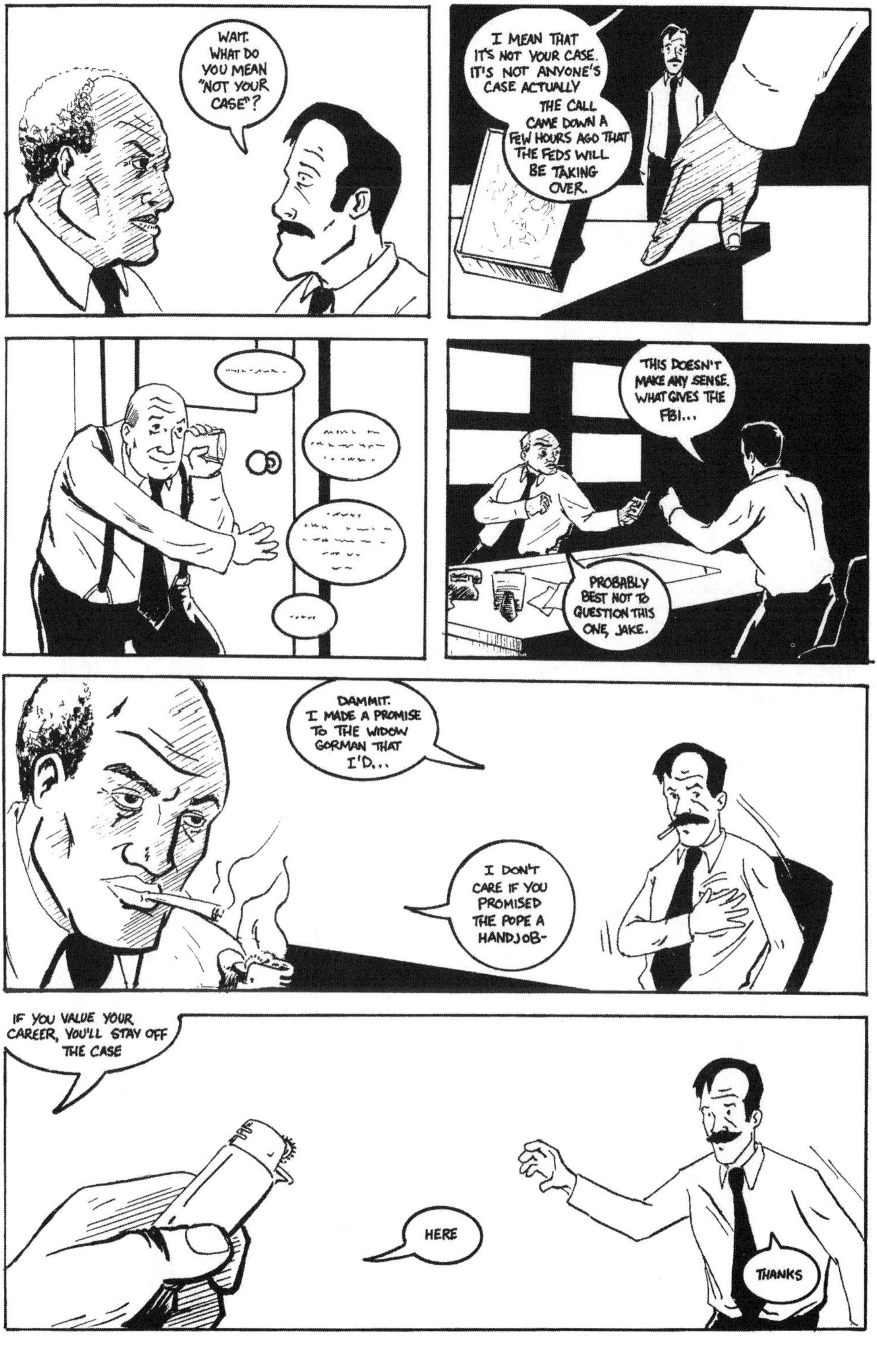
WAIT. WHAT DO YOU MEAN "NOT YOUR CASE"?
I MEAN THAT IT'S NOT YOUR CASE. IT'S NOT ANYONE'S CASE ACTUALLY
THE CALL CAME DOWN A FEW HOURS AGO THAT THE FEDS WILL BE TAKING OVER.
THIS DOESN'T MAKE ANY SENSE. WHAT GIVES THE FBI...
PROBABLY BEST NOT TO QUESTION THIS ONE, JAKE.
DAMMIT. I MADE A PROMISE TO THE WIDOW GORMAN THAT I'D...
I DON'T CARE IF YOU PROMISED THE POPE A HANDJOB-
IF YOU VALUE YOUR CAREER, YOU'LL STAY OFF THE CASE
HERE
THANKS

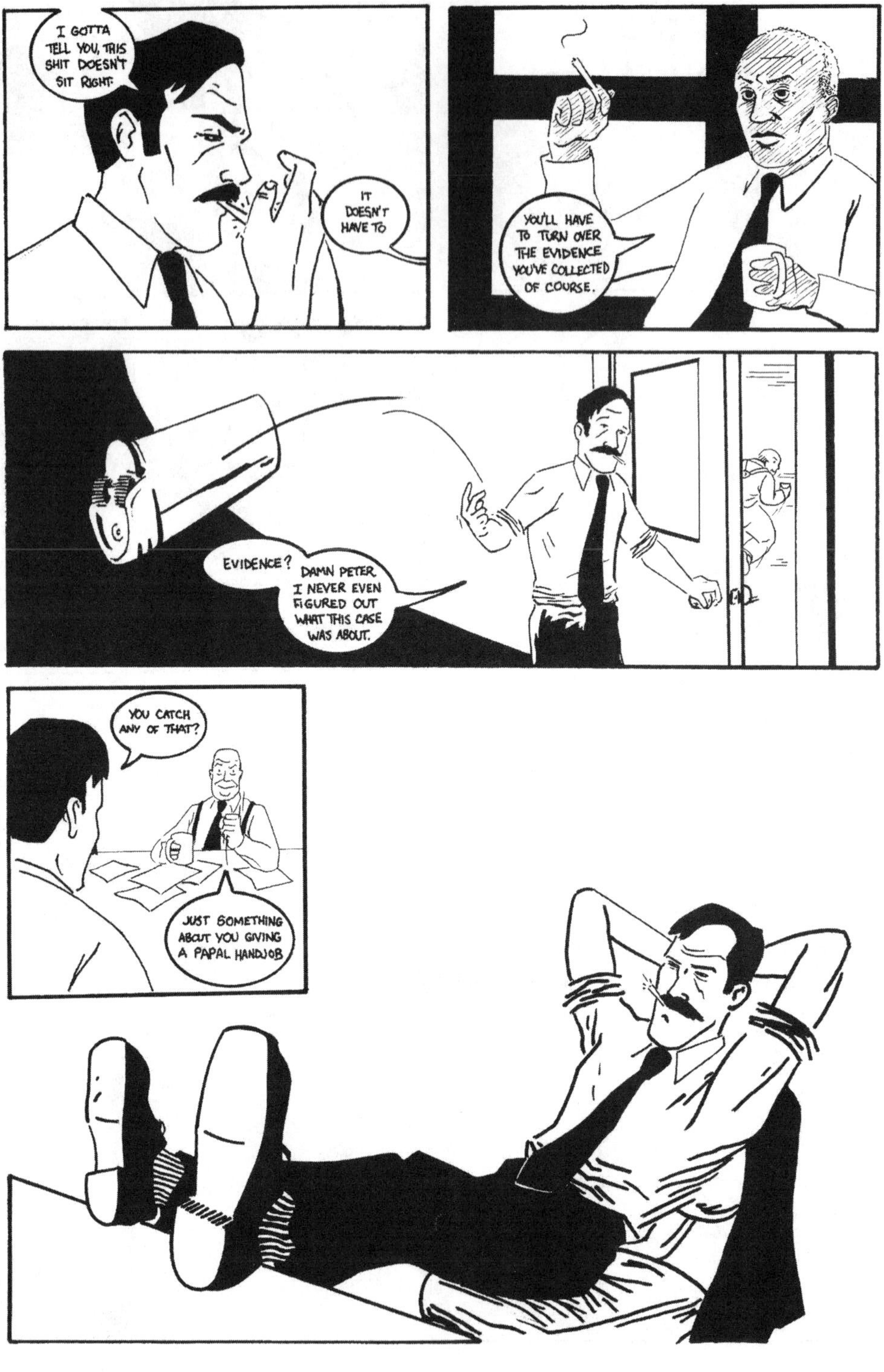
I GOTTA TELL YOU, THIS SHIT DOESN'T SIT RIGHT.
IT DOESN'T HAVE TO
YOU'LL HAVE TO TURN OVER THE EVIDENCE YOU'VE COLLECTED OF COURSE.
EVIDENCE?
DAMN PETER. I NEVER EVEN FIGURED OUT WHAT THIS CASE WAS ABOUT.
YOU CATCH ANY OF THAT?
JUST SOMETHING ABOUT YOU GIVING A PAPAL HANDJOB

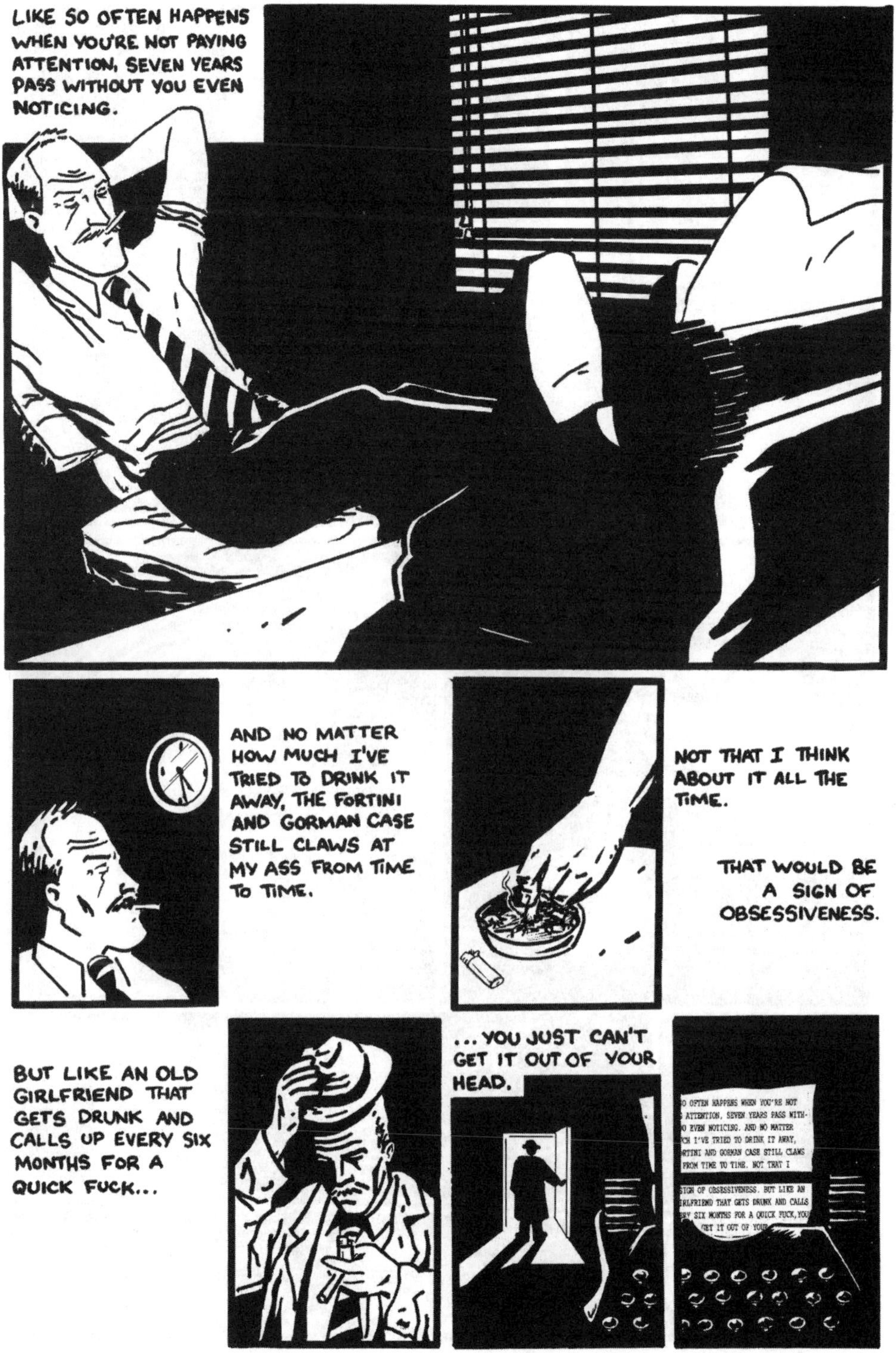
LIKE SO OFTEN HAPPENS WHEN YOU'RE NOT PAYING ATTENTION, SEVEN YEARS PASS WITHOUT YOU EVEN NOTICING.
AND NO MATTER HOW MUCH I'VE TRIED TO DRINK IT AWAY, THE FORTINI AND GORMAN CASE STILL CLAWS AT MY ASS FROM TIME TO TIME.
NOT THAT I THINK ABOUT IT ALL THE TIME.
THAT WOULD BE A SIGN OF OBSESSIVENESS.
BUT LIKE AN OLD GIRLFRIEND THAT GETS DRUNK AND CALLS UP EVERY SIX MONTHS FOR A QUICK FUCK...
...YOU JUST CAN'T GET IT OUT OF YOUR HEAD.
O OFTEN HAPPENS WHEN YOU'RE NOT
ATTENTION, SEVEN YEARS PASS WITH-
O EVEN NOTICING. AND NO MATTER
CH I'VE TRIED TO DRINK IT AWAY,
RTINI AND GORMAN CASE STILL CLAWS
FROM TIME TO TIME. NOT THAT I
IGN OF OBSESSIVENESS. BUT LIKE AN
IRLFRIEND THAT GETS DRUNK AND CALLS
Y SIX MONTHS FOR A QUICK FUCK, YOU
ET IT OUT OF YOUR

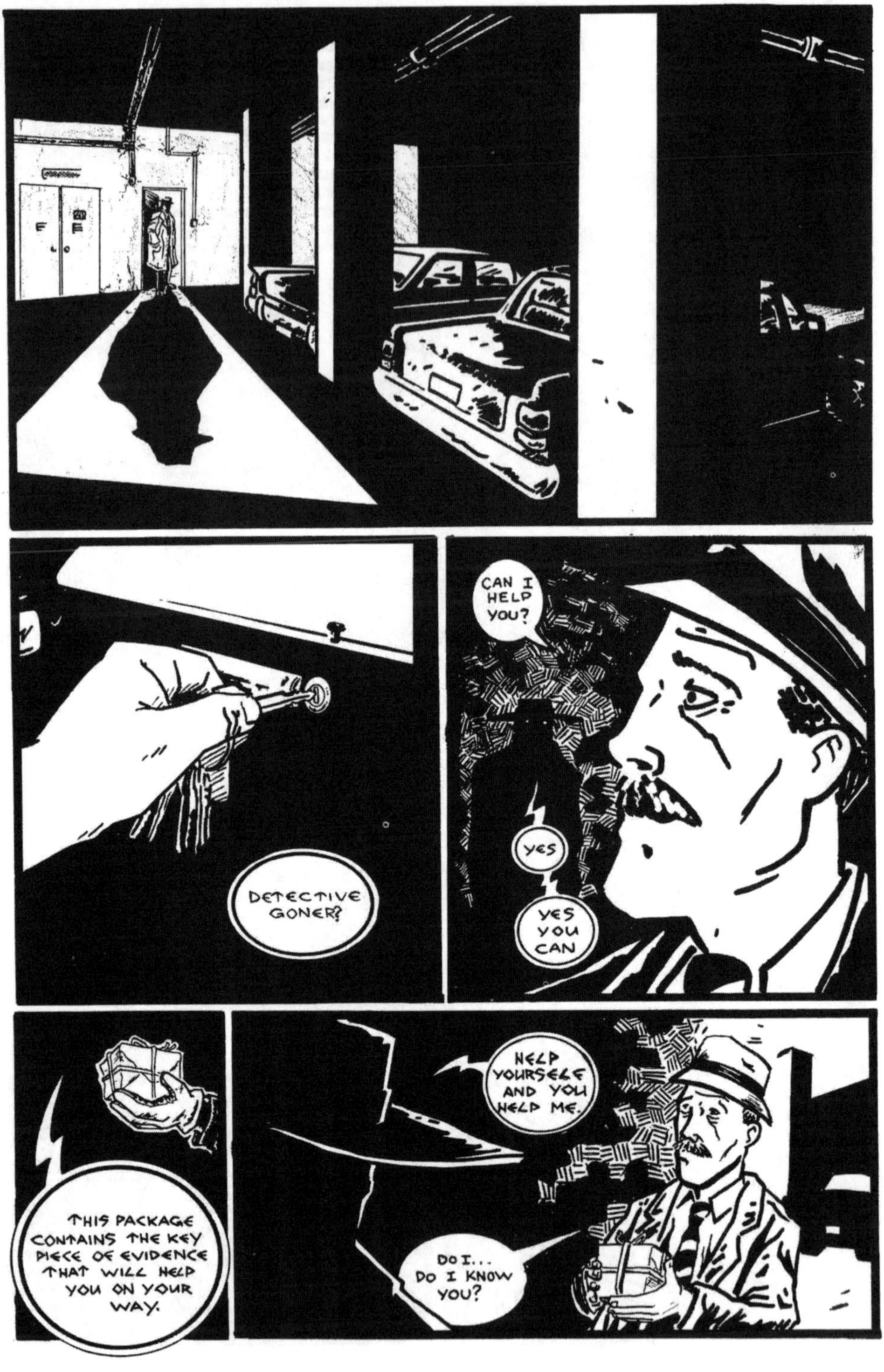
DETECTIVE GONER?
CAN I HELP YOU?
YES
YES YOU CAN
THIS PACKAGE CONTAINS THE KEY PIECE OF EVIDENCE THAT WILL HELP YOU ON YOUR WAY.
HELP YOURSELF AND YOU HELP ME.
DO I... DO I KNOW YOU?

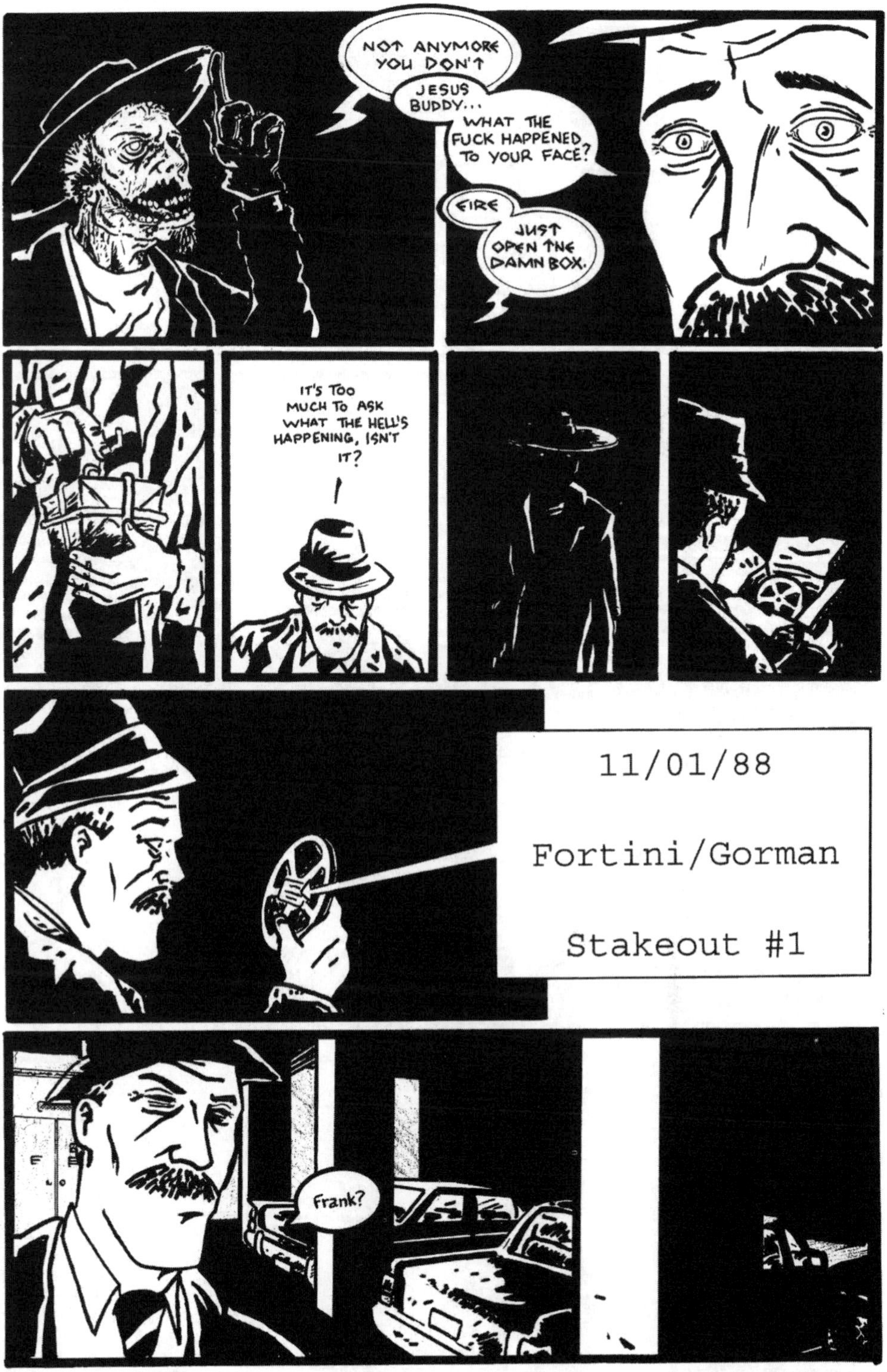
NOT ANYMORE YOU DON'T
JESUS BUDDY... WHAT THE FUCK HAPPENED TO YOUR FACE?
FIRE
JUST OPEN THE DAMN BOX.
IT'S TOO MUCH TO ASK WHAT THE HELL'S HAPPENING, ISN'T IT?
11/01/88
Fortini/Gorman
Stakeout #1
Frank?

I MAKE A QUICK CALL TO CARL AND HAVE HIM MEET ME IN THE CRIME LAB.

YES, WE HAVE A CRIME LAB.

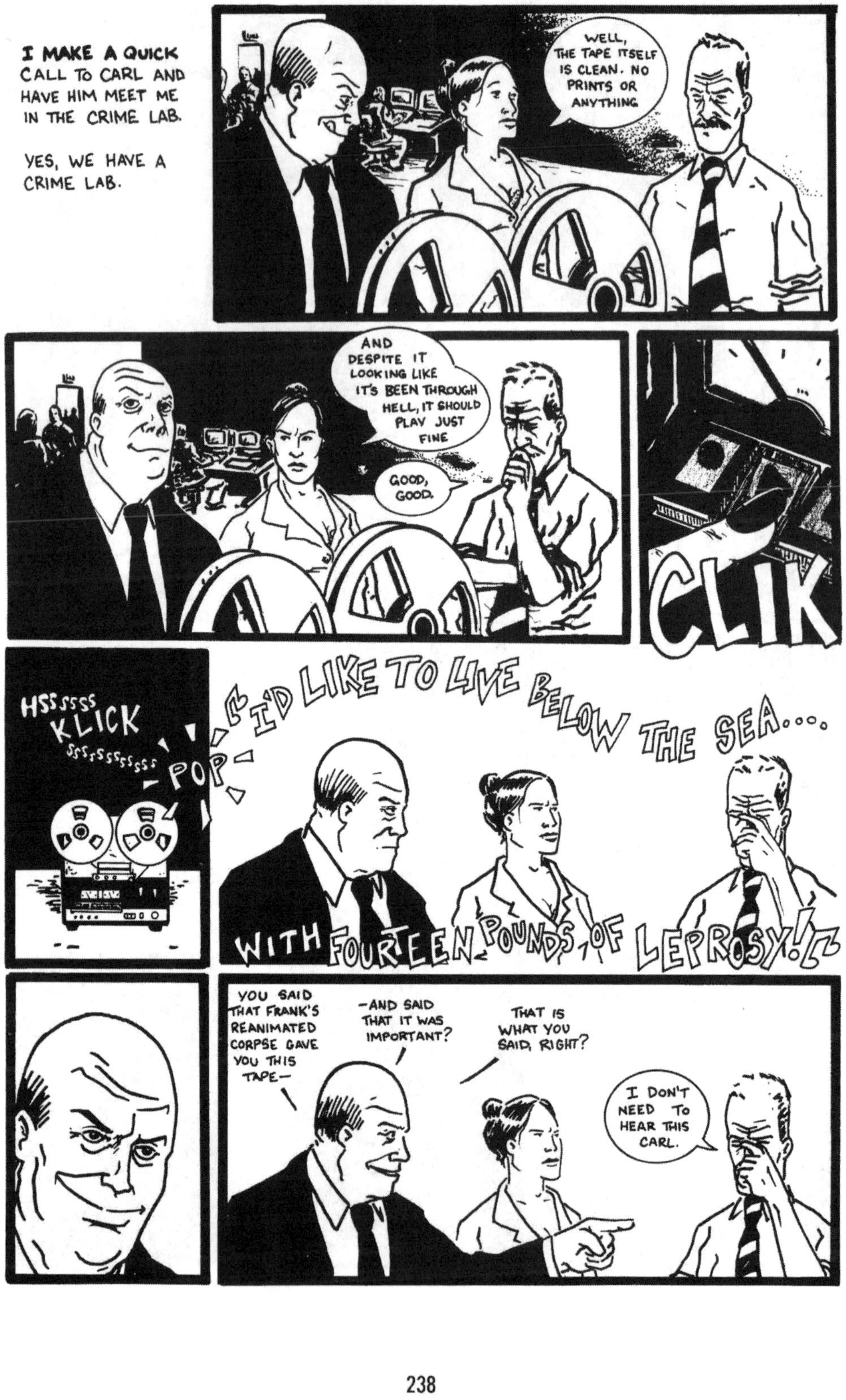
WELL, THE TAPE ITSELF IS CLEAN. NO PRINTS OR ANYTHING
AND DESPITE IT LOOKING LIKE IT'S BEEN THROUGH HELL, IT SHOULD PLAY JUST FINE
GOOD, GOOD.
CLIK
HSSSSSS
KLICK
SSSSSSSSSSSS
POP
"I'D LIKE TO LIVE BELOW THE SEA....
WITH FOURTEEN POUNDS OF LEPROSY!"
YOU SAID THAT FRANK'S REANIMATED CORPSE GAVE YOU THIS TAPE—
—AND SAID THAT IT WAS IMPORTANT?
THAT IS WHAT YOU SAID, RIGHT?
I DON'T NEED TO HEAR THIS CARL.

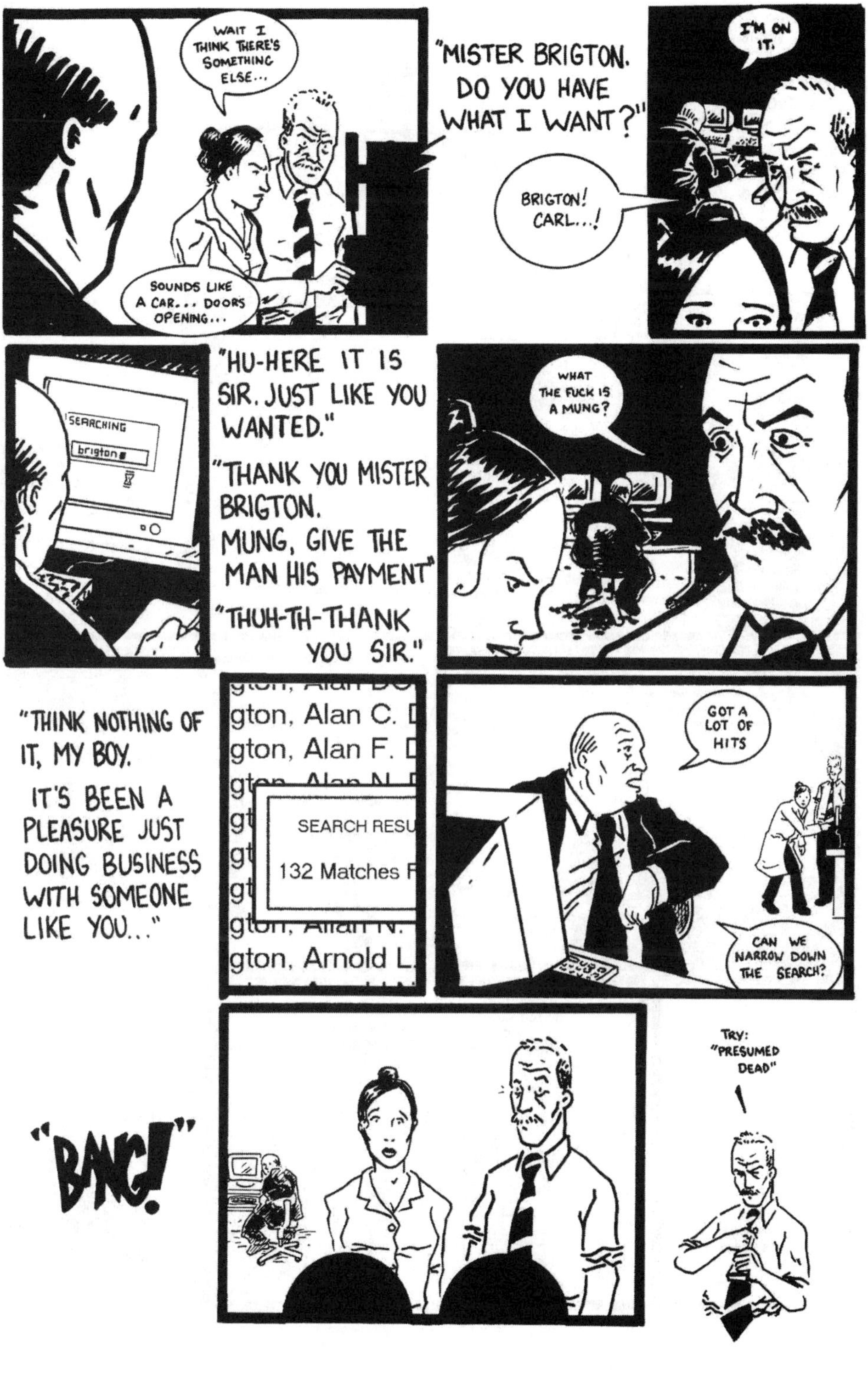
WAIT I THINK THERE'S SOMETHING ELSE...
SOUNDS LIKE A CAR... DOORS OPENING...
"MISTER BRIGTON. DO YOU HAVE WHAT I WANT?"
I'M ON IT.
BRIGTON! CARL...!
SEARCHING
brigton
"HU-HERE IT IS SIR. JUST LIKE YOU WANTED."
"THANK YOU MISTER BRIGTON. MUNG, GIVE THE MAN HIS PAYMENT"
"THUH-TH-THANK YOU SIR."
WHAT THE FUCK IS A MUNG?
"THINK NOTHING OF IT, MY BOY.
IT'S BEEN A PLEASURE JUST DOING BUSINESS WITH SOMEONE LIKE YOU..."
gton, Alan C. D
gton, Alan F. D
SEARCH RESU
132 Matches F
gton, Arnold L.
GOT A LOT OF HITS
CAN WE NARROW DOWN THE SEARCH?
"BANG!"
TRY: "PRESUMED DEAD"

CARL COMES UP WITH A SINGLE NAME AFTER THAT ONE CHARLES BRIGTON MISSING AND PRESUMED DECEASED. TURNS OUT THAT ALL OF BRIGTON'S FAMILY HAS DIED IN THE PAST SEVEN YEARS AND NO ONE AT ANY OF HIS PREVIOUS RESIDENCES SEEMS TO REMEMBER HIM.

HOLMDEL
MEDICAL CENTER

WHICH BRINGS US TO NEW JERSEY

OKAY SO BRIGTON WORKED HERE FROM '84 TO EARLY '88...

...WHEN HE QUIT OR GOT FIRED. THIS PLACE HAS A BUNCH OF DOCTORS WORKING THEIR PRACTICES...

...BRIGTON WAS A GENERAL WORKER AND DID SMALL JOBS FOR MOST OF THE DOCTORS THAT WERE WORKING HERE AT THE TIME. THING IS, ONLY ONE OF THOSE DOCTORS IS STILL WORKING HERE.

AKUTSU, S.   504
GENERAL PRACTICE

BAKER, J.   729
PARAPSYCHOLOGY

BANNON, M.   417
CHILD PSYCHOLOGY

BE   523
G   CHOLOGY

                             104
CIAN

T, W.   22
PH
TON
LD P

YKOWSKI, C.   506
OPHTHALMOLOGY

I CALLED AHEAD AND MADE AN APPOINTMENT.

DETECTIVE BRECKENRIDGE I PRESUME? MARY BANNON.

OH... I'M DETECTIVE GONER ACTUALLY. DETECTIVE BRECKENRIDGE IS...

PLEASE MA'AM, MY FRIENDS CALL ME CARL.

OH... I....

DR. BANNON? IS THERE SOMEWHERE WE CAN TALK?

240

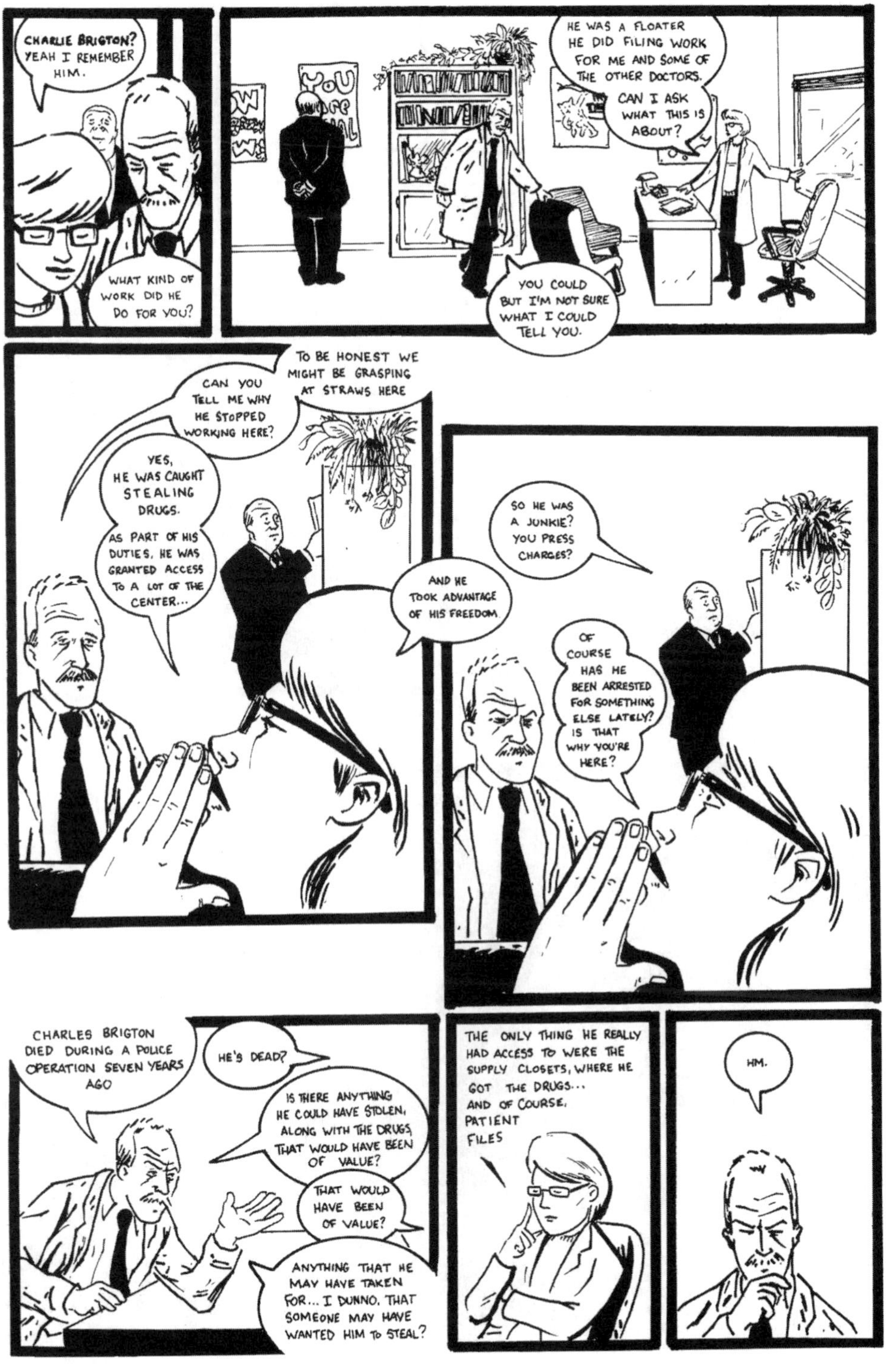
CHARLIE BRIGTON? YEAH I REMEMBER HIM.
WHAT KIND OF WORK DID HE DO FOR YOU?
HE WAS A FLOATER HE DID FILING WORK FOR ME AND SOME OF THE OTHER DOCTORS.
CAN I ASK WHAT THIS IS ABOUT?
YOU COULD BUT I'M NOT SURE WHAT I COULD TELL YOU.
CAN YOU TELL ME WHY HE STOPPED WORKING HERE?
TO BE HONEST WE MIGHT BE GRASPING AT STRAWS HERE
YES, HE WAS CAUGHT STEALING DRUGS.
AS PART OF HIS DUTIES, HE WAS GRANTED ACCESS TO A LOT OF THE CENTER...
AND HE TOOK ADVANTAGE OF HIS FREEDOM.
SO HE WAS A JUNKIE? YOU PRESS CHARGES?
OF COURSE HAS HE BEEN ARRESTED FOR SOMETHING ELSE LATELY? IS THAT WHY YOU'RE HERE?
CHARLES BRIGTON DIED DURING A POLICE OPERATION SEVEN YEARS AGO
HE'S DEAD?
IS THERE ANYTHING HE COULD HAVE STOLEN, ALONG WITH THE DRUGS, THAT WOULD HAVE BEEN OF VALUE?
THAT WOULD HAVE BEEN OF VALUE?
ANYTHING THAT HE MAY HAVE TAKEN FOR... I DUNNO. THAT SOMEONE MAY HAVE WANTED HIM TO STEAL?
THE ONLY THING HE REALLY HAD ACCESS TO WERE THE SUPPLY CLOSETS, WHERE HE GOT THE DRUGS... AND OF COURSE, PATIENT FILES
HM.

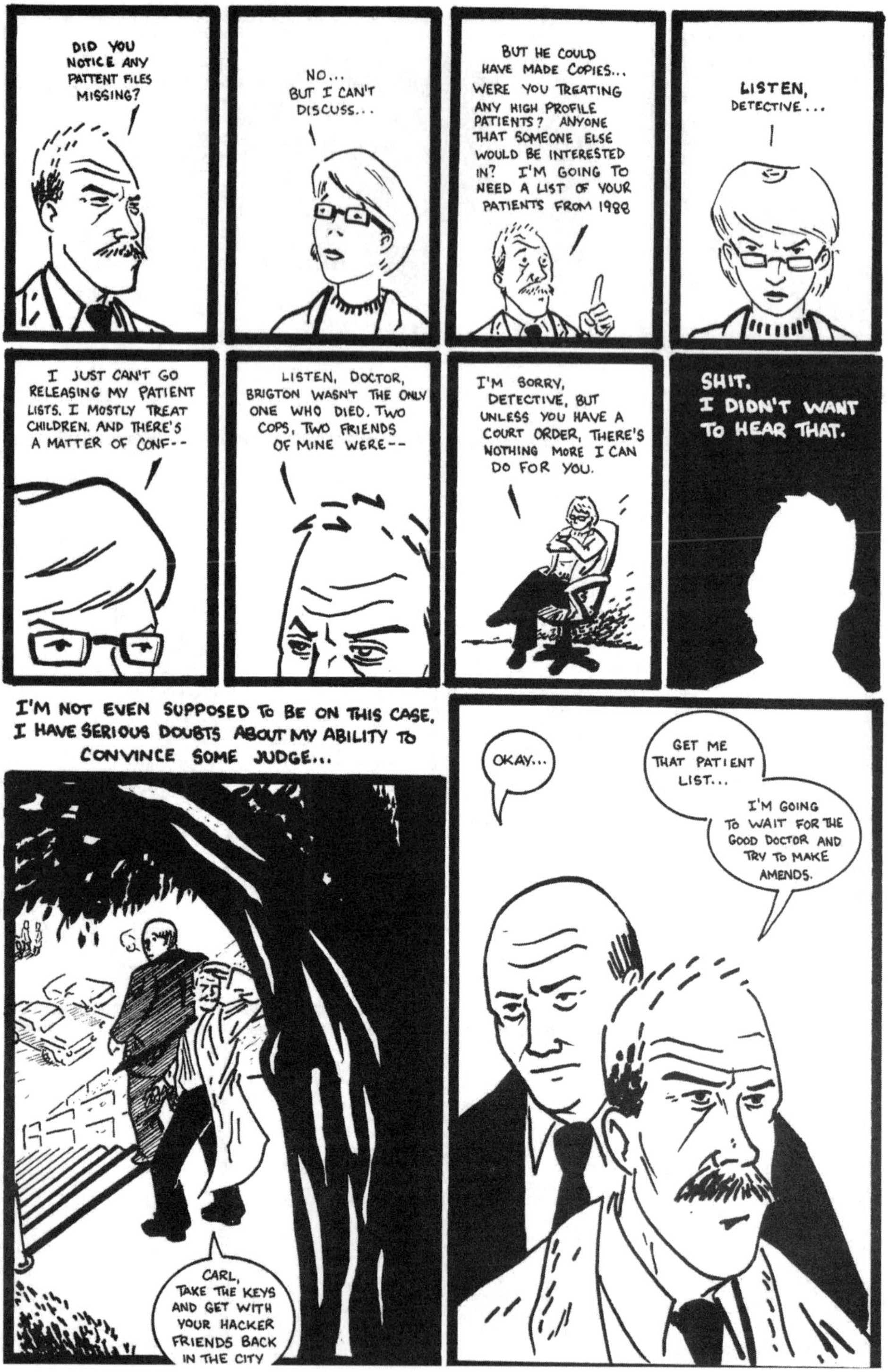
DID YOU NOTICE ANY PATIENT FILES MISSING?
NO... BUT I CAN'T DISCUSS...
BUT HE COULD HAVE MADE COPIES... WERE YOU TREATING ANY HIGH PROFILE PATIENTS? ANYONE THAT SOMEONE ELSE WOULD BE INTERESTED IN? I'M GOING TO NEED A LIST OF YOUR PATIENTS FROM 1988
LISTEN, DETECTIVE...
I JUST CAN'T GO RELEASING MY PATIENT LISTS. I MOSTLY TREAT CHILDREN. AND THERE'S A MATTER OF CONF--
LISTEN, DOCTOR, BRIGTON WASN'T THE ONLY ONE WHO DIED. TWO COPS, TWO FRIENDS OF MINE WERE--
I'M SORRY, DETECTIVE, BUT UNLESS YOU HAVE A COURT ORDER, THERE'S NOTHING MORE I CAN DO FOR YOU.
SHIT. I DIDN'T WANT TO HEAR THAT.
I'M NOT EVEN SUPPOSED TO BE ON THIS CASE. I HAVE SERIOUS DOUBTS ABOUT MY ABILITY TO CONVINCE SOME JUDGE...
CARL, TAKE THE KEYS AND GET WITH YOUR HACKER FRIENDS BACK IN THE CITY
OKAY...
GET ME THAT PATIENT LIST...
I'M GOING TO WAIT FOR THE GOOD DOCTOR AND TRY TO MAKE AMENDS.

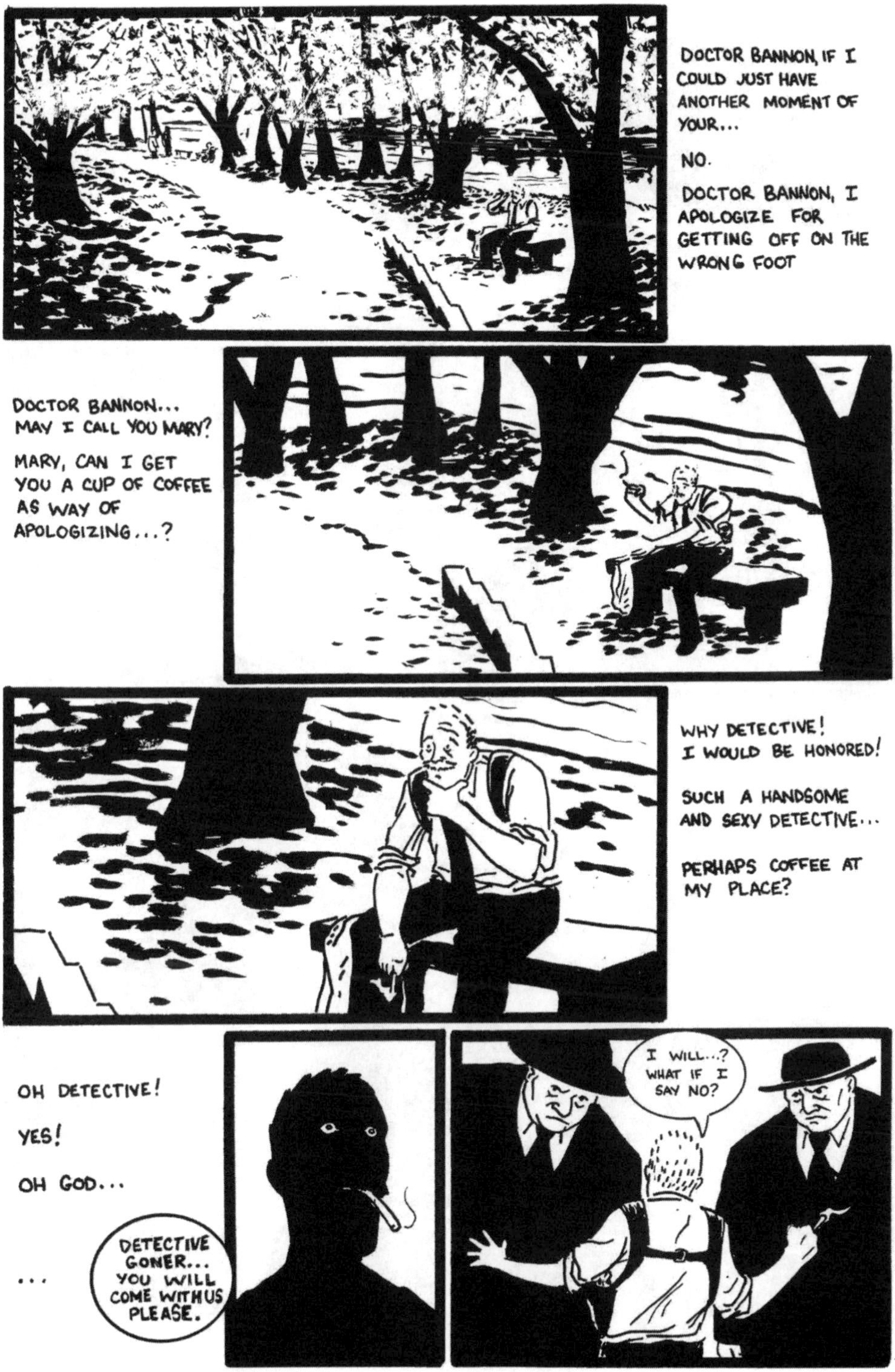
DOCTOR BANNON, IF I COULD JUST HAVE ANOTHER MOMENT OF YOUR...
NO.
DOCTOR BANNON, I APOLOGIZE FOR GETTING OFF ON THE WRONG FOOT
DOCTOR BANNON... MAY I CALL YOU MARY?
MARY, CAN I GET YOU A CUP OF COFFEE AS WAY OF APOLOGIZING...?
WHY DETECTIVE! I WOULD BE HONORED!
SUCH A HANDSOME AND SEXY DETECTIVE...
PERHAPS COFFEE AT MY PLACE?
OH DETECTIVE!
YES!
OH GOD...
...
DETECTIVE GONER... YOU WILL COME WITH US PLEASE.
I WILL...? WHAT IF I SAY NO?

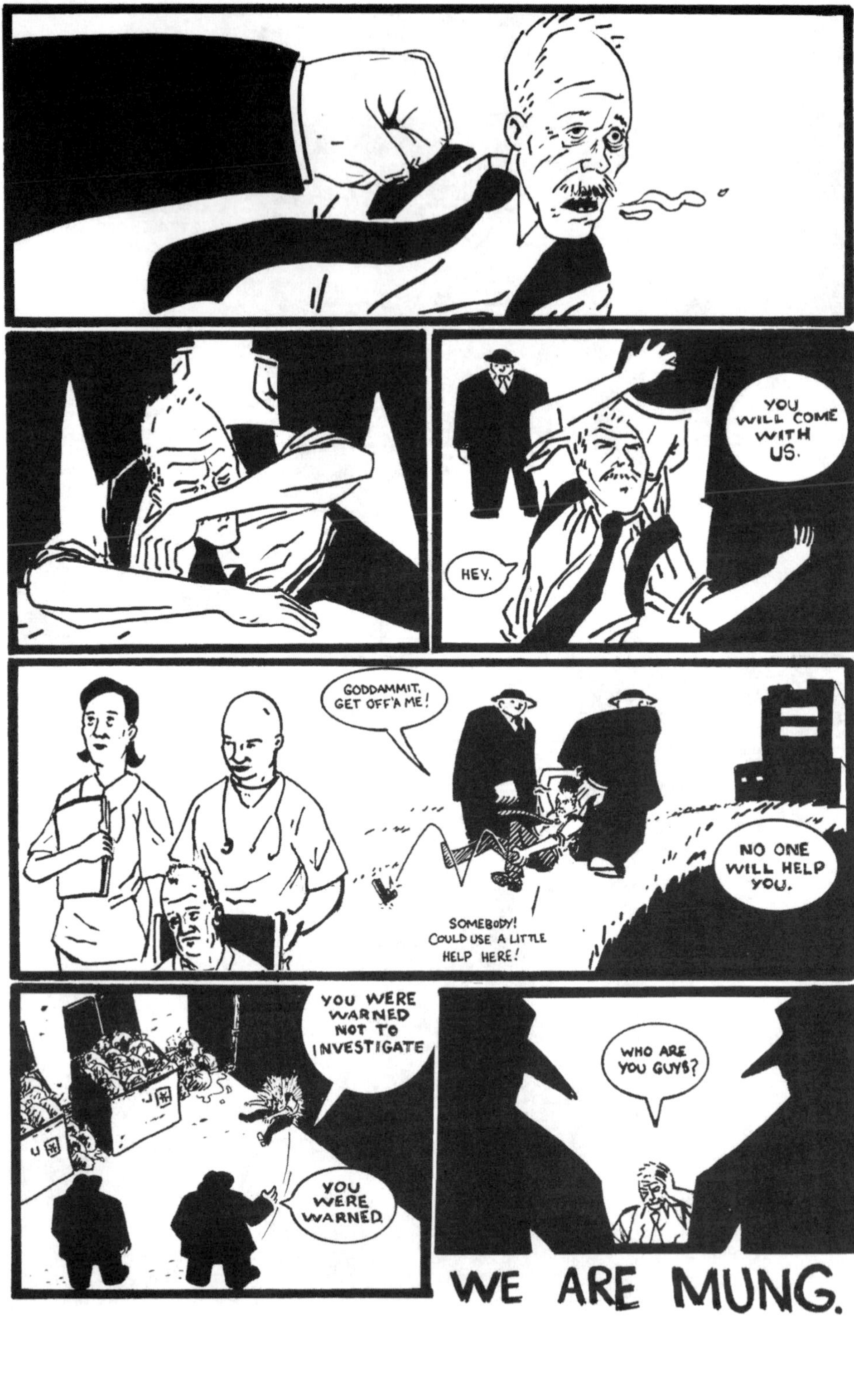
YOU WILL COME WITH US.
HEY.
GODDAMMIT, GET OFF'A ME!
NO ONE WILL HELP YOU.
SOMEBODY! COULD USE A LITTLE HELP HERE!
YOU WERE WARNED NOT TO INVESTIGATE
YOU WERE WARNED.
WHO ARE YOU GUYS?
WE ARE MUNG.

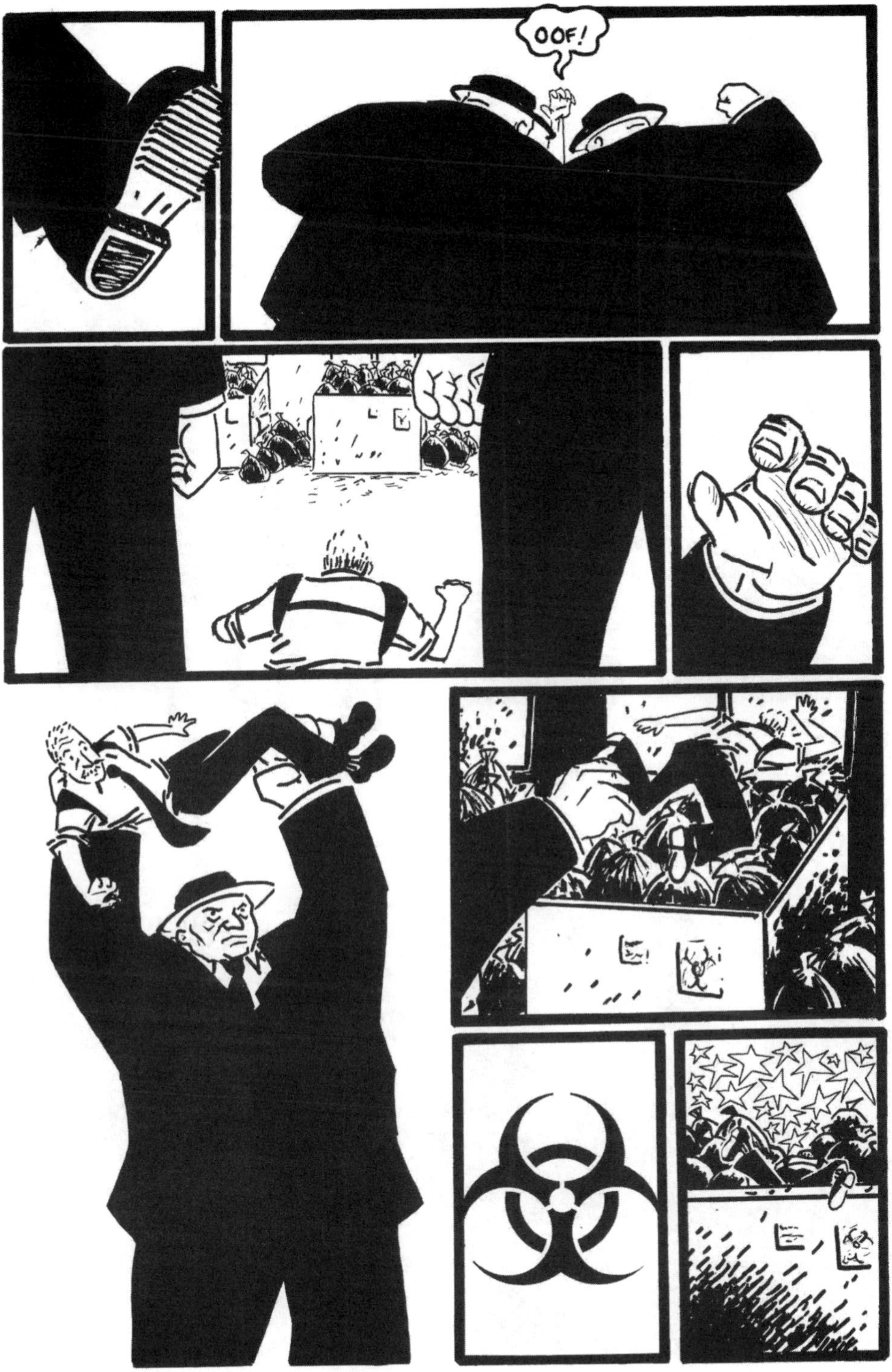
OOF!

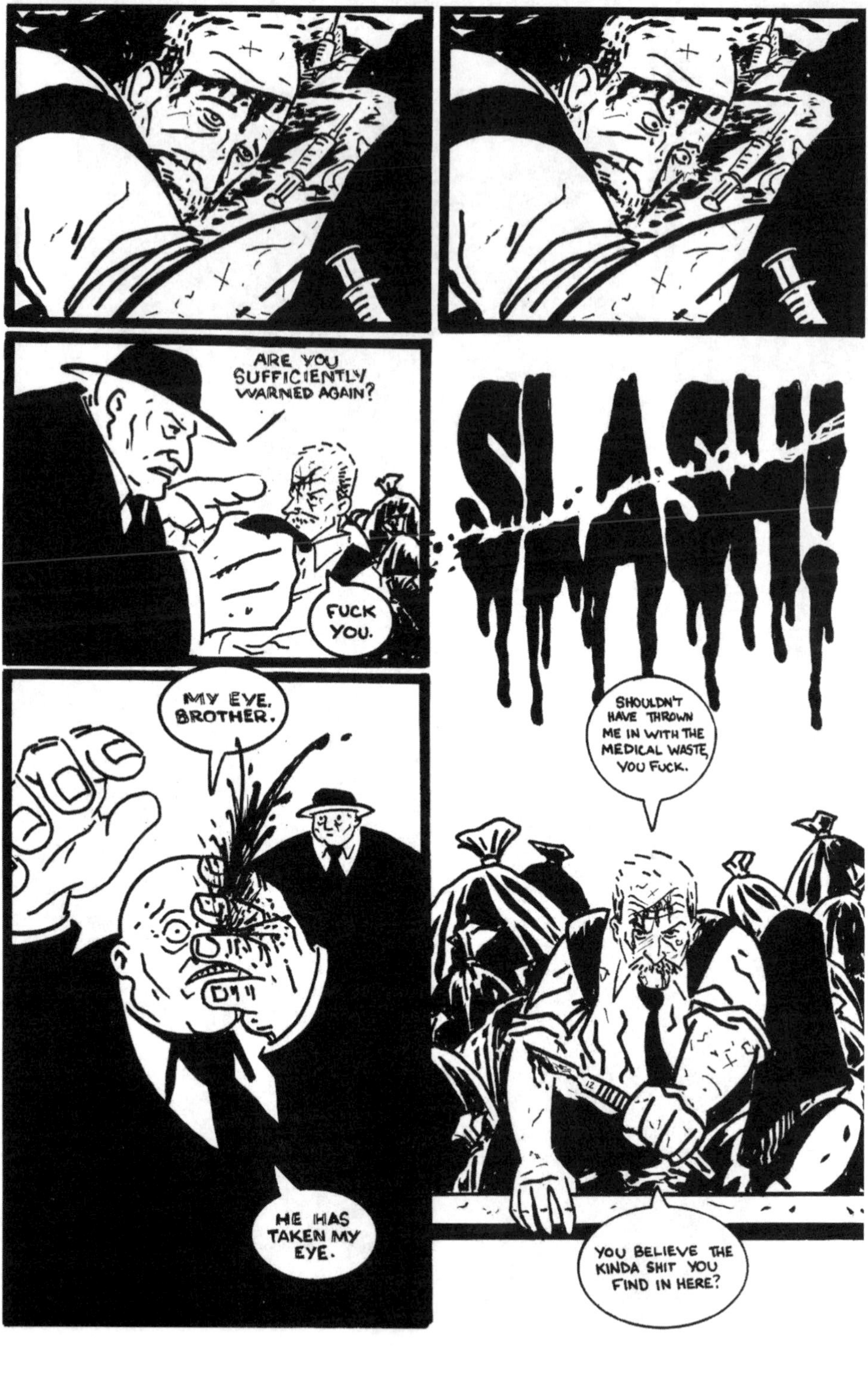
ARE YOU SUFFICIENTLY WARNED AGAIN?
FUCK YOU.
SLASH!
MY EYE, BROTHER.
HE HAS TAKEN MY EYE.
SHOULDN'T HAVE THROWN ME IN WITH THE MEDICAL WASTE, YOU FUCK.
YOU BELIEVE THE KINDA SHIT YOU FIND IN HERE?

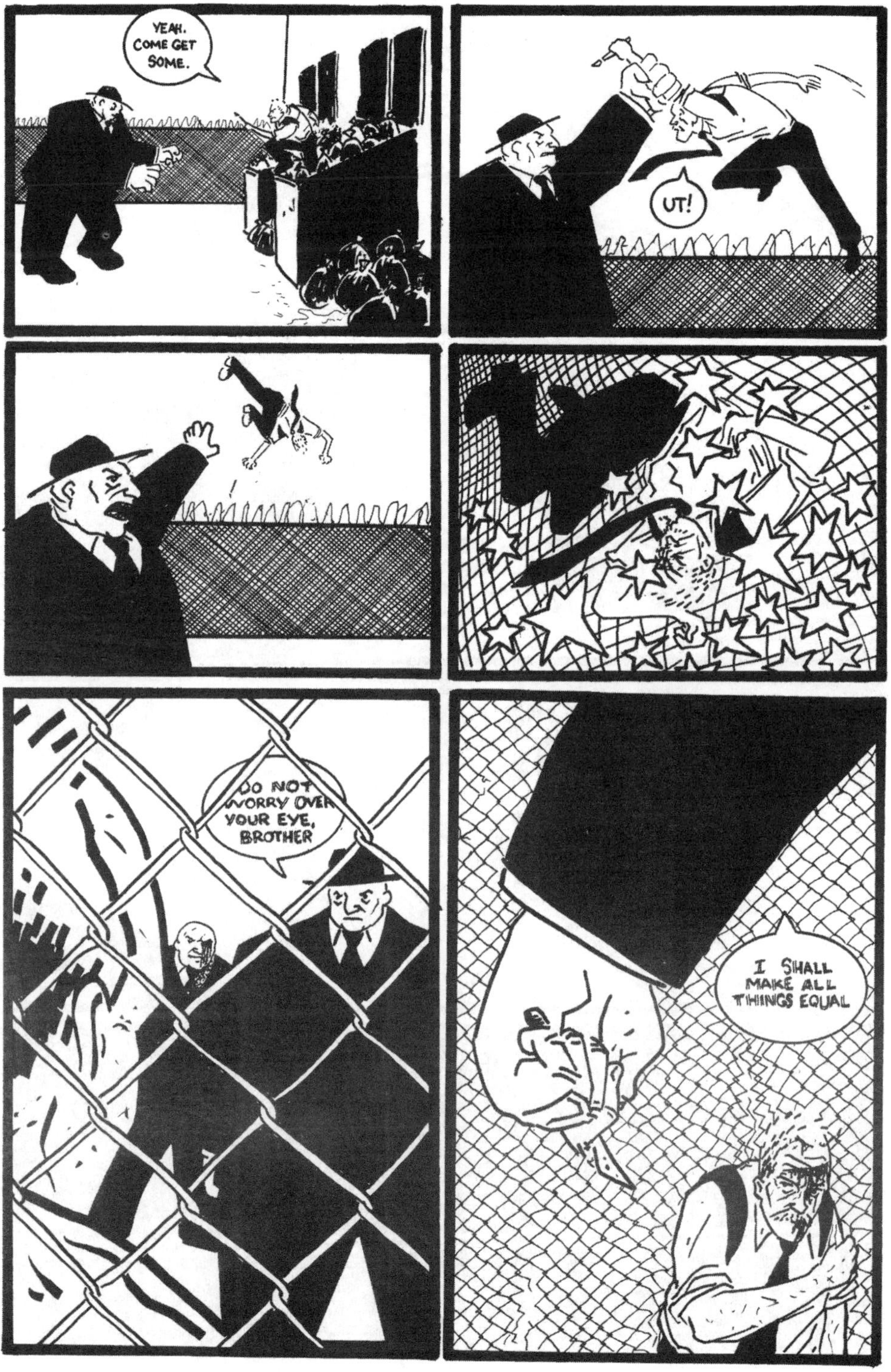
YEAH. COME GET SOME.
UT!
DO NOT WORRY OVER YOUR EYE, BROTHER
I SHALL MAKE ALL THINGS EQUAL

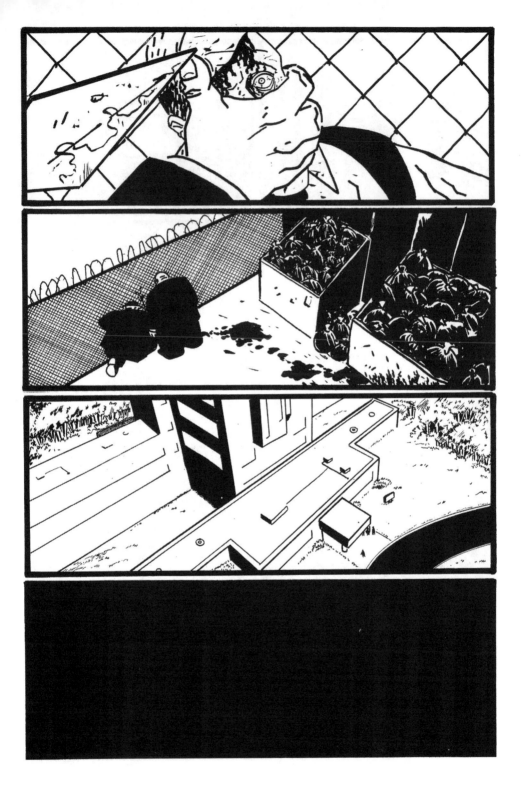

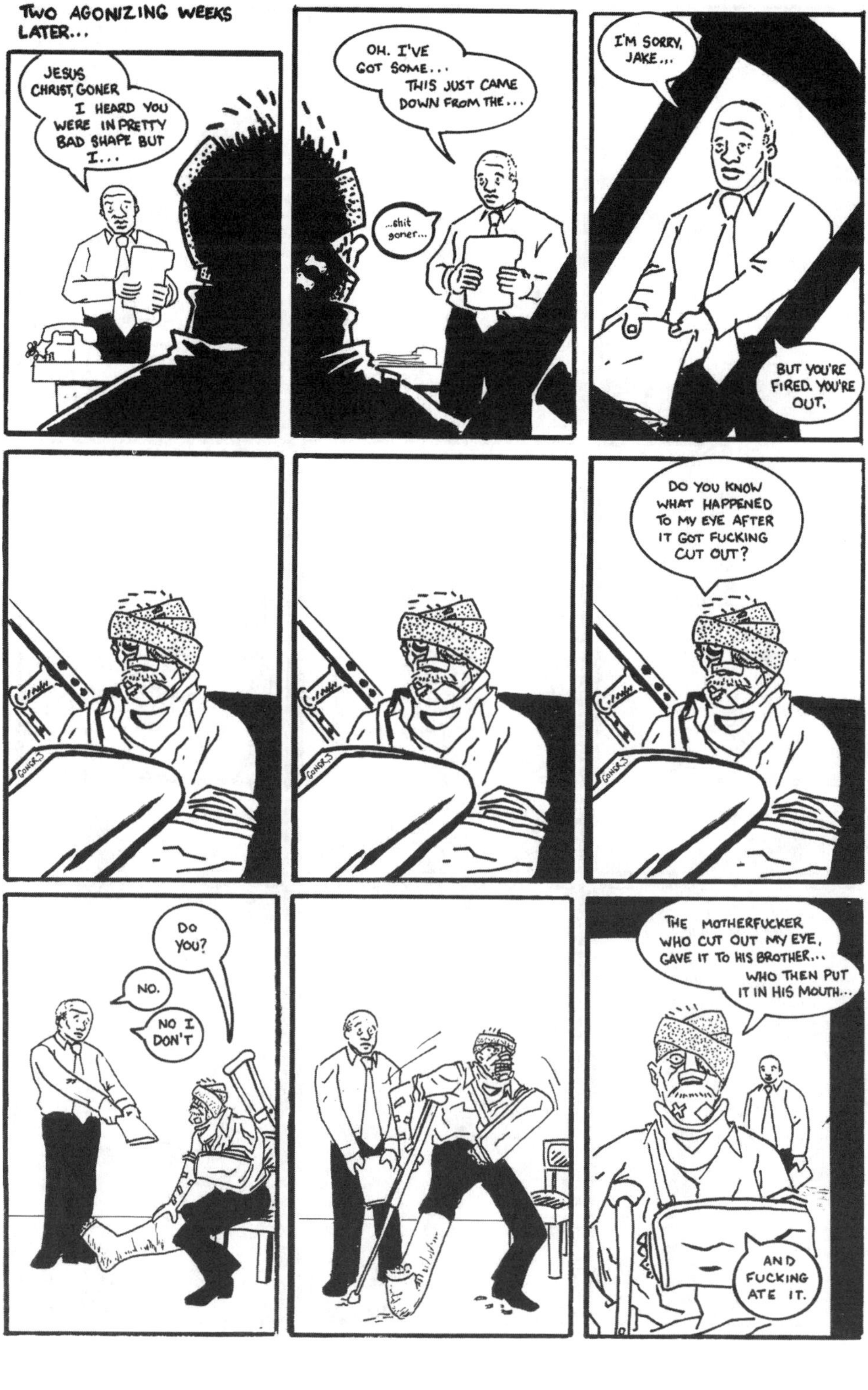
TWO AGONIZING WEEKS LATER...
JESUS CHRIST, GONER I HEARD YOU WERE IN PRETTY BAD SHAPE BUT I...
OH. I'VE GOT SOME... THIS JUST CAME DOWN FROM THE...
...shit goner...
I'M SORRY, JAKE...
BUT YOU'RE FIRED. YOU'RE OUT.
DO YOU KNOW WHAT HAPPENED TO MY EYE AFTER IT GOT FUCKING CUT OUT?
DO YOU?
NO.
NO I DON'T
THE MOTHERFUCKER WHO CUT OUT MY EYE, GAVE IT TO HIS BROTHER... WHO THEN PUT IT IN HIS MOUTH...
AND FUCKING ATE IT.

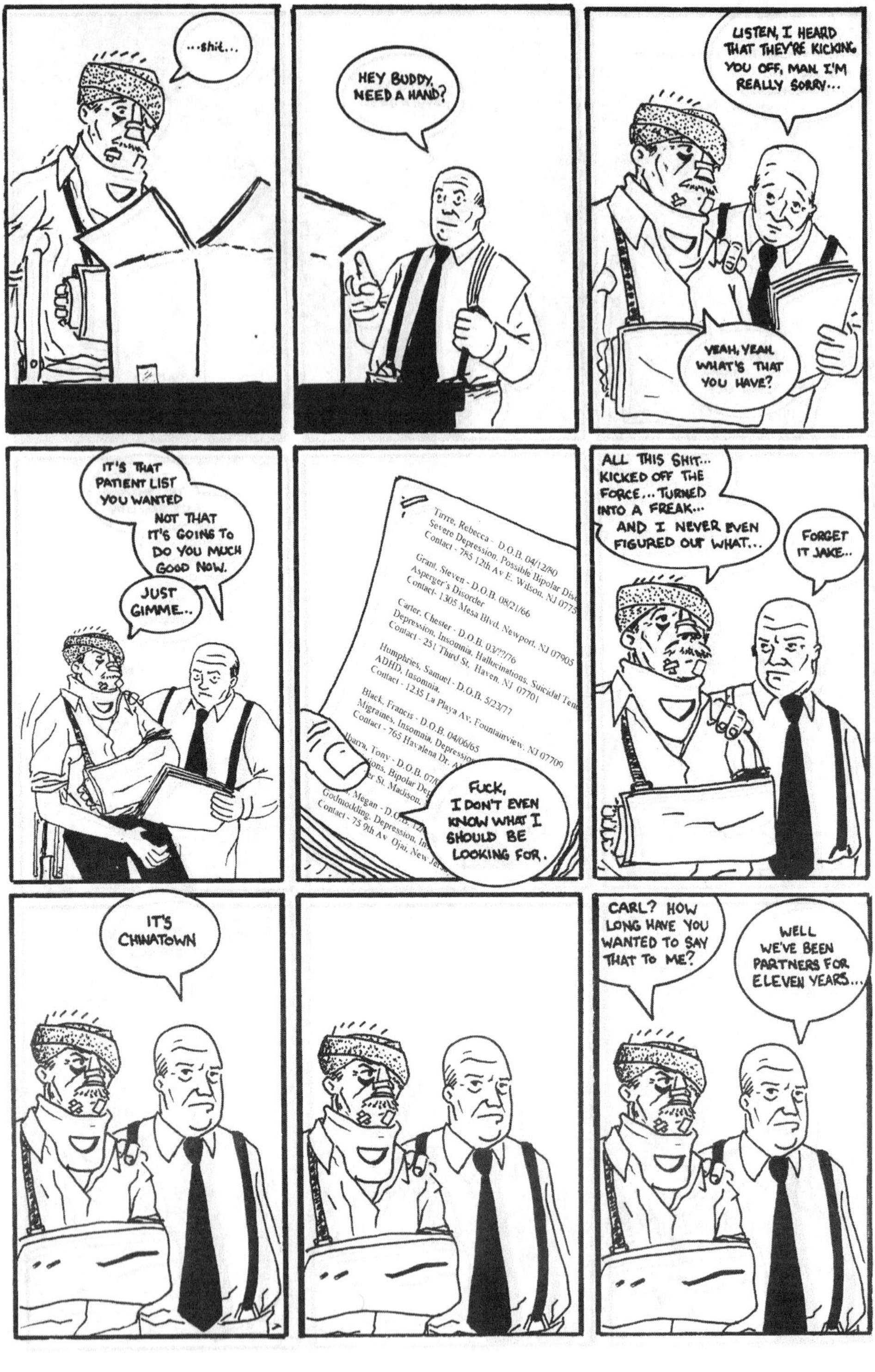
...shit...
HEY BUDDY, NEED A HAND?
LISTEN, I HEARD THAT THEY'RE KICKING YOU OFF, MAN. I'M REALLY SORRY...
YEAH, YEAH. WHAT'S THAT YOU HAVE?
IT'S THAT PATIENT LIST YOU WANTED
NOT THAT IT'S GOING TO DO YOU MUCH GOOD NOW.
JUST GIMME...
Tirre, Rebecca - D.O.B. 04/12/80
Severe Depression, Possible Bipolar
Contact - 785 12th Av E. Wilson, NJ
Grant, Steven - D.O.B. 08/21/66
Asperger's Disorder
Contact- 1305 Mesa Blvd, Newport, NJ 07905
Carter, Chester - D.O.B. 03/??/76
Depression, Insomnia, Hallucinations, Suicidal
Contact - 251 Third St. Haven, NJ 07701
Humphries, Samuel - D.O.B. 5/23/77
ADHD, Insomnia.
Contact - 1235 La Playa Av, Fountainview, NJ 07709
Black, Francis - D.O.B. 04/06/65
Migraines, Insomnia, Depression
Contact - 765 Havalena Dr.
Contact - 75 9th Av Ojai,
FUCK, I DON'T EVEN KNOW WHAT I SHOULD BE LOOKING FOR.
ALL THIS SHIT... KICKED OFF THE FORCE... TURNED INTO A FREAK...
AND I NEVER EVEN FIGURED OUT WHAT...
FORGET IT JAKE...
IT'S CHINATOWN
CARL? HOW LONG HAVE YOU WANTED TO SAY THAT TO ME?
WELL WE'VE BEEN PARTNERS FOR ELEVEN YEARS...

chapter twelve: time like a 3–legged turtle

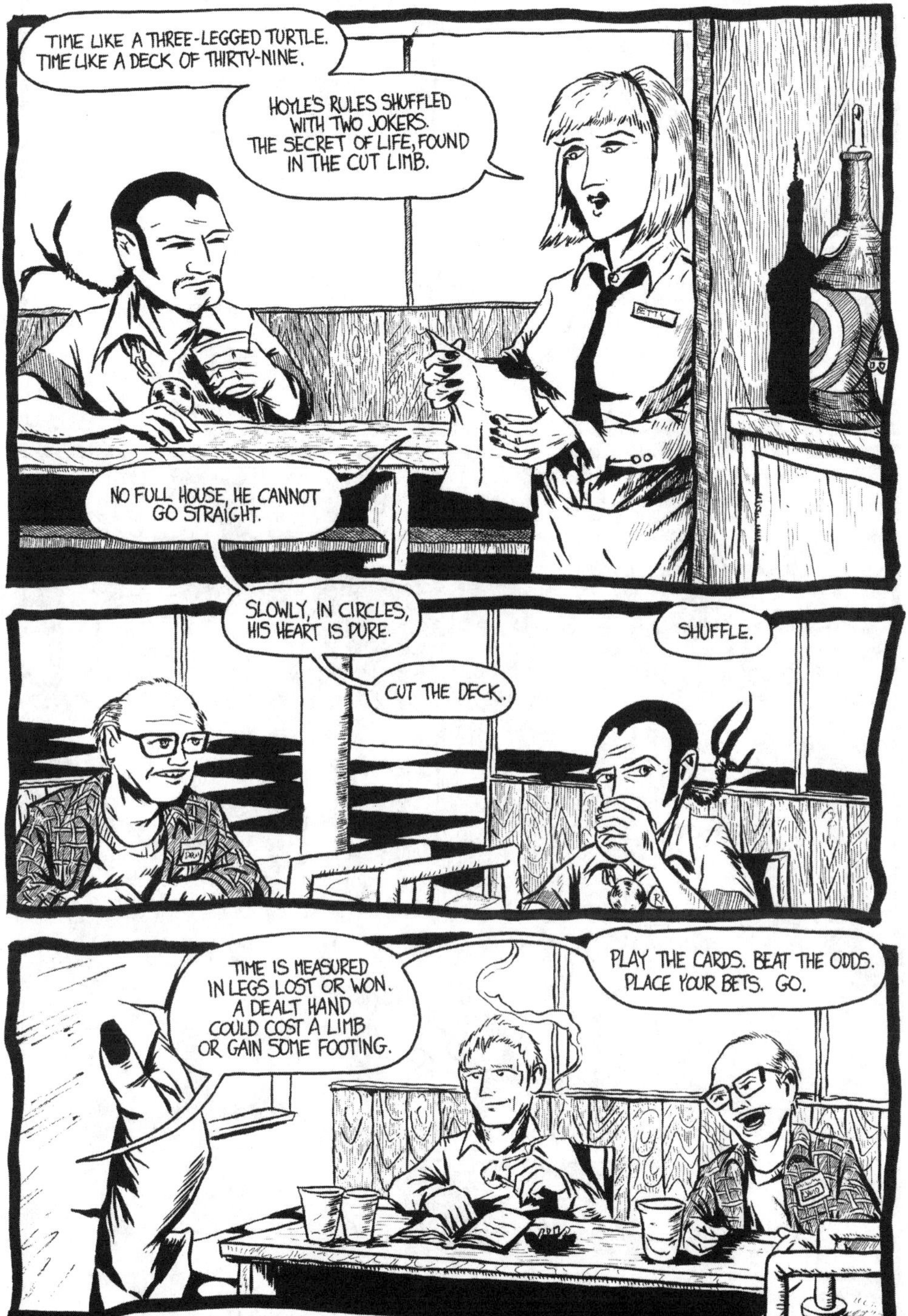

TIME LIKE A THREE-LEGGED TURTLE. TIME LIKE A DECK OF THIRTY-NINE.
HOYLE'S RULES SHUFFLED WITH TWO JOKERS. THE SECRET OF LIFE, FOUND IN THE CUT LIMB.
NO FULL HOUSE, HE CANNOT GO STRAIGHT.
SLOWLY, IN CIRCLES, HIS HEART IS PURE.
CUT THE DECK.
SHUFFLE.
TIME IS MEASURED IN LEGS LOST OR WON. A DEALT HAND COULD COST A LIMB OR GAIN SOME FOOTING.
PLAY THE CARDS. BEAT THE ODDS. PLACE YOUR BETS. GO.

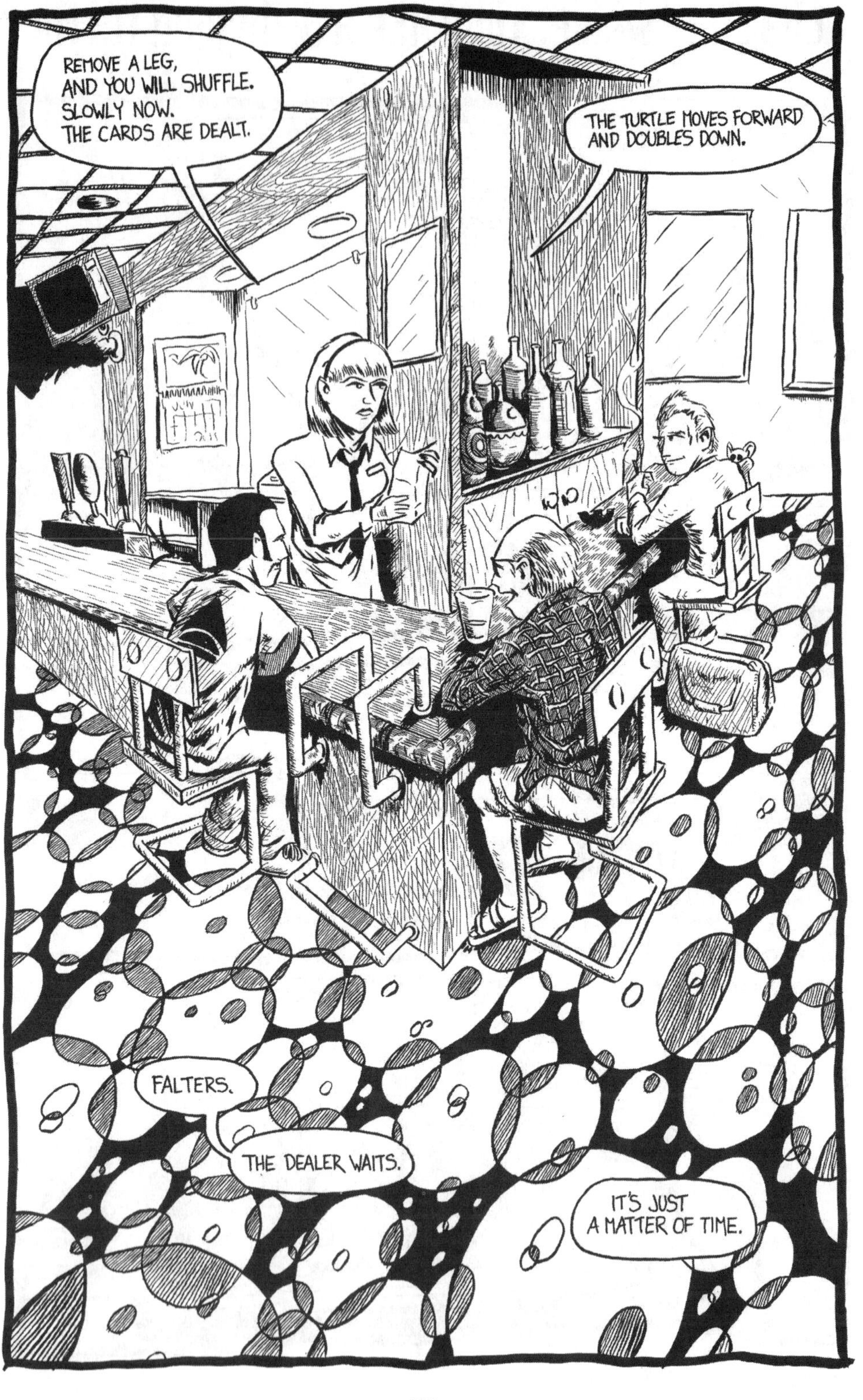
REMOVE A LEG,
AND YOU WILL SHUFFLE.
SLOWLY NOW.
THE CARDS ARE DEALT.
THE TURTLE MOVES FORWARD
AND DOUBLES DOWN.
FALTERS.
THE DEALER WAITS.
IT'S JUST
A MATTER OF TIME.

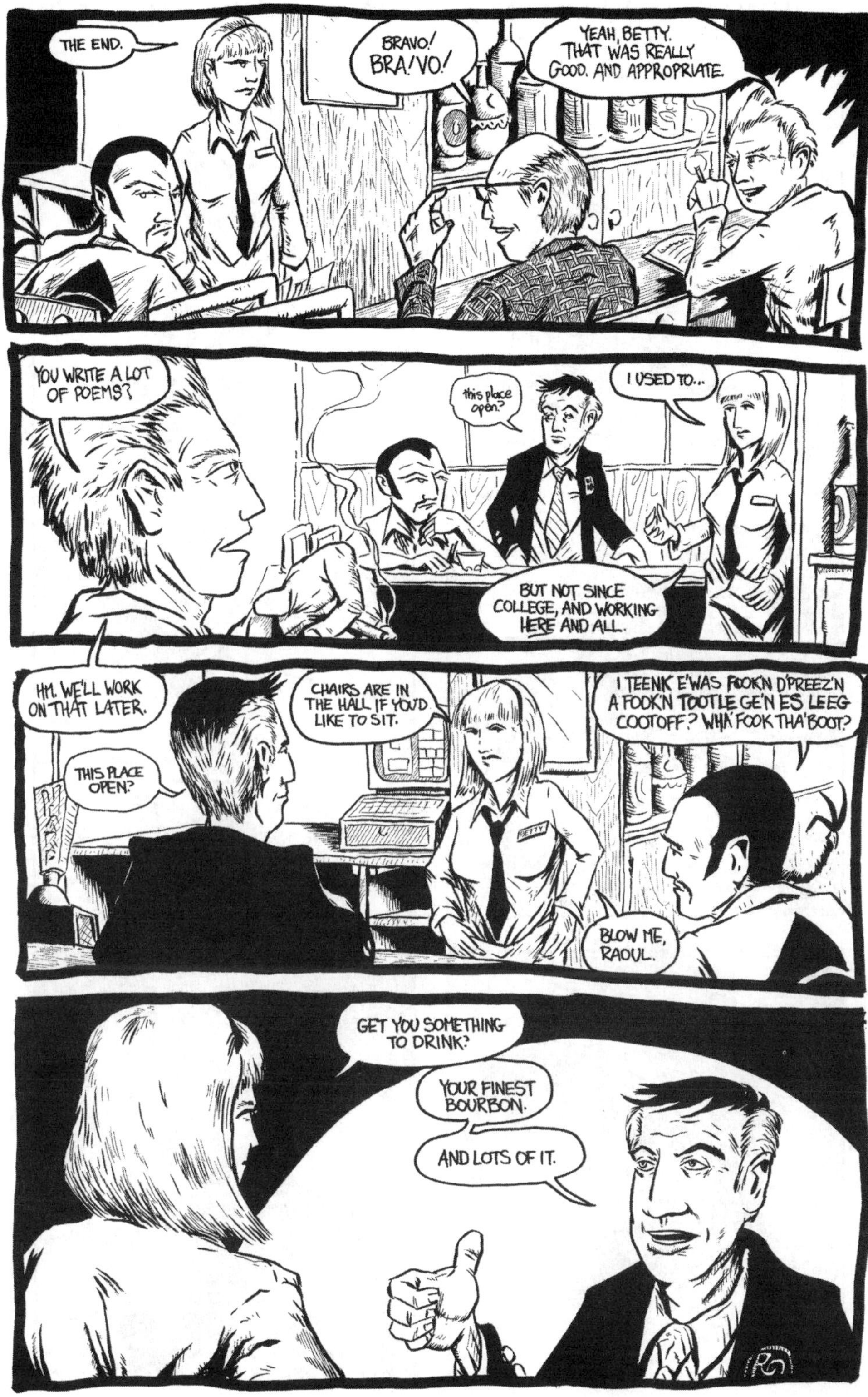

THE END.
BRAVO! BRA!VO!
YEAH, BETTY. THAT WAS REALLY GOOD. AND APPROPRIATE.
YOU WRITE A LOT OF POEMS?
this place open?
I USED TO...
BUT NOT SINCE COLLEGE, AND WORKING HERE AND ALL.
HM. WE'LL WORK ON THAT LATER.
THIS PLACE OPEN?
CHAIRS ARE IN THE HALL IF YOU'D LIKE TO SIT.
I TEENK E'WAS FOOK'N D'PREEZ'N A FOOK'N TOOTLE GE'N ES LEEG COOTOFF? WHA' FOOK THA'BOOT?
BLOW ME, RAOUL.
GET YOU SOMETHING TO DRINK?
YOUR FINEST BOURBON.
AND LOTS OF IT.

chapter thirteen: people's choice (pt. 2)

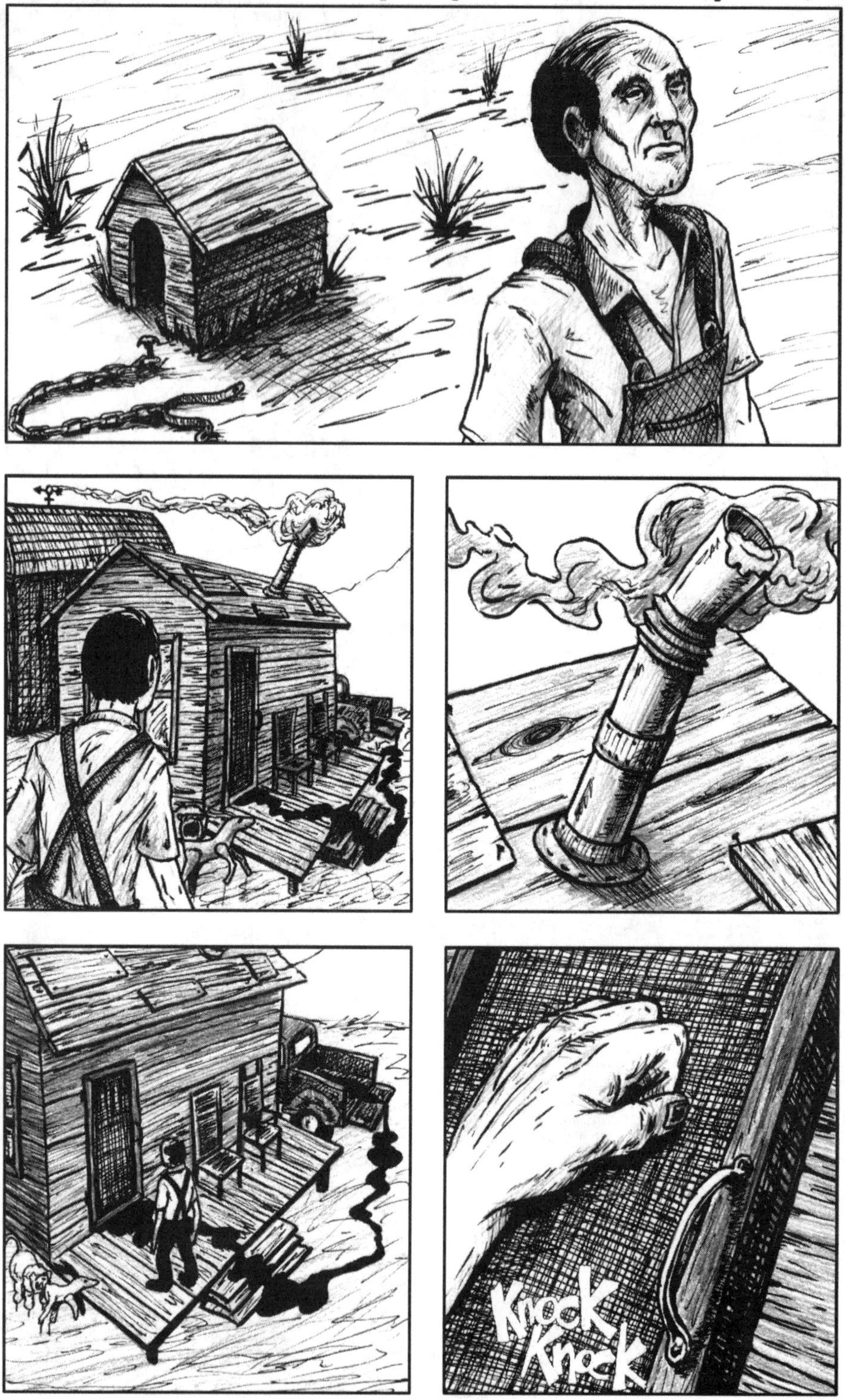
Knock
Knock

art by dave morgan

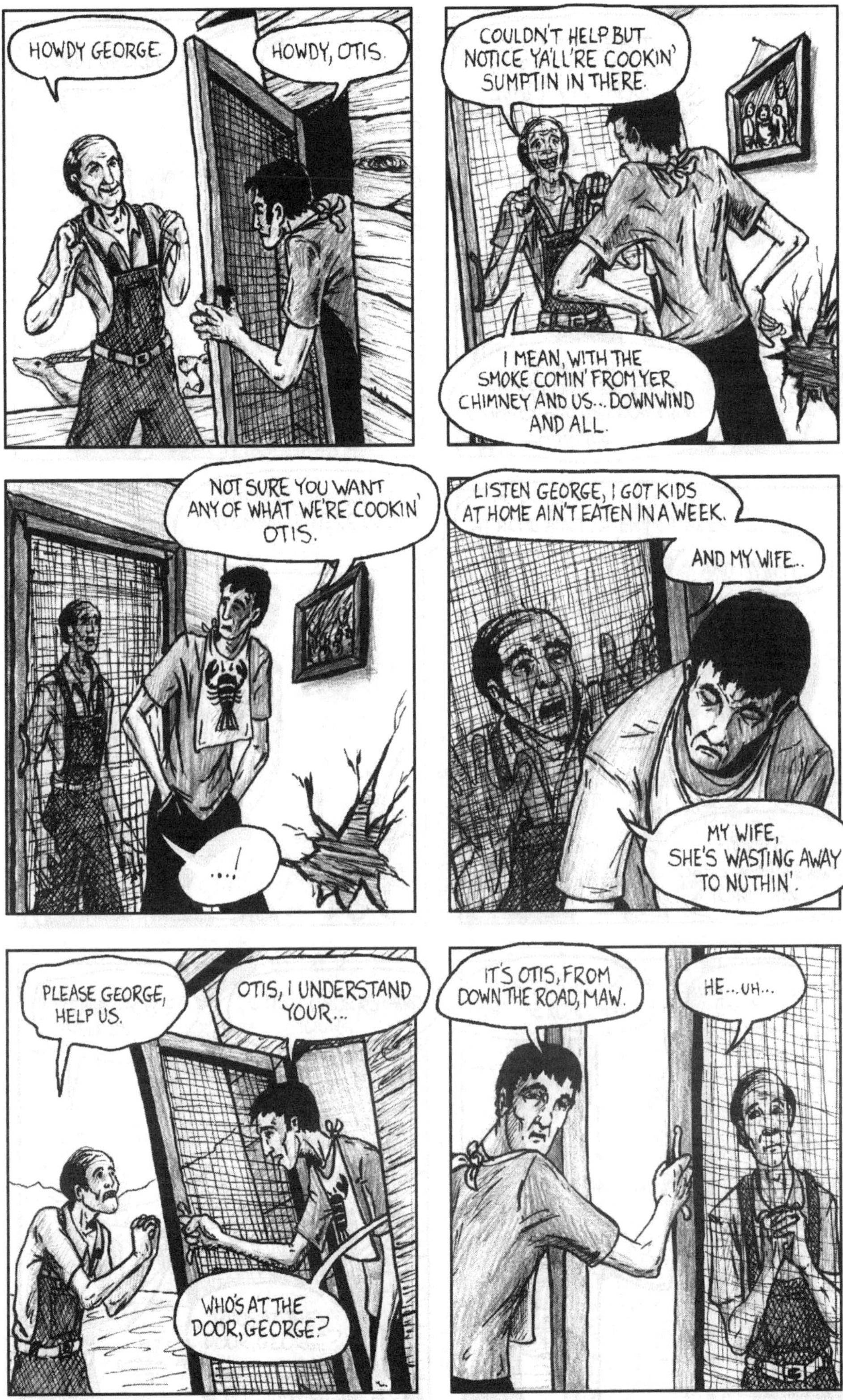
HOWDY GEORGE.
HOWDY, OTIS.
COULDN'T HELP BUT NOTICE YA'LL'RE COOKIN' SUMPTIN IN THERE.
I MEAN, WITH THE SMOKE COMIN' FROM YER CHIMNEY AND US... DOWNWIND AND ALL.
NOT SURE YOU WANT ANY OF WHAT WE'RE COOKIN' OTIS.
...!
LISTEN GEORGE, I GOT KIDS AT HOME AIN'T EATEN IN A WEEK.
AND MY WIFE...
MY WIFE, SHE'S WASTING AWAY TO NUTHIN'.
PLEASE GEORGE, HELP US.
OTIS, I UNDERSTAND YOUR...
WHO'S AT THE DOOR, GEORGE?
IT'S OTIS, FROM DOWN THE ROAD, MAW.
HE... UH...

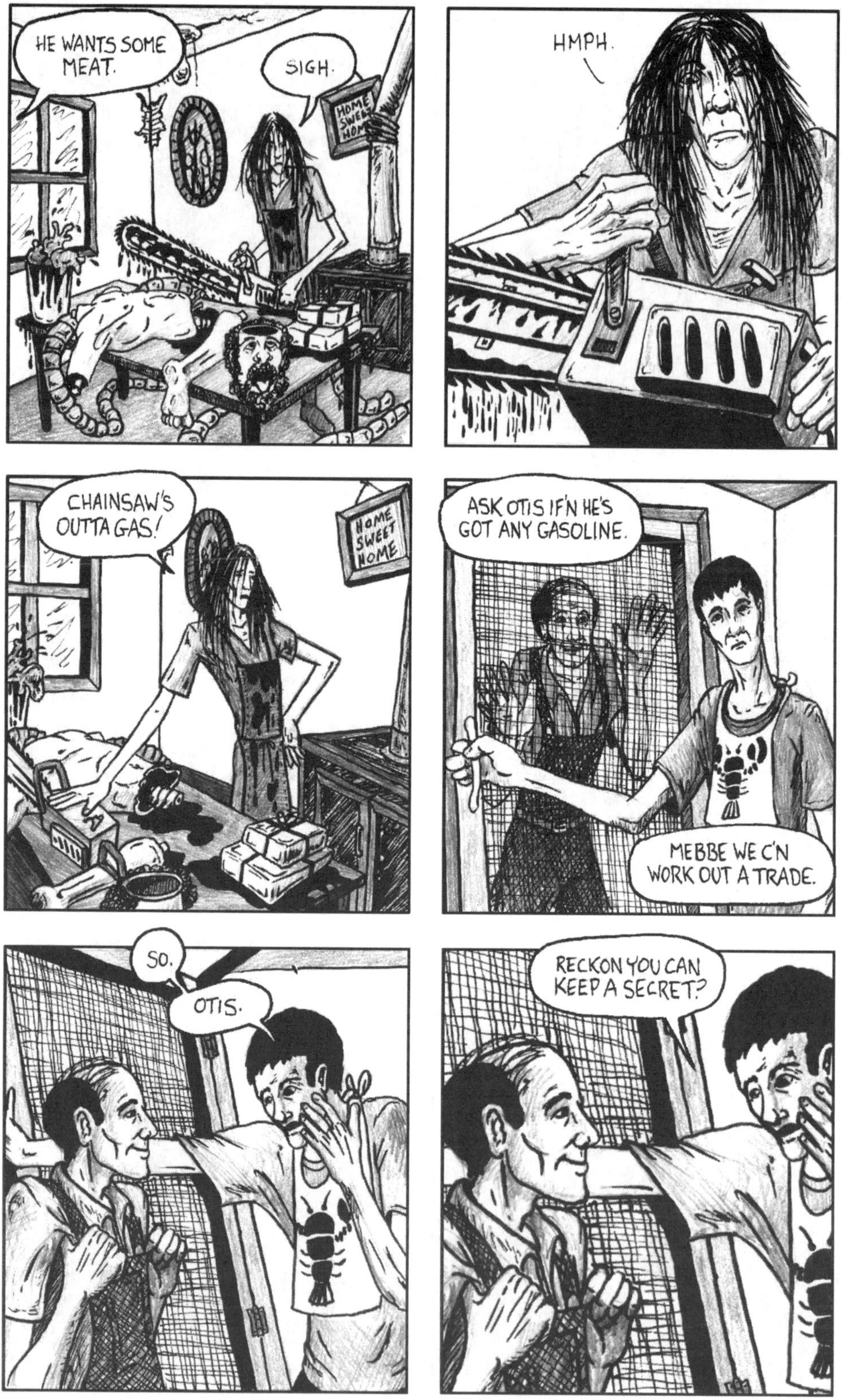
HE WANTS SOME MEAT.
SIGH.
HOME SWEET HOME
HMPH.
CHAINSAW'S OUTTA GAS!
HOME SWEET HOME
ASK OTIS IF'N HE'S GOT ANY GASOLINE.
MEBBE WE C'N WORK OUT A TRADE.
SO.
OTIS.
RECKON YOU CAN KEEP A SECRET?

chapter fourteen: bannon gets it

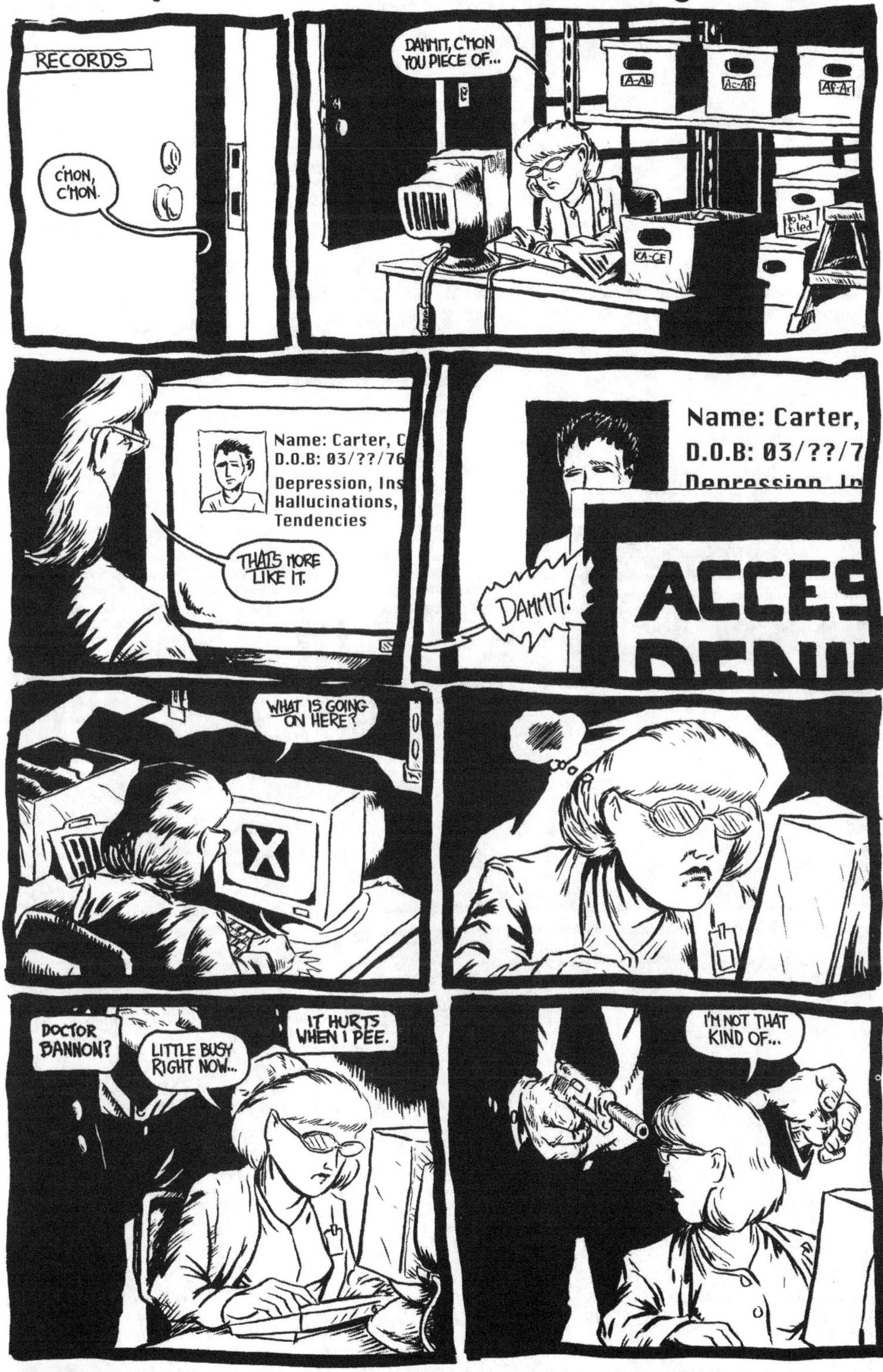
RECORDS
C'MON, C'MON.
DAMMIT, C'MON YOU PIECE OF...
A-Ab
Ac-Af
Af-Ar
KA-CE
To be filed
Name: Carter, C
D.O.B: 03/??/76
Depression, Ins
Hallucinations,
Tendencies
THAT'S MORE LIKE IT.
Name: Carter,
D.O.B: 03/??/7
DAMMIT!
ACCES
WHAT IS GOING ON HERE?
DOCTOR BANNON?
LITTLE BUSY RIGHT NOW...
IT HURTS WHEN I PEE.
I'M NOT THAT KIND OF...

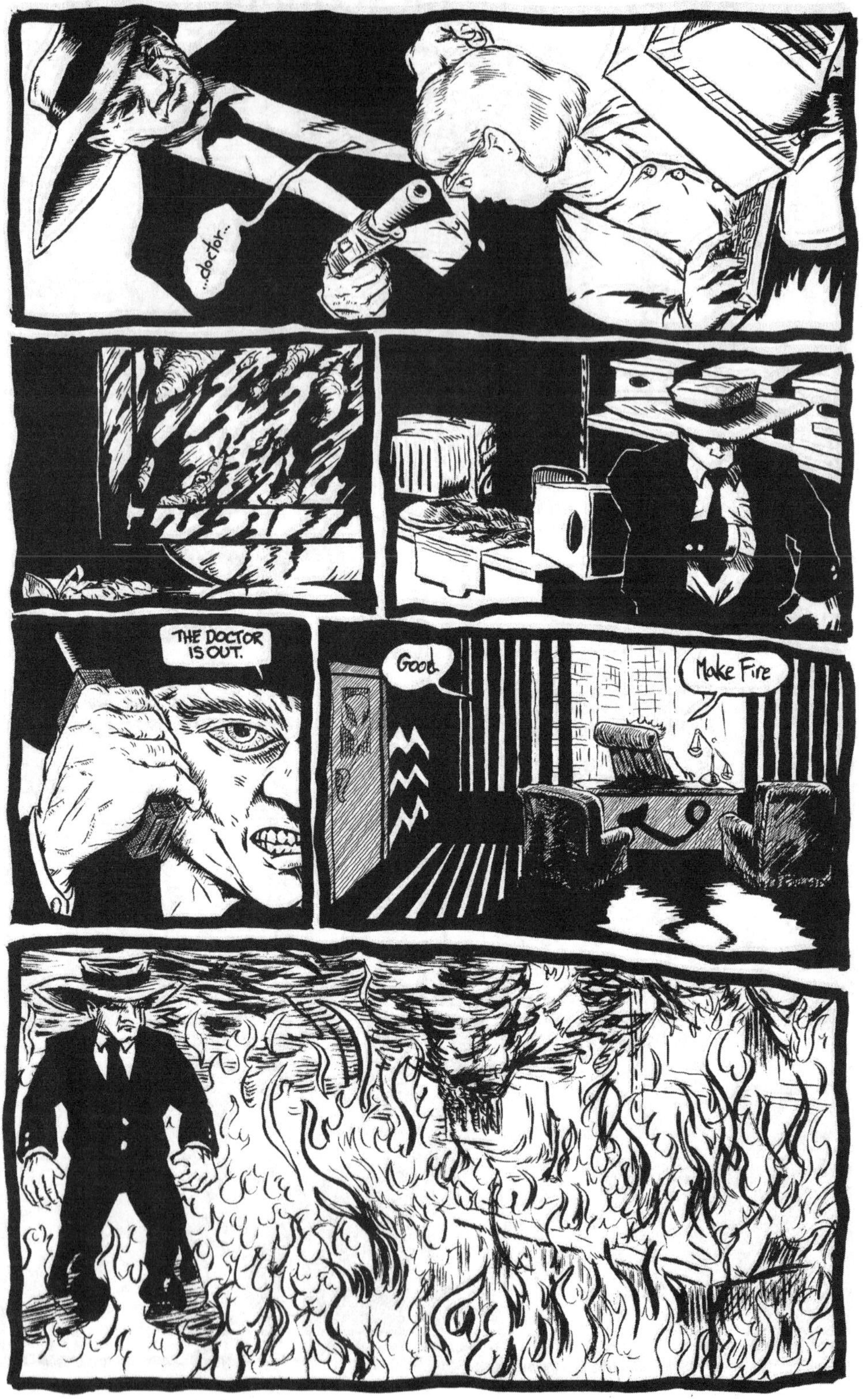
...doctor...
THE DOCTOR IS OUT.
Good.
Make Fire

chapter fifteen: jack on the beach

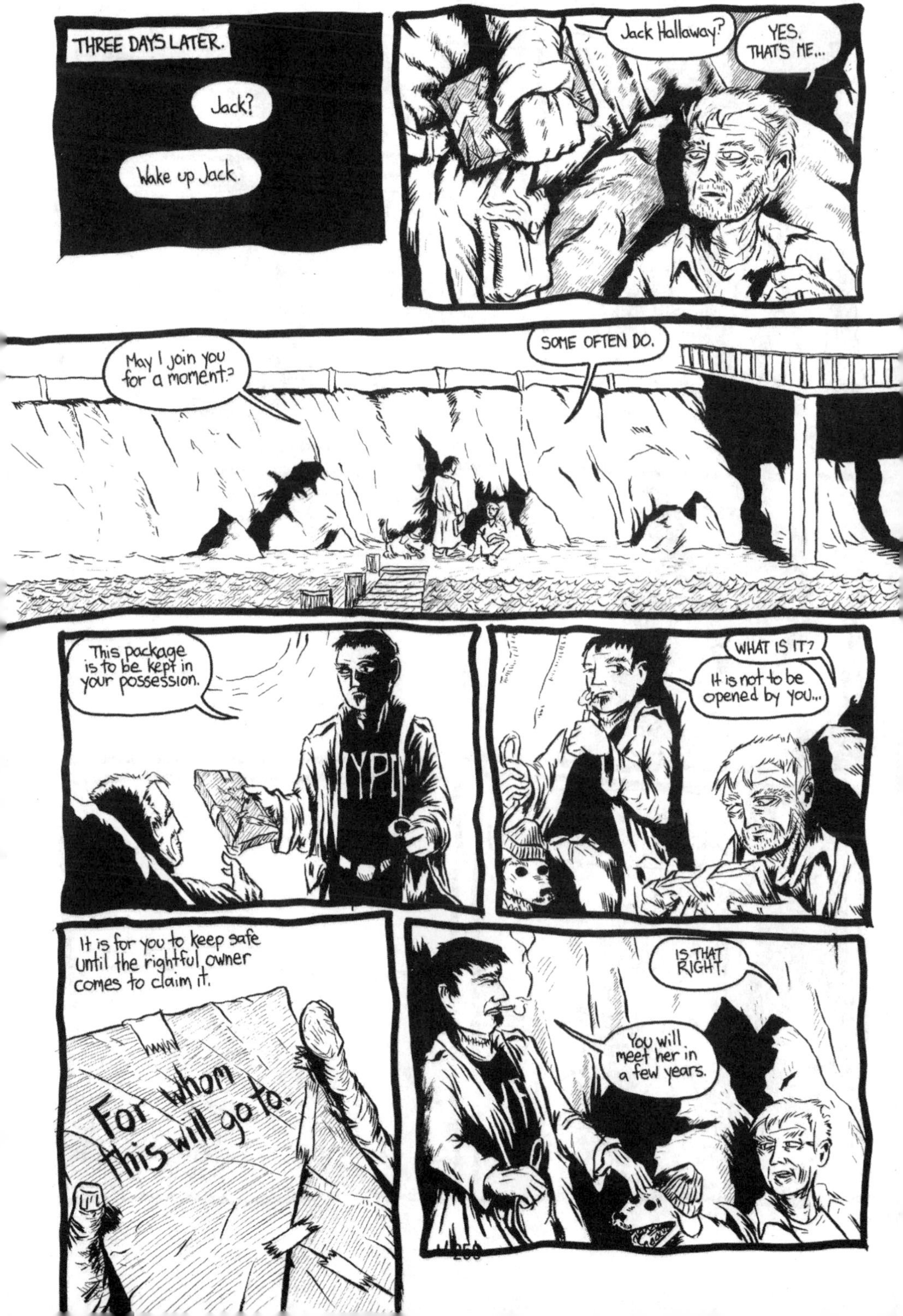
THREE DAYS LATER.
Jack?
Wake up Jack.
Jack Hallaway?
YES. THAT'S ME...
May I join you for a moment?
SOME OFTEN DO.
This package is to be kept in your possession.
WHAT IS IT?
It is not to be opened by you...
It is for you to keep safe until the rightful owner comes to claim it.
For whom this will go to.
IS THAT RIGHT.
You will meet her in a few years.

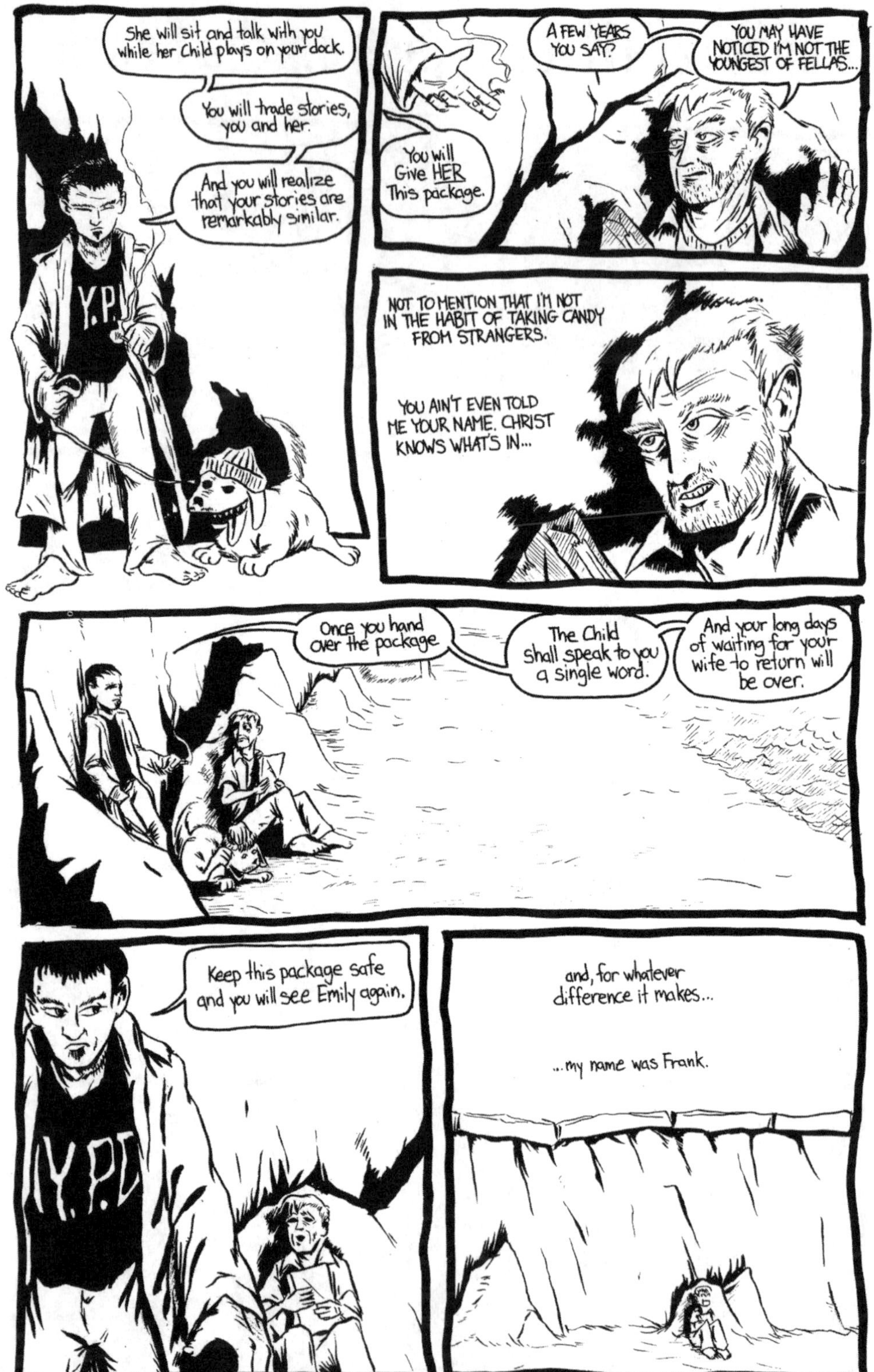
She will sit and talk with you while her Child plays on your dock.
You will trade stories, you and her.
And you will realize that your stories are remarkably similar.
You will Give HER This package.
A FEW YEARS YOU SAY?
YOU MAY HAVE NOTICED I'M NOT THE YOUNGEST OF FELLAS...
NOT TO MENTION THAT I'M NOT IN THE HABIT OF TAKING CANDY FROM STRANGERS.
YOU AIN'T EVEN TOLD ME YOUR NAME. CHRIST KNOWS WHAT'S IN...
Once you hand over the package
The Child shall speak to you a single word.
And your long days of waiting for your wife to return will be over.
Keep this package safe and you will see Emily again.
and, for whatever difference it makes...
...my name was Frank.

chapter sixteen: the flavor of my love

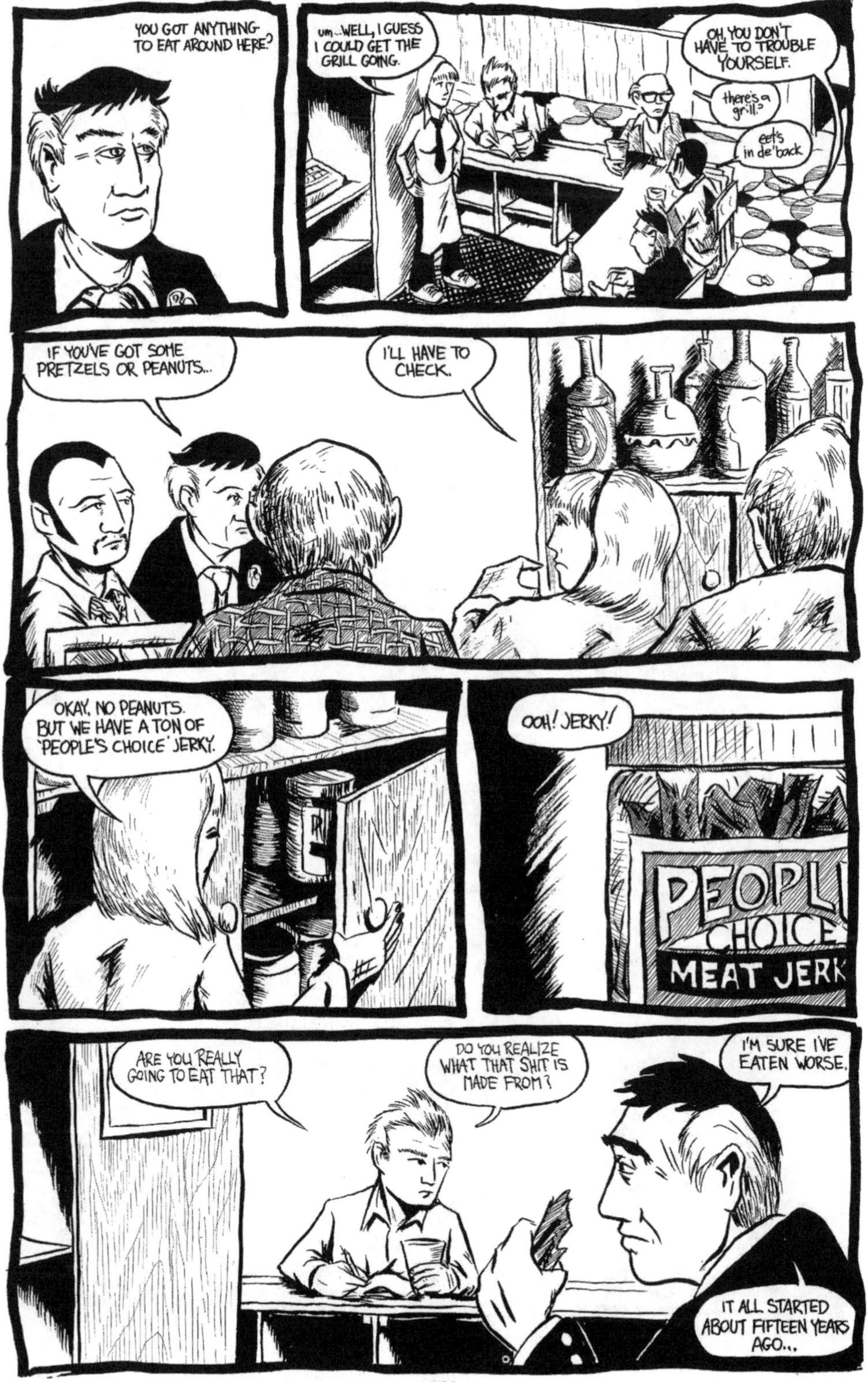

YOU GOT ANYTHING TO EAT AROUND HERE?
um... WELL, I GUESS I COULD GET THE GRILL GOING.
OH, YOU DON'T HAVE TO TROUBLE YOURSELF.
there's a grill?
eet's in de' back
IF YOU'VE GOT SOME PRETZELS OR PEANUTS...
I'LL HAVE TO CHECK.
OKAY, NO PEANUTS. BUT WE HAVE A TON OF 'PEOPLE'S CHOICE' JERKY.
OOH! JERKY!
PEOPL CHOICE MEAT JERK
ARE YOU REALLY GOING TO EAT THAT?
DO YOU REALIZE WHAT THAT SHIT IS MADE FROM?
I'M SURE I'VE EATEN WORSE.
IT ALL STARTED ABOUT FIFTEEN YEARS AGO...

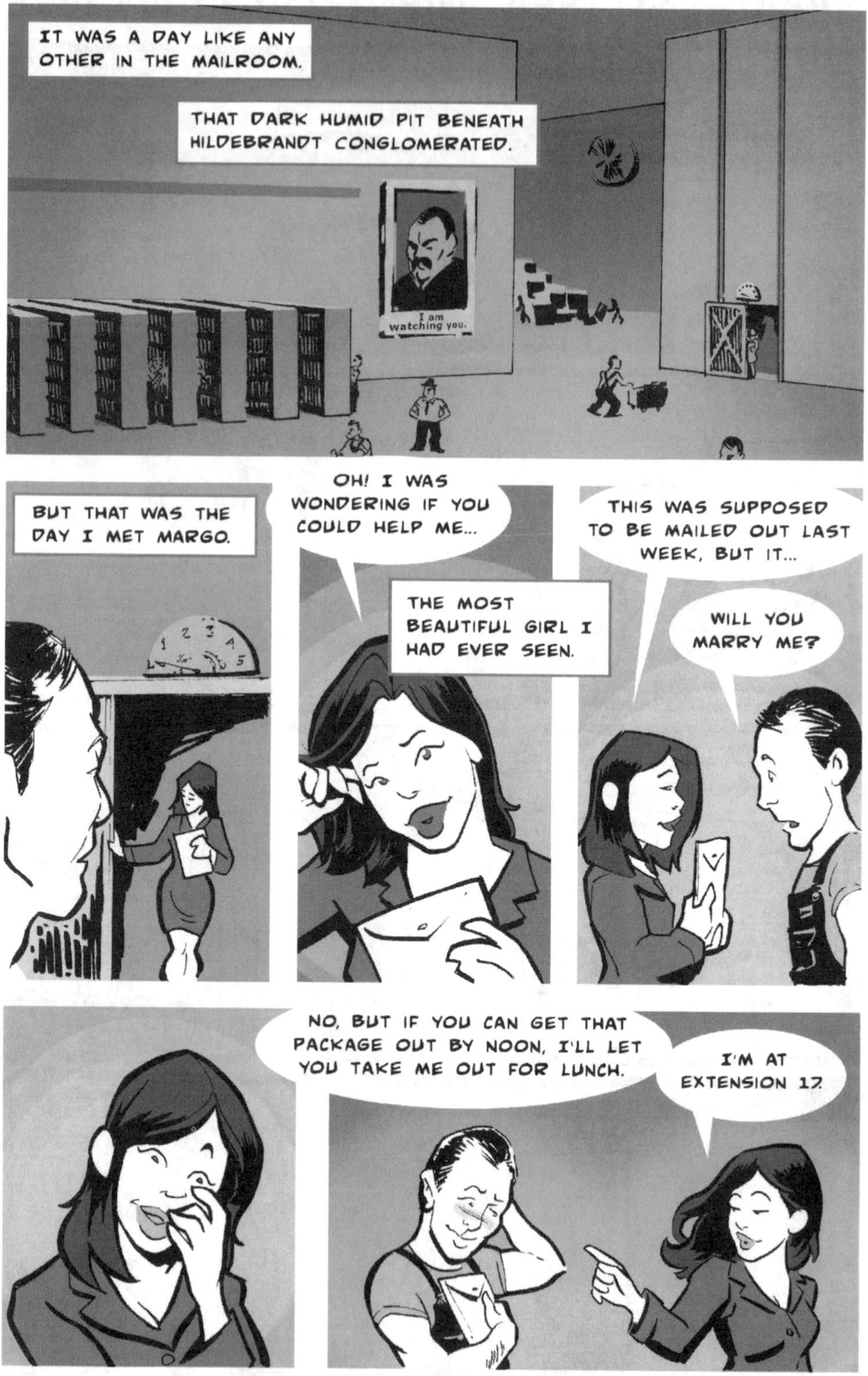
IT WAS A DAY LIKE ANY OTHER IN THE MAILROOM.
THAT DARK HUMID PIT BENEATH HILDEBRANDT CONGLOMERATED.
I am watching you.
BUT THAT WAS THE DAY I MET MARGO.
OH! I WAS WONDERING IF YOU COULD HELP ME...
THE MOST BEAUTIFUL GIRL I HAD EVER SEEN.
THIS WAS SUPPOSED TO BE MAILED OUT LAST WEEK, BUT IT...
WILL YOU MARRY ME?
NO, BUT IF YOU CAN GET THAT PACKAGE OUT BY NOON, I'LL LET YOU TAKE ME OUT FOR LUNCH.
I'M AT EXTENSION 17.

art by danielle corsetto

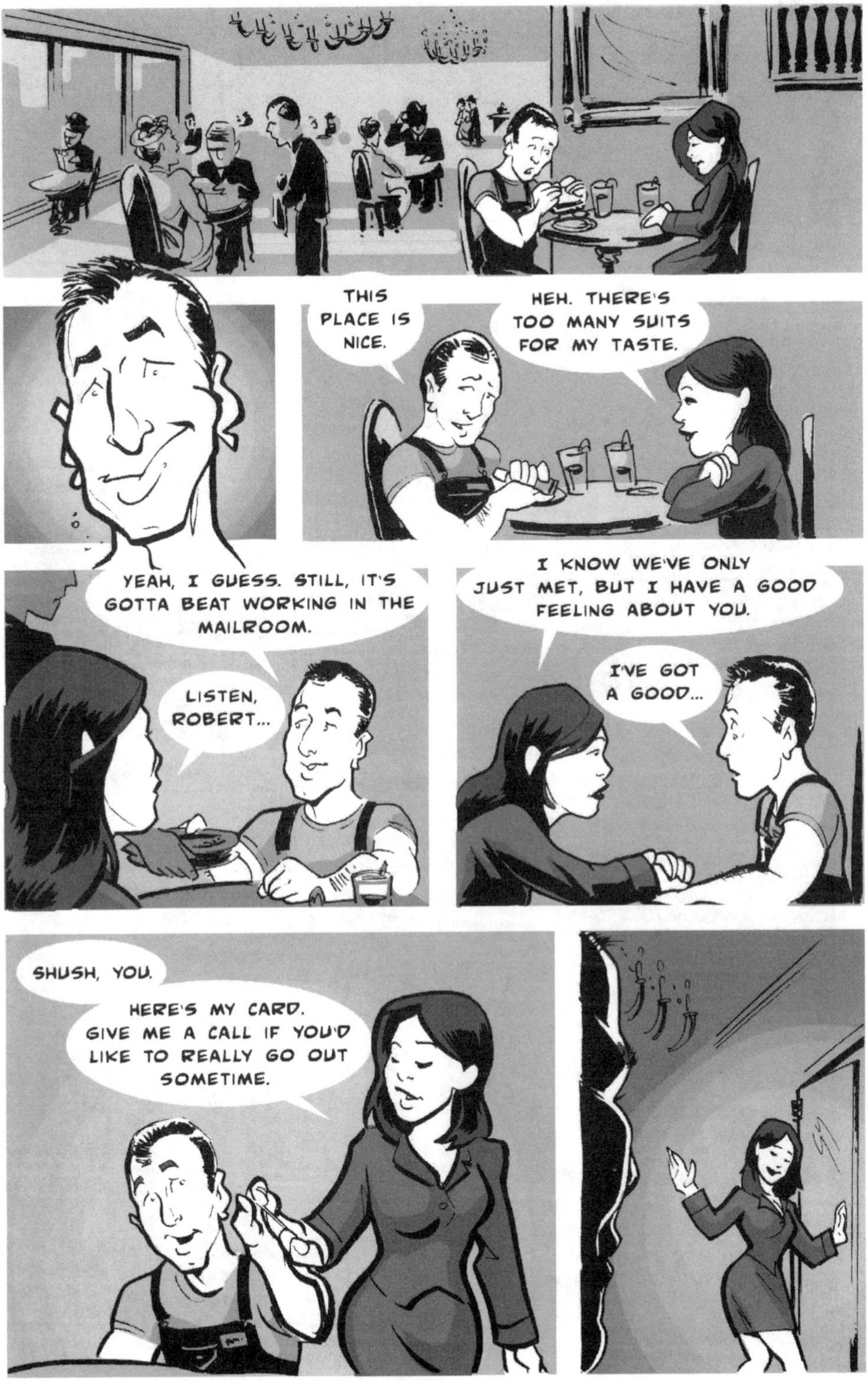
THIS PLACE IS NICE.
HEH. THERE'S TOO MANY SUITS FOR MY TASTE.
YEAH, I GUESS. STILL, IT'S GOTTA BEAT WORKING IN THE MAILROOM.
LISTEN, ROBERT...
I KNOW WE'VE ONLY JUST MET, BUT I HAVE A GOOD FEELING ABOUT YOU.
I'VE GOT A GOOD...
SHUSH, YOU.
HERE'S MY CARD. GIVE ME A CALL IF YOU'D LIKE TO REALLY GO OUT SOMETIME.

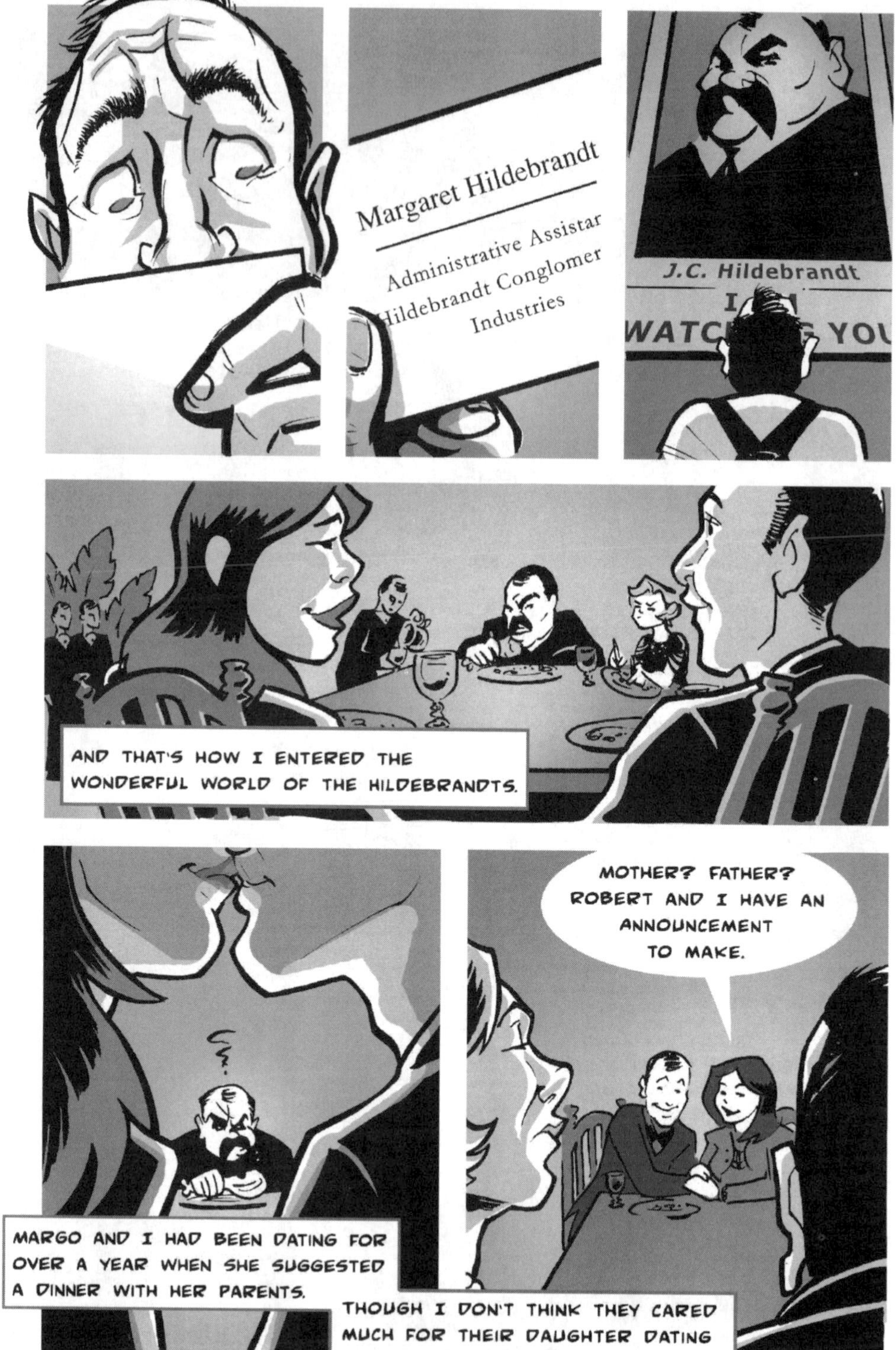
Margaret Hildebrandt
Administrative Assistar
Hildebrandt Conglomer
Industries
J.C. Hildebrandt
WATC
YOU
AND THAT'S HOW I ENTERED THE WONDERFUL WORLD OF THE HILDEBRANDTS.
MARGO AND I HAD BEEN DATING FOR OVER A YEAR WHEN SHE SUGGESTED A DINNER WITH HER PARENTS.
MOTHER? FATHER? ROBERT AND I HAVE AN ANNOUNCEMENT TO MAKE.
THOUGH I DON'T THINK THEY CARED MUCH FOR THEIR DAUGHTER DATING A POOR MAILROOM WORKER.

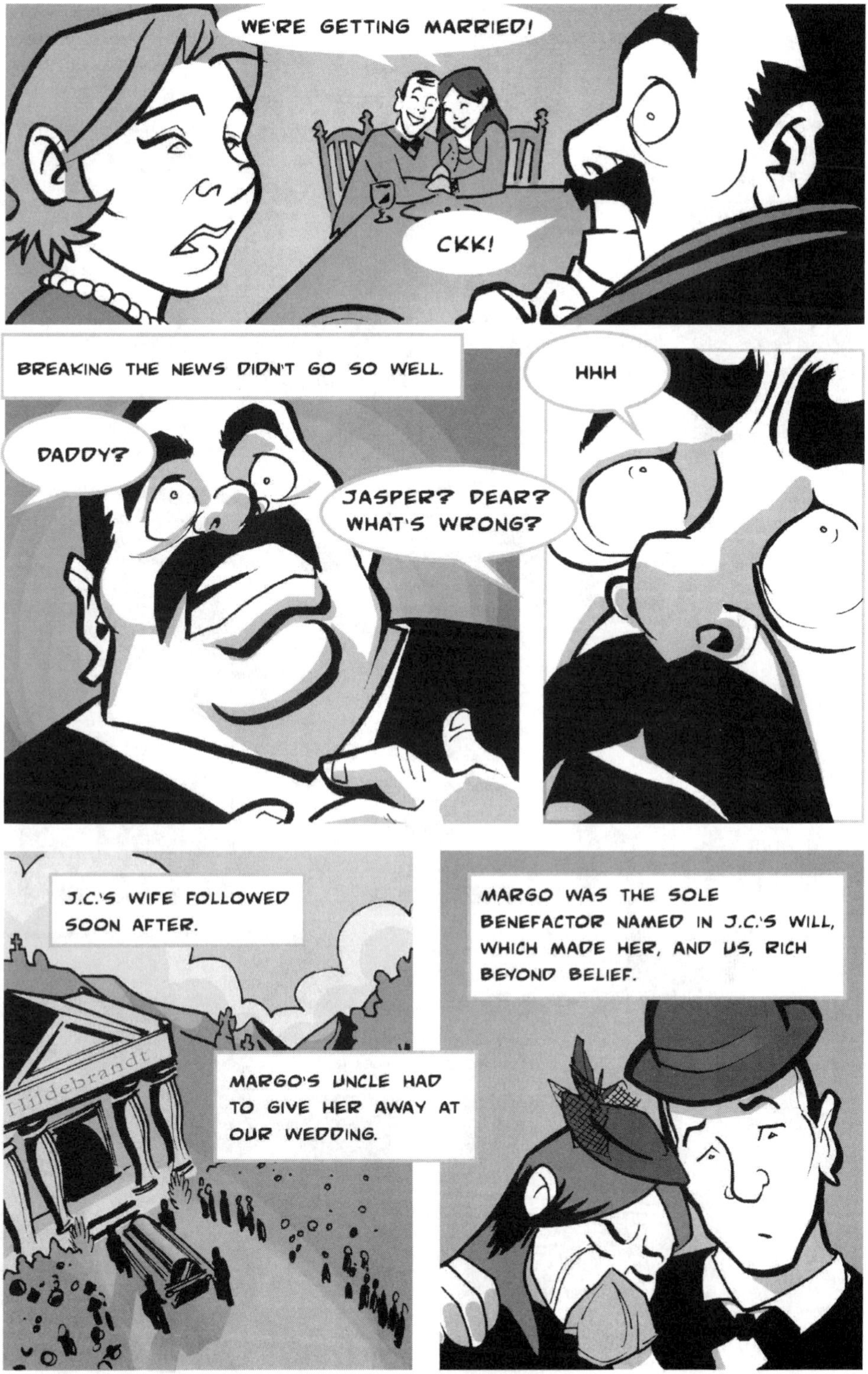
WE'RE GETTING MARRIED!
CKK!
BREAKING THE NEWS DIDN'T GO SO WELL.
DADDY?
JASPER? DEAR? WHAT'S WRONG?
HHH
J.C.'S WIFE FOLLOWED SOON AFTER.
Hildebrandt
MARGO'S UNCLE HAD TO GIVE HER AWAY AT OUR WEDDING.
MARGO WAS THE SOLE BENEFACTOR NAMED IN J.C.'S WILL, WHICH MADE HER, AND US, RICH BEYOND BELIEF.

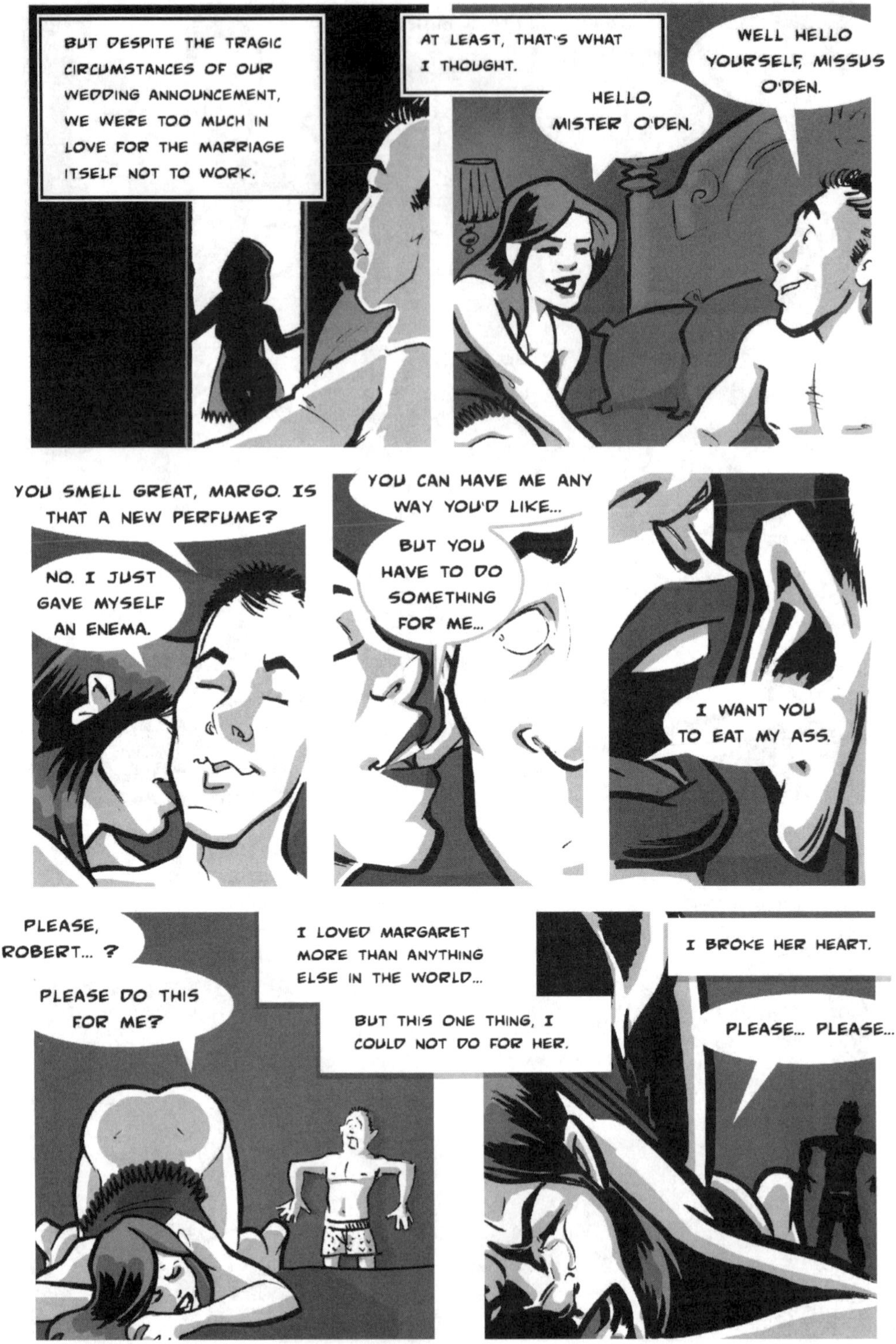

BUT DESPITE THE TRAGIC CIRCUMSTANCES OF OUR WEDDING ANNOUNCEMENT, WE WERE TOO MUCH IN LOVE FOR THE MARRIAGE ITSELF NOT TO WORK.
AT LEAST, THAT'S WHAT I THOUGHT.
HELLO, MISTER O'DEN.
WELL HELLO YOURSELF, MISSUS O'DEN.
YOU SMELL GREAT, MARGO. IS THAT A NEW PERFUME?
NO. I JUST GAVE MYSELF AN ENEMA.
YOU CAN HAVE ME ANY WAY YOU'D LIKE...
BUT YOU HAVE TO DO SOMETHING FOR ME...
I WANT YOU TO EAT MY ASS.
PLEASE, ROBERT... ?
PLEASE DO THIS FOR ME?
I LOVED MARGARET MORE THAN ANYTHING ELSE IN THE WORLD...
BUT THIS ONE THING, I COULD NOT DO FOR HER.
I BROKE HER HEART.
PLEASE... PLEASE...

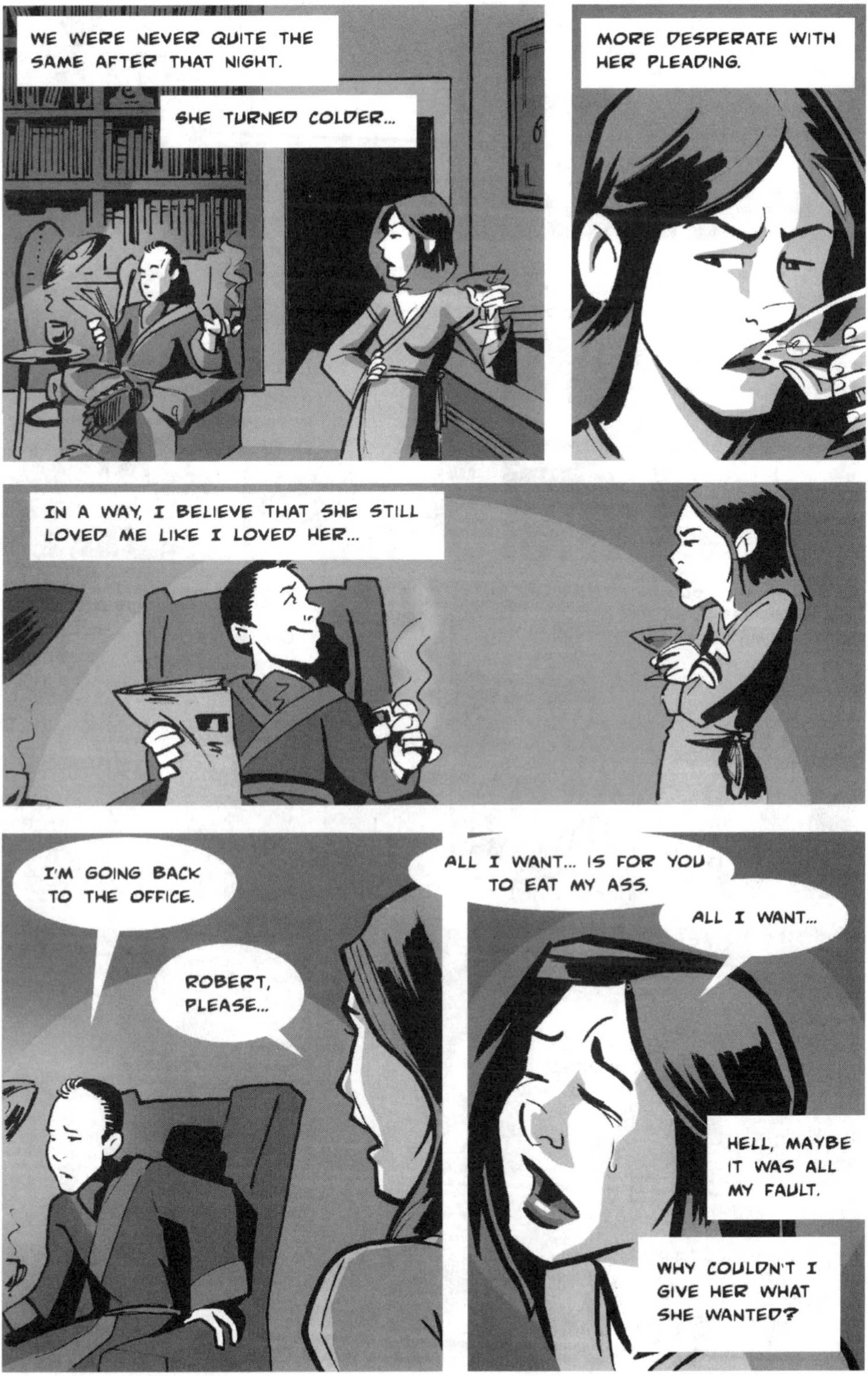
WE WERE NEVER QUITE THE SAME AFTER THAT NIGHT.
SHE TURNED COLDER...
MORE DESPERATE WITH HER PLEADING.
IN A WAY, I BELIEVE THAT SHE STILL LOVED ME LIKE I LOVED HER...
I'M GOING BACK TO THE OFFICE.
ROBERT, PLEASE...
ALL I WANT... IS FOR YOU TO EAT MY ASS.
ALL I WANT...
HELL, MAYBE IT WAS ALL MY FAULT.
WHY COULDN'T I GIVE HER WHAT SHE WANTED?

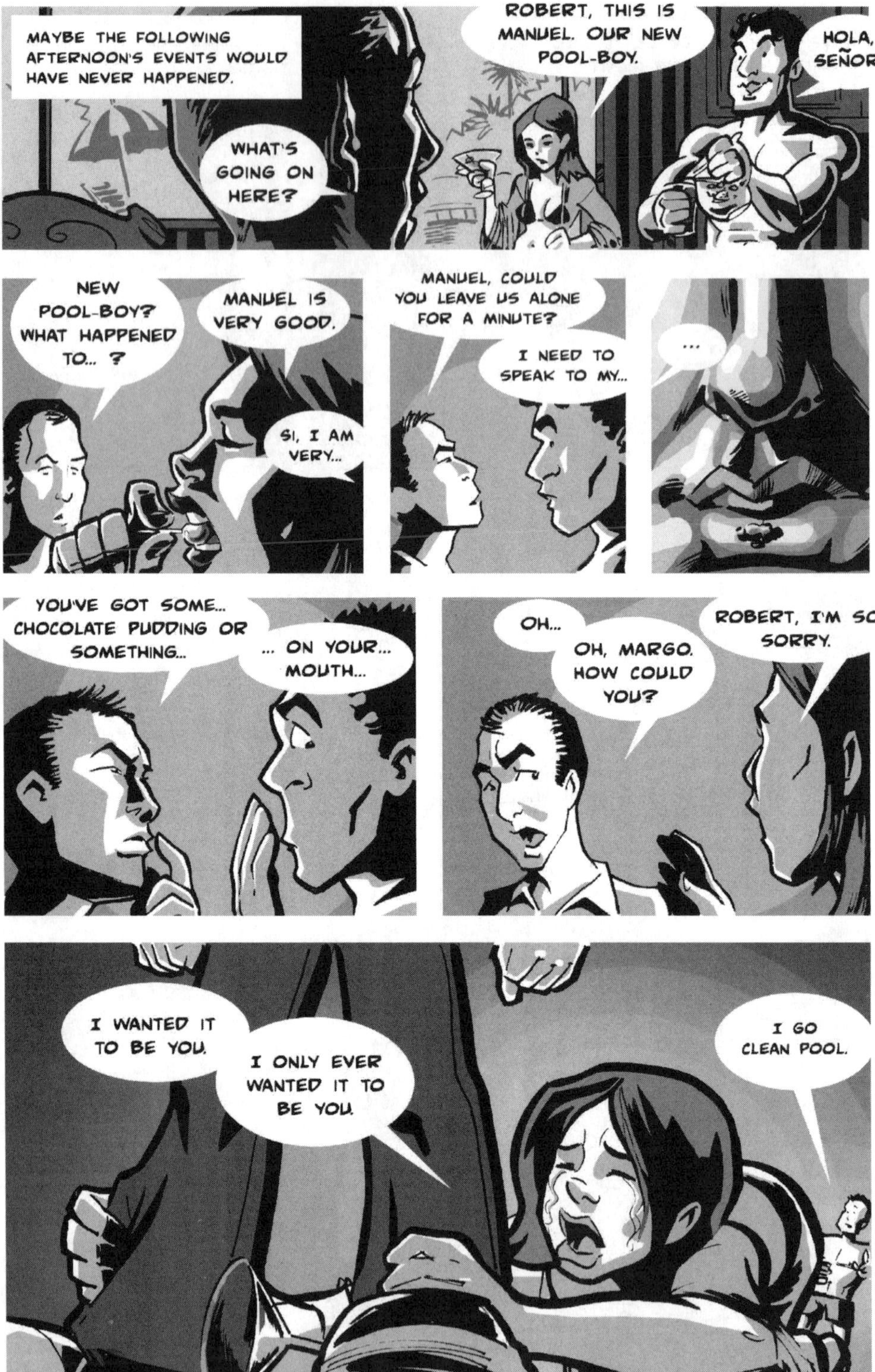

MAYBE THE FOLLOWING AFTERNOON'S EVENTS WOULD HAVE NEVER HAPPENED.
WHAT'S GOING ON HERE?
ROBERT, THIS IS MANUEL. OUR NEW POOL-BOY.
HOLA, SEÑOR.
NEW POOL-BOY? WHAT HAPPENED TO... ?
MANUEL IS VERY GOOD.
SI, I AM VERY...
MANUEL, COULD YOU LEAVE US ALONE FOR A MINUTE?
I NEED TO SPEAK TO MY...
...
YOU'VE GOT SOME... CHOCOLATE PUDDING OR SOMETHING...
... ON YOUR... MOUTH...
OH...
OH, MARGO. HOW COULD YOU?
ROBERT, I'M SO SORRY.
I WANTED IT TO BE YOU.
I ONLY EVER WANTED IT TO BE YOU.
I GO CLEAN POOL.

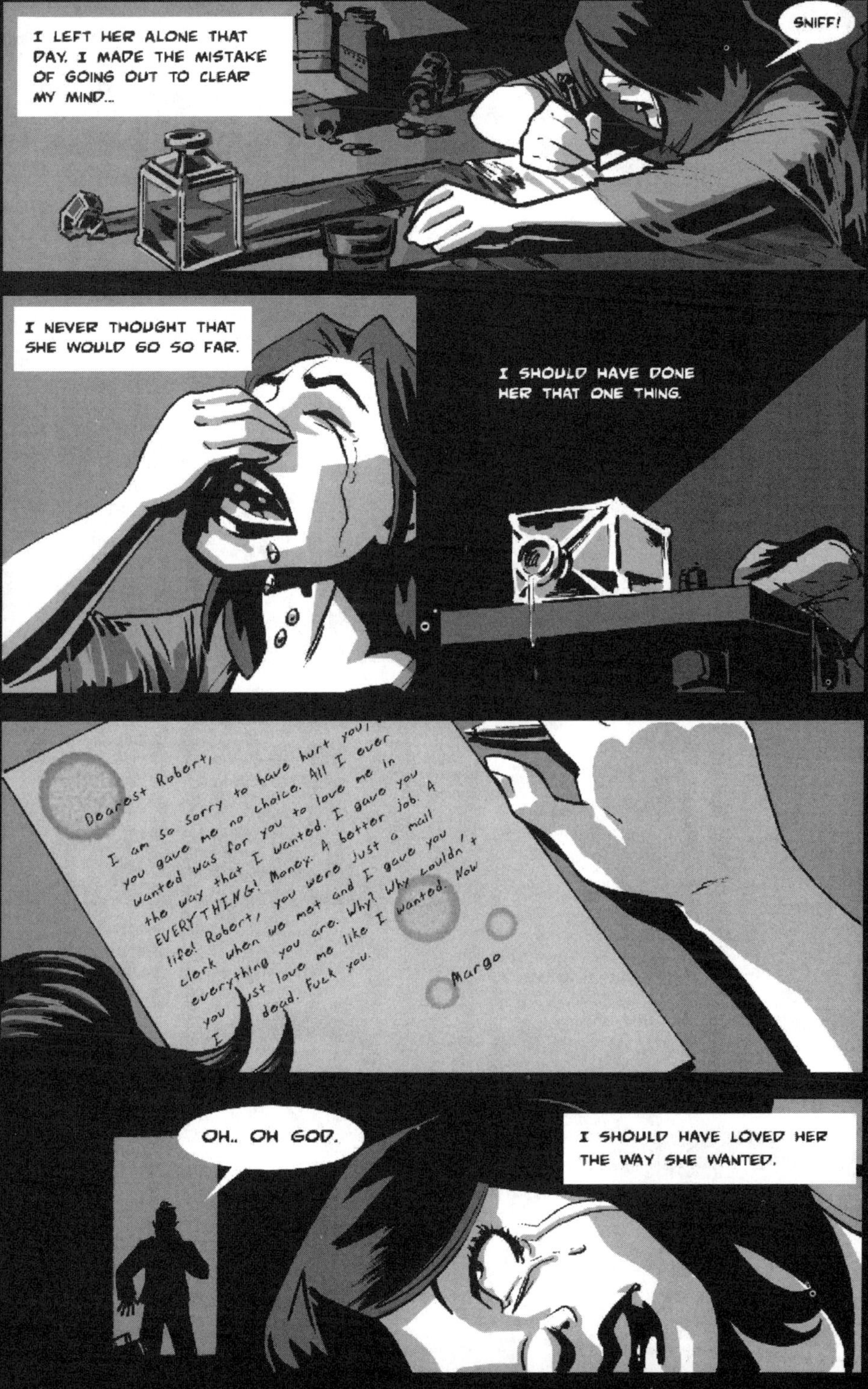

I LEFT HER ALONE THAT DAY. I MADE THE MISTAKE OF GOING OUT TO CLEAR MY MIND...
SNIFF!
I NEVER THOUGHT THAT SHE WOULD GO SO FAR.
I SHOULD HAVE DONE HER THAT ONE THING.
Dearest Robert,
I am so sorry to have hurt you,
you gave me no choice. All I ever
wanted was for you to love me in
the way that I wanted. I gave you
EVERYTHING! Money. A better job. A
life! Robert, you were just a mall
clerk when we met and I gave you
everything you are. Why? Why couldn't
you ust love me like I wanted. Now
I dead. Fuck you.
Margo
OH.. OH GOD.
I SHOULD HAVE LOVED HER THE WAY SHE WANTED.

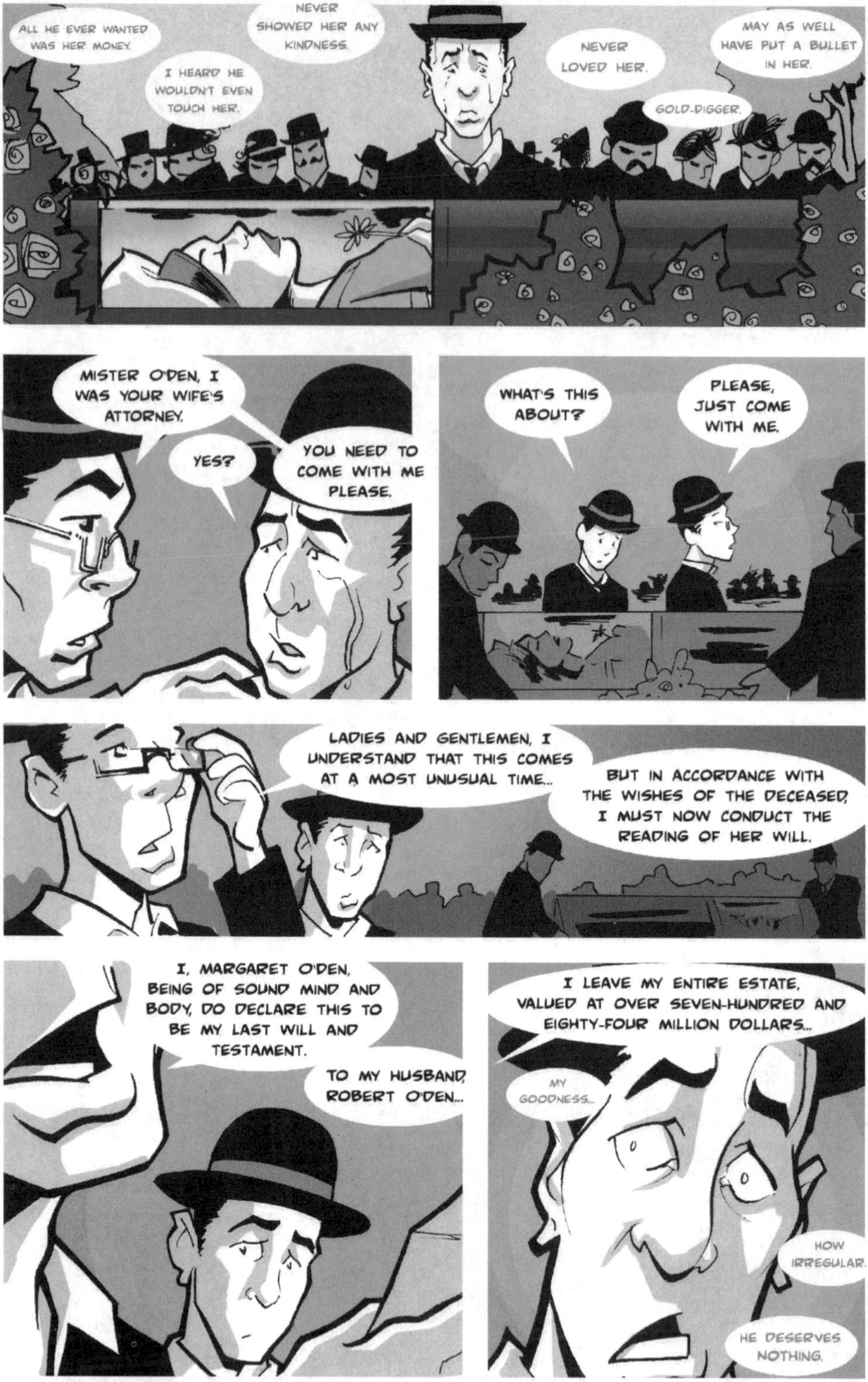
ALL HE EVER WANTED WAS HER MONEY.
I HEARD HE WOULDN'T EVEN TOUCH HER.
NEVER SHOWED HER ANY KINDNESS.
NEVER LOVED HER.
GOLD-DIGGER.
MAY AS WELL HAVE PUT A BULLET IN HER.
MISTER O'DEN, I WAS YOUR WIFE'S ATTORNEY.
YES?
YOU NEED TO COME WITH ME PLEASE.
WHAT'S THIS ABOUT?
PLEASE, JUST COME WITH ME.
LADIES AND GENTLEMEN, I UNDERSTAND THAT THIS COMES AT A MOST UNUSUAL TIME...
BUT IN ACCORDANCE WITH THE WISHES OF THE DECEASED, I MUST NOW CONDUCT THE READING OF HER WILL.
I, MARGARET O'DEN, BEING OF SOUND MIND AND BODY, DO DECLARE THIS TO BE MY LAST WILL AND TESTAMENT.
TO MY HUSBAND, ROBERT O'DEN...
I LEAVE MY ENTIRE ESTATE, VALUED AT OVER SEVEN-HUNDRED AND EIGHTY-FOUR MILLION DOLLARS...
MY GOODNESS...
HOW IRREGULAR.
HE DESERVES NOTHING.

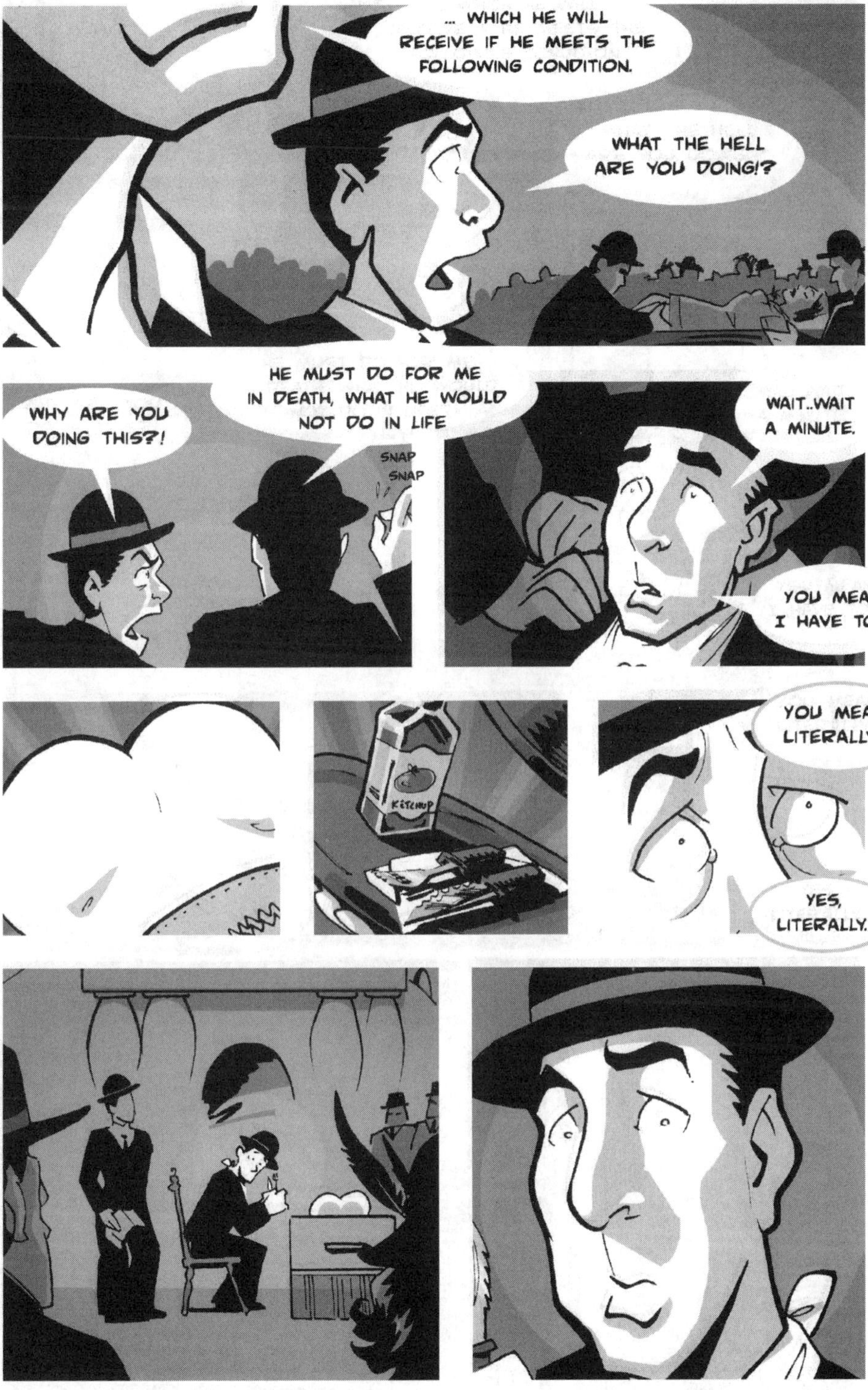
... WHICH HE WILL RECEIVE IF HE MEETS THE FOLLOWING CONDITION.
WHAT THE HELL ARE YOU DOING!?
WHY ARE YOU DOING THIS?!
HE MUST DO FOR ME IN DEATH, WHAT HE WOULD NOT DO IN LIFE
SNAP
SNAP
WAIT..WAIT A MINUTE.
YOU MEAN I HAVE TO...
KETCHUP
YOU MEAN... LITERALLY?
YES, LITERALLY.

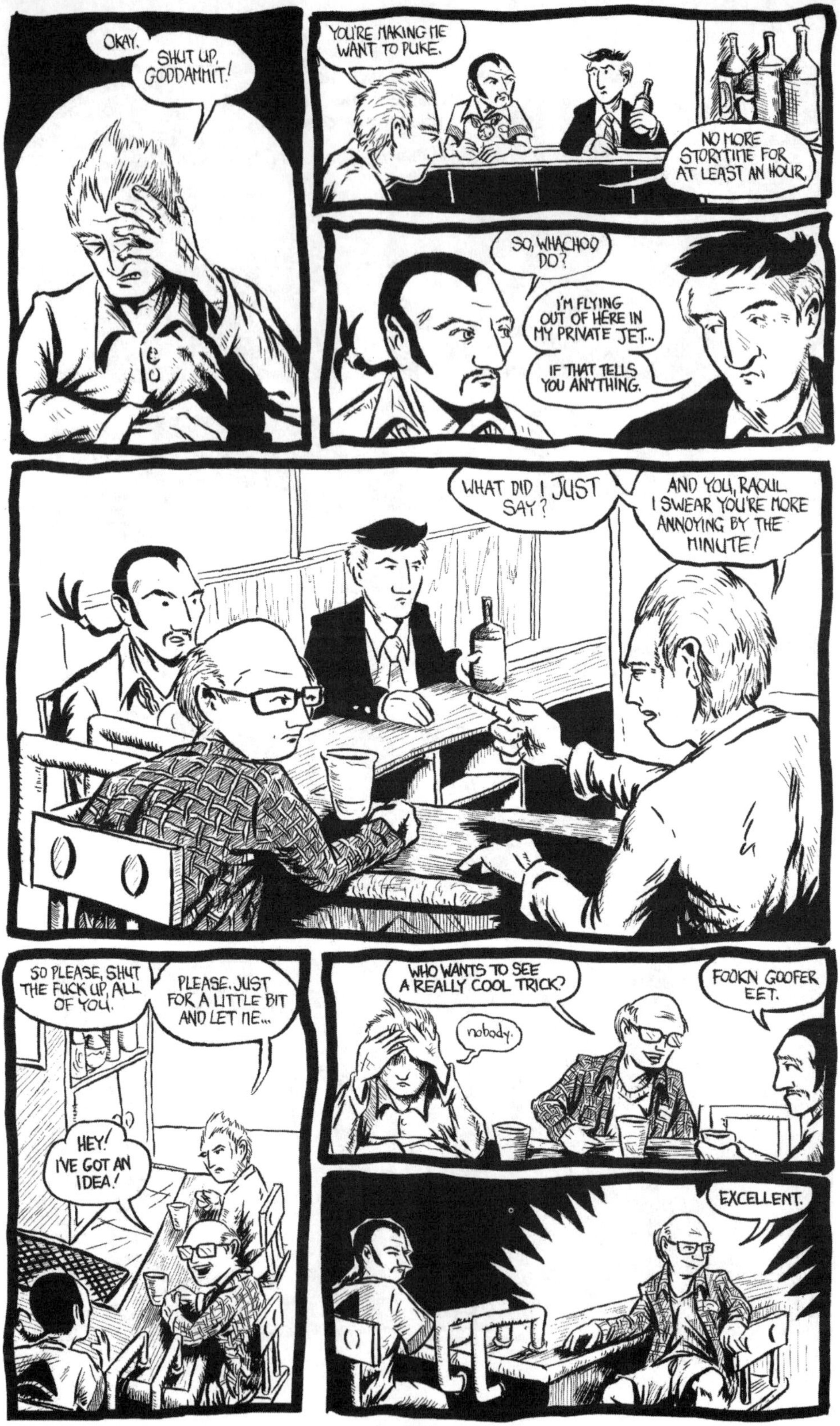
OKAY.
SHUT UP, GODDAMMIT!
YOU'RE MAKING ME WANT TO PUKE.
NO MORE STORYTIME FOR AT LEAST AN HOUR.
SO, WHACHOO DO?
I'M FLYING OUT OF HERE IN MY PRIVATE JET...
IF THAT TELLS YOU ANYTHING.
WHAT DID I JUST SAY?
AND YOU, RAOUL I SWEAR YOU'RE MORE ANNOYING BY THE MINUTE!
SO PLEASE, SHUT THE FUCK UP, ALL OF YOU.
PLEASE, JUST FOR A LITTLE BIT AND LET ME...
HEY! I'VE GOT AN IDEA!
WHO WANTS TO SEE A REALLY COOL TRICK?
nobody.
FOOKN GOOFER EET.
EXCELLENT.

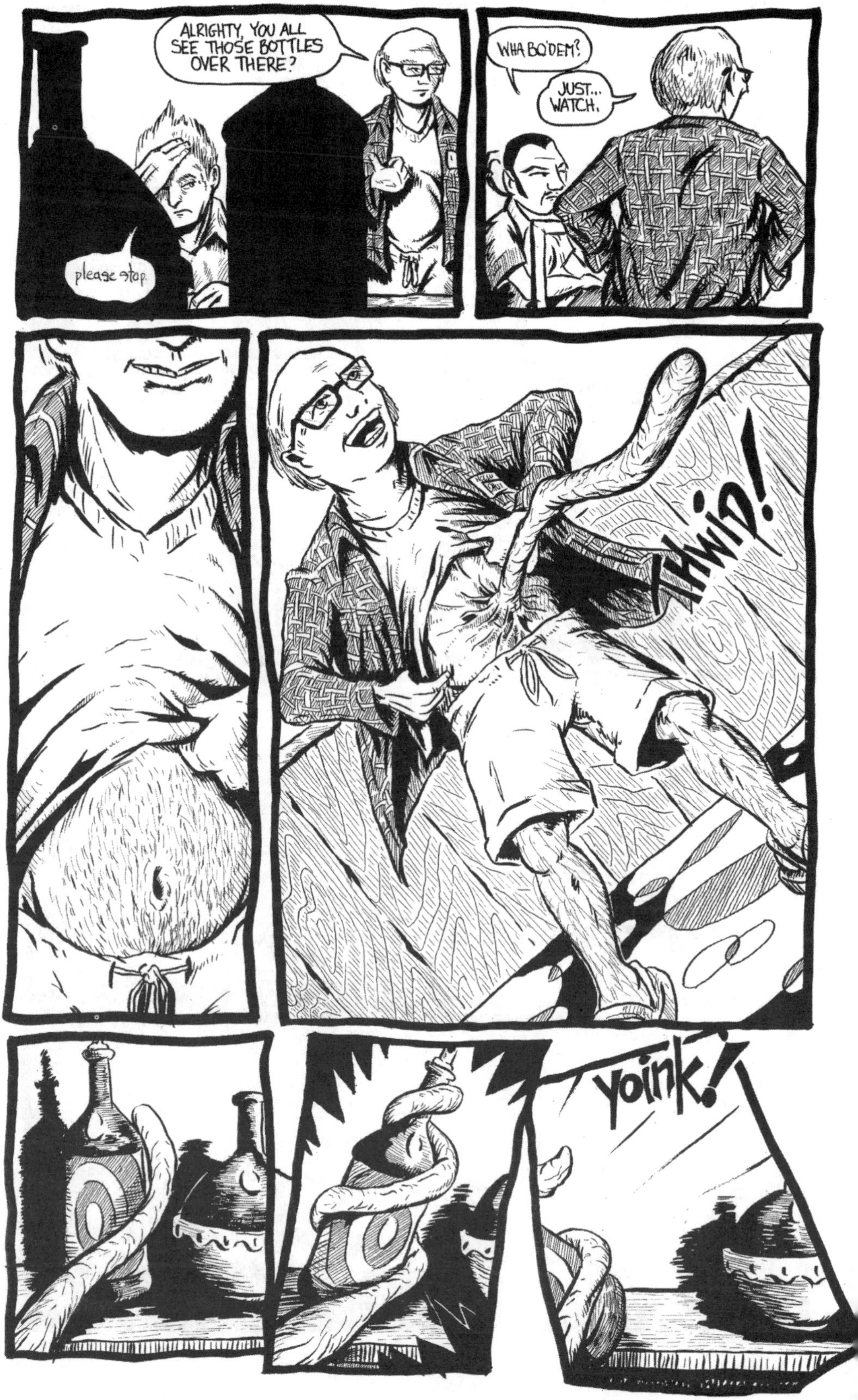
ALRIGHTY, YOU ALL SEE THOSE BOTTLES OVER THERE?
please stop.
WHA BO'DEM?
JUST... WATCH.
THWIP!
yoink!

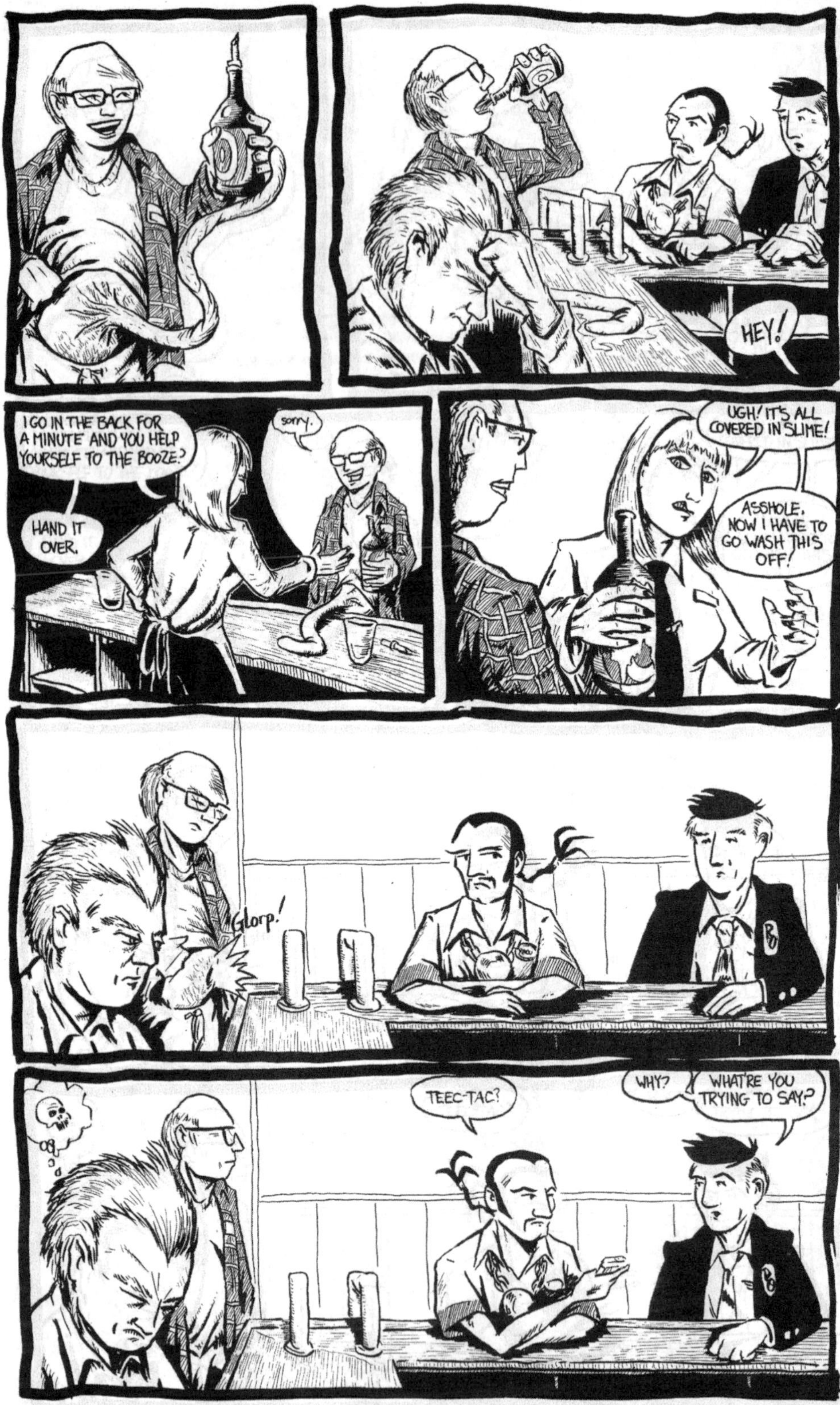
HEY!
I GO IN THE BACK FOR A MINUTE AND YOU HELP YOURSELF TO THE BOOZE?
sorry.
HAND IT OVER.
UGH! IT'S ALL COVERED IN SLIME!
ASSHOLE. NOW I HAVE TO GO WASH THIS OFF!
Glorp!
TEEC-TAC?
WHY?
WHAT'RE YOU TRYING TO SAY?

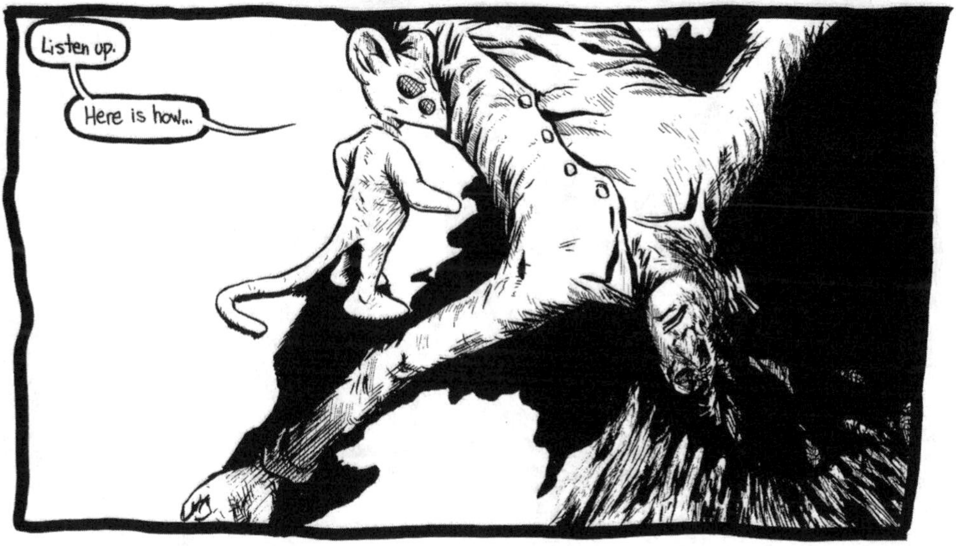
Listen up.
Here is how...

Concoction Seventeen: Madame Selina and The Man In The Bunny Suit

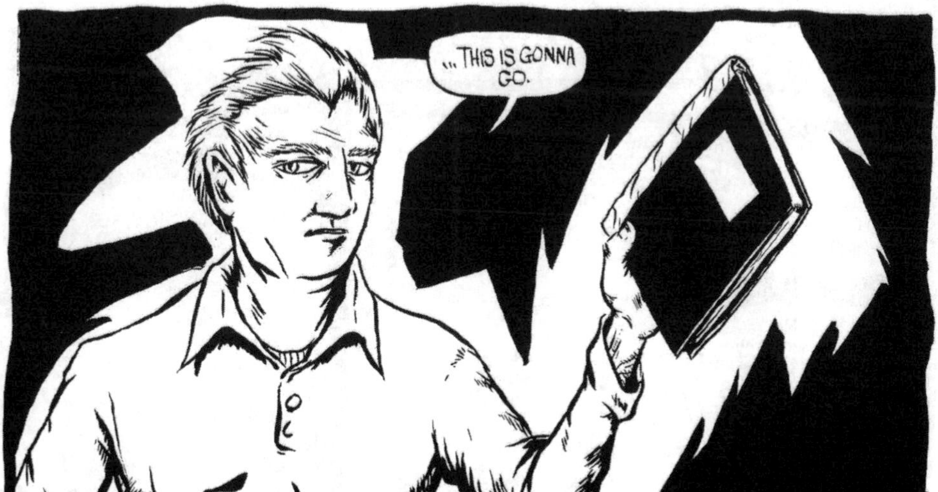
...THIS IS GONNA GO.

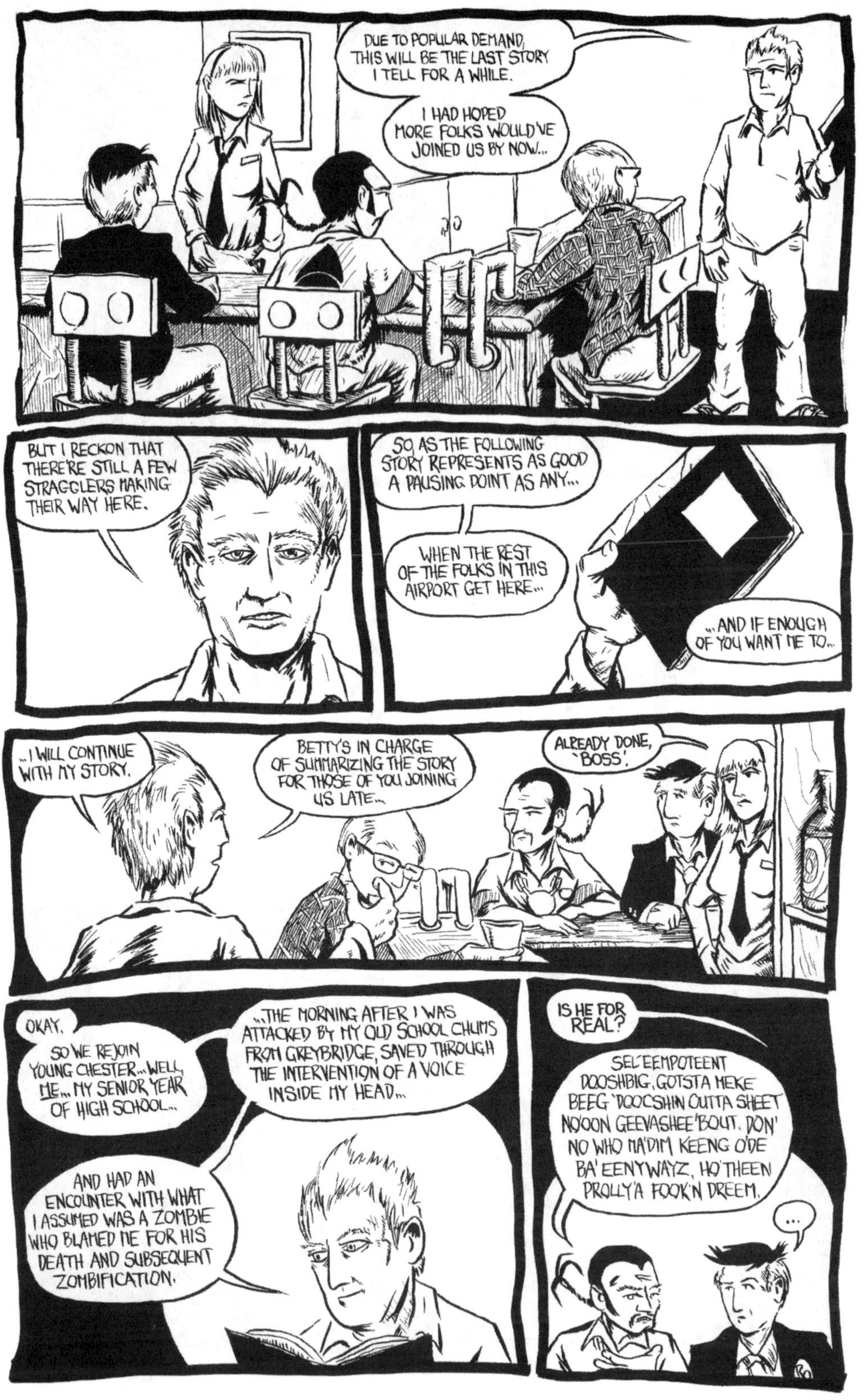
DUE TO POPULAR DEMAND, THIS WILL BE THE LAST STORY I TELL FOR A WHILE.
I HAD HOPED MORE FOLKS WOULD'VE JOINED US BY NOW...
BUT I RECKON THAT THERE'RE STILL A FEW STRAGGLERS MAKING THEIR WAY HERE.
SO, AS THE FOLLOWING STORY REPRESENTS AS GOOD A PAUSING POINT AS ANY...
WHEN THE REST OF THE FOLKS IN THIS AIRPORT GET HERE...
...AND IF ENOUGH OF YOU WANT ME TO...
...I WILL CONTINUE WITH MY STORY.
BETTY'S IN CHARGE OF SUMMARIZING THE STORY FOR THOSE OF YOU JOINING US LATE...
ALREADY DONE, 'BOSS'.
OKAY.
SO WE REJOIN YOUNG CHESTER...WELL, ME... MY SENIOR YEAR OF HIGH SCHOOL...
...THE MORNING AFTER I WAS ATTACKED BY MY OLD SCHOOL CHUMS FROM GREYBRIDGE, SAVED THROUGH THE INTERVENTION OF A VOICE INSIDE MY HEAD...
AND HAD AN ENCOUNTER WITH WHAT I ASSUMED WAS A ZOMBIE WHO BLAMED ME FOR HIS DEATH AND SUBSEQUENT ZOMBIFICATION.
IS HE FOR REAL?
SEL'EEMPOTEENT DOOSHBIG, GOTSTA MEKE BEEG 'DOOCSHIN OUTTA SHEET NO'OON GEEVASHEE 'BOUT. DON' NO WHO MA'DIM KEENG O'DE BA' EENYWAYZ. HO'THEEN PROLLY'A FOOK'N DREEM.
...

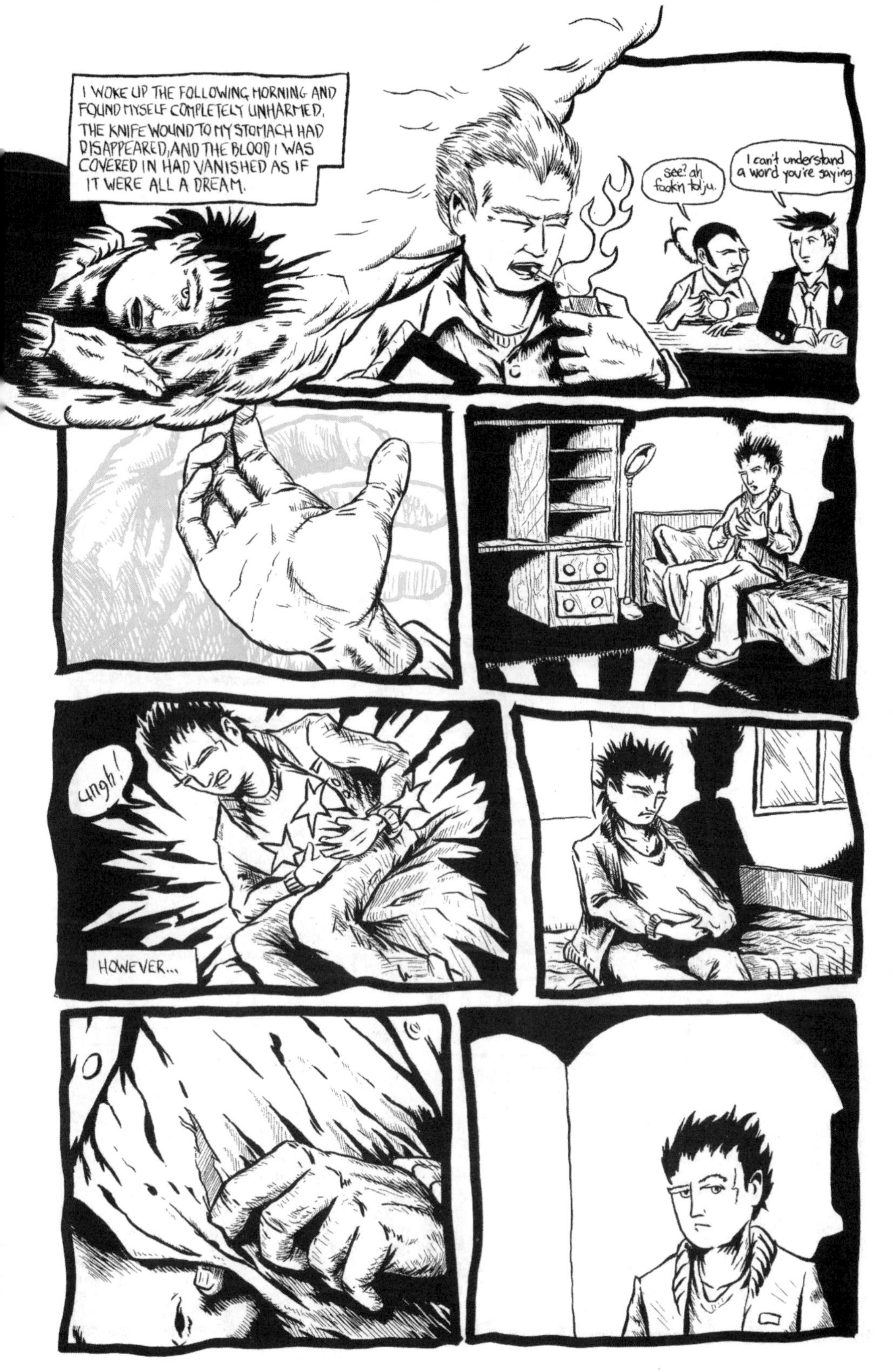
I WOKE UP THE FOLLOWING MORNING AND FOUND MYSELF COMPLETELY UNHARMED. THE KNIFE WOUND TO MY STOMACH HAD DISAPPEARED, AND THE BLOOD I WAS COVERED IN HAD VANISHED AS IF IT WERE ALL A DREAM.
see? ah fookin tolju.
I can't understand a word you're saying.
ungh!
HOWEVER...

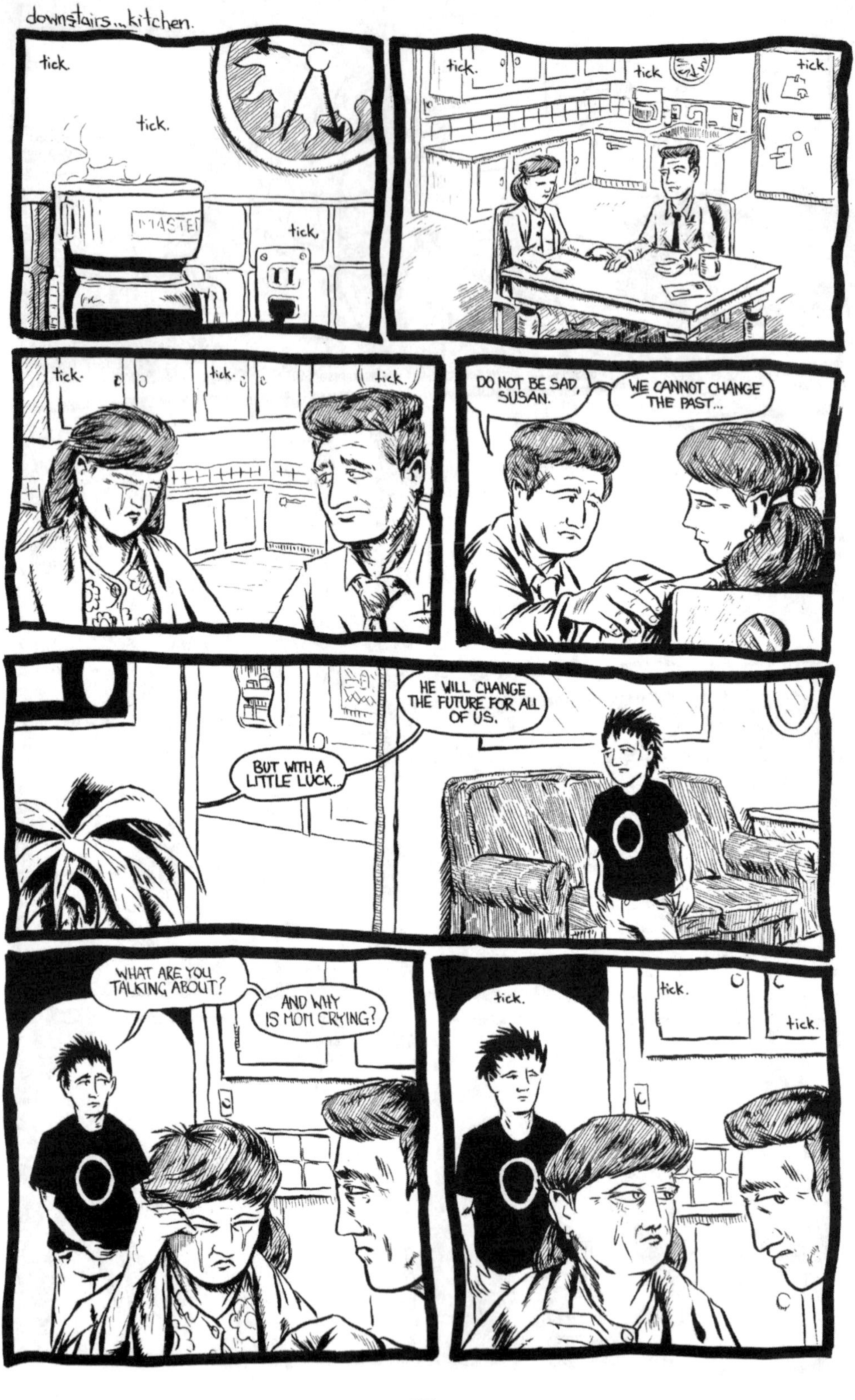
downstairs... kitchen.
tick.
tick.
MASTER
tick.
tick.
tick
tick.
tick.
tick.
tick.
DO NOT BE SAD, SUSAN.
WE CANNOT CHANGE THE PAST...
BUT WITH A LITTLE LUCK...
HE WILL CHANGE THE FUTURE FOR ALL OF US.
WHAT ARE YOU TALKING ABOUT?
AND WHY IS MOM CRYING?
tick.
tick.
tick.

OH! CHESTER, YOU GOT A LETTER FROM LENSCOM UNIVERSITY YESTERDAY

IT'S FROM ADMISSIONS...

WHEN DID I APPLY HERE?

Lenscom University
of South Carolina

Chester Thomson
251 Third Street
Haven, NJ 0770

Thomson,
e pleased to announced that you have been ACCEPT
University in South Carolina. Lenscom University
ith open arms, and trust that you will find
finest education that money can bu
e use and abuse. Madness
ge creatures, insa
(realiz

HUH. I GOT IN.

BUT SOUTH CAROLINA IS SO FAR AWAY.

YES. IT IS.

CHESTER, YOUR FOSTER FATHER AND I AGREE THAT WHILE WE LOVE YOU AND WOULD MISS YOU LIKE CRAZY...

LENSCOM WOULD BE A GREAT OPPORTUNITY FOR YOU.

JUST PROMISE THAT YOU'LL THINK ABOUT IT, OKAY?

I... I SHOULD GET TO WORK.

Scene of the crime...

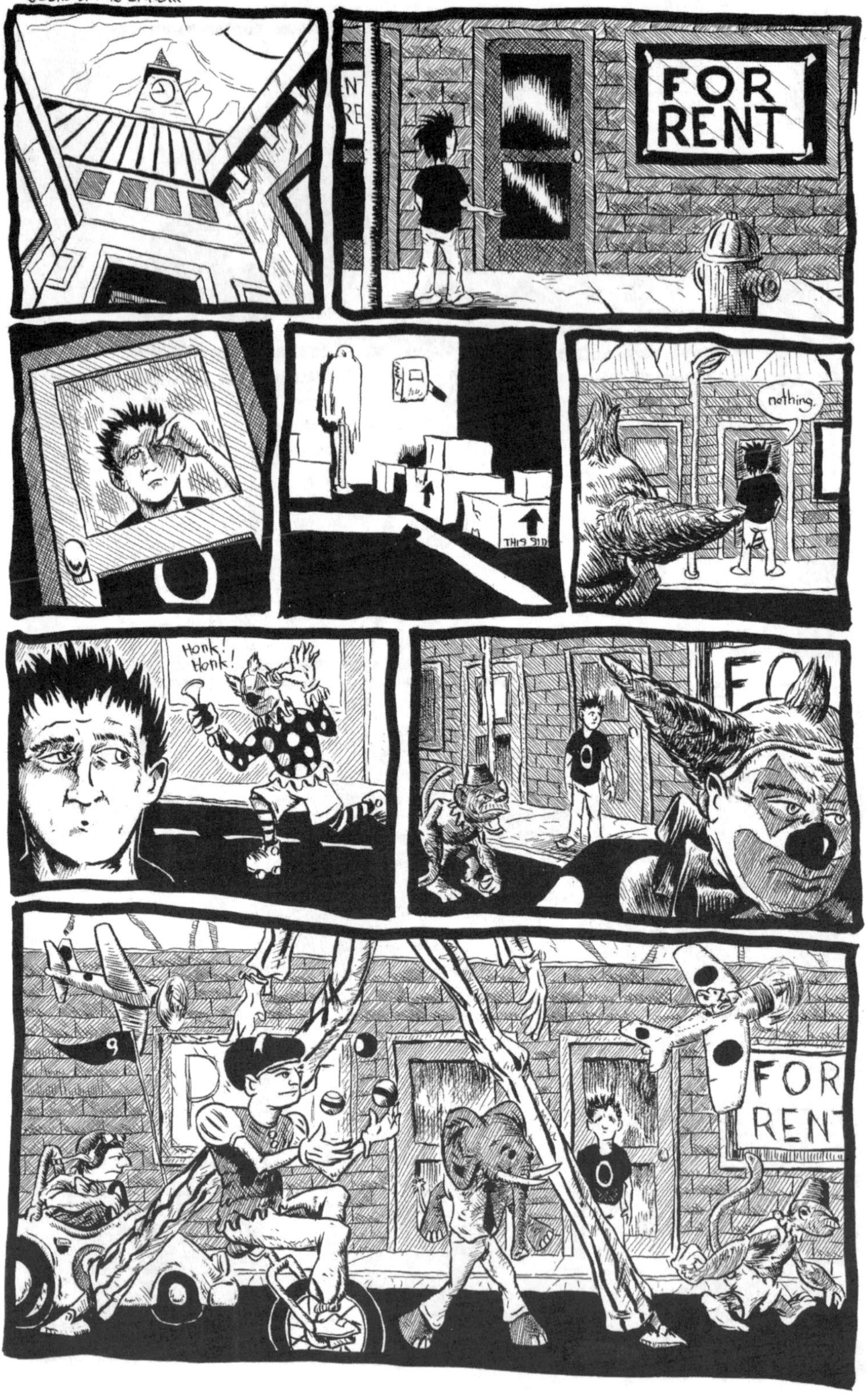
FOR RENT
nothing.
THIS SID
Honk! Honk!
FO
FOR RENT

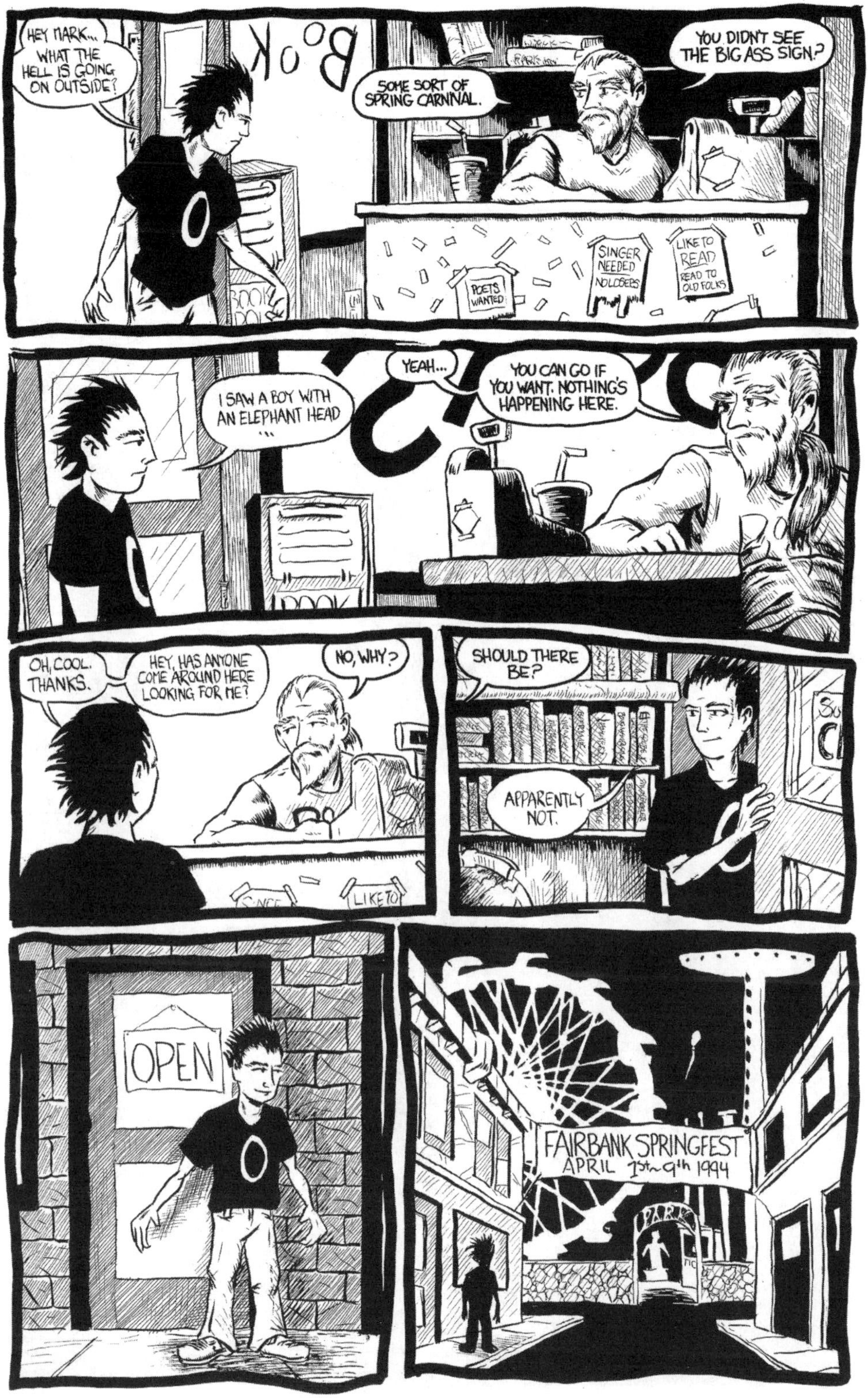

BOOK
HEY MARK...
WHAT THE
HELL IS GOING
ON OUTSIDE?
SOME SORT OF
SPRING CARNIVAL.
YOU DIDN'T SEE
THE BIG ASS SIGN?
POETS
WANTED
SINGER
NEEDED
NO LOSERS
LIKE TO
READ
READ TO
OLD FOLKS
I SAW A BOY WITH
AN ELEPHANT HEAD
...
YEAH...
YOU CAN GO IF
YOU WANT. NOTHING'S
HAPPENING HERE.
OH, COOL.
THANKS.
HEY, HAS ANYONE
COME AROUND HERE
LOOKING FOR ME?
NO, WHY?
SHOULD THERE
BE?
APPARENTLY
NOT.
OPEN
FAIRBANK SPRINGFEST
APRIL 1st~9th 1994

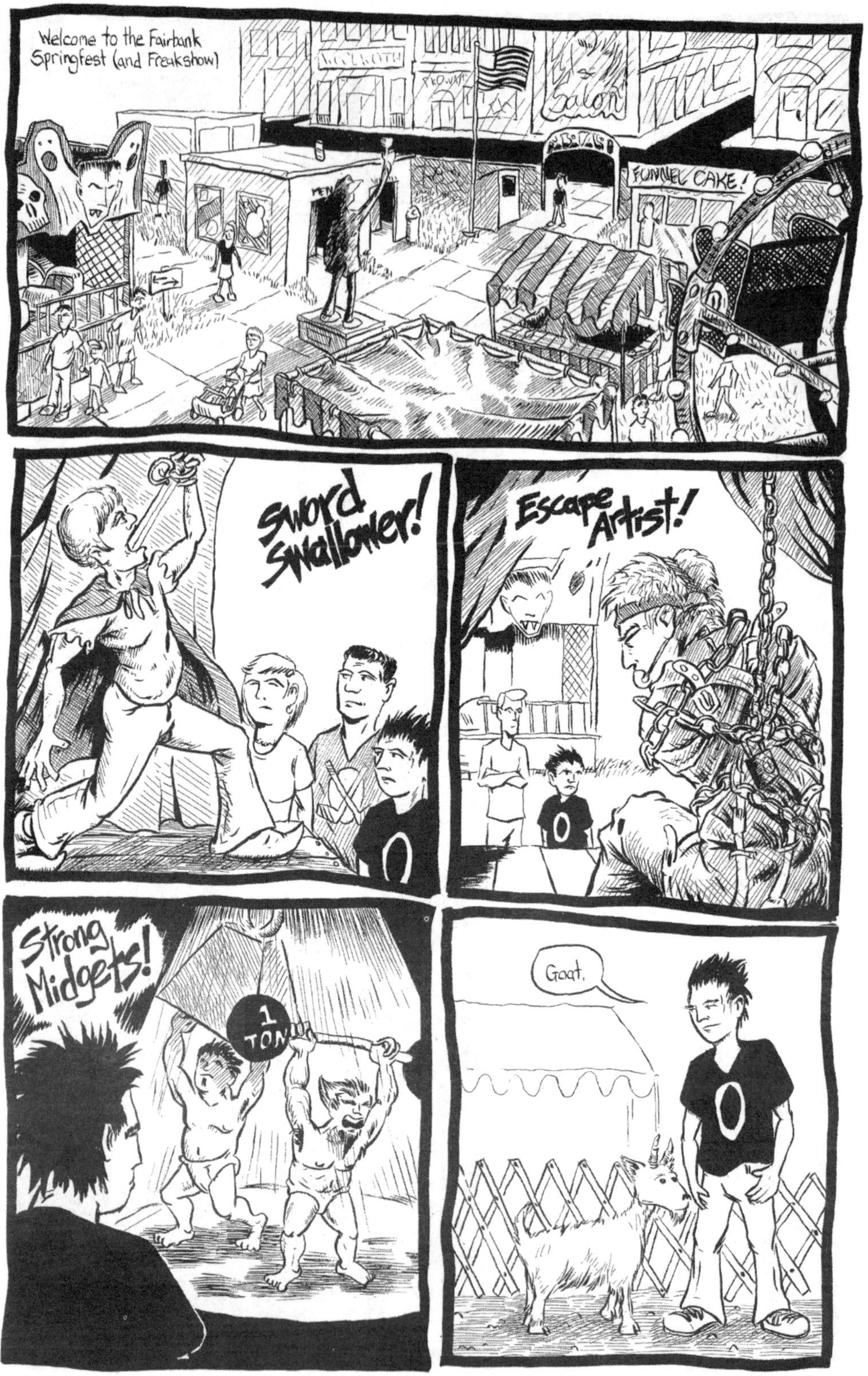

Welcome to the Fairbank Springfest (and Freakshow)
FUNNEL CAKE!
Salon
Sword Swallower!
Escape Artist!
Strong Midgets!
1 TON
Goat.

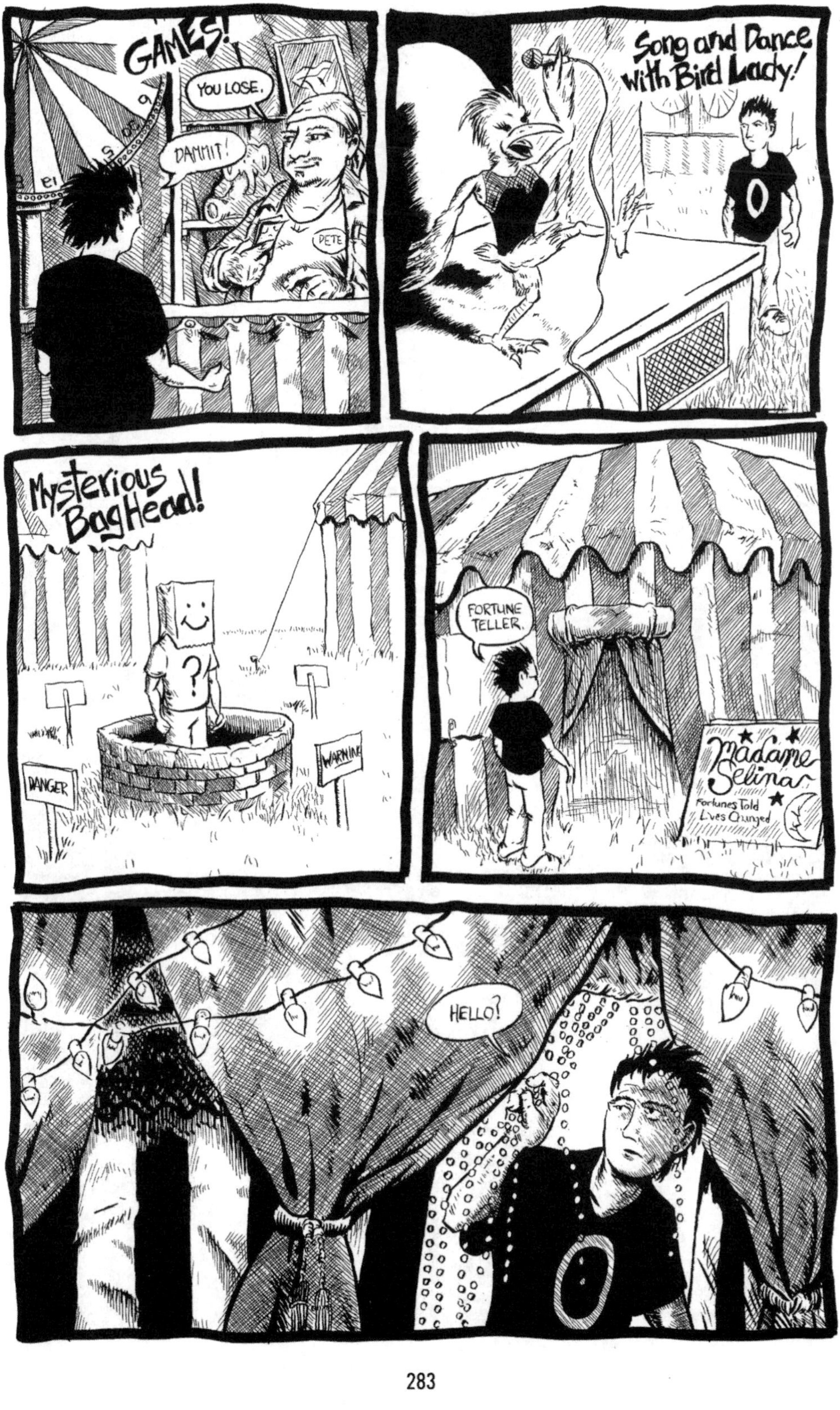
GAMES!
YOU LOSE.
DAMMIT!
PETE
Song and Dance with Bird Lady!
Mysterious Bag Head!
?
DANGER
WARNING
FORTUNE TELLER.
Madame Selina
Fortunes Told
Lives Changed
HELLO?

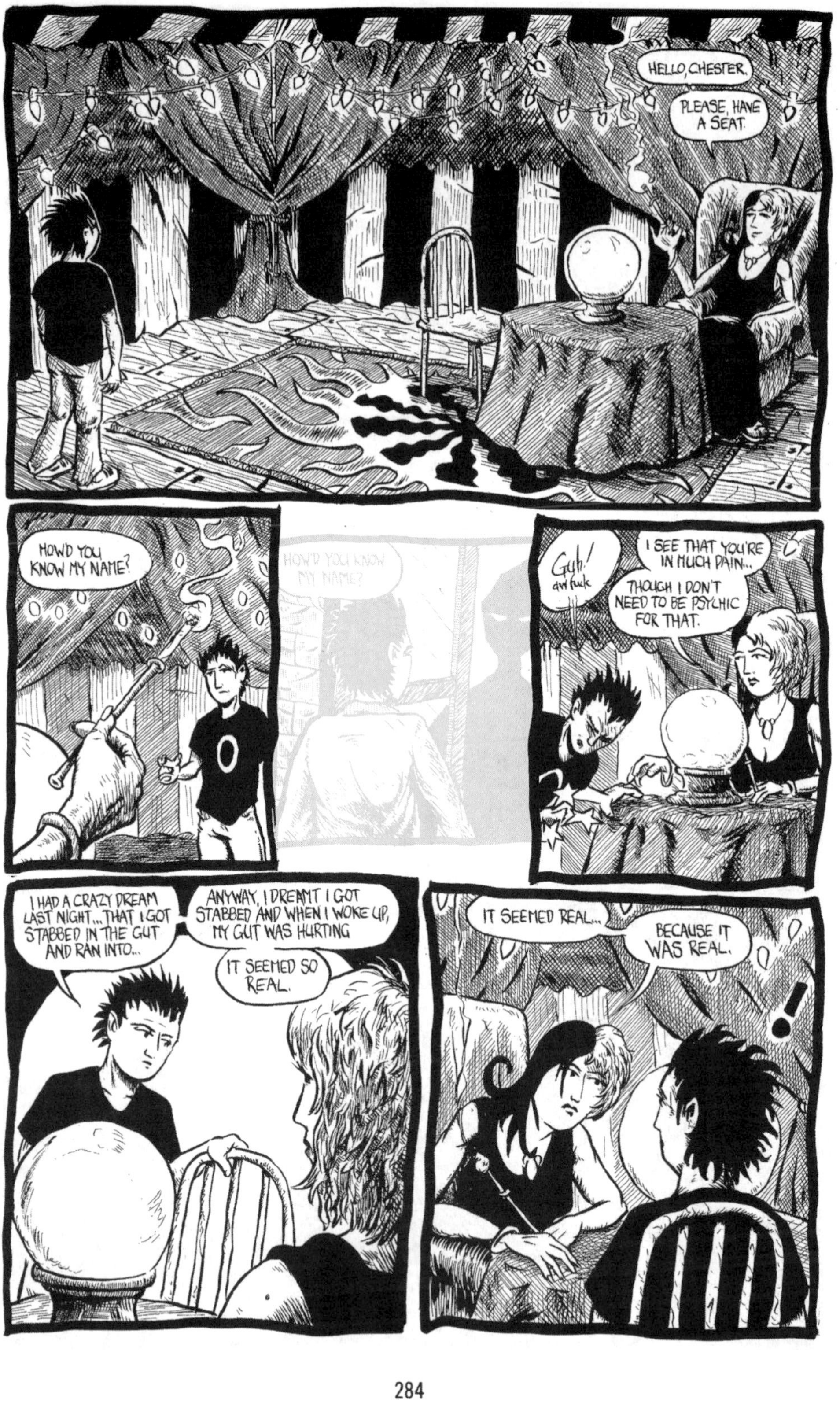
HELLO, CHESTER.
PLEASE, HAVE A SEAT.
HOW'D YOU KNOW MY NAME?
HOW'D YOU KNOW MY NAME?
Guh! aw fuck
I SEE THAT YOU'RE IN MUCH PAIN...
THOUGH I DON'T NEED TO BE PSYCHIC FOR THAT.
I HAD A CRAZY DREAM LAST NIGHT... THAT I GOT STABBED IN THE GUT AND RAN INTO...
ANYWAY, I DREAMT I GOT STABBED AND WHEN I WOKE UP, MY GUT WAS HURTING
IT SEEMED SO REAL.
IT SEEMED REAL...
BECAUSE IT WAS REAL.

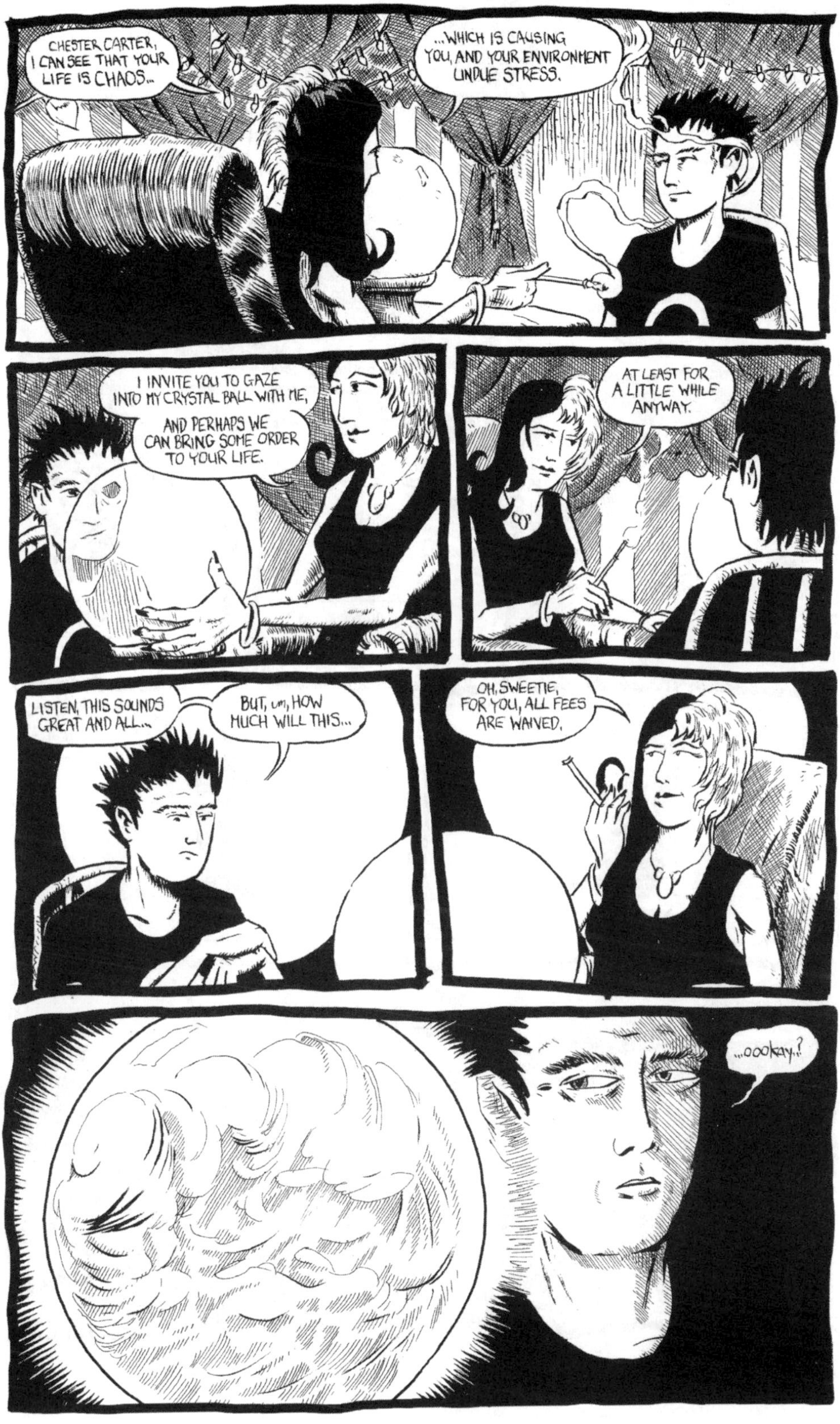
CHESTER CARTER, I CAN SEE THAT YOUR LIFE IS CHAOS...
...WHICH IS CAUSING YOU, AND YOUR ENVIRONMENT UNDUE STRESS.
I INVITE YOU TO GAZE INTO MY CRYSTAL BALL WITH ME,
AND PERHAPS WE CAN BRING SOME ORDER TO YOUR LIFE.
AT LEAST FOR A LITTLE WHILE ANYWAY.
LISTEN, THIS SOUNDS GREAT AND ALL...
BUT, um, HOW MUCH WILL THIS...
OH, SWEETIE, FOR YOU, ALL FEES ARE WAIVED.
...oookay..?

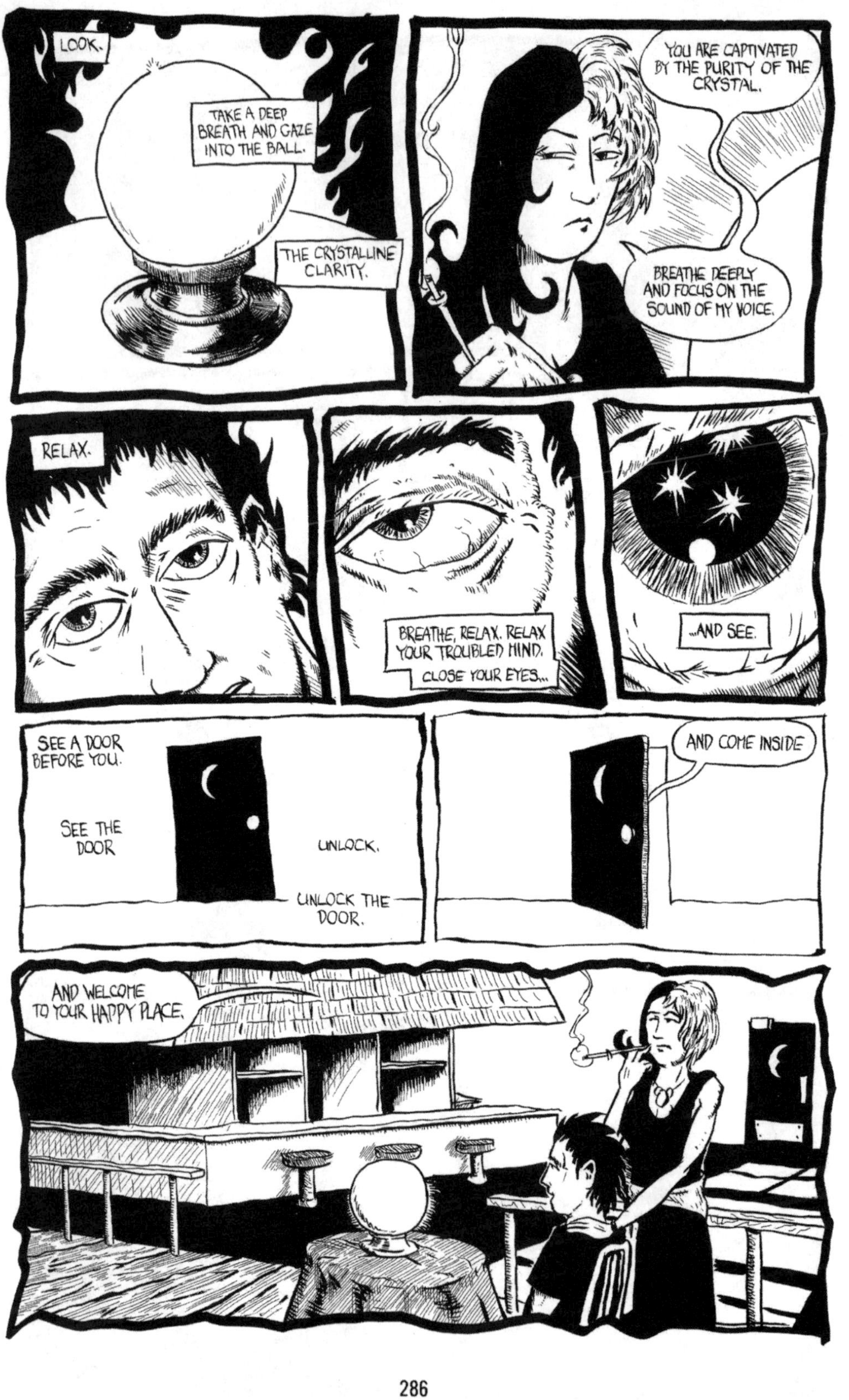
LOOK.
TAKE A DEEP BREATH AND GAZE INTO THE BALL.
THE CRYSTALLINE CLARITY.
YOU ARE CAPTIVATED BY THE PURITY OF THE CRYSTAL.
BREATHE DEEPLY AND FOCUS ON THE SOUND OF MY VOICE.
RELAX.
BREATHE, RELAX. RELAX YOUR TROUBLED MIND.
CLOSE YOUR EYES...
...AND SEE.
SEE A DOOR BEFORE YOU.
SEE THE DOOR
UNLOCK.
UNLOCK THE DOOR.
AND COME INSIDE
AND WELCOME TO YOUR HAPPY PLACE.

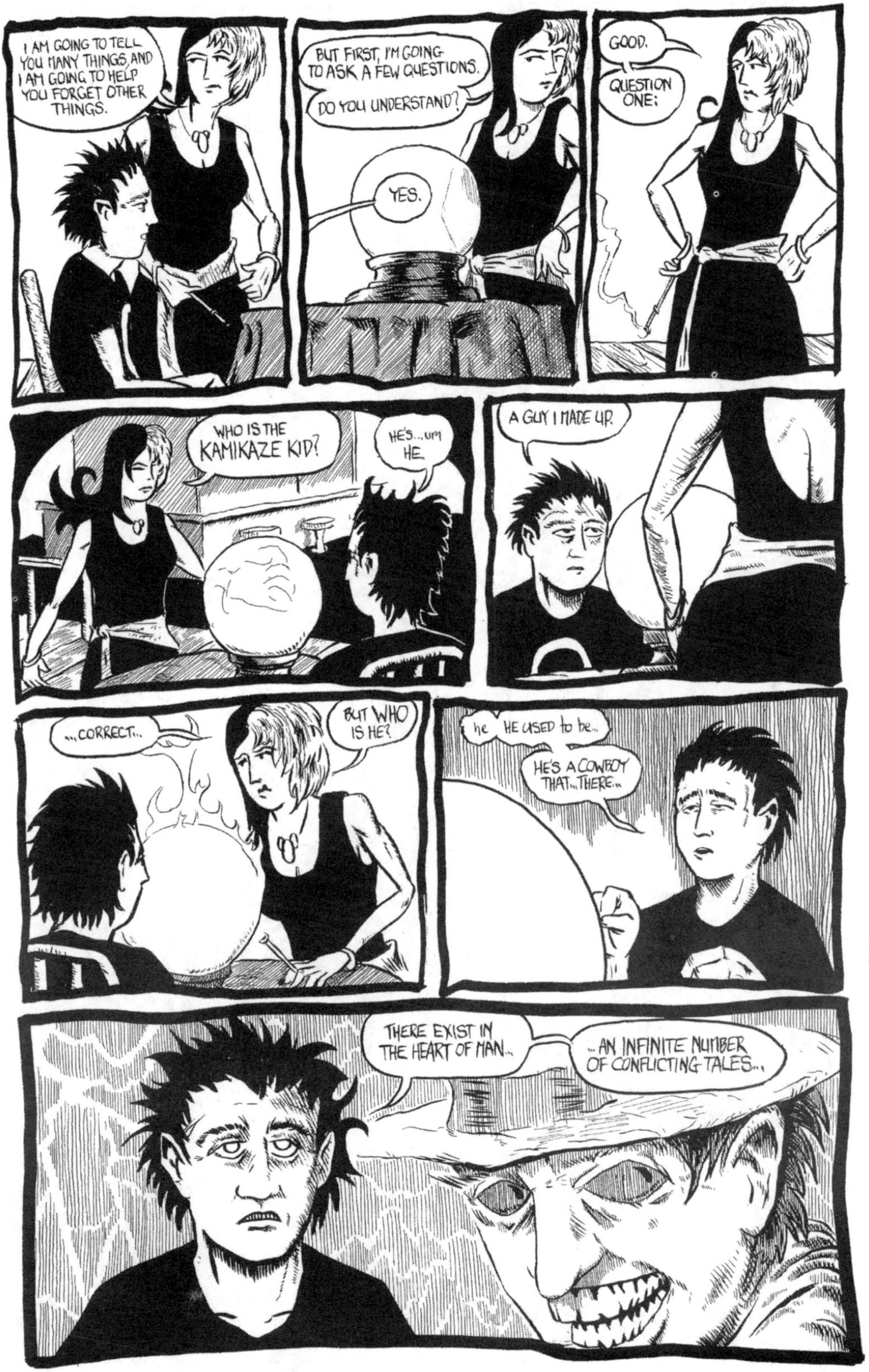
I AM GOING TO TELL YOU MANY THINGS, AND I AM GOING TO HELP YOU FORGET OTHER THINGS.
BUT FIRST, I'M GOING TO ASK A FEW QUESTIONS.
DO YOU UNDERSTAND?
YES.
GOOD.
QUESTION ONE:
WHO IS THE KAMIKAZE KID?
HE'S...um HE.
A GUY I MADE UP.
...CORRECT...
BUT WHO IS HE?
he HE USED to be...
HE'S A COWBOY THAT...THERE...
THERE EXIST IN THE HEART OF MAN...
...AN INFINITE NUMBER OF CONFLICTING TALES...

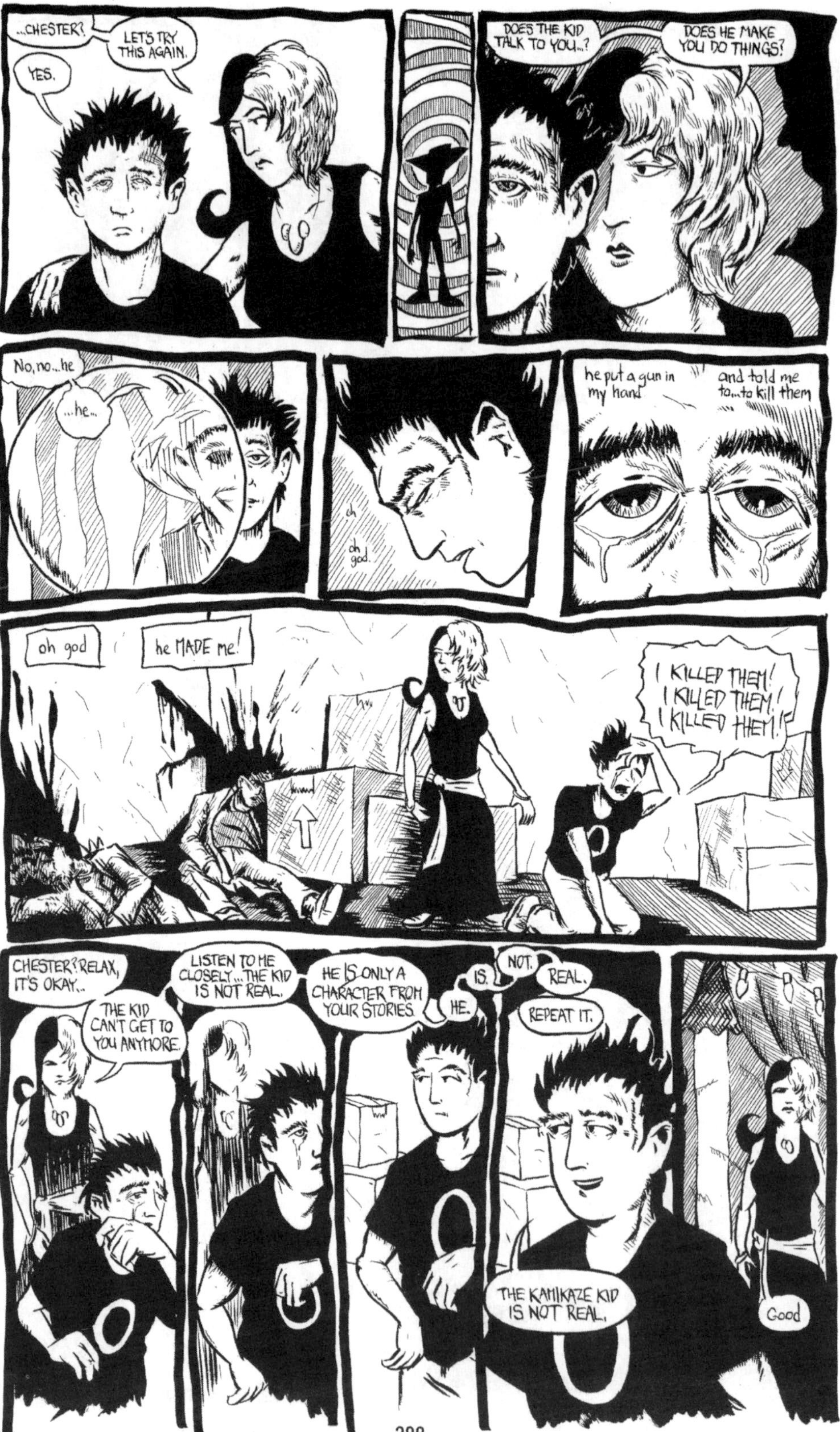
...CHESTER?
LET'S TRY THIS AGAIN.
YES.
DOES THE KID TALK TO YOU...?
DOES HE MAKE YOU DO THINGS?
No, no...he
...he...
oh
oh god.
he put a gun in my hand
and told me to...to kill them
oh god
he MADE me!
I KILLED THEM! I KILLED THEM! I KILLED THEM!
CHESTER? RELAX, IT'S OKAY...
THE KID CAN'T GET TO YOU ANYMORE.
LISTEN TO ME CLOSELY... THE KID IS NOT REAL.
HE IS ONLY A CHARACTER FROM YOUR STORIES.
HE.
IS.
NOT.
REAL.
REPEAT IT.
THE KAMIKAZE KID IS NOT REAL.
Good

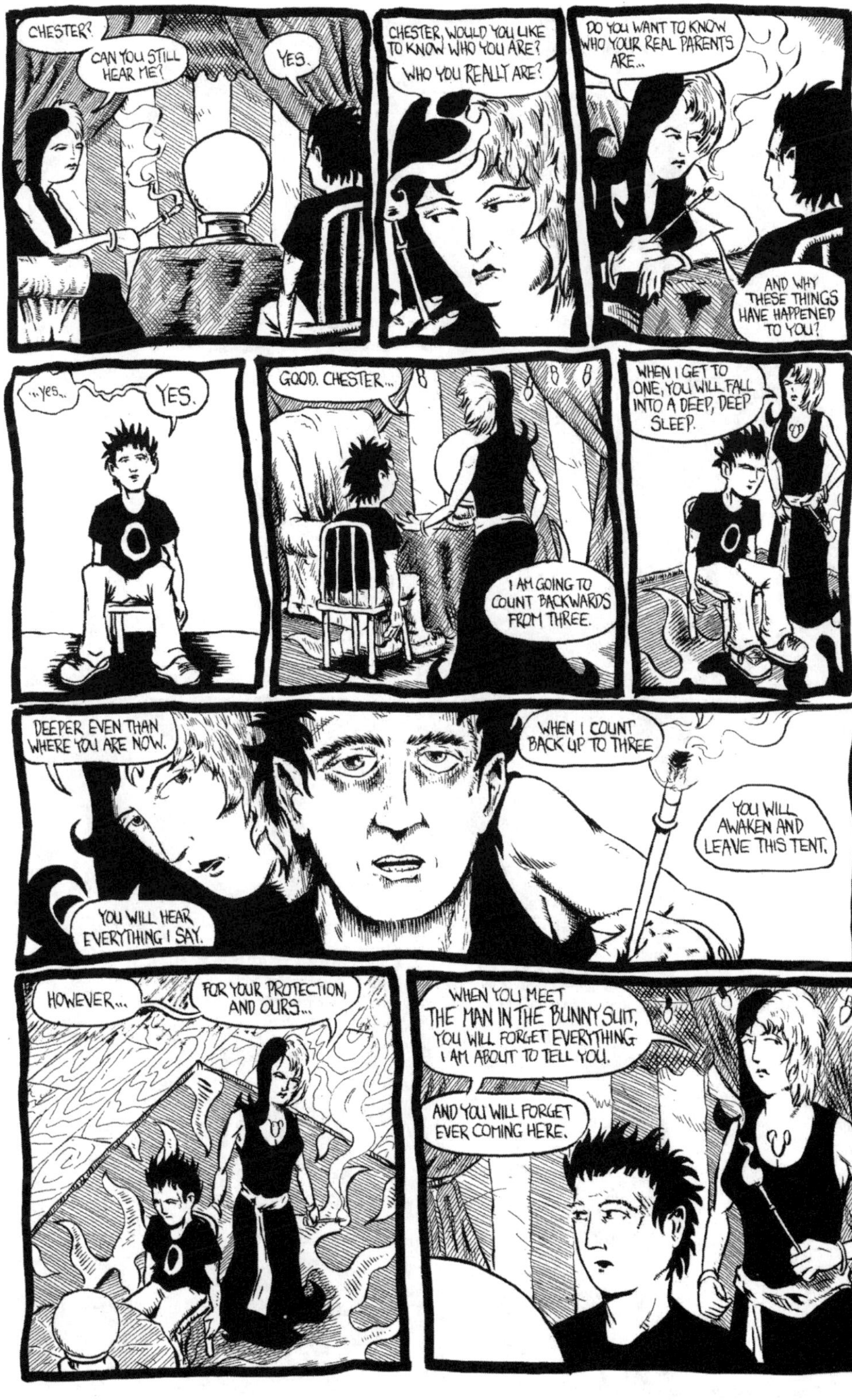
CHESTER?
CAN YOU STILL HEAR ME?
YES.
CHESTER, WOULD YOU LIKE TO KNOW WHO YOU ARE?
WHO YOU REALLY ARE?
DO YOU WANT TO KNOW WHO YOUR REAL PARENTS ARE...
AND WHY THESE THINGS HAVE HAPPENED TO YOU?
...YES...
YES.
GOOD. CHESTER...
I AM GOING TO COUNT BACKWARDS FROM THREE.
WHEN I GET TO ONE, YOU WILL FALL INTO A DEEP, DEEP SLEEP.
DEEPER EVEN THAN WHERE YOU ARE NOW.
YOU WILL HEAR EVERYTHING I SAY.
WHEN I COUNT BACK UP TO THREE
YOU WILL AWAKEN AND LEAVE THIS TENT.
HOWEVER...
FOR YOUR PROTECTION, AND OURS...
WHEN YOU MEET THE MAN IN THE BUNNY SUIT, YOU WILL FORGET EVERYTHING I AM ABOUT TO TELL YOU.
AND YOU WILL FORGET EVER COMING HERE.

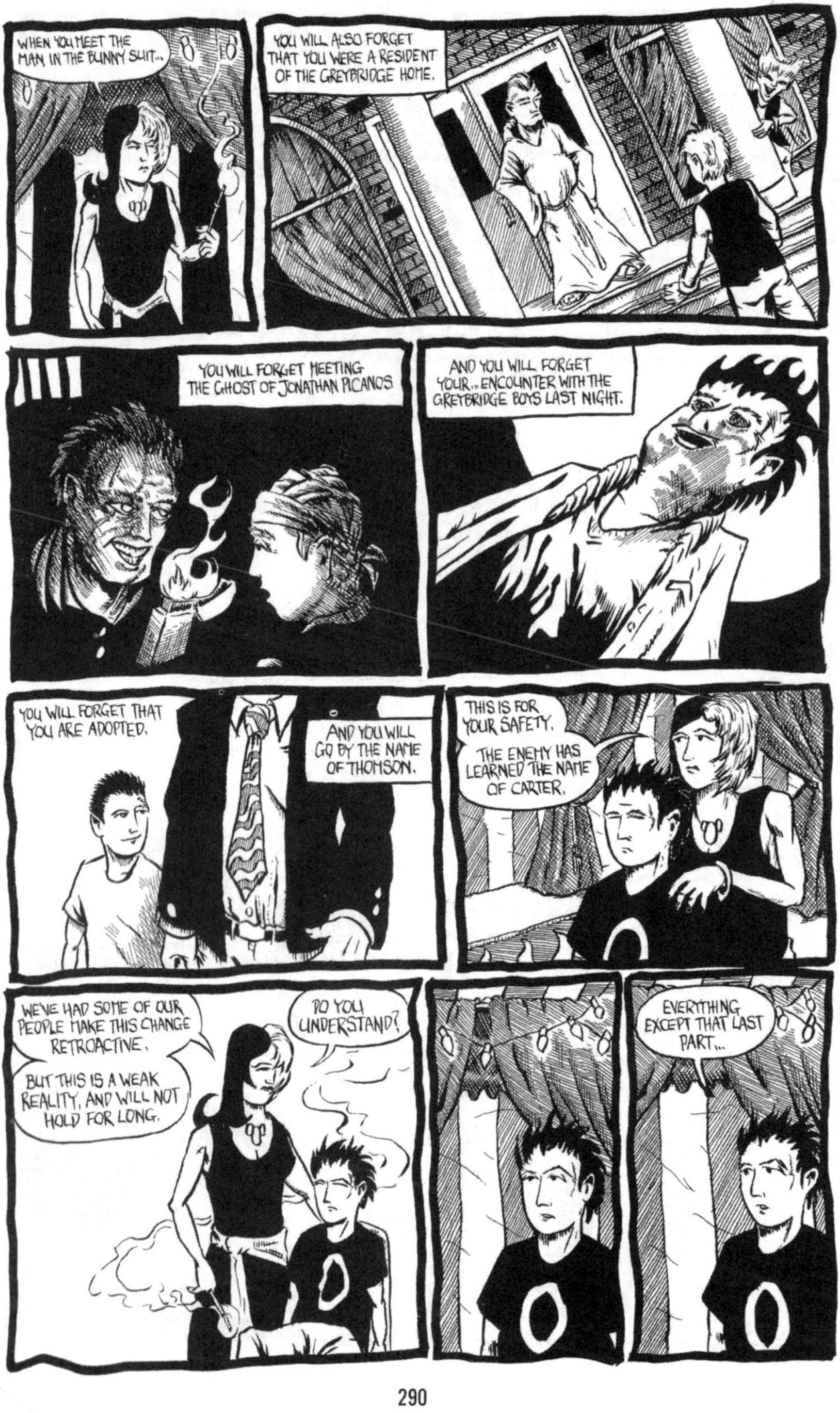
WHEN YOU MEET THE MAN IN THE BUNNY SUIT...
YOU WILL ALSO FORGET THAT YOU WERE A RESIDENT OF THE GREYBRIDGE HOME.
YOU WILL FORGET MEETING THE GHOST OF JONATHAN PICANOS
AND YOU WILL FORGET YOUR... ENCOUNTER WITH THE GREYBRIDGE BOYS LAST NIGHT.
YOU WILL FORGET THAT YOU ARE ADOPTED.
AND YOU WILL GO BY THE NAME OF THOMSON.
THIS IS FOR YOUR SAFETY.
THE ENEMY HAS LEARNED THE NAME OF CARTER.
WE'VE HAD SOME OF OUR PEOPLE MAKE THIS CHANGE RETROACTIVE.
BUT THIS IS A WEAK REALITY, AND WILL NOT HOLD FOR LONG.
DO YOU UNDERSTAND?
EVERYTHING EXCEPT THAT LAST PART...

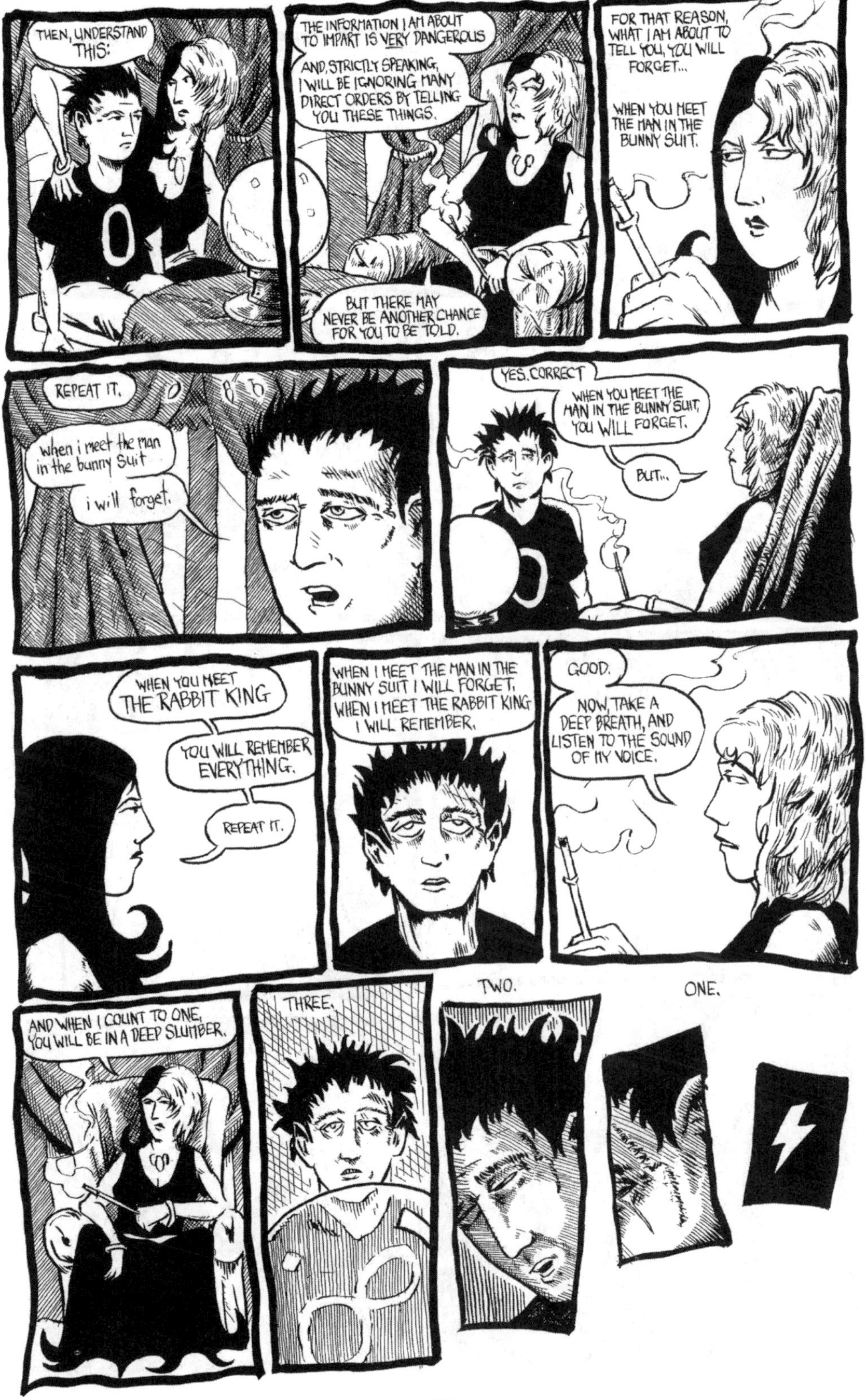
THEN, UNDERSTAND THIS:
THE INFORMATION I AM ABOUT TO IMPART IS VERY DANGEROUS
AND, STRICTLY SPEAKING, I WILL BE IGNORING MANY DIRECT ORDERS BY TELLING YOU THESE THINGS.
BUT THERE MAY NEVER BE ANOTHER CHANCE FOR YOU TO BE TOLD.
FOR THAT REASON, WHAT I AM ABOUT TO TELL YOU, YOU WILL FORGET...
WHEN YOU MEET THE MAN IN THE BUNNY SUIT.
REPEAT IT.
when i meet the man in the bunny suit
i will forget.
YES, CORRECT
WHEN YOU MEET THE MAN IN THE BUNNY SUIT, YOU WILL FORGET.
BUT...
WHEN YOU MEET THE RABBIT KING
YOU WILL REMEMBER EVERYTHING.
REPEAT IT.
WHEN I MEET THE MAN IN THE BUNNY SUIT I WILL FORGET, WHEN I MEET THE RABBIT KING I WILL REMEMBER.
GOOD.
NOW, TAKE A DEEP BREATH, AND LISTEN TO THE SOUND OF MY VOICE.
AND WHEN I COUNT TO ONE, YOU WILL BE IN A DEEP SLUMBER.
THREE.
TWO.
ONE.

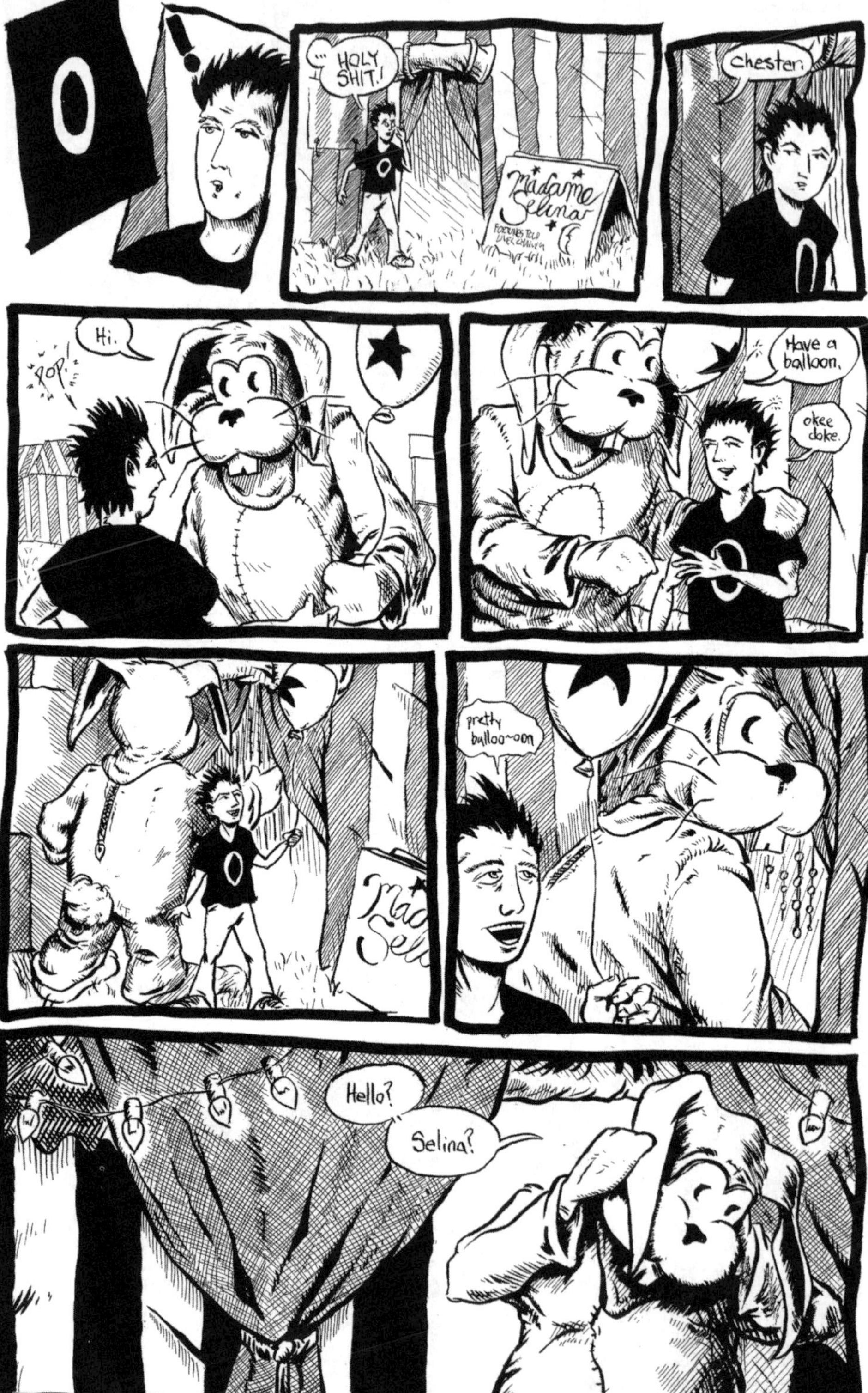

... HOLY SHIT!
Madame Selina
Chester.
POP!
Hi.
Have a balloon.
okee doke.
pretty balloo~oon
Hello?
Selina?

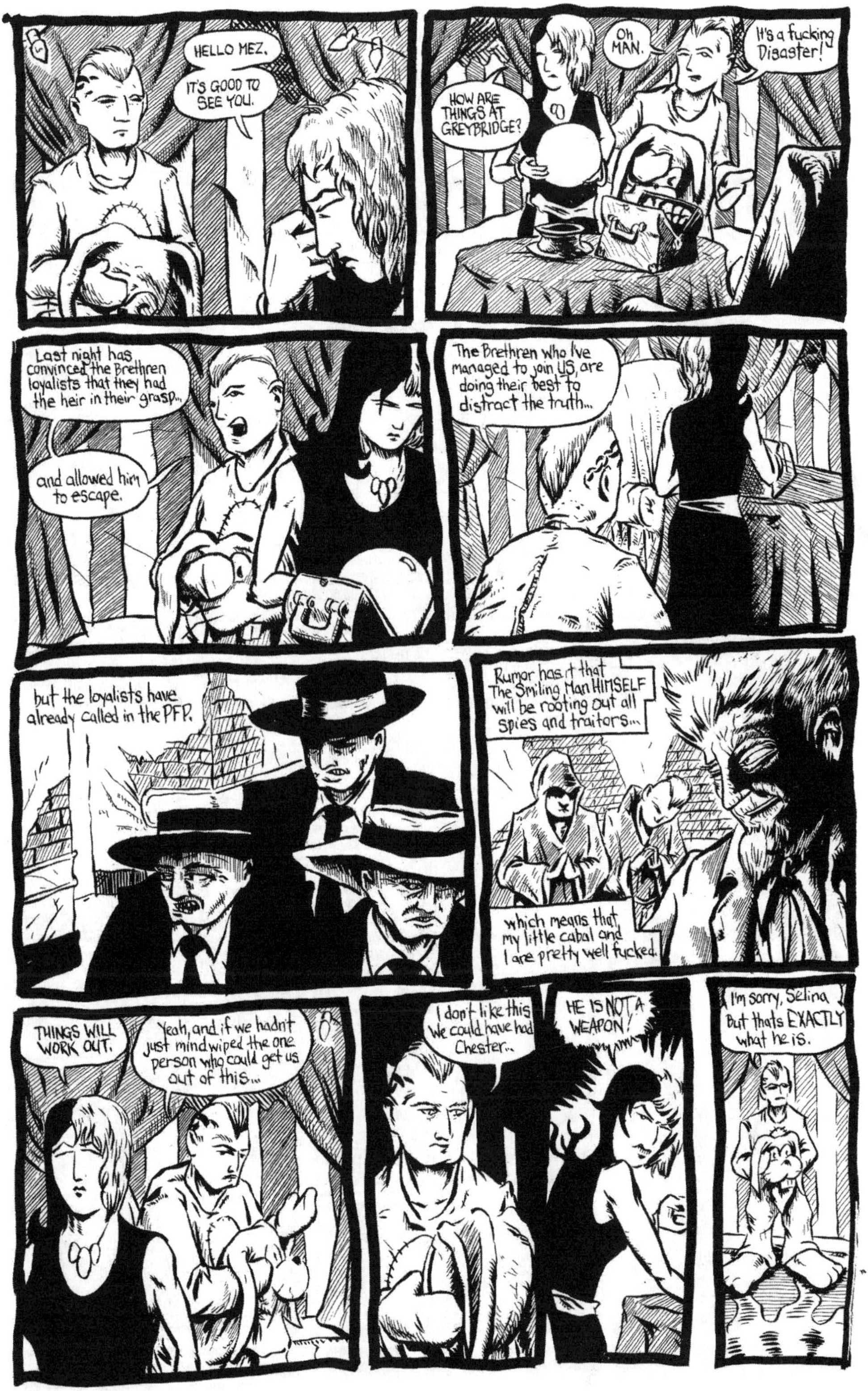
HELLO MEZ.
IT'S GOOD TO SEE YOU.
HOW ARE THINGS AT GREYBRIDGE?
Oh MAN.
It's a fucking Disaster!
Last night has convinced the Brethren loyalists that they had the heir in their grasp...
and allowed him to escape.
The Brethren who I've managed to join US, are doing their best to distract the truth...
but the loyalists have already called in the PFP.
Rumor has it that The Smiling Man HIMSELF will be rooting out all spies and traitors...
which means that my little cabal and I are pretty well fucked.
THINGS WILL WORK OUT.
Yeah, and if we hadn't just mindwiped the one person who could get us out of this...
I don't like this We could have had Chester...
HE IS NOT A WEAPON!
I'm sorry, Selina But thats EXACTLY what he is.

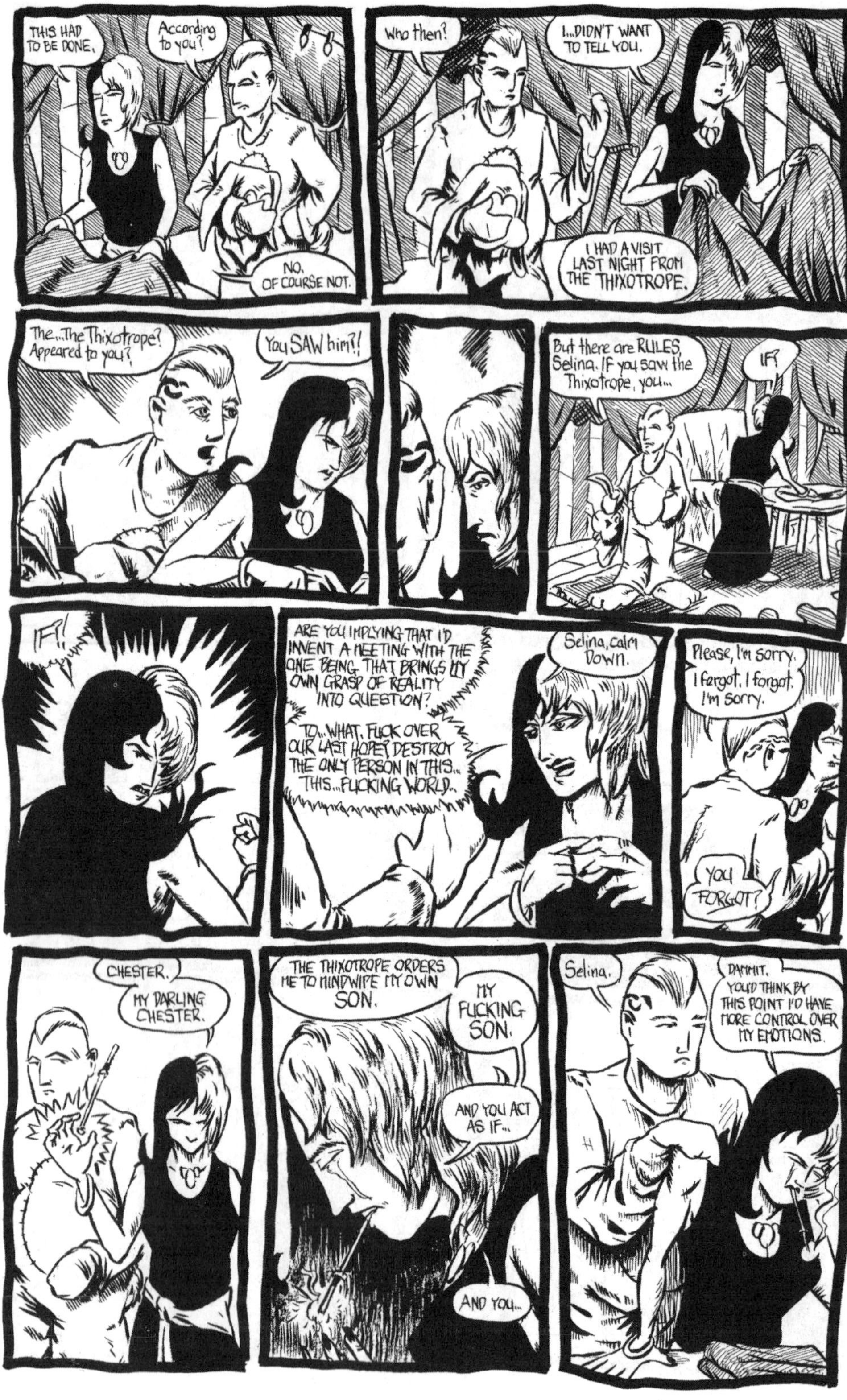
THIS HAD TO BE DONE.
According to you?
NO. OF COURSE NOT.
Who then?
I...DIDN'T WANT TO TELL YOU.
I HAD A VISIT LAST NIGHT FROM THE THIXOTROPE.
The...The Thixotrope? Appeared to you?
You SAW him?!
But there are RULES, Selina. If you saw the Thixotrope, you...
IF?
IF?!
ARE YOU IMPLYING THAT I'D INVENT A MEETING WITH THE ONE BEING THAT BRINGS MY OWN GRASP OF REALITY INTO QUESTION?
TO...WHAT, FUCK OVER OUR LAST HOPE? DESTROY THE ONLY PERSON IN THIS... THIS...FUCKING WORLD...
Selina, calm Down.
Please, I'm sorry. I forgot, I forgot. I'm sorry.
YOU FORGOT?
CHESTER.
MY DARLING CHESTER.
THE THIXOTROPE ORDERS ME TO MINDWIPE MY OWN SON.
MY FUCKING SON.
AND YOU ACT AS IF...
AND YOU...
Selina.
DAMMIT. YOU'D THINK BY THIS POINT I'D HAVE MORE CONTROL OVER MY EMOTIONS.

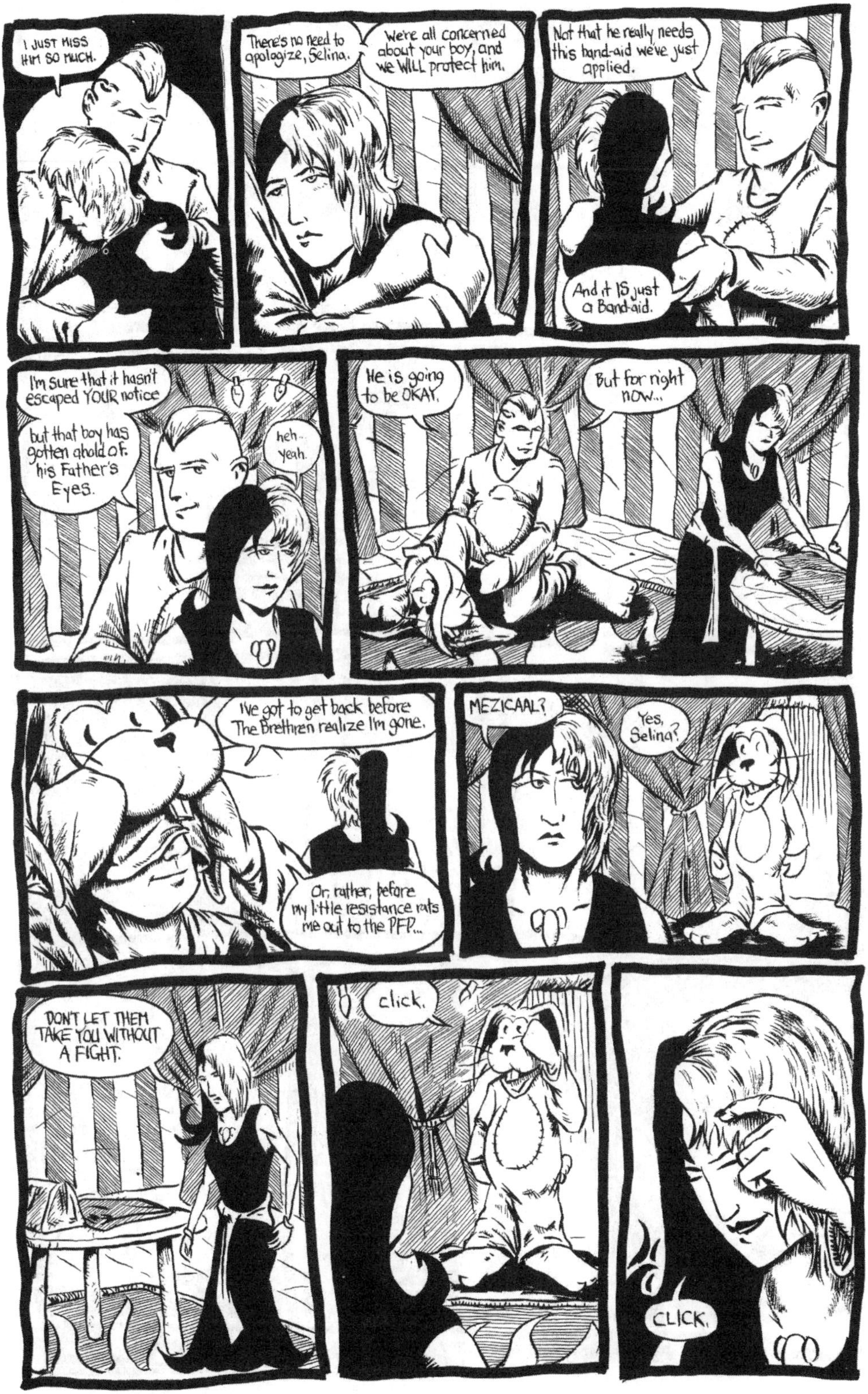
I JUST MISS HIM SO MUCH.
There's no need to apologize, Selina.
We're all concerned about your boy, and we WILL protect him.
Not that he really needs this band-aid we've just applied.
And it IS just a Band-aid.
I'm sure that it hasn't escaped YOUR notice
but that boy has gotten ahold of his Father's Eyes.
heh.. yeah.
He is going to be OKAY.
But for right now...
I've got to get back before The Brethren realize I'm gone.
Or, rather, before my little resistance rats me out to the PFP...
MEZICAAL?
Yes, Selina?
DON'T LET THEM TAKE YOU WITHOUT A FIGHT.
click.
CLICK.

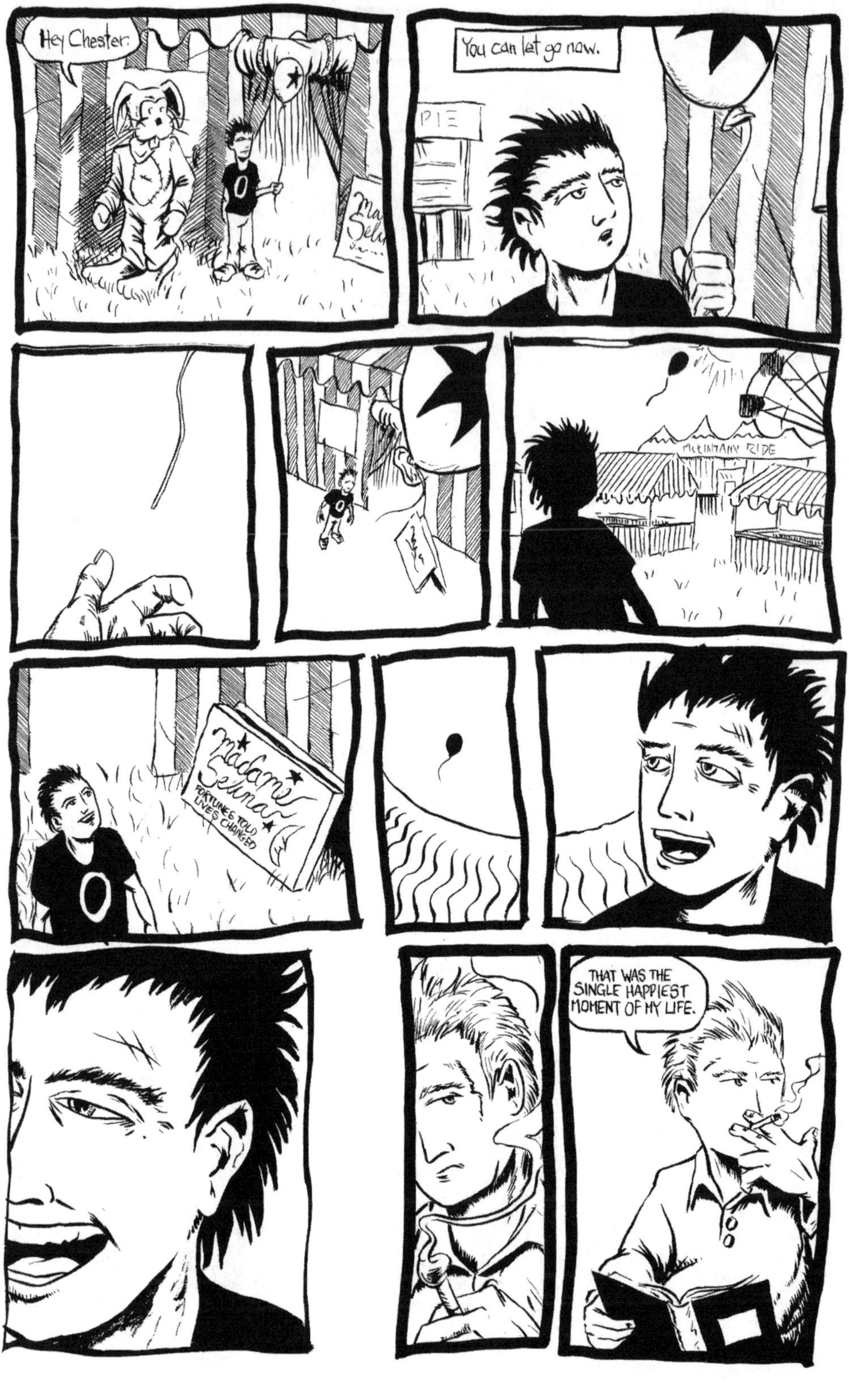
Hey Chester.
You can let go now.
PIE
MOUNTAIN RIDE
Madame Selma
FORTUNES TOLD
LIVES CHANGED
THAT WAS THE SINGLE HAPPIEST MOMENT OF MY LIFE.

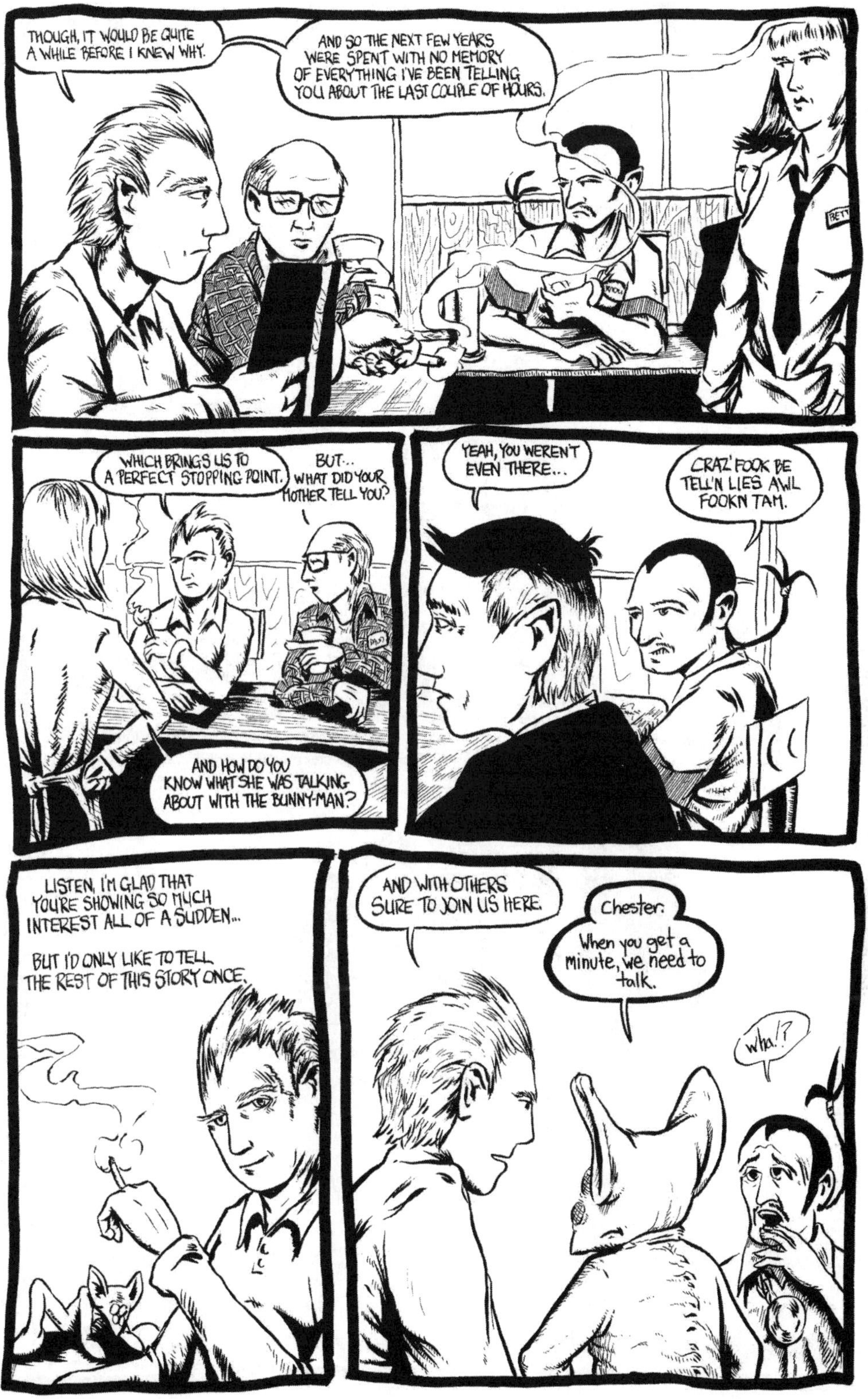
THOUGH, IT WOULD BE QUITE A WHILE BEFORE I KNEW WHY.
AND SO THE NEXT FEW YEARS WERE SPENT WITH NO MEMORY OF EVERYTHING I'VE BEEN TELLING YOU ABOUT THE LAST COUPLE OF HOURS.
WHICH BRINGS US TO A PERFECT STOPPING POINT.
BUT... WHAT DID YOUR MOTHER TELL YOU?
AND HOW DO YOU KNOW WHAT SHE WAS TALKING ABOUT WITH THE BUNNY-MAN?
YEAH, YOU WEREN'T EVEN THERE...
CRAZ' FOOK BE TELL'N LIES AWL FOOKN TAM.
LISTEN, I'M GLAD THAT YOU'RE SHOWING SO MUCH INTEREST ALL OF A SUDDEN...
BUT I'D ONLY LIKE TO TELL THE REST OF THIS STORY ONCE.
AND WITH OTHERS SURE TO JOIN US HERE.
Chester:
When you get a minute, we need to talk.
wha!?

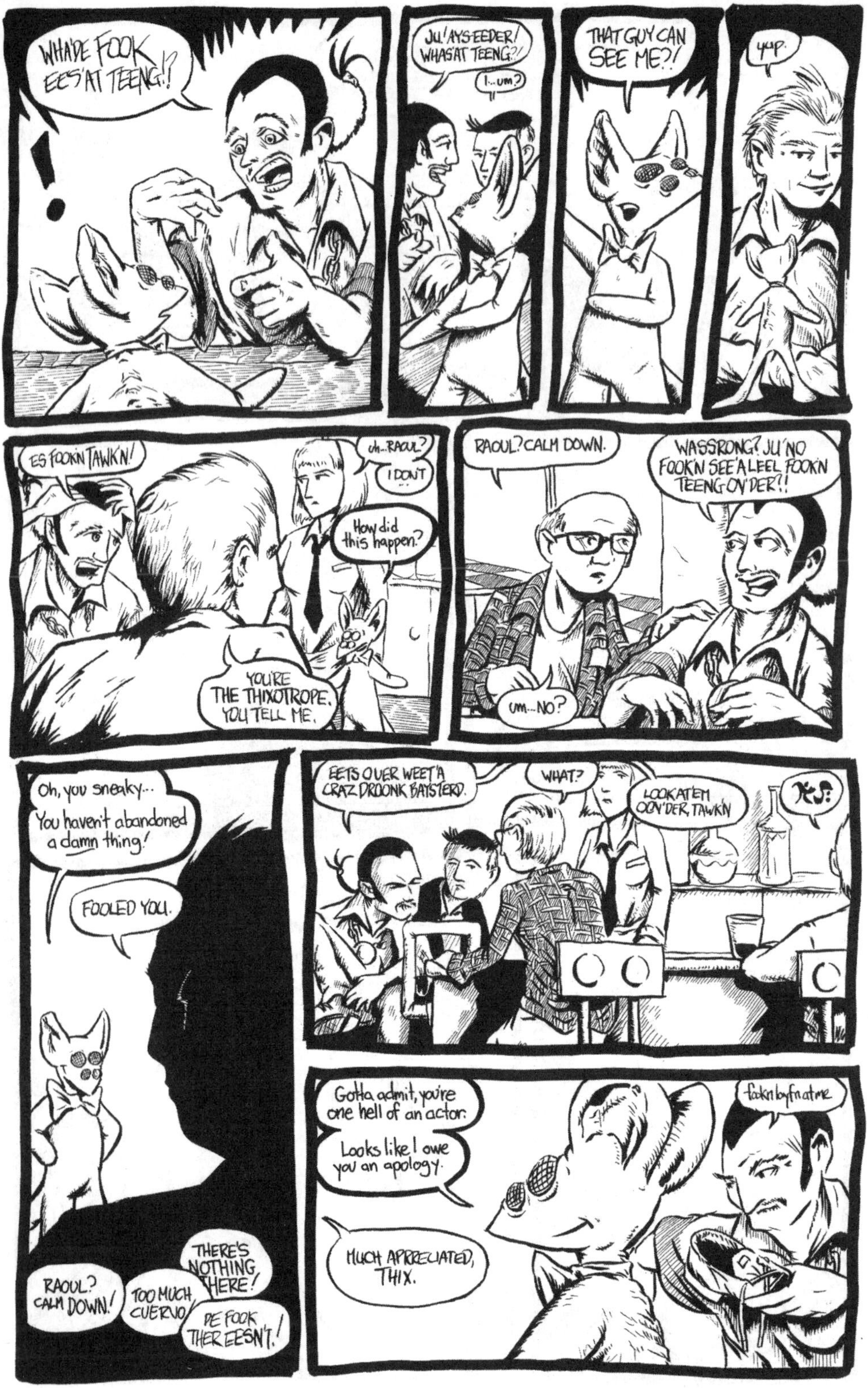
WHA'DE FOOK EES'AT TEENG!?
JU! AYS EEDER! WHASAT TEENG?!
I...um?
THAT GUY CAN SEE ME?!
Yup.
ES FOOK'N TAWK'N!
uh... RAOUL?
I DON'T
How did this happen?
YOU'RE THE THIXOTROPE. YOU TELL ME.
RAOUL? CALM DOWN.
WASSRONG? JU'NO FOOK'N SEE'A LEEL FOOK'N TEENG OV'DER?!
UM... NO?
Oh, you sneaky...
You haven't abandoned a damn thing!
FOOLED YOU.
RAOUL? CALM DOWN!
TOO MUCH CUERVO
THERE'S NOTHING THERE!
DE FOOK THER EESN'T!
EETS OVER WEET'A CRAZ DROONK BAYSTERD.
WHAT?
LOOK AT'EM OOV'DER, TAWK'N
Gotta admit, you're one hell of an actor.
Looks like I owe you an apology.
MUCH APPRECIATED, THIX.
fookn boyfrn at me

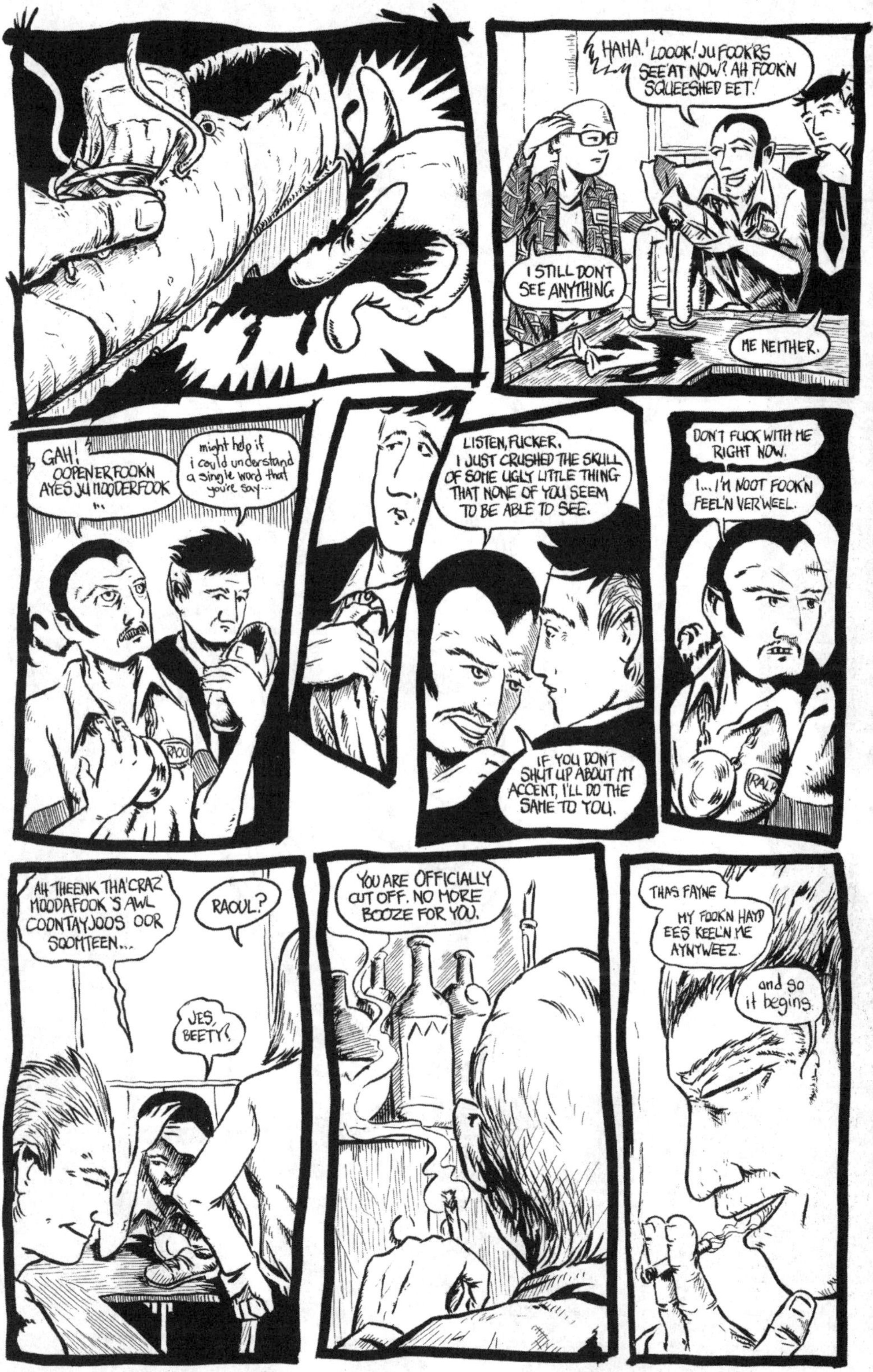
HAHA!
LOOOK! JU FOOK'RS SEE'AT NOW? AH FOOK'N SQUEESHED EET!
I STILL DON'T SEE ANYTHING
ME NEITHER.
GAH! OOPENER FOOK'N AYES JU MOODERFOOK ...
might help if i could understand a single word that you're say...
RAOUL
LISTEN, FUCKER. I JUST CRUSHED THE SKULL OF SOME UGLY LITTLE THING THAT NONE OF YOU SEEM TO BE ABLE TO SEE.
IF YOU DON'T SHUT UP ABOUT MY ACCENT, I'LL DO THE SAME TO YOU.
DON'T FUCK WITH ME RIGHT NOW.
I... I'M NOOT FOOK'N FEEL'N VER'WEEL.
RALPH
AH THEENK THA'CRAZ' MOODAFOOK 'S AWL COONTAYJOOS OOR SOOMTEEN...
RAOUL?
JES, BEETY?
YOU ARE OFFICIALLY CUT OFF. NO MORE BOOZE FOR YOU.
THAS FAYNE
MY FOOK'N HAYD EES KEEL'N ME AYNYWEEZ.
and so it begins.

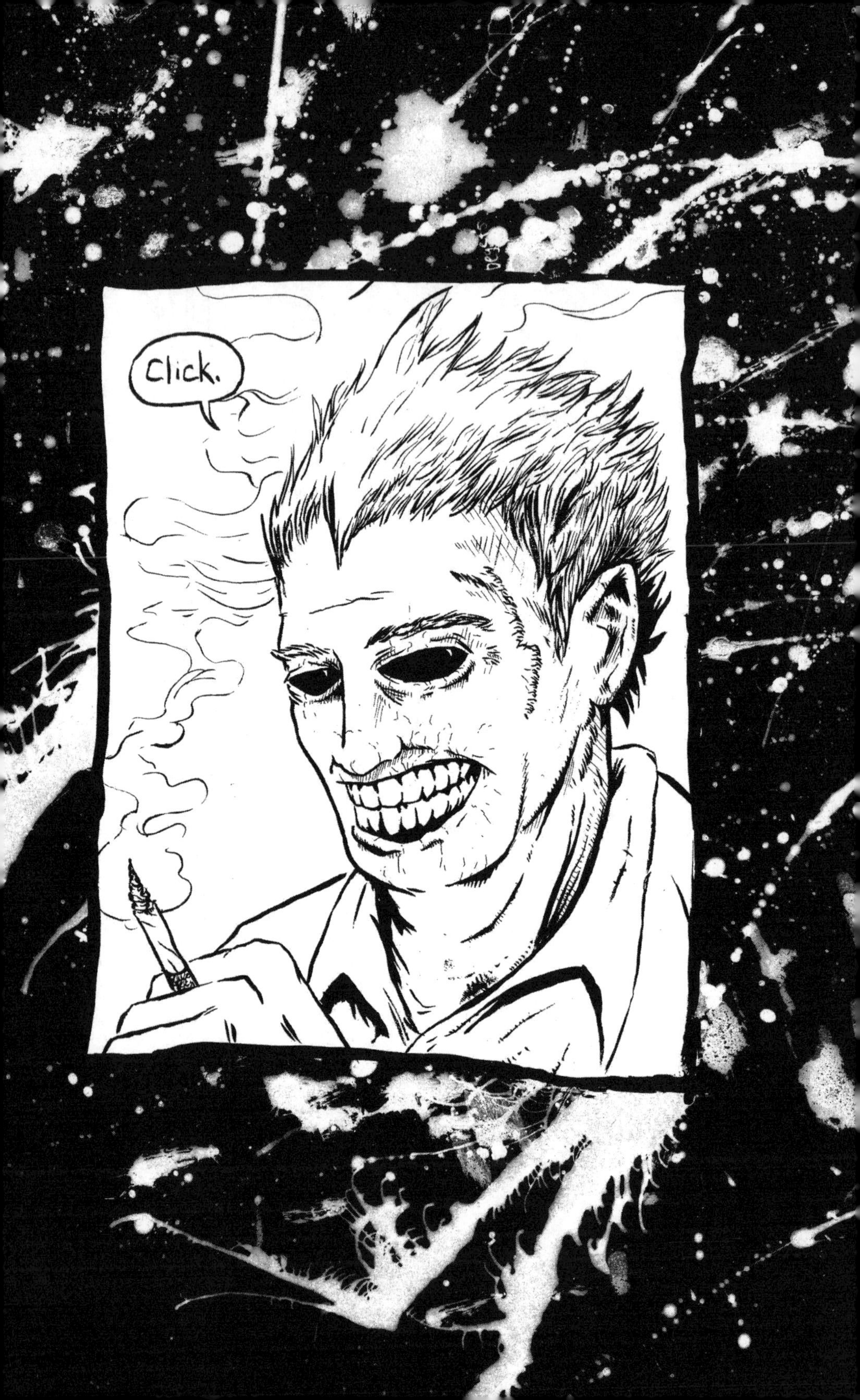
Click.

end of part one

Plastic Farm Part One:
Sowing Seeds on Fertile Soil was brought to you by:

Rafer Roberts
Writer and artist

The Reverend Rafer Roberts has been making comics since the fourth grade, when he and his friend Tom founded Tablet Comics. Tablet Comics was a light in the darkness, an angelic choir of art and vision rolled into a giant cupcake of peace and harmony. Such comics as "Monster Mash", "Killer Razor Blades" and "Attack of the Killer Toilet Bowls" united a nation, brought stability to the universe, and became the raw material that would one day become Plastic Farm. In college, during those rare moments of sobriety, Rafer and a man named Jeff created a philosophical clothing line designed to lay waste to the minds and belief systems of those who would not wear their brand of fashion. Rafer is married to his muse, and along with their multitude of retarded cats, live the life of nomads.

Danielle Corsetto is the artist and creator of the hit webcomic "Girls With Slingshots," a dramedy that updates five times a week and features two girls, a bar, and a talking cactus. She's also the former artist/writer on "The New Adventures of Bat Boy" featured in the Weekly World News. Danielle lives in an old farmhouse in Shepherdstown, West Virginia with her two cats, a goldfish, and a billion pounds of tea.

Danielle Corsetto
Artist, chapter 16

Wendi Strang-Frost
Artist, chapter 10

Wendi Strang-Frost is the artist of Johnny Public, an on-going mini comic serial about this poor guy with a lot of other people in his head and a whole lot of hurt in his future. Wendi's work has previously appeared in Revolving Hammer published by Cyberosa Publishing, and ElfQuest published by Warp Graphics. Wendi runs two companies, HULA CAT COMICS, for the publishing of stories, and STRANG-FROST PRODUCTIONS, for the making of illustrations. In 2004, Hula Cat Comics published Dope Fiends of the Zombie Cafe which was written by her husband Sean and illustrated by some guy named Rafer. Wendi, Sean and the entire 2000 person Hula Cat staff plan on releasing a trade paperback collection of Johnny Public. Wendi Strang-Frost can be visited online, and her books can be purchased at http://www.hulacatcomics.com and http://www.sfpro.com

Dave Morgan
Artist, chapters 2 and 13

House plant psychiatrist, Latvian pop star, professional cat juggler. Dave doesn't know which of these paths he'll follow next, but for the time being he grinds away working for "The Man" alongside Rafer. Dave is a sedentary life-style enthusiast, and is considered by many to be one of the greatest minds and most provocative sex symbols of our time. His artistic talent mainly lies neglected until called upon to contribute a little something to the world of Plastic Farm.

Dennis Culver

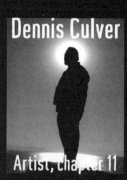

Dennis Culver is the artist for True Tales of Roller Derby 2 and Odd Schnozz and The Odd Squad. He has also written and rendered stories that have appeared in Plastic Farm 4, The Black Diamond 1, and Jam! Tales From The World of Roller Derby. He is currently co-writing and illustrating The Agents of S.A.N.T.A. from Oni Press.

Artist, chapter 11

Jacob Warrenfeltz lives in Takoma Park, Maryland. He's the creator of two amazing children and a whole slew of comics, as well as tattoo designs, album cover art, and t-shirt designs.

Jake Warrenfeltz
Artist, chapters 3, 5, 7

Nan Roberts
Muse, Poet, Editor

Nan Roberts was born in a very small town. She was raised by a wise woman who allowed her to become fairly independent and adventurous. She has had two books of poetry published by Plastic Farm Press, and has hopes of putting more together when her life isn't filled with everything else. In addition to her work for Plastic Farm, she is a phenomenal petsitter, a great catmom, and does other jobs to pay the bills.

Timeline of Major Events
covering chapters 1-17 and prologue

August, 1963 ~ George and Martha, two farmers on the brink of starvation, resort to cannibalism. Their newfound food source does not go unnoticed by their equally hungry neighbors.

March, 1967 ~ Jack Hallaway and Emily Watson, students at Haven High School, fall in love.

1968 ~ Jack Hallaway's plane is shot down over Vietnam.

1972 ~ Although presumed dead, Jack Hallaway returns from Vietnam and marries Emily.

1974 ~ Jonathan Picanos, a convicted serial killer, is sent to Greybridge State Psychiatric Hospital. He spends less than a year in captivity before making a daring escape in mid-1975. He is re-apprehended and executed. Greybridge closes due to the scandal.

December, 1975 ~ Greybridge Hospital is purchased by The Brethren, a strict fringe religious group. Greybridge is converted and re-opened as a school for "troubled youth".

March, 1976 ~ Chester Carter is born.

April, 1976 ~ Baby Chester is abandoned and ends up at the new Greybridge School.

May, 1988 ~ The offspring of released mental patients come to Greybridge School where they beat the shit out of Chester. Chester copes by writing stories about The Kamikaze Kid, a cowboy who he also dreams about.

September, 1988 ~ Chester meets the Ghost of Jonathan Picanos. Later, he attempts suicide.

November, 1988 ~ Detectives Frank Gorman and Benito Fortini stakeout a hand-off of medical files to a man known only as "The Big Guy". The stake-out ends badly as both Gorman and Fortini are killed. Detective Jake Goner begins an investigation into Frank and Benny's deaths, but is quickly removed from the case when it is handed over to the federal government.

1989-1994
Jack and Emily Hallaway have been married for 17 years. One morning, Emily disappears after taking their seaplane out during a sudden storm. Jack, convinced that she is still alive, begins a long vigil awaiting her return.

Chester is adopted by Fred and Susan Thomson. He attends Haven High School, has few friends, works at a used bookstore, and despite the aid of social worker Mary Bannon, has trouble dealing with the pressures of everyday life. In 1994, he is attacked and nearly killed by three Greybridge "students". With the help of a strange voice inside his head, Chester escapes his attackers, possibly killing them, then meets Detectives Frank and Benny, who appear to be zombies. Later that evening, Chester dreams of The Kamikaze Kid who kills some potato monsters, discusses the true nature of reality, and gets his head exploded by The Thixotrope. Chester's birth mother shows up the following day and alters his mind and reality so that he has no recollection of having ever been in Greybridge, the events of the previous evening, or that he is even adopted. Also, Chester gets accepted into college.

Spring, 1995 ~ Det. Jake Goner, visited by Frank Gorman (deceased), resumes his investigation after a seven-year hiatus. The trail leads to social worker Mary Bannon, but before any further progress is made, Goner is attacked by a pair of Mungs, and is fired from the NYPD. Bannon is later killed by a Mung.

June, 1997 ~ Doug Hoffman graduates from college and leaves his almost-fiance Sean MacInery behind. She gets a dog and names it Stuart.

Valentine's Day, 1998 ~ Eliza Dorne, reporting to a man known only as "The Reverend" completes a seven-month long sting operation to create a blackmail situation against U.S. Senator John MacGonagle.

June, 1998 ~ Chester wakes up after a night of heavy drinking, presumably caused by his obsession over a girl named Sean, and discovers that he has wrecked his car. He attempts to come to terms with the fact that The Kamikaze Kid may be real.

2002-2003 ~ David Ects discovers the ability to "inflate" his belly-button. This begins his meteoric rise, subsequent fall, and phoenix-like rebirth with fame.

Summer, 2003 ~ Ralph Baker, a college professor short on money, submits to a questionable medical experiment that leaves him with super human strength. Hunted by Mungs, Ralph adopts the identity of Raoul, an airline baggage handler with an unintelligible fake accent.

"About fifteen years earlier" ~ Robert O'Den meets Margo Hildebrandt.

"The Future" ~ Chester sits in a nameless airport bar during a blizzard and tells his life story to people who really couldn't care less. Chester's madness has already begun to change them one by one.

"Three Days Later" ~ Jack Hallaway is visited by Frank Gorman who delivers a mysterious package.

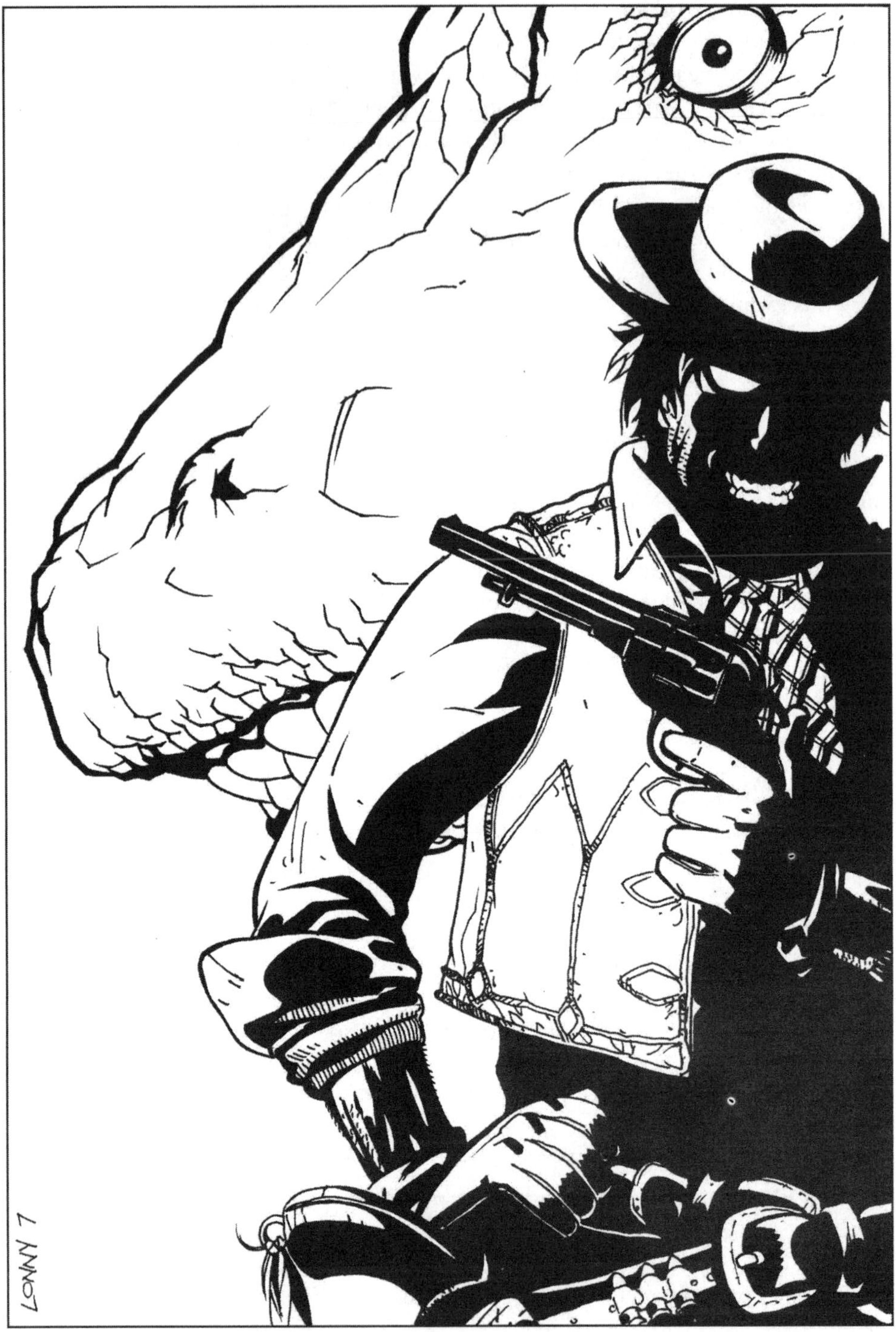
LONNY 7

pinup by lonny chant

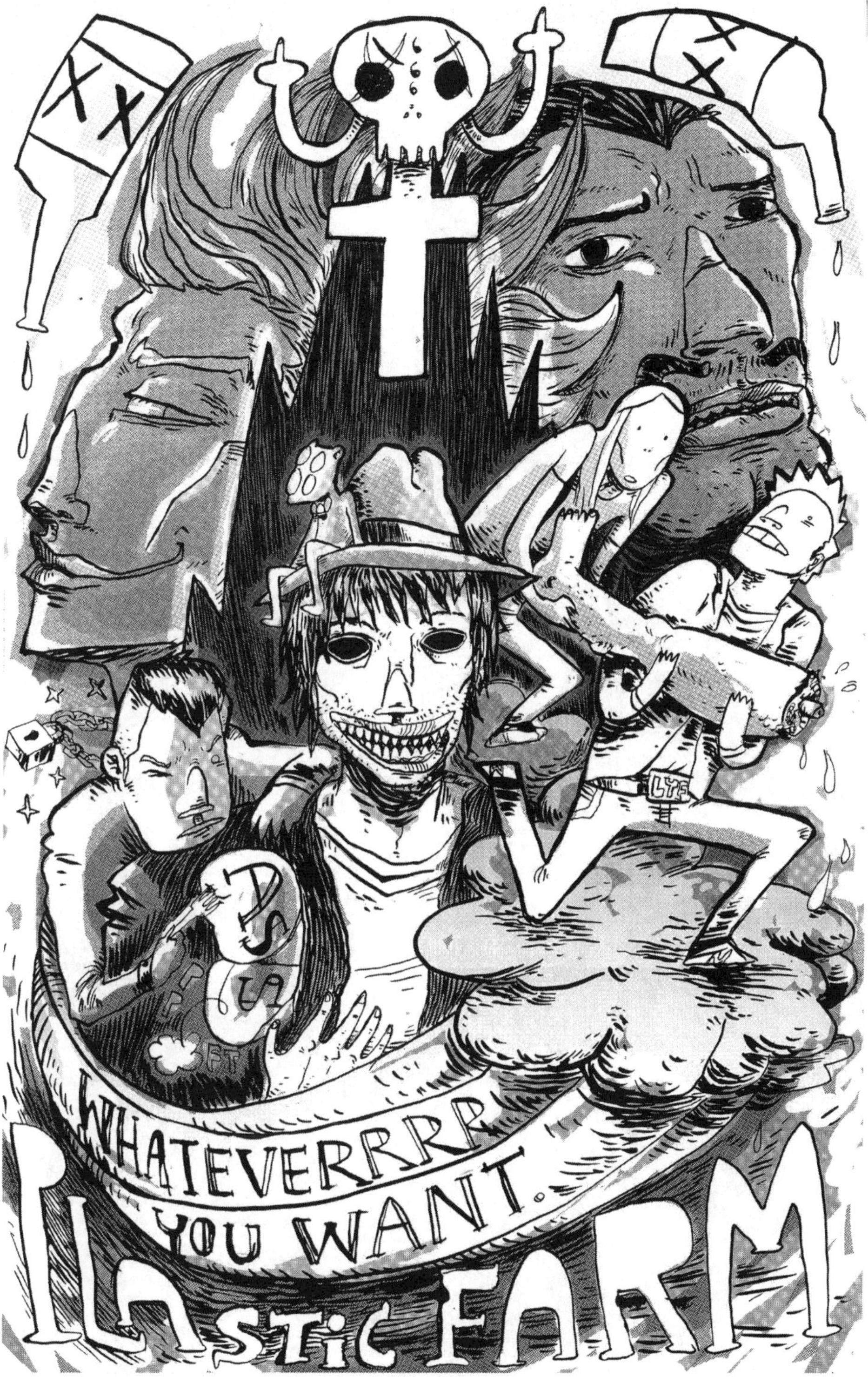
WHATEVERRRR YOU WANT.
PLASTIC FARM

pinup by michaela collette zacchilli

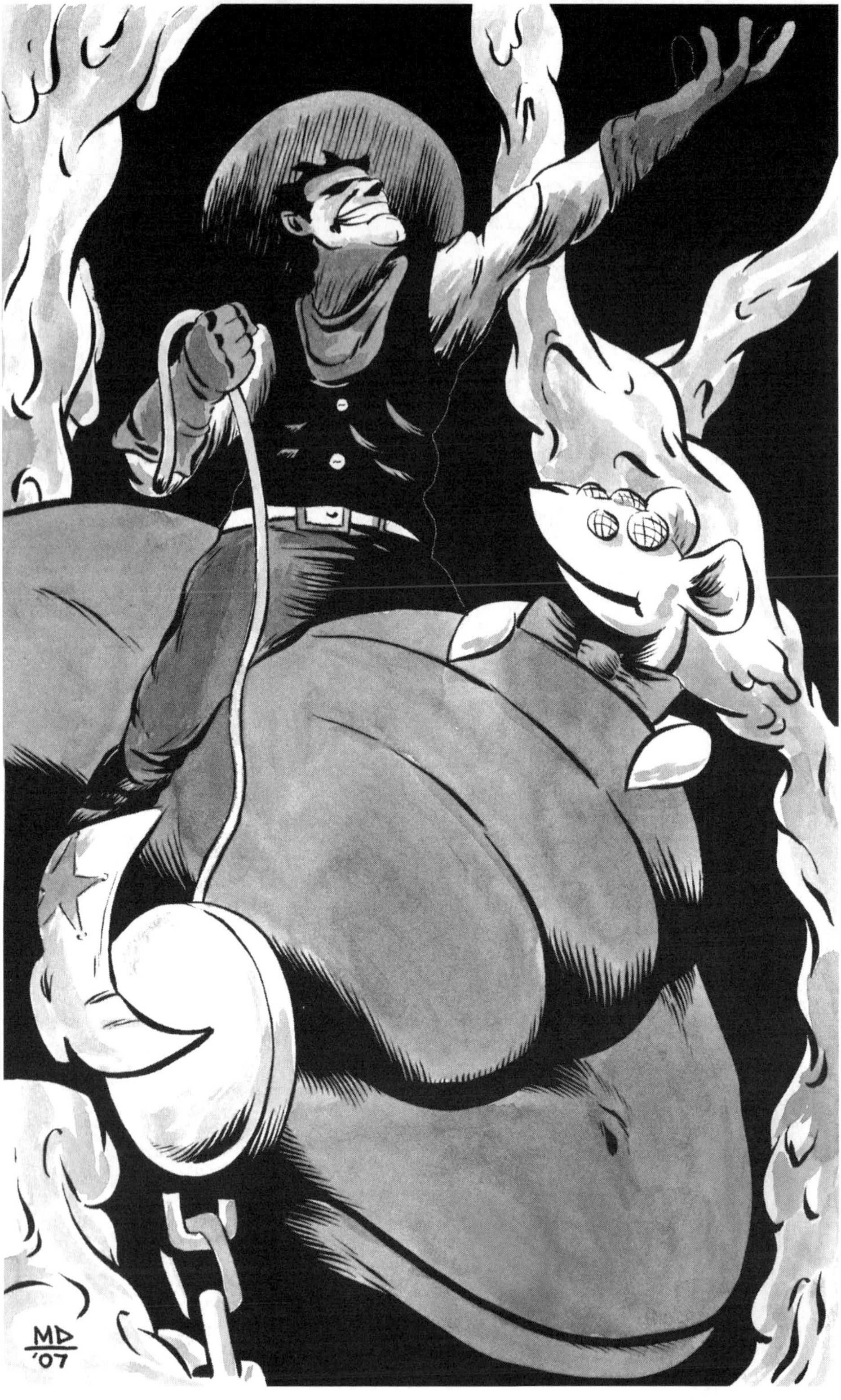
MD
'07

pinup by matt dembicki

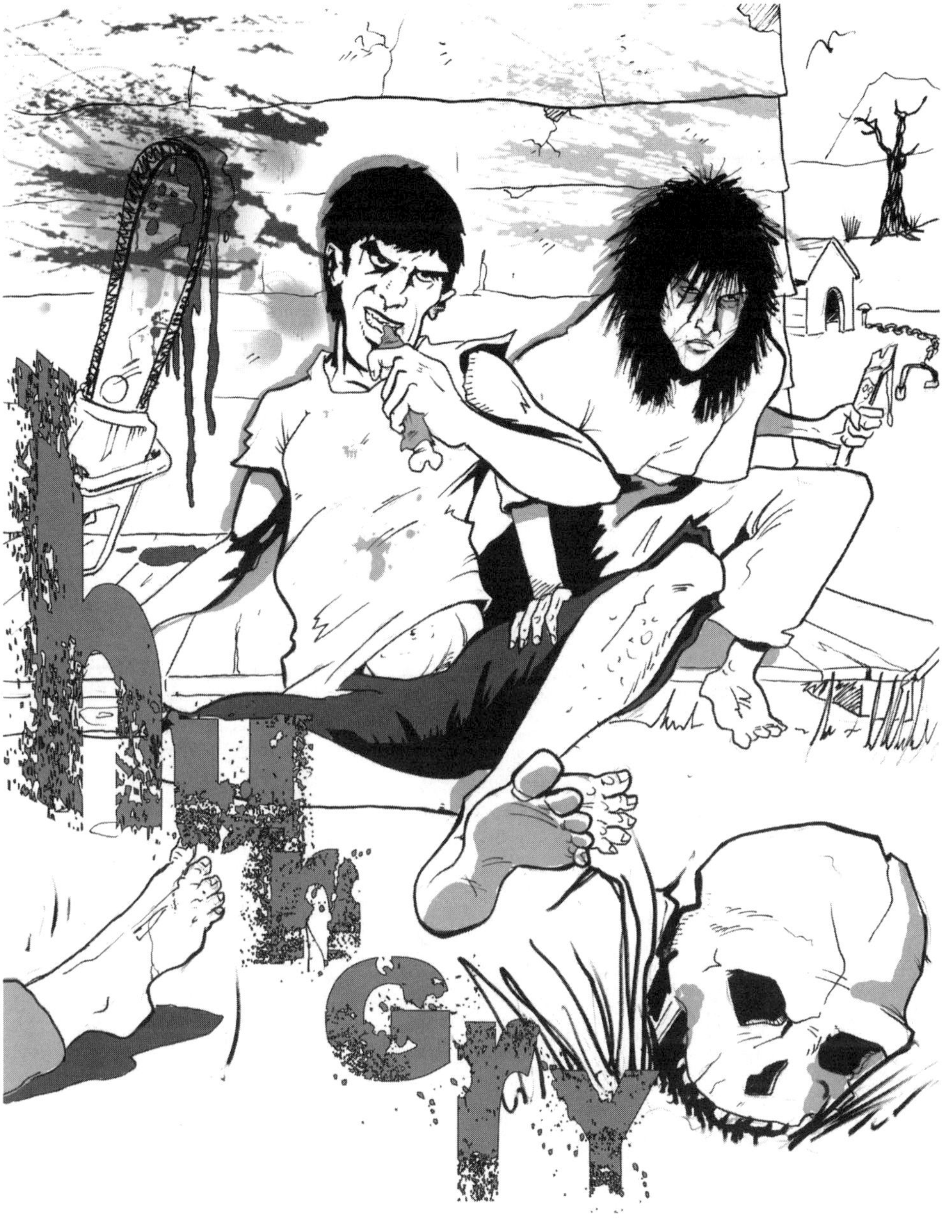
hungry

pinup by marc haines

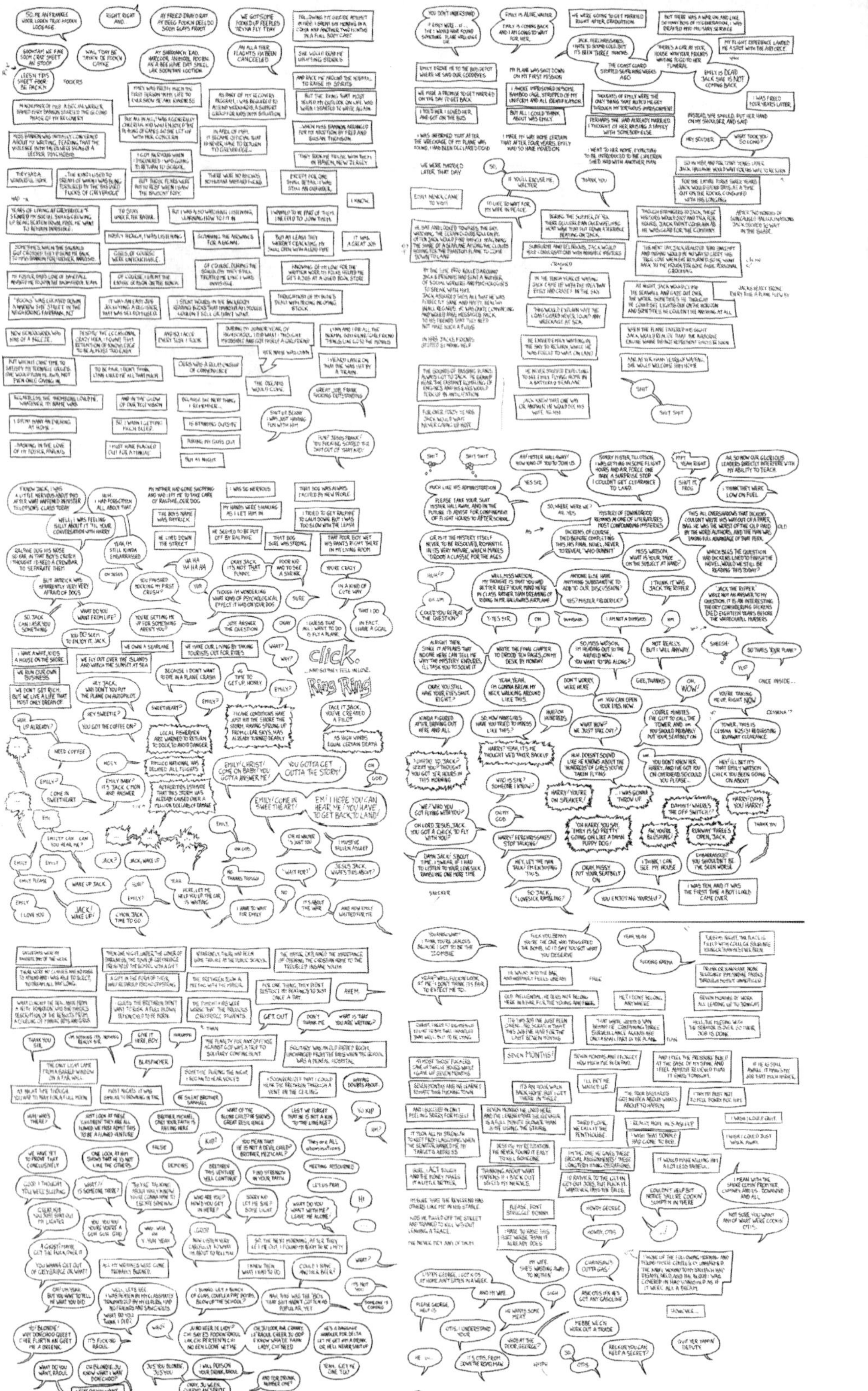

SO ME AN FRANKEE
RIGHT RIGHT AND...
AY FREEZ-DRAY'D RAT. AY BEEG FOOKN DEEL DO SOOM GLAYS FROOT
WE GOT SOME FOOKED UP PEEPLES TRYNA FLY TDAY
IN A FULL BODY CAST
AN ALL A THER FLAGHTS HA BEEN CANCEELED
SHE WOULD READ ME UPLIFTING STORIES
WAL TDAY BE TAYK'N DE FOOK'N CAYKE
AND BACK ME AROUND THE HOSPITAL TO RAISE MY SPIRITS
BUT THE THING THAT MOST HELPED MY OUTLOOK ON LIFE WAS WHEN I STARTED TO WRITE AGAIN.
IN APRIL OF 1981, IT BECAME OFFICIAL THAT I'D NEVER HAVE TO RETURN TO GREYBRIDGE...
...WHEN MISS BANNON ARRANGED FOR MY ADOPTION BY FRED AND SUSAN THOMSON.
THEY TOOK ME TO LIVE WITH THEM IN HAVEN, NEW JERSEY.
I GOT NERVOUS WHEN I DISCOVERED I WAS GOING TO RETURN TO SCHOOL...
THEY HAD A WONDERFUL HOME.
...THE KIND I USED TO DREAM OF WHEN I WAS BEING TORTURED BY THE BASTARD FUCKS OF GREYBRIDGE
BUT THOSE FEARS WERE PUT TO REST WHEN I SAW THE BRIGHT TOY.
EXCEPT FOR ONE SMALL DETAIL: I WAS STILL AN OUTSIDER.
I KNOW.
TO STAY UNDER THE RADAR.
I WANTED TO BE PART OF THEM. I NEEDED TO JOIN THEM.
BUT AT LEAST THEY WEREN'T CRACKING MY SKULL OPEN WITH A LEAD PIPE
IT WAS A GREAT JOB
SCANNING THE AIRWAVES FOR A SIGNAL.
GIRLS, OF COURSE, WERE UNTOUCHABLE.
OF COURSE, I SPENT THE ENTIRE SEASON ON THE BENCH.
KNOWING OF MY LOVE FOR THE WRITTEN WORD, MY FOLKS HELPED ME GET A JOB AT A USED BOOK STORE

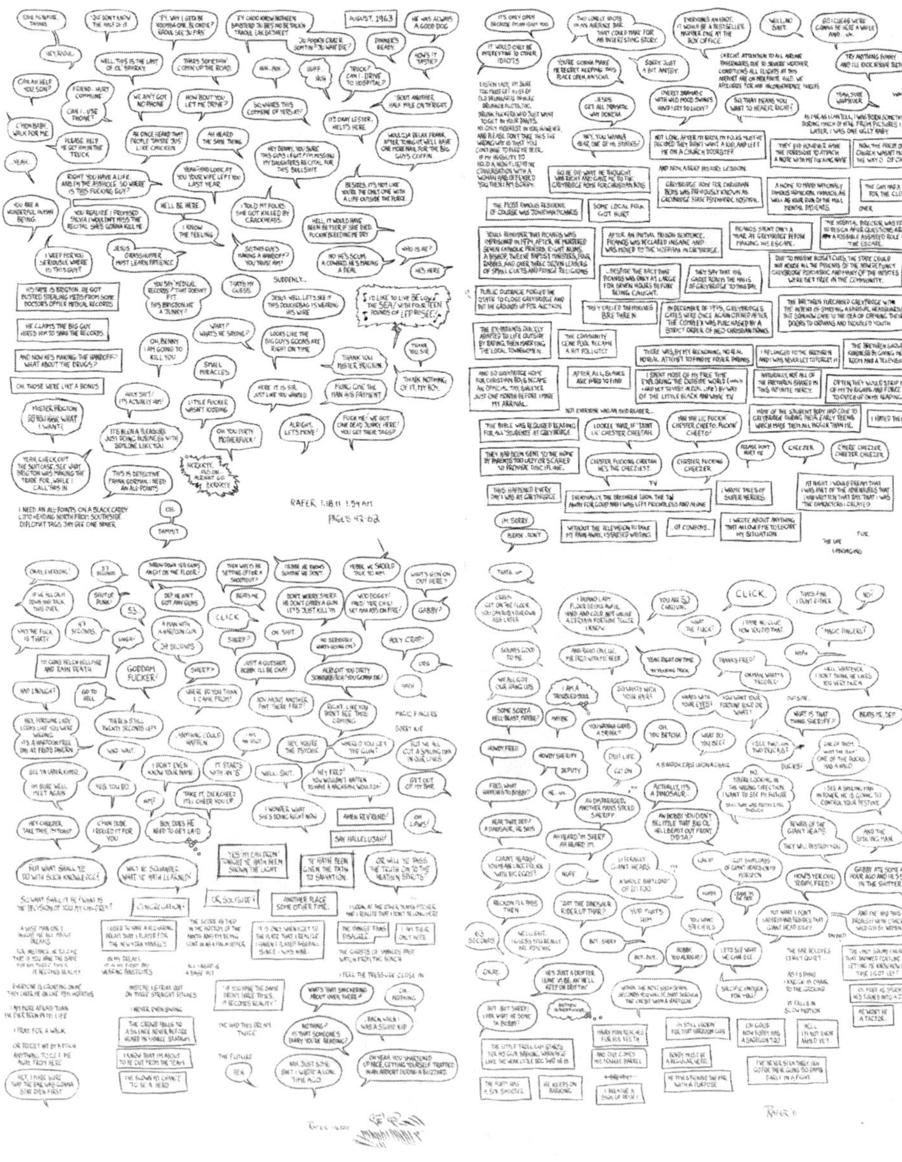

I letter directly on the artwork, so re-lettering these older comics was a bit of a pain in the ass. On these two pages are 10 of the sheets of new lettering. I used an actual T-square and Ames Lettering Guide to hand letter, then scanned these in for placement over the old lettering. In most cases the new word balloons were slightly larger than the old ones (or the backgrounds were non-existent) and all I had to do was put the balloons in place. In some cases I had to clone new artwork where the old balloon was showing through. On the next two pages are a few before and after examples which I hope exemplify the need for this re-lettering and the effort put into it.

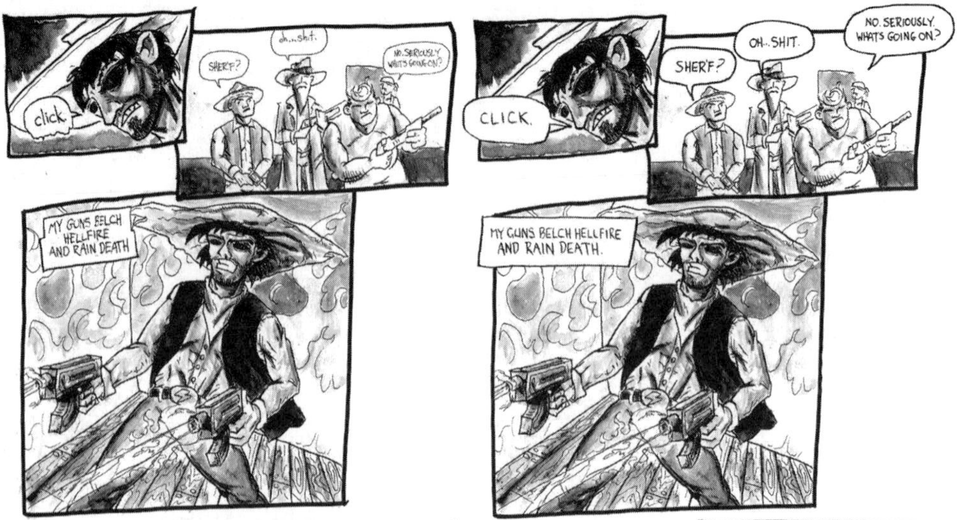
click.
SHER'F?
oh...shit.
NO. SERIOUSLY WHAT'S GOING ON?
MY GUNS BELCH HELLFIRE AND RAIN DEATH
CLICK.
SHER'F?
OH.. SHIT.
NO. SERIOUSLY. WHATS GOING ON?
MY GUNS BELCH HELLFIRE AND RAIN DEATH.

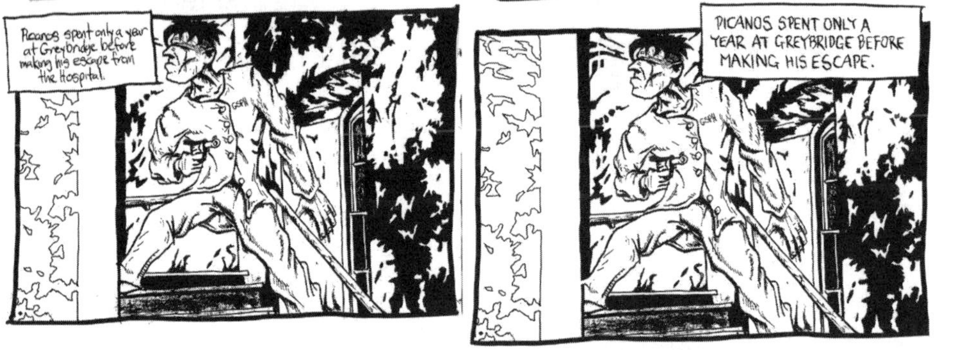
Picanos spent only a year at Greybridge before making his escape from the Hospital.
PICANOS SPENT ONLY A YEAR AT GREYBRIDGE BEFORE MAKING HIS ESCAPE.

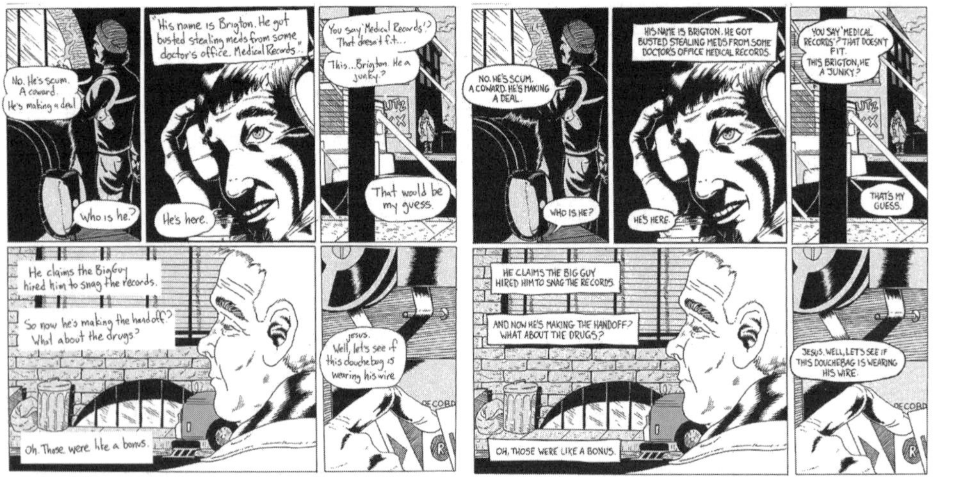
No. He's scum. A coward. He's making a deal.
Who is he?
His name is Brigton. He got busted stealing meds from some doctor's office. Medical Records.
He's here.
You say 'Medical Records'? That doesn't fit...
This...Brigton. He a junky?
That would be my guess.
He claims the Big Guy hired him to snag the records.
So now he's making the handoff? What about the drugs?
Oh. Those were like a bonus.
Jesus. Well, let's see if this douchebag is wearing his wire.
NO. HE'S SCUM. A COWARD. HE'S MAKING A DEAL.
WHO IS HE?
HIS NAME IS BRIGTON. HE GOT BUSTED STEALING MEDS FROM SOME DOCTOR'S OFFICE MEDICAL RECORDS.
HE'S HERE.
YOU SAY 'MEDICAL RECORDS'? THAT DOESN'T FIT.
THIS BRIGTON, HE A JUNKY?
THAT'S MY GUESS.
HE CLAIMS THE BIG GUY HIRED HIM TO SNAG THE RECORDS.
AND NOW HE'S MAKING THE HANDOFF? WHAT ABOUT THE DRUGS?
OH, THOSE WERE LIKE A BONUS.
JESUS. WELL, LETS SEE IF THIS DOUCHEBAG IS WEARING HIS WIRE.

First row: Page 20. Note how in the "after" panels you can read what the trio of gunfighters is saying compared to the"before" panels. Also note the positioning of the "MY GUNS..." caption box in the before and after, and the cloning needed for the new placement.
Second row: Page 30. Speaking of redrawing, when I moved the caption box from the left to the right of the panel I had to draw in everything that was "under" the old caption. Hopefully you didn't even notice.
Third row: Page 58. The original lettering was just really shitty.

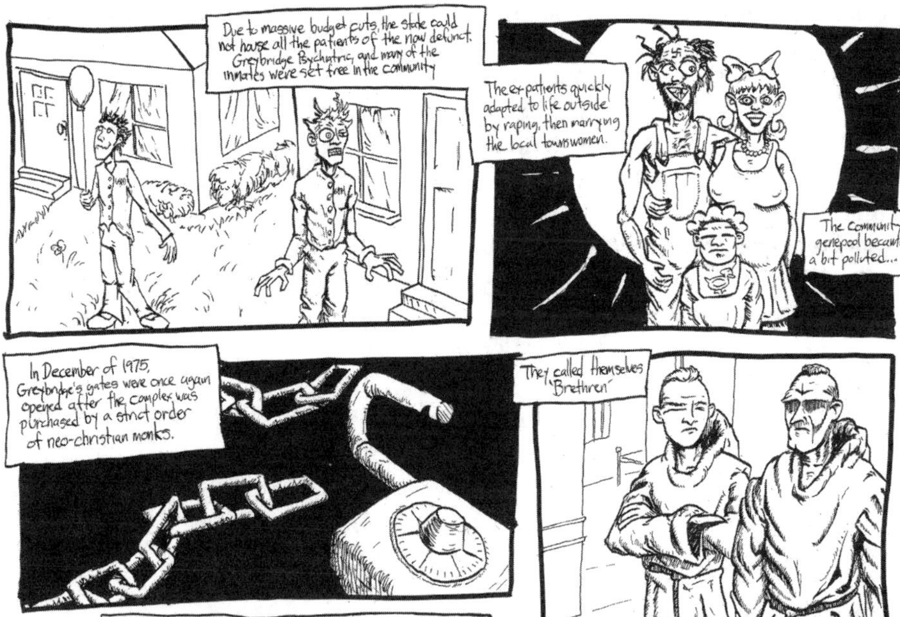
Due to massive budget cuts, the state could not house all the patients of the now defunct Greybridge Psychatric, and many of the inmates were set free in the community
The ex-patients quickly adapted to life outside by raping, then marrying the local townswomen.
The community genepool became a bit polluted...
In December of 1975, Greybridge's gates were once again opened after the complex was purchased by a strict order of neo-christian monks.
They called themselves "Brethren"

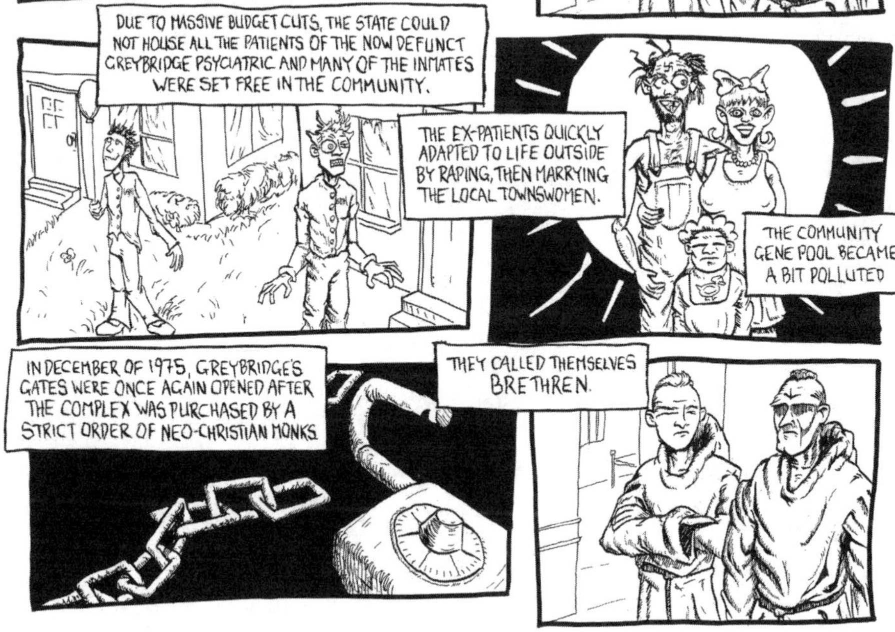
DUE TO MASSIVE BUDGET CUTS, THE STATE COULD NOT HOUSE ALL THE PATIENTS OF THE NOW DEFUNCT GREYBRIDGE PSYCIATRIC AND MANY OF THE INMATES WERE SET FREE IN THE COMMUNITY.
THE EX-PATIENTS QUICKLY ADAPTED TO LIFE OUTSIDE BY RAPING, THEN MARRYING THE LOCAL TOWNSWOMEN.
THE COMMUNITY GENE POOL BECAME A BIT POLLUTED
IN DECEMBER OF 1975, GREYBRIDGE'S GATES WERE ONCE AGAIN OPENED AFTER THE COMPLEX WAS PURCHASED BY A STRICT ORDER OF NEO-CHRISTIAN MONKS
THEY CALLED THEMSELVES BRETHREN.

Page 31. I consider this to have been one of the worst lettered pages in the original Plastic Farm. Obviously I had to cover up more artwork to fit the new lettering, but at least there was a lot of non-essential space for me to work with. There are other instances in this new edition where I barely left enough room for the original shitty lettering and a small amount of compromise was needed. See the prologue for most of these small compromises.

I know, more than anyone, that the new lettering isn't perfect. Short of redrawing the old comics, it never could be. I hope that you'll agree that despite whatever flaws still exist, this is still an improvement.

Here are a couple of script excerpts from this first part of Plastic Farm, as well as a plot breakdown so I could keep track of where the hell I was. Included in this breakdown you will notice a reference to a story that did not appear in Plastic Farm part one. Basically, as I was writing Chapter Ten and plotting out some future parts of Plastic Farm I discovered who Frank and Benny are. I realized that due to their future interactions with Chester, the scene referenced made no sense, so it got cut. At some point I toyed with the idea of including within the series of really short chapters that originally appeared in issue eleven a few pages of nothing but The Kamikaze Kid laying bleeding from where he was left at the end of Chapter Nine, his skull slowly healing. But then I really really wanted the last chapter of the book to be 17, so I could rename it Concoction Seventeen.

And yes, I have the entire series outlined just like this. But in much greater detail. No, you can't read it yet.

Prologue
Chapter One: Chester done
Chapter Two: People's Choice done
Chapter Three: Be Prepared done
Chapter Four Bookends done
Chapter Five: Sean - Script done
Chapter Six: CSGC - done
Chapter Seven: Ins and Outs- done
Chapter Eight: Eliza Day: Assassin – rr done
CH 9 - Kamikaze Kid dream sequence rr (issue eight)
Chapter 10 - Chester and Raoul go for chairs –rr and
WSF (issue 9)
CH 11 - Private Detective on the Grin beat. (Jake
Garner) Bannon gets killed. culver (issue 10)
Issue 11- A few short stories
Betty talking to recent bar arrivals, Chester freaks in bg.
Mung kills Bannon.
Offering of "People's Choice Jerky". "Jesus, do you have any idea what's in that?
The ass munch story in the airport bar
and...
Ch goes to bathroom talks with Frank and Benny.
(What were you doing with Raoul? I thought you were on my side.)
CH 13- Ch last days before college/waking up from dream/watching parade/MADE TO
FORGET
"You will believe that you were adopted shortly after you were born. Your suicide attempt a few years ago was caused by normal early teen stress. You will have never been to the Greybridge Home, you never met Picanos's ghost, you were never attacked by those boys." The man in the rabbit suit is one of the brethren. The fortune teller is Chester's mother.
(issue 12)

A few scenes from Chapter Five. This was one of the first scripts I ever wrote, and the first one of any substantial length. You can tell that I had no idea what I was doing in terms of proper formatting. Still, I like this story and other than a few instances of painful dialogue I'm not sure I would change a thing. (Note: I changed the character of Pete to Paul in the final comic.)

PAGE SIX:

P1

Some people at the party, sitting on the couch, drinking. A man with a woman on both sides of him. Man is ignoring the two women and is looking towards Sean, infatuated. Woman on left, annoyed, asks, "Who the hell are these people. How does Rupert know these people?" Man responds, "I…don't know." Woman on right is looking at man, slightly pissed that he is not paying attention to her.

P2

Sean doing some dance moves and the prepboys around her doing the white boy dance.

P3

Doug has taken a beer from Paul and is cracking it open. The melon tucked under his arm (if possible, otherwise it's on a nearby table. Pete has since taken out a grocery bag of sorts and is filling it with the beer.

P4

Bongo Betty is in the Kitchen. Two rather young and handsome prep boys, and one rather homely preppy chick are with her. She is telling them a story about why they should never snort Benadryl. One of the prep boys asks if they can get her a drink.

P5

Betty replies that she'll get the drinks as she walks towards the fridge.

P6

Sean again, she has one finger raised (somewhat seductively) at one of the boys. She is smiling, as are the other boys. Her expression implies a "Hold on a second. Let me show you something."

PAGE SEVEN:

P1

Betty is pouring two drinks. Most possibly two martinis, but they can be any mixed drink. It doesn't matter. But she is pouring two drinks.

P2

Sean has pulled out a cassette tape from her pocket. She is holding it up as if she has conjured it up from thin air rather than taking it from her pocket. This is what she was referencing earlier. This is what she wanted to show the boys.

P3

Doug and Paul. Paul says, "Uh oh, she's got the tape out already." Doug is smiling, "That's my girl."

P4

Betty drops a pill (probably a roofie) in one of the mixed drinks.

P5

She walks back over to the two guys and the girl and hands the girl the drink with the roofie in it. "Here you go sweetie," says Betty. "Thank you" says the girl.

P6

Girl takes a sip of the drink. Betty has a subtle evil smile as she looks towards the boys. "I hope you guys have fun tonight," she says.

P7

Sean is putting the tape into the player. We can see the label on the tape says "Mephiska-pheles Party Mix"

Page Eight

P1

(The song playing is Saba by Mephiskapheles. I'll see if'n I can't find it for you. But anyway, the song starts out slow, melodic, a nice sexy slow dance. It eventually builds up to a crescendo of guitars and Skanking) As the first strains of music start to play, Sean begins a sultry dance.

P2

From the kitchen, Betty can hear the music playing. "Well, that's my cue" she says. The girl is now, in the 30 seconds since taking a sip of the drink, trashed. Her glass is empty.

P3

Sean dancing. Preppy boys dancing with, and on her.

P4

Betty has joined Doug and Paul. "Battle Stations," she says. Doug, his eyes never leaving Sean says "Pete was just about to get the car ready."

P5

We can now see that a good half of the party is now dancing to the music. Slow nasty grinding (in a shallow, rich kid kinda way) There are probably groups of two guys dancing with one girl, and groups of two chicks dancing. Everyone not dancing is watching the dancing occur.

P6

Sean is getting into her dancing and smiling as a hand taps her on her shoulder.

P7

She turns and sees the first preppy boy, the one who let them in the house, standing there with his hand extended. "May I have this dance?" he asks

P8

Sean smiles, flipping her hair (or she would be if here hair were of the right length or style) "I thought you'd never ask."

PAGE NINE

P1

Doug standing alone. He has polished off another beer. There are three or four empties sitting around him. He has picked up the watermelon and is examining it.

P2

Sean dancing with preppy boys. Betty is coming to join her.

P3

Sean screams in delight when she sees Betty. Sean grabs her hand to pull her into the tight dance group that has formed.

P4

Longer shot of living room. Everybody is now up and dancing. Sean is dancing with Betty. Dancing in a cock-tease sorta way, all grinding on each other.

P5

Closeup of Sean's face. Her eyes are looking up, as if she is looking at the music playing. She wears a slight crooked smile. She knows that the music is about to change tempo and the final phase of the plan is about to begin. "Three..." she says.

P6

Mid close-up on Doug who is holding the watermelon in his outstretched hand as if he were holding a basketball. With his other hand he is wiping his mouth which is now a full smile. "Two..." he says.

P7

Close-up on Bongo Betty. Her eyes are wild. A great big grin is on her face. She is ready to do some damage. "One..." she says.

Page Ten
P1
Loud guitar cranks out of the stereo, (big iconic jagged notes, force lines coming from speakers) physically pushing partygoers back. Some are holding their ears, one or two people spill their drinks. Sean and Betty are standing in the middle of it all facing each other. They have both arms above their heads making the "Rock!" symbol with their hands. They are both grinning, laughing. They are shouting "Fuck Yeah!" "Rock!"
P2
Sean has jumped on the living room coffee table and is jumping up and down, stomping the fuck out of it. She looks crazy. Anything that was on the table is crashing to the floor, or is being stomped by Sean.
P3
The table collapses. Sean almost falls on her ass. Partygoers are still in shock from the music. Some are still holding their ears, some are watching Sean, hands over their mouths in shock. They do not know what to do.
P4
Betty is grabbing a piece of framed artwork off the wall. Also smiling crazily.
P5
She smashes the art against the wall. People dive out of the way.
P6-7
Doug is stomp-kicking people as they try to run by.

****

PAGE 20
P1
Doug has now sat up indian style at Sean's feet. She still eating and talking at the same time. Sean: "Hm, I wish I had waken up earl…" Doug: " Listen baby, I hope you don't mind…"
P2
Just Sean in panel, waist up. Her mouth is full of food and again has a full fork ready to go. Offpanel, Doug: "…but I got you a present" Sean, mouth full can only mumble a response.
P3
View from foot of bed. Doug has turned and is looking towards bedroom door. He has his fingers in his mouth and emits a loud whistle. Sean is looking at him like he's lost his mind.
P4
Similar panel as previous. Doug has turned back to Sean who is still looking at him like he" crazy. Doug: "I really hope you don't mind, but I hated thinking I was leaving you all unprotected." Sean responds "What did you do?"
P5
From literally out of nowhere the puppy makes his entrance. He is a small Pit Bull / Doberman mix. Brown. He enters by jumping right on the tray of food scaring the bejeezus out of Sean. The dog is cuter than all fuck and if dogs could smile, this dog would be grinning. The food is getting spilled.
P6
The dog is now licking Sean's face and she is holding him and laughing. The tray of food has fallen to the floor. The coffee has spilled on the bed.

PAGE 21

P1

Sean is laughing as she plays with the dog who is still licking her face. Doug is smiling when he sees that she loves the puppy. Sean, through laughter. "Oh my god! He's so fucking cute!"

P2

Doug is beaming, looking at Sean. The dog has stopped licking and is standing with is ears perked up on Seans lap. He has just realized that there is FOOD! And it's ALL OVER THE FLOOR! And he can EAT THE FOOD! YAY! (Tail is wagging) Doug:" I went out early this morning and picked him up. He's been waiting for a week for me to come get him."

P3

Eye level with dog. Dog has jumped down to floor and has started devouring the food. Sean and Doug can be seen on bed above, looking down on ravenous canine. Sean: "Doug, this is the best thing you've ever gotten me. What's his name?" Doug: "That's up to you."

P4

Sean is smiling and looking at Doug who is returning her gaze and expression. Doug: "I'm glad you like him, baby." Sean: "Oh, I love it!"

P5

Another big passionate kiss.

P6

The kiss stops suddenly. Sean has turned to look in the dog's direction (dog is off panel) and she wears a quizzical look on her face. "What's that smell?" she asks.

PAGE 22

P1

It is now an hour (or so) later. From inside apartment looking out. Sean is on front step and has back to camera and has dog on leash. We can see Doug standing next to his 77 Lincoln Continental. The driver's side door is open and he is ready to get in. No dialogue.

P2

From behind Doug, looking back at Sean in doorway with dog. Sean is still wearing same thing she woke up in. White shirt shows food stains. Sean: "How long do you think it'll take?" Doug: "I dunno. Ten, twelve hours? Hartford's like eleven hundred miles away."

P3

Sean has walked out to the car with the dog. She isn't looking at doug but at dog. Sean: "Well, take a break if you get tired. Drive safe..." Doug is trying to look her in the face.

P4

Doug has put his hand under Sean's chin to force her to face him (gentle-like). Doug: "Baby, you know me. I'm always careful" new balloon "And besides..."

P5

Doug is all smiles, but you can see that he may be starting to well up. "...I can always put in one of your mix tapes if I get sleepy."

P6

They embrace. A hug similar to that one pin-up you drew, except that their whole figures are in frame. Doug and his gargantuan physique nearly swallows Sean whole, but you can see that she is hugging him back.

Sean is still holding onto the dog leash and the dog has it pulled tight as he as seen a squirrel (off panel) and his trying to get to it.

PAGE 23

P1

Close up of Doug's hand turning the key in his car. On key chain is an average looking
bottle opener, three other average looking keys, and a pewter skull and crossbones.

P2 - 3

Foreground: Sean standing on front step waving goodbye to Doug as he drives away. Dog
is trying to jump up on her. Distance: The Continental drives off. Big plumes of black
smoke follow. (this is a 2 panel deal. The car is out of view in second panel, suggesting
that Sean has watched him until she couldn't see him anymore.)

P4

Largest panel on page.

Sean standing inside apartment and has her hand on the doorknob as she has just shut the
door. She is looking around the living room which is in pretty much the same condition
as the bedroom, except that there are more empty bottles, more ashtrays, and less clothes.
Artwork is basic starving artist cheap paintings. No magazine cutouts (those are reserved
for the bedroom). No TV, but there is a small single component stereo on a small table up
against a wall next to a ratty looking couch. A pile of cd cases, some open, some closed,
and some uncased cds lay around it. The dog is still leaping up on Sean who has a somewhat blank look on her face.

P5

Smaller panel. Sean has bent down and is unhooking the dog from his leash. Dog looks
very happy.

PAGE 24

P1

Sean has flumped down on couch, head on one of the armests, one leg up on couch, the
other foot flat on floor. Dog is running around, sniffing stuff.

P2

Dog has come up to couch (still on floor) and is nuzzling Sean's hand which is dangling
off the couch. Sean is looking at the dog, semi-seriously. She obviously has things on her
mind, but her face is a mystery. "So little puppy, my great big protector, whatever shall I
name you?"

P3

Side shot of Sean looking down at dog who is sitting on floor looking at Sean. They
almost look as if they are communicating telepathically. Like the dog was trying to tell
Sean what his name is.

P4

Camera on floor. Dog in foreground, Sean above. She has half rolled over so that she is
now on her side looking at dog. One eyebrow raised because an unexpected name has
popped into her head. From the dog, perhaps? "Chester?" she says, trying out the sound
of it.

P5

Sean's pov of dog, sitting on floor looking up at her. He is really fucking cute and is smiling, wagging his tail. The dog appears to be saying YES.

P6

Same as P4, which is important for the punchline. "No." says Sean. "That's a stupid
name. Your name is Stuart."

Here are a few selected pages of the script for Chapter Ten. I want you to pay attention to the hell I must have put Wendi through with these descriptions of fucking staircases and tenement hallways. I like this script a lot and I think Wendi knocked it out of the ballpark. Gotta admit, it was fun making her draw hardcore violence. Also, a lot of people don't like Raoul. This story is for those people.

PAGE ONE-205

Panel 1
Raoul, who will be referred to as Ralph for the duration of this script, is walking up to his shitty apartment building. From the outside we can see an alleyway on the side with a fire escape. The building, which is no more than a tenement, stands perhaps six stories tall. Old crap air conditioners protrude from a few of the front windows. The front entrance is a set of double glass doors. The glass is cracked in one of them. The sign in front of the building reads in large type: MODULAR ARMS APTS. In smaller type below it LUXURY DWELLINGS. Ralph wears a thrift store suit, the style the type an eighty-year-old would wear to go and play chess in the park. (Think Willy Loman) It doesn't quite fit him and hangs on his frame like it was hanging from a clothesline. Raoul is carrying a beat up briefcase. He is coming from a job interview for a job he knows that he has not gotten.
CAPTION: IT WAS THE SUMMER OF 2003

Panel 2
Ralph enters the building.
The hallway extends before him as he lightly closes the door behind him. A small amount of litter lays about the hallway floor (bits of paper, a fast food wrapper, a smushed Jack o'Lantern, whatever you think would be kinda funny). He doesn't want to make a sound to alert his landlord to his presence. The landlord's office, door open, is to the right of the front door. A small sign indicates that this is the landlord's office. Next to the door, built in the hallway wall, is a dropbox. The sign above that reads in printed letters RENT DUE THE FIRST OF THE MONTH Handwritten below that reads NO EXCUSES! Ralph, lightly closes the front door behind him, and has his gaze nervously fixed towards the door.
CAPTION: I HAD JUST BEEN LAID OFF FROM MY TEACHING GIG AT A LOCAL COLLEGE AND MONEY WAS TIGHT.

Panel 3
Ralph tiptoes, comically, past the landlord's door. Inside the office, we can see the back of the landlord as he sits in his la-z-boy recliner watching Maury Povich on TV. To one side of the recliner, there is one of those standup ashtrays that you use to see in hotel lobbies. Cigarette butts lay scattered on the floor below it.
CAPTION: I HAD BEEN TEACHING A COURSE ON BUSINESS ETHICS IN THE 21ST CENTURY...

Panel 4
Ralph has reached the stairs at the end of the hall; we can see the hallway behind him. Ralph wipes a bead of sweat from his forehead with the hand that isn't holding a suitcase. A look of relief is on his face. The stairs are old but look like they were fancy and ornate about 100 years previously. Large wooden handrails with subtle carved patterns. What

other decorations may have ordained this once magnificent staircase are now broken or in a state of disrepair. If we can see the stairs themselves, they too have a bit of trash on them.

CAPTION: BUT SOMEONE HIGHER UP DECIDED THAT THERE WAS NO LONGER ANY NEED FOR SUCH A CLASS.
CAPTION: STUPID FUCKS.

****

PAGE FOUR-208

Panel 1
Ralph walks down a dirty old street with his hands deep in his pockets, looking down at his feet. The stores around him are all pawn shops and all in a state of disrepair. Metal bars, the jail cell type, cover most of the windows. Through the windows we can see pawned typewriters, jewelry, baby strollers, musical instruments, and a collection of mounted monkey heads. Sitting on the sidewalk next to one of the shops is a homeless man holding a sign which reads: MY FIFTEEN MINUTES ARE UP. (Note, this is homeless David Ects from Chapter Seven. You don't HAVE to draw him exactly like Jake did, but he should look similar. I told Jake to draw him like David Cross.)

****

PAGE THIRTEEN-217

Panel 1
Similar shot as the last two panels on the previous page. But now Ralph has awakened, and boy has he ever! His eyes wide, not with fear, but with unrepressed rage. His mouth open, his lips pulled back to reveal all of this teeth, The muscles in his face are all pulled tight. Imagine like Ralph was "Hulking-Out", but he's not really as he's not getting any bigger. He just has Hulk-like rage. God, I am such a nerd. This is so silly. Anyway, it's really scary. Ralph mad!

Panel 2
Ka-Pow! Ralph tears his arms free from the straps. (His neck, waist and ankle straps remain...for now) Ralph's face is filled with that same hate Hulk rage.
RALPH (BIG BOLD LETTERING): GRAAAAAHHHH!

Panel 3
Ralph in foreground as he tears at his neck strap, which is already starting to give. Super angry face, teeth gritted shut in angry determination. Background, door has flown open. Frank and Benny are almost falling back into the room. (as if they had run back down the hall to see what the commotion was). Their mouths are agape. At this point, I should probably mention again that besides the rage, and perhaps some veins now showing through, Ralph looks no different. He has not gained any muscle mass. He has not gotten any taller. He doesn't even really look like a threat. He is the same old Ralph, but madder and more filled with blood-lust. This, I hope, adds to the absurdity of the following pages of action.

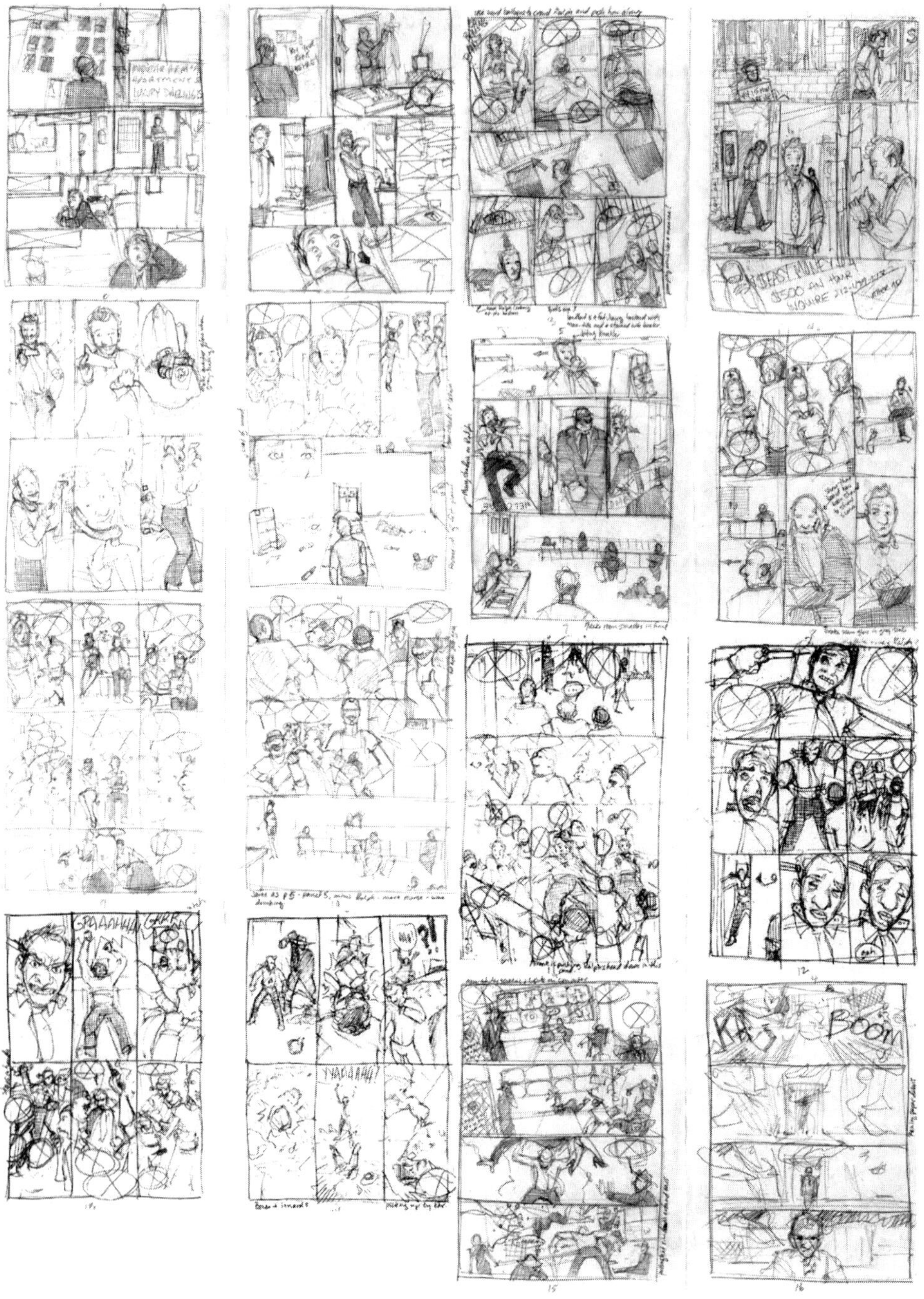
$500 AN HOUR
BOOM

Wendi's thumbnails from Chapter Ten. She nailed this from the get-go.

RALPH: GRRRRR
BENNY: HOLY SHIT!

Panel 4
Oh my god! Ralph has torn his neck strap loose! And now he's looking at the pair of fake doctors that originally strapped him down! He looks like he wants to kill them both...no, that's too light. He looks like he wants to jump up and down on their bodies, over and over, until there's nothing left but a fine red powder. Meanwhile, Frank and Benny are terrified. They're freaking out! Benny is pointing towards Ralph Monster and screaming at Frank. Frank has pulled out a radio and is screaming into it.
BENNY: JESUS! HE RIPPED OFF THAT STRAP LIKE IT WAS NOTHING!
FRANK: I'M GONNA NEED THE TRANQ CART DOWN HERE RIGHT FUCKING NOW!
RALPH: YOU!

Panel 5
Ralph has leaned down, causing the waist restraint to burst, and has ripped off his ankle restraints. He has done this all never taking his anger filled eyes off of the two doctors who are shaking in fear. However, neither doctor is really looking at him. Benny continues to yell at Frank, while Frank is half turned screaming into the radio.
RALPH: KILL YOU!
BENNY: FRANK! WE GOTTA GET THE FUCK OUT OF HERE!
FRANK: GODAMMIT! WE NEED THAT CART NOW!

Panel 6
Ralph has come up from behind and PUNCHED OFF FRANK'S HEAD! Benny can only duck backwards, watching his partner's head sail through the air. Ralph is in the follow through of the punch, screaming in rage.
RALPH: GAHH!
BENNY: OH JESUS!

****

Which brings us to Chapter Eleven. Saying nothing else about any of the other chapters of Plastic Farm, or commenting on the authors, this was probably the best script I had written up to this point. Dennis did a great job in showing the tone, and as awesome as my script was, he improved upon it by his splitting up of action over more panels than I indicated. What follows are some prime examples.

PAGE 14 - The Crime Lab
The crime lab is a small, dark (again) room. There are at least five computers spread across the room (remember, this is 1995), and a chainlink fence separating the room in two. The fence serves to create an equipment/evidence locker, which is filled with shelves of random shit. In the center of the room is one of those lab tables like everyone had in high school physics. It's got a sink, a gas spigot and bunsen burner etc. There is also a big ass microscope and a reel-to-reel tape player. The lab tech, let's call her...Laura, wears a white lab coat, her hair back in a bun, plastic safety goggles rest on top of her head. She's cute in a she-can-totallykick- your-ass-if-she-wanted-to kinda way.

PANEL ONE:

Decent establishing shot of lab. Goner, Carl and Laura are gathered around the reel-to-reel tape player. all looking intensely at it. Actually, Carl is trying to look down the front of Laura's jacket.

NARRATION: I MAKE A QUICK CALL TO CARL AND HAVE HIM MEET ME IN THE CRIME LAB.

NARRATION: YES, WE HAVE A CRIME LAB.

LAURA: WELL, THE TAPE ITSELF IS CLEAN. NO PRINTS OR ANYTHING...

PANEL TWO:

Laura presses play on the player. Goner crosses his left arm across his chest, and puts his right hand up to his mouth, because that's what people do when they're preparing to listen to things I guess. He's intent and curious about what might be on the tape. While pressing play, Laura is at the same time looking over at Carl who is now looking away from Laura's chest and trying to look innocent.

LAURA: AND, DESPITE IT LOOKING LIKE IT'S BEEN THROUGH HELL

LAURA: IT SHOULD PLAY JUST FINE.

GONER: GOOD, GOOD.

PANEL THREE:

The trio stand motionless above the now playing tape, waiting intently for it to give up its secrets.SFX coming from tape deck speakers: HSSSS..KLICK....SSS...POP...

PANEL FOUR:

Same exact layout as previous panel. except now Laura and Carl are looking at Goner with raised eyebrows and general "I can't believe you dragged us down here for this shit" expressions. Goner is wincing and squeezing the bridge of his nose.

FROM TAPE DECK (SINGING): I'D LIKE TO LIVE BELOW THE SEA, WITH FOURTEEN POUNDS OF LEPROSY!

PANEL FIVE:

You may as well photocopy the previous panel.

CARL: YOU SAID THAT FRANK'S REANIMATED ZOMBIE CORPSE GAVE YOU THIS TAPE AND TOLD YOU THAT IT WAS IMPORTANT? THAT IS WHAT YOU SAID, RIGHT?

GONER: I DON'T NEED TO HEAR THIS, CARL...

PAGE FIFTEEN - THE CRIME LAB AGAIN.

PANEL ONE

Laura has turned back to the tape deck and is adjusting the knobs. The volume, probably. Turning it up. She looks a little excited. Goner has reopened his eyes and dropped his hand just a little bit away from his face. He looks a bit more excited. Carl almost seems excited too.

LAURA: WAIT A MINUTE, I THINK THERE'S SOMETHING ELSE...

LAURA: SOUNDS LIKE A CAR...DOORS OPENING...

PANEL TWO

Excitement as the tape gives up a clue. Laura is still focused on the tape, but Goner is barking an order at Carl and pointing at one of the computers in the room. Carl is already halfway to one of them

TAPE DECK: MISTER BRIGTON. DO YOU HAVE WHAT I WANT?

GONER: BRIGTON! CARL....!

CARL: I'M ON IT.

PANEL THREE

We're looking over Carl's shoulder as he sits at the computer. He is bathed in the glow of the monitor and we can see a "Search Database" window open. He has already typed in the name "Brigton". The tape continues to play off panel.

TAPE DECK: HU-HERE IT IS SIR. J-JUST LIKE YOU WANTED.

TAPE DECK: THANK YOU MISTER BRIGTON.

PANEL FOUR

Laura and Goner still at the tape deck. Carl is in the background at the computer. Goner and Laura are still listening intently.

TAPE DECK: MUNG, GIVE THE MAN HIS PAYMENT.

TAPE DECK: THU-THUH. THANK YOU SIR.

GONER: WHAT THE FUCK IS A MUNG?

PANEL FIVE

The tape continues to play as Carl, still seated, has turned back towards Goner and Laura. On the monitor we can see a long list of names. A pop-up window over the names reads "132 Matches Found". Laura and Goner are turned away from the deck, looking towards Carl.

TAPE DECK: THINK NOTHING OF IT, MY BOY.

TAPE DECK: IT'S BEEN A PLEASURE JUST DOING BUSINESS WITH SOMEONE LIKE YOU...

CARL: GOT A LOT OF HITS. CAN WE NARROW DOWN THE SEARCH?

PANEL SIX

Everyone looks shocked at the tape deck as the recorded sound of Brigton getting his brains blown out ring out. Laura has nearly jumped out of her chair, it startled her so much. Goner's eyes are wide.

TAPE DECK: BLAM!

PANEL SEVEN

Same layout as previous. Carl still half turned around and watching Laura and Goner. Laura has her hand covering her mouth, still a little shocked. Goner, body still facing tape deck, has his head turned around slightly towards Carl.

GONER: TRY "PRESUMED DEAD".

I think that I wrote a kick-ass fight scene right here:

PAGE TWENTY-ONE

PANEL ONE
Mung Two kicks Goner in his ribs at full force. Goner is crumpled over in pain, his eyes bulging.
GONER: OOF!

PANEL TWO
Foreground - The Mungs watch as Goner tries to crawl away. He is crawling in the direction of one of the dumpsters. (The dumpster is marked with the symbol for medical waste, and has an OPEN LID.)

PANEL THREE
Mung One, bent over, grabs Goner's collar with his left hand, and at Goner's belt with his right. Goner is wincing in pain.
PANEL FOUR
Like King Kong picking up a bus, Mung One has lifted Goner over his head by his collar and belt. We can see the open dumpster looming in the background. Goner is NOW scared. He's not really flailing around like a jerk though. He's a tough cop, and though he's terrified, he's not going to start acting like a fucking baby.

PANEL FIVE
Mung throws Goner against the back of the open dumpster lid. Goner should be shown hitting the back of the lid, face first, with big impact lines. Mung should be seen in follow-through of the hard toss.
SFX: SLAM!

PANEL SIX
Top view of Goner lying in the open, and very full dumpster amongst big trash bags filled with god knows what kind of biological waste. He now has a huge cut on his forehead. His feet dangle out over the side of the dumpster. if you're feeling goofy, maybe some stars circling Goner's head.

PAGE TWENTY-TWO
PANEL ONE
Close up on Goner's face. He's dazed and bleeding. His face looks straight forward, but his eyes look off to his left at a trashbag.

PANEL TWO
Same shot, Goner still looking over, but now he has a slight smile, and his eyes are alive again. He sees something in the trash that'll help him fight back, but we can't see it yet.

PANEL THREE
Mung One is at the dumpster, pulling Goner up my the front of his shirt. Goner's left hand is hidden inside the dumpster, but Goner is grinning like an Elvis smirk.
MUNG ONE: ARE YOU SUFFICIENTLY WARNED AGAIN?
GONER: FUCK YOU.

PANEL FOUR

a Dave Sim style sound effect panel. Bloody letters, reading vertically, slashed down through the center.

SLASH!

PANEL FIVE

Mung One has staggered back, holding both of his hands over his left eye. Blood gushes from between his fingers. Mung Two has joined his brother, and looks just a little concerned.

MUNG ONE: MY EYE, BROTHER.

MUNG ONE: HE HAS TAKEN MY EYE.

PANEL SIX

A badass dramatic shot of Goner climbing out of the dumpster. He is crouched, his left foot on the edge, holding onto the edge with his right hand. His left arm and hand are extended outward, triumphantly brandishing the scalpel that he found in the trash. It is now blood splattered and the blood is trickling down his hand. Goner is looking straight ahead, covered in his own blood and the filth of the dumpster. He's a fucking mess, but he's pissed and now he has a scalpel.

GONER: SHOULDN'T HAVE THROWN ME IN WITH THE MEDICAL WASTE, YOU FUCK.

GONER: YOU BELIEVE THE KINDA SHIT YOU FIND IN HERE?

PAGE TWENTY-THREE

PANEL ONE:

Mung Two, foreground, angrily marches towards Goner and the dumpster, background. Goner has his left arm back, and he's ready to pounce. Mung Two shows no signs of being at all afraid of this little man.

GONER: YEAH, COME GET SOME.

PANEL TWO

Goner has leapt at Mung Two, but Mung Two, using his right hand thumb and forefinger pointing down, has caught Goner in midair by his scalpel wielding left wrist. Mung Two snarls like a gorilla. Goner looks shocked as this was not part of his plan. How the hell can this Mung thing be so impossibly strong?

GONER: UT!

PANEL THREE

It should be like this is all one motion from the grab in the previous panel. Mung Two is tossing Goner towards the chainlink fence using only his right arm. Goner is like a ragdoll in the hands of this madman. The scalpel can be seen dropping from his hand. Mung Two is even more bestial in expression now. Maybe Mung One can be seen in the background, or foreground depending on how you best think the panel should be laid out, hands no longer covering his missing eye, approaching the melee.

PANEL FOUR

Crash! Goner hits the chainlink fence hard! Same sorta effect as when he hit the dumpster.

PANEL FIVE

Through the fence, as if we were in the woods watching this, Goner, crumpled on the ground at the base of the fencing, looks upward at Mung Two. Mung One is definitely in this panel, hands away from his face, joining his brother. Goner is nearly dead, his arm is broken. The Mungs have their expressionless faces on again.

MUNG TWO: DO NOT WORRY OVER YOUR EYE, BROTHER...

PANEL SIX

The Sergio Leone gunfight style panel. Mung Two's hand hangs in the foreground holding the bloodstained scalpel, Goner, nearly dead, beaten to the point that he can no longer fight back, all he can do is watch, eyes the scalpel with numb fear.

MUNG TWO: I SHALL MAKE ALL THINGS EQUAL.

PAGE TWENTY-FOUR

Four quarter page horizontal panels. Like a crane shot pulling back.

PANEL ONE

Close up on Goner's face. We can see his left eye, wide in fear as Mung moves the scalpel to it. Mung has his free hand on Goner's face, pulling down on his cheek, forcing the eye to remain open.

PANEL TWO

We're twenty feet over the three men. Mung Two is hunched over Goner in such a way that we cannot see most of Goner above the waist. Goner's arms are, if we can make it out, clawing at Mung Two's face, trying to push him off. Mung One stands back and watches. We should be able to see a good amount of the back alley as well. Probably some blood stains on the ground, on the wall, on the dumpster...

PANEL THREE

We're way overhead. We can see much of the Medical center, people who look like ants milling around in front, the back alley filled with three tightly close together ants.

PANEL FOUR

Solid black

And now, in the last of the full script department, I present Flavor Of My Love. I have been told that Danielle cannot show this story to her parents. I begin this excerpt at the good bit to let her off the hook. Danielle, just show your folks this, and tell them it was all my fault.

PAGE FIVE

Panel One:

The Honeymoon suite at a ritzy hotel. Robert lies on top of the covers, wearing only silk boxers. Margo stands, seductively, in the bathroom doorway, wearing sexy lingerie. She is backlit by the bathroom light.

CAPTION: BUT DESPITE THE TRAGIC CIRCUMSTANCES OF OUR WEDDING ANNOUNCEMENT, WE WERE TOO MUCH IN LOVE FOR THE MARRIAGE ITSELF NOT TO WORK.

Panel Two:

Margo climbs, catlike onto the bed. She is grinning sexily at Robert, who is quite excited to see this figure of beauty coming towards him.

CAPTION: AT LEAST, THAT'S WHAT I THOUGHT.

MARGO: HELLO, MISTER O'DEN.

ROBERT: WELL HELLO YOURSELF, MISSUS O'DEN.

Panel Three:

Robert and Margo in bed. We can see the pair from Robert's chest up. Margo has snuggled herself up against Robert, kissing his neck, overcome with lust. Robert's not having such a bad time himself.

ROBERT: YOU SMELL GREAT, MARGO. IS THAT A NEW PERFUME?

MARGO: NO. I JUST GAVE MYSELF AN ENEMA.

Panel Four:

Similar panel as P3. Robert has stopped having such a great time and is now stonefaced, facing forward but looking at Margo out of the corner of his eyes. Margo has begun to nibble on Robert's earlobe.

MARGO (WHISPERING): You can have me any way you'd like...

MARGO (WHISPERING): but you have to do something for me...

Panel Five:

Close up on Margo's lips next to Robert's ear as she whispers her strange sexual request.

MARGO'S LIPS (WHISPERING): I want you to eat my ass.

Panel Six:

Robert is out of bed, standing up against a wall, looking back aghast at his new bride. Robert has his eyes wide, his hand over his mouth. Margo is on the bed, kneeling like a Muslim at worship, her ass in the air aimed at Robert.

MARGO: PLEASE, ROBERT...?

MARGO: PLEASE DO THIS FOR ME?

CAPTION: I LOVED MARGARET MORE THAN ANYTHING ELSE IN THE WORLD...

CAPTION: BUT THIS ONE THING, I COULD NOT DO FOR HER.

Panel Seven:

Close up on Margo's face, lying sideways on the bed as she maintains her position. She is crying, her eyes closed, makeup running.

CAPTION: I BROKE HER HEART.

MARGO (CRYING): please...please...

PAGE SIX

Panel One:

In their mansion. Living room. Evening. There's a bar built into the wall, and a large glass double door leading out to a pool. Feels like four years later. Margo leans against the bar setup, holding a martini glass, scowling at Robert who is sitting in a recliner smoking a pipe. There is tension in the air, all directed at Robert.

CAPTION: WE WERE NEVER QUITE THE SAME AFTER THAT NIGHT.

CAPTION: SHE TURNED COLDER...

Panel Two:
Close up of Margo scowling, taking a sip of her martini.
CAPTION: MORE DESPERATE WITH HER PLEADING.

Panel Three:
Robert has taken the pipe out of his mouth, and is turned towards his scowling wife, giving her a loving smile...which is not reciprocated.
CAPTION: IN A WAY, I BELIEVE THAT SHE STILL LOVED ME LIKE I LOVED HER...

Panel Four:
Robert, sadly, has stood up and has begun to walk away. Margo's scowl disappears, and she looks pleadingly after he husband.
ROBERT: I'M GOING BACK TO THE OFFICE.
MARGO: ROBERT, PLEASE...

Panel Five:
Robert is out of the panel. Margo has begun to cry, and has her free hand up to her eyes. She is slumping in her sadness, the martini spilling from her other hand.
MARGO: ALL I WANT...IS FOR YOU TO EAT MY ASS.
MARGO: ALL I WANT...
CAPTION: HELL, MAYBE IT WAS ALL MY FAULT.
CAPTION: WHY COULDN'T I GIVE HER WHAT SHE WANTED?

PAGE SEVEN
Panel One
Afternoon. The kitchen. Robert has just walked in wearing a business suit, carrying a briefcase. The pool-boy, Manuel, super-muscular, stands in the kitchen wearing nothing but a pair of bermuda shorts. He's a big buff pretty boy. He's got a splotch of something on his lower lip and is pouring himself a glass of lemonade. Margo stands in an opposite doorway, dressed in an open robe. Underneath, a skimpy bikini. She is holding a cocktail glass, an olive on a toothpick floats inside the glass.
CAPTION: MAYBE THE FOLLOWING AFTERNOON'S EVENTS WOULD NEVER HAVE HAPPENED.
ROBERT: WHAT'S GOING ON HERE?
MARGO: ROBERT, THIS IS MANUEL. OUR NEW POOL-BOY.
MANUEL: HOLA, SENOR.

Panel Two
Robert looks suspiciously at his wife, who has taken out the tooth-picked olive and is biting down on it. Manuel looks on.
ROBERT: NEW POOL-BOY? WHAT HAPPENED TO...?
MARGO: MANUEL IS VERY GOOD.
MANUEL: SI, I AM VERY...

Panel Three
Robert, growing more angry, turns to Manuel. Manuel has the pretty boy "who, me?" look upon his face.
ROBERT: MANUEL. COULD YOU LEAVE US ALONE FOR A MINUTE?
ROBERT: I NEED TO SPEAK TO MY...

Panel Four

Close-up on Manuel's face, highlighting the splotch on his lower lip. Manuel still looks innocent.

ROBERT (FROM OFF-PANEL): ...

Panel Five

Same layout as panel three. Robert, still slightly angry. Manuel now wears an "oops" face.

ROBERT: YOU'VE GOT SOME...CHOCOLATE PUDDING OR SOMETHING...

ROBERT: ...ON YOUR...MOUTH...

Panel Six

Robert has turned to look at Margo. He is sad, disappointed. She is crying again, apologetic in her sadness, reaching out to him. Robert has both arms at his side. He has no intention of going to her. Manuel in the background, wiping his face with a dishtowel.

ROBERT: OH...

ROBERT: OH, MARGO. HOW COULD YOU?

MARGO: ROBERT, I'M SO SORRY.

Panel Seven

Margo has fallen at Robert's feet, a crying disheveled mess, but he does not look at her, does not try to comfort her. He stares straight ahead, emotionless. Manuel sneaks out behind them.

MARGO: I WANTED IT TO BE YOU.

MARGO: I ONLY EVER WANTED IT TO BE YOU.

MANUEL: I GO CLEAN POOL.

PAGE EIGHT

Panel one-later that evening

Margo, mascara running down her face, sits at the living room table. She has not changed clothes since that afternoon. On the table are numerous prescription bottles, some open and lying on their sides, spilling some of their contents. There is a bottle of expensive whisky, half empty. She is crying as she writes her note. The room is dark, the shadows menacing.

CAPTION: I LEFT HER ALONE THAT DAY. I MADE THE MISTAKE OF GOING OUT TO CLEAR MY MIND...

Panel Two

Margo shoves a handful of pills into her mouth with one hand, holds the bottle of whisky with the other.

CAPTION: I NEVER THOUGHT THAT SHE WOULD GO SO FAR.

Panel Three

Margo, falling into her final sleep, rests her head on her limp arm on the table. Her other hand, limp, has knocked over the whisky which is spilled over the table.

CAPTION: I SHOULD HAVE DONE HER THAT ONE THING.

Panel Four

Overhead, upside-down, close-up of her dead hand lying over her suicide note. The handwriting on the note is scrawly, sloppy, and tear stains can be seen blotting some of the ink. Part of the note is obscured, so some of the writing cannot be seen. But the complete thing reads:

"Dearest Robert,

I am so sorry to have hurt you, but you gave me no choice. All I ever wanted was for you to love me in the way that I wanted. I gave you EVERYTHING! Money. A better job. A life! Robert, you were just a mail clerk when we met and I gave you everything you are. Why? Why couldn't you just love me like I wanted.

Now I am dead. Fuck you.

Margo"

CAPTION: I SHOULD HAVE LOVED HER THE WAY SHE DESERVED.

Panel Five

Robert stands in the doorway to the dining room, silhouetted, framed by the doorway. He has a hand over his mouth, in shock at seeing his dead wife. Margo is close-up in the foreground, Robert the background. Margo looks like she's been dead for a while, her glassy eyes open, bloodshot, a trickle of blood from her mouth. His briefcase dropped to the ground.

ROBERT: OH..OH GOD.

CAPTION: I SHOULD HAVE LOVED HER THE WAY SHE WANTED.

PAGE NINE

Panel One

The funeral home. It's Margo's wake. Open coffin. She looks so pretty, surrounded by flowers, wreaths, pictures of her. The grieving relatives all in black, the same fatcat aristocrats we've seen before. Robert sits in the front row, directly in front of the coffin, tear-stained eyes. The grieving relatives whispering behind his back. Their tail-less word balloons float over the crowd, with tiny whispered lettering

WHISPER #1: ALL HE EVER WANTED WAS HER MONEY.

WHISPER #2: I HEARD HE WOULDN'T EVEN TOUCH HER.

WHISPER #3: NEVER SHOWED HER ANY KINDNESS.

WHISPER #4: NEVER LOVED HER.

WHISPER #5: GOLD-DIGGER.

WHISPER #6: MAY AS WELL HAVE PUT A BULLET IN HER.

Panel Two:

A lawyerly looking fellow has come over to Robert and put his hand on Robert's shoulder. The lawyer has a look of compassion. Robert looks up at him.

LAWYER: MISTER O'DEN, I WAS YOUR WIFE'S ATTORNEY.

ROBERT: YES?

LAWYER: YOU NEED TO COME WITH ME PLEASE.

Panel Three:

Robert has stood up and is following the lawyer up to Margo's coffin. Two funeral workers now flank the coffin, one at the head and one at the foot. Robert looks confused.

ROBERT: WHAT'S THIS ABOUT?

LAWYER: PLEASE, JUST COME WITH ME.

Panel Four:

Lawyer and Robert stand behind the coffin (which is still flanked). Lawyer is now holding an official looking piece of paper and is putting on a pair of reading glasses as he begins to address the crowd.

LAWYER: LADIES AND GENTLEMEN, I UNDERSTAND THAT THIS COMES AT A MOST UNUSUAL TIME...

LAWYER: BUT IN ACCORDANCE WITH THE WISHES OF THE DECEASED, I MUST NOW CONDUCT THE READING OF HER WILL.

Panel Five:

Robert looks at the lawyer in shock. The crowd is aghast, silently murmuring to each other. But the lawyer is ignoring this change in protocol and begins to read.

LAWYER: I, MARGARET O'DEN, BEING OF SOUND MIND AND BODY, DO DECLARE THIS TO BE MY LAST WILL AND TESTAMENT.

LAWYER: TO MY HUSBAND, ROBERT O'DEN...

Panel Six:

Just Robert. He's agape. His teary eyes wide. He is not happy to hear the news. More in shock, as is the entire congregation off-panel.

LAWYER: I LEAVE MY ENTIRE ESTATE, VALUED AT OVER SEVEN-HUNDRED AND EIGHTY-FOUR MILLION DOLLARS...

OFF-PANEL#1: MY GOODNESS.

OFF-PANEL #2: HOW IRREGULAR.

OFF-PANEL #3: HE DESERVES NOTHING.

PAGE TEN

Panel One

We've pulled the camera back and can see that the two funeral workers have the coffin completely open, and are in the process of lifting Margo's corpse out. (One is at her head, and one has her feet.) Robert is beyond confused. He is questioning the two workers, angrily. (To make life easier, let's say that this is a special coffin that has a lid that comes completely off, not hinged like regular coffins. The lid is now on the ground.)

LAWYER: ...WHICH HE WILL RECEIVE IF HE MEETS THE FOLLOWING CONDITION.

ROBERT: WHAT THE HELL ARE YOU DOING!?

Panel two

The two works have flipped Margo over and are putting her back in the coffin FACE DOWN. Robert is now aghast, not listening to the lawyer. The lawyer is snapping his fingers at an off-panel person, like he was calling for a waiter.

ROBERT: WHY ARE YOU DOING THIS?!

LAWYER: HE MUST DO FOR ME IN DEATH, WHAT HE WOULD NOT DO IN LIFE.

Panel three

Funeral workers stand behind Robert as he stands over the coffin and his face-down wife. One worker is tying a lobster bib on him, another puts down a chair for Robert to sit on, a third holds a tray containing silverware (a fork and a big steak knife) and a bottle of ketchup. Robert is no longer angry, but very confused.

ROBERT: WAIT..WAIT A MINUTE.
ROBERT: YOU MEAN I HAVE TO...

Panel Four - small quick panel
Robert looks at Margo's butt.

Panel Five - small quick panel
He eyes the silverware.

Panel Six- small quick panel
Robert looks up at the lawyer, confused. The lawyer shows no sign of emotion.
ROBERT: YOU MEAN...LITERALLY?
LAWYER: YES, LITERALLY.

Panel Seven:
Robert, fork in one hand, knife in the other, is sitting behind the coffin, in line with Margo's ass. The lawyer stands to one side, the funeral workers behind him. In the foreground, the shocked congregation stares at him in disbelief. Robert shares that emotion as he looks back out at them.

Panel Eight:
Robert, from the waist up, holding the knife and fork out in front of him. He's turned his head to look right in the camera, breaking the third wall, addressing the audience. He has one eyebrow raised, as if to ask "well, what the fuck would YOU do?"

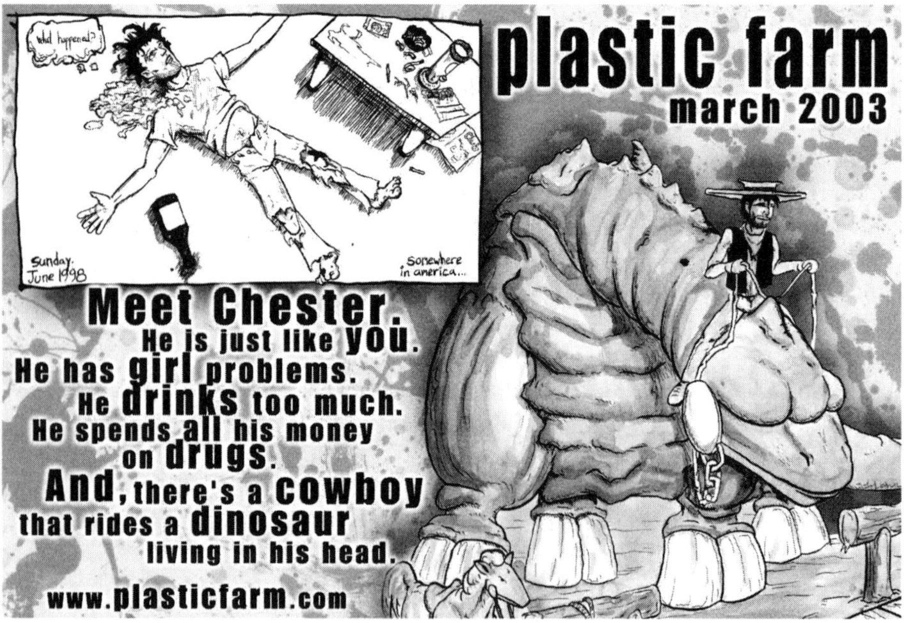
what happened?
Sunday.
June 1998
Somewhere
in america...
plastic farm
march 2003
Meet Chester.
He is just like you.
He has girl problems.
He drinks too much.
He spends all his money
on drugs.
And, there's a cowboy
that rides a dinosaur
living in his head.
www.plasticfarm.com

An ad for the first non-mini comic issue of Plastic Farm.

The following article originally appeared on comicon.com's The Pulse on June 16th, 2003. It is reprinted with permission. http://www.comicon.com/pulse

Life on the Plastic Farm - BY JENNIFER M. CONTINO

Plastic Farm tells the story of Chester Carter, a man who's led an eclectic, crazy, hectic life, mixed in reality and steeped with fantasy. It's a tale that will unfold over time and is meant to be cryptic and confusing. The creator, Rafer Roberts was influenced by David Lynch and hopes to craft a series that is akin to the best elements of Lynch's creations.

Plastic Farm began life as a series of mini comics, but now is being published in full comic's size containing some of the art from the minis and lots of new content. "Plastic Farm is the comic that I've been building up to for as long as I've been doing comics, so it's hard to peg one specific thing that has inspired this book," said Rafer Roberts, when asked about some of the elements that led him to create Plastic Farm. "It's got bits and pieces culled from other books that I've done and stuck them together, so it's almost like a greatest hits collection of the various ideas that I've been writing about for a long time."

Roberts continued, "There are also parts of Plastic Farm that are a little bit autobiographical. The opening scene of issue one, for example, where Chester wakes up after a night of heavy drinking and discovers that he's wrecked his car. That really happened. I just thought it would be a good way to start the book off. Y'know, take one of the lowest moments of my life and turn it into the introduction to a surreal western. It seemed like a good idea at the time."

"Beyond that, I'm a big David Lynch fan. I've gotten a few reviews comparing the book to stuff that Mr. Lynch has done, so I suppose I hide that influence very poorly."

Like a lot of other independent comics, this series started out in the mini-comics format. After whetting his feet in that format, Roberts branched out to full size comics. "Plastic Farm started out as a series of tabloid-sized mini-comics," explained Roberts. "I put out four issues of the book in that format then decided that I'd be happier doing the book as a regular comic. I went back and rescanned a lot of the art for the first two issues, cleaned up a lot of the artwork, and got the thing professionally printed. Story-wise, even people who have read all four of the original books don't know what Plastic Farm is really about. At this point in the story that slight confusion is kind of the idea. I've always been interested in stories where at a certain point everything just falls into place, and the reader who up to that point may have only partially understood the narrative, reaches perfect understanding of the story and can see the story with perfect clarity.At issue two however, we're still in chaos mode."

Although the story may be confusing and seem a little mixed up, Roberts has a definite plan for the series. "Plastic Farm is the tale of Chester 'Cheezer' Carter and his slow descent into complete insanity," explained Roberts. "When we first meet Chester in issue one, it's during the exact middle of his story. He's first starting to really come to terms with his mental problems, when he first realizes that he may not be quite right in the head. To get more specific, Chester has come to accept that there is a cowboy that rides a dinosaur living inside of his head that makes him do bad things."

"In issue two we meet Chester again, though it's many years later and chronologically towards the end of his story," continued the creator. "He proceeds to tell the story of his life from the very beginning, detailing his childhood and the events that help cause his mental illness. The part of Plastic Farm that I think throws most people is that Chester, the main character, doesn't appear in most of the first ten issues. The other issues deal more with the world where Chester lives, rather than Chester himself. However, these seemingly random tales are just as much a part of the overall story of Plastic Farm as Chester's tale is. Chapter three, for example, deals with two cops on a stakeout that goes all sorts of wrong. Their story eventually intersects with Chester's, but when first introduced it looks like a nice little self-contained standalone story."

"Plastic Farm, and Chester's story,will be told in three parts of approximately 15 issues each.This first part, the chaos part of the book which we're currently at the beginning of, randomly introduces every character for the entire series and will, in all honesty, confuse a lot of people. I believe that a lot of people think that I'm making this all up as I go along, but I honestly have a plan."

Like anyone working on a project, there are easy parts and the not-so-easy parts. Roberts faced several challenges while creating Plastic Farm. "In terms of story, making sure that I don't screw myself on one of these random chapters," said Roberts. "I've got a timeline-style outline that helps me to keep track of where each character is supposed to be during a given time, but I get urges in the middle of drawing a book to deviate from the plan. There's also the challenge of finding enough time to draw all of this. I work full-time on the night shift and I try to draw pretty much constantly when off the clock. I would go weeks without going out into the sunlight. If not for my wife, I'd probably go insane working my job and doing this book. And, I'll admit, my lettering could be cleaner."

"It's very difficult to professionally put out a comic book all by yourself. It's much easier with the help of your wife, friends and family. It's also hard to cheerfully sell comics at a con when you are suffering from a terrible hangover."

Issue two is available now and it reveals a lot about Chester Carter's past. "Issue two begins Chester's story in earnest," explained Roberts. "We learn that he's grown up in an orphanage built on the grounds of an old mental hospital. It's run by this intense group of religious monks and is possibly haunted by an ex-patient."

Roberts promises a unique experience with each issue. "I don't think that there is another comic on the market quite like Plastic Farm," Roberts stated. "I mean, where else are you going to find an invisible demon spider-monkey, a dinosaur-riding cowboy, the heartbreaking story of a young woman and her crumbling relationship with her boyfriend, and a guy who can turn his belly-button from an innie to an outie all under one title."

"Plastic Farm started because it's a story that I wanted to read, but that no one was writing for me. I'd like to think that there are other folks out there who share my tastes in stories, and so I'm probably writing the book for them as well. Also, and I make this promise. Plastic Farm will never be boring. I have way too many different kinds of stories to write for it to ever get old."

next:
Plastic Farm: Fertilizer
an interlude in three aprils

There are an infinite number of tales to tell from the world of Plastic Farm. These are three of them.

April, 1972. Living on a compound surrounded by those who have rejected the reality that modern society has imposed upon us all, Jonathan Picanos has begun to experiment with new forms of meditation and self-mutilation. His friends, while recognizing that Jonathan has become adept at his mastery over nature, do not realize the depths to which he has gone. When a new threat to their way of life emerges from the shadows, will Jonathan's mastery over reality save his friends and family, or will he lead them all to death and damnation?

April, 1998. Eliza Dorne is an assassin and, while she is quite good at her job, wishes to retire. She has completed what she hoped was her final mission, but her employer (a man known by many names, but most commonly known as The Reverend or The Smiling Man) is not so eager to let her go.

April, 1994. Frank and Benny were two honest cops killed while staking out the handoff of medical files between a junkie and The Smiling Man. Now they find themselves resurrected and performing menial tasks as an undead zombie-like janitorial staff.

Three seemingly unrelated tales detailing three separate events that will reshape the lives and realities of all who dare enter the world of Plastic Farm.

and then, after that:
Plastic Farm Part Two
Seasons of Growth in the Fields of Despair

This second part of PLASTIC FARM picks up young Chester's life a few months after the events of SOWING SEEDS ON FERTILE SOIL, details his college years, and further explores his descent into madness.

Over the course of Part Two, we'll reunite with The Thixotrope, Frank, Benny, the starving farmers, and The Smiling Man. We'll finally get a chance to get to know Chester's roomate Steve, and get introduced to bandito Ed Erbmas. Of course, we'll also return to the Nameless Airport Bar to meet a few more stranded travellers who have arrived in time to have their sanities tested by a certain storytelling madman.

But mostly, and it won't seem like it at first, this is about Chester and Sean.

And Doug. And Eliza. And Jake.

visit http://www.plasticfarm.com for more information

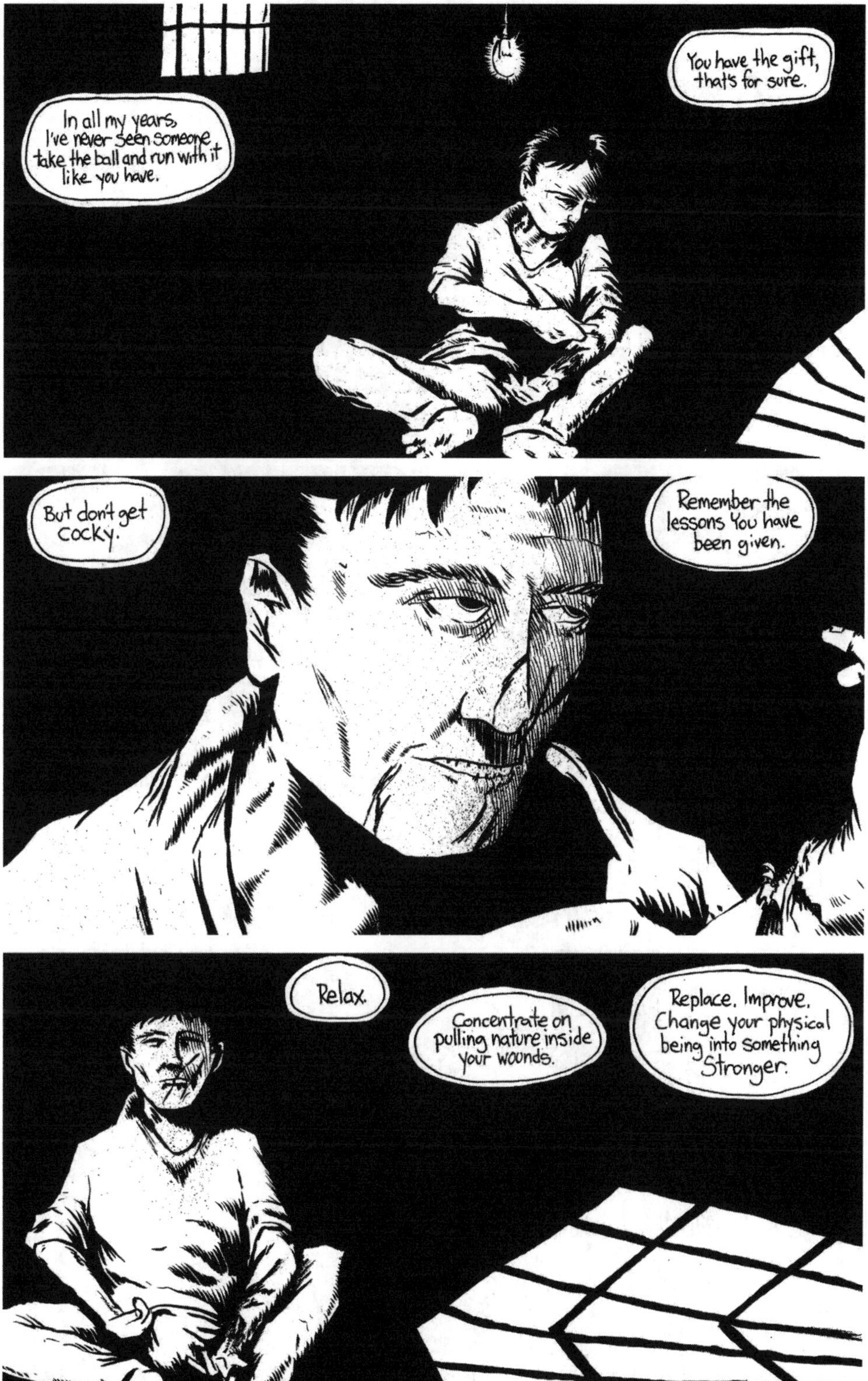
In all my years, I've never seen someone take the ball and run with it like you have.
You have the gift, that's for sure.
But don't get cocky.
Remember the lessons You have been given.
Relax.
Concentrate on pulling nature inside your wounds.
Replace. Improve. Change your physical being into something Stronger.

from Plastic Farm: Fertilizer

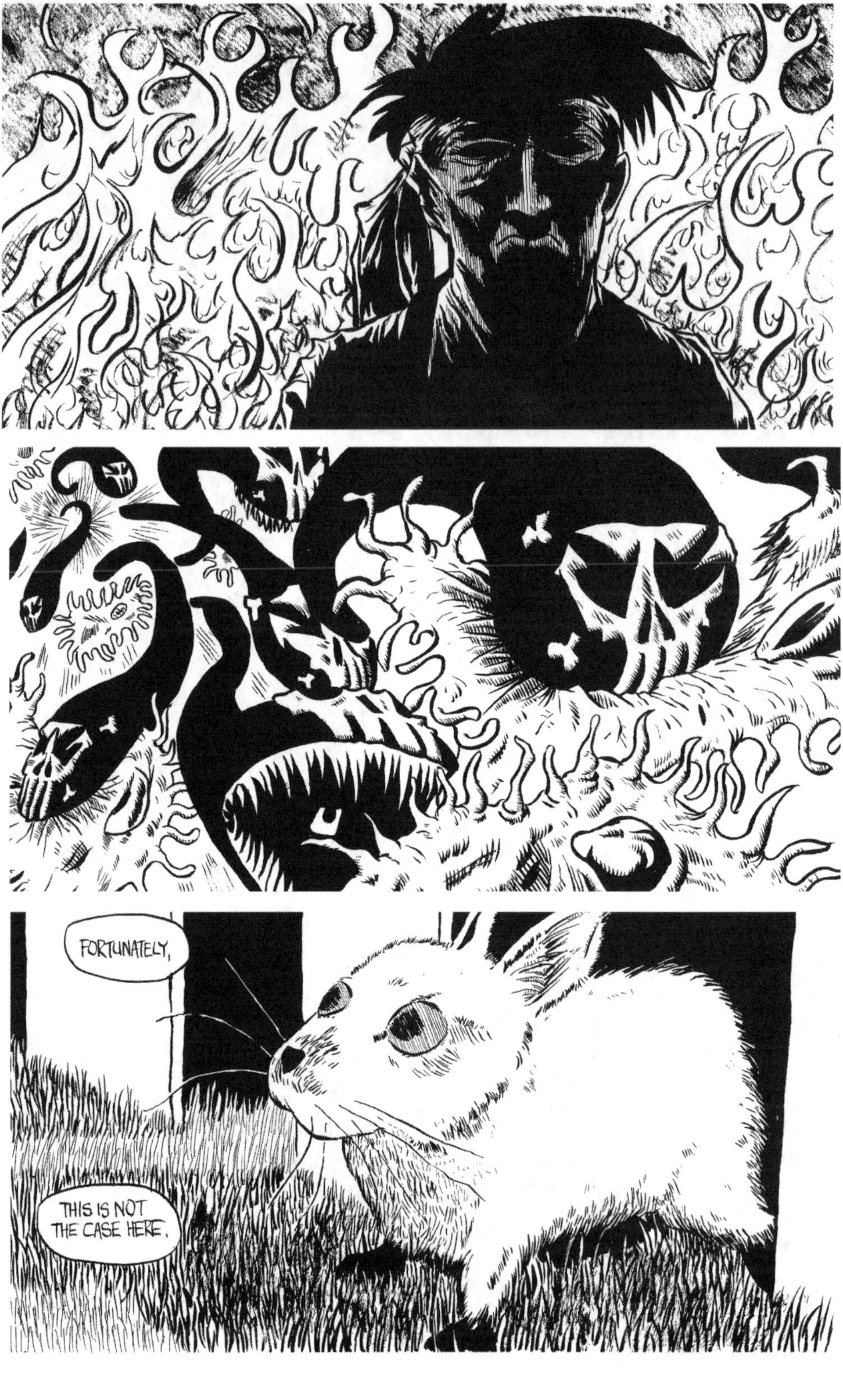
FORTUNATELY,
THIS IS NOT THE CASE HERE.

from Plastic Farm: Fertilizer

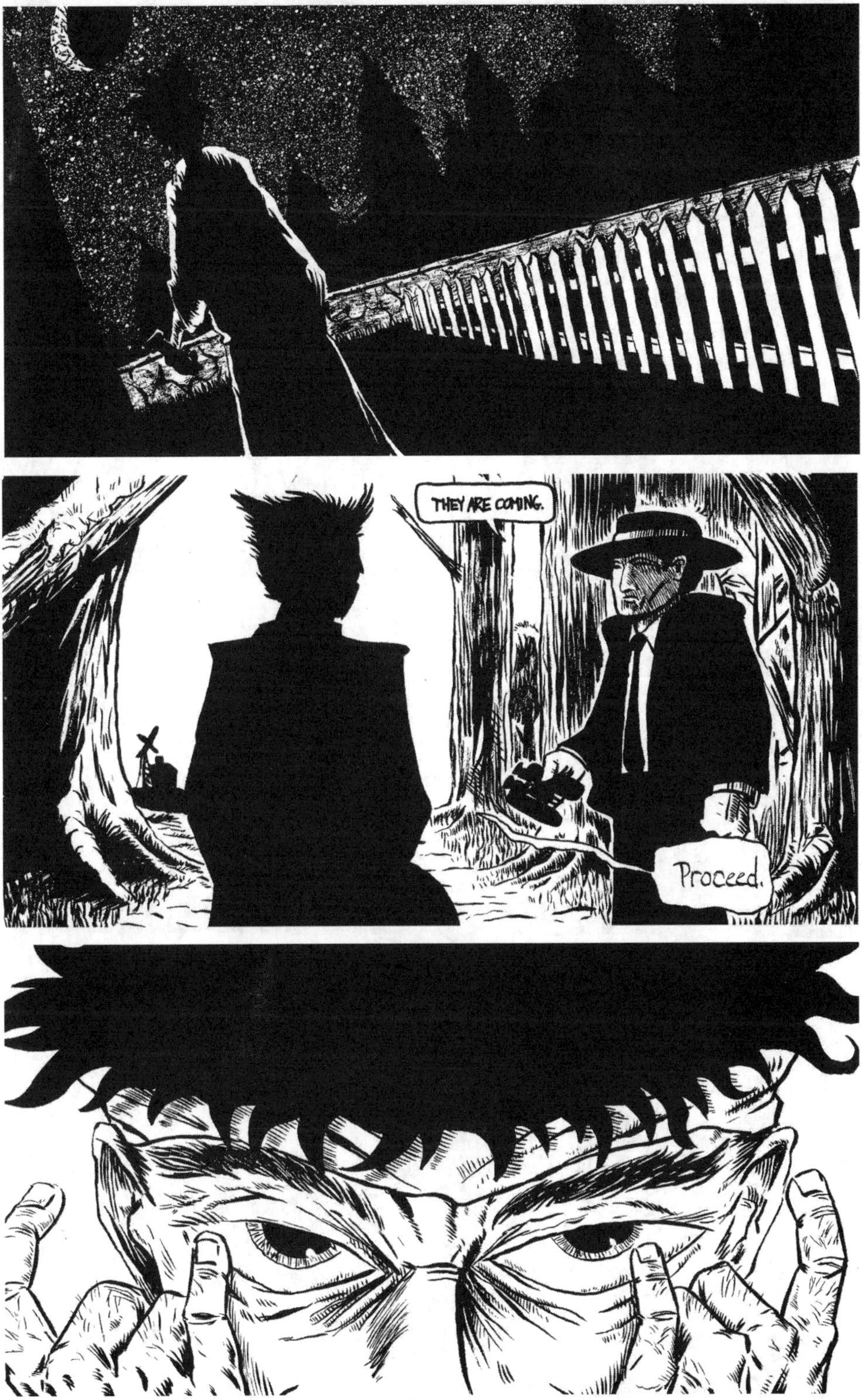
THEY ARE COMING.
Proceed.

from Plastic Farm: Fertilizer

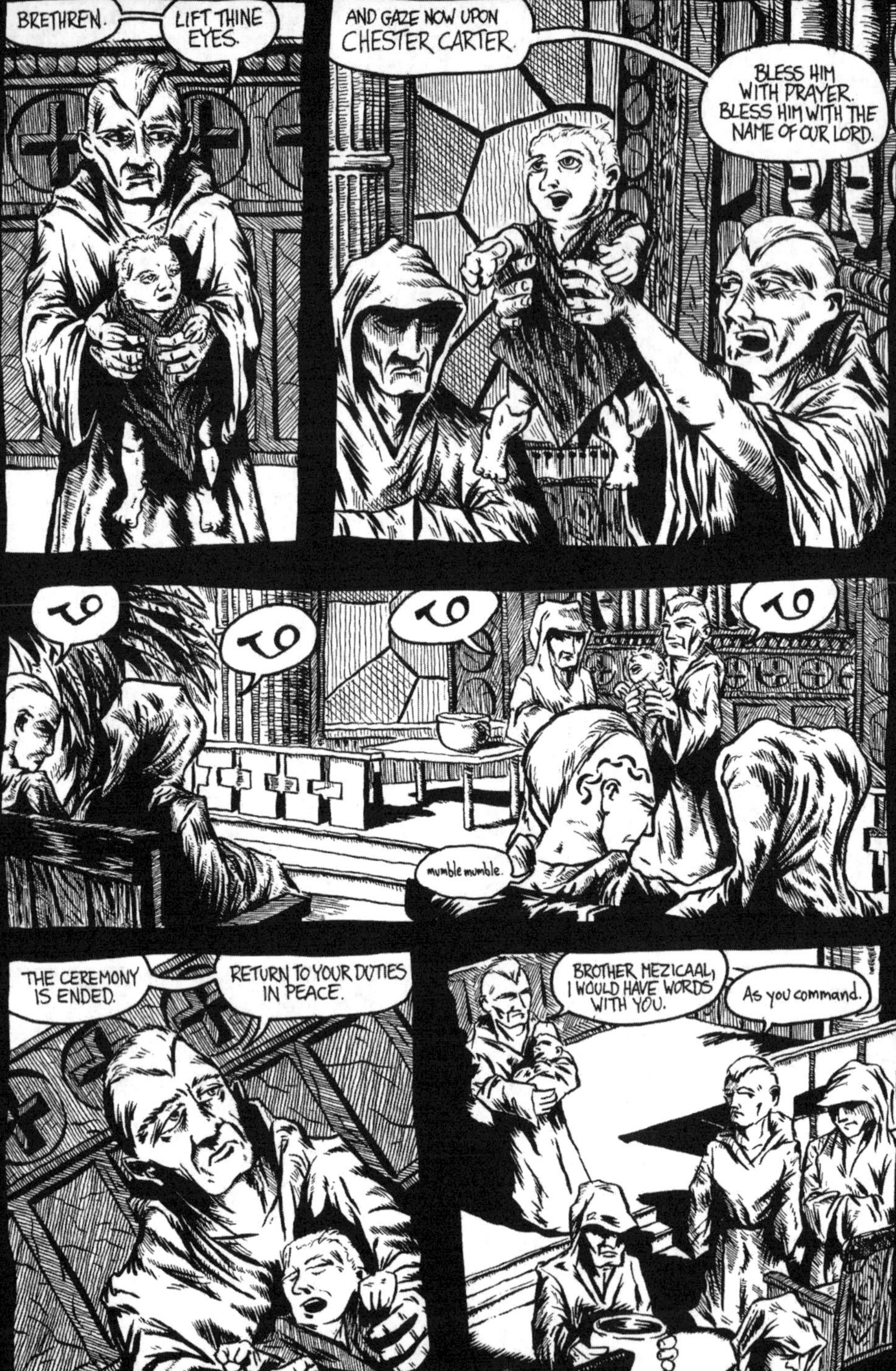
BRETHREN.
LIFT THINE EYES.
AND GAZE NOW UPON CHESTER CARTER.
BLESS HIM WITH PRAYER. BLESS HIM WITH THE NAME OF OUR LORD.
mumble mumble.
THE CEREMONY IS ENDED.
RETURN TO YOUR DUTIES IN PEACE.
BROTHER MEZICAAL, I WOULD HAVE WORDS WITH YOU.
As you command.

from Plastic Farm: Seasons of Growth on the Fields of Despair

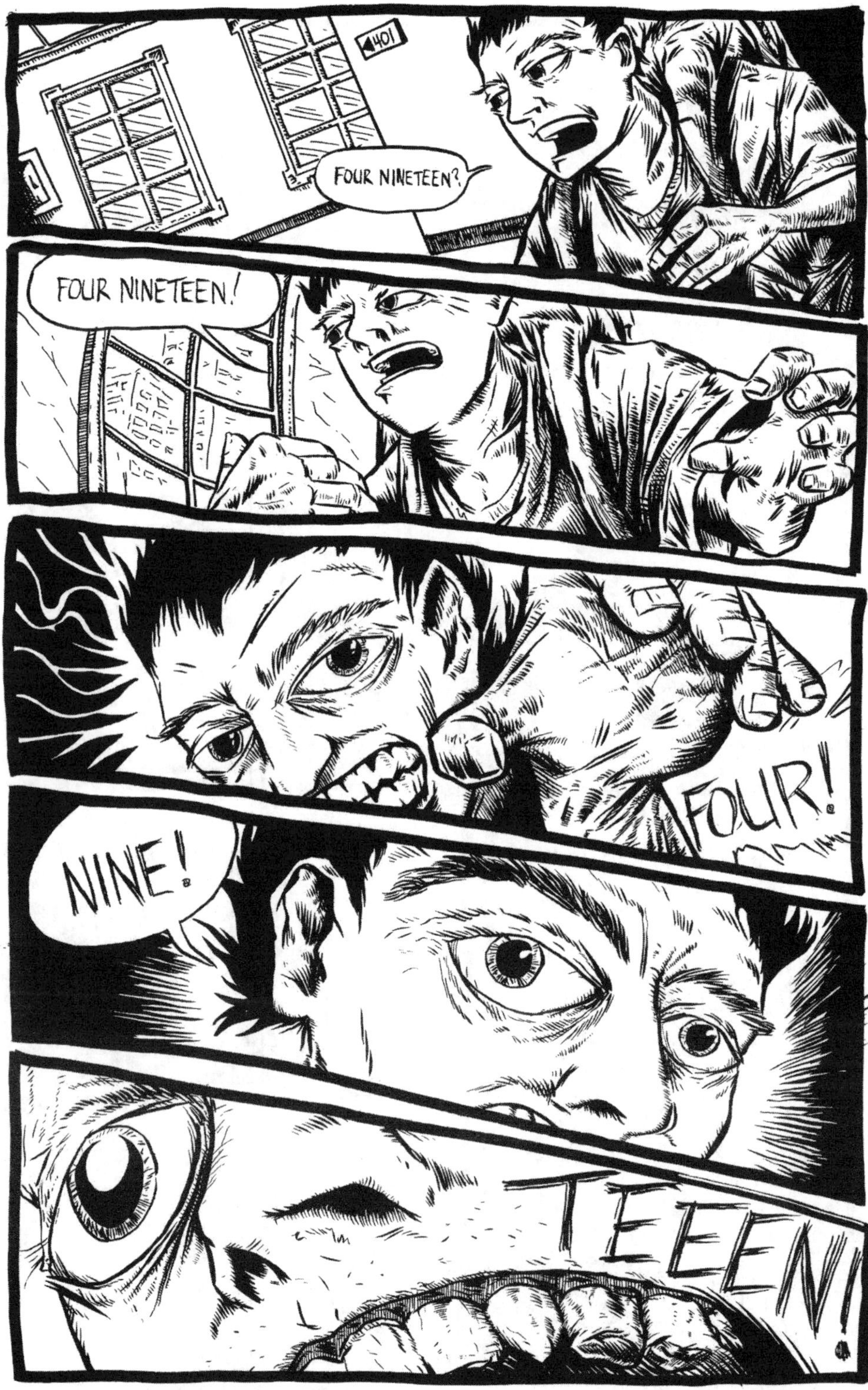
401
FOUR NINETEEN?
FOUR NINETEEN!
FOUR!
NINE!
TEEEN!

from Plastic Farm: Seasons of Growth on the Fields of Despair

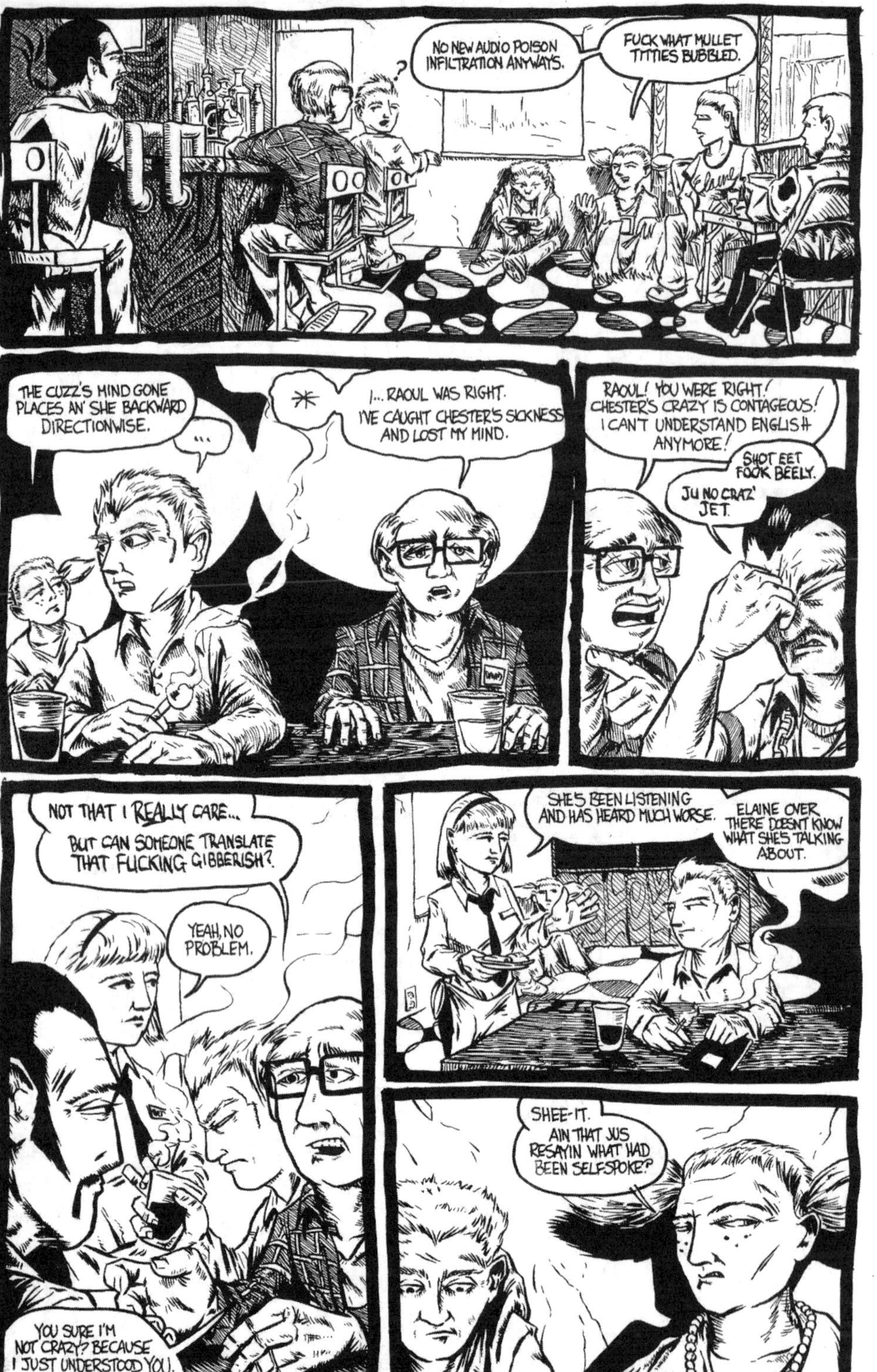
NO NEW AUDIO POISON INFILTRATION ANYWAYS.
FUCK WHAT MULLET TITTIES BUBBLED.
THE CUZZ'S MIND GONE PLACES AN' SHE BACKWARD DIRECTIONWISE.
...
I... RAOUL WAS RIGHT. I'VE CAUGHT CHESTER'S SICKNESS AND LOST MY MIND.
RAOUL! YOU WERE RIGHT! CHESTER'S CRAZY IS CONTAGEOUS! I CAN'T UNDERSTAND ENGLISH ANYMORE!
SHOT EET FOOK BEELY.
JU NO CRAZ' JET.
NOT THAT I REALLY CARE... BUT CAN SOMEONE TRANSLATE THAT FUCKING GIBBERISH?
YEAH, NO PROBLEM.
YOU SURE I'M NOT CRAZY? BECAUSE I JUST UNDERSTOOD YOU.
SHE'S BEEN LISTENING AND HAS HEARD MUCH WORSE.
ELAINE OVER THERE DOESN'T KNOW WHAT SHE'S TALKING ABOUT.
SHEE-IT. AIN THAT JUS RESAYIN WHAT HAD BEEN SELFSPOKE?

from Plastic Farm: Seasons of Growth on the Fields of Despair